Modeling, Analysis, and Applications in Metaheuristic Computing:
Advancements and Trends

Peng-Yeng Yin
National Chi Nan University, Taiwan

Managing Director:	Lindsay Johnston
Senior Editorial Director:	Heather Probst
Book Production Manager:	Sean Woznicki
Development Manager:	Joel Gamon
Development Editor:	Heather Probst
Acquisitions Editor:	Erika Gallagher
Typesetter:	Russell A. Spangler
Cover Design:	Nick Newcomer, Lisandro Gonzalez

Published in the United States of America by
Information Science Reference (an imprint of IGI Global)
701 E. Chocolate Avenue
Hershey PA 17033
Tel: 717-533-8845
Fax: 717-533-8661
E-mail: cust@igi-global.com
Web site: http://www.igi-global.com

Library of Congress Cataloging-in-Publication Data

Modeling, analysis, and applications in metaheuristic computing: advancements and trends / Peng-Yeng Yin, editor.
    p. cm.
 Includes bibliographical references and index.
 Summary: "This book is a collection of the latest developments, models, and applications within the transdisciplinary fields related to metaheuristic computing, providing readers with insight into a wide range of topics such as genetic algorithms, differential evolution, and ant colony optimization"--Provided by publisher.
 ISBN 978-1-4666-0270-0 (hardcover) -- ISBN 978-1-4666-0271-7 (ebook) -- ISBN 978-1-4666-0272-4 (print & perpetual access) 1. Heuristic algorithms. 2. Computer simulation. I. Yin, Peng-Yeng, 1966-
 T57.84.M58 2012
 003'.3--dc23
                         2011048473

British Cataloguing in Publication Data
A Cataloguing in Publication record for this book is available from the British Library.

All work contributed to this book is new, previously-unpublished material. The views expressed in this book are those of the authors, but not necessarily of the publisher.

Table of Contents

Detailed Table of Contents

Chapter 1

Fred Glover, OptTek Systems, Inc., USA
Saïd Hanafi, Universite de Valenciennes, France

Recent adaptive memory and evolutionary metaheuristics for mixed integer programming have included proposals for introducing inequalities and target objectives to guide the search. These guidance approaches are useful in intensification and diversification strategies related to fixing subsets of variables at particular values, and in strategies that use linear programming to generate trial solutions whose variables are induced to receive integer values. In Part I (the present paper), we show how to improve such approaches by new inequalities that dominate those previously proposed and by associated target objectives that underlie the creation of both inequalities and trial solutions. Part I focuses on exploiting inequalities in target solution strategies by including partial vectors and more general target objectives. We also propose procedures for generating target objectives and solutions by exploiting proximity in original space or projected space. Part II of this study (to appear in a subsequent issue) focuses on supplementary linear programming models that exploit the new inequalities for intensification and diversification, and introduce additional inequalities from sets of elite solutions that enlarge the scope of these models. Part II indicates more advanced approaches for generating the target objective based on exploiting the mutually reinforcing notions of reaction and resistance. Our work in the concluding segment, building on the foundation laid in Part I, examines ways our framework can be exploited in generating target objectives, employing both older adaptive memory ideas of tabu search and newer ones proposed here for the first time.

Chapter 2

Fred Glover, OptTek Systems, Inc., USA
Saïd Hanafi, University of Lille -Nord de France, UVHC, and LAMIH, France

Recent metaheuristics for mixed integer programming have included proposals for introducing inequalities and target objectives to guide this search. These guidance approaches are useful in intensification and diversification strategies related to fixing subsets of variables at particular values. The authors' preceding Part I study demonstrated how to improve such approaches by new inequalities that dominate those previously proposed. In Part II, the authors review the fundamental concepts underlying weighted pseudo cuts for generating guiding inequalities, including the use of target objective strategies. Building on these foundations, this paper develops a more advanced approach for generating the target objective based on exploiting the mutually reinforcing notions of reaction and resistance. The authors demonstrate how to produce new inequalities by "mining" reference sets of elite solutions to extract characteristics these solutions exhibit in common. Additionally, a model embedded memory is integrated to provide a range of recency and frequency memory structures for achieving goals associated with short term and long term solution strategies. Finally, supplementary linear programming models that exploit the new inequalities for intensification and diversification are proposed.

Chapter 3

Ender Özcan, University of Nottingham, UK
Mustafa Mısır, Yeditepe University, Turkey
Gabriela Ochoa, University of Nottingham, UK
Edmund K. Burke, University of Nottingham, UK

Hyper-heuristics can be identified as methodologies that search the space generated by a finite set of low level heuristics for solving search problems. An iterative hyper-heuristic framework can be thought of as requiring a single candidate solution and multiple perturbation low level heuristics. An initially generated complete solution goes through two successive processes (heuristic selection and move acceptance) until a set of termination criteria is satisfied. A motivating goal of hyper-heuristic research is to create automated techniques that are applicable to a wide range of problems with different characteristics. Some previous studies show that different combinations of heuristic selection and move acceptance as hyper-heuristic components might yield different performances. This study investigates whether learning heuristic selection can improve the performance of a great deluge based hyper-heuristic using an examination timetabling problem as a case study.

Chapter 4

Ahmed Mellouli, University of Sfax, Tunisia
Faouzi Masmoudi, University of Sfax, Tunisia
Imed Kacem, University Paul Verlaine - Metz, LITA, France
Mohamed Haddar, University of Sfax, Tunisia

In this paper, the authors present a hybrid genetic approach for the two-dimensional rectangular guillotine oriented cutting-stock problem. In this method, the genetic algorithm is used to select a set of cutting patterns while the linear programming model permits one to create the lengths to produce with each cutting pattern to fulfill the customer orders with minimal production cost. The effectiveness of the hybrid genetic approach has been evaluated through a set of instances which are both randomly generated and collected from the literature.

Chapter 5

Dennis Weyland, Istituto Dalle Molle di Studi sull'Intelligenza Artificiale (IDSIA), Switzerland

In recent years a lot of novel (mostly naturally inspired) search heuristics have been proposed. Among those approaches is Harmony Search. After its introduction in 2000, positive results and improvements over existing approaches have been reported. In this paper, the authors give a review of the developments of Harmony Search during the past decade and perform a rigorous analysis of this approach. This paper compares Harmony Search to the well-known search heuristic called Evolution Strategies. Harmony Search is a special case of Evolution Strategies in which the authors give compelling evidence for the thesis that research in Harmony is fundamentally misguided. The overarching question is how such a method could be inaccurately portrayed as a significant innovation without confronting a respectable challenge of its content or credentials. The authors examine possible answers to this question, and implications for evaluating other procedures by disclosing the way in which limitations of the method have been systematically overlooked.

Chapter 6

Recently a paper was published which claims "harmony search is equivalent to evolution strategies and because the latter is not popular currently, the former has no future. Also, research community was misguided by the former's disguised novelty." This paper is written to rebut the original paper's claims by saying 1) harmony search is different from evolution strategies because each has its own uniqueness, 2) performance, rather than novelty, is an algorithm's survival factor, and 3) the original paper was biased to mislead into a predefined conclusion. Also, the shortcomings of current review system, citation system, and funding system are briefly mentioned.

Chapter 7

Metaheuristic algorithms will gain more and more popularity in the future as optimization problems are increasing in size and complexity. In order to record experiences and allow project to be replicated, a standard process as a methodology for designing and implementing metaheuristic algorithms is necessary. To the best of the authors' knowledge, no methodology has been proposed in literature for this purpose. This paper presents a Design and Implementation Methodology for Metaheuristic Algorithms, named DIMMA. The proposed methodology consists of three main phases and each phase has several steps in which activities that must be carried out are clearly defined in this paper. In addition, design and implementation of tabu search metaheuristic for travelling salesman problem is done as a case study to illustrate applicability of DIMMA.

Chapter 8

Particle Swarm Optimization (PSO) is one of the most effective metaheuristics algorithms, with many successful real-world applications. The reason for the success of PSO is the movement behavior, which allows the swarm to effectively explore the search space. Unfortunately, the original PSO algorithm is only suitable for single objective optimization problems. In this paper, three movement strategies are discussed for multi-objective PSO (MOPSO) and popular test problems are used to confirm their effectiveness. In addition, these algorithms are also applied to solve the engineering design and portfolio optimization problems. Results show that the algorithms are effective with both direct and indirect encoding schemes.

Many real-world problems are dynamic and require an optimization algorithm that is able to continuously track a changing optimum over time. In this paper, a new multiagent algorithm is proposed to solve dynamic problems. This algorithm is based on multiple trajectory searches and saving the optima found to use them when a change is detected in the environment. The proposed algorithm is analyzed using the Moving Peaks Benchmark, and its performances are compared to competing dynamic optimization algorithms on several instances of this benchmark. The obtained results show the efficiency of the proposed algorithm, even in multimodal environments.

This paper presents the optimal design of a switched current sigma delta modulator. The Multi-objective Particle Swarm Optimization technique is adopted to optimize performances of the embryonic cell forming the modulator, that is, a class AB grounded gate switched current memory cell. The embryonic cell was optimized regarding to its main performances such as sampling frequency and signal to noise ratio. The optimized memory cell was used to design the switched current modulator which operates at a 100 MHz sampling frequency and the output signal spectrum presents a 45.75 dB signal to noise ratio.

This paper discusses a particular "packing" problem, namely the two dimensional strip packing problem, where a finite set of objects have to be located in a strip of fixed width and infinite height. The variant studied considers regular items, rectangular to be precise, that must be packed without overlap, not allowing rotations. The objective is to minimize the height of the resulting packing. In this regard, the authors present a local search algorithm based on the well-known tabu search metaheuristic. Two important components of the presented tabu search strategy are reinforced in attempting to include problem knowledge. The fitness function incorporates a measure related to the empty spaces, while the diversification relies on a set of historically "frozen" objects. The resulting reinforced tabu search approach is evaluated on a set of well-known hard benchmark instances and compared with state-of-the-art algorithms.

The authors present an experimental investigation of tabu search (TS) to solve the 3-coloring problem (3-COL). Computational results reveal that a basic TS algorithm is able to find proper 3-colorings for random 3-colorable graphs with up to 11000 vertices and beyond when instances follow the uniform or equipartite well-known models, and up to 1500 vertices for the hardest class of flat graphs. This study also validates and reinforces some existing phase transition thresholds for 3-COL.

In graph theory, a graceful labeling of a graph $G = (V, E)$ with n vertices and m edges is a labeling of its vertices with distinct integers between 0 and m inclusive, such that each edge is uniquely identified by the absolute difference between its endpoints. In this paper, the well-known graceful labeling problem of graphs is represented as an optimization problem, and an algorithm based on Ant Colony Optimization metaheuristic is proposed for finding its solutions. In this regard, the proposed algorithm is applied to different classes of graphs and the results are compared with the few existing methods inside of different literature.

The use of Evolutionary Algorithms to perform data reduction tasks has become an effective approach to improve the performance of data mining algorithms. Many proposals in the literature have shown that Evolutionary Algorithms obtain excellent results in their application as Instance Selection and Instance Generation procedures. The purpose of this paper is to present a survey on the application of Evolutionary Algorithms to Instance Selection and Generation process. It will cover approaches applied to the enhancement of the nearest neighbor rule, as well as other approaches focused on the improvement of the models extracted by some well-known data mining algorithms. Furthermore, some proposals developed to tackle two emerging problems in data mining, Scaling Up and Imbalance Data Sets, also are reviewed.

In studies of genetic algorithms, evolutionary computing, and ant colony mechanisms, it is recognized that the higher-order forms of collective intelligence play an important role in metaheuristic computing and computational intelligence. Collective intelligence is an integration of collective behaviors of individuals in social groups or collective functions of components in computational intelligent systems. This paper presents the properties of collective intelligence and their applications in metaheuristic computing. A social psychological perspective on collected intelligence is elaborated toward the studies on the structure, organization, operation, and development of collective intelligence. The collective behaviors underpinning collective intelligence in groups and societies are analyzed via the fundamental phenomenon of the basic human needs. A key question on how collective intelligence is constrained by social environment and group settings is explained by a formal motivation/attitude-driven behavioral model. Then, a metaheuristic computational model for a generic cognitive process of human problem solving is developed. This work helps to explain the cognitive and collective intelligent foundations of metaheuristic computing and its engineering applications.

Modern metaheuristic methodologies rely on well defined neighborhood structures and efficient means for evaluating potential moves within these structures. Move mechanisms range in complexity from simple 1-flip procedures where binary variables are "flipped" one at a time, to more expensive, but more powerful, r-flip approaches where "r" variables are simultaneously flipped. These multi-exchange neighborhood search strategies have proven to be effective approaches for solving a variety of combinatorial optimization problems. In this paper, we present a series of theorems based on partial derivatives that can be readily adopted to form the essential part of r-flip heuristic search methods for Pseudo-Boolean optimization. To illustrate the use of these results, we present preliminary results obtained from four simple heuristics designed to solve a set of Max 3-SAT problems.

Chapter 17

The graph coloring problem (GCP) is a widely studied combinatorial optimization problem due to its numerous applications in many areas, including time tabling, frequency assignment, and register allocation. The need for more efficient algorithms has led to the development of several GC solvers. In this paper, the authors introduce a team of Finite Learning Automata, combined with the random walk algorithm, using Boolean satisfiability encoding for the GCP. The authors present an experimental analysis of the new algorithm's performance compared to the random walk technique, using a benchmark set containing SAT-encoding graph coloring test sets.

Chapter 18

Book-embedding of graph G involves embedding its vertices along the spine of the book and assigning its edges to pages of the book such that no two edges cross on the same page. The pagenumber of G is the minimum number of pages in a book-embedding of G. In this paper, the authors also examine the treewidth TW(G), which is the minimum k such that G is a subgraph of a k-tree. The authors then study the relationship between pagenumber and treewidth. Results show that PN(G)≤ TW(G), which proves a conjecture of Ganley and Heath showing that some known upper bounds for the pagenumber can be improved.

In this paper, simple and general Order-Up-To (OUT) models with Minimum Mean Square Error (MMSE) forecast for the AR(1) demand pattern are introduced in the control engineering perspective. Important insights about lead-time misidentification are derived from the analysis of variance discrepancy. By applying the Final Value Theorem (FVI), a final value offset (i.e., inventory drift) is proved to exist and can be measured even though the actual lead-time is known. In this regard, to eliminate the inherent offset and keep the system variances acceptable, two kinds of zero inventory drift variants based on the general OUT model are presented. The analysis of variance amplification suggests lead-times should always be estimated conservatively in variant models. The stability conditions for zero inventory drift variants are evaluated in succession and some valuable attributes of the new variants are illustrated via spreadsheet simulation under the assumption that lead-time misidentification is inevitable.

Reversible logic became a promising alternative to traditional circuits because of its applications in emerging technologies such as quantum computing, low-power design, DNA computing, or nanotechnologies. As a result, synthesis of the respective circuits is an intensely studied topic. However, most synthesis methods are limited, because they rely on a truth table representation of the function to be synthesized. In this paper, the authors present a synthesis approach that is based on Binary Decision Diagrams (BDDs). The authors propose a technique to derive reversible or quantum circuits from BDDs by substituting all nodes of the BDD with a cascade of Toffoli or quantum gates, respectively. Boolean functions containing more than a hundred of variables can efficiently be synthesized. More precisely, a circuit can be obtained from a given BDD using an algorithm with linear worst case behavior regarding run-time and space requirements. Furthermore, using the proposed approach, theoretical results known from BDDs can be transferred to reversible circuits. Experiments show better results (with respect to the circuit cost) and a significantly better scalability in comparison to previous synthesis approaches.

Preface

TOWARDS MORE EFFECTIVE METAHEURISTIC COMPUTING

1. INTRODUCTION

The engineering and business problems we face today have become more impenetrable and unstructured, making the design of a satisfactory algorithm nontrivial. Traditionally, researchers strive to formulate the problems as a mathematical model by relaxing, if necessary, hard objectives and constraints. The exact solution to this formulated version can be obtained through manipulations of mathematical programming such as integer linear programming, branch-and-bound and dynamic programming. However, due to the enumeration nature of these methods, mathematical programming techniques are limited to the applications with small problem size. As an alternative, approximation solutions are targeted by problem-specific heuristics which analyze the properties and structures of the underlying problems and greedily construct a feasible solution. The quality of the generated solution varies significantly upon problem instances, though the greedy heuristics are usually computationally fast. It has been a dilemma for the choice between the mathematical programming techniques and heuristic approaches. A notion of levering the two solution methods has created the regime of *metaheuristic* which was first coined by Fred Glover (1986). The metaheuristic approach guides the course of a heuristic to search beyond the local optimality by taking full advantage of strategic level problem solving using memory manipulations without a hassle to design problem-specific operations each time a new application shows up and still inheriting the computational efficiency from the embedded heuristic. Metaheuristic has built its foundations on multidiscipilary research findings ranging from phylogenetic evolution, sociocognition, gestalt psychology, social insects foraging, to strategic level problem solving. From a broader perspective, *nature-inspired metaheuristics* focusing on metaphors share its name with evolutionary algorithms, artificial immune systems, memetic algorithm, simulated annealing, ant colony optimization, particle swarm optimization, etc (Holland, 1975; Kirkpatrick et al., 1983; Dorigo, 1992; Kennedy & Eberhart, 1995). *Strategic level metaheuristics* incorporate higher level problem solving mechanisms from artificial intelligence relying on rules and memory. Typical renowned methods at least include tabu search, scatter search, GRASP, variable neighbourhood search (Glover, 1989; Laguna & Marti, 2003; Feo & Resende, 1995; Mladenovic & Hansen, 1997).

With technologies and conceptions emerging over the years, the development of metaheuristic has come to a new era. Researchers and practitioners intend to identify the primitive components contained in metaheuristics and try to develop the so-called hybrid metaheuristics towards more effective metaheuristic computing. In light of this, several innovations have been proposed under variable categories such as *Matheuristic, Hyper-heuristic*, and *Cyber-heuristic*. These methodologies do not stick to a particular metaheuristic method, instead, an abstract model is defined. A hybrid metaheuristic algorithm can be automatically constructed or evolved using the abstract model. These innovative ideas advance the research of metaheuristic computing into a new generation. Another desired result of the intensive research on fundamentals of metaheuristics is the provision of unified development frameworks for constructing various forms of metaheuristics. These frameworks are easy enough for practitioners to construct a main-stream metaheuristic program, and are also flexible for researchers to create a sophisticated metaheuristic algorithm.

The remainder of this chapter is organized as follows. Section 2 reviews principal metaheuristics according to the classification of nature-inspired computation vs. strategic level problem solving. In Section 3 we disclose the research trend in metaheuristics hybridizations. Section 4 presents the notion for establishing unified development frameworks for metaheuristics. Finally, conclusions are made in Section 5.

2. NATURE-INSPIRED COMPUTATION VS. STRATEGIC LEVEL PROBLEM-SOLVING

In this section we present the most important metaheuristics according to the nature-inspired computation vs. strategic level problem solving classification.

2.1 Nature-Inspired Metaheuristics

Metaheuristic algorithms based on natural metaphors are easy to describe and likely to catch the attention of wide audiences. Since the advent of evolutionary algorithms inspired by Darwinian Theory, the research of nature-inspired metaheuristics has grown at a fast speed with an overwhelming number of metaphors ranging from ants, termites, birds, fish, immune systems, bacteria, and jazz harmony, to most recent ones such as honey bees, fireflies, monkeys, and cuckoos. We briefly review some of the important ones in the following.

2.1.1 Evolutionary Algorithm

Evolutionary algorithms (EA) (Bäck, 1996) may be the earliest form of metaheuristics taking advantage of nature metaphors. The famous selection principle, survival of the fittest, from Darwinian Theory was easily introduced into computation field for evolving elite solutions of perplexing problems. The simplest form of EA proceeds as follows (see Figure 1). A population of random solutions is initiated as the gene pool. The generational cycle consisting of selection, crossover, and mutation is iterated to accomplish the genetic functions of selecting the fitter individuals for reproduction. Representative EAs have been recognized as genetic algorithm, evolutionary programming, genetic programming, and evolutionary strategy. A later form of EA called memetic algorithm embeds a local search procedure into the generational cycle such that the evolution is more directly guided towards fitter genes.

Figure 1. Summary of the EA conception

```
Initialize
    Generate the initial population at random
Repeat
    Evaluate the fitness of each individual
    Peform selection principle to create parent population
    Conduct crossover between the selected parents to produce offspring
        population
    Conduct mutation on the offspring
Until the stopping criterion is satisfied
Output the overall best individual
```

2.1.2 Ant Colony Optimization

The ant colony optimization (ACO) algorithm (Dorigo, 1992) is inspired by the research on the real ant behavior during food foraging. Ethologists observed that ants are able to construct the shortest path from their colony to the feeding source through the use of pheromone trails as follows. An ant leaves some quantities of pheromone as it walks and marks the path by a trail of this substance. The next ant will sniff the pheromone laid on different paths and choose the walking direction with a probability proportional to the amount of pheromone on it. The ant then traverses the chosen path and leaves its own pheromone. This is an autocatalytic (positive feedback) process which favors the shorter path along which more ants have previously traversed. ACO simulates this process to solve an optimization problem as summarized in Figure 2 by considering a better solution as a shorter path.

2.1.3 Particle Swarm Optimization

Kennedy and Eberhart (1995) gave the first particle swarm optimization (PSO) proposal for continuous function optimization. The theory on which the PSO is founded is *sociocognition*, which states that social cognition happens in the interactions among individuals in such a manner that each individual learns from its neighbors' behavioral models/patterns, especially from those learning experiences that are rewarded. Cognition emerges from the convergence of individuals' beliefs. PSO is also biologically inspired, drawing on the observation that a swarm of birds (or particles, using the terminology of PSO) flock synchronously, change direction suddenly, scatter and regroup iteratively, and finally perch on a target. Each individual particle benefits from the experience of its own and that of the other particles of the swarm during the foraging process. This form of social intelligence not only increases the success rate for food foraging but also expedites the process. The baseline PSO proceeds as follows. Given an optimization problem, a swarm of particles representing candidate solutions is generated at random. Each particle iteratively moves in the solution space by reference to best experiences. In the baseline PSO, a particle remembers its best position visited so far and the best position observed overall by its neighbors. Figure 3 summarizes the process of a baseline PSO.

Figure 2. Summary of the ACO conception

```
Initialize
        Encode the solution space by a connected weighted graph
        Set initial pheromone for each edge
Repeat
        For each ant do
            Randomly select a starting node
            Repeat
                Move to the next node according to the node transition rule
            Until a solution is constructed
        For each edge do
            Update the pheromone intensity using the pheromone updating rule
Until the stopping criterion is satisfied
Output the overall best solution
```

2.2 Strategic Level Problem Solving Metaheuristics

The major difference between the strategic level problem solving metaheuristics and the nature-inspired metaheuristics is that the former takes a higher degree of memory utilization. With varying forms of memory structure, purposeful strategies can be devised to enhance the balance between intensification and diversification types of search. In this section we introduce a prevailing set of strategic level problem solving metaheuristics.

2.2.1 Iterative Local Search

Iterative local search (ILS) (Tounsi & Ouis, 2008) could be the simplest strategy to target the global optimum in a given search space. ILS conducts a single-point (trajectory) search strategy which iteratively performs local search at different starting solution chosen strategically. Figure 4 summarizes the

Figure 3. Summary of the PSO conception

```
Initialize
        Generate a swarm of particles at random
Repeat
        Evaluate the fitness of each particle
        Determine the personal best position visited so far by each particle
        Determine the best position visited so far by the particle's neighbors
        Update particles' positions by reference to best experiences
Until the stopping criterion is satisfied
Output the overall best solution
```

conception of ILS. The home base keeps track of the local search region of which the local optimum will be sought by a local search procedure. Once the local optimum is identified, it is compared to the current home base in order to decide the next region of interest according to an acceptance function. The acceptance function can be designed in variable forms, such as: (1) always accept the local optimum as the new home base, (2) accept the local optimum as the new home base if it's better than the current home base, and (3) conditionally accept the local optimum according to the Metropolitan criterion. The Restarting feature of the ILS is an important strategy that is the central idea adopted in recent strategic level problem solving metaheuristics.

2.2.2 Tabu Search

"Tabu" comes from Tongan, a language of Polynesia, where it indicates things that cannot be touched because they are sacred, and the word now means prohibition. Tabu search (TS) (Glover, 1989) forbids the reverse search to solutions already visited. TS starts with an initial solution configuration chosen at random, and then moves iteratively from one configuration to another until a given stopping criterion is satisfied. At each iteration, a set of candidate moves are considered and thus identify a neighborhood of the current configuration. When a move is taken this move is recorded in the tabu list and will not be reversed in next few iterations. Glover pointed out that there is no value in choosing a poor move except for avoiding a visited path being re-examined. Hence, all candidate moves are sorted in decreasing order according to the quality of their resulting solutions, and one could execute the best nontabu move or the best tabu move that meets the aspiration level and consider the resulting solution as the new current configuration. Upon termination, the best configuration visited overall is considered as the best solution. The conception of TS is illustrated in Figure 5.

2.2.3 Greedy Randomized Adaptive Search Procedure

Greedy randomized adaptive search procedure (GRASP) (Feo & Resende, 1995) is a restart or iterative search process, where each iteration consists of two phases: greedy randomized construction phase and local search phase (see Figure 6). The greedy randomized construction phase starts with an empty solution and incrementally constructs the solution by repeatedly adding an element selected from the restricted

Figure 4. Summary of the ILS conception

Initialize
    Generate an initial solution at random
    Set the home base optimum to the initial solution
Repeat
    Apply a local search on the current solution and return a local optimum
    Determine the new home base according to an acceptance function
    Generate a new solution based on the home base
Until the stopping criterion is satisfied
Output the overall best solution

candidate list (RCL) which stores the elements whose insertion would cause an increment cost under a quality restriction criterion α, where $\alpha = 0$ corresponds to a pure greedy selection (i.e., the element with the minimal increment cost is always selected), and $\alpha = 1$ is equivalent to a random solution construction (any element without destroying the solution feasibility can be selected). In the local search phase, the neighborhood of the solution obtained from the greedy randomized construction phase is investigated until a local minimum is found. The two phases are restarted repetitively until a stopping criterion is met. Upon termination, the best overall solution is kept as the final result.

3. METAHEURISTICS HYBRIDIZATIONS

The obvious advantage of hybridizing metaheuristics is the potential for enhancing the intensification/ diversification synergy and improving the selection for regions to be explored in the course of the search. Often, hybrid algorithms exhibit better performance when solving complex problems, such as the optimization of difficult multimodal functions. These mechanisms are mainly combinations of using metaheuristics, low-level heuristics, mathematical programming techniques, direct search methods, etc.

Many successful metaheuristics hybridizations have been proposed. The capability in enhancing exploitation search has made direct search methods as popular alternatives to be combined with metaheuristics. Hedar and Fukushima (2006) proposes the Directed Tabu Search (DTS) method by employing the Nelder & Mead Method to intensify the search in the promising areas identified by the tabu search. They have shown the superiority of DTS over several TS variants on a set of benchmark test functions. Vaz and Vicente (2007) introduces a hybridization of pattern search (another form of direct search) with PSO. The pattern search is used to improve the best particle in the swarm with a length-decreasing mesh structure.

Another viable thinking is to create a hybridization by marrying metaheuristic methods with mathematical programming techniques. The motivation is that metaheuristics are good at exploring large space

Figure 5. Summary of the TS conception

```
Initialize
        Encode an initial solution into a configuration
        Set the tabu list (TL) to empty
Repeat
        Generate a candidate list (CL) of neighbors by applying the move
                function to the current configuration
        Sort the members contained in CL according to solution quality
        Choose from the CL the best nontabu neighbor or the best tabu
                neighbor that satisfies the aspiration criterion
        Replace the current configuration by the selected neighbor
        Tally the performed move into TL with a tabu tenure
Until the stopping criterion is satisfied
Output the overall best solution
```

Figure 6. Summary of the GRASP conception

```
Repeat
    //Greedy randomized construction phase//
    Repeat
        Establish an RCL which stores the solution elements whose insertion
        would cause an increment cost satisfying a quality restriction criterion α
        Insert an element randomly selected from the RCL into the current partial
        solution
    Until a complete solution is obtained

    //Local search phase//
    Investigate the neighborhood of the solution obtained from the previous phase
        until a local minimum is found
Until the stopping criterion is satisfied
Output the overall best solution
```

and identifying promising regions or directions where the global optimum might exist and mathematical programming techniques are efficient and effective in solving structured problems with small search regions. Plateau et al. (2002) hybridized path relinking technique with the interior point method for solving 0–1 linear programs. It is seen in Backer et al. (2000) that the constraint programming is combined with tabu search to tackle the vehicle routing problem. Both references indicated the significant benefit of this model-based metaheuristic framework.

Multiple metaheuristics can cooperatively work in a framework to create synergism. Talbi and Bachelet (2006) proposes the COSEARCH approach which manages the cooperation of tabu search and a genetic algorithm for solving large scale instances of the quadratic assignment problem (QAP). Wang et al. (2007) enhances the diversification capability of PSO by setting the less fit attributes contained in the global best solution as tabu-active and repelling the particles from the tabu area. Shen et al. (2008) proposes an approach called HPSOTS which enables the PSO to leap over local optima by restraining the particle movement based on the use of tabu conditions.

Among the many possible plans for creating hybridizations, three emerging frameworks, namely, Matheuristics, Hyper-heuristics, and Cyber-heuristics, have attracted a broad attention from the research community. We highlight the features of each framework in the following sections.

3.1 Matheuristics

From the perspective of history, there seems to be a departure between the development of mathematical programming and metaheuristics. At one end, mathematical programming techniques (e.g., primal and dual forms, Lagrangean method, branch-and-bound, dynamic programming, linear/nonlinear programming, constraint programming, goal programming) can derive exact solutions of underlying problems; however, they are constrained to the applications that involve small or moderately sized problems. At the other end, metaheuristic techniques (e.g., TS, ACO, PSO, GRASP) trade the solution quality to run time, and thus they are able to report near-optimal solutions in acceptable times. Only few literature references have disclosed that the knowledge from mathematical programming can be integrated into metaheuristics, and few attempts have been intended to incorporate metaheuristic components into the mathematical programming framework. However, a notion of *mathematical programming aware metaheuristic* (matheuristic) proposed recently has shown that it may be beneficial to marry the two paradigms. On the one hand, the derived intermediate solutions by mathematical programming techniques can be used to help metaheuristics handle complex constraints and reduce the search space. On the other hand, the mechanism of metaheuristics, if appropriately embedded into the framework of mathematical programming, can expedite the process of locating promising regions (e.g., by deriving a better bound for cutting).

A type of matheuristic methodology is to decompose the given problem into several restricted subordinate problems, and to solve each subordinate problem by using a mathematical programming approach. This form of "meta-exact" method not only takes full advantage of mathematical programming to solve the subordinate problems to optimality but also relies on the diversification capability of metaheuristics to well explore the large problem space. In a similar vein, the composition can be done by using a mathematical programming model to define the neighborhood (search corridor) of the incumbent solution of focus to the mastering metaheuristic algorithm. Another type of matheuristic methodology is to employ metaheuristic scheme as the column generation and cut generation in the branch and cut framework. The metaheuristic techniques are in general more efficient and effective in finding an initial feasible solution than classic mathematical programming approaches, thus having an opportunity to find a better branching variable and quality bound.

A number of successful applications for Matheuristics have been reported. Glover and Hanafi (2010) exploits the advantages of using metaheuristic methods as supplements to classical mixed integer programming (MIP) approaches. It indicates the ways for generating inequalities in reference to target solutions and target objectives to supplement the basic functions of metaheuristic methods as evidenced by the experience of applying classical MIP approaches. It also focuses on supplementary linear programming model embedding these inequalities in special intensification and diversification processes and proposes more advanced approaches for generating the target objectives. Plateau et al. (2002) hybridized interior point processes and metaheuristics for solving 0–1 linear programs. The interior points generated are combined by a path relinking template. Computational experiments are reported on 0–1 multiconstraint knapsack problems. Backer et al. (2000) combines constraint programming with several meta-heuristics ranging from a simple tabu search to guided local search and applies the technique to vehicle routing problems. The experimental result manifests significant benefit. Mostaghim et al. (2006) combines linear programming technique with PSO to solve continuous optimization with linear constraints. They first compute the basic feasible solutions through linear programming and use these solutions as the initial swarm of particles. A random set of feasible solutions (particles) are used to update the particles so that they never get infeasible. Talbi (2002) proposes a taxonomy of hybrid metaheuristics which also claims an emerging trend in developing a generic hybrid that combines exact algorithms with metaheuristics. Croce et al. (2011) presents a matheuristic procedure based on integer programming formulation to deal with the total completion time 2-machines flow shop problem. Puchinger and Raidl (2005) compiles a comprehensive survey discussing different state-of-the-art approaches of combining mathematical programming techniques and metaheuristics to solve combinatorial optimization problems. It introduced several works disclosing the usefulness and strong potential of the research direction of matheuristics.

3.2 Hyper-Heuristic

Denzinger et al. first coined the term Hyper-heuristic in 1997. Hyper-heuristic is an abstract model that describes how to select, combine, or generate more primitive heuristics to create an effective solution method for the given type of problems (Cowling et al., 2001; Burke et al., 2003; Özcan et al., 2008). It is thus representing a class of algorithms instead of a single one. The abstract model will generate a metaheuristic that is able to adapt to the characteristics of the given problem class. In conception, a set of feasible heuristics (constructive or perturbative) are identified and implemented. Then a learning engine would repeatedly generate higher-level heuristics by selecting or combining the primitive ones. Each produced higher-level heuristic is evaluated by performing to solve a training class of problems. The performance evaluation is then used to update the selection or combination probabilities. As a result, Hyper-heuristic can be thought of a heuristic for choosing heuristics, and it works in the heuristics space as a contrary to metaheuristic which usually works in the solution space of the problem at hand.

Hyper-heuristic can be performed in either macro-level or micro-level. The macro-level Hyper-heuristic automatically selects or combines known heuristics that were already designed for solving the given class of problems, while the micro-level Hyper-heuristic generates a generic new heuristic by working on the space of primitive components of known heuristics. The Hyper-heuristic model can be implemented using machine learning approaches (e.g., C4.5 and reinforcement learning) or evolutionary computation techniques (e.g., genetic programming and tabu search). It is not necessary to know intensive knowledge about the problem domain for constructing a Hyper-heuristic because the domain knowledge is encapsulated in the selected or combined heuristics.

Figure 7 shows an abstract model using Hyper-heuristic. The process repeatedly selects a pre-implemented heuristic element E_i according to an estimate of probability $p_i = \vartheta(s, E_i)$ for performing element E_i at a given state s. The state is then changed to a new state by $s' = \delta(s, E_i)$ as a consequence of the performed heuristics. The selection of the element can be practiced in various ways. The *first-best* scheme chooses the first element that leads to an improvement on the value of the estimate of merit. The *overall-best* scheme selects the element that gives the best value of the estimate of merit. *Probability* scheme associates each element with a selection probability based on the estimate of merit. *Random* scheme simply chooses an arbitrary element without biased probability. The *hybrid* scheme combines multiple alternatives above noted.

We have observed a number of successful applications for Hyper-heuristic. Cano-Belmán et al. (2010) proposes a scatter search based hyper-heuristic for addressing an assembly-line sequencing problem with work overload minimization. In the low-level, the procedure makes use of priority rules through a constructive procedure. In the strategic-level, the scatter search is used to select most suitable low-level heuristics to construct a new heuristics. Experimental results show that the proposed hyper-heuristics overcomes existing heuristics. Ouelhadj and Petrovic (2010) investigates the cooperation between low-level heuristics within a hyper-heuristic framework. Low-level heuristics perform local search through the same solution space, and the cooperative hyper-heuristic makes use of a pool of the solutions of the low-level heuristics for the overall selection of the low-level heuristics and the exchange of solutions. The experiment results show that the cooperative hyper-heuristics outperforms sequential hyper-heuristics. Burke et al. (2003) evaluates a hyper-heuristic approach on various instances of two distinct timetabling and rostering problems. The strategic-level hyper-heuristics selects low-level heuristics based on the reinforcement learning framework. A tabu list of heuristics is also maintained which pre-

Figure 7. An abstract model of Hyper-heuristic

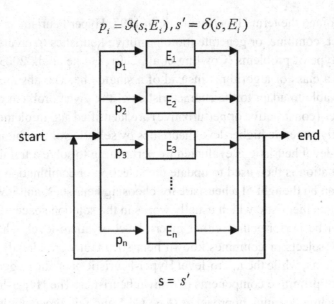

$$p_i = \vartheta(s, E_i), s' = \delta(s, E_i)$$

vents certain heuristics from being chosen at certain times during the search. The proposed hyper-heuristics is capable of producing solutions that are competitive with those obtained using state-of-the-art problem-specific techniques. Özcan et al. (2010) proposes a hyper-heuristic framework which combines successive stages of heuristic selection and move acceptance. The heuristic selection is automatically controlled by the reinforcement learning technique, while the great deluge is employed to implement the acceptance function of the solution move.

3.3 Cyber-Heuristic

Before the mid-1990 most nature-inspired metaheuristics made use of metaphors for combining solutions. But today there is a major emphasis to generate new solutions using high-level problem-solving strategies. These strategies may involve complex neighborhood concepts, memory structure, and adaptive search prinicples, mainly drawn from the field of Tabu Search. The reason for this paradigm shift is that although natural metaphors are useful to describe the rationale of solution reproduction, it may create a biased perspective about preferred forms of methods and also cause valuable alternative strategies to be overlooked.

The aim of developing Cyber-heuristic algorithms is to marry strategic-level problem solving metaheuristic approaches with nature-inspired metaheuristics to create additional benefits that cannot be obtained using either one of them alone. The adjective "Cyber" emphasizes the connection between the nature-inspired metaheuristics and the intelligent learning provided by the Scatter Search /Path Relinking (SS/PR) components, which in turn draw upon the adaptive memory programming suite. Following this vein, a number of metaheuristics hybridizations can be developed such as Cyber-EA, Cyber-ACO, Cyber-PSO, etc.

Omran (2011) edited a special issue on Scatter Search and Path Relinking methods which addresses the contributions of SS/PR components for swarm methods. The contrasting features of the two parties are that SS/PR utilizes systematic solution construction rather than using randomization, and that SS/PR employs adaptive memory strategies to select influencial solutions instead of drawing metaphors from nature. This difference creates a potential to marry them together and achieve synergism. Several successful hybridizations of SS/PR and swarm methods were proposed in this special issue, searving a good reference for further extensions.

Yin et al. (2010) introduces the Cyber Swarm Algorithm which gives more substance to the PSO metaphors by adapting them to refer to social interactions among humans as well as interactions among lower organisms. The conception of the Cyber Swarm Algorithm is summarized as follows. In this algorithm, the social learning of a particle is not restricted to the interaction with the previous best of its neighbors but instead, the learning is involved with members from a dynamically maintained reference set, a notion from Scatter Search, containing the best solutions found overall in history by reference to quality and diversity. The use of dynamic social network can provide more fertile information in guidance than the static social network. Path relinking diversification strategies are introduced to locate quality solutions that are diverse in various ways from those seen in the normal search course.

4. UNIFIED DEVELOPMENT FRAMEWORK

As most metaheuristics and their hybrids are described by an abstract model, it would be beneficial to create a metaheuristics development framework to assist researchers and practitioners to develop a metaheuristic algorithm customized to their underlying problems. We observed a number of program callable libraries provided by relevant research centers and institutes. Primitive functions and operators for varying metaheuristics were implemented and the users only need to define their problem and construct the desired solution method.

Among others, GAlib (Wall, 1996) is a framework for developing genetic algorithms. MAFRA (Krasnogor & Smith, 2000) allows the users to insert a local search procedure into an evolutionary algorithm, resulting in a memetic algorithm. Hotframe (Fink, Voss, & Woodruff, 1999) is for implementing trajectory-based (single solution) evolutionary algorithms. iOpt (Voudouris et al. 2001) is a framework for genetic algorithm and extended hybrid approaches. CIlib (Cloete, Engelbrecht, & Pampar, 2008) is a callable library for constructing many swarm-based and evolutionary algorithms. Particle Swarm Center (http://www.particleswarm.info/Programs.html) contains a number of useful sources for obtaining variable versions of Particle Swarm Optimization. MetaYourHeuristic (http://intelligence.im.ncnu.edu.tw) can facilitate flexible course of metaheuristic construction, including GA, ACO, PSO, SA, TS, SS, GRASP, and Hyper-heuristics. ParadiseEO (http://paradiseo.gforge.inria.fr) can handle multiobjective optimization problems and KanGAL (http://www.iitk.ac.in/kangal/codes.shtml) provides source codes for single and multiobjective GAs.

Yaghini et al. (2010) proposed a framework called DIMMA for standardizing the design, implementation, and evaluation of variable metaheuristic algorithms. From the perspective of software engineering, DIMMA divides the time axis of metaheuristics development into three phases, initialization, blueprint, and construction. Each phase requires various domains of disciplines, such as problem definition, heuristic strategies and components, parameter optimization, performance testing metrics, etc.

A general conceptual diagram for a unified development framework of metaheuristic algorithms can be depicted in Figure 8. There are four main components constituting this flexible framework. The *problem characterization* component allows the user to describe the addressed problem in a documentary and then to define the problem according to a formal definition language such as AMPL and GAMS. This could be nontrivial because the addressed problem may have more than one possible formulation and the merit of each formulation should be evaluated with the used (meta)heuristic method and the employed solution configuration, and one needs to conduct a design of experiment (DOE) approach in order to seek a good combination.

The *callable library* component contains computation procedures and operations that are frequently used in variable mathematical programming techniques and (meta)heuristic methods. Useful mathematical programming techniques include linear programming, branch and bound, dynamic programming, constraint programming, and the like. The common core procedures and operations used in many (meta) heuristics involve initialization heuristics, neighborhood search heuristics, solution selection, information sharing, solution combination, solution improvement, adaptive memory strategy, constraint handling, diversity control, among others. Moreover, the solution configuration representation is another matter of concern. The formulated problem is not restricted to a fixed solution configuration. The solution may appear in a form of array, tree, path, or any particular graph. Different solution configurations would affect the selection of applied (meta)heuristics.

The *interface* component plays a central role in this development framework. First, it separates the framework into three levels, namely, the problem abstract level, solution operation level, and system performance level. Each level is transparent to the others. In other words, the modification of codes in any level would not affect those in the rest of the framework. Second, the interface component encapsu-

Figure 8. Unified development framework of metaheuristic algorithms

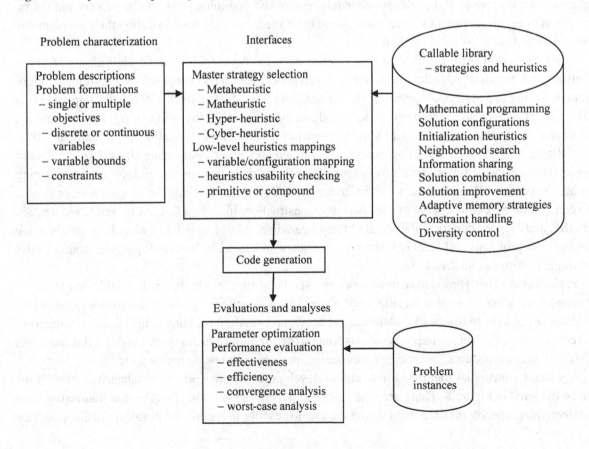

lates high-level problem solving strategies which purposefully organize the procedures and operations called from the library. For instance, a Metaheuristic strategy will require the user to specify the values of appropriate parameters for calling the procedures and operations of the indicated method (GA, SA, TS, SS, etc.) A Matheuristic strategy may activate a problem decomposition technique and calls the linear programming procedure to solve the subordinate problem. Hyper-heuristic strategy usually needs to specify a heuristic selection method and a function to decide whether to accept the selected heuristic. The heuristic selection method ranges from random selection, performance proportional, rank truncation, to any metaheuristics and machine learning techniques. The criteria used by the acceptance function include accept all, accept on solution improvement, accept on Metropolitan criterion, to name a few. The Cyber-heuristic strategy should indicate the nature-inspired metaheuristic method as the inhabited and the embedding search strategies introduced in the Scatter Search and Path Relinking (SS/PR) template. Third, the interface component deals with the mapping between solution feasibility and operation applicability. As previously mentioned, there may exist more than one solution configuration form for a given problem formulation. Some configurations may be easier to handle the solution constraints and in essence reduce the search space. The low-level heuristic operations are usually dependent on the problem constraints and the solution configurations. The applicability of various heuristics should be taken into account in anticipation of the interface mapping selection. Another issue is the selection for primitive or compound operations for construction and perturbation of the solution at hand. There is yet no theoretic or empirical proof showing that either the compound operations are favorable or individual primitive operations are prevailing. Further, there could exist some correlations between the operations employed in the same framework. Some operations may be preferably performed in a sequence, but some operations could deteriorate the performance if they are bound in the same method. The optimization problems having similar properties in the objectives, variables, and constraints may benefit from similar patterns in adopting the heuristic operations. Finally, all viable interface mappings are evaluated using the DOE approach and the one with the best performance is realized.

The *evaluations and analyses* component provides a systematic way of deciding the final appropriate form of the established metaheuristic algorithm. One should evaluate and analyze the strengths and weaknesses of each mapping between interested problem formulations, solution configurations, and applied heuristics. For a tentative mapping, a sequence of experiments is advised. The parameter optimization experiment evaluates the mapping on an orthogonal set of parameter value combinations and analyzes the result with appropriate statistical tests. To obtain good generalization of the developed metaheuristic algorithm, a representative set of problem instances should be prepared and experimented with. The performance evaluation experiment then proceeds with the best parameter values identified in the previous phase and is conducted with a suite of performance metrics such as effectiveness, efficiency, convergence, and worst-case analyses. The effectiveness evaluation asserts the quality of the objective value obtained by the applied metaheuristics. One can compare the objective value obtained by competing metaheuristics given the same stopping criterion. Another popular measure for effectiveness is, the number of times a compared metaheuristic algorithm can produce a solution satisfying a target level. The efficiency analysis measures the computational time consumed by the metaheuristics to reach the target objective value. Since metaheuristics usually involve randomization, some statistics (mean, standard deviation, minimum, maximum, median) on the computational times across a larger number of repetitive nuns are favorable. The convergence of the tested metaheuristic algorithm can be analyzed by measuring the information gain during successions of iterations. As the number of iterations increases, the metaheuristic algorithm collects more information through exploration of the solution space and gradually resorts to some promising regions. The information entropy or variation metrics are suitable for analyzing the convergence. To provide a good Quality of Service (QoS), it is crucial to analyze the worst optimal performance we can obtain using the applied metaheuristics with various numbers of repetitive runs. As such different levels of quality guarantee can be facilitated.

More advanced schemes for selecting the appropriate mapping can be implemented based on self-adaption or meta-evolution. The space of variable mappings is explored using machine learning techniques or metaheuristic computing methods, while for each tentative mapping the principles of the implied method are used to guide the search for optimal solutions.

5. CONCLUSION

Many real-world problems are unstructured or semi-structured, making the design of a satisfactory algorithm nontrivial. Metaheuristic algorithms have emerged as viable solution methods for solving the problems to which the traditional mathematical programming and heuristics are ill-suited. The metaheuristic approach guides the course of a heuristics to search beyond the local optimality by taking full advantage of nature metaphores or problem-solving strategies. With our recent survey on metaheuristic algorithms, this chapter discloses two research trends that might make metaheuristics more effective. The first trend constitutes various proposals of metaheurisitcs hybridizations. Matheuristics, hyper-heuristics, and cyber-heuristics are notable among others. The second trend is the birth of many metaheuristics development frameworks. We present a unified development framework as a general conception for varying models. It would be beneficial for both practitioners and researchers to develop their metaheuristic algorithms by reference to this unified development model such that many possible plans for formulating problem, selecting search strategy, and performance evaluation can be systematically explored. The chapter has shown the great potentials of metaheuristic computing and invited more fruitful strategies from other domains to be injected into this ever exciting field.

Peng-Yeng Yin
National Chi Nan University

REFERENCES

Bäck, T. (1996). *Evolutionary Algorithms in Theory and Practice: Evolution Strategies, Evolutionary Programming, Genetic Algorithms*. Oxford Univ. Press.

Backer, B. D., Furnon, V., Shaw, P., Kilby, P., & Prosser, P. (2000). Solving vehicle routing problems using constraint programming and metaheuristics. *Journal of Heuristics*, 6(4), 501–523. doi:10.1023/A:1009621410177

Burke, E. K., Kendall, G., & Soubeiga, E. (2003). A tabu-search hyper-heuristic for timetabling and rostering. *Journal of Heuristics*, 9(6), 451–470. doi:10.1023/B:HEUR.0000012446.94732.b6

Cano-Belmán, J., Ríos-Mercado, R. Z., & Bautista, J. (2010). A scatter search based hyper-heuristic for sequencing a mixed-model assembly line. *Journal of Heuristics, 16,* 749–770. doi:10.1007/s10732-009-9118-2

Cloete, T., Engelbrecht, A. P., & Pampar, G. (2008). *CIlib: A collaborative framework for computational intelligence algorithms – part I,* IJCNN 2008. *IEEE World Congress on Computational Intelligence.*

Cowling, P., Kendall, G., & Soubeiga, E. (2001). A Hyper-heuristic approach to scheduling a sales summit. *Lecture Notes in Computer Science, 2079,* 176–190. doi:10.1007/3-540-44629-X_11

Croce, F. D., Grosso, A., & Salassa, F. (2011). Lecture Notes in Computer Science: *Vol. 6622. A matheuristic approach for the total completion time two-machines permutation flow shop problem* (pp. 38–47).

Dorigo, M. (1992). *Optimization, learning, and natural algorithms,* Ph.D. Thesis, Dip. Elettronica e Informazione, Politecnico di Milano, Italy.

Feo, T. A., & Resende, M. G. C. (1995). Greedy randomized adaptive search procedures. *Journal of Global Optimization, 6,* 109–133. doi:10.1007/BF01096763

Fink, A., Voss, S., & Woodruff, D. L. (1999). Building reusable software components for heuristic search. In Kall, P., & Luthi, H. J. (Eds.), *Operations Research Proceedings* (pp. 210–219). Heidelberg: Springer.

Glover, F. (1986). Future paths for integer programming and links to artificial intelligence. *Computers & Operations Research, 13,* 533–549. doi:10.1016/0305-0548(86)90048-1

Glover, F. (1989). Tabu search - Part I, *ORSA J. Comput., 1,* 190–206.

Glover, F., & Hanafi, S. (2010). Metaheuristic search with inequalities and target objectives for mixed binary optimization part I: exploiting proximity. *International Journal of Applied Metaheuristic Computing, 1*(1), 1–15. doi:10.4018/jamc.2010102601

Hedar, A., & Fukushima, M. (2006). Tabu search directed by direct search methods for nonlinear global optimization. *European Journal of Operational Research, 170*(2), 329–349. doi:10.1016/j.ejor.2004.05.033

Holland, J. (1975). *Adaptation in natural and artificial systems: an introductory analysis with applications to biology, control, and artificial intelligence* (pp. 175–177). Ann Arbor: University of Michigan.

Kennedy, J., & Eberhart, R. C. (1995). Particle swarm optimization, *Proceedings of the IEEE International Conference on Neural Networks, IV,* 1942-1948.

Kirkpatrick, S., Gelatt, C., & Vecchi, M. (1983). Optimization by simulated annealing. *Science, 220,* 671–680. doi:10.1126/science.220.4598.671

Krasnogor, N., & Smith, J. (2000). MAFRA: a Java memetic algorithms framework. In Freitas, A. A., Hart, W., Krasnogor, N., & Smith, J. (Eds.), *Data Mining with Evolutionary Algorithms* (pp. 125–131). Las Vegas, NV.

Laguna, M., & Marti, R. (2003). *Scatter Search.* Boston: Kluwer Academic Publishers.

Mladenovic, N., & Hansen, P. (1997). Variable neighborhood search. *Computers & Operations Research, 24*, 1097–1100. doi:10.1016/S0305-0548(97)00031-2

Mostaghim, S., Halter, W. E., & Wille, A. (2006). Linear multi-objective particle swarm optimization, *Stigmergy optimization, 31*, 209-237.

Omran, M. (2011). Special Issue on Scatter Search and Path Relinking Methods. *International Journal of Swarm Intelligence Research, 2*(2).

Ouelhadj, D., & Petrovic, S. (2010). A cooperative hyper-heuristic search framework. *Journal of Heuristics, 16*, 835–857. doi:10.1007/s10732-009-9122-6

Özcan, E., Bilgin, B., & Korkmaz, E. E. (2008). A comprehensive analysis of hyper-heuristics. *Intelligent Data Analysis, 12*(1), 3–23.

Özcan, E., Misir, M., Ochoa, G., & Burke, E. K. (2010). A reinforcement learning - great-deluge hyper-heuristic for examination timetabling. *International Journal of Applied Metaheuristic Computing, 1*(1), 39–59. doi:10.4018/jamc.2010102603

Plateau, A., Tachat, D., & Tolla, P. (2002). A hybrid search combining interior point methods and metaheuristics for 0-1 programming. *International Transactions in Operational Research, 9*(6), 731–746. doi:10.1111/1475-3995.00385

Puchinger, J., & Raidl, G. (2005). Combining metaheuristics and exact algorithms in combinatorial optimization: a survey and classification. *Lecture Notes in Computer Science, 3562*, 41–53. doi:10.1007/11499305_5

Shen, Q., Shi, W. M., & Kong, W. (2008). Hybrid particle swarm optimization and tabu search approach for selecting genes for tumor classification using gene expression data. *Computational Biology and Chemistry, 32*(1), 52–59. doi:10.1016/j.compbiolchem.2007.10.001

Talbi, E. G. (2002). A taxonomy of hybrid metaheuristics. *Journal of Heuristics, 8*(5), 541–564. doi:10.1023/A:1016540724870

Talbi, E. G., & Bachelet, V. (2006). COSEARCH: a parallel cooperative metaheuristic. *Journal of Mathematical Modelling and Algorithms, 5*(1), 5–22. doi:10.1007/s10852-005-9029-7

Tounsi, M., & Ouis, S. (2008). An iterative local-search framework for solving constraint satisfaction problem. *Proceedings of Appl. Soft Computing, n.d.*, 1530–1535.

Vaz, A. I. F., & Vicente, L. N. (2007). A particle swarm pattern search method for bound constrained global optimization. *Journal of Global Optimization, 39*, 197–219. doi:10.1007/s10898-007-9133-5

Voudouris, C., Dorne, R., Lesaint, D., & Liret, A. (2001). iOpt: a software toolkit for heuristic search methods, In *CP '01 7th International Conference on Principles and Practice of Constraint Programming*: LNCS Vol. 2239 (pp. 716–729), Springer.

Wall, M. (1996). *GAlib: A C++ library of genetic algorithm components (Technical Report)*. USA: Mechanical Engineering Department, Massachusetts Institute of Technology.

Yaghini, M., & Kazemzadeh, M. (2010). DIMMA: a design and implementation methodology for metaheuristic algorithms – a perspective from software development. *International Journal of Applied Metaheuristic Computing, 1*(4), 57–74. doi:10.4018/jamc.2010100104

Yin, P. Y., Glover, F., Laguna, M., & Zhu, J. X. (2010). Cyber swarm algorithms – improving particle swarm optimization using adaptive memory strategies. *European Journal of Operational Research, 201*(2), 377–389. doi:10.1016/j.ejor.2009.03.035

Chapter 1
Metaheuristic Search with Inequalities and Target Objectives for Mixed Binary Optimization Part I:
Exploiting Proximity

Fred Glover
OptTek Systems, Inc., USA

Saïd Hanafi
Universite de Valenciennes, France

ABSTRACT

Recent adaptive memory and evolutionary metaheuristics for mixed integer programming have included proposals for introducing inequalities and target objectives to guide the search. These guidance approaches are useful in intensification and diversification strategies related to fixing subsets of variables at particular values, and in strategies that use linear programming to generate trial solutions whose variables are induced to receive integer values. In Part I (the present paper), we show how to improve such approaches by new inequalities that dominate those previously proposed and by associated target objectives that underlie the creation of both inequalities and trial solutions. Part I focuses on exploiting inequalities in target solution strategies by including partial vectors and more general target objectives. We also propose procedures for generating target objectives and solutions by exploiting proximity in original space or projected space. Part II of this study (to appear in a subsequent issue) focuses on supplementary linear programming models that exploit the new inequalities for intensification and diversification, and introduce additional inequalities from sets of elite solutions that enlarge the scope of these models. Part II indicates more advanced approaches for generating the target objective based on exploiting the mutually reinforcing notions of reaction and resistance. Our work in the concluding segment, building on the foundation laid in Part I, examines ways our framework can be exploited in generating target objectives, employing both older adaptive memory ideas of tabu search and newer ones proposed here for the first time.

DOI: 10.4018/978-1-4666-0270-0.ch001

1. NOTATION AND PROBLEM FORMULATION

We represent the mixed integer programming problem in the form

$$(\text{MIP}) \begin{cases} Minimize & x_0 = fx + gy \\ subject\ to & (x,y) \in Z = \{(x,y) : Ax + Dy \geq b \\ & x\ \text{int}eger \end{cases}$$

We assume that $Ax + Dy \geq b$ includes the inequalities $U_j \geq x_j \geq 0, j \in N = \{1, ..., N\}$, where some components of U_j may be infinite. The linear programming relaxation of (MIP) that results by dropping the integer requirement on x is denoted by (LP). We further assume $Ax + Dy \geq b$ includes an objective function constraint $x_0 \leq U_0$, where the bound U_0 is manipulated as part of a search strategy for solving (MIP), subject to maintaining $U_0 < x_0^*$, where x_0^* is the x_0 value for the currently best known solution x^* to (MIP).

The current paper focuses on the zero-one version of (MIP) denoted by (MIP:0-1), in which $U_j = 1$ for all $j \in N$. We refer to the LP relaxation of (MIP:0-1) likewise as (LP), since the identity of (LP) will be clear from the context,

In the following we make reference to two types of search strategies: those that fix subsets of variables to particular values within approaches for exploiting strongly determined and consistent variables, and those that make use of solution targeting procedures. As developed here, the latter solve a linear programming problem $\text{LP}(x',c')^1$ that includes the constraints of (LP) (and additional bounding constraints in the general (MIP) case) while replacing the objective function x_0 by a linear function $v_0 = c'x$. The vector x' is called a *target solution*, and the vector c' consists of integer coefficients c_j' that seek to induce assignments $x_j = x_j'$ for different variables with varying degrees of emphasis.

We adopt the convention that each instance of $\text{LP}(x', c')$ implicitly includes the (LP) objective of minimizing the function $x_0 = fx + gy$ as a secondary objective, dominated by the objective of minimizing $v_0 = c'x$, so that the true objective function consists of minimizing $\omega_0 = Mv_0 + x_0$, where M is a large positive number. As an alternative to working with ω_0 in the form specified, it can be advantageous to solve $\text{LP}(x',c')$ in two stages. The first stage minimizes $v_0 = c'x$ to yield an optimal solution $x = x''$ (with objective function value $v_0'' = c'x''$), and the second stage enforces $v_0 = v_0''$ to solve the residual problem of minimizing $x_0 = fx + gy.^2$

A second convention involves an interpretation of the problem constraints. Selected instances of inequalities generated by approaches of the following sections will be understood to be included among the constraints $Ax + Dy \geq b$ of (LP). In our definition of $\text{LP}(x', c')$ and other linear programs related to (LP), we take the liberty of representing the currently updated form of the constraints $Ax + Dy \geq b$ by the compact representation $x \in X = \{x: (x,y) \in Z\}$, recognizing that this involves a slight distortion in view of the fact that we implicitly minimize a function of y as well as x in these linear programs.[3]

To launch our investigation of the problem (MIP:0-1) we first review previous ideas for generating guiding inequalities for this problem in Section 2 and associated target objective strategies using partial vectors and more general target objectives in Section 3. We then present new inequalities in Section 4 that improve on those previously proposed. The fundamental issue of creating the target objectives that can be used to generate the new inequalities and that lead to trial solutions for (MIP: 0-1) by exploiting proximity is addressed in Section 5. Concluding remarks are given in Section 6.

2. EXPLOITING INEQUALITIES IN TARGET SOLUTION STRATEGIES

Let x' denote an arbitrary solution, and define the associated index sets

$N(x', v) = \{j \in N: x_j' = v\}$ for $v \in \{0, 1\}$, $N(x')$ = $\{j \in N: x_j' \in \{0, 1\}\}$ and $N^*(x') = \{j \in N: x_j' \in]0, 1[\}$, we have $N = N(x') \cup N^*(x')$. For any real number z, $\lceil z \rceil$ and $\lfloor z \rfloor$ respectively identify the least integer $\geq z$ and the greatest integer $\leq z$.

Define

$$\delta\left(x', x\right) = \sum_{j \in N} x_j\left(1 - x_j'\right) + x_j'\left(1 - x_j\right) \tag{1}$$

Proposition 1. Let x' denote an arbitrary binary solution. Then the inequality

$$\delta(x', x) \geq 1 \tag{1.1}$$

eliminates the assignment $x = x'$ as a feasible solution, but admits all other binary x vectors.

Proof: It is evident that $\delta(x', x) = \| x - x' \|_1 = \| x - x' \|_2$, so for all $x \neq x'$, we have $\delta(x', x) > 0$. The proposition follows from the fact that the value $\delta(x', x)$ is integer.

Remark 1: The inequality (1.1) has been used, for example, to produce 0-1 "short hot starts" for branch and bound by Spielberg and Guignard (2000) and Guignard and Spielberg (2003).

The constraint (1.1) is called *canonical cut* on the unit hypercube by Balas and Jeroslow (1972). The constraint (1.1) has also been used by Soyster et al. (1978), Hanafi and Wilbaut (2006) and Wilbaut and Hanafi (2006).

Proposition 1 has the following consequence.

Corollary 1. Let x' denote an arbitrary binary solution. Then the inequality

$$\delta(x', x) \leq n - 1 \tag{1.2}$$

eliminates the assignment $x = e - x'$ (the complement of x') as a feasible solution, but admits all other binary x vectors.

Proof: Immediate from the proof on Proposition 1, by using $e - x'$. □

We make use of solutions such as x' by assigning them the role of *target solutions*. In this approach, instead of imposing the inequality (1.1) we adopt the strategy of first seeing how close we can get to satisfying $x = x'$ by solving the LP problem[4]

LP(x'): Minimize $\{\delta(x', x): x \in X\}$

whereas earlier, $X = \{x: (x, y) \in Z\}$. We call x' the *target solution* for this problem. Let x'' denote an optimal solution to LP(x'). If the target solution x' is feasible for LP(x') then it is also uniquely optimal for LP(x') and hence $x'' = x'$, yielding $\delta(x', x'') = 0$. In such a case, upon testing x' for feasibility in (MIP:0-1) we can impose the inequality (1.1) as indicated earlier in order to avoid examining the solution again. However, in the case where x' is not feasible for LP(x'), an optimal solution x'' will yield $\delta(x', x'') > 0$ and since the distance $\delta(x, x')$ is an integer value we may impose the valid inequality

$$\delta(x, x') \geq \lceil \delta(x', x'') \rceil \tag{2.1}$$

The fact that $\delta(x', x'') > 0$ discloses that (2.1) is at least as strong as (1.1). In addition, if the solution x'' is a binary vector that differs from x', we can also test x'' for feasibility in (MIP:0-1) and then redefine $x' = x''$, to additionally append the constraint (1.1) for this new x'. Consequently, regardless of whether x'' is binary, we eliminate x'' from the collection of feasible solutions as well as obtaining an inequality (2.1) when $\delta(x', x'')$ is fractional that dominates the original inequality (1.1).

Upon generating the inequality (2.1) (and an associated new form of (1.1) if x'' is binary), we continue to follow the policy of incorporating newly generated inequalities among the constraints defining X, and hence those defining Z of (MIP:0-1). Consequently, we assure that X excludes both the original x' and the solution x''. This allows the problem LP(x') to be re-solved, either for x' as initially defined or for a new target vector (which can be also be x'' if the latter is binary), to obtain another solution x'' and a new (2.1).

Remark 2: The same observations can be made to eliminate the complement of x', i.e. ($e - x'$), by solving the following LP problem:

LP⁺(x'): Maximize ($\delta(x', x)$: $x \in X$)

Let $x^{+\prime\prime}$ denote an optimal solution to LP⁺(x'). If the complement of the target solution x' is feasible for LP⁺(x') then it is also uniquely optimal for LP⁺(x') and hence $x^{+\prime\prime} = e - x'$, yielding $\delta(x', x^{+\prime\prime}) = n$. In such a case, upon testing $e - x'$ for feasibility in (MIP:0-1) we can impose the inequality (1.2) as indicated earlier in order to avoid examining the solution again. However, in the case where $e - x'$ is not feasible for LP⁺(x'), an optimal solution $x^{+\prime\prime}$ will yield $\delta(x', x^{+\prime\prime}) < n$ and we may impose the valid inequality

$$\delta(x', x) \leq \lfloor \delta(x', x^{+\prime\prime}) \rfloor \qquad (2.2)$$

The fact that $\delta(x', x^{+\prime\prime}) < n$ discloses that (2.2) is at least as strong as (1.2).

It is worthwhile to use simple forms of tabu search memory based on recency and frequency in such processes to decide when to drop previously introduced inequalities, in order to prevent the collection of constraints from becoming unduly large. Such approaches can be organized in a natural fashion to encourage the removal of older constraints and to discourage the removal of constraints that have more recently or frequently been binding in the solutions to the LP(x') problems

produced (see Glover & Laguna, 1997; Glover & Hanafi, 2002). Older constraints can also be replaced by one or several surrogate constraints.

The strategy for generating a succession of target vectors x' plays a critical role in exploiting such a process. The feasibility pump approach of Fischetti, Glover and Lodi (2005) applies a randomized variant of nearest neighbor rounding to each non-binary solution x'' to generate the next x', but does not make use of associated inequalities such as (1.x) and (2.x). In subsequent sections we show how to identify more effective inequalities and associated target objectives to help drive such processes.

3. GENERALIZATION TO INCLUDE PARTIAL VECTORS AND MORE GENERAL TARGET OBJECTIVES

We extend the preceding ideas in two ways, drawing on ideas of parametric branch and bound and parametric tabu search (Glover, 1978, 2006a). First we consider *partial x vectors* that may not have all components x_j determined, in the sense of being fixed by assignment or by the imposition of bounds. Such vectors are relevant in approaches where some variables are compelled or induced to receive particular values, while others remain free or are subject to imposed bounds that are not binding.

Let x' denote an arbitrary solution and $J \subseteq N(x')$ define the associated set

$$F(J, x') = \{x \in [0,1]^n : x_j = x_j' \text{ for } j \in J\}$$

Let x, x' two arbitrary binary solutions and $J \subseteq N$, define

$$\delta\left(J, x', x\right) = \sum\nolimits_{j \in J} x_j\left(1 - x_j'\right) + x_j'\left(1 - x_j\right) \qquad (3)$$

Proposition 2. Let x' denote an arbitrary binary solution and $J' \subseteq N(x')$. Then the inequality

$$\delta(J', x', x) \geq 1 \qquad (3.1)$$

eliminates all solutions in $F(J', x')$ as a feasible solution, but admits all other binary x vectors.

Proof: It is evident that for all $x \in F(J', x')$, we have $\delta(J', x', x) = 0$. $\square$

Proposition 2 has the following consequence.

Corollary 2. Let x' denote an arbitrary binary solution and $J' \subseteq N(e - x')$. Then the inequality

$$\delta(J', x', x) \leq |J'| - 1 \qquad (3.2)$$

eliminates all solutions in $F(J', e - x')$ as a feasible solution, but admits all other binary x vectors.

Proof: Immediate from the proof on Proposition 2, by using $e - x'$.

We couple the target solution x' with the associated set $J' \subseteq N(x')$ to yield the problem

LP(x',J'): Minimize $(\delta(J', x', x): x \in X)$.

An optimal solution to LP(x', J'), as a generalization of LP(x'), will likewise be denoted by x''. We obtain the inequality

$$\delta(J', x', x) \geq \lceil \delta(J', x', x\text{-}'') \rceil \qquad (4.1)$$

By an analysis similar to the derivation of (2.1), we observe that (4.1) is a valid inequality, i.e., it is satisfied by all binary vectors that are feasible for (MIP:0-1) (and more specifically by all such vectors that are feasible for LP(x', J')), with the exception of those ruled out by previous examination.

Remark 3: The same observations can be made to eliminate all solutions in $F(J', e - x')$ as a feasible solution by solving the following LP problem:

LP$^+$(x',J'): Maximize $(\delta(J', x, x'): x \in X)$.

We obtain the inequality

$$\delta(J', x', x) \leq \lfloor \delta(J', x', x^{+''}) \rfloor \qquad (4.2)$$

where $x^{+''}$ is an optimal solution to LP$^+$(x', J').

In the special case where $J' = N(x')$, we have the following properties. Let $x' \in [0,1]^n$ define the associated set

$$F(x') = F(x', N(x')) = \{x \in [0,1]^n: x_j = x_j' \text{ for } j \in N(x')\}.$$

Let k be an integer satisfying $0 \leq k \leq n - |N(x')|$, the canonical hyperplane associated to the solution x', denoted $H(x', k)$ is defined by

$$H(x', k) = \{ x \in [0,1]^n: \delta(N(x'), x', x) = k\}.$$

Proposition 3. $x \in H(x', k) \cap \{0,1\}^n \Leftrightarrow \delta(x, F(x') \cap \{0,1\}^n) = k$

where $\delta(x, F) = \min\{\delta(x, y): y \in F\}$

Proof: i) Necessity: if $x \in H(x', k) \cap \{0,1\}^n$ this imply that $\delta(N(x'), x', x) = k$. Moreover if $y \in F(x') \cap \{0,1\}^n$ thus $\delta(N(x'), x', y) = 0$ which imply that $y(N(x')) = x'(N(x'))$ where $x(J) = (x_j)_{j \in J}$. Hence, we have

$$\delta(x, y) = \delta(N(x'), x, y) + \delta(N-N(x'), x, y)$$
$$= \delta(N(x'), x, x') + \delta(N-N(x'), x, y)$$
$$= k + \delta(N-N(x'), x, y) \geq k.$$

Let $y' \in \{0,1\}^n$ such that $y'(N(x')) = x'(N(x'))$ and $y'(N-N(x')) = x(N-N(x'))$. Then we have $y' \in$

$F(x')$ and $\delta(x, y') = k$. Hence, $\delta(x, F(x') \cap \{0,1\}^n)$ $= \min\{\delta(x, y): y \in F(x') \cap \{0,1\}^n \} = k$.

ii) Sufficiency: Let $y' \in F(x') \cap \{0,1\}^n$ such that $\delta(x, y') = \delta(x, F(x') \cap \{0,1\}^n) = k$. To simplify the notion let $F' = F(x') \cap \{0,1\}^n = \{x \in \{0,1\}^n: x_j = x_j'$ for $j \in N(x')\}$. Hence, we have $\delta(N\text{-}N(x'), x, F') = 0$ which implies that $\delta(N\text{-}N(x'), x, y') = 0$. Moreover if $y' \in F(x')$ we have $y'(N(x')) = x'(N(x'))$. Thus $\delta(N(x'), x, x') = k$. This implies that $x \in H(x', k) \cap \{0,1\}^n$. which completes the proof of this proposition.

In the next proposition, we state relation between half-spaces associated to the canonical hyperplanes. Let $H(x', k)$ be the half-space associated with the canonical hyperplane $H(x', k)$ defined by

$$H(x', k) = \{ x \in [0,1]^n: \delta(N(x'), x', x) \leq k\}$$

Proposition 4. Let x' and x'' be two arbitrary solutions. Then

$$H(x', k) \cup H(x'', k) \subseteq H((x' + x'')/2, k).$$

Proof: Immediate from the fact that $N(x') \subseteq N((x' + x'')/2)$ and $N(x'') \subseteq N((x' + x'')/2)$.

Proposition 5. $Co(H(x', k) \cap \{0,1\}^n) = H(x', k)$, where $Co(X)$ is the convex hull of the set X.

Proof: The inclusion $Co(H(x',k) \cap \{0,1\}^n) \subseteq H(x', k)$ is obvious for any solution x' and integer k. To prove the inclusion

$$H(x', k) \subseteq Co(H(x', k) \cap \{0,1\}^n), \qquad (5.1)$$

let $y \in H(x', k)$ and observe that $\delta(N(x'), x', y) = \delta(N(x') \cap N(y), x', y) + \delta(N(x') \cap N^*(y), x', y) = k$. Now, we show by induction the second inclusion (4.3) on $p = \delta(N(x') \cap N^*(y), x', y)$. The statement

is evident for $p = 0$. We assume that the statement is true for $\delta(N(x') \cap N^*(y), x', y) = p$. To show that it is also true for $\delta(N(x') \cap N^*(y), x', y) = p+1$, consider the subset $J \subseteq N(x') \cap N^*(y)$ such that

$$\delta\left(J, x', y\right) = \sum\nolimits_{j \in J} \delta\left(j, x', y\right) = 1 \qquad (5.2)$$

Thus we have $\delta(N(x'), x', y) = \delta(J, x', y) + \delta((N\text{-}J) \cap (N(x') \cap N^*(y)), x', y) = k$. For all $j \in J$, define the vector y^j such that

$$y^j(N\text{-}J) = y(N\text{-}J)$$
$$y^j(J\text{-}\{j\}) = x'(J\text{-}\{j\}) \text{ and} \qquad (5.3)$$
$$y^j(\{j\}) = 1 - x_j'.$$

Now we show that

$$\sum\nolimits_{j \in J} \delta\left(j, x', y\right) y^j = y. \qquad (5.4)$$

From (5.3) and (5.2), for all $q \notin J$ we have

$$\sum\nolimits_{j \in J} \delta\left(j, x', y\right) y_q^j =$$
$$y_q \sum\nolimits_{j \in J} \delta\left(j, x', y\right) y_q^j = y_q.$$

For all $q \in J$, from (5.3) and (5.2) and since $(1 - 2x_q')^2 = 1$ and $x_q'(1 - x_q') = 0$ for all $x_q' \in \{0,1\}$, we have

$$\sum\nolimits_{j \in J} \delta\left(j, x', y\right) y_q^j = \sum\nolimits_{j \in J-\{q\}} \delta\left(j, x', y\right) y_q^j +$$
$$\delta\left(q, x', y\right) y_q^q$$
$$= \sum\nolimits_{j \in J-\{q\}} \delta\left(j, x', y\right) x_q' +$$
$$\delta\left(q, x', y\right)\left(1 - x_q'\right)$$
$$= \sum\nolimits_{j \in J} \delta\left(j, x', y\right) x_q' +$$
$$\delta\left(q, x', y\right)\left(1 - 2x_q'\right)$$
$$= x_q' \sum\nolimits_{j \in J} \delta\left(j, x', y\right) +$$
$$\delta\left(q, x', y\right)\left(1 - 2x_q'\right)$$
$$= x_q' + \delta\left(q, x', y\right)\left(1 - 2x_q'\right)$$
$$= x_q' + \left(\left(1 - 2x_q'\right) y_q + x_q'\right)\left(1 - 2x_q'\right)$$
$$= \left(1 - 2x_q'\right)^2 y_q + 2x_q'\left(1 - x_q'\right)$$
$$= y_q$$

Hence y is on the convex hull of the vector y^j for $j \in J$ (see 5.4) and it is easy to see that

$$\delta(N(x') \cap N^*(y^j), x', y) = p \text{ for all } j \in J.$$

By applying the hypothesis of the induction, we conclude that each vector y^j is also on the convex hull of binary solutions in $H(x', k)$. This completes the proof of the second inclusion (5.1).

The proposition then follows from the two inclusions.

Proposition 5 is related to Theorem 1 of Balas and Jeroslow.

Let x' denote an arbitrary solution and $c \in IN^n$ define the associated set

$$F(x', c) = \{x \in [0,1]^n: c_j(x_j - x_j') = 0 \text{ for } j \in N(x')\}$$

Let x, x° be two arbitrary binary solutions and let c be an integer vector ($c \in IN^n$). Define

$$\delta\left(c, x', x\right) = \sum_{j \in N} c_j\left(x_j\left(1 - x_j'\right) + x_j'\left(1 - x_j\right)\right).$$

Remark 4: $\delta(e, x', x) = \| x - x' \|_1 = \| x - x' \|_2$

$$B(c) = \{x \in [0,1]^n: c_j x_j (1 - x_j) = 0\}.$$

Remark 5: $\delta(c, x', x) = \delta(J', x', x)$ if $c_j = 1$ if $j \in J'$ otherwise $c_j = 0$.

Remark 6: $B(e) = \{0,1\}^n$ and $B(0) = [0,1]^n$

$$C(x) = \{c \in IN^n_+: c_j x_j (1 - x_j) = 0\}.$$

Proposition 6. Let x' denote an arbitrary solution and $c \in C(x')$. Then the inequality

$$\delta(c, x', x) \geq 1 \qquad (6.1)$$

eliminates the solutions in $F(x', c)$ as a feasible solution, but admits all other binary x vectors.

The inequality

$$\delta(c, x', x) \leq ce - 1 \qquad (6.2)$$

eliminates the solutions in $F(e - x', c)$ as a feasible solution, but admits all other binary x vectors.

Proof: Immediate from the proof on Proposition 2 and Corollary 2 by by setting $J' = \{c \in N: c_j \neq 0\}$.

We couple the target solution x' with the associated vector $c \in C(x')$ to yield the two problems

LP(x', c): Minimize ($\delta(c, x', x): x \in X$).

LP$^+$(x', c): Maximize ($\delta(c, x', x): x \in X$).

An optimal solution to LP(x', c) (resp. LP$^+$(x', c)), as a generalization of LP(x') (resp. LP$^+$(x'), will likewise be denoted by x'' (resp. $x^{+''}$). Finally, we obtain the inequalities

$$\delta(c, x', x) \geq \lceil \delta(c, x', x'') \rceil \qquad (7.1)$$

$$\delta(c, x', x) \leq \lfloor \delta(c, x', x^{+''}) \rfloor \qquad (7.2)$$

4. STRONGER INEQUALITIES AND ADDITIONAL VALID INEQUALITIES FROM BASIC FEASIBLE LP SOLUTIONS

Our approach to generate inequalities that dominate those of (7) is also able to produce additional valid inequalities from related basic feasible solution to the LP problem LP(x',c), expanding the range of solution strategies for exploiting the use of target solutions. We refer specifically to the class of basic feasible solutions that may be called *y-optimal* solutions, which are dual feasible in the continuous variables y (including in y any continuous slack variables that may be added to the formulation), disregarding dual feasibility relative to the x variables. Such y-optimal solutions can be easily generated in the vicinity of an optimal LP solution by pivoting to bring one or more non-basic x variables into the basis, and then applying a restricted version of the primal simplex method that re-optimizes (if necessary) to establish dual feasibility relative only to the continuous variables, ignoring pivots that would bring x variables into the basis. By this means, instead of generating a single valid inequality from a given LP formulation such as LP(x',c), we can generate a collection of such inequalities from a series of basic feasible y-optimal solutions produced by a series of pivots to visit some number of such solutions in the vicinity of an optimal solution.

As a foundation for these results, we assume x'' (or more precisely, (x'', y'')) has been obtained as a y-optimal basic feasible solution to LP(x',c) by the bounded variable simplex method (see, e.g., Dantzig, 1963). By reference to the linear programming basis that produces x'', which we will call the x'' basis, define $B = \{j \in N: x_j'' \text{ is basic}\}$ and $NB = \{j \in N: x_j'' \text{ is non-basic}\}$. We subdivide NB to identify the two subsets $NB(0) = \{j \in NB: x_j'' = 0\}$, $NB(1) = \{j \in NB: x_j'' = 1\}$. These sets have no necessary relation to the sets $N'(0)$ and $N'(1)$, though in the case where x'' is an optimal basic solution[5] to LP(x',c), we would normally expect from the definition of c in relation to the target vector x' that there would be some overlap between $NB(0)$ and $N'(0)$ and similarly between $NB(1)$ and $N'(1)$.

To simplify the notation, we find it convenient to give $\delta(c, x', x)$ an alternative representation.

$$\delta(c, x', x) = c'x + cx' \text{ with } c_j' = c_j(1 - 2x_j'), j \in N$$

The new inequality that dominates (6) results by taking account of the reduced costs derived from the x'' basis. Letting rc denote the reduced cost to an arbitrary y-optimal basic feasible solution x'' for LP(x',c). Finally, to identify the new inequality, define the vector d' by

$$d' = \lfloor c - rc \rfloor$$

We then express the inequality as

$$\delta(d', x', x) \geq \lceil \delta(d', x', x'') \rceil \tag{8}$$

We first show that (8) is valid when generated from an arbitrary y-optimal basic feasible solution, and then demonstrate in addition that it dominates (7) in the case where (8) is a valid inequality (i.e., where (8) is derived from an optimal basic feasible solution). By our previously stated convention, it is understood that X (and (MIP:0-1)) may be modified by incorporating previously generated inequalities that exclude some binary solutions originally admitted as feasible.

Our results concerning (8) are based on identifying properties of basic solutions in reference to the problem

LP(x', d'): Minimize $(\delta(d', x', x): x \in X)$

Proposition 7. The inequality (8) derived from an arbitrary y-optimal basic feasible solution x'' for LP(x', c) is satisfied by all binary vectors $x \in X$, and excludes the solution $x = x''$ when $\delta(c, x', x'')$ is fractional.

Proof: We first show that the basic solution x'' for LP(x', c) is an optimal solution to LP(x', d'). Let rd denote the reduced cost for the objective function $\delta(d', x', x)$ for LP(x', d') relative to the x'' basis. Assume $X = \{x: Ax \geq b, x \geq 0\}$ and let B the basis associated to the basic solution x''. From the definitions the reduced cost $rc = c' - c'_B(A^B)^{-1}A$, and of $d' = \lfloor c - rc \rfloor$, it follows that

$$d' = \lfloor c'_B(A^B)^{-1}A \rfloor \text{ and } d'_B = c'_B \tag{8.1}$$

thus the reduced costs rd is null; i.e.,

$$rd' = d' - d'_B(A^B)^{-1}A = \lfloor c'_B(A^B)^{-1}A \rfloor - d'_B(A^B)^{-1}A$$
$$= \lfloor c'_B(A^B)^{-1}A \rfloor - c'_B(A^B)^{-1}A \leq 0.$$

This establishes the optimality of x'' for LP(x', d').

Since the d_j' coefficients are all integers, we therefore obtain the valid inequality

$$\delta(d', x', x) \geq \lceil \delta(d', x', x'') \rceil.$$

The definition of d' yields

$$\delta(d', x', x'') = \delta(c, x', x'') + \delta(\lfloor -rc \rfloor, x', x'').$$

The $\delta(\lfloor -rc \rfloor, x', x'')$ value is integer, since $x'' \in B(\lfloor -rc \rfloor)$. Thus, $\delta(d', x', x'')$ is fractional if and only if $\delta(c', x', x'')$ is fractional, and we also have

$$\lceil \delta(d', x', x'') \rceil = \lceil \delta(c, x', x'') \rceil + \delta(\lfloor -rc \rfloor, x', x'').$$

The proposition then follows from the definitions of (7) and (8).

Proposition 7 has the following novel consequence.

Corollary 3. The inequality (8) is independent of the c_j values for the non-basic x variables. In particular, for any y-feasible basic solution and specified values c_j for $j \in B$, the coefficients d_j' of d' are identical for every choice of the integer coefficients $c_j, j \in NB$.

Proof: The Corollary follows from the arguments of the Proof of Proposition 7 (see 8.1) thus showing that these changes cancel out, to produce the same final d_o' and d' after implementing the changes that existed previously. □

In effect, since Corollary 1 applies to the situation where $c_j = 0$ for $j \in NB$, it also allows each d_j' coefficient for $j \in NB$ to be identified by reference to the quantity that results by multiplying the vector of optimal dual values by the corresponding column A^j of the matrix A defining the constraints of (MIP), excluding rows of A corresponding to the inequalities $1 \geq x_j \geq 0$. (We continue to assume this matrix is enlarged by reference to additional inequalities such as (7) or (8) that may currently be included in defining $x \in X$.)

Now we establish the result that (8) is at least as strong as (7).

Proposition 8. If the basic solution x'' for LP(x', c) is optimal, and thus yields a valid inequality (7), then the inequality (8) dominates (7).

Proof: We use the fact that x'' is optimal for LP(x', d') as established by Proposition 7. When x'' is optimal for LP(x', c) from the optimal condition of the corresponding dual we have

$$rc \, x'' \leq rc \, x \text{ for all } x \geq 0$$

Thus we have

$$\lfloor -rc \rfloor \, x'' \geq \lfloor -rc \rfloor \, x \text{ for all } x \geq 0 \qquad (8.2)$$

Since

$$\delta(\lfloor -rc \rfloor, x', x'') = \lfloor -rc \rfloor' x'' + \lfloor -rc \rfloor x'$$
$$\delta(\lfloor -rc \rfloor, x', x) = \lfloor -rc \rfloor' x + \lfloor -rc \rfloor x'$$

This with (8.2) implies that

$$\delta(\lfloor -rc \rfloor, x', x'') - \delta(\lfloor -rc \rfloor, x', x) = \lfloor -rc \rfloor' x'' - \lfloor -rc \rfloor' x \geq 0 \qquad (8.3)$$

Moreover we have

$$\delta(d', x', x'') = \delta(c, x', x'') + \delta(\lfloor -rc \rfloor, x', x''). \qquad (8.4)$$

$$\delta(d', x', x) = \delta(c, x', x) + \delta(\lfloor -rc \rfloor, x', x). \qquad (8.5)$$

Hence by substituting (8.4) and (8.5) in the inequality (8) we obtain

$$\delta(c, x', x) + \delta(\lfloor -rc \rfloor, x', x) \geq \lceil \delta(c, x', x'') + \delta(\lfloor -rc \rfloor, x', x'') \rceil = \delta(c, x', x'') + \delta(\lfloor -rc \rfloor, x', x'').$$

Thus by using (8.3) we obtain (7). Consequently, this establishes that (8) implies (7).

Corollary 4. If the basic solution x'' for LP(x',c) is optimal then

$$\delta(d', x', x) - \lceil \delta(d', x', x'') \rceil = \delta(c, x', x) - \lceil \delta(c, x', x'') \rceil.$$

Proof. If the basic solution x'' for LP(x',c) is optimal then $\delta(\lfloor -rc \rfloor, x', x'')$ is integer so

$\delta(\lfloor -rc \rfloor, x', x'') = \lceil \delta(\lfloor -rc \rfloor, x', x'') \rceil$ which implies that $\delta(d', x', x) - \lceil \delta(d', x', x'') \rceil = \delta(c, x', x) - \lceil \delta(c, x', x'') \rceil$.

As in the use of the inequality (7), if a basic solution x'' that generates (8) is a binary vector that differs from x', then we can also test x'' for feasibility in (MIP:0-1) and then redefine $x' = x''$, to additionally append the constraint (1.1) for this new x'.

The combined arguments of the proofs of Propositions 7 and 8 lead to a still stronger conclusion. Consider a linear program LP(x', h') given by

LP(x',h'): Minimize $(\delta(h', x', x): x \in X)$.

where the coefficients $h_j' = d_j'$ (and hence $= c_j$) for $j \in B$ and, as before, B is defined relative to a given y-optimal basic feasible solution x''. Subject to this condition, the only restriction on the h_j' coefficients for $j \in NB$ is that they be integers. Then we can state the following result.

Corollary 5. The x'' basis is an optimal LP basis for LP(x', h') if and only if

$$h_j' \geq d_j' \text{ for } j \in NB$$

and the inequality (8) dominates the corresponding inequality derived by reference to LP(x', h').

Proof. Immediate from the proofs on Propositions 7 and 8.

The importance of Corollary 5 is the demonstration that (8) is the strongest possible valid inequality from those that can be generated by reference to a given y-optimal basic solution x'' and an objective function that shares the same coefficients for the basic variables.

It is to be noted that if (MIP:0-1) contains an integer valued slack variable s_i upon converting the associated inequality $A_i x + D_i y \geq b_i$ of the system $Ax + Dy \geq b$ into an equation – hence if A_i and b_i consist only of integers and D_i is the 0 vector – then s_i may be treated as one of the components of the vector x in deriving (8), and this inclusion serves to sharpen the resulting inequality. In the special case where all slack variables have this form, i.e., where (MIP:0-1) is a pure integer problem having no continuous variables and all data are integers, then it can be shown that the inclusion of the slack variables within x yields an instance of (8) that is equivalent to a fractional Gomory cut, and a stronger inequality can be derived by means of the foundation-penalty cuts of Glover and Sherali (2003). Consequently, the primary relevance of (8) comes from the fact that it applies to mixed integer as well as pure integer problems, and more particularly provides a useful means for enhancing target objective strategies for these problems. As an instance of this, we now examine methods that take advantage of (8) in additional ways by extension of ideas proposed with parametric tabu search.

5. GENERATING TARGET OBJECTIVES AND SOLUTIONS BY EXPLOITING PROXIMITY

We now examine the issue of creating the target solution x' and associated target objective $\delta(c, x', x)$ that underlies the inequalities of the preceding sections. This is a key determinant of the effectiveness of targeting strategies, since it determines how quickly and effectively such a strategy can lead to new integer feasible solutions.

In this section, we propose a relatively simple approach for generating the vector c of the target objective by exploiting proximity. The proximity procedure for generating target solutions x' and associated target objectives $\delta(c, x', x)$ begins by solving the initial problem (LP), and then solves a succession of problems $LP(x', c)$ by progressively modifying x' and c. Beginning from the linear programming solution x'' to (LP) (and subsequently to $LP(x', c)$), the new target solution x' is derived from x'' simply by setting $x_j' = \langle x_j'' \rangle, j \in N$, where $\langle v \rangle$ denotes the nearest integer neighbour of v. (The value $\langle .5 \rangle$ can be either 0 or 1, by employing an arbitrary tie-breaking rule.)

Since the resulting vector x' of nearest integer neighbors is unlikely to be feasible for (MIP:0-1), the critical element is to generate the target objective $\delta(c, x', x)$ so that the solutions x'' to successively generated problems $LP(x', c)$ will become progressively closer to satisfying integer feasibility.

If one or more integer feasible solutions is obtained during this approach, each such solution qualifies as a new best solution x^*, due to the incorporation of the objective function constraint $x_0 \leq U_0 < x_0^*$.

The criterion of the proximity procedure that selects the target solution x' as a nearest integer neighbor of x'' is evidently myopic. Consequently, the procedure is intended to be executed for only a limited number of iterations. However, the possibility exists that for some problems the target objectives of this approach may quickly lead to new integer solutions without invoking more advanced rules. To accommodate this eventuality, we include the option of allowing the procedure to continue its execution as long as it finds progressively improved solutions.

The proximity procedure is based on the principle that some variables x_j should be more strongly induced to receive their nearest neighbor target values x_j' than other variables. In the absence of other information, we may tentatively suppose that a variable whose LP solution value x_j'' is already an integer or is close to being an integer is more likely to receive that integer value in a feasible integer solution. Consequently, we are motivated to choose a target objective $\delta(c, x', x)$ that will more strongly encourage such a variable to receive its associated value x_j'. However, the relevance of being close to an integer value needs to be considered from more than one perspective.

5.1 Batwing Function for Proximity

The targeting of $x_j = x_j'$ for variables whose values x_j'' already equal or almost equal x_j' does not exert a great deal of influence on the solution of the new $LP(x', c)$, in the sense that such a targeting does not drive this solution to differ substantially from the solution to the previous $LP(x', c)$. A more influential targeting occurs by emphasizing the variables x_j whose x_j'' values are more "highly fractional," and hence which differ from their integer neighbours x_j' by a greater amount. There are evidently trade-offs to be considered in the pursuit of influence, since a variable whose x_j'' value lies close to .5, and hence whose integer target may be more influential, has the deficiency that the likelihood of this integer target being the "right" target is less certain. A compromise targeting criterion is therefore to give greater emphasis to driving x_j to an integer value if x_j'' lies "moderately" (but not exceedingly) close to an integer value. Such a criterion affords an improved chance that the targeted value will be appropriate, without abandoning the quest to identify targets that exert a useful degree of influence. Consequently, we select values λ_0 and $\lambda_1 = 1 - \lambda_0$ that lie moderately (but not exceedingly) close to 0 and 1, such as $\lambda_0 = 1/5$ and $\lambda_1 = 4/5$, or $\lambda_0 = 1/4$ and $\lambda_1 = 3/4$, and generate c_j coefficients that give greater emphasis to driving variables to 0 and 1 whose x_j'' values lie close to λ_0 and λ_1.

The following rule creates a target objective $\delta(c, x', x)$ based on this compromise criterion, arbitrarily choosing a range of 1 to 21 for the coefficient c_j. (From the standpoint of solving the problem $LP(x', c)$, this range is equivalent to any other range over positive values from v to $21v$, except for the necessity to round the c_j coefficients to integers.)

Proximity Rule for Generating c_j:

Choose λ_0 from the range $.1 \le \lambda_0 \le .4$, and let $\lambda_1 = 1 - \lambda_0$.

If $x_j' = 0$ (hence $x_j'' \le .5$) then
If $x_j'' \le \lambda_0$, set $c_j = 1 + 20x_j''/\lambda_0$
Else set $c_j = 1 + 20(.5 - x_j'')/(.5 - \lambda_0)$
Else if $x_j' = 1$ (hence $x_j'' \ge .5$) then
If $x_j'' \le \lambda_1$, set $c_j = 1 + 20(x_j'' - .5)/(\lambda_1 - .5)$
Else set $c_j = 1 + 20(1 - x_j'')/(1 - \lambda_1)$
End if

Finally, replace the specified value of c_j by its nearest integer neighbour $\langle c_j \rangle$

Remark 7: $c_j = 1$ if $x_j' = x_j''$.

The values of c_j coefficients produced by the preceding rule describe what may be called a *batwing* function – a piecewise linear function resembling the wings of a bat, with shoulders at $x_j'' = .5$, wing tips at $x_j'' = 0$ and $x_j'' = 1$, and the angular joints of the wings at $x_j'' = \lambda_0$ and $x_j'' = \lambda_1$. Over the x_j'' domain from the left wing tip at 0 to the first joint at λ_0, the function ranges from 1 to 21, and then from this joint to the left shoulder at .5 the function ranges from 21 back to 1. Similarly, from right shoulder, also at .5, to the second joint at λ_1, the function ranges from 1 to 21, and then from this joint to the right wing tip at 1 the function ranges likewise from 21 to 1. (The coefficient c_j takes the negative of these absolute values from the right shoulder to the right wing tip.).

In general, if we let *Tip*, *Joint* and *Shoulder* denote the c_j values to be assigned at these junctures (where typically *Joint* > *Tip*, *Shoulder*), then the generic form of a batwing function results by replacing the four successive c_j values in the preceding method by

$c_j = Tip + (Joint - Tip)x_j''/\lambda_0$,
$c_j = Shoulder + (Joint - Shoulder)(.5 - x_j'')/(.5 - \lambda_0)$,
$c_j = Shoulder + (Joint - Shoulder)(x_j'' - .5)/(\lambda_1 - .5)$
$c_j = Tip + (Joint - Tip)(1 - x_j'')/(1 - \lambda_1)$

The values of c_j coefficients called a *batwing* function can also be expressed as follows:

$c_j = Tip + (Joint - Tip)\, \delta(j, x', x'')/\lambda_0$, if $x_j'' \notin]\lambda_0, 1 - \lambda_0]$
$c_j = Shoulder + (Joint - Shoulder)(.5 - \delta(j, x', x''))/(.5 - \lambda_0)$, otherwise

The image of such a function more nearly resembles a bat in flight as the value of Tip is increased in relation to the value of Shoulder, and more nearly resembles a bat at rest in the opposite case. The function can be turned into a piecewise convex function that more strongly targets the values λ_0 and λ_1 by raising the absolute value of c_j to a power $p > 1$ (affixing a negative sign to yield c_j over the range from the right shoulder to the right wing tip). Such a function (e.g., a quadratic function) more strongly resembles a bat wing than the linear function.[6]

5.2 Design of the Proximity Procedure

We allow the proximity procedure that incorporates the foregoing rule for generating c_j the option of choosing a single fixed λ_0 value, or of choosing different values from the specified interval to generate a greater variety of outcomes. A subinterval for λ_0 centred around .2 or .25 is anticipated to lead to the best outcomes, but it can be useful to periodically choose values outside this range for diversification purposes.

We employ a stopping criterion for the proximity procedure that limits the total number of iterations or the number of iterations since finding the last feasible integer solution. In each instance where a feasible integer solution is obtained, the method re-solves the problem (LP), which is updated to incorporate both the objective function constraint $x_o \leq U_o < x_o^*$ and inequalities such as (8) that are generated in the course of solving various problems LP(x', c). The instruction "Update the Problem Inequalities" is included within the proximity procedure to refer to this process of adding inequalities to LP(x', c) and (LP), and to the associated process of dropping inequalities by criteria indicated in Section 2.

Proximity Procedure

1. Solve (LP). (If the solution x'' to the first instance of (LP) is integer feasible, the method stops with an optimal solution for (MIP:0-1).)
2. Construct the target solution x' derived from x'' by setting $x_j' = \langle x_j'' \rangle$, for $j \in N$. Apply the Rule for Generating c_j, to each $j \in N$, to produce the vector c.
3. Solve LP(x', c), yielding the solution x''. Update the Problem Inequalities.
4. If x'' is integer feasible: update the best solution $(x^*, y^*) = (x'', y'')$, update $U_o < x_o^*$, and return to Step 1. Otherwise, return to Step 2.

A preferred variant of the proximity procedure does not change all the components of c each time a new target objective is produced, but changes only a subset consisting of k of these components, for a value k somewhat smaller than N. For example, a reasonable default value for k is given by $k = 5$. Alternatively, the procedure may begin with $k = n$ and gradually reduce k to its default value.

This variant results by the following modification. Let c^o identify the form of c produced by the Proximity Rule for Generating c_j, as applied in Step 2 of the Proximity Procedure. Re-index

the x_j variables so that $c_1^o \geq c_2^o \geq \dots \geq c_n^o$, and let $J(k) = \{1, \dots, k\}$, thus identifying the variables x_j, $j \in J(k)$, as those having the k largest c_j^o values. Then proximity procedure is amended by setting $c = 0$ in Step 1 and then setting $c_j = c_j^o$ for $j \in J(k)$ in Step 2, without modifying the c_j values for $j \in N - J(k)$. Relevant issues for research involve the determination of whether it is better to begin with k restricted or to gradually reduce it throughout the search, or to allow it to oscillate around a preferred value. Different classes of problems will undoubtedly afford different answers to such questions, and may be susceptible to exploitation by different forms of the batwing function (allowing different magnitudes for the Tip, Joint and Shoulder, and possibly allowing the location of the shoulders to be different than the .5 midpoint, with the locations of the joints likewise asymmetric).

6. CONCLUSION

Branch-and-bound (*B&B*) and branch-and-cut (*B&C*) methods have long been considered the methods of choice for solving mixed integer programming problems. This orientation has resulted in eliciting contributions to these classical methods from many researchers, and has led to successive improvements in these methods extending over a period of several decades. In recent years, these efforts to create improved *B&B* and *B&C* solution approaches have intensified and have produced significant benefits, as evidenced by the existence of MIP procedures that are appreciably more effective than their predecessors.

It remains true, however, that many MIP problems resist solution by the best current *B&B* and *B&C* methods. It is not uncommon to encounter problems that confound the leading commercial solvers, resulting in situations where these solvers are unable to find even moderately good feasible solutions after hours, days, or weeks of computational effort. As a consequence, metaheuristic methods have attracted attention as possible alternatives or supplements to the more classical approaches. Yet to date, the amount of effort devoted to developing good metaheuristics for MIP problems is almost negligible compared to the effort being devoted to developing refined versions of the classical methods.

The view adopted in this paper is that metaheuristic approaches can benefit from a change of perspective in order to perform at their best in the MIP setting. Drawing on lessons learned from applying classical methods, we anticipate that metaheuristics can likewise profit from generating inequalities to supplement their basic functions. However, we propose that these inequalities be used in ways not employed in classical MIP methods, and indicate two principal avenues for doing this: first by generating the inequalities in reference to strategically created target solutions and target objectives, as in the current Part I, and second by embedding these inequalities in special intensification and diversification processes, as described in Part II.

ACKNOWLEDGMENT

The present research work has been supported by International Campus on Safety and Intermodality in Transportation, the Nord-Pas-de-Calais Region, the European Community, the Regional Delegation for Research and Technology, the Ministry of Higher Education and Research, the National Center for Scientific Research, and by a "Chaire d'excellence" from "Pays de la Loire" Region (France). A restricted (preliminary) version of this work appeared in Glover (2008).

REFERENCES

Balas, E., & Jeroslow, R. (1972). Canonical cuts on the unit hypercube. *SIAM Journal on Applied Mathematics*, *23*(1), 60–69. doi:10.1137/0123007

Dantzig, G. (1963). *Linear programming and extensions*. NJ: Princeton University Press.

Fischetti, M., Glover, F., & Lodi, A. (2005). Feasibility pump. *Mathematical Programming - Series A*, *104*, 91–104. doi:10.1007/s10107-004-0570-3

Glover, F. (1978). Parametric branch and bound. *OMEGA. The International Journal of Management Science*, *6*(2), 145–152.

Glover, F. (2005). Adaptive memory projection methods for integer programming. In Rego, C., & Alidaee, B. (Eds.), *Metaheuristic optimization via memory and evolution: Tabu search and scatter search* (pp. 425–440). Dordecht, The Netherlands: Kluwer Academic Publishers. doi:10.1007/0-387-23667-8_19

Glover, F. (2006a). Parametric tabu search for mixed integer programs. *Computers & Operations Research*, *33*(9), 2449–2494. doi:10.1016/j.cor.2005.07.009

Glover, F. (2006b). *Satisfiability data mining for binary data classification problems*. Boulder: University of Colorado.

Glover, F. (2007). Infeasible/feasible search trajectories and directional rounding in integer programming. *Journal of Heuristics*, *13*(6), 505–542. doi:10.1007/s10732-007-9029-z

Glover, F. (2008). Inequalities and target objectives for metaheuristic search – part I: Mixed binary optimization. In Siarry, P., & Michalewicz, Z. (Eds.), *Advances in metaheuristics for hard optimization* (pp. 439–474). New York: Springer. doi:10.1007/978-3-540-72960-0_21

Glover, F., & Greenberg, H. (1989). New approaches for heuristic search: A bilateral linkage with artificial intelligence. *European Journal of Operational Research*, *39*(2), 119–130. doi:10.1016/0377-2217(89)90185-9

Glover, F., & Hanafi, S. (2002). Tabu search and finite convergence. *Discrete Applied Mathematics, 119*, 3–36. doi:10.1016/S0166-218X(01)00263-3

Glover, F., & Laguna, M. (1997). *Tabu search*. Dordecht, The Netherlands: Kluwer Academic Publishers. doi:10.1007/978-1-4615-6089-0

Glover, F., & Sherali, H. D. (2003). Foundation-penalty cuts for mixed-integer programs. *Operations Research Letters, 31*, 245–253. doi:10.1016/S0167-6377(03)00014-2

Guignard, M., & Spielberg, K. (2003). *Double contraction, double probing, short starts and bb-probing cuts for mixed (0, 1) programming*. Philadelphia: Wharton School of the University of Pennsylvania.

Hanafi, S., & Wilbaut, C. (2006). Improved convergent heuristics for the 0-1 multidimensional knapsack problem. *Annals of Operations Research*. doi:10.1007/s10479-009-0546-z

Hvattum, L. M., Lokketangen, A., & Glover, F. (2004). Adaptive memory search for boolean optimization problems. *Discrete Applied Mathematics, 142*, 99–109. doi:10.1016/j.dam.2003.06.006

Nowicki, E., & Smutnicki, C. (1996). A fast taboo search algorithm for the job shop problem. *Management Science, 42*(6), 797–813. doi:10.1287/mnsc.42.6.797

Soyster, A. L., Lev, B., & Slivka, W. (1978). Zero–one programming with many variables and few constraints. *European Journal of Operational Research, 2*(3), 195–201. doi:10.1016/0377-2217(78)90093-0

Spielberg, K., & Guignard, M. (2000). *A sequential (quasi) hot start method for bb (0,1) mixed integer programming*. Paper presented at the Mathematical Programming Symposium, Atlanta.

Ursulenko, A. (2006). *Notes on the global equilibrium search*. College Station, TX: Texas A&M University.

Wilbaut, C., & Hanafi, S. (2009). New convergent heuristics for 0-1 mixed integer programming. *European Journal of Operational Research, 195*, 62–74. doi:10.1016/j.ejor.2008.01.044

ENDNOTES

[1] The vector c' depends on x'. As will be seen, we define several different linear programs that are treated as described here in reference to the problem LP(x', c').

[2] An effective way to enforce $v_o = v_o''$ is to fix all non-basic variables having non-zero reduced costs to compel these variables to receive their optimal first stage values throughout the second stage. This can be implemented by masking the columns for these variables in the optimal first stage basis, and then to continue the second stage from this starting basis while ignoring the masked variables and their columns. (The masked non-basic variables may incorporate components of both x and y, and will generally include slack variables for some of the inequalities embodied in $Ax + Dy \geq b$.) The resulting residual problem for the second stage can be significantly smaller than the first stage problem, allowing the problem for the second stage to be solved very efficiently.

[3] In some problem settings, the inclusion of the secondary objective x_o in $v_{oo} = Mv_o + x_o$ is unimportant, and in these cases our notation is accurate in referring to the explicit minimization of $v_o = c'x$.

[4] This strategy is utilized in the parametric branch and bound approach of Glover (1978) and in the feasibility pump approach of Fischetti, Glover and Lodi (2005).

[5] We continue to apply the convention of referring to just the x-component x'' of a solution (x'', y''), understanding the y component to be implicit.

6   Calibration to determine a batwing structure, either piecewise linear or nonlinear, that proves more effective than other alternatives within Phase 1 would provide an interesting study.

This work was previously published in International Journal of Applied Metaheuristic Computing, Volume 1, Issue 1, edited by Peng-Yeng Yin, pp. 1-15, copyright 2010 by IGI Publishing (an imprint of IGI Global).

Chapter 2
Metaheuristic Search with Inequalities and Target Objectives for Mixed Binary Optimization – Part II:
Exploiting Reaction and Resistance

Fred Glover
OptTek Systems, Inc., USA

Saïd Hanafi
University of Lille -Nord de France, UVHC, and LAMIH, France

ABSTRACT

Recent metaheuristics for mixed integer programming have included proposals for introducing inequalities and target objectives to guide this search. These guidance approaches are useful in intensification and diversification strategies related to fixing subsets of variables at particular values. The authors' preceding Part I study demonstrated how to improve such approaches by new inequalities that dominate those previously proposed. In Part II, the authors review the fundamental concepts underlying weighted pseudo cuts for generating guiding inequalities, including the use of target objective strategies. Building on these foundations, this paper develops a more advanced approach for generating the target objective based on exploiting the mutually reinforcing notions of reaction and resistance. The authors demonstrate how to produce new inequalities by "mining" reference sets of elite solutions to extract characteristics these solutions exhibit in common. Additionally, a model embedded memory is integrated to provide a range of recency and frequency memory structures for achieving goals associated with short term and long term solution strategies. Finally, supplementary linear programming models that exploit the new inequalities for intensification and diversification are proposed.

DOI: 10.4018/978-1-4666-0270-0.ch002

1. INTRODUCTION

We represent the zero-one mixed integer programming problem in the form

$$(P)$$

$$\begin{cases} Minimize\ z_0 = fx + gy \\ subject\ to\ (x,y) \in Z = \{(x,y) : Ax + Dy \geq b\} \\ \qquad x\ integer \end{cases}$$

We assume that $Ax + Dy \geq b$ includes the inequalities $1 \geq x_j \geq 0, j \in N = \{1, ..., n\}$. The linear programming relaxation of P that results by dropping the integer requirement on x is denoted by LP. We further assume $Ax + Dy \geq b$ includes an objective function constraint $z_0 \leq u_0$, where the bound u_0 is manipulated as part of a search strategy for solving P, subject to maintaining $u_0 < z_0^*$, where z_0^* is the z_0 value for the currently best known solution z^* to P.

Recent adaptive memory and evolutionary metaheuristics for mixed integer programming have included proposals for introducing inequalities and target objectives to guide the search. These guidance approaches are useful in intensification and diversification strategies related to fixing subsets of variables at particular values, and in strategies that use linear programming to generate trial solutions whose variables are induced to receive integer values.

In this paper we make reference to two types of search strategies: those that fix subsets of variables to particular values within approaches for exploiting strongly determined and consistent variables, and those that make use of solution *targeting* procedures. Those targeting procedures solve a linear programming problem LP(x', c') where the objective vector c' depends on the target solution x'. LP(x', c') includes the constraints of LP (and additional bounding constraints) while replacing the objective function z_0 by a linear function $v_0 = c'x$. Given a *target solution* x', the objective vector c' consists of integer coefficients c'_j that seek to induce assignments $x_j = x'_j$ for different variables

with varying degrees of emphasis. We adopt the convention that each instance of LP(x', c') implicitly includes the LP objective of minimizing the function $z_0 = fx + gy$ as a secondary objective, dominated by the objective of minimizing $v_0 = c'x$, so that the true objective function consists of minimizing $\omega_0 = Mv_0 + z_0$, where M is a large positive number.

A useful alternative to working with ω_0 in the form specified is to solve LP(x', c') in two stages. The first stage minimizes $v_0 = c'x$ to yield an optimal solution $x = x''$, and the second stage enforces $v_0 = c'x''$ to solve the residual problem of minimizing $z_0 = fx + gy$. An effective way to enforce $v_0 = c'x''$ is to fix all non-basic variables having non-zero reduced costs to compel these variables to receive their optimal first stage values throughout the second stage. This can be implemented by masking the columns for these variables in the optimal first stage basis, and then to continue the second stage from this starting basis while ignoring the masked variables and their columns. The resulting residual problem for the second stage can be significantly smaller than the first stage problem, allowing the problem for the second stage to be solved efficiently.

A second convention involves an interpretation of the problem constraints. Selected instances of inequalities generated by approaches of the following sections will be understood to be included among the constraints $Ax + Dy \geq b$ of (LP). In our definition of LP(x', c') and other linear programs related to (LP), we take the liberty of representing the currently updated form of the constraints $Ax + Dy \geq b$ by the compact representation $x \in X = \{x: (x,y) \in Z\}$, recognizing that this involves a slight distortion in view of the fact that we implicitly minimize a function of y as well as x in these linear programs.[1]

In Part I (Glover & Hanafi, 2010), we proposed procedures for generating target objectives and solutions by exploiting proximity in the original space or projected space. To launch our investigation we first review weighted pseudo cuts for generating guiding inequalities for this problem and associated target objective strategies by exploiting proximity with embedded memory in Section 2. Section 3 indicates more advanced approaches for generating the target objective based on exploiting the mutually reinforcing notions of reaction and resistance. The term "reaction" refers to the change in the value of a variable as a result of creating a target objective and solving the resulting linear programming problem. We show how to generate additional inequalities by "mining" reference sets of elite solutions to extract characteristics these solutions exhibit in common. Section 4 describes models that use embedded memory, as proposed in parametric tabu search (Glover, 1978, 2006), which offers a range of recency and frequency memory structures for achieving goals associated with short term and long term solution strategies. We examine ways this framework can be exploited in generating target objectives, employing both older adaptive memory ideas and newer ones proposed here for the first time. Section 5 focuses on supplementary linear programming models that exploit the new inequalities for intensification and diversification, and introduce additional inequalities from sets of elite solutions that enlarge the scope of these models. Concluding remarks are given in Section 6.

2. TARGET OBJECTIVES BY EXPLOITING PROXIMITY WITH EMBEDDED MEMORY

To develop the basic ideas, let x' denote an arbitrary solution, and define the associated index sets

$$N(x', v) = \{j \in N: x'_j = v\} \text{ for } v \in \{0, 1\},$$

$$N(x') = \{j \in N: x'_j \in \{0, 1\}\} = \{j \in N: x_j(1 - x_j) = 0\} = N(x', 0) \cup N(x', 1)$$

$$N^*(x') = \{j \in N: x'_j \in]0, 1[\} = \{j \in N: x_j(1 - x_j) \neq 0\} \text{ (hence } N = N(x') \cup N^*(x'))$$

$$C(x') = \{ c \in IN^m_+ : c_j x'_j (1 - x'_j) = 0\}.$$

Let x, x' be two arbitrary binary solutions and let c' be an integer vector in $C(x')$. Define

$$\delta(c', x', x) = \sum_{j \in N} c'_j x_j (1 - x_j) + c'_j x'_j (1 - x_j). \tag{1}$$

The following result is proved in Part I.

Proposition 1. Let x' denote an arbitrary target solution with the associated vector $c' \in C(x')$. Let x'' denoted an optimal solution to the following LP problem

LP(x', c'): Minimize $\{\delta(c', x', x): x \in X\}$.

Then the inequality

$$\delta(c', x', x) \geq \max\{1, \lceil \delta(c', x', x'') \rceil^2\} \tag{2}$$

eliminates all solutions in $F(x', c') = \{x \in [0,1]^n: c'_j(x_j - x'_j) = 0 \text{ for } j \in N(x')\}$ as a feasible solution, but admits all other binary x vectors.

We observe that (2) is a valid inequality, i.e., it is satisfied by all binary vectors that are feasible for (P) (and more specifically by all such vectors that are feasible for LP(x', c')), with the exception of those ruled out by previous examination. We make use of solutions such as x' by assigning them the role of *target solutions and* by c' assigning them the role of *target objective vectors*.

Remark 1: The special case of the inequality (2) where $c' = e$ has been used, for example, to produce 0-1 "short hot starts" for branch and bound by Spielberg and Guignard (2000) and Guignard and Spielberg (2003). This special inequality is called a *canonical cut* on the unit hypercube by Balas and Jeroslow (1972). The inequality (2) also generalizes the partial pseudo cuts used by Soyster et al. (1978), Hanafi and Wilbaut (2009) and

Wilbaut and Hanafi (2009). The partial pseudo cuts are generated from a subset J' $\subseteq N(x')$, by using the partial distance

$$\delta(J', x', x) = \sum_{j \in J'} x_j(1 - x_j') + x_j'(1 - x_j)$$

(3)

The distance $\delta(J', x', x) = \delta(c', x', x)$ where $c_j' = 1$ if $j \in J'$ otherwise $c_j' = 0$.

In Part I, we identified a relatively simple approach for generating the vector c' of the target objective by exploiting proximity. The proximity procedure for generating target solutions x' and associated target objectives $\delta(c', x', x)$ begins by solving the initial problem (LP), and then solves a succession of problems $LP(x', c')$ by progressively modifying x' and c'. Beginning from the linear programming solution x'' to (LP) (and subsequently to $LP(x', c')$), the new target solution x' is derived from x'' simply by setting $x_j' = \langle x_j'' \rangle, j \in N$, where $\langle v \rangle$ denotes the nearest integer neighbour of v. (The value $\langle .5 \rangle$ can be either 0 or 1, by employing an arbitrary tie-breaking rule.)

Proximity Procedure

1. Solve (LP). (If the solution x'' to the first instance of (LP) is integer feasible, the method stops with an optimal solution for (P).)
2. Construct the target solution x' derived from x'' by setting $x_j' = \langle x_j'' \rangle$, for $j \in N$. Apply the Rule for Generating c_j', to each $j \in N$, to produce the vector c'.
3. Solve $LP(x', c')$, yielding the solution x''. Update the Problem Inequalities.
4. If x'' is integer feasible: update the best solution $(x^*, y^*) = (x'', y'')$, update $u_0 < z_0^*$, and return to Step 1. Otherwise, return to Step 2.

The targeting of $x_j = x_j'$ for variables whose values x_j'' already equal or almost equal x_j' does not exert a great deal of influence on the solution of the new (updated) $LP(x', c')$, in the sense that such a targeting does not drive this solution to differ substantially from the solution to the previous $LP(x', c')$. A more influential targeting occurs by emphasizing the variables x_j whose x_j'' values are more "highly fractional," and hence which differ from their integer neighbours x_j' by a greater amount.

The following rule creates a target objective $\delta(c', x', x)$ based on this compromise criterion, arbitrarily choosing a range of 1 to $BaseCost + 1$ for the coefficient c_j'.

Proximity Rule for Generating c_j'

Choose λ_0 from the range $.1 \leq \lambda_0 \leq .4$. For $j \in N$ do

$c_j' = 1 + BaseCost\,(1-2x_j')(.5 - x_j'')/(.5 - \lambda_0)$ if $x_j'' \notin]\lambda_0, 1 - \lambda_0]$

$c_j' = 1 + BaseCost\,(x_j' - x_j'')/\lambda_0$ otherwise

The values of c_j' coefficients produced by the preceding rule describe what may be called a *batwing* function. Figure 1 shows the shape of this function.

We may modify the specification of the c_j' values by using model embedded memory, as proposed in parametric tabu search. For this, we replace the constant value $BaseCost$ in the c_j' generation rules by a changing $BaseCost$ value which is increased on each successive iteration, thus causing the new c_j' values to grow as the number of iterations increases. The influence of these values in driving variables to reach their targets will thus become successively greater, and targets that have been created more recently will be less likely to be violated than those created earlier. (The larger value of c_j' the more likely it will be that x_j will not resist its target value x_j' by becoming fractional.)

Figure 1. Batwing function

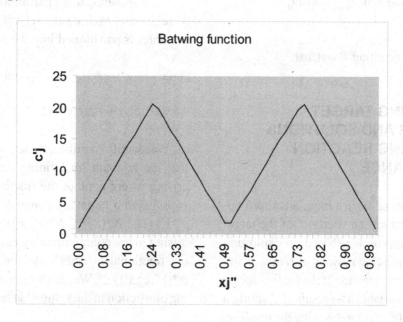

Consequently, as the values c'_j grow from one iteration to the next, the variables that were given new targets farther in the past will tend to be the ones that become resistors and candidates to receive new target values. As a result, the c'_j coefficients produced by progressively increasing *BaseCost* emulate a tabu search recency memory that seeks more strongly to prevent assignments from changing the more recently that they have been made.

The determination of the c'_j values can be accomplished by starting with *BaseCost* = 20 in Step 1 of the proximity procedure, and updating the value of *BaseCost* each time *iter* is incremented by 1 in Step 3 to give *BaseCost*:= $\lambda BaseCost$, where the parameter λ is chosen from the interval $\lambda \in$ [1.1,1.3]. (This value of λ can be made the same for all iterations, or can be selected randomly from such an interval at each iteration.)

To prevent the c'_j values from becoming excessively large, the current c'_j values can be reduced once *BaseCost* reaches a specified limit by the applying following rule.

1) Reset *BaseCost* = 20 and index the variables $x_j, j \in N(x')$ so that

$c'_1 \geq c'_2 \geq ... \geq c'_p$ where $p = |N(x')|$.

2)   Define $\Delta_j = c'_j - c'_{j+1}$ for $j = 1, ..., p$ -1 and select $\lambda \in$ [1.1,1.3].

3)   Set c'_p:= *BaseCost* and c'_j:= $\text{Min}(c'_{j+1} + \Delta_j, \lambda c'_{j+1})$ for $j = p$ -1, ..., 1.

4)   Finally, reset *BaseCost*:= c'_1 (= $\text{Max}(c'_j, j \in N(x'))$.

Remark 2: An equivalent implementation is obtained by replacing instruction 3 with

3-a) Set c'_p:= *BaseCost* and $\Delta = c'_{p-1} - c'_p$;
3-b) for $j = p$ -1, ..., 1 do{ $\Delta' = c'_{j-1} - c'_j$; c'_j:= $\text{Min}(c'_{j+1} + \Delta, \lambda c'_{j+1}); \Delta = \Delta';$}

The new c_j values produced by this rule will retain the same ordering as the original ones.

In a departure for diversification purposes, the foregoing rule can be changed by modifying the next to last step to become

Set $|c'_1| := BaseCost$ and $|c'_{j+1}| := Min(|c'_j| + \Delta_j, \lambda|c'_j|)$ for $j =, \ldots, p - 1$

and conclude by resetting $BaseCost := |c'_p|$.

3. GENERATING TARGET OBJECTIVES AND SOLUTIONS BY EXPLOITING REACTION AND RESISTANCE

In this section, we propose a more advanced approach for generating the vector c' of the target objective. This approach is based on exploiting the mutually reinforcing notions of *reaction* and *resistance*. The term "reaction" refers to the change in the value of a variable as a result of creating a target objective $\delta(c', x', x)$ and solving the resulting problem $LP(x', c')$. The term "resistance" refers to the degree to which a variable fails to react to a non-zero c_j coefficient by receiving a fractional value rather than being driven to 0 or 1.

Relative to a given vector x' and a target vector c' we consider the partition of N into the sets

$$N(c', x') = \{j \in N: c'_j \neq 0 \text{ and } x_j(1 - x_j) = 0\} \text{ and}$$

$$N^*(c', x') = \{j \in N: c'_j = 0 \text{ or } x_j(1 - x_j) \neq 0\}.$$

i.e. $N = N(c', x') \cup N^*(c', x')$. Note that the set $N^*(c', x')$ contains the indexes of variables that are not subject to a binding constraint or incorporated into a target affecting their values. The set $N(c', x')$ identifies the variables that have been assigned target values x'_j. (Equivalently, $N(c', x') = N - N^*(c', x')$.)

Remark 3: $N^*(e, x') = N^*(x') = \{j \in N: 0 < x'_j < 1\}$ is the set of variables that receive fractional values in the solution x'. (Similarly, we note $N(e, x') = N(x')$.)

Corresponding to the partition of N into the sets $N^*(c', x')$ and $N(c', x')$, the set $N^*(x'')$ of fractional variables is partitioned into the sets

$$N^*(x'', c', x') = N^*(x'') \cap N(c', x') \text{ and}$$

$$N^{**}(x'', c', x') = N^*(x'') \cap N^*(c', x').$$

We identify two different sets of circumstances that are relevant to defining reaction, the first arising where none of the fractional variables x_j is assigned a target x'_j, hence $N^*(x'') = N^{**}(x'', c', x')$ (i.e., $N^*(x'') \subseteq N^*(c', x')$), and the second arising in the complementary case where at least one fractional variable is assigned a target, hence $N^*(x'', c', x') \neq \varnothing$. We start by examining the meaning of reaction in the somewhat simpler first case.

3.1. Reaction When No Fractional Variables Have Targets

Our initial goal is to create a measure of reaction for the situation where $N^*(x'') = N^{**}(x'', c', x')$, i.e., where all of the fractional variables are unassigned (hence, none of these variables have targets). In this context we define reaction to be measured by the change in the value x''_j of a fractional variable x_j relative to the value x^o_j received by x_j in an optimal solution x^o to (LP), as given by

$$\Delta_j = x^o_j - x''_j.$$

We observe there is some ambiguity in this Δ_j definition since (LP) changes as a result of introducing new inequalities and updating the value u_o of the inequality $z_o \leq u_o$. To remove this ambiguity, we understand the definition of Δ_j to refer to the solution x^o obtained by the most recent effort to solve (LP), though this (LP) may be to some extent out of date, since additional inequalities may have been introduced since it was solved. For reasons that will become clear in the context of resistance, we also allow the alternative of designating x^o to be the solution to the most recent problem $LP(x',$

c') preceding the current one; i.e., the problem solved before creating the latest target vector c'.

The reaction measure Δ_j is used to determine the new target objective by re-indexing the variables $x_j, j \in N^*(x'') = N^{**}(x'', c', x')$, so that the absolute values $|\Delta_j|$ are in descending order, thus yielding $|\Delta_1| \geq |\Delta_2| \geq \ldots$. We then identify the k-element subset $N(k) = \{1, 2, \ldots, k\}$ of $N^*(x'')$ that references the k largest $|\Delta_j|$ values, where $k = \mathrm{Min}(|N^*(x'')|, k_{max})$. We suggest the parameter k_{max} be chosen at most 5 and gradually decreased to 1 as the method progresses.

The c_j coefficients are then determined for the variables $x_j, j \in N(k)$, by the following rule. (The constant *BaseCost* is the same one used to generate c'_j values in the Proximity procedure, and $\langle v \rangle$ again denotes the nearest integer neighbor of v.)

$N^{**}(x'', c', x')$ *Rule for Generating c'_j and x'_j, $j \in N(k)$ (for $N(k) \subset N^*(x'') = N^{**}(x'', c', x')$):*

Set $c'_j = 1 + \langle BaseCost\, |\Delta_j|\, /|\Delta_1| \rangle$ and $x'_j = \mathrm{sign}(\Delta_j)$.

When $\Delta_j = 0$, a tie-breaking rule can be used to determine which of the two options should apply, and in the special case where $\Delta_1 = 0$ (hence all $\Delta_j = 0$), the c'_j assignment is taken to be 1 for all $j \in N(k)$.

To determine a measure of reaction for the complementary case $N^*(x'', c', x') \neq \varnothing$, we first introduce the notion of resistance.

3.2. Resistance

A *resisting variable* (or *resistor*) x_j is one that is assigned a target value x'_j but fails to satisfy $x_j = x'_j$ in the solution x'' to $\mathrm{LP}(x', c')$. Accordingly the index set for resisting variables may be represented by

$$NR = \{j \in N(c', x'): x''_j \neq x'_j\}$$

$$NR = \{j \in N: c'_j(x''_j - x'_j) \neq 0 \text{ and } x'_j(1 - x'_j) = 0\}$$

$$NR = \{j \in N: c'_j \delta(j, x', x'') \neq 0\}$$

If x''_j is fractional and $j \in N(c', x')$ then clearly $j \in NR$ (i.e., $N^*(x'', c', x') \subset NR$). Consequently, the situation $N^*(x'', c', x') \neq \varnothing$ previously identified as complementary to $N^*(x'') = N^{**}(x'', c', x')$ corresponds to the presence of at least one fractional resistor.

If a resistor x_j is not fractional, i.e., if the value x''_j is the integer $1 - x'_j$, we say that x_j *blatantly resists* its targeted value x'_j. Blatant resistors x_j are automatically removed from NR and placed in the unassigned set $N^*(c', x')$ by setting $c'_j = 0$. (Alternatively, a blatant resistor may be placed in $N(x', 1 - x'_j)$ by setting $x'_j := 1 - x'_j$.)

After executing this operation, we are left with $NR = N^*(x'', c', x')$, and hence the condition $N^*(x'', c', x') \neq \varnothing$ (which complements the condition $N^*(x'') = N^{**}(x'', c', x')$) becomes equivalent to $NR \neq \varnothing$.

We use the quantity $\delta(j, x', x'')$ to define a *resistance measure* RM_j for each resisting variable $x_j, j \in NR$, that identifies how strongly x_j resists its targeted value x'_j. Two simple measures are given by

$$RM_j = \delta(j, x', x'') \text{ or } RM_j = c'_j \delta(j, x', x'') \text{ for } j \in NR.$$

The resistance measure RM_j is used in two ways: (a) to select specific variables x_j that will receive new x'_j and c'_j values in creating the next target objective; (b) to determine the relative magnitudes of the resulting c'_j values. For this purpose, it is necessary to extend the notion of resistance by making reference to *potentially resisting* variables (or *potential resistors*) $x_j, j \in N(c', x') - NR$, i.e., the variables that have been assigned target values x'_j and hence non-zero objective function coefficients c'_j, but which yield $x''_j = x'_j$ in the solution x'' to $\mathrm{LP}(x', c')$. We identify a resistance measure RM_j° for potential resistors by reference to their reduced cost values rc_j (as identified in Section 4):

$$RM_j^\circ = (2x_j' - 1)\, rc_j \text{ for } j \in N(c', x') - NR$$

We note that this definition implies $RM_j^\circ \le 0$ for potentially resisting variables. (Otherwise, x_j would be a non-basic variable yielding $x_j'' = 1$ in the case where $j \in N(x', 0)$, or yielding $x_j'' = 0$ in the case where $j \in N(x', 1)$, thus qualifying as a blatant resistor and hence implying $j \in NR$.) The closer that RM_j° is to 0, the closer x_j is to qualifying to enter the basis and potentially to escape the influence of the coefficient c_j' that seeks to drive it to the value 0 or 1. Thus larger values of RM_j° indicate greater potential resistance. Since the resistance measures RM_j are positive for resisting variables x_j, we see that there is an automatic ordering whereby $RM_p > RM_q^\circ$ for a resisting variable x_p and a potentially resisting variable x_q.

3.3. Combining Measures of Resistance and Reaction

The notion of reaction is relevant for variables x_j assigned target values x_j' ($j \in N(c', x')$) as well as for those not assigned such values ($j \in N^*(c', x')$). In the case of variables having explicit targets (hence that qualify either as resistors or potential resistors) we combine measures of resistance and reaction to determine which of these variables should receive new targets x_j' and new coefficients c_j'.

Let x° refer to the solution x'' to the instance of the problem $LP(x', c')$ that was solved immediately before the current instance;[3] hence the difference between x_j° and x_j'' identifies the reaction of x_j to the most recent assignment of c_j' values. In particular, we define this reaction for resistors and potential resistors by

$$\delta_j = (1 - x_j')(x_j'' - x_j^\circ) + x_j'(x_j^\circ - x_j'') \ (j \in N(c', x'))$$

$$\delta_j = \delta(j, x', x'') - \delta(j, x', x^\circ)$$

If we use the measure of resistance $RM_j = \delta(j, x', x'')$, which identifies how far x_j lies from its target value, a positive δ_j implies that the resistance of x_j has increased as a result of the latest assignment of c_j' values, and a negative δ_j implies that the resistance of x_j has decreased as a result of this assignment. Just as the resistance measure RM_j is defined to be either $\delta(j, x', x'')$ or $c_j'\delta(j, x', x'')$, the corresponding reaction measure $R\delta_j$ can be defined by either

$$R\delta_j = \delta_j \text{ or } R\delta_j = \delta_j\, c_j'.$$

$$R\delta_j = \delta(j, x', x'') - \delta(j, x', x^\circ) \text{ or } R\delta_j = c_j'(\delta(j, x', x'') - \delta(j, x', x^\circ)).$$

Based on this we define a composite resistance-reaction measure RR_j for resisting variables as a convex combination of RM_j and $R\delta_j$; *i.e.*, for a chosen value of $\lambda \in [0,1]$:

$$RR_j = \lambda RM_j + (1 - \lambda)R\delta_j, j \in NR.$$

$$RR_j = \lambda\delta(j, x', x'') + (1 - \lambda)(\delta(j, x', x'') - \delta(j, x', x^\circ)), j \in NR.$$

$$RR_j = \delta(j, x', x'') + (\lambda - 1)\delta(j, x', x^\circ), j \in NR.$$

Similarly, for implicitly resisting variables, we define a corresponding composite measure RR_j° by

$$RR_j^\circ = \lambda RM_j^\circ + (1 - \lambda)R\delta_j, j \in N(c', x') - NR$$

In order to make the interpretation of λ more consistent, it is appropriate first to scale the values of RM_j, RM_j° and $R\delta_j$. If v_j takes the role of each of these three values in turn, then v_j may be replaced by the scaled value $v_j := v_j/|Mean(v_j)|$ (bypassing the scaling in the situation where $|Mean(v_j)| = 0$).

To give an effective rule for determining RR_j and RR_j°, a few simple tests can be performed to determine a working value for λ, as by limiting λ to a small number of default values (e.g., the three values 0, 1 and .5, or the five values that include .25 and .75).

3.4. Including Reference to a Tabu List

A key feature in using both RR_j and RR_j° to determine new target objectives is to make use of a simple tabu list T to avoid cycling and insure a useful degree of variation in the process. We specify in the next section a procedure for creating and updating T, which we treat both as an ordered list and as a set. (We sometimes speak of a variable x_j as belonging to T, with the evident interpretation that $j \in T$.) It suffices at present to stipulate that we always refer to non-tabu elements of $N(c', x')$, and hence we restrict attention to values RR_j and RR_j° for which $j \in N(c', x') - T$. The rules for generating new target objectives make use of these values in the following manner.

Because RR_j and RR_j° in general are not assured to be either positive or negative, we treat their ordering for the purpose of generating c'_j coefficients as a rank ordering. We want each RR_j value (for a resistor) to be assigned a higher rank than that assigned to any RR_j° value (for a potential resistor). An easy way to do this is to define a value RR_j for each potential resistor given by

$$RR_j = RR_j^\circ - RR_1^\circ + 1 - Min(RR_j : j \in NR), j \in N(c', x') - NR.$$

$$RR_j = RR_j^\circ - Max(RR_j^\circ : j \in N(c', x') - NR) - 1 + Min(RR_j : j \in NR), j \in N(c', x') - NR.$$

The set of RR_j values over $j \in N(c', x')$ then satisfies the desired ordering for both resistors ($j \in NR$) and potential resistors ($j \in N(c', x') - NR$). (Recall that $NR = N^*(x'', c', x')$ by having previously disposed of blatant resistors.)

For the subset $N(k)$ of k non-tabu elements of $N(c', x')$ (hence of $N(c', x') - T$) that we seek to generate, the ordering over the subset $NR - T$

thus comes ahead of the ordering over the subset $(N(c', x') - NR) - T$, This allows both resistors and potential resistors to be included among those elements to be assigned new coefficients c'_j and new target values x'_j, where the new c'_j coefficients for resistors always have larger absolute values than the c'_j coefficients for potential resistors. If the set of non-tabu resistors $NR - T$ already contains at least k elements, then no potential resistors will be assigned new c'_j or x'_j values.

3.5. Overview of the Resistance and Reaction Procedure

The rule for generating the target objective $\delta(c', x', x)$ that lies at the heart of the Resistance & Reaction procedure is based on carrying out the following preliminary steps, where the value k_{max} is determined as previously indicated: (a) re-index the variables $x_j, j \in N(c', x') - T$, so that the values RR_j are in descending order, thus yielding $RR_1 \geq RR_2 \geq \ldots$; (b) identify the subset $N(k) = \{1, 2, \ldots, k\}$ of NR that references the k largest RR_j values, where $k = Min(|N(c', x') - T|, k_{max})$; (c) create a rank ordering by letting $R_p, p = 1, \ldots, r$ denote the distinct values among the $RR_j, j \in N(k)$, where $R_1 > R_2 > \ldots > R_r (r \geq 1)$.

Then the rule to determine the c'_j and x'_j values for the variables $x_j, j \in N(k)$, is given as follows:

$N(c', x') - T$ *Rule for Generating* c'_j *and* $x_j', j \in N(k)$ *(for* $NR = N^*(x'', c', x') \neq \varnothing$*):*

If $RR_j = R_p$, set $c'_j = \langle 1 + BaseCost(r + 1 - p)/r \rangle$ and $x'_j = 1 - x'_j$.

We see that this rule assigns c'_j coefficients so that the c'_j values are the positive integers $\langle 1 + BaseCost(1/r) \rangle$, $\langle 1 + BaseCost(2/r) \rangle, \ldots, \langle 1 + BaseCost(r/r) \rangle = 1 + BaseCost$.

We are now ready to specify the Resistance & Reaction procedure in overview, which incorporates its main elements except for the creation and updating of the tabu list T.

Resistance and Reaction Procedure in Overview

0. Initialize the current problem P to be the (MIP:0-1) problem.

1. Solve LP(P) yielding the optimal solution x^o. (Stop if the first instance of (LP) yields an integer feasible solution x^o, which therefore is optimal for (MIP:0-1).)

2. Construct the target solution x' derived from x^o by setting $x'_j = \langle x^o_j \rangle$, for $j \in N$. Apply the Rule of the Proximity Procedure for Generating c'_j (to each j in N) to produce the vector c'.

3. Solve LP(x', c'), yielding the solution x''. Set $x^{oo} = x''$. Update the current problem by adding the inequality derived from c' (i.e., $P = P \mid \delta(c', x', x) \geq \lceil v(LP(x', c')) \rceil + 1$).

4. Let $N^*(x'') = \{j \in N: 0 < x_j'' < 1\}$, $N^*(c', x') = \{j \in N: c'_j = 0$ or $0 < x_j' < 1\}$, $N(c', x') = N - N^*(c', x')$, $N^{**}(x'', c', x') = N^*(x'') \cap N^*(c', x')$ and $N^*(x'', c', x') = N^*(x'') \cap N(c', x')$, $NR = \{j \in N: c'_j \delta(j, x', x'') \neq 0\}$.

5. There exists at least one fractional variable ($N^*(x'') \neq \varnothing$). Remove blatant resistors x_j, if any exist, from NR and transfer them to $N^*(c', x')$ (or to $N(x', 1-x'_j)$) so $NR = N^*(x'', c', x')$.

   a. If $N^*(x'') = N^{**}(x'', c', x')$ (hence $NR = \varnothing$), apply the $N^{**}(x'', c', x')$ Rule for Generating c'_j and x'_j, $j \in N(k)$ to produce the new target objective $\delta(c', x', x)$ and associated target vector x':

Set $c'_j = 1 + \langle BaseCost|\Delta_j| /|\Delta_1|\rangle$ and $x'_j = \text{sign}(\Delta_j)$, where $\Delta_j = x^o_j - x''_j$.

   b. If instead $NR \neq \varnothing$, then apply the $N(c', x') - T$ Rule for Generating $c'j$ and $x'j$, $j \in N(k)$, to produce the new target objective $\delta(c', x', x)$ and associated target vector x':

If $RR_j = R_p$, set $c'_j = \langle 1 + BaseCost(r + 1 - p)/r\rangle$ and $x'_j = 1 - x'_j$.

6. Set $x^{oo} = x''$ and solve LP(x', c'), yielding the solution x''. Update the current problem P by adding the inequality derived from c' (i.e., $P = P \mid \delta(c', x', x) \geq \lceil v(LP(x', c')) \rceil + 1$).

7. If x'' is integer feasible: update the best solution $(x^*, y^*) = (x'', y'')$, update the current problem P by adding $u_o < z_o^*$, (i.e., $P = P \mid u_o < z_o^*$) and return to Step 1. Otherwise, return to Step 4.

This design is completed by the processes described in the next section.

4. CREATING AND MANAGING THE TABU LIST T – RESISTANCE & REACTION PROCEDURE COMPLETED

We propose an approach for creating the tabu list T that is relatively simple but offers useful features within the present context. As in a variety of constructions for handling a recency-based tabu memory, we update T by adding a new element j to the first position of the list when a variable x_j becomes tabu (as a result of assigning it a new target value x'_j and coefficient c'_j), and by dropping the "oldest" element that lies in the last position of T when its tabu status expires.

Our present construction employs a rule that may add and drop more than one element from T at the same time. The checking of tabu status is facilitated by using a vector $Tabu(j)$ that is updated by setting $Tabu(j) = true$ when j is added to T and by setting $Tabu(j) = false$ when j is dropped from T. (Tabu status is often monitored by using a vector $TabuEnd(j)$ that identifies the last iteration that element j qualifies as tabu, without bothering to explicitly store the list T, but the current method of creating and removing tabu status makes the indicated handling of T preferable.)

We first describe the method for the case where $k = 1$, i.e., only a single variable x_j is assigned a new target value (and thereby becomes tabu) on a given iteration. The modification for handling the case $k > 1$ is straightforward, as subsequently indicated. Two parameters T_{min} and T_{max} govern the generation of T, where $T_{max} > T_{min} \geq 1$. For simplicity we suggest the default values $T_{min} = 2$ and $T_{max} = n^{.6}$. (In general, appropriate values are anticipated to result by selecting T_{min} from the interval between 1 and 3 and T_{max} from the interval between $n^{.5}$ and $n^{.7}$.) The small value of T_{min} accords with an intensification focus, and larger values may be selected for diversification.

The target value x'_j and coefficient c'_j do not automatically change when j is dropped from T and x_j becomes non-tabu. Consequently, we employ one other parameter AssignSpan that limits the duration that x_j may be assigned the same x'_j and c'_j values, after which x_j is released from the restrictions induced by this assignment. To make use of *AssignSpan*, we keep track of when x_j most recently was added to T by setting *TabuAdd(j)* = *iter*, where *iter* denotes the current iteration value (in this case, the iteration when the addition occurred). Then, when *TabuAdd(j)* + *AssignSpan* < *iter*, x_j is released from the influence of x'_j and c'_j by removing j from the set $N(c', x')$ and adding it to the unassigned set $N^*(c', x')$. As long as x_j is actively being assigned new x'_j and c'_j values, *TabuAdd(j)* is repeatedly being assigned new values of iter, and hence the transfer of j to $N^*(c', x')$ is postponed. We suggest a default value for *AssignSpan* between $1.5T_{max}$ and $3T_{max}$; e.g., *AssignSpan* = $2T_{max}$.

To manage the updating of T itself, we maintain an array denoted *TabuRefresh(j)* that is initialized by setting *TabuRefresh(j)* = 0 for all $j \in N$. Then on any iteration when j is added to T, *TabuRefresh(j)* is checked to see if *TabuRefresh(j)* < *iter* (which automatically holds the first time j is added to T). When the condition is satisfied, a *refreshing operation* is performed, after adding j to the front of T, that consists of two steps: (a) the list T is

reduced in size to yield $|T| = T_{min}$ (more precisely, $|T| \leq T_{min}$) by dropping all but the T_{min} first elements of T; (b) *TabuRefresh(j)* is updated by setting *TabuRefresh(j)* = *iter* + v, where v is a number randomly chosen from the interval [*AssignSpan*, 2*AssignSpan*]. These operations assure that future steps of adding this particular element j to T will not again shrink T to contain T_{min} elements until *iter* reaches a value that exceeds *TabuRefresh(j)*. Barring the occurrence of such a refreshing operation, T is allowed to grow without dropping any of its elements until it reaches a size of T_{max}. Once $|T| = T_{max}$, the oldest j is removed from the end of T each time a new element j is added to the front of T, and hence T is stabilized at the size T_{max} until a new refreshing operation occurs.

This approach for updating T is motivated by the following observation. The first time j is added to T (when *TabuRefresh(j)* = 0) T may acceptably be reduced in size to contain not just T_{min} elements, but in fact to contain only 1 element, and no matter what element is added on the next iteration the composition of $N(c', x')$ cannot duplicate any previous composition. Moreover, following such a step, the composition of $N(c', x')$ will likewise not be duplicated as long as T continues to grow without dropping any elements. Thus, by relying on intervening refreshing operations with *TabuRefresh(j)* = 0 and $T_{min} = 1$, we could conceivably allow T to grow even until reaching a size $T_{max} = n$. (Typically, a considerable number of iterations would pass before reaching such a state.) In general, however, by allowing T to reach a size $T_{max} = n$ the restrictiveness of preventing targets from being reassigned for T_{max} iterations would be too severe. Consequently we employ two mechanisms to avoid such an overly restrictive state: (i) choosing $T_{max} < n$ and (ii) performing a refreshing operation that allows each j to shrink T more than once (whenever *iter* grows to exceed the updated value of *TabuRefresh(j)*) The combination of these two mechanisms provides a flexible tabu list that is self-calibrating in the sense of automatically adjusting its size in response to varying patterns of assigning target values to elements.

The addition of multiple elements to the front of T follows essentially the same design, subject to the restriction of adding only up to T_{min} new indexes j of $N(k)$ to T on any iteration, should k be greater than T_{min}. We slightly extend the earlier suggestion $T_{min} = 2$ to propose $T_{min} = 3$ for $k_{max} \geq 3$.

Note that the organization of the method assures $T \subset N(c', x')$ and typically a good portion of $N(c', x')$ lies outside T. If exceptional circumstances result in $T = N(c', x')$, the method drops the last element of T so that $N(c', x')$ contains at least one non-tabu element.

Drawing on these observations, the detailed form of the Resistance & Reaction Procedure that includes instructions for managing the tabu list is specified below, employing the stopping criterion indicated earlier of limiting the computation to a specified maximum number of iterations. (These iterations differ from those counted by *iter*, which is re-set to 0 each time a new solution is found and the method returns to solve the updated (LP),)

Complete Resistance and Reaction Procedure

0. Choose the values T_{min}, T_{max} and *AssignSpan*.
1. Solve (LP). (Stop if the first instance of (LP) yields an integer feasible solution x″, which therefore is optimal for (MIP:0-1).) Set TabuRefresh(j) = 0 for all j ∈ N and set iter = 0.
2. There exists at least one fractional variable $(N^*(x'') \neq \emptyset)$. Remove each blatant resistor x_j, if any exists, from NR and transfer it to $N^*(c', x')$ (or to $N'(1 - x'_j)$), yielding $NR = N^*(x'', c', x')$. If j is transferred to $N^*(c', x')$ and $j \in T$, drop j from T. Also, if $T = N(c', x')$, then drop the last element from T.
   (a) If $N^*(x'') = N^{**}(x'', c', x')$ (hence $NR = \emptyset$), apply the $N^{**}(x'', c', x')$ Rule for Generating c'_j and x'_j, $j \in N(k)$.

(b) If instead $NR \neq \emptyset$, then apply the $N(c', x') - T$ Rule for Generating c'_j and x'_j, $j \in N(k)$.

(c) Set *iter*: = *iter* + 1. Using the indexing that produces $N(k)$ in (a) or (b), add the elements $j = 1, 2, \ldots min(T_{min}, k)$ to the front of T (so that $T = (1, 2, \ldots)$ after the addition). If *TabuRefresh*(j) < *iter* for any added element j, set *TabuRefresh*(j) = *iter* + v, for v randomly chosen between *AsignLength* and 2*AssignSpan* (for each such j) and then reduce T to at most T_{min} elements by dropping all elements in positions > T_{min}.

3. Solve LP(x′, c′), yielding the solution x″. Update the Problem Inequalities.
4. If x″ is integer feasible: update the best solution $(x^*, y^*) = (x'', y'')$, update $u_o < z_o^*$, and return to Step 1. Otherwise, return to Step 2.

The inequalities introduced in Sections 3 and 4 provide a useful component of this method, but the method is organized to operate even in the absence of such inequalities. The intensification and diversification strategies proposed in Section 5 can be incorporated for solving more difficult problems.

5. INTENSIFICATION AND DIVERSIFICATION BASED ON STRATEGIC INEQUALITIES

More generally, for any positive integer k satisfying $n \geq k \geq 1$, the binary vectors x that lie at least a Hamming distance k from x' are precisely those that satisfy the inequality

$$\delta(e, x', x) \geq k \tag{4}$$

The inequality (4) has been introduced within the context of adaptive memory search strategies

(Glover, 2005) to compel new solutions x to be separated from a given solution x' by a desired distance. In particular, upon identifying a reference set $R = \{x^r, r \in R_l\}$, which consists of elite and diverse solutions generated during prior search, the approach consists of launching a diversification strategy that requires new solutions x to satisfy the associated set of inequalities

$$\delta(e, x^r, x) \geq k^r, r \in R_l \tag{5}$$

This system also gives a mechanism for implementing a proposal of Shylo (1999)[4] to separate new binary solutions by a minimum specified Hamming distance from a set of solutions previously encountered.

The inequalities of (5) constitute a form of *model embedded memory* for adaptive memory search methods where they are introduced for two purposes: (a) to generate new starting solutions and (b) to restrict a search process to visiting solutions that remain at specified distances from previous solutions. A diversification phase that employs the strategy (b) operates by eventually reducing the e_o^r values to 1, in order to transition from diversification to intensification. One approach for doing this is to use tabu penalties to discourage moves that lead to solutions violating (5). We discuss another approach in the next section.

A more limiting variant of (5) arises in the context of exploiting strongly determined and consistent variables, and in associated adaptive memory *projection* strategies that iteratively select various subsets of variable to hold fixed at specific values, or to be constrained to lie within specific bounds (Glover, 2005). This variant occurs by identifying sub-sets $J^{r1}, J^{r2}, \ldots,$ of N for the solutions x^r to produce the inequalities

$$\delta(J^{rh}, x^r, x) \geq k^{rh}, r \in R_l, h = 1, 2 \ldots \tag{6}$$

The inequalities of (6) are evidently more restrictive than those of (5), if the sum of the values k^{rh} over h is strictly greater than the values k^r (i.e., if $\sum_h k^{rh} > k^r$ for each r).

The inequalities (6) find application within two main contexts. The first occurs within a diversification segment of alternating intensification and diversification phases, where each intensification phase holds certain variables fixed and the ensuing diversification divides the index of variables N of each x^r into two sub-sets J^{r1} and J^{r2} that respectively contain the components of x^r held fixed (i.e., this arise by setting $k^{r1} = 0$) and the components permitted to be free during the preceding intensification phase. For example, the heuristic based on the LP-relaxation considers x^r which is an optimal solution of LP-relaxtion of a current problem and divides the set N into two sub-sets J^{r1} and J^{r2} that respectively contain the components of x^r held basis variables and the components no basis. Then a reduced problem is generated where the no basic variables are fixed to their values in x^r (i.e. this arise by setting $k^{r2} = 0$) and the components in J^{r1} permitted to be free. The heuristic solves approximatily or exactly the corresponding reduced problem (see Soyster et al., 1978; Hanafi & Wilbaut, 2009). Another example is the Local Branching proposed by Fischetti and Lodi (2003), at each iteration r, the set J^{r1} corresponds to the set of variables over which branching has already been occured (those variables held fixed i.e., $k^{r1} = 0$) and J^{r2} contains the components of x^r permitted to be separated from a given solution x' by a desired distance k^{r2}. In Relaxation Induced Neighborhood Search for solving the MIP proposed by Danna et al. (2005), they use $J^{r1} = N((\bar{x} + x^*)/2)$ and $J^{r2} = N - J^{r1}$ where x^* is the current incumbent feasible solution and $\bar{x}$ is an optimal solution of the LP-relaxation.

The second area of application occurs in conjunction with frequency memory by choosing three sub-sets J^{r1}, J^{r2} and J^{r3} (for example) to consist of components of solution x^r that have received particular values with high, middle and low frequencies, relative to a specified set of previously visited solutions. (The same frequency vector, and hence the same way of sub-dividing the x^r vectors, may be relevant for all x^r solutions generated during a given phase of search.)[5]

Our following ideas can be implemented to enhance these adaptive memory projection strategies as well as the other strategies previously described.

5.1 An Intensification Procedure

Consider an indexed collection of inequalities of the form of (2) given by

$$\delta(c^p, x', x) \geq \lceil \delta(c^p, x', x'') \rceil, p \in P \qquad (7)$$

We introduce an intensification procedure that makes use of (7) by basing the inequalities indexed by P on a collection of high quality binary target solutions x'. Such solutions can be obtained from past search history or from approaches for rounding an optimal solution to a linear programming relaxation (LP) of (P), using penalties to account for infeasibility in ranking the quality of such solutions. The solutions x' do not have to be feasible to be used as target solutions or to generate inequalities. In Section 6 we give specific approaches for creating such target solutions and the associated target objectives $\delta(c', x', x)$ that serve as a foundation for producing the underlying inequalities.

Our goal from an intensification perspective is to find a new solution that is close to those in the collection of high quality solutions that give rise to (7). We introduce slack variables s_p, $p \in P$, to permit the system (7) to be expressed equivalently as

$$\delta(c^p, x', x) - s_p = \lceil \delta(c^p, x', x'') \rceil, s_p \geq 0, p \in P \qquad (8)$$

Then, assuming the set X includes reference to the constraints (8), we create an *Intensified LP Relaxation*

Minimize $(s_0 = \sum_{p \in P} W_p S_p : x \in X)$ where the weights w_p for the variables s_p are selected to be positive integers.

An important variation is to seek a solution that minimizes the maximum deviation of x from solutions giving rise to (7). This can be accomplished by introducing the inequalities

$$s_0 \geq \lceil \delta(c^p, x', x'') \rceil - \delta(c^p, x', x), p \in P \qquad (9)$$

Assuming these inequalities are likewise incorporated into X,[6] the Min(Max) goal is achieved by solving the problem

Minimize $(s_0 : x \in X)$

An optimal solution to either of these two indicated objectives can then be used as a starting point for an intensified solution pass, performing all-at-once or successive rounding to replace its fractional components by integers.[7]

5.2 A Diversification Analog

To create a diversification procedure for generating new starting solutions, we seek an objective function to drive the search to lie as far as possible from solutions in the region defined by (7). For this purpose we introduce the variables s_p as in (8), but utilize a maximization objective rather than a minimization objective to produce the problem

Maximize $(s_0 = \sum_{p \in P} W_p S_p : x \in X)$

The weights w_p are once again chosen to be positive.

A principal alternative in this case consists of maximizing the minimum deviation of x from solutions giving rise to (7). For this, we additionally include the inequalities

$$s_0 \leq \lceil \delta(c^p, x', x'') \rceil - \delta(c^p, x', x), p \in P \qquad (10)$$

giving rise to the problem

Maximize $(s_0 : x \in X)$.

The variable s_0 introduced in (10) differs from its counterpart in (9). In the case where the degree of diversification provided by this approach is excessive, by driving solutions too far away from solutions expected to be good, control can be exerted through bounding X with other constraints, and in particular by manipulating the bound z_0 identified in Section 1.

6. CONCLUSION

Branch-and-bound ($B\&B$) and branch-and-cut ($B\&C$) methods have long been considered the methods of choice for solving mixed integer programming problems. In recent years, efforts to create improved $B\&B$ and $B\&C$ solution approaches have intensified and have produced significant benefits, as evidenced by the existence of MIP procedures that are appreciably more effective than their predecessors. It remains true, however, that many MIP problems resist solution by the best current $B\&B$ and $B\&C$ methods. As a consequence, metaheuristic methods have attracted attention as possible alternatives or supplements to the more classical approaches. Yet to date, the amount of effort devoted to developing good metaheuristics for MIP problems is almost negligible compared to the effort being devoted to developing refined versions of the classical methods.

The view adopted in Part I and II is that metaheuristic approaches can benefit from a change of perspective in order to perform at their best in the MIP setting. Drawing on lessons learned from applying classical methods, we anticipate that metaheuristics can likewise profit from generating inequalities to supplement their basic functions. However, we propose that these inequalities be used in ways not employed in classical MIP methods, and indicate two principal avenues for doing this: first by generating the inequalities in reference to strategically created target solutions and target objectives, as in Part I, and second by embedding these inequalities in special intensification and diversification processes, as described in this Part II. The use of such strategies raises the issue of how to compose the target solutions and objectives themselves. Classical MIP methods such as $B\&B$ and $B\&C$ again provide a clue to be heeded, by demonstrating that memory is relevant to effective solution procedures. However, we suggest that gains can be made by going beyond the rigidly structured memory employed in $B\&B$ and $B\&C$ procedures. Thus we make use of the type of adaptive memory framework introduced in tabu search, which offers a range of recency and frequency memory structures for achieving goals associated with short term and long term solution strategies.

ACKNOWLEDGMENT

The present research work has been supported by International Campus on Safety and Intermodality in Transportation, the Nord-Pas-de-Calais Region, the European Community, the Regional Delegation for Research and Technology, the Ministry of Higher Education and Research, the National Center for Scientific Research. A restricted (preliminary) version of this work appeared in Glover (2008).

REFERENCES

Balas, E., & Jeroslow, R. (1972). Canonical Cuts on the Unit Hypercube. *SIAM Journal on Applied Mathematics, 23*(1), 60–69. doi:10.1137/0123007

Blum, C., & Roli, A. (2003). Metaheuristics in Combinatorial Optimization: Overview and Conceptual Comparison. *ACM Journal, 35*(3), 268–308.

Crainic, T. G., & Toulouse, M. (2003). Parallel Strategies for Meta-Heuristics. In Kochenberger, G., & Glover, F. (Eds.), *Handbook of Metaheuristics*. Dordrecht, The Netherlands: Kluwer Academic Publishers.

Dantzig, G. (1963). *Linear Programming and Extensions*. Princeton, NJ: Princeton University Press.

Davoine, T., Hammer, P. L., & Vizvári, B. (2003). A Heuristic for Boolean optimization problems. *Journal of Heuristics, 9*, 229–247. doi:10.1023/A:1023717307746

Fischetti, M., Glover, F., & Lodi, A. (2005). Feasibility Pump. *Mathematical Programming - Series A, 104*, 91–104. doi:10.1007/s10107-004-0570-3

Fischetti, M., Glover, F., Lodi, A., & Monaci, M. (2006). *Feasibility Net*.

Glover, F. (1978). Parametric Branch and Bound. *OMEGA. The International Journal of Management Science, 6*(2), 145–152.

Glover, F. (2005). Adaptive Memory Projection Methods for Integer Programming. In C. Rego & B. Alidaee (Eds.), *Metaheuristic Optimization Via Memory and Evolution: Tabu Search and Scatter Search* (pp. 425-440). Dordrecht, The Netherland: Kluwer Academic Publishers.

Glover, F. (2006). Parametric Tabu Search for Mixed Integer Programs. *Computers & Operations Research, 33*(9), 2449–2494. doi:10.1016/j.cor.2005.07.009

Glover, F. (2006a). *Satisfiability Data Mining for Binary Data Classification Problems (Tech. Rep.)*. Boulder, CO: University of Colorado, Boulder.

Glover, F. (2007). Infeasible/Feasible Search Trajectories and Directional Rounding in Integer Programming. *Journal of Heuristics*.

Glover, F., & Greenberg, H. (1989). New Approaches for Heuristic Search: A Bilateral Linkage with Artificial Intelligence. *European Journal of Operational Research, 39*(2), 119–130. doi:10.1016/0377-2217(89)90185-9

Glover, F., & Hanafi, S. (2002). Tabu Search and Finite Convergence. *Discrete Applied Mathematics, 119*, 3–36. doi:10.1016/S0166-218X(01)00263-3

Glover, F., & Hanafi, S. (2010). Metaheuristic Search with Inequalities and Target Objectives for Mixed Binary Optimization Part I: Exploiting Proximity. *International Journal of Applied Metaheuristic Computing, 1*(1), 1–15.

Glover, F., & Laguna, M. (1997). *Tabu Search*. Dordrecht, The Netherlands: Kluwer Academic Publishers.

Glover, F., & Sherali, H. D. (2003). Foundation-Penalty Cuts for Mixed-Integer Programs. *Operations Research Letters, 31*, 245–253. doi:10.1016/S0167-6377(03)00014-2

Guignard, M., & Spielberg, K. (2003). *Double Contraction, Double Probing, Short Starts and BB-Probing Cuts for Mixed (0,1) Programming (Tech. Rep.)*. Philadelphia, PA: University of Pennsylvania, Wharton School.

Hanafi, S., & Wilbaut, C. (2006). Improved Convergent Heuristic for 0-1 Mixed Integer Programming. *Annals of Operations Research*. doi:. doi:10.1007/s10479-009-0546-z

Hvattum, L. M., Lokketangen, A., & Glover, F. (2004). Adaptive Memory Search for Boolean Optimization Problems. *Discrete Applied Mathematics, 142*, 99–109. doi:10.1016/j.dam.2003.06.006

Nediak, M., & Eckstein, J. (2007). Pivot, Cut, and Dive: A Heuristic for Mixed 0-1 Integer Programming. *Journal of Heuristics, 13*, 471–503. doi:10.1007/s10732-007-9021-7

Nowicki, E., & Smutnicki, C. (1996). A Fast Taboo Search Algorithm for the Job Shop Problem. *Management Science, 42*(6), 797–813. doi:10.1287/mnsc.42.6.797

Pardalos, P. S., & Shylo, O. V. (2006). *An algorithm for Job Shop Scheduling based on Global Equilibrium Search Techniques. Computational Management Science. DOI: 10.1007/s10287-006-0023-y Patel, J., & Chinneck, J. W. (2006). Active-Constraint Variable Ordering for Faster Feasibility of Mixed Integer Linear Programs.* Mathematical Programming.

Pedroso, J. P. (2005). Tabu search for mixed integer programming. In Rego, C., & Alidaee, B. (Eds.), *Metaheuristic Optimization via Memory and Evolution: Tabu Search and Scatter Search.* Dordrecht, The Netherlands: Kluwer Academic Publishers. doi:10.1007/0-387-23667-8_11

Shylo, O. V. (1999). A Global Equilibrium Search Method. *Kybernetika I Systemniy Analys, 1,* 74–80.

Soyster, A. L., Lev, B., & Slivka, W. (1978). Zero–one programming with many variables and few constraints. *European Journal of Operational Research, 2*(3), 195–201. doi:10.1016/0377-2217(78)90093-0

Spielberg, K., & Guignard, M. (2000). A Sequential (Quasi) Hot Start Method for BB (0,1) Mixed Integer Programming. In *Proceedings of the Mathematical Programming Symposium,* Atlanta.

Ursulenko, A. (2006). *Notes on the Global Equilibrium Search (Tech. Rep.).* Al Paso, TX: Texas A & M University.

Wilbaut, C., & Hanafi, S. (2009). New Convergent Heuristics for 0-1 Mixed Integer Programming. *European Journal of Operational Research, 195,* 62–74. doi:10.1016/j.ejor.2008.01.044

ENDNOTES

[1] In some problem settings, the inclusion of the secondary objective x_0 in a primary objective $v_{00} = Mv_0 + x_0$ is unimportant, and in these cases our notation is accurate in referring to the explicit minimization of $v_0 = c'x$.

[2] For any real number α, $\lceil \alpha \rceil$ and $\lfloor \alpha \rfloor$ respectively identify the least integer $\geq \alpha$ and the greatest integer $\leq \alpha$.

[3] This is the "alternative definition" of x^o indicated earlier.

[4] See also Pardalos and Shylo (2006) and Ursulenko (2006).

[5] The formulas of Glover (2005) apply more generally to arbitrary integer solution vectors.

[6] The inclusion of (8) and (9) is solely for the purpose of solving the associated linear programs, and these temporarily accessed constraints do not have to be incorporated among those defining Z.

[7] Successive rounding normally updates the LP solution after rounding each variable in order to determine the effects on other variables and thereby take advantage of modified rounding options.

This work was previously published in International Journal of Applied Metaheuristic Computing, Volume 1, Issue 2, edited by Peng-Yeng Yin, pp. 1-17, copyright 2010 by IGI Publishing (an imprint of IGI Global).

Chapter 3

A Reinforcement Learning:
Great-Deluge Hyper-Heuristic
for Examination Timetabling

Ender Özcan
University of Nottingham, UK

Mustafa Mısır
Yeditepe University, Turkey

Gabriela Ochoa
University of Nottingham, UK

Edmund K. Burke
University of Nottingham, UK

ABSTRACT

Hyper-heuristics can be identified as methodologies that search the space generated by a finite set of low level heuristics for solving search problems. An iterative hyper-heuristic framework can be thought of as requiring a single candidate solution and multiple perturbation low level heuristics. An initially generated complete solution goes through two successive processes (heuristic selection and move acceptance) until a set of termination criteria is satisfied. A motivating goal of hyper-heuristic research is to create automated techniques that are applicable to a wide range of problems with different characteristics. Some previous studies show that different combinations of heuristic selection and move acceptance as hyper-heuristic components might yield different performances. This study investigates whether learning heuristic selection can improve the performance of a great deluge based hyper-heuristic using an examination timetabling problem as a case study.

DOI: 10.4018/978-1-4666-0270-0.ch003

1. INTRODUCTION

Meta-heuristics have been widely and successfully applied to many different problems. However, significant development effort is often needed to produce fine tuned techniques for the particular problem or even instance that is under investigation. Hyper-heuristics represent an increasingly popular research direction in search and optimisation (Burke et al., 2003a; Ross, 2005; Chakhlevitch et al., 2008; Özcan et al., 2008; Burke et al. 2009a, 2009b). One of the aims is to at produce more general problem solving techniques, which can potentially be applied to different problems or instances with little development effort. The idea is that a hyper-heuristic approach should able to intelligently choose an appropriate low-level heuristic (from a given repository of heuristics) to be applied at any given time. Thus, in hyper-heuristics, we are interested in adaptively finding solution methods, rather than directly producing a solution for whichever search problem we are studying.

Several hyper-heuristics approaches have been proposed in the literature. It is possible to consider methodologies based on *perturbation* low-level heuristics and those based on *construction* low-level heuristics. The latter type builds a solution incrementally, starting with a blank solution and using construction heuristics to gradually build a complete solution. They have been successfully investigated for several combinatorial optimisation problems such as: bin-packing (Tereshima-Marin et al., 2007), timetabling (Terashima-Marin et al., 1999; Burke et al., 2007, Qu et al., 2008), production scheduling (Vazquez-Rodriguez et al., 2007), and cutting stock (Terashima-Marin et al., 2005). On the other hand, approaches based on perturbation heuristics find a reasonable initial solution by some straightforward means (either randomly or using a simple construction heuristic) and then use heuristics, such as shift and swap to perturb solution components with the aim of finding improved solutions. In other words, they start from a complete solution and then search or select among a set of neighbourhoods for better solutions. A class of the most commonly used hyper-heuristics based on perturbation (improvement) low level heuristics is the *choice* hyper-heuristics (heuristic selection methodologies). They have been applied to real world problems, such as, personnel scheduling (Cowling et al., 2001; Burke et al., 2003b), timetabling (Burke et al., 2003b; Dowsland et al., 2007), and vehicle routing problems (Pisinger et al., 2007). In a choice hyper-heuristic framework based on perturbation low level heuristics, search is mostly performed using a single candidate solution. Such hyper-heuristics, iteratively, attempt to improve a given solution throughout two consecutive phases: *heuristic selection* and *move acceptance* as illustrated in Figure 1.

In Figure 1, a candidate solution (S_t) at a given time (t) is modified into a new solution (or solutions) using a chosen heuristic (or heuristics). Then, a move acceptance method is employed to decide whether to accept or reject a resultant solution (R_t). This process is repeated until a predefined stopping condition is met. Only problem independent information flow is allowed between the problem domain and hyper-heuristic layers. Unless, we specifically say otherwise, a choice hyper-heuristic refers to a hyper-heuristic that operates on a set of perturbation low level heuristics from this point onwards. Moreover, such a hyper-heuristic will be denoted as *heuristic selection − move acceptance* based on its components.

Great deluge is a well-known acceptance strategy (Dueck, 1993; Burke et al., 2003). Bilgin et al. (2007) reported that hyper-heuristics formed by different combinations of heuristic selection and move acceptance methods might yield different performances. Moreover, simple random−great deluge delivered a similar performance to the best approach; namely, choice function − simulated annealing for examination timetabling. Obviously, simple random receives no feedback at all during

Figure 1. A hyper-heuristic framework based on a single point search, where S_t denotes a candidate solution at time t, H_i is the ith low level heuristic, R_t is the resultant solution after applying a set of selected low level heuristics that goes into the move acceptance process

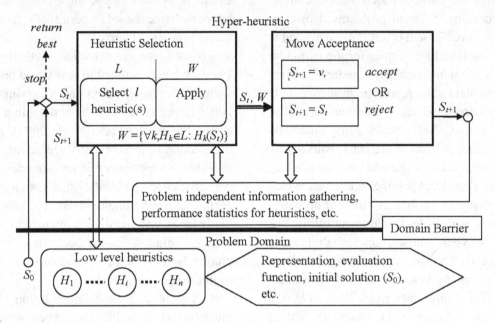

the search to improve upon the heuristic selection process. Hence, in this study, *great-deluge* is preferred as the move acceptance component within a choice hyper-heuristic framework to investigate the effect of learning heuristic selection on its overall performance for solving the same examination timetabling problem as formulated in Bilgin et al. (2007). The learning mechanisms, inspired by the work by Nareyek (2003), are based on weight adaptation.

2. Hyper-Heuristics and Learning

Although hyper-heuristic as a term has been introduced recently (Denzinger et al., 1997), the origins of the idea date back to the early 1960s (Fisher et al., 1961). A hyper-heuristic operates at a high level by managing or generating low level heuristics which operate on the problem domain. Meta-heuristics have been commonly used as hyper-heuristics. A hyper-heuristic can conduct a single point or multi-point search. Population based meta-heuristics which perform multi-

point search, such as learning classifier systems (Marín-Blázquez and Schulenburg, 2005), evolutionary algorithms (Cowling et al., 2002; Han et al., 2003; Pillay and Banzhaf, 2008), genetic programming (Keller et al., 2007; Burke et al., 2009a), ant colony optimisation (Cuesta-Canada et al., 2005; Chen et al., 2007) have been applied to a variety of combinatorial optimisation problems as hyper-heuristics. Distributed computing methods can also be used to perform multi-point search (Rattadilok et al., 2004; Rattadilok et al., 2005; Ouelhadj et al., 2008). Özcan et al. (2008) presented different hyper-heuristic frameworks showing that a matching performance to memetic algorithms can be achieved. In this study, the choice hyper-heuristic framework as presented in Figure 1 is studied. The primary components of such hyper-heuristics are heuristic selection and move acceptance.

A major motivating feature of hyper-heuristic research is the aim to facilitate applicability to different problem instances having different characteristics as well as different problem domains. With this goal in mind, machine learning techniques are vital for hyper-heuristics to make the right choices during the heuristic selection process. Learning can be achieved in an *offline* or *online* manner. An offline learning hyper-heuristic requires training over a set of problems, before it is used to solve the unseen problem instances. For example, Burke et al. (2006) use a case based reasoning system as a hyper-heuristic for solving course and examination timetabling problems. An online learning hyper-heuristic learns through the feedback obtained during the search process while solving a given problem. Most of the existing online learning hyper-heuristics incorporate *reinforcement learning* (Kaelbling et al., 1996; Sutton et al., 1998). A reinforcement learning system interacts with the environment and changes its state via a selected action in such a way as to increase some notion of long term reward. Hence, a learning hyper-heuristic maintains a utility value obtained through predetermined reward and punishment schemes for each low level heuristic. A heuristic is selected based on the utility values of the low level heuristics in hand at each step. Remembering and forgetting represent core ingredients of learning. Remembering can be achieved through reward and punishment schemes. Forgetting can be achieved through the use of lower and upper bounds on the utility values. Some reinforcement learning methods use weighted average of the learnt utility values. A dynamic weighting scheme can be employed which favours the outcome of the most recent actions or choices. Reward and punishment schemes are allowed to use different adaptation rates in the case of an improving and worsening move, respectively. For example, the utility value of a selected heuristic can be increased at a constant rate linearly whenever there is an improvement after it is employed, otherwise the utility value can be decreased at a different rate, or it can even be kept constant. Initialisation of the utility values, lower and upper bounds for them along with a memory adjustment scheme (weight-

ing) represent the remainder of the constituents for a reinforcement learning based hyper-heuristic.

Some previously studied heuristic selection methods are summarised in Table 1. Simple random, random gradient, random permutation gradient, greedy and choice function heuristic selection methods are presented in Cowling et al. (2001a). All these approaches can be considered to be learning heuristic selection methods, except simple random. In Cowling et al. (2001b), a parameter-free choice function was presented. As a problem domain, sales summit scheduling was used in both studies. Cowling and Chakhlevitch (2003) investigated peckish heuristic selection strategies that eliminated the selection and application of all low level heuristics as in greedy heuristic selection.

Nareyek (2003) investigated reinforcement learning using different reward/penalty schemes and heuristic selection strategies on the Orc Quest problem and in the logistics domain. Additive/subtractive adaptation rates combined with heuristic selection using the maximal utility generated better results as opposed to a fair random choice (softmax, roulette wheel). All heuristics were assigned to a utility value of 0 initially and raw utility values were maintained. Upper and lower bounds were defined for the utility values. In Burke et al. (2003b), reinforcement learning was combined with tabu search in a hyper-heuristic and applied to the personnel rostering and timetabling problems. The aim of this modification was to prevent the selection of some heuristics for a while by inserting them into a variable-length tabu list. A non-tabu heuristic with the highest utility value was chosen at each step.

Some studies concentrate on move acceptance in hyper-heuristics rather than upon heuristic selection methods, as accepting a move turns out to be an extremely important decision. In Cowling et al. (2001), heuristic selection methods are combined with either all moves accepted or with only an improving moves accepted strategy. On the other hand, Ayob and Kendall (2003) proposed

Table 1. Description of a set of heuristic selection methods used within choice hyper-heuristics

Name	Description
Simple Random	Choose a low level heuristic randomly
Random Descent	Choose a low level heuristic randomly and employ the same heuristic as long as the candidate solution in hand is improved
Random Permutation Descent	Generate a random permutation of low level heuristics and form a cyclic list. Starting from the first heuristic, employ it repeatedly until a worsening move is hit, then go to the next heuristic in the list.
Greedy	Apply all low level heuristics to the same candidate solution separately and choose the heuristic that generates the best change in the objective value
Peckish	Apply a subset of all low level heuristics to the same candidate solution and choose the heuristic that generates the best change in the objective value
Choice Function	Dynamically score each heuristic weighing their individual performance, combined performance with the previously invoked heuristic and time passed since the last call to the heuristic at a given step. Then, a heuristic is chosen based on these scores.
Reinforcement Learning	Each heuristic carries a utility value and heuristic selection is performed based on these values. This value gets updated at each step based on the success of the chosen heuristic. An improving move is rewarded, while a worsening move is punished using a preselected adaptation rate.
Tabu Search	This method employs the same strategy as Reinforcement Learning and uses a tabu list to keep track of the heuristics causing worsening moves. A heuristic is selected which is not in the tabu list.

three different Monte Carlo move acceptance strategies based on the objective value change due to the move, time (units), number of consecutive non-improving moves. Simple random was used as a heuristic selection within the hyper-heuristic for solving the component placement problem. The best move acceptance turned out to be *exponential Monte Carlo with counter*. One of the well known move acceptance strategies is *simulated annealing* (SA) (Kirkpatrick, 1983). The improving moves or the moves that generate an equal quality solution are accepted, while a worsening move is not rejected immediately. Acceptance of a given candidate solution is based on a probabilistic framework that depends on the objective value change and a temperature that decreases in time (cooling). The difference between exponential Monte Carlo with counter and the simulated annealing is that the latter one uses this *cooling schedule* while the former does not. Bai and Kendall (2003) investigated the performance of a simple random – simulated annealing hyper-heuristic on a shelf space allocation problem. Anagnostopoulos et al. (2006) applied a similar

hyper-heuristic to a set of travelling tournament problem instances embedding a reheating scheme into the simulated annealing move acceptance. In Bai et al. (2007a), a reinforcement learning scheme is combined with simulated annealing with reheating as a hyper-heuristic and applied to three different problem domains: nurse rostering, course timetabling and 1D bin packing.

In (Dueck, 1993), two move acceptance strategies, namely *great deluge* (GD) and *record-to-record travel* that accept worsening moves based on a dynamic threshold value were presented. Kendall and Mohamad (2004) utilised a simple random – great deluge hyper-heuristic to solve a mobile telecommunication network problem. Great deluge uses a threshold that decreases in time at a given rate (e.g., linearly) to determine an acceptance range for the solution qualities based on three main parameters: (i) the maximum number of iterations (or total time), (ii) the number of iterations (or time) passed, and (iii) an expected range for the maximum fitness change between the initial and final objective value (e.g., lower bound). In the case of an improving move, it is accepted, while a worsening move is accepted only if the objective value of the resultant candidate solution is less than the computed threshold at a given iteration. Kendall and Mohamad (2004) used an iteration based threshold formula with a maximum number of iterations as a termination criterion aiming a quadratic running time for the overall algorithm.

Bilgin et al. (2007) employed different heuristic selection and move acceptance mechanisms and used their combinations as hyper-heuristics. The results showed that a simple random – great deluge hyper-heuristic was the second best after choice function – simulated annealing, considering the average performance of all hyper-heuristics over a set of examination timetabling problems. Consequently, a hyper-heuristic without learning delivered a comparable performance to another one with a learning mechanism. Therefore, in this study, reinforcement learning is combined with great deluge to observe the effect of learning heuristic selection on the overall performance of the hyper-heuristic for solving the same problem. All the runs during the experiments in (Bilgin et al., 2007) were restricted to 600 seconds; hence, the threshold is computed based on the CPU time within the great deluge move acceptance strategy. If a heuristic takes less time, then the threshold value will be lower as compared to the one that takes longer time. This hyper-heuristic differs from the one that Kendall and Hussin (2005) have investigated, as their hyper-heuristic embeds a tabu list approach to keep the chosen heuristic from getting selected again for a number of steps (tabu duration) into reinforcement learning as a heuristic selection. Moreover, the low level heuristics contained a mixture of thirteen different construction and perturbation low level heuristics.

Özcan et al. (2009) combined different heuristic selection methods with a late acceptance strategy, a new method that is initially presented as a local search for solving examination timetabling problems. Late acceptance requires a single parameter and it is a memory based approach. A trial solution is compared with a previously visited solution at a fixed distance apart from the current step in contrast to the conventional approaches that usually compare the trial solution with a current one. The trial solution is accepted, if there is an improvement over this previously visited solution. The results showed that reinforcement learning, reinforcement learning with tabu list or choice function heuristic selection methods did not improve the performance of the hyper-heuristic if late acceptance is used. Choosing a heuristic randomly at each step performed the best. More on hyper-heuristics can be found in Burke et al. (2003a), Ross (2005), Özcan et al. (2008), Chakhlevitch and Cowling (2008), Burke et al. (2009a, 2009b, 2009c).

3. THE EXAMINATION TIMETABLING PROBLEM

Examination timetabling is a challenging real world problem addressed by educational institutions. The goal is to find the best assignment of available timeslots and possibly other resources, such as rooms for each examination subject to a range of constraints. There are two types of constraints: hard and soft constraints. Hard constraints must not be violated under any circumstances and a solution which satisfies them is called a feasible solution. For example, a student cannot take any pair of his/her examinations at the same time. Soft constraints reflect preferences and their violation is allowed, but the goal is to minimise it. For example, a number of timeslots might be preferred in between the examinations of a student scheduled to the same day.

3.1 Previous Work

Researchers have been studying various aspects of examination timetabling problems since the early 1960s (Cole, 1964; Broder, 1964). Examination timetabling problems are NP-complete (Even,

Table 2. Different approaches to examination timetabling

Approach	Representative Reference(s)
Decomposition and/or construction heuristics	Qu and Burke (2007);
Simulated annealing	Thompson and Dowsland (1998); Merlot et al. (2002);
Genetic algorithms and constraint satisfaction	Marin (1998)
Grouping genetic algorithm	Erben (2001)
Iterative greedy algorithm	Caramia et al. (2001)
Tabu search	Di Gaspero and Schaerf (2001); Burke et al. (2005)
Multiobjective evolutionary algorithm	Paquete and Fonseca (2001); Cheong et al. (2007)
Greedy randomised adaptive search procedure	Casey and Thompson (2003)
Adaptive heuristic ordering strategies	Burke and Newall, (2004)
Very large neighbourhood search	Abdullah et al. (2007)
Fuzzy reasoning	Petrovic et al. (2005)
Variable neighbourhood search	Qu and Burke (2005)
Ant colony optimisation	Dowsland and Thompson (2005)
Hybrid heuristics	Azimi (2005), Ersoy et al. (2007)
Neural network	Corr et al. (2006)
Case based reasoning based investigations	Petrovic et al. (2007)
Alternating stochastic-deterministic local search	Caramia and Dell'Olmo (2007)
Hyper-heuristics	Burke et al. (2006), Pillay and Banzhaf (2008)

1976). Since the search space of candidate solutions grows exponentially with respect to the number examinations to be scheduled, many different non-traditional approaches (e.g., meta-heuristics) have been investigated for solving a variety of examination timetabling problems. Tables 2 and 3 provide some illustrative examples of these approaches.

Many examination timetabling problems are studied from a practical point of view, as they arise due to practical needs within institutions. It is worth pointing out that different institutions have very different requirements (Burke et al., 1996a). One consequence of this is that there is a variety of examination timetabling problems in the literature (Table 3; see Qu et al., 2009). Carter et al. (1996b) introduced one of the widely used examination timetabling data sets which was originally made up of 13 real world problems. Özcan et al. (2005) introduced an examination

timetabling problem at Yeditepe University. In this initial study, different memetic algorithms were described. A type of violation directed hill climbing (Alkan and Özcan, 2003) was also in-

Table 3. Some examination timetabling problems from different universities and the initial approaches proposed to solve them

Institution	Reference	Approach
University of Nottingham	Burke et al. (1995)	Memetic algorithm
Middle East Technical University	Ergul (1996)	Genetic algorithm
École de Technologie Supérieure	Wong et al. (2002)	Genetic algorithm
University of Melbourne	Merlot et al. (2002)	A multi-phase hybrid algorithm
University of Technology MARA	Kendall and Hussin (2005)	Hyper-heuristic
Yeditepe University	Özcan et al. (2005)	Memetic algorithm

vestigated as a part of the memetic algorithm which turned out to be the best choice. A survey on examination timetabling is provided by Qu et al. (2009). Carter (1986) and Carter et al. (1996a, 1996b) provide earlier surveys on examination timetabling.

3.2 Problem Description

In this study, we deal with the examination timetabling problem at Yeditepe University. This specific problem requires finding the best timeslots for a given set of examinations under four hard constraints and a soft constraint. The hard constraints are as follows:

- **Scheduled examination restriction:** Each examination must be assigned to a timeslot only once.
- **Unscheduled examination restriction:** All the examinations must be scheduled.
- **Examination clash restriction (C_1):** A student cannot enter into more than one examination at a given time.
- **Seating capacity restriction (C_2):** The number of students seated for all exams at a timeslot cannot be more than a given capacity.

The soft constraint is as follows:

- **Examination spread preference (C_3):** A student should have at least a single timeslot in between his/her examinations in the same day.

Let E represent the set of examinations $E=\{e_1,\ldots, e_j,\ldots,e_n\}$ and let S denotes the ordered list of timeslots to be assigned to the examinations, $S=\{t_1,\ldots, t_k,\ldots,t_p\}$. An array $A=\{a_1,\ldots, a_j,\ldots,a_n\}$ is used as a direct representation of a candidate solution, where each entry $a_j=t_k$, $t_k \in S$,

indicates that e_j is assigned to a timeslot t_k in S. Hence, scheduled and unscheduled examination restrictions are resolved by using this direct and complete representation that encodes a timeslot for each given examination. The quality of a given timetable (TT) with respect to a set of students and the courses upon which they enrolled (SR) is determined by calculating the weighted average of constraint violations.

$$quality(TT) = \frac{-1}{1 + \sum_{\forall i} violations(C_i, TT, SR)\ w_i}$$

(1)

where $i=\{1,2,3\}$ and *violations* measures the violations due to a constraint C_i in TT considering SR.

The performances of a set of Reinforcement Learning – Great Deluge hyper-heuristics are investigated over the Yeditepe University and Toronto benchmarks (Carter et al., 1996b). Yeditepe University (Faculty of Engineering) data set contains real problem instances from each semester in three consecutive years. Bilgin et al. (2007) modified the initial data set provided in Özcan et al. (2005) with new properties and also generated a variant of Toronto benchmarks that fits into the problem formulation. The Yeditepe University data sets and Toronto benchmarks can be obtained from http://www.cs.nott.ac.uk/~exo/research/TTML/ and http://www.cs.nott.ac.uk/~rxq/data.htm, respectively. The number of exams determines the size of the search space to be explored, but the difficulty of a given problem might change with respect to some other characteristics, such as the number of students or conflict density (ratio of the number of examination pairs that should not clash to the total number of examination pairs) that might implicitly or explicitly restrict the search space containing feasible solutions. Such properties for each experimental data are provided in Table 4.

Table 4. Properties of Yeditepe and modified Toronto benchmark problem instances

Data Set	Instance	Exams	Students	Enrolment	Conflict Density	Days	Capacity
Yeditepe	yue20011	126	559	3486	0.18	6	450
	yue20012	141	591	3708	0.18	6	450
	yue20013	26	234	447	0.25	2	150
	yue20021	162	826	5755	0.18	7	550
	yue20022	182	869	5687	0.17	7	550
	yue20023	38	420	790	0.20	2	150
	yue20031	174	1125	6714	0.15	6	550
	yue20032	210	1185	6833	0.14	6	550
Toronto	car91 I	682	16925	56877	0.13	17	1550
	car92 I	543	18419	55522	0.14	12	2000
	ear83 I	190	1125	8109	0.27	8	350
	hecs92 I	81	2823	10632	0.42	6	650
	kfu93	461	5349	25118	0.06	7	1955
	lse91	381	2726	10918	0.06	6	635
	pur93 I	2419	30029	120681	0.03	10	5000
	rye92	486	11483	45051	0.07	8	2055
	sta83 I	139	611	5751	0.14	4	3024
	tre92	261	4360	14901	0.18	10	655
	uta92 I	622	21266	58979	0.13	12	2800
	ute92	184	2749	11793	0.08	3	1240
	yor83 I	181	941	6034	0.29	7	300

4. THE REINFORCEMENT LEARNING – GREAT DELUGE HYPER-HEURISTIC

Reinforcement Learning (RL) is a general term for a set of widely used approaches that provide a way to learn how to behave when an action comes or "*how to map situations to actions*" (Sutton and Barto, 1998) through *trail-and-error* interactions (Kaelbling et al., 1996). A choice hyper-heuristic combining reinforcement learning heuristic selection and great deluge move acceptance is implemented as shown in Figure 2. As suggested in Nareyek (2003), additive adaptation rate that increments the utility value of the low level heu-

ristic is used in the case of an improvement as a reward at step 14. This value is tested against three different negative adaptation rates, namely subtractive, divisional and root, denoted as r_1, r_2 and r_3, respectively for the punishment of a heuristic causing a worsening move at step 17, where u_i is the utility value of the ith low level heuristic:

$$r_1 : u_i = u_i - 1 \tag{2}$$

$$r_2 : u_i = u_i / 2 \tag{3}$$

$$r_3 : u_i = \sqrt{u_i} \tag{4}$$

Figure 2. Pseudocode of the Reinforcement Learning – Great Deluge hyper-heuristic

RL–GD ALGORITHM
Input – *n*: number of heuristics, *u*: array holding utility value for each heuristic, *totalTime*
1. // initialisation
2. Generate a random complete solution $S_{current}$;
3. Initialise utility values;
4. $f_{current} = f_0 = quality(\ S_{current}\ )$;
5. $startTime = t = time()$; $level = f_{current}$
6. // main loop executes until total running time allowed is exceeded
7. **while** ($t < totalTime$) {
8. // heuristic selection
9. $i = selectHeuristic(\ u\ )$; // select a heuristic using the utility values
10. $S_{temp} = applyHeuristic(\ i\ )$;
11. $f_{temp} = quality(\ S_{temp}\ )$;
12. $t = time() - startTime$;
13. // move acceptance
14. **if** ($f_{temp} < f_{current}$) **then** {
15. $u_i = reward(\ u_i\ )$; // improving move
16. $S_{current} = S_{temp}$;
17. } **else** {
18. $u_i = punish(\ u_i\ )$; // worsening move
19. **if** ($f_{temp} < qualityLB + (f_0 - qualityLB)(1 - t/totalTime)$) **then**
20. $S_{current} = S_{temp}$; // accept the move else reject the move
21. }
22. }

RL–GD ALGORITHM

Input – *n*: number of heuristics, *u*: array holding
utility value for each heuristic, *totalTime*
// initialisation
Generate a random complete solution $S_{current}$;
Initialise utility values;
$f_{current} = f_0 = quality(S_{current})$;
$startTime = t = time()$; $level = f_{current}$
// main loop executes until total running time allowed is exceeded
while ($t < totalTime$) {
// heuristic selection
i $= selectHeuristic(u)$; // select a heuristic using the utility values
$S_{temp} = applyHeuristic(i)$;
$f_{temp} = quality(S_{temp})$;
t $= time() - startTime$;
// move acceptance
if ($f_{temp} < f_{current}$) **then** {
$u_i = reward(u_i)$; // improving move

$S_{current} = S_{temp}$;
} **else** {
$u_i = punish(u_i)$; // worsening move
if($f_{temp} == f_{current} \| f_{temp} < qualityLB + (f_0 - qualityLB)(1 - t/totalTime)$)
then
$S_{current} = S_{temp}$; // accept the move else reject the move
}
}

Memory length is implemented not only in terms of adaptation rates, but also by using a lower and an upper bound on the utility values. We experimented with four different ranges in [0,*number_of_heuristics*×(5*i*)], *i*={1,2,3,4}. It is assumed that these bounds are checked during steps 14 and 17. Optimistic initial utility values are utilised and all utilities are set to $\lfloor 0.75 \times upper\ bound \rfloor$ at step 3 to support exploration. As the environment might change dynamically, bounds on the utility values are essential in order to encourage exploration in further steps. Reinforcement learning is based on the idea that heuristics obtaining large rewards should be more likely to be selected again, while heuristics getting small rewards should be less likely to be selected again. The reinforcement scheme used returns the same reward for all heuristic choices and we use the maximal utility value to select a heuristic. Note that selecting the heuristic with this strategy (denoted as *max*) is reported in (Nareyek, 2003) to be the best choice for step 9. If there are multiple low level heuristics under consideration, since their utility values are the same, then a random choice is made. Another approach to decide whether a given total reward is small or large can be achieved by comparing that value to a relative *reference reward*, such as the average of all utility values. In addition to the maximal utility, another heuristic selection scheme that chooses a low level heuristic randomly from the ones that are over (and equal to) the average, denoted as *overAvr* is implemented. The lower bound (*qualityLB*) is set to -1 at step 19 considering the evaluation function (Equation 1) during the experiments. The reinforcement learning heuristic selection methods using the negative adaptation rates r_1, r_2 and r_3 are referred to as RL_1, RL_2 and RL_3, respectively.

In this study, we employed four low level heuristics (Bilgin et al., 2007). Three of them H_1, H_2 and H_3 are associated with three constraints C_1, C_2 and C_3, respectively. They probe constraint based neighbourhoods using tournament selection to resolve violations of a corresponding constraint only. Each low level heuristic operates as follows:

1. **H_1 ($H(x)$):** This heuristic chooses a number of examinations randomly that violate $x=C_1$ and this number is referred to as *toursize*1. Then, the examination causing the largest number of violations is selected. This examination is reassigned to a timeslot from a randomly selected set of timeslots (*toursize*2) which generates the least number of $x=C_1$ violations.

2. **H_2:** Using a tournament strategy, a number of timeslots (*toursize*3) with capacity constraint violations are selected. Examinations in the timeslot that has the largest number of violations are marked for further processing. The examination with the largest number of enrolled students is rescheduled. Then, this examination is reassigned to a timeslot from a randomly selected set of timeslots (*toursize*4) which generates the least amount of C_2 violations.

3. **H_3:** This heuristic employs the same strategy as described in $H(x)$ with $x=C_3$.

4. **H_4:** This heuristic makes a pass over all the examinations and reschedules the examination under consideration with a probability of $1/number\_of\_examinations$.

5. EXPERIMENTAL RESULTS

The experiments were performed on a Pentium IV 3 GHz LINUX (Fedora Core 8) PC with 2 GB memory. Each hyper-heuristic is tested on each instance for 50 trials and each trial is terminated after 600 CPU seconds. Initial experiments were performed for parameter tuning. Unless mentioned otherwise, the utility value upper bound is fixed as 40 and *max* is used as the utility based heuristic selection strategy within the reinforcement learning hyper-heuristics. A sample run is performed for sta83 I using a reinforcement learning – great deluge hyper-heuristic. Figure 3 illustrates the change in utility for each low level heuristic and the improvement based on different negative adaptation rates for this run. If a low level heuristic worsens the solution after a number of successive improving moves, the best heuristic still gets a chance to operate on the candidate solution. The frequency of that chance is determined by the negative adaptation rate. For example, H_3 gets selected more frequently when the adaptation

Figure 3. Plot of utility value for each low level heuristic and quality versus iteration on sta83 I using the reinforcement learning – great deluge hyper-heuristic based on (a) subtractive, (b) divisional and (c) root negative adaptation rates with max, utility upper bound=40, respectively

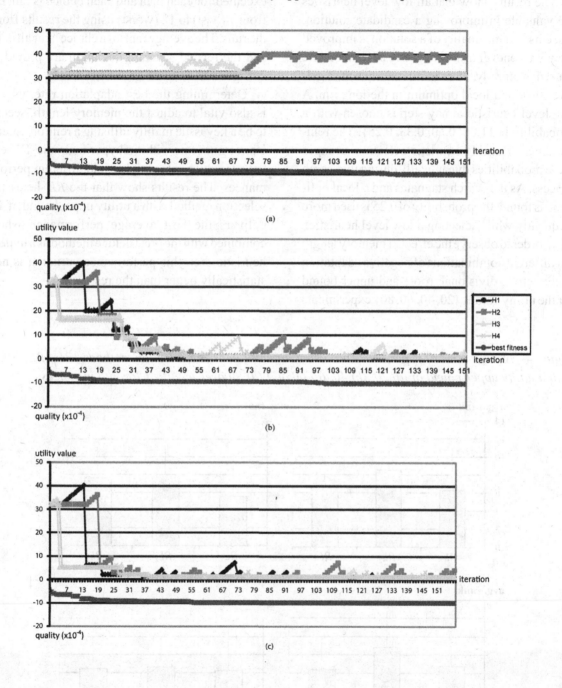

rate is subtractive(/divisional) as compared to divisional(/root) before the optimistic utility values of all heuristics reduces toward the lower bound (see Figure 3). The more severe (high) this rate

is, the more exploration of different heuristics is favoured. All the low level heuristics get invoked within tens of steps while using divisional and root adaptation rates (Figure 3. (b) and (c)), whereas only two heuristics get invoked while using a subtractive adaptation rate (Figure 3. (a)).

The results show that all low level heuristics are valuable in improving a candidate solution. It seems that the quality of a solution is improved slowly whenever a slow negative adaptation rate is used. Naturally, there is still the chance of getting stuck at a local optimum in the long run. A low level heuristic at any step is chosen with a probability in {1.00, 0.50, 0.33, 0.25}. The reinforcement learning heuristic selection arranges these probabilities dynamically during the search process. As the search stagnates and a local optimum is found, the probability of 0.25 is used more frequently while selecting a low level heuristic.

In order to observe the effect of memory length via different combinations of negative adaptation {subtractive, divisional, root} and upper bound for the utility values {20, 40, 60, 80} experiments have been performed on modified Toronto problem instances. As a total twelve different choices are executed for each data and each choice is ranked from 1 (best) to 12 (worst) using the results from the runs. The average rank of a choice over all data and the related standard deviation are provided in Figure 4.

Determining the best adaptation rate, which is also vital to adjust the memory length, seems to be a key issue in fully utilising a reinforcement learning scheme within a hyper-heuristic. Different adaptation rates might yield different performances. The results show that the RL_1 heuristic selection method with a utility upper bound of 40 delivers the best average performance when combined with the great deluge method as a hyper-heuristic. Yet, this performance variation is not statistically better than the rest.

Figure 4. Average rank of hyper-heuristics using different heuristic selection methods {RL_1, RL_2, RL_3} with a utility upper bound of (a) 20, (b) 40, (c) 60 and (d) 80 over modified Toronto instances

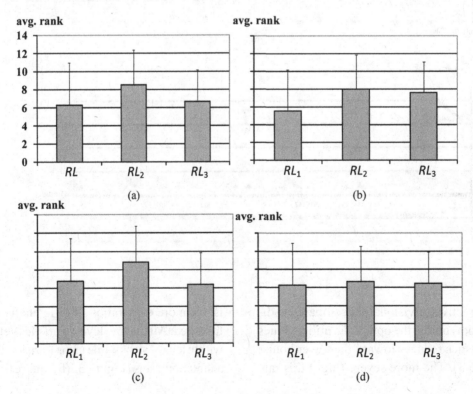

Figure 5. Comparison of utility value based heuristic selection schemes over modified Toronto instances based on their average ranks

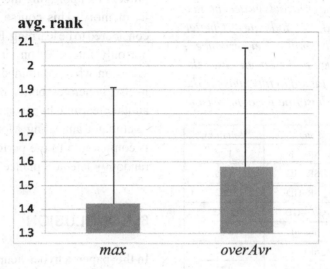

Using the best configuration from the previous set of experiments, another experiment is performed over modified Toronto problem instances to compare the average performances of utility based heuristic selection schemes; *max* and *overAvr*. Figure 5 summarises the experimental results. Maximal utility selection performs slightly better than *overAvr* with an average rank of 1.42 for the modified problem instances {car91 I, car92 I, kfu93, lse91, pur93 I, rye92, ute92}. There is a tie for sta83 I. Still, the performance difference between *max* and *overAvr* is not statistically significant. There might still be potential for a future use of this approach, as, in general, *overAvr* shows success in solving problem instances with relatively high conflict densities.

The reinforcement learning heuristic selection method, which is referred to as RL_1, utilises additive reward and subtractive punishment schemes with a utility upper bound of 40 and *max*. RL_1 is combined with great deluge and tested against simple random – great deluge hyper-heuristic during the final set of experiments. The results are provided in Table 5. The percentage improvement in the table uses whichever approach generates a better result (average best of fifty trials) as the baseline for comparison. The simple random – great deluge hyper-heuristic generates better average performance for eight problem instances. It is especially successful in solving the Yeditepe problem instances which are smaller and have low conflict densities when compared with the modified Toronto instances. Yet, RL_1 improves the performance of simple random hyper-heuristic with the great deluge move acceptance on eleven problem instances (out of twenty one problem instances), and for two problem instances there is a tie.

Finally, RL_1 – great deluge is compared to two previous studies. Bilgin et al. (2007) showed that the choice function – simulated annealing hyper-heuristic, out of thirty five approaches, performs the best for examination timetabling. In a recent study, Özcan et al. (2009) introduced a new move acceptance strategy that can be used in hyper-heuristics. The experiments resulted in the success of a simple random – late acceptance hyper-heuristic, performing even better than choice function – simulated annealing. Both of these approaches are compared to the RL_1 – great deluge in Table 6.

Table 5. Comparison of reinforcement learning and simple random heuristic selection within a hyper-heuristic using the great deluge acceptance move method. "≥" and "≈" indicate "is better than" and "delivers a similar performance", respectively. 'Percentage improvement' uses the average best quality obtained in fifty runs for the better approach as the baseline for comparison.

Instance	Comparison	%-improv.
car91 I	RL_1–GD ≥ SR–GD	1.70
car92 I	RL_1–GD ≥ SR–GD	1.68
ear83 I	RL_1–GD ≥ SR–GD	2.02
hecs92 I	**SR–GD ≥ RL_1–GD**	**11.85**
kfu93	RL_1–GD ≥ SR–GD	2.09
lse91	RL_1–GD ≥ SR–GD	2.47
pur93 I	**SR–GD ≥ RL_1–GD**	**0.32**
rye92	RL_1–GD ≥ SR–GD	3.43
sta83 I	RL_1–GD ≥ SR–GD	0.06
tre92	**SR–GD ≥ RL_1–GD**	**5.05**
uta92 I	**SR–GD ≥ RL_1–GD**	**0.23**
ute92	RL_1–GD ≥ SR–GD	0.28
yor83 I	RL_1–GD ≥ SR–GD	1.13
yue20011	RL_1–GD ≈ SR–GD	0.00
yue20012	RL_1–GD ≥ SR–GD	0.53
yue20013	RL_1–GD ≈ SR–GD	0.00
yue20021	**SR–GD ≥ RL_1–GD**	**1.49**
yue20022	**SR–GD ≥ RL_1–GD**	**0.83**
yue20023	**SR–GD ≥ RL_1–GD**	**0.71**
yue20031	RL_1–GD ≥ SR–GD	5.26
yue20032	**SR–GD ≥ RL_1–GD**	**0.88**

A hyper-heuristic learns how to make *good* moves through both heuristic selection and move acceptance. If a move is rejected, then the selected heuristic is annulled. Hence, if a hyper-heuristic uses a simple random heuristic selection, it does not imply that there is no learning within that hyper-heuristic. The late acceptance strategy uses a fixed length memory to hold the quality of some previously visited solutions. Simple random heuristic selection diversifies the search, while the late acceptance strategy intensifies the search process by approving the better moves based on its memory. This course of action can also be considered to be learning. Reinforcement learning not only improves on simple random heuristic selection when combined with great deluge but it also generates better results as compared to another learning hyper-heuristic; choice function – simulated annealing. Moreover, its performance is comparable to the performance of the simple random – late acceptance hyper-heuristic.

6. CONCLUSION

In this paper, a hyper-heuristic can be thought of as a methodology that guides the search process at a high level by controlling a set of perturbation low level heuristics. A single point search hyper-heuristic framework that combines successive stages of heuristic selection and move acceptance is employed during the experiments. It has been observed in Bilgin et al. (2007) that simple random heuristic selection in a great deluge based hyper-heuristic performed well for solving an examination timetabling problem encountered at Yeditepe University every semester. The same problem is used as a case study to investigate reinforcement learning with different components as heuristic selection methods in place of simple random.

There are different ways of implementing the great deluge move acceptance. In this study, a linear decreasing rate is adopted as suggested in previous studies (Bilgin et al., 2007; Kendal and Mohamad, 2004). Additionally, CPU time is used as a termination criterion and hence, CPU time is used as a part of the *level* decreasing scheme. This level sets a goal for the chosen heuristic in the case of a worsening move after its invocation. The resultant *bad* move is required to have a better quality than the goal, otherwise it is rejected. Using CPU time within the great deluge provides an additional side benefit. The running times of low level heuristics might be different. If a heuristic

Table 6. Comparison of RL_1 – great deluge to the previous studies; (1) choice function – simulated annealing (Bilgin et al., 2007), (2) simple random – late acceptance (Özcan et al., 2009). Each approach is ranked from 1 (best) to 3 (worst) for each modified Toronto problem instance.

Instance	RL_1–GD	(1) CF–SA`	(2) SR–LAS
car91 I	2	3	1
car92 I	1	3	2
ear83 I	1	2	3
hecs92 I	1	3	2
kfu93	1	3	2
lse91	2	3	1
pur93 I	2	3	1
rye92	2	3	1
sta83 I	1	3	2
tre92	1	3	2
uta92 I	2	3	1
ute92	3	1	2
yor83 I	2	3	1
avg.	1.62	2.77	1.62

takes a short time to execute, then the expectation on the quality of the resultant move is lower as compared to a heuristic which takes a longer time to execute. This strategy seems to be viable and great deluge based on this strategy performs well as a hyper-heuristic component (Bilgin et al., 2007; Özcan et al., 2008).

A learning hyper-heuristic usually attempts to follow the best moves within a given period of time using some type of memory to make better future decisions. Bai et al. (2007b) observed that memory length is vital in learning and that the use of a learning mechanism with *short* term memory combined with a simulated annealing move acceptance generated the best results in their experiments over a set of course timetabling problems. They used weighted adaptation and tested various *learning rates* that adjust the influence of rewards compiled at different stages of

search. In this study, other factors regarding the memory that affect the learning process, such as adaptation rate, lower and upper bounds on the utility values are identified and tested using relatively short memory lengths as suggested before. Furthermore, two different heuristic selection strategies, based on the utility values, are assessed. Considering only the adaptation rates, the results support the previous findings in Nareyek (2003). The combination of slow adaptation rates (additive/subtractive) seems to perform the best. The reinforcement learning – great deluge hyper-heuristic with the settings {lower bound=0, upper bound=40, heuristic selection strategy=*max*, positive adaptation rate=*additive*, negative adaptation rate=*subtractive*} improves the performance of the simple random – great deluge hyper-heuristic for solving the examination timetabling problem instances studied in this paper.

The choice of reinforcement learning heuristic selection components affects the memory length which in turn also affects the intensification and diversification processes during the search. The set of low level heuristics contains neighbourhood operators that attempt to resolve conflicts due to a specific constraint type without considering whether the move will cause other constraint violations or not. The reinforcement heuristic selection chooses a constraint based heuristic as long as a given solution is improved in terms of overall quality. If the same heuristic starts generating worsening moves, the reinforcement learning heuristic selection method still supports the selection of the same heuristic until its utility value decreases to the same value as another one (or others). As soon as there is more than one low level heuristic with the same utility value, one of them is chosen randomly to give (another) chance to the other heuristic(s) for improving the candidate solution in hand. The intensification and diversification processes over the problem domain occur as a result of a dynamic interaction between heuristic selection, move acceptance and low level heuristics. The intensification process is activated whenever an improving move is accepted and continues as long as an improvement in the overall quality is achieved. Diversification arises in three ways which is mainly based on the great deluge move acceptance. Firstly, whenever there is a worsening move, the intensification phase ends. This worsening move might still be accepted by the great deluge allowing a jump to other promising regions of the search space. Secondly, a low level heuristic is included within the hyper-heuristic that perturbs a given candidate solution randomly using a small step size. If this heuristic is selected for invocation, it acts as a diversification mechanism. Finally, the random choice, in the case of equal utility values, provides an additional diversification mechanism. The reinforcement learning – great deluge hyper-heuristic with the given low level heuristics attempts to balance intensification and diversification automatically. It turns out to be successful in this attempt as this hyper-heuristic delivers a good performance over the Yeditepe University examination timetabling problem.

REFERENCES

Abdullah, S., Ahmadi, S., Burke, E. K., & Dror, M. (2007). Investigating Ahuja-Orlins large neighbourhood search for examination timetabling. *OR-Spektrum*, *29*(2), 351–372. doi:10.1007/s00291-006-0034-7

Alkan, A., & Özcan, E. (2003). Memetic algorithms for timetabling. In *Proceedings of 2003 IEEE Congress on Evolutionary Computation* (pp. 1796-1802).

Anagnostopoulos, A., Michel, L., Hentenryck, P. V., & Vergados, Y. (2006). A simulated annealing approach to the traveling tournament problem. *Journal of Scheduling*, *9*, 177–193. doi:10.1007/s10951-006-7187-8

Ayob, M., & Kendall, G. (2003). A monte carlo hyper-Heuristic to optimise component placement sequencing for multi head placement machine. In *Proceedings of the International Conference on Intelligent Technologies (InTech '03)* (pp. 132-141).

Azimi, Z. N. (2005). Hybrid heuristics for examination timetabling problem. *Applied Mathematics and Computation*, *163*(2), 705–733. doi:10.1016/j.amc.2003.10.061

Bai, R., Blazewicz, J., Burke, E., Kendall, G., & McCollum, B. (2007a). *A simulated annealing hyper-heuristic methodology for flexible decision support* (Computer Science Tech. Rep. No. NOTTCS-TR-2007-8). Nottingham, UK: University of Nottingham.

Bai, R., Burke, E. K., Kendall, G., & McCollum, B. (2007b). Memory length in hyper-heuristics: an empirical study. In *Proceedings of 2007 IEEE Symposium on Computational Intelligence in Scheduling (CISched2007)* (pp. 173-178).

Bai, R., & Kendall, G. (2003). An investigation of automated planograms using a simulated annealing based hyper-heuristics. In T. Ibaraki, K. Nonobe, & M. Yagiura (Ed.), *Meta-heuristics: Progress as Real Problem Solvers, selected papers from the 5th Metaheuristics International Conference (MIC '03)* (pp. 87-108). New York: Springer.

Bilgin, B., Özcan, E., & Korkmaz, E. E. (2007). An experimental study on hyper-heuristics and exam scheduling. In *Proceedings of the 6th International Conference on the Practice and Theory of Automated Timetabling (PATAT '06)* (LNCS 3867, pp. 394-412).

Broder, S. (1964). Final examination scheduling. *Communications of the ACM*, *7*(8), 494–498. doi:10.1145/355586.364824

Burke, E., Bykov, Y., Newall, J. P., & Petrovic, S. (2003). A time-predefined approach to course timetabling. [YUJOR]. *Yugoslav Journal of Operations Research, 13*(2), 139–151. doi:10.2298/YJOR0302139B

Burke, E., Hyde, M., Kendall, G., Ochoa, G., Özcan, E., & Rong, Q. (2009b). *A survey of hyper-heuristics* (Computer Science Tech. Rep. No. NOTTCS-TR-SUB-0906241418-2747). Nottingham, UK: University of Nottingham.

Burke, E., Hyde, M., Kendall, G., Ochoa, G., Özcan, E., & Woodward, J. R. (2009a). Exploring hyper-heuristic methodologies with genetic programming. In C. L. Mumford & L. C. Jain (Eds.), *Computational intelligence: Collaboration, fusion and emergence* (pp. 177-201). New York: Springer.

Burke, E., Hyde, M., Kendall, G., Ochoa, G., Özcan, E., & Woodward, J. R. (2009c). *A classification of hyper-heuristic appraoches* (Computer Science Tech. Rep. No. NOTTCS-TR-SUB-0907061259-5808). Nottingham, UK: University of Nottingham.

Burke, E., Kendall, G., Newall, J., Hart, E., Ross, P., & Schulenburg, S. (2003a). Hyper-heuristics: An emerging direction in modern search technology. In F. W. Glover & G. A. Kochenberger (Ed.), *Handbook of Metaheuristics* (Vol. 57, pp. 457-474). Dordrecht, The Netherlands: Kluwer International Publishing.

Burke, E., Kendall, G., & Soubeiga, E. (2003b). A tabu-search hyper-heuristic for timetabling and rostering. *Journal of Heuristics, 9,* 451–470. doi:10.1023/B:HEUR.0000012446.94732.b6

Burke, E. K., Dror, M., Petrovic, S., & Qu, R. (2005). Hybrid graph heuristics within a hyper-heuristic approach to exam timetabling problems. In B. L. Golden, S. Raghavan, & E. A. Wasil (Ed.), *The next wave in computing, optimization, and decision technologies: Proceedings of the 9th Informs Computing Society Conference* (pp. 79-91). Springer.

Burke, E. K., Elliman, D. G., Ford, P. H., & Weare, R. F. (1996a). Examination timetabling in British universities - a survey. In E. K. Burke & P. Ross (Eds.), *Selected Papers from the 1st International Conference on the Practice and Theory of Automated Timetabling,* Edinburgh (LNCS 1153, pp.76-92).

Burke, E. K., McCollum, B., Meisels, A., Petrovic, S., & Qu, R. (2007). A graph-based hyper-heuristic for educational timetabling problems. *European Journal of Operational Research, 176*(1), 177–192. doi:10.1016/j.ejor.2005.08.012

Burke, E. K., & Newall, J. P. (2004). Solving examination timetabling problems through adaption of heuristic orderings: Models and algorithms for planning and scheduling problems. *Annals of Operations Research, 129,* 107–134. doi:10.1023/B:ANOR.0000030684.30824.08

Burke, E. K., Newall, J. P., & Weare, R. F. (1996b). A memetic algorithm for university exam timetabling. In E. K. Burke & P. Ross (Eds.), *Selected Papers from the 1st International Conference on the Practice and Theory of Automated Timetabling,* Edinburgh (LNCS 1153, pp. 241-250).

Burke, E. K., Petrovic, S., & Qu, R. (2006). Case based heuristic selection for timetabling problems. *Journal of Scheduling, 9,* 115–132. doi:10.1007/s10951-006-6775-y

Caramia, M., & Dell'Olmo, P. (2007). Coupling stochastic and deterministic local search in examination timetabling. *Operations Research, 55*(2). doi:10.1287/opre.1060.0354

Caramia, M., DellOlmo, P., & Italiano, G. F. (2001). New algorithms for examination timetabling. In S. Naher & D. Wagner (Eds.), *Algorithm Engineering 4th International Workshop (WAE'00)* (LNCS 1982, pp. 230-241).

Carter, M. W. (1986). A survey of practical applications of examination timetabling algorithms. *Operations Research, 34*, 193–202. doi:10.1287/opre.34.2.193

Carter, M. W., & Laporte, G. (1996a). Recent developments in practical examination timetabling. In E. K. Burke & P. Ross (Eds.), *Selected Papers from the 1st International Conference on the Practice and Theory of Automated Timetabling*, Edinburgh (LNCS 1153, pp. 3-21).

Carter, M. W., Laporte, G., & Lee, S. (1996b). Examination timetabling: Algorithmic strategies and applications. *The Journal of the Operational Research Society, 47*(3), 373–383.

Casey, S., & Thompson, J. (2003). GRASPing the examination scheduling problem. In E. K. Burke & P. De Causmaecker (Eds.), *Practice and theory of automated timetabling: Selected Papers from the 4th International Conference* (LNCS 2740, pp. 232-244).

Chakhlevitch, K., & Cowling, P. I. (2008). Hyperheuristics: Recent developments. In *Adaptive and Multilevel Metaheuristics* (pp. 3-29).

Chen, P.-C., Kendall, G., & Berghe, G. V. (2007). An ant based hyper-heuristic for the travelling tournament problem. In *Proceedings of IEEE Symposium of Computational Intelligence in Scheduling (CISched'07)* (pp. 19-26).

Cheong, C. Y., Tan, K. C., & Veeravalli, B. (2007). Solving the exam timetabling problem via a multi-objective evolutionary algorithm – a more general approach. In *Proceedings of the IEEE Symposium on Computational Intelligence in Scheduling (CISched'07)* (pp. 165-172).

Cole, A. J. (1964). The preparation of examination timetables using a small-store computer. *The Computer Journal, 7*, 117–121. doi:10.1093/comjnl/7.2.117

Corr, P. H., McCollum, B., McGreevy, M. A. J., & McMullan, P. (2006). A new neural network based construction heuristic for the examination timetabling problem. In T. P. Runarsson et al. (Eds.), *PPSN IX* (LNCS 4193, pp. 392-401).

Cowling, P., & Chakhlevitch, K. (2003). Hyperheuristics for managing a large collection of low level heuristics to schedule personnel. In *Proceedings of the IEEE Congress on Evolutionary Computation (CEC'03)* (pp. 1214-1221).

Cowling, P., Kendall, G., & Han, L. (2002). An investigation of a hyperheuristic genetic algorithm applied to a trainer scheduling problem. In *Proceedings of the IEEE Congress on Evolutionary Computation (CEC'02)* (pp. 1185-1190).

Cowling, P., Kendall, G., & Soubeiga, E. (2001a). A hyperheuristic approach to scheduling a sales summit. In *Proceedings of the 3rd International Conference on Practice and Theory of Automated Timetabling (PATAT'00)* (pp. 176-190). Springer-Verlag.

Cowling, P., Kendall, G., & Soubeiga, E. (2001b). A parameter-free hyperheuristic for scheduling a sales summit. In *Proceedings of 4th Metaheuristics International Conference (MIC'01)* (pp. 127-131).

Cuesta-Canada, A., Garrido, L., & Terashima-Marin, H. (2005). Building hyper-heuristics through ant colony optimization for the 2d bin packing problem. In *Proceedings of the 9th International Conference on Knowledge-Based Intelligent Information and Engineering Systems (KES'05)* (LNCS 3684, pp. 654-660).

Denzinger, J., Fuchs, M., & Fuchs, M. (1997). High performance ATP systems by combining several ai methods. In *Proceedings of the Fifteenth International Joint Conference on Artificial Intelligence (IJCAI 97)* (pp. 102-107).

Di Gaspero, L., & Schaerf, A. (2001). Tabu search techniques for examination timetabling. In E. K. Burke & W. Erben (Eds.), *Selected Papers from the 3rd International Conference on the Practice and Theory of Automated Timetabling (PATAT'00)* (LNCS 2079, pp. 104-117).

Dowsland, K., & Thompson, J. (2005). Ant colony optimization for the examination scheduling problem. *The Journal of the Operational Research Society*, *56*(4), 426–438. doi:10.1057/palgrave. jors.2601830

Dowsland, K. A., Soubeiga, E., & Burke, E. (2007). A simulated annealing hyper-heuristic for determining shipper sizes. *European Journal of Operational Research*, *179*(3), 759–774. doi:10.1016/j.ejor.2005.03.058

Dueck, G. (1993). New optimization heuristics: the great deluge algorithm and the record-to-record travel. *Journal of Computational Physics*, *104*, 86–92. doi:10.1006/jcph.1993.1010

Erben, W. (2001). A grouping genetic algorithm for graph colouring and exam timetabling. In K. Burke & W. Erben (Eds.), *Proceedings of the 3rd International Conference on the Practice and Theory of Automated Timetabling (PATAT'00)* (LNCS 2079, pp. 132-156).

Ergul, A. (1996). GA-based examination scheduling experience at Middle East Technical University. In E. K. Burke & P. Ross (Eds.), *Selected Papers from the 1st International Conference on the Practice and Theory of Automated Timetabling*, Edinburgh (LNCS 1153, pp. 212-226).

Ersoy, E., Özcan, E., & Uyar, S. (2007). Memetic algorithms and hyperhill-climbers. In *Proceedings of the 3rd Multidisciplinary International Scheduling Conference: Theory and Applications (MISTA'07)* (pp. 156-166).

Even, S., Itai, A., & Shamir, A. (1976). On the complexity of timetable and multicommodity Flow problems. *SIAM Journal on Computing*, *5*(4), 691–703. doi:10.1137/0205048

Fisher, H., & Thompson, G. L. (1961). *Probabilistic learning combinations of local job-shop scheduling rules*. Paper presented at the *Factory Scheduling Conference*, Carnegie Institue of Technology.

Han, L., & Kendall, G. (2003). An investigation of a tabu assisted hyper-heuristic genetic algorithm. *Proceedings of the IEEE Congress on Evolutionary Computation (CEC'03)*, *3*, (pp. 2230-2237).

Kaelbling, L. P., Littman, M., & Moore, A. (1996). Reinforcement learning: A survey. *Journal of Artificial Intelligence Research*, *4*, 237–285.

Keller, R. E., & Poli, R. (2007). Cost-benefit investigation of a genetic-programming hyper-heuristic. In *Proceedings of the 8th International Conference on Artificial Evolution (EA'07)*, Tours, France (pp. 13-24).

Kendall, G., & Hussin, N. M. (2005). Tabu search hyper-heuristic approach to the examination timetabling problem at university of technology MARA. In E. K. Burke and M. Trick (Eds.), *Proceedings of the 5th International Conference on the Practice and Theory of Automated Timetabling (PATAT'04)* (LNCS 3616, pp. 270-293).

Kendall, G., & Mohamad, M. (2004). Channel assignment in cellular communication using a great deluge hyper-heuristic. In *Proceedings of the 12th IEEE International Conference on Network (ICON'04)* (pp. 769-773).

Kirkpatrick, S., Gelatt, C., & Vecchi, M. (1983). Optimization by simulated annealing. *Science, 220*, 671–680. doi:10.1126/science.220.4598.671

Marin, H. T. (1998). *Combinations of GAs and CSP strategies for solving examination timetabling problems*. Unpublished PhD thesis, Instituto Tecnologico y de Estudios Superiores de Monterrey.

Marín-Blázquez, J., & Schulenburg, S. (2005). A hyper-heuristic framework with XCS: Learning to create novel problem-solving algorithms constructed from simpler algorithmic ingredients. In T. Kovacs, X. Llorà, K. Takadama, P. Lanzi, W. Stolzmann, & S. Wilson (Eds.), *Proceedings of the 8th International Workshop on Learning Classifier Systems (IWLCS'05)* (LNCS 4399, pp. 193-218).

Merlot, L. T. G., Boland, N., Hughes, B. D., & Stuckey, P. J. (2002). A hybrid algorithm for the examination timetabling problem. In E. K. Burke & P. De Causmaecker (Eds.), *Proceedings of the 4th International Conference on the Practice and Theory of Automated Timetabling (PATAT'02)* (LNCS 1153, pp. 207-231).

Nareyek, A. (2003). Choosing search heuristics by non-stationary reinforcement learning. In *Metaheuristics: Computer decision-making* (pp. 523-544). Dordrecht, The Netherlands: Kluwer Academic Publishers.

Ouelhadj, D., & Petrovic, S. (2008). A cooperative distributed hyper-heuristic framework for scheduling. In *Proceedings of the IEEE International Conference on Systems, Man, and Cybernetics (SMC'08)* (pp. 2560-2565).

Özcan, E., Bilgin, B., & Korkmaz, E. E. (2008). A comprehensive analysis of hyper-heuristics. *Intelligent Data Analysis, 12*, 3–23.

Özcan, E., Bykov, Y., Birben, M., & Burke, K. E. (2009). Examination timetabling using late acceptance hyper-heuristics. In *Proceedings of the 2009 IEEE Congress on Evolutionary Computation (CEC'09)* (pp. 997-1004).

Özcan, E., & Ersoy, E. (2005). Final exam scheduler – FES. In *Proceedings of the IEEE Congress on Evolutionary Computation (CEC'05)* (Vol. 2, pp. 1356-1363).

Paquete, L. F., & Fonseca, C. M. (2001). A study of examination timetabling with multiobjective evolutionary algorithms. In *Proceedings of the 4th Metaheuristics International Conference (MIC'01)* (pp. 149-154).

Petrovic, S., Patel, V., & Yang, Y. (2005). Examination timetabling with fuzzy constraints. In E. K. Burke & M. Trick (Eds.), *Proceedings of the 5th International Conference on the Practice and Theory of Automated Timetabling (PATAT'05)* (LNCS 3616, pp. 313-333), Springer.

Petrovic, S., Yang, Y., & Dror, M. (2007). Case-based selection of initialisation heuristics for meta-heuristic examination timetabling. *Expert Systems with Applications: An International Journal, 33*(3), 772–785. doi:10.1016/j.eswa.2006.06.017

Pillay, N., & Banzhaf, W. (2008). A study of heuristic combinations for hyper-heuristic systems for the uncapacitated examination timetabling problem. *European Journal of Operational Research*. doi:.doi:10.1016/j.ejor.2008.07.023

Qu, R., Burke, E. K., & McCollum, B. (2008). Adaptive automated construction of hybrid heuristics for exam timetabling and graph colouring problems. *European Journal of Operational Research, 198*(2), 392–404. doi:10.1016/j.ejor.2008.10.001

Qu, R., Burke, E. K., McCollum, B., Merlot, L. T., & Lee, S. Y. (2009). A survey of search methodologies and automated system development for examination timetabling. *Journal of Scheduling, 12*(1), 55–89. doi:10.1007/s10951-008-0077-5

Rattadilok, P., Gaw, A., & Kwan, R. (2005). Distributed choice function hyper-heuristics for timetabling and scheduling. In *Proceedings of the 5th International Conference on the Practice and Theory of Automated Timetabling (PATAT'2004)* (pp. 51-67).

Ross, P. (2005). Hyper-heuristics. In: E. K. Burke & G. Kendall (Eds.), *Search methodologies: Introductory tutorials in optimization and decision support techniques* (Ch. 17, pp. 529-556). New York: Springer.

Sutton, R. S., & Barto, A. G. (1998). *Reinforcement learning: An introduction.* Cambridge, MA: MIT Press.

Terashima-Marin, H. T., Moran-Saavedra, A., & Ross, P. (2005). Forming hyper-heuristics with GAs when solving 2D-regular cutting stock problems. In *Proceedings of the 2005 IEEE Congress on Evolutionary Computation* (Vol. 2, pp. 1104-1110).

Terashima-Marin, H. T., Ross, P., & Valenzuela-Rendon, M. (1999). Evolution of constraint satisfaction strategies in examination timetabling. In *Proceedings of the Genetic and Evolutionary Computation Conference (GECCO'99)* (pp. 635-642).

Tereshima-Marin, H. T., Zarate, C. J. F., Ross, P., & Valenzuela-Rendon, M. (2007). Comparing two models to generate hyper-heuristics for the 2d-regular bin-packing problem. In *Proceedings of the 9th Annual Conference on Genetic and Evolutionary Computation (GECCO'07)* (pp. 2182-2189).

Thompson, J. M., & Dowsland, K. A. (1998). A robust simulated annealing based examination timetabling system. *Computers & Operations Research, 25,* 637–648. doi:10.1016/S0305-0548(97)00101-9

Vazquez-Rodriguez, J. A., Petrovic, S., & Salhi, A. (2007). A combined meta-heuristic with hyper-heuristic approach to the scheduling of the hybrid flow shop with sequence dependent setup times and uniform machines. In P. Baptiste, G. Kendall, A. Munier-Kordon, & F. Sourd (Eds.), *Proceedings of the 3rd Multi-disciplinary International Scheduling Conference: Theory and Applications (MISTA'07),* Paris (pp. 506-513).

Wong, T., Cote, P., & Gely, P. (2002). Final exam timetabling: a practical approach. In *Proceedings of the IEEE Canadian Conference on Electrical and Computer Engineering, 2,* 726–731.

This work was previously published in International Journal of Applied Metaheuristic Computing, Volume 1, Issue 1, edited by Peng-Yeng Yin, pp. 40-60, copyright 2010 by IGI Publishing (an imprint of IGI Global).

Chapter 4
A Hybrid Genetic Algorithm for Optimization of Two–Dimensional Cutting–Stock Problem

Ahmed Mellouli
University of Sfax, Tunisia

Faouzi Masmoudi
University of Sfax, Tunisia

Imed Kacem
University Paul Verlaine - Metz, LITA, France

Mohamed Haddar
University of Sfax, Tunisia

ABSTRACT

In this paper, the authors present a hybrid genetic approach for the two-dimensional rectangular guillotine oriented cutting-stock problem. In this method, the genetic algorithm is used to select a set of cutting patterns while the linear programming model permits one to create the lengths to produce with each cutting pattern to fulfill the customer orders with minimal production cost. The effectiveness of the hybrid genetic approach has been evaluated through a set of instances which are both randomly generated and collected from the literature.

INTRODUCTION

Cutting problems are encountered in several industries with different objectives and constraints. The ship building, textile and leather industry (Farley, 1988) are mainly concerned with the cutting of irregular shapes, whereas in the glass wood and paper industry, regular shapes are to be cut. In particular, rectangular shape which can be obtained through guillotine or non guillotine cut and oriented or non-oriented cut. A guillotine cut means that each cut must go from one side of a rectangle straight to the opposite. Then, each cut

DOI: 10.4018/978-1-4666-0270-0.ch004

produces two sub-rectangles. An oriented cutting means that the lengths of rectangles are aligned parallel to lengths of the stock sheet or roll. Hence, a piece of length l and width w is different from a piece of length w and width l when $l \neq w$.

In order to classify the types of constraints with other specifications such as types of pieces, types of containers and objectives, previous typologies were defined (Wascher, Haussner, & Schumann, 2007; Dyckhoff, 1990). Beside, extensive survey of two dimensional cutting problems can be found in Lodi, Martello, and Monaci (2002).

In this paper the two-dimensional rectangular guillotine oriented cutting-stock problem is considered, with the objective of minimizing the production cost. Before providing the details of this problem and the details of the elaborated algorithm, we briefly review the resolution techniques available in the literature.

The two-dimensional cutting-stock problem is NP-hard and a solution can be found either by exact methods that require large amounts of computational time (Martello, Monaci, & Vigo, 2003; Fekete, Schepers, & Veen, 2007) or by heuristic algorithms whose solutions can be very far from the optimal ones. Many heuristic algorithms have been developed, ranging from simple constructive algorithms to complex meta-heuristic procedures such as evolutionary algorithms, which are known as powerful tools for NP-hard problems. However, due to the complexity of these problems, special chromosome structures are needed. In Esbensen (1992) and Kado, Ross, and Corne (1995), chromosomes are used with some specific designed genetic operations. However, they, in turn generate many difficulties in handing the geometrical constraints of these problems and the efficiency of these algorithms is greatly affected.

In Leo and Wallace (2004), Jakops (1996), Gomez (2000) and Yeung and Tang (2004), a combination of genetic algorithms and constructive methods were proposed. By applying a constructive method such as Bottom Left (BL) and Lowest-Fit-Left-Right-Balanced (LFLRB)

heuristic methods, the cutting problem is transformed into a simple permutation problem, which can be effectively solved by genetic algorithms.

In this paper, a hybrid genetic approach which combines a genetic algorithm with a linear programming model is elaborated. The genetic algorithm is used to select a set of cutting patterns while the linear programming model allows us to determine the lengths to produce with each cutting pattern in order to satisfy the customer orders with the minimal production cost. This paper is organized as follows. The first section describes the problem and the mathematical formulation proposed. The hybrid approach with the details of the genetic algorithm is then presented and the experimental results are illustrated. Finally, concluding remarks are given.

PROBLEM FORMULATION

In this paper, we study the two-dimensional rectangular guillotine oriented cutting-stock problem. This problem can be stated as follows. N customer orders of rectangular pieces with dimensions $w_i \, l_i$ ($i=1,\ldots,N$) are requested with quantity d_i ($i=1,\ldots,N$). d_i is usually a very large number, greater than one hundred, and it is to be cut from K rolls of material with standard width W_k ($k=1,\ldots,K$), each in sufficient length to satisfy the entire demand.

A set of rectangular pieces with dimensions $w_i \, l_i$ ($i=1,\ldots,N$) are requested with quantity d_i ($i=1,\ldots,N$). d_i is usually a very large number, greater than one hundred, and it is to be cut from rolls of material with standard width W_k ($k=1,\ldots,K$), each in sufficient length to satisfy the entire demand. The cutting patterns must satisfy the following technological constraints. First, the pieces are obtained from oriented guillotine cuts. Second, the number of transversal cuts cannot exceed the number of knives available in the machine, in this case the number is equal to six (see Figure 1.). For this problem it is required to determine the production schedule that minimizes the total production cost while satisfying the given demand. The production cost represents the sum of the material needed cost and the set-up cost.

In order to formulate the mathematical model of this problem the following notations related to cutting orders, roll sizes and cutting patterns are introduced.

Sets and parameters

$\lfloor x \rfloor$: Greatest integer lower than x

$\lceil x \rceil$: Lowest integer greater than x

N: Number of order pieces to be fulfilled

K: Number of available width rolls in stock

w_i: Width of the ith order pieces ($i=1,\dots,N$)

l_i: Length of the ith order pieces ($i=1,\dots,N$)

d_i: Demand of the ith order pieces ($i=1,\dots,N$)

W_k: Width of the kth width roll ($k=1,\dots,K$)

V_{kji}: Number of units of width w_i being cut according to the jth pattern from the kth width roll

V_{kj}: j^{th} pattern from the kth width roll

L_{kj}: Length produced with the pattern V_{kj}.

Y_{kj}: Equal to 1, if the pattern V_{kj} is used ($L_{kj}>0$) and 0 otherwise ($L_{kj}=0$)

X_{kji}: If $V_{kji}>0$, X_{kji} denote the integer value $\lfloor L_{kj}/l_i \rfloor$, so that $X_{kji}V_{kji}$ represents the number of pieces of width w_i contained in the pattern V_{kj} through the length L_{kj}.

J_k: Number of patterns of W_k width roll

C_{USM}: Cost of the unit square meter of material

C_S: Cost of the set-up machine to prepare a new configuration

M: Large positive constant, which can be calculated as $M = \sum\limits_{i=1}^{N} l_i\, d_i$

This problem can be formulated as follows:

Minimize

$$C_{USM} \left(\sum_{k=1}^{K} W_k \sum_{j=1}^{J_k} L_{kj} \right) + C_S \left(\sum_{k=1}^{K} \sum_{j=1}^{J_k} Y_{kj} \right) \tag{1}$$

Subject to

$$\sum_{k=1}^{K} \sum_{j=1}^{J_k} X_{kji} V_{kji} \geq d_i \quad (i=1,2\dots,N) \tag{2}$$

$$l_i\, X_{kji} \leq L_{kj} \quad (k=1,2\dots,K, j=1,2\dots,J_k, i=1,2\dots,N) \tag{3}$$

$$L_{kj} \leq M\, Y_{kj} \quad (k=1,2\dots,K, j=1,2\dots,J_k) \tag{4}$$

$$L_{kj} \geq 0 \quad X_{kji} \in \mathbb{Z}_+ \quad Y_{kj} \in \{0,1\} \tag{5}$$

Figure 1. Schematic representation of cutting process

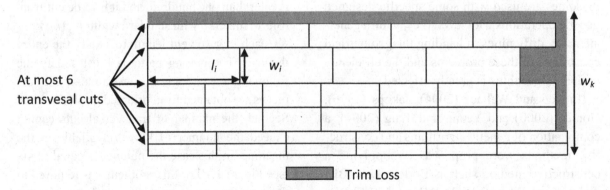

At most 6 transvesal cuts

l_i w_i w_k

Trim Loss

Were the patterns V_{kj} must satisfy:

$$\sum_{i=1}^{N} V_{kji} \leq 6 \quad (k=1, 2 \dots, K, j=1, 2 \dots, J_k)$$

(6)

$$W_{k+1} < \sum_{i=1}^{N} V_{kji} w_i \leq W_k \quad (k=1, 2 \dots, K-1, \\ j=1, 2 \dots, J_k)$$

(7)

$$\sum_{i=1}^{N} V_{Kji} w_i \leq W_K \quad (j=1, 2 \dots, J_k)$$

(8)

The objective function (1) represents the total production cost which represents the sum of the area of the material needed multiplied by the cost of one unit square meter of material and the number of configurations used multiplied by the cost of one set-up machine. The constraints have the following meaning. Constraints (2) ensure that the demand of each type of items is satisfied. Constraints (3) imply that the variables L_{kj} assume the appropriate values which respect the corresponding integer variables X_{kji}. If any cutting pattern V_{kj} is used with a length L_{kj} greater than zero, constraints (4) impose to Y_{kj} to be equal to one. On the other hand, the minimization of the objective function will impose to Y_{kj} to be equal

Table 1. Example data

Item number	Width w_i	Length l_i	Demand d_i
1	1.3	2.2	650
2	1.2	2.3	600
3	0.5	1.4	380

to zero when the cutting pattern V_{kj} is not used. Constraints (5) introduce non-negativity and integrality conditions. Constraints (6) specify that the number of transversal cuts in each pattern cannot exceed the number of knives available in the machine (in this case, the number is equal to six). Finally, constraints (7) and (8) reduce the number of patterns by selecting for each pattern width the closest feasible roll. To explain the mathematical formulation, the following example is used.

Illustrative example: Four rectangular pieces with the specifications shown in Table 1 are to be cut from rolls with two widths: $W_1 = 2.5m$; $W_2 = 2m$. The cost of the unit square meter of material is equal to 1 \$ and the cost of the set-up machine to prepare a new configuration is equal to 100 \$.

The feasible patterns of different widths which satisfy the set of constraints (6), (7) and (8) and the associated roll widths are presented respectively in the following matrix A and C (Mellouli & Dammak, 2008) (see Exhibit 1).

Exhibit 1.

	V_{11}	V_{12}	V_{21}	V_{13}	V_{14}	V_{22}	V_{15}	V_{23}
$A=$	1	1	1	0	0	0	0	0
	1	0	0	2	1	1	0	0
	0	2	1	0	2	1	5	4
$C=$	2.5	2.5	2	2.5	2.5	2	2.5	2

The mathematical formulation of this problem is as follows:

Minimise

$$1(2.5(L_{11} + L_{12} + L_{13} + L_{14} + L_{15}) + 2(L_{21} + L_{22} + L_{23})) + 100(Y_{11} + Y_{12} + Y_{13} + Y_{14} + Y_{15} + Y_{21} + Y_{22} + Y_{23}) \qquad (9)$$

Subject to

$$X_{111} + X_{121} + X_{211} \geq 650 \qquad (10)$$

$$X_{112} + 2X_{132} + X_{142} + X_{222} \geq 600 \qquad (11)$$

$$2X_{123} + X_{213} + 2X_{143} + X_{223} + 5X_{153} + 4X_{233} \geq 380 \qquad (12)$$

$$2.2X_{1j1} \leq L'_{1j} \ (j=1, 2, 3, 4, 5) \qquad (13)$$

$$2.2X_{2j1} \leq L_{2j} \ (j=1, 2, 3) \qquad (14)$$

$$2.3X_{1j2} \leq L_{1j} \ (j=1, 2, 3, 4, 5) \qquad (15)$$

$$2.3X_{2j2} \leq L_{2j} \ (j=1, 2, 3) \qquad (16)$$

$$1.4X_{1j3} \leq L_{1j} \ (j=1, 2, 3, 4, 5) \qquad (17)$$

$$1.4X_{2j3} \leq L_{2j} \ (j=1, 2, 3) \qquad (18)$$

$$L_{1j} \leq M \ Y_{1j} \ (j=1, 2, 3, 4, 5) \qquad (19)$$

$$L_{2j} \leq M \ Y_{2j} \ (j=1, 2, 3) \qquad (20)$$

$$L_{kj} \geq 0 \quad X_{kji} \in Z_{+} \quad Y_{kj} \in \{0,1\} \qquad (21)$$

The optimal solution presented in Figure 2 is obtained through a Mixed Integer Linear Programming model.

$$L_{11} = 1430 \ Y_{11} = 1 \ X_{111} = \lfloor L_{11} / l_1 \rfloor = 650 \ X_{112} = \lfloor L_{11} / l_2 \rfloor = 621$$

$$L_{15} = 106 \ Y_{15} = 1 \ X_{153} = \lfloor L_{15} / l_3 \rfloor = 76$$

Objective = (2.5 x (1430 + 106)) + (100 x 2) = 4041\$

For this problem with only 3 customer orders and 2 available width rolls it is necessary to solve a Mixed Integer Linear Problem (MILP) with 8 continuous variables, 24 integer variables, 8 boolean variables and 35 constraints. This task need a high computing time especially with problems with medium and large sizes. That is why the use of heuristics and meta-heuristics such as genetic algorithm are necessary to solve this class of problems.

Figure 2. Optimal solution

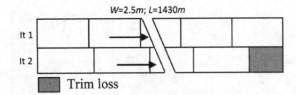

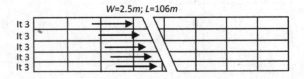

THE GENETIC ALGORITHM

To solve this problem in a reasonable time, a genetic algorithm and a linear program model are elaborated. The main idea of this algorithm is to generate the initial population. Each individual of this population is formed by a few cutting patterns which can generate a feasible solution. Through a linear program model the associated production length of each cutting pattern is calculated to fulfill all the customer orders with the minimal area of material. Then, the production cost which represents the sum of the material cost and the set-ups cost is calculated. The following step is to use the genetic algorithm tools such as crossover, mutation, evaluation and a linear program model in order to mix the individuals of the initial population and better populations. These steps will be executed until the stopping condition holds.

In this section, the different steps in producing a genetic algorithm are presented: chromosome representation, initial generation, repairing of an infeasible solution, evaluation of a solution, calculation of the fitness, selection, crossover and mutation operators and stopping condition.

Chromosome Representation

Although traditional genetic algorithms, operating on fixed-length character strings, can solve a large number of problems, they may not be suitable for the two-dimensional cutting-stock problem. Indeed, because every solution has a different number of cutting configurations and then a different number of design parameters.

In this work, a solution is represented by a nonnegative integer value matrix where the number of columns is the number of cutting patterns T, and the number of rows is the number of customer orders N. For the example presented in Figure 3 the size of the matrix is (3, 2), 3 customer orders and 2 cutting patterns.

Initial Generation

We create the initial population based on some prior knowledge on the problem. Knowing that a solution may have a number of cutting patterns T greater than T_{min} (the minimal number of cutting patterns that allows the generation of a feasible solution), we suggest limiting our decision space to solution having a number of cutting patterns between T_{min} and N. Then, we can obtain $(N-T_{min}+1)$ candidates with different numbers of

Figure 3. Chromosome representation

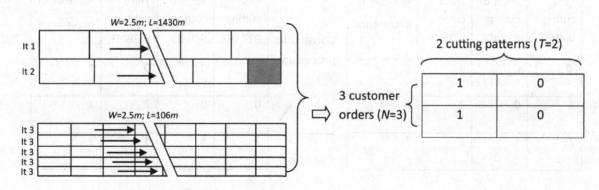

Solution with 2 cutting patterns   Chromosome Encoding

cutting patterns, which we call a packet of ($N-T_{min}+1$) solutions.

Starting with initializing a solution with T_{min} cutting patterns, the number of cutting patterns will be incremented with each newly initialized individual. Another packet of solutions will then be generated until individuals required in the population are obtained. Thus, we can guarantee a diversity of the search space of each kind of solutions.

To determine T_{min} it is necessary to solve a bin packing problem (Alves & Carvalhoa, 2007; Crainica, Perbolib, Pezzutob, & Tadeib, 2007). This task needs a high computing time, especially for problems of a large size which affect negatively the computation time of the genetic algorithm. To undergo this weakness a sequential approach is elaborated to estimate the value of T_{min}.

Note that E represents the set of orders not assigned to any cutting pattern.

Step 1. Initialize T_{min} and E ($T_{min} = 0$; $E = \left\{ w_i \ , \ i = 1, \ 2 \ ..., \ N \right\}$).

Step 2. Arrange the customer orders in E in decreasing widths. Go to step 3.

Step 3. If $E \neq \varphi$, then $T_{min} = T_{min} + 1$, go to step 4, otherwise go to step 6.

Step 4. Generate a new cutting pattern by placing the width available in the set E one after one with respect to the following technological constraints: The sum of the elements placed cannot be greater than the number of knives in the machine (for this problem the number is equal to six), and the sum of the widths placed cannot exceed the greatest available roll width W_1. Go to step 5.

Step 5. Update E. Go to step 3.

Step 6. End.

Feasibility and Correction

In our algorithm the set of cutting patterns for each individual are randomly generated. First, the width roll is chosen randomly from the set of available width rolls. Second, a set of width customer orders are randomly generated and respectively integrated one after one in the cutting pattern from the way that the sum of the width customer orders chosen does not exceed the width of the roll. Since in our algorithm the recombination operators applied cannot guarantee the feasibility of the solutions, the number of non-feasible solutions in a population may easily grow as the algorithm progresses. Thus, we propose that non-feasible solutions be repaired instead of

Figure 4. Correction procedure

First cutting pattern	Second cutting pattern	Third cutting pattern	Number of occurrence
0	0	0	0
1	0	2	3
2	4	1	7

Correction procedure →

First cutting pattern	Second cutting pattern	Third cutting pattern	Number of occurrence
1	0	0	1
0	0	2	2
2	4	1	7

Non-feasible solution   Feasible solution

Figure 5. Crossover operator

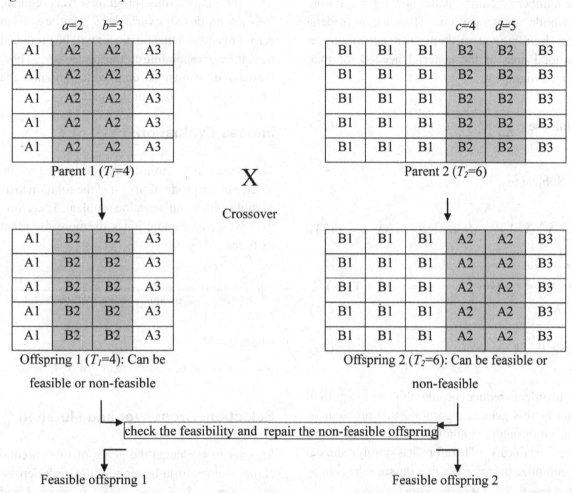

being rejected. To ensure a feasible solution, it is enough, considering the chromosome representation adopted in our algorithm, that each type of customer order appears at least one time on a cutting pattern. Once a missing type is found in a given solution, a correction procedure is called upon to repair it (Figure 4.).

First, we calculate the number of occurrences of each width customer order in the matrix and construct two sets A and NA formed respectively by the orders which appear more than once and do not appear. Second, we try for each cutting pattern from the matrix to eliminate the elements that belong to the set A and replace them by one

or more elements from the set NA from the way that the sum of the widths of the new elements does not exceed the greatest width roll. For each step the two set A and NA are updated. Third, if the set $NA \neq \varphi$ it is necessary to create one or more additional cutting patterns to integrate the remainder elements in the set NA.

Evaluation

Considering the chromosome representation (Figure 3.) of a given solution, we can generate the corresponding values L_{kj} and X_{kji}. Knowing the number of cutting patterns T for a solution and the details of repartition of the customer orders on each cutting pattern, the problem is to minimize the total area of the material needed for that given assignment.

$$\text{Minimise } \left(\sum_{k=1}^{K} W_k \sum_{j=1}^{T} L_{kj}\right) \tag{22}$$

Subject to

$$\sum_{k=1}^{K} \sum_{j=1}^{T} X_{kji} V_{kji} \geq d_i \quad (i=1, 2 \ldots, N) \tag{23}$$

$$l_i X_{kji} \leq L_{kj} \ (k=1, 2 \ldots, K, j=1, 2 \ldots, T, i=1, 2 \ldots, N) \tag{24}$$

$$L_{kj} \geq 0 \quad X_{kji} \in Z_+ \tag{25}$$

In order to reduce considerably the computing time of this genetic algorithm, this problem is relaxed through the elimination of the set of integer variables X_{kji}. Therefore, it is simply reduced to minimize the total area that satisfies the cumulated length $l_i d_i$ for each customer order.

$$\text{Minimise } \left(\sum_{k=1}^{K} W_k \sum_{j=1}^{T} L_{kj}\right) \tag{26}$$

Subject to

$$\sum_{k=1}^{K} \sum_{j=1}^{T} L_{kj} V_{kji} \geq l_i d_i \quad (i=1, 2 \ldots, N) \tag{27}$$

$$L_{kj} \geq 0 \tag{28}$$

It should be noted that this mathematical formulation has N constraints and at most N variables.

After using the linear program solver (Teghem, 1996), some decision variables L_{kj} may be equal to zero. This means that no pieces will be produced from the corresponding cutting patterns V_{kj}. Then, these patterns must be removed to guarantee the survival of only good cutting patterns.

Fitness Evaluation

The fitness of a chromosome is defined as the inverse of the production cost of the solution to be suitable with a minimization problem. Therefore, the lowest cost the solution is, the more important its fitness.

$$Fit\,(solution) = \frac{1}{production\ \cos t\ of\ the\ solution}$$

where

$$production\ \cos t\ of\ the\ solution = C_{USM} \left(\sum_{k=1}^{K} W_k \sum_{j=1}^{T} L_{kj}\right) + C_S(T).$$

Selection, Crossover and Mutation

In order to exchange the genes of two parental chromosomes for a better solution, order crossover (Hertez & Kobler, 2000) is adopted and an example is given in Figure 5. First, parents are chosen through the roulette wheel selection (RWS) (Rennera., & Ekart, 2003). Second, parents are divided into three portions based on two randomly selection points. Third, the middle portions are exchanged between the two parents to generate two offspring. Fourth, a procedure is called to check the feasibility and to repair the non-feasible offspring.

It should be noted that crossover may change the number of columns for the two offspring compared to the two parents, which may lead in a set of cases to generate offspring with a number of columns smaller than T_{min} or greater than N. To avoid this problem the selection crossover points

Table 2. Genetic parameters

Population size	100
Evaluation number	10 000
Crossover rate	0.95
Mutation rate	0.1

Table 3. Experimental parameters

Parameters (unit measure)	Values
Min. width of pieces (*m*)	0.3
Max. width of pieces (*m*)	1.7
Min. length of pieces (*m*)	$0.9w_i$
Max. length of pieces (*m*)	$2 w_i$
Min. width of rolls (*m*)	1.7
Max. width of rolls (*m*)	2.5
Cost of the unit square meter of the material ($)	1
Cost of the set-up of the machine to prepare a new configuration ($)	200

are generated from the way that the middle portions of the two parents have the same size.

$$a = 1 + \left\lfloor (T_1 - 1).(random[0,1]) \right\rfloor \qquad (29)$$

$$M = Min((T_1 - a), T_2) \qquad (30)$$

$$b = a + \left\lfloor M \cdot (random[0,1]) \right\rfloor \qquad (31)$$

$$c = 1 + \left\lfloor (T_2 - (b - a) - 1).(randon[0,1] \right\rfloor \qquad (32)$$

$$d = c + (b - a) \qquad (33)$$

where *a* and *b* represent the two selection points for the first parent, *c* and *d* the two selection points for the second parent.

In order to introduce genetic diversity, mutation is designed with one of the two following possibilities:

- Replace a cutting pattern by another one which is randomly generated.
- If the number of cutting patterns is greater than T_{min} eliminate one from the matrix.

After mutation the procedure described above is called to check the feasibility of the solutions and repair the unfeasible ones.

Stopping Criteria

The algorithm is stopped after 10 000 evaluations of the fitness function, then for a population of 100 individuals, the algorithm is stopped after 100 generations and returns the best solution.

Implementation and Experimental Results

In this section the performances of this algorithm were evaluated through the following experimental study. The proposed hybrid genetic approach has been implemented with MATLAB 6.5. All experiments were run in the Windows XP environment on desktop PC with Intel Core 2 Duo Processor T5270, 1.4 GHz. Note that this algorithm was executed for only one run for each instance of problem. The typical genetic parameters are set as in Table 2. The operational rates of crossover and mutation are relatively high, as to improve the intensification and the diversification of the search.

The quality of the solutions obtained through the hybrid genetic approach has been evaluated through the value of the relative error which represents a comparison between the solutions presented by our algorithm and the optimal solutions obtained through a Mixed Integer Linear Program solver.

Table 4. Experimental results

Problem number	N	K	Hybrid genetic approach		Exact algorithm		VRE (%)
			VSHGA	Average CPU (sec)	VOS	Average CPU (sec)	
1	5	1	24024,6		24018,7		0,02
2	5	1	25130,3		25129,6		0,00
3	5	2	22716,4		22625,5		0,40
4	5	2	22051,4		22045,7		0,03
5	5	3	19744,2	27,88	19587,1	30,09	0,80
6	5	3	20879,5		20792,7		0,42
7	5	4	20161,2		20090,2		0,35
8	5	4	20797,9		20794		0,02
9	10	1	73167		73159,3		0,01
10	10	1	83151,5		83149,3		0,00
11	10	2	66101,4		65906,3		0,30
12	10	2	75984,7		75977,4		0,01
13	10	3	63857,1	53,38	62959,9	80,56	1,41
14	10	3	71393,4		71388,7		0,01
15	10	4	62622,8		61978,5		1,03
16	10	4	71245,1		70807,1		0,61
17	15	1	95762,3		95326,4		0,46
18	15	1	69015,4		68477,6		0,78
19	15	2	88166,9		86823,7		1,52
20	15	2	66997,3		65880,2		1,67
21	15	3	83579,2	71,38	82876,6	11828,1	0,84
22	15	3	66602,1		65491,7		1,67
23	15	4	83514,7		82478,4		1,24
24	15	4	65923		OM		-
25	20	1	98444,2		96789,6		1,68
26	20	1	124065,3		OM		-
27	20	2	96163,4		94975,5		1,24
28	20	2	109466,9		108842,8		0,57
29	20	3	93632,7	86,5	91791	7870,375	1,97
30	20	3	101021,1		99958,7		1,05
31	20	4	92733,7		92049,3		0,74
32	20	4	99338,4		98701,9		0,64

continued on the following page

Table 4. Continued

Problem number	N	K	Hybrid genetic approach		Exact algorithm		VRE (%)
			VSHGA	Average CPU (sec)	VOS	Average CPU (sec)	
33	25	1	159957,6		OM		-
34	25	1	102558,9		OM		-
35	25	2	146092,8		OM		-
36	25	2	98739,4	103,5	OM	-	-
37	25	3	136952,1		OM		-
38	25	3	100363,3		OM		-
39	25	4	136401,9		OM		-
40	25	4	97719,4		OM		-

OM: Out of Memory

Figure 6. Average computation time

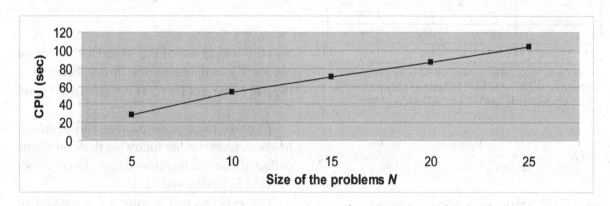

Figure 7. Evolution of solution costs for P1-A1, P2-A1 and P3-B1

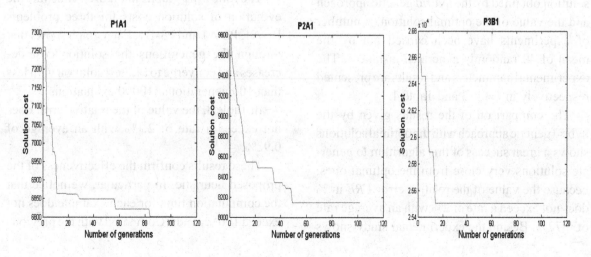

Table 5. Problem 1 data

Item number	Width w_i	Length l_i	Demand d_i
1	0.8	1.03	300
2	0.4	0.51	200
3	0.66	0.55	100
4	1.035	1.27	300
5	0.324	0.46	200
6	0.233	1.07	600
7	0.615	0.724	100
8	0.8	1.03	300
9	0.7	0.9	200
10	0.77	1.03	1000
11	0.37	0.45	2000
12	0.3	0.4	1000
13	0.55	0.65	2000
14	0.8	1.05	1000
15	0.388	0.51	100
16	0.605	0.73	100
17	0.795	1.03	100

The test has been carried out with the following sets of roll widths: A1 = (1.33), A2 = (1.33 ; 1.25), A3 = (1.33 ; 1.25 ; 0.77), B1= (1.15), B2 = (1.15 ; 1.05), B3 = (1.15 ; 1.05 ; 1.01)

$$VRE = \frac{VSHGA - VOS}{VSHGA}$$

where *VRE*, *VSHGA* and *VOS* denote respectively, the value of the relative error, the value of the solution obtained by the hybrid genetic approach and the value of the optimal solution. A number of experiments have been carried out by the mean of 40 randomly generated instances. The experimental parameters and results are presented respectively in Table 3 and Table 4.

The comparison of the results given by the hybrid genetic approach with the optimal solutions shows a great success of this algorithm to generate solutions very close from the optimal ones, because the value of the relative error *VRE* in % does not exceed a rate of 2% with an average rate of 0.72%. Beside the experimental study shows

Table 6. Problem 2 data

Item number	Width w_i	Length l_i	Demand d_i
1	0.37	0.45	2000
2	0.24	0.3	500
3	0.3	0.4	3000
4	0.35	0.45	4000
5	0.4	0.5	4000
6	0.4	0.512	4000
7	0.5	0.6	500
8	0.55	0.65	6000
9	0.4	0.51	2000
10	0.415	0.521	1000
11	0.52	0.64	600
12	1.05	0.5	500

The problem has been tested with the same sets of rolls as in Problem 1.

also the robustness of the suggested algorithm because the computation time grows linearly with the size of the problem *N* as it is shown in Figure 6.

To prove these performances, this approach has been tested on the following three problems collected from the literature Benati (1997) shown in Table 5, Table 6 and Table 7.

The experimental results are presented in Table 8.

The following graphs in Figure 7 illustrate the evolution of solution costs for three problems P1-A1, P2-A1 and P3-B1. Each graph shows that through the generations the solution cost decreases and converge to the best solution with less than 100 generations (10000 evaluations).

In Table 8, the value of the relative error does not exceed a rate of 2.1% with an average of 0.92%.

These results confirm the effectiveness of the proposed heuristic. In particular, we notice that the computation time for each example does not exceed 100 seconds. Compared with the previous

Table 7. Problem 3 data

Item number	Width w_i	Length l_i	Demand d_i
1	1.05	1.315	400
2	0.78	1.08	200
3	0.82	1.03	500
4	0.4	0.51	2000
5	0.37	0.45	2000
6	0.74	0.935	3000
7	0.8	1.05	3000
8	0.55	0.65	5000
9	0.6	0.8	500
10	0.615	0.73	3000
11	0.72	1	3000
12	0.77	1.03	2000
13	0.55	0.65	2000
14	0.4	0.5	2000
15	0.605	0.73	500
16	0.388	0.51	500
17	0.55	0.65	500
18	0.37	0.45	1000
19	0.43	0.57	500
20	0.72	0.72	1500
21	1	0.7	500
22	0.8	1	300

For this problem, roll widths are the following: C1=(1.33), C2=(1.33;1.12), C3=(1.33;1.12;1.05) and then B1, B2, B3.

works which have near the same technological constraints, this combined approach is competitive. For example Rinaldi & Franz (2007) elaborated a heuristic with 2% average VRE.

CONCLUSION

In this work, a hybrid genetic approach is proposed for solving an industrial application of a two-dimensional guillotine oriented cutting-stock problem. Through the proposed strategy which combines a genetic algorithm with a linear pro-

Table 8. Experimental results

Code	VSHGA	VOS	VRE (%)
P1-A1	6800,8	6731,4	1,02
P1-A2	6688,1	6560,8	1,90
P1-A3	6560,8	6560,3	0,01
P1-B1	7044,9	7044,9	0,00
P1-B2	6832,2	6832,2	0,00
P1-B3	6810,1	6810,1	0,00
P2-A1	8144,3	8007,3	1,68
P2-A2	8058,8	7890,7	2,09
P2-A3	7980,9	7890,6	1,13
P2-B1	8142,1	8142,1	0,00
P2-B2	8079,1	8078,7	0,00
P2-B3	8247,9	8074,5	2,10
P3-B1	25503,6	25118,1	1,51
P3-B2	24476,5	24175,4	1,23
P3-B3	23949,7	23681,9	1,12
P3-C1	23570,9	OM	-
P3-C2	22324,9	OM	-
P3-C3	22535,8	OM	-

OM: Out of Memory

gramming model, the complicated geometrically constraints of this problem are converted into a simple selection of a set of cutting patterns (by the means of a genetic algorithm followed by a linear programming model to determine the associated length of each cutting pattern in order to satisfy the customer orders with the least production cost). This algorithm has been tested on a set of problems which are both randomly generated and collected from the literature. The experimental work shows the following performances of the hybrid genetic approach for every problem tested: a good quality of the solution (the average of *VRE* is 0.72%) and a short computation time. Further developments of this work are related to the optimisation of the algorithm structure and parameters. Such as the use of crossover with unequal-length segments exchange.

REFERENCES

Alves, C., & Carvalhoa, J. M. V. (2007). Accelerating column generation for variable sized bin-packing problems. *European Journal of Operational Research*, *183*(3), 1333–1352. doi:10.1016/j.ejor.2005.07.033

Benati, S. (1997). An algorithm for a cutting stock problem on a strip. *The Journal of the Operational Research Society*, *48*, 288–294.

Crainica, T. G., Perbolib, G., Pezzutob, M., & Tadeib, R. (2007). Computing the asymptotic worst-case of bin packing lower bounds. *European Journal of Operational Research*, *183*(3), 1295–1303.doi:10.1016/j.ejor.2005.07.032

Dyckhoff, H. (1990). A typology of cutting and packing problems. *European Journal of Operational Research*, *44*(2), 145–159. doi:10.1016/0377-2217(90)90350-K

Esbensen, H. (1992). Genetic algorithm for macro cell placement. In *Proceedings of the European Design Automation Conference (EUDO-VHDL)* (pp. 52-57).

Farley, A. (1988). Mathematical programming models for cutting stock problems in the clothing industry. *The Journal of the Operational Research Society*, *39*, 41–53.

Fekete, S. P., Schepers, J., & Veen, J. C. V. D. (2007). An exact algorithm for higher-dimensional orthogonal packing. *Operations Research*, *55*, 569–587.doi:10.1287/opre.1060.0369

Gomez, A. (2000). Resolution of strip-packing problems with genetic algorithms. *The Journal of the Operational Research Society*, *51*, 1289–1295.

Hertez, A., & Kobler, D. (2000). A framework for the description of evolutionary algorithms. *European Journal of Operational Research*, *126*, 1–12.doi:10.1016/S0377-2217(99)00435-X

Jakops, S. (1996). On genetic algorithms for the packing of polygons. *European Journal of Operational Research*, *88*(1), 165–181. doi:10.1016/0377-2217(94)00166-9

Kado, K., Ross, P., & Corne, D. (1995). A study of genetic algorithm hybrids for facility layout problem. In *Proceedings of the Sixth International Conference on Genetic Algorithms* (pp. 498-505).

Leo, H. W. Y., & Wallace, K. S. T. (2004). Strip packing using hybrid genetic approach. *Engineering Applications of Artificial Intelligence*, *17*, 169–177.doi:10.1016/j.engappai.2004.02.003

Lodi, A., Martello, S., & Monaci, M. (2002). Two-dimensional packing problems. *European Journal of Operational Research*, *141*(2), 241–252. doi:10.1016/S0377-2217(02)00123-6

Martello, S., Monaci, M., & Vigo, D. (2003). An exact approach to the strip packing problem. *INFORMS Journal on Computing*, *15*(3), 310–319. doi:10.1287/ijoc.15.3.310.16082

Mellouli, A., & Dammak, A. (2008). An algorithm for the two-dimensional cutting-stock problem based on a pattern generation procedure. *International Journal of Information and Management Sciences*, *19*(2), 201–218.

Rennera, G., & Ekart, A. (2003). Genetic algorithms in computer aided design. *Computer Aided Design*, *35*, 709–726.doi:10.1016/S0010-4485(03)00003-4

Rinaldi, F., & Franz, A. F. (2007). A two-dimensional strip cutting problem with sequencing constraint. *European Journal of Operational Research*, *183*(3), 1371–1384.doi:10.1016/j.ejor.2005.12.050

Teghem, J. (1996). Programmation linéaire. *Editions Ellipses*, 51-62.

Wascher, G., Haussner, H., & Schumann, H. (2007). An improved typology of cutting and packing problems. *European Journal of Operational Research*, *183*(3), 1109–1130. doi:10.1016/j.ejor.2005.12.047

Yeung, H. L. W., & Tang, W. K. S. (2004). Strip-packing using hybrid genetic approach. *Engineering Applications of Artificial Intelligence*, *17*, 169–177. doi:10.1016/j.engappai.2004.02.003

Chapter 5

A Rigorous Analysis of the Harmony Search Algorithm:
How the Research Community can be Misled by a "Novel" Methodology

Dennis Weyland
Istituto Dalle Molle di Studi sull'Intelligenza Artificiale (IDSIA), Switzerland

ABSTRACT

In recent years a lot of novel (mostly naturally inspired) search heuristics have been proposed. Among those approaches is Harmony Search. After its introduction in 2000, positive results and improvements over existing approaches have been reported. In this paper, the authors give a review of the developments of Harmony Search during the past decade and perform a rigorous analysis of this approach. This paper compares Harmony Search to the well-known search heuristic called Evolution Strategies. Harmony Search is a special case of Evolution Strategies in which the authors give compelling evidence for the thesis that research in Harmony is fundamentally misguided. The overarching question is how such a method could be inaccurately portrayed as a significant innovation without confronting a respectable challenge of its content or credentials. The authors examine possible answers to this question, and implications for evaluating other procedures by disclosing the way in which limitations of the method have been systematically overlooked.

1. INTRODUCTION

Recent years have witnessed the introduction of numerous search heuristics, many of them inspired by metaphors from nature, physics and life. One of these, *Harmony Search*, has attracted considerable attention through its reported success based on the metaphor of jazz music improvisation, where jazz musicians try to improve harmonies over time. Since its introduction in the year 2000, *Harmony Search* has been the subject of many publications. At the time this paper was written, Google Scholar (http://scholar.google.com) gave a total of 586 hits for *"Harmony Search"*, with 329 hits for publications since 2007 and even a book about this method has been published recently (Geem, 2010). A lot of positive results and improvements over existing approaches

DOI: 10.4018/978-1-4666-0270-0.ch005

have been reported, which suggest that *Harmony Search* could be a promising method with a lot of potential for future improvements. In this paper we take a closer look at *Harmony Search* and try to understand what is really behind the metaphor of jazz improvisation and this presumably novel search heuristic.

The remaining part of the paper is organized as follows. In the next section we give a formal introduction of *Harmony Search* together with an overview about the developments regarding this heuristic in the last decade. Section 3 is dedicated to the well known and established search heuristic *Evolution Strategies* and to a rigorous comparison between *Evolution Strategies* and *Harmony Search*. With the background knowledge obtained in that part, we discuss in section 4 some representative publications regarding *Harmony Search* more in detail. We finish the paper with an extensive discussion in section 5 as well as with conclusions and an outlook about possible further work in section 6.

2. HARMONY SEARCH

Harmony Search (HS) is a search heuristic based on the improvisation process of jazz musicians (Geem et al., 2001). In jazz music the different musicians try to adjust their pitches, such that the overall harmonies are optimized due to aesthetic objectives. Starting with some harmonies, they attempt to achieve better harmonies by improvisation. This analogy can be used to derive search heuristics, which can be used to optimize a given objective function instead of harmonies. Here the musicians are identified with the decision variables and the harmonies correspond to solutions. Like jazz musicians create new harmonies by improvisation, the HS algorithm creates iteratively new solutions based on past solutions and on random modifications. While this framework leaves a lot of space for interpretation, the basic

HS algorithm is always described in the literature in the following way.

The HS algorithm initializes the Harmony Memory (HM) with randomly generated solutions. The number of solutions stored in the HM is defined by the Harmony Memory Size (HMS). Then iteratively a new solution is created as follows. Each decision variable is generated either on memory consideration and a possible additional modification, or on random selection. The parameters that are used in the generation process of a new solution are called Harmony Memory Considering Rate (HMCR) and Pitch Adjusting Rate (PAR). Each decision variable is set to the value of the corresponding variable of one of the solutions in the HM with a probability of HMCR, and an additional modification of this value is performed with a probability of PAR. Otherwise (with a probability of 1-HMCR), the decision variable is set to a random value. After a new solution has been created, it is evaluated and compared to the worst solution in the HM. If its objective value is better than that of the worst solution, it replaces the worst solution in the HM. This process is repeated, until a termination criterion is fulfilled. More detailed descriptions of this algorithm can be found in Geem et al. (2005c), Mahdavi et al. (2007), and Geem (2005a). Algorithm 1 gives an overview about the HS algorithm using pseudo code.

Since its introduction in the year 2000, *Harmony Search* has been subject of many publications. It has been applied to pipe network design (Geem et al., 2000; Geem et al., 2002), the design of water distribution networks (Geem, 2000; Geem, 2006a; Geem, 2007b; Geem, 2008), vehicle routing (Geem et al., 2005a; Geem, 2005b), the generalized orienteering problem (Geem et al., 2005c), the geometry design of geodesic domes (Saka, 2007), satellite heat pipe design (Geem & Hwangbo, 2006), the design of steel sway frames (Degertekin, 2008; Saka, 2009), the design of grillage systems (Erdal & Saka, 2006; Erdal & Saka, 2008), university course timetabling (Al-

Algorithm 1. Harmony Search Algorithm

```
1: Initialize the HM with HMS randomly generated solutions
2: repeat
    3: Create a new solution in the following way
    4: for all decision variables do
        5: With probability HMCR use a value of one of the solutions in the
           harmony memory and additionally change this value slightly with
           probability PAR
        6: Otherwise (with probability 1 - HMCR) use a random value for this
           decision variable
    7: end for
    8: if the new solution is better than the worst solution in the harmony memory then
        9: Replace the worst solution by the new one
    10: end if
11: until Termination criterion is fulfilled
12: return The best solution in the harmony memory
```

Betar et al., 2008), scheduling of a multiple dam system (Geem, 2007c), bandwidth-delay-constrained least-cost multicast routing (Forsati et al., 2008a), the minimal covering species problem (Geem & Williams, 2007), mooring cost optimization (Ryu et al., 2007), multi-pass face-milling (Zarei et al., 2009), web page clustering (Forsati et al., 2008b), solving sudoku (Geem, 2007a) and music composition (Geem & Choi, 2007). Various extensions to the basic algorithm have been proposed, e.g. dynamic algorithm parameters (Mahdavi et al., 2007), more bias to the current best solution (Omran & Mahdavi, 2008), modeling dependencies between decision variables (Geem, 2006b), a multi-objective variant (Geem & Hwangbo, 2006) and a hybridization with sequential quadratic programming (Fesanghary et al., 2008). Even some theoretical work has been published (Lee & Geem, 2005; Mukhopadhyay et al., 2008).

In almost all publications regarding *Harmony Search* positive results have been reported. Together with the increasing number of publications, it suggests that HS is an adequate and promising search heuristic with a lot of potential for further research work. We clarify this statement in the remaining part of this paper, starting with a rigorous analysis of the HS algorithm in the next section.

3. COMPARISON TO EVOLUTION STRATEGIES

In this section we give a short description of the well known and established search heuristic *Evolution Strategies* (ES). We then perform a rigorous comparison between ES and the HS algorithm.

The history of *Evolution Strategies* dates back to the 60s. At the beginning these algorithms were used to automatically adjust variables for a series of consecutive experiments. When computers became available at universities in the early 70s, those methods were used for the optimization of parameters within simulation models. Since then *Evolution Strategies* have been successfully applied to numerous optimization problems and a lot of extensions and improvements of those methods have been proposed. For a detailed historical review the interested reader is referred to (Beyer & Schwefel, 2002).

In this paper we focus on the so called (μ+1) *Evolution Strategy* (Rechenberg, 1973), a method introduced in the early 70s, almost 30 years before the first *Harmony Search* publication was released. This algorithm uses a population of μ randomly generated solutions. In each iteration a new solution is generated from the existing solutions by using recombination and mutation operators. If this solution is better than the worst solution in the current population, it replaces the

Algorithm 2. (μ+1) Evolution Strategy

1: Initialize the population with μ randomly generated solutions
2: **repeat**
   3: Create a new solution using recombination and mutation operators
   4: **if** the new solution is better than the worst solution in the population **then**
      5: Replace the worst solution by the new one
   6: **end if**
7: **until** Termination criterion is fulfilled
8: **return** The best solution in the population

---

worst solution. This iterative process continues, until a termination criterion is met. An overview about this method is given in algorithm 2.

Of course this is a very generic model and we have to define more concretely how new solutions are generated. In the past a huge variety of different recombination and mutation operators have been proposed in the evolutionary computation community (Beyer & Schwefel, 2002; Bäck et al., 2000a; Bäck et al., 2000b). One choice for the recombination operator could be the global discrete recombination (Bäck et al., 1991; Bäck et al., 1993; Bäck & Schwefel, 1993). Here each decision variable of the new solution uses the value of the corresponding decision variable of an arbitrarily (e.g., uniformly) selected solution in the current population. As a subsequent mutation operator the following strategy could be used for each decision variable. With a probability of p_1 we perform a small modification of the decision variable. In a second step we set the value of the decision variable with a probability of p_2 to a random value. Those are both common choices for mutation operators (Rechenberg, 1973; Schwefel, 1981; Fogel & Atmar, 1990; Michalewicz et al., 1992; Bäck & Schwefel, 1993; Michalewicz, 1996).

Now let us compare both heuristics, *Harmony Search* and the (μ+1) *Evolution Strategy*, step by step. Both algorithms use a population of a fixed size. In case of the ES, the population is of size μ, in case of the HS algorithm; the population is called Harmony Memory and is of size HMS. Both algorithms are working iteratively and create exactly one new solution in each iteration. If this solution is better than the worst solution in the

current population, the worst solution is replaced by the new one. This process continues, until finally a termination criterion is fulfilled. In all these steps both algorithms are completely identical. The only thing, in which they could differ, is the way, in which the new solutions are created.

Both algorithms handle all decision variables independently, so it is sufficient to focus on one decision variable. The HS algorithm uses the so called memory consideration with a probability of HMCR. In this case it sets the value of the decision variable to the value of the corresponding decision variable of a uniformly selected solution in the HM, and performs a small modification of that value afterwards with a probability of PAR. Otherwise (with a probability of 1-HMCR), the value of the decision variable is set to a completely random value. The ES discussed here performs a population wide uniform crossover and therefore sets the value of each decision variable to the value of the corresponding decision variable of a uniformly selected solution in the current population. Then with probability p_1 a first mutation operator modifies the value of the decision variable slightly. After that a second mutation operator sets the value of the decision variable to a completely random value with probability p_2. It is easy to see that the methods used to create the new solutions in both algorithms are equivalent. Given parameters HMCR and PAR for the HS algorithm, we can set $p_1 = $ PAR and $p_2 = 1 - $ HMCR to obtain the same method of creating solutions for the ES. On the other hand, given parameters p_1 and p_2 for the ES, we can set HMCR $= 1 - p_2$ and PAR $= p_1$ and in this case we obtain the same method of creating solutions for the HS algorithm.

This means that *Harmony Search* is a special case of the $(\mu+1)$ *Evolution Strategy*, and therefore the best ES is at least as good as the HS algorithm. In other words: The HS algorithm is not able to outperform the best ES. Although HS is derived from a completely different metaphor, it is in its basic variant not a novel approach. For the moment, this does not mean that the concept of HS is not useful at all. There are a lot of publications regarding HS reporting positive results, and there is the possibility that there are other properties of jazz music and improvisation, which could probably lead to new concepts or ideas for search heuristics and optimization. To resolve those issues, we take a closer look at some representative HS publications in the next section, and pose the question of whether the studies that proclaim the virtues of the method have been carried out in a prudent manner.

4. REPRESENTATIVE PUBLICATIONS IN DETAIL

In this section we give a detailed presentation of some publications regarding *Harmony Search* and discuss the results in-depth. For this purpose we have chosen publications which are available online via Google Scholar (http://scholar.google.com). We start with those publications that focus on the applications of HS, then we present those publications that use modifications of the HS algorithm and we finish this section with one publication about theoretical results regarding HS. We should emphasize that the authors involved in the studies cited have undoubtedly proceeded in good faith, apparently with no knowledge of the fact that the ground they were covering was already well-traveled. As we later discuss, this gives reason to take action that will help future authors avoid similar mistakes.

Applications of Harmony Search

We have seen that the *Harmony Search* algorithm is a special case of the $(\mu+1)$ *Evolution Strategy*. In this section we want to clarify the question of how the numerous positive results in literature could be obtained. It is clear that the best ES is at least as good as HS. This means that there exists at least one well known method, which cannot be outperformed by HS. So it is even more surprising that literature is full of publications reporting positive results using the HS algorithm. Examples for such publications are (Degertekin, 2008; Erdal & Saka, 2008; Geem et al., 2005b; Geem et al., 2005c; Geem & Williams, 2007; Al-Betar et al., 2008; Geem & Choi, 2007; Ryu et al., 2007; Geem, 2005b; Geem et al., 2005a; Geem, 2007c; Geem et al., 2000; Geem, 2005a; Geem & Hwangbo, 2006), which are used in this section. In all those papers empirical experiments regarding HS and other methods are performed. In the remaining part of this section we analyze those experiments based on *Guidelines for designing and reporting on computational experiments with heuristic methods* (Barr et al., 2001).

When performing empirical experiments with heuristic methods, the goal is usually to show that a specific method performs better than other methods on a class of problem instances with respect to some predefined objective, which is usually computational time and/or solution quality. Instead of using a class of problem instances, or a randomly sampled subset, in all the publications experiments are performed only on a few instances (Geem et al., 2000; Geem & Choi, 2007; Al-Betar et al., 2008; Erdal & Saka, 2006; Degertekin, 2008), or even on a single instance (Geem & Hwangbo, 2006; Geem, 2005a; Geem, 2007c; Geem et al., 2005a; Geem, 2005b; Ryu et al., 2007; Geem & Williams, 2007; Geem et al., 2005c; Geem et al., 2005b). The majority of experiments are performed on a single instance, all but one of the experiments are performed on at most 5 instances and only in one experiment 11 instances are used.

Another problem is the size of the (few) instances used in the experiments. Heuristics are mainly used in scenarios, where it is not possible to use approximation algorithms or exact approaches for some reason. This usually implies that the sizes of the problems, which are tackled by heuristics, are rather large. In almost all of the publications mentioned above, the instance sizes are relatively small, which means that less than 50 decision variables are used. The most extreme publications here are (Geem et al., 2005c) with 27, (Geem et al., 2000) with 12, (Geem, 2005b; Geem et al., 2005a) with 10, (Ryu et al., 2007) with 6 and (Geem & Hwangbo, 2006) with 5 decision variables.

The next issue deals with the comparison to other methods. The best way to show that a new method is really successful is to demonstrate that it outperforms state-of-the-art approaches. In all of the publications mentioned above it is not clear whether a state-of-the-art method has been used for the comparisons or not. Another way to show that the new method is at least competitive or interesting could be to demonstrate that it outperforms some standard approaches. There are plenty of different established search heuristics, like *Local Search*, *Tabu Search*, *Simulated Annealing*, *Evolution Strategies*, *Genetic Algorithms*, *Ant Colony Optimization* and *Particle Swarm Optimization*. All of them could be used for such a comparison. Unfortunately in most of the publications the HS algorithm is only compared to a few other approaches. In (Geem & Hwangbo, 2006; Geem et al., 2000; Geem et al., 2005b; Degertekin, 2008) 2 other approaches are used for the comparison and in (Geem & Williams, 2007; Geem, 2007c; Geem et al., 2005c; Geem et al., 2005a; Geem, 2005b) the HS algorithm is only compared to a single other approach. Even more dramatic is the fact that in (Erdal & Saka, 2006; Geem & Choi, 2007; Ryu et al., 2007) no comparisons are performed at all. Each of these publications can at most be used to demonstrate that HS can be used to tackle the problem (or instance) under consideration.

There are some other issues, which we do not discuss in detail here. For example, the experimental conditions are not completely clear in most of the publications, sometimes best solutions are used for comparisons instead of average solutions and statistical tests are not performed in any of the publications.

All in all, it is not possible to support the conclusions presented in those publications, using the inadequate experimental setups, which were discussed in this section.

Improvements of Harmony Search

So far we have not clarified whether the basic metaphor of the HS algorithm, the improvisation process in jazz music, can lead to any new and promising concepts for the field of optimization. Therefore we focus in this section on publications that introduce modifications of the HS algorithm (Mahdavi et al., 2007; Omran & Mahdavi, 2008; Geem, 2006b; Fesanghary et al., 2008). Here we want to clarify whether the modifications of the HS algorithm presented in those publications are new ideas or concepts. The question of whether we can expect any new and promising concepts for the future, or not, is postponed to section 5. Although most of the issues from the previous section also hold for the publications considered here, we only focus on the way in which the original HS algorithm is modified.

In (Mahdavi et al., 2007) the authors claim that the use of fixed parameters is a limitation to the HS algorithm. Instead of using fixed parameters, the parameters are changed in a predefined way. The dynamic adjustment of parameters is not a new concept and has been used successfully for many years (Bäck, 1992).

The journal article (Omran & Mahdavi, 2008) deals with another modification of HS. Here the authors modify the algorithm in a way that decision variables are set to the value of the corresponding variable in the best solution found so far with a higher probability than in the standard approach. This idea is not new; there are plenty of methods that use a stronger bias to the best solution found so far. An explicit example is given by the search process in *Particle Swarm Optimization* (Eberhart & Kennedy, 1995), an implicit example is given by different parent selection mechanisms in *Evolution Strategies* or *Genetic Algorithms* (Bäck et al., 2000a; Bäck et al., 2000b).

In (Geem, 2006b) the HS algorithm is extended in such a way that dependencies between pairs of decision variables are considered. The idea of modeling dependencies between decision variables exists since several years. For example, it is used implicitly by population based heuristics and explicitly in some Estimation of Distribution Algorithms (Pelikan & Mühlenbein, 1999; Mühlenbein & Mahnig, 1999).

The last publication in this subsection is (Fesanghary et al., 2008). In this work the authors hybridize the HS algorithm with sequential quadratic programming. The concept of combining different problem solving methods on a more abstract (meta heuristic) level or in concrete hybrid approaches is also not new in the field of optimization (Davis, 1990; Berger et al., 1998).

All in all, there are no new ideas or concepts used in the modifications of the *Harmony Search* algorithm, which are presented in this section.

Theory about Harmony Search

Perhaps we can get new insights about *Harmony Search* from (Mukhopadhyay et al., 2008). Here some theoretical results for the HS algorithm are presented. It is interesting to note that the results are based on similar analyses for *Evolution Strategies* (Beyer, 1998). The authors want to illustrate the explorative power of the HS algorithm. For this purpose they modify the algorithm in the following way. Instead of creating one solution in each iteration, HMS many solutions are created. Those new solutions then completely replace the old population. It is obvious that this variant has nothing to do with the original HS algorithm, and it is hard to transfer any conclusions from this variant to the original HS algorithm. Additionally the results which are obtained in (Mukhopadhyay et al., 2008) cannot be valid. The authors *prove* that the sample variance between the solutions in the population grows exponentially, if some specific parameter values are used for the algorithm. Since they assume that the decision variables are bounded within an interval, the variance is bounded as well and cannot grow arbitrarily large. Therefore their results are simply incorrect.

In short, this work does not help us to identify any promising ideas or concepts, which are related to the metaphor used for the HS algorithm.

5. DISCUSSION

In this section we discuss the results obtained in the previous section, together with their impacts. We begin with a short summary of the results. After that we explain which future development can be expected regarding the HS algorithm. We finish our discussion with some possible explanations for our results.

We started with a formal definition of the *Harmony Search* algorithm in section 2. In section 3 we compared this algorithm to a specific (not uncommon or exotic) *Evolution Strategy*. We showed that HS is completely equivalent to this well known and established ES. This result raises two questions. Why are there so many positive results about HS in the literature, if this is not really a new approach? And are there any other properties of jazz music and improvisation which could probably lead to new concepts or ideas for search heuristics and optimization in the future?

The first question can be answered easily. We analyzed different publications, which report positive results regarding *Harmony Search*. We showed that the experimental setups used in the experiments for those publications are inadequate.

The few results that were obtained in those experiments cannot be used to support the conclusions presented in those publications.

It is a little bit more complicated to answer the second question. We examined four publications, which use modifications of the HS algorithm, and one publication, which deals with theoretical aspects of the HS algorithm. The modifications proposed in those publications are all well known and used for many years in the context of other search heuristics. It seems that only ideas and concepts, which have been applied successfully to other search heuristics, are used for HS. For example, there is a kind of parallel between the development of modifications for the HS algorithm and the development of modifications for *Evolutionary Algorithms* in the past. For both algorithms a bias towards better solutions in the population has been introduced and for both algorithms dynamic parameters have been used instead of fixed ones. It is only a matter of time until concepts like self adaptation for the HS algorithms will be proposed. But since the HS algorithm is itself an ES, the usefulness of such results will be limited. Also the theoretical paper could not help us to identify promising concepts of the HS algorithm. Of course, we cannot prove that there are no properties of jazz music and improvisation which might be usefully incorporated into search heuristics and for optimization. But in the last decade no new concept has been derived from this metaphor and the probability that this will ever happen appears on this basis to be rather low.

Before we finish the paper we want to discuss possible explanations for our findings. We do not state that they are in fact the true explanations, but in our opinion they are in general of high interest for the whole community and could also be relevant for this paper.

It is quite obvious that we, the whole research community, are operating in a completely antiquated and fallible framework. The scientific publication system as it is now has a lot of inherent defects, which handicap and slow down research. First of all there are a lot of financial concerns involved in the current system which leave a lot of space for misusage. Additionally the most widely used method to judge scientific publications, called peer reviewing, requires idealistic behavior on the part of the people participating in that process, and we can not rely on the assumption that such behavior will manifest itself gratuitously, especially if there are plenty of personal and career concerns involved. Furthermore the publication system has scarcely been affected by the rapid technological progress of the last decades. For example, we still have no comprehensive public access to scientific publications, although this would be easily realizable, and release durations are extremely long in some cases for no obvious reasons. We do not want to go into greater detail here and for people who are more interested in the defects of the scientific publication system, the article *Science's journal and conference system - a joke that got old* (http://www.math.temple.edu/~wds/homepage/refereeing) is strongly recommended.

Since not all people can be expected to behave in an idealistic way, it is not very surprising to find that a system which is not well-designed and carefully regulated can be subject to abuse. But the key issue is whether we should tolerate this situation, by continuing to operate within a system of scientific publication whose design and regulation is conspicuously deficient. In our opinion it is of the greatest importance to bend our efforts to correcting the defects of the current system.

6. CONCLUSION

In this paper we performed a rigorous analysis of the search heuristic *Harmony Search*. We showed that this heuristic is in fact a special case of an *Evolution Strategy* and we gave strong arguments for the theses that research in *Harmony Search* is fundamentally misguided and that future research effort could better be devoted to more promising areas.

There are some other purportedly novel approaches proposed in the literature, which could fall into the same category as *Harmony Search*. Admittedly, it is not entirely fair to single out HS as the sole representative of this category. Our goal is not to belabor the shortcomings of a single method, but to sensitize other researches to the existence of the situation in which such shortcomings can prevail, and to encourage a response that can lead to producing something better. We operate in an antiquated and fallible framework, and there is no remedy in sight as long as the number of an author's publications is considered more important than the quality of those publications, and as long as we use a reviewing system which is inherently inconsistent.

ACKNOWLEDGMENT

The author is grateful to the anonymous reviewers for their helpful comments and remarks. The author's research has been supported by the Swiss National Science Foundation, grant 200021-120039/1.

REFERENCES

Al-Betar, M., Khader, A., & Gani, T. (2008). A harmony search algorithm for university course timetabling. In *Proceedings of the 7th International Conference on the Practice and Theory of Automated Timetabling (PATAT 2008)*, Montreal, Canada.

Bäck, T. (1992). Self-adaptation in genetic algorithms. In *Proceedings Toward a practice of autonomous systems: the First European Conference on Artificial Life* (pp. 263-271).

Bäck, T., Fogel, D., & Michalewicz, Z. (2000a). *Evolutionary Computation 1*. Bristol, UK: Institute of Physics Publishing.

Bäck, T., Fogel, D., & Michalewicz, Z. (2000b). *Evolutionary Computation 2: Advanced algorithms and operators*. Bristol, UK: Institute of Physics Publishing.

Bäck, T., Hoffmeister, F., & Schwefel, H. (1991). A survey of evolution strategies. In *Proceedings of the Fourth International Conference on Genetic Algorithms*.

Bäck, T., Rudolph, G., & Schwefel, H. (1993). Evolutionary programming and evolution strategies: Similarities and differences. In *Proceedings of the Second Annual Conference on Evolutionary Programming* (pp. 11-22).

Bäck, T., & Schwefel, H. (1993). An overview of evolutionary algorithms for parameter optimization. *Evolutionary Computation*, *1*(1), 1–23. doi:10.1162/evco.1993.1.1.1

Barr, R., Golden, B., Kelly, J., Steward, W., & Resende, M. (2001). Guidelines for designing and reporting on computational experiments with heuristic methods. In *Proceedings of International Conference on Metaheuristics for Optimization* (pp. 1-17). Dordrecht, The Netherlands: Kluwer.

Berger, J., Salois, M., & Begin, R. (1998). *A hybrid genetic algorithm for the vehicle routing problem with time windows. LNCS, 1418*, 114–127.

Beyer, H. (1998). *On the "explorative power" of ES/EP-like algorithms* (pp. 323–334). LNCS.

Beyer, H., & Schwefel, H. (2002). Evolution strategies – A comprehensive introduction. *Natural Computing*, *1*(1), 3–52. doi:10.1023/A:1015059928466

Davis, L. (1990). Hybrid genetic algorithms for machine learning. In *Proceedings of IEE Colloquium on Machine Learning* (pp. 9).

Degertekin, S. (2008). Optimum design of steel frames using harmony search algorithm. *Structural and Multidisciplinary Optimization, 36*(4), 393–401. doi:10.1007/s00158-007-0177-4

Eberhart, R., & Kennedy, J. (1995). A new optimizer using particle swarm theory. In *Proceedings of the Sixth Symposium on Micro Machine and Human Science* (pp. 39-43).

Erdal, F., & Saka, M. (2006). Optimum design of grillage systems using harmony search algorithm. In *Proceedings of 8th International Conference on Computational Structures Technology (CST 2006)*, Las Palmas de Gran Canaria, Spain.

Erdal, F., & Saka, M. (2008). Effect of beam spacing in the harmony search based optimum design of grillages. *Asian Journal of Civil Engineering, 9*(3), 215–228.

Fesanghary, M., Mahdavi, M., Minary-Jolandan, M., & Alizadeh, Y. (2008). Hybridizing harmony search algorithm with sequential quadratic programming for engineering optimization problems. *Computer Methods in Applied Mechanics and Engineering, 197*(33-40), 3080-3091.

Fogel, D., & Atmar, J. (1990). Comparing genetic operators with Gaussian mutations in simulated evolutionary processes using linear systems. *Biological Cybernetics, 63*(2), 111–114. doi:10.1007/BF00203032

Forsati, R., Haghighat, A., & Mahdavi, M. (2008a). *Harmony search based algorithms for bandwidth-delay-constrained least-cost multicast routing.* Computer Communications.

Forsati, R., Mahdavi, M., Kangavari, M., & Safarkhani, B. (2008b). Web page clustering using harmony search optimization. In *Proceedings of Electrical and Computer Engineering (CCECE 2008)* (pp. 1601-1604).

Geem, Z. (2000). *Optimal design of water distribution networks using harmony search.* Unpublished doctoral dissertation, Korea University, Seoul, South Korea.

Geem, Z. (2005a). *Harmony search in water pump switching problem. LNCS, 3612,* 751.

Geem, Z. (2005b). School bus routing using harmony search. In *Proceedings of the Genetic and Evolutionary Computation Conference (GECCO 2005)*, Washington, DC.

Geem, Z. (2006a). *Comparison Harmony Search with Other Meta-Heuristics in Water Distribution Network Design.* Reston, VA: ASCE.

Geem, Z. (2006b). *Improved harmony search from ensemble of music players* (*Lecture Notes in Computer Science*, 4251:86.

Geem, Z. (2007a). *Harmony search algorithm for solving Sudoku. LNCS, 4692,* 371.

Geem, Z. (2007b). Harmony search algorithm for the optimal design of largescale water distribution network. In *Proceedings of the 7th International IWA Symposium on Systems Analysis and Integrated Assessment in Water Management (Watermatex 2007)*, Washington, DC.

Geem, Z. (2007c). *Optimal scheduling of multiple dam system using harmony search algorithm. LNCS, 4507,* 316.

Geem, Z. (2008). *Harmony search optimisation to the pump-included water distribution network design.* Civil Engineering and Environmental Systems.

Geem, Z. (2010). *Recent advances in harmony search algorithm.*

Geem, Z., & Choi, J. (2007). *Music composition using harmony search algorithm. LNCS, 4448,* 593.

Geem, Z., & Hwangbo, H. (2006). Application of harmony search to multi-objective optimization for satellite heat pipe design. In *Proceedings of US-Korea Conference on Science, Technology, and Entrepreneurship (UKC 2006)*, Teaneck, NJ.

Geem, Z., & Kim, J. (2001). A new heuristic optimization algorithm: harmony search. *Simulation, 76*(2), 60. doi:10.1177/003754970107600201

Geem, Z., Kim, J., & Loganathan, G. (2002). Harmony search optimization: Application to pipe network design. *International Journal of Modelling & Simulation, 22*(2), 125–133.

Geem, Z., Kim, J., & Yoon, Y. (2000). Optimal layout of pipe networks using harmony search. In *Proceedings of 4th International Conference on Hydro-Science and Engineering*, Seoul, South Korea.

Geem, Z., Lee, K., & Park, Y. (2005a). Application of harmony search to vehicle routing. *American Journal of Applied Sciences, 2*(12), 1552–1557. doi:10.3844/ajassp.2005.1552.1557

Geem, Z., Lee, K., & Tseng, C. (2005b). Harmony search for structural design. In *Proceedings of the 2005 conference on Genetic and evolutionary computation* (pp. 651-652). New York: ACM.

Geem, Z., Tseng, C., & Park, Y. (2005c). *Harmony search for generalized orienteering problem: best touring in China* (LNCS 3612, p. 741).

Geem, Z., & Williams, J. (2007). Harmony search and ecological optimization. *International Journal of Energy and Environment, 1*, 150–154.

Lee, K., & Geem, Z. (2005). A new meta-heuristic algorithm for continuous engineering optimization: harmony search theory and practice. *Computer Methods in Applied Mechanics and Engineering, 194*(36-38), 3902–3933. doi:10.1016/j.cma.2004.09.007

Mahdavi, M., Fesanghary, M., & Damangir, E. (2007). An improved harmony search algorithm for solving optimization problems. *Applied Mathematics and Computation, 188*(2), 1567–1579. doi:10.1016/j.amc.2006.11.033

Michalewicz, Z. (1996). *Genetic algorithms+ data structures*. New York: Springer.

Michalewicz, Z. (1992). A modified genetic algorithm for optimal control problems. *Computers & Mathematics with Applications (Oxford, England), 23*(12), 83–94. doi:10.1016/0898-1221(92)90094-X

Mühlenbein, H., & Mahnig, T. (1999). FDA-A scalable evolutionary algorithm for the optimization of additively decomposed functions. *Evolutionary Computation, 7*(4), 353–376. doi:10.1162/evco.1999.7.4.353

Mukhopadhyay, A., Roy, A., Das, S., & Abraham, A. (2008). Population-variance and explorative power of harmony search: an analysis. In *Proceedings of the Second National Conference on Mathematical Techniques: Emerging Paradigms for Electronics and IT Industries (MATEIT 2008)*, New Delhi, India.

Omran, M., & Mahdavi, M. (2008). Global-best harmony search. *Applied Mathematics and Computation, 198*(2), 643–656. doi:10.1016/j.amc.2007.09.004

Pelikan, M., & Mühlenbein, H. (1999). *The bivariate marginal distribution algorithm* (pp. 521–535). Advances in Soft Computing-Engineering Design and Manufacturing.

Rechenberg, I. (1973). *Evolutionsstrategie: Optimierung technischer Systeme nach Prinzipien der biologischen Evolution*.

Ryu, S., Duggal, A., Heyl, C., & Geem, Z. (2007). Mooring cost optimization via harmony search. In *Proceedings of the 26th ASME International Conference on Offshore Mechanics and Arctic Engineering*.

Saka, M. (2007). Optimum geometry design of geodesic domes using harmony search algorithm. *Advances in Structural Engineering, 10*(6), 595–606. doi:10.1260/136943307783571445

Saka, M. (2009). Optimum design of steel sway frames to BS5950 using harmony search algorithm. *Journal of Constructional Steel Research, 65*(1), 36–43. doi:10.1016/j.jcsr.2008.02.005

Schwefel, H. (1981). *Numerical optimization of computer models*. New York: John Wiley & Sons, Inc.

Zarei, O., Fesanghary, M., Farshi, B., Saffar, R., & Razfar, M. (2009). Optimization of multi-pass face-milling via harmony search algorithm. *Journal of Materials Processing Technology, 209*(5), 2386–2392. doi:10.1016/j.jmatprotec.2008.05.029

Chapter 6

RESEARCH COMMENTARY
Survival of the Fittest Algorithm or the Novelest Algorithm?
The Existence Reason of the Harmony Search Algorithm

Zong Woo Geem
iGlobal University, USA

ABSTRACT

Recently a paper was published which claims "harmony search is equivalent to evolution strategies and because the latter is not popular currently, the former has no future. Also, research community was misguided by the former's disguised novelty." This paper is written to rebut the original paper's claims by saying 1) harmony search is different from evolution strategies because each has its own uniqueness, 2) performance, rather than novelty, is an algorithm's survival factor, and 3) the original paper was biased to mislead into a predefined conclusion. Also, the shortcomings of current review system, citation system, and funding system are briefly mentioned.

INTRODUCTION

Recently I happened to read a paper (Weyland, 2010) with shocking title "how the research community can be misled by a 'novel' methodology." The paper claimed that the harmony search (HS) algorithm is similar to the evolution strategies (ES) algorithm (the author in the paper even said HS is "completely equivalent" to ES), and that the research community was misguided by the "fake" novelty of the HS algorithm. Did the (original paper's) author really intend to write a

DOI: 10.4018/978-1-4666-0270-0.ch006

good paper or a *veto-ergo-sum* (I protest, therefore I exist) paper?

As the original developer of the HS algorithm, I feel like writing a rebuttal because the research community will be "really" misguided otherwise.

Is HS Equivalent to ES?

Although I do not know much about ES (this algorithm is not very popular in my research area), based on my literature review when I wrote the original HS paper (Geem et al., 2001), ES was developed to solve continuous-valued problem such as parameter calibration (Schwefel, 1994) using standard deviation (Fogel, 1995) while HS was originally developed to solve discrete-valued problem such as traveling salesperson problem without using any statistical information. I cannot imagine how the author concluded that HS equals ES with these different problem set and algorithm structure.

The author claims that because both HS and ES use solution population and produce one solution per iteration, HS is equivalent to ES if the latter is tweaked.

I'd like to rebut this musically. People may easily tell Schöberg's from Haydn's. However, sometimes people may not be able to tell Haydn's from Mozart's because they share similarity (e.g., Sonata structure). Or, religiously speaking, people may hardly tell the difference between two denominations under Christianity. If we tweak the liturgy of Denomination A, it may become that of Denomination B. In this case, can we say A equals B? (If someone is ecumenical, (s)he may say so though).

Likewise, every meta-heuristic algorithm possesses similarity as well as uniqueness, and there exists the possibility that the discrepancy between HS and ES is greater than that between ES and another nature-inspired algorithm. Also, there is a chance for HS to become a general form of another algorithm.

More fundamentally, every meta-heuristic algorithm contains only two basic features: global search and local search. The key factor to an algorithm's success is how efficiently two features are handled using certain number of operation categories (sometimes different algorithms share the identical operation). As an "evolutionary" algorithm which is a similar term to meta-heuristic algorithm, any algorithm can be survived as long as it is the fittest or at least fitter than others instead of being novel.

Most importantly, when I searched Wikipedia, I could not find the structure $(\mu+1)$-ES which, the author claimed, equals that of HS. Instead, Wikipedia says: $(1+\lambda)$-ES is a general form which has the opposite structure (multiple children from one parent) of HS; $(1+1)$-ES is the simplest form; and $(\mu+\lambda)$-ES is the contemporary form. Maybe $(\mu+1)$-ES is possible, but appears not popular.

Thus, HS and ES normally have opposite structures and they were originally developed for opposite variable-type (discrete and continuous) problems. I cannot compare more details because Wikipedia does not provide any details of ES.

When I further investigate ES by reading a comprehensive introduction paper written by one of the original ES developers (Beyer & Schwefel, 2002), I found only a brief description of $(\mu+1)$-ES. But it still selects parents (two of μ are chosen at random and recombined to give life to an offspring) while HS never does this. In other words, I never found any exact match between ES and HS with respect to the algorithm structure, not to mention details.

Is Novelty Everything?

If the author still wants to focus on similarity between HS and ES rather than their own uniqueness, I'd like to ask this question: Why is ES not popular in one of my research areas (more specifically, hydraulic and hydrologic optimization field)?

For the optimal design of hydraulic networks as an example, ES was not utilized in major literature while other algorithms such as genetic algorithm (GA), simulated annealing, tabu search, shuffled frog-leaping algorithm, ant colony optimization algorithm, cross entropy, scatter search, and HS have been used (Geem, 2009).

Now, the author may think "because HS claimed the novelty, it was included." Is this really true? As far as I know, high-level engineering community does not accept an algorithm just because it appears novel. Rather, its performance such as solution quality and computational effort is the key factor to accept. I believe HS was selected because it has performed better than other algorithms instead of novelty. From time to time, researchers claim better performance with fake solutions (e.g., constraint-violated solutions) in order to be published. Experienced reviewers, however, easily detect it by replicating proposed solutions.

With an analogy in music, every day so many musicians produce numerous "novel" music pieces all over the world. But only a few go to a music chart based on audience' preference rather than novelty.

If ES really equals HS, it should be more popular in major literature because of its performance regardless of its novelty. But, reality is not the case. Also, if ES equals HS, GA also equals HS after tweaking GA (uniform crossover, neighboring mutation, multiple parents (polygamy?), etc). But, why did the author insist ES = HS rather than GA = HS? Is this because GA is still popular while ES is not?

Moreover, how can the author explain the reason HS has outperformed even GA in most of my papers? For the example of a large-scale water network design (number of variables = 454 discrete variables; and number of possible solutions = 10^{454}), HS found a better design only after 0.62% of function evaluations that GA (uniform crossover, mutation, reproduction plan of steady-state-delete-worst, etc) used (Geem, 2009); for the example of a multiple-dam operation (number of variables = 48 integer variables; and number of

possible solutions = 6.87×10^{34}), HS found five different global optima that share the identical objective function value while GA (binary, gray, and real-value representations; tournament selection; one-point, two-point, and uniform crossovers; and uniform and modified uniform mutations) could not reach any global optimum after 35,000 function evaluations (Geem, 2007); and for the example of a pipeline optimization (number of variables = 40 binary variables; and number of possible solutions = 2^{40}) which was originally tackled by Prof. Goldberg, HS obtained the energy consumption of 11,169.4 HP which outperforms GA (11,263.2 HP) (Geem, 2005; because the best solution vector with 40 binary variables was also provided in the paper, I always welcome any algorithm's tackle to the problem).

Again, any algorithm, which performs better, is naturally selected by the research community instead of being rejected by an unverified author who pretends to be an Ultimate Being.

Who Misleads What?

Although the author claims the research community is misled, I'd like to point out how the author misleads the research community.

The author mentioned HS has been applied only to small size problems and the most extreme case has 27 variables. Is this true? Actually HS has been applied to large-scale real-world problems such as hydraulic network design (Geem, 2009) with 454 discrete variables and ecological reserve planning (Geem & Williams, 2007) with 441 binary variables. The author omitted to mention these large-scale applications.

More strangely, the author included those large-scale problem references in his paper although he omitted mentioning. Did the author intentionally mislead the community by omitting them or just cite without reading them? Whether the former case is true (I do not think so though) or the latter is true, it is another problem of peer reviewing system as the author also mentioned.

Also, the author tried to exclude cutting-edge and challenging references such as stochastic partial derivative of HS (Geem, 2008). Is this because he could not access to major research databases or because these references are obstacles to his predefined conclusion? I guess that the author was pressed to publish a paper using predefined conclusion and biased bases.

Another point that the author misleads is the fact that he pretends to be a representative of the whole research community. He claims that the whole research community is vulnerable to novelty. However, as far as I know, that is not true. My research community is not that much vulnerable. Although novelty is one of important factors, it disappears after couple publications and performance instead becomes the survival fuel for long-term success. In other words, any algorithm's success depends upon the rule "survival of the fittest" rather than "survival of the novelest."

The author claims that the number of instances is too few in HS publications. If research community means algorithm field, it may be true. But if research community means engineering application field for example, the author cannot say that deterministically. Sometimes, just introducing a meta-heuristic technique into a problem can be a contribution (although I've tried to compare every algorithm which tackled the problem so far, I did not want to make the results of the other algorithms by myself because I am not good at the other algorithms especially in terms of "proper" parameter setting. Also, sometimes I could not compare HS with other algorithms just because I created the problem for the first time (Geem & Choi, 2007)). In other words, an application-oriented community, whose major interest is practical usefulness rather than theoretical clearness, can be also the subset of the whole research community. Certain application-oriented community wants "simple-but-easy-to-use" algorithms for large-variable technically-constrained problems while the algorithm-oriented community wants complicated algorithms for less-variable-but-ideal problems.

Finally, the author claims that there is no new concept in modifications of HS because the concepts of adjusting parameter dynamically, combining two algorithms, and considering inter-variable relationship were already used in previous researches. Actually, the authors of those papers never claimed the novelty of the concepts. Instead, they claimed that their approaches were first attempts with HS. Also, the author appears to misunderstand the concept of musical properties that may enrich the algorithm in the future.

DISCUSSIONS AND CONCLUSION

In this paper, I tried to briefly demonstrate how fictitiously the author wrote a "novel". His logic is "HS equals ES. Because ES is not popular currently, HS has no future" without any rigorous analysis such as theoretical proof or numerical example. However, if the author wants to write a real paper, his logic should be "HS shares similarity with ES in term of X. Thus, HS correspondingly shares the weakness of ES, and it was supported by numerical results. In order to overcome this weakness, HS should be reinforced with Y feature."

In reality, while the author insists to devote readers' efforts to more promising area than HS, I really do not know where it is because HS is one of the best methods among various meta-heuristic algorithms in my research fields (*Quo Vadis*?). That is why I really hate this kind of *veto-ergo-sum* and hoax paper although I am open to any constructive criticism. Anyhow, this kind of growing pain for rookie method appears very natural because even well-established methods such as Fourier series and genetic algorithm have been once rejected by research societies in their early ages.

Even if any limitation of HS is found in the future, I do not think it is a deadlock because I believe the maxim "where there is a will (of overcoming the limitation), there is a way (to solve)." I imagine this overcoming process is similar to a breakthrough moment of local optimum. On the contrary, the author appears to have a negative attitude to novel approaches and to stick to well-established algorithms. In my opinion, any novel approach can be a global search as long as it has better performance than current local optima of existing algorithms.

Here, I'd like to point out that not only reviewing system but also citation system is not perfect because I do not like to cite any non-constructive paper even when I have to do. Also, I think the author's research patron (Swiss National Science Foundation) would be much happier if the author wrote a more constructive paper rather than publication-oriented paper under the financial benefit and time duration. If the author really wants to criticize a theory, he should use academic way (mathematical proof or numerical results) rather than malediction with predefined conclusion and biased supports. Only in that way, the real chance for the author to write a good paper is given.

In conclusion, while the author claimed that HS equals ES but HS succeeded because of fake novelty, I explained why his paper is incorrect by the following reasons: 1) there is no structural match between HS and ES even in a lengthy paper of an original ES inventor; and 2) the author tried to distort the performance (this is the success factor of any algorithm) of HS by excluding major HS references.

Anyhow, I appreciate the author to allow me to explore different aspects of the algorithm. My last wish is that the author becomes Paul rather than Saul of HS, or that he becomes the president of a new algorithm rather than the sniper of the existing algorithm (I do not want to mention another academic vandalism by the IP which locates the author's region).

REFERENCES

Beyer, H.-G., & Schwefel, H.-P. (2002). Evolution strategies: A comprehensive introduction. *Natural Computing*, *1*(1), 3–52. doi:10.1023/A:1015059928466

Fogel, D. B. (1995). A Comparison of Evolutionary Programming and Genetic Algorithms on Selected Constrained Optimization Problems. *Simulation*, *64*(6), 399–406. doi:10.1177/003754979506400605

Geem, Z. W. (2005). Harmony Search in Water Pump Switching Problem. *Lecture Notes in Computer Science*, *3612*, 751–760. doi:10.1007/11539902_92

Geem, Z. W. (2007). Optimal Scheduling of Multiple Dam System Using Harmony Search Algorithm. *Lecture Notes in Computer Science*, *4507*, 316–323. doi:10.1007/978-3-540-73007-1_39

Geem, Z. W. (2008). Novel Derivative of Harmony Search Algorithm for Discrete Design Variables. *Applied Mathematics and Computation*, *199*(1), 223–230. doi:10.1016/j.amc.2007.09.049

Geem, Z. W. (2009). Particle-Swarm Harmony Search for Water Network Design. *Engineering Optimization*, *41*(4), 297–311. doi:10.1080/03052150802449227

Geem, Z. W., & Choi, J. Y. (2007). Music Composition Using Harmony Search Algorithm. *Lecture Notes in Computer Science*, *4448*, 593–600. doi:10.1007/978-3-540-71805-5_65

Geem, Z. W., Kim, J. H., & Loganathan, G. V. (2001). A New Heuristic Optimization Algorithm: Harmony Search. *Simulation*, *76*(2), 60–68. doi:10.1177/003754970107600201

Geem, Z. W., & Williams, J. C. (2007). Harmony Search and Ecological Optimization. *International Journal of Energy and Environment*, 1(2), 150–154.

Schwefel, H.-P. (1994). On the Evolution of Evolutionary Computation. In Zurada, J., Marks, R., & Robinson, C. (Eds.), *Computational Intelligence: Imitating Life* (pp. 116–124). Washington, DC: IEEE Press.

Weyland, D. (2010). A Rigorous Analysis of the Harmony Search Algorithm: How the Research Community can be Misled by a 'Novel' Methodology. *International Journal of Applied Metaheuristic Computing*, 1(2), 50–60.

This work was previously published in International Journal of Applied Metaheuristic Computing, Volume 1, Issue 4, edited by Peng-Yeng Yin, pp. 76-80, copyright 2010 by IGI Publishing (an imprint of IGI Global).

Chapter 7
DIMMA:
A Design and Implementation Methodology for Metaheuristic Algorithms – A Perspective from Software Development

Masoud Yaghini
Iran University of Science and Technology, Iran

Mohammad Rahim Akhavan Kazemzadeh
Iran University of Science and Technology, Iran

ABSTRACT

Metaheuristic algorithms will gain more and more popularity in the future as optimization problems are increasing in size and complexity. In order to record experiences and allow project to be replicated, a standard process as a methodology for designing and implementing metaheuristic algorithms is necessary. To the best of the authors' knowledge, no methodology has been proposed in literature for this purpose. This paper presents a Design and Implementation Methodology for Metaheuristic Algorithms, named DIMMA. The proposed methodology consists of three main phases and each phase has several steps in which activities that must be carried out are clearly defined in this paper. In addition, design and implementation of tabu search metaheuristic for travelling salesman problem is done as a case study to illustrate applicability of DIMMA.

1. INTRODUCTION

Optimization problems, which occur in real world applications, are sometimes NP-hard. In the case of NP-hard problems, exact algorithms need, in the worst case, exponential time to find the optimum. Metaheuristics or *modern heuristics* deal with these problems by introducing systematic rules to escape from local optima. Metaheuristics are applicable to a wide range of optimization problems (Doreo et al., 2006; Morago, DePuy, & Whitehouse, 2006). Some popular population-based metaheuristic methods are genetic algorithm

DOI: 10.4018/978-1-4666-0270-0.ch007

(Goldberg, 1989) and ant colony optimization (Dorigo & Stützle, 2004) in which collective intelligence play the important role (Wang, 2010). Tabu search (Glover & Laguna, 1997) and simulated annealing (Kirkpatrick, Gelatt, & Vecchi, 1983) are the two popular single-solution based metaheuristics that improve a single solution in an iterative algorithm.

With growing scale and complexity of optimization problems, metaheuristics will gain more and more popular. According to significant growth in using metaheuristics as optimization tools, there must be a standard methodology for design and implementing them. Such a methodology is used for recording experience and allows projects to be replicated. Moreover, this standard methodology can be a comfort factor for new adopters with little metaheuristic experience, and can show the guidelines to everyone who want to design and implement metaheuristics.

To the best of our knowledge, no methodology has been proposed in literature for design and implementation metaheuristic algorithms. There are many software frameworks in the literature for metaheuristics (Voss & Woodruff, 2002; Fink et al., 1999), in which framework means reusable programming codes and components for metaheuristics (Talbi, 2009). Hence, the meaning of frameworks in these references is different from our proposed methodology. Although there are several tutorials as lectures on how to design meheuristics (Thierens, 2008), they are sometimes for special metaheuristic and do not consider this process as a whole.

The proposed methodology in this paper, a *Design and Implementation Methodology for Metaheuristic Algorithms (DIMMA)*, shows guidelines to everyone who wants to design and implement a metaheuristic algorithm. Webster's collegiate dictionary defines methodology as "a body of methods, rules, and postulate employed by a discipline" or "the analysis of the principles or procedures of inquiry in a particular field" (Merriam-Webster, 1997).

DIMMA includes several phases, steps, disciplines, and principles to design and implement a specific metaheuristic for a given optimization problem. In other words, DIMMA refers to the methodology that is used to standardize process of design and implementing a metaheuristic algorithm. In Sections 2-5 we explain the architecture of DIMMA and its phases and steps, In Section 6 we followed by a description of each step of DIMMA using design and implementation of Tabu Search (TS) metaheuristic for Travelling Salesman Problem (TSP) as a case study.

2. ARCHITECTURE OF DIMMA

The architecture of DIMMA has been inspired from *Rational Unified Process* (RUP) which is a methodology for software engineering (Kroll & Krutchten, 2003). DIMMA has two dimensions including *dynamic* and *discipline* dimension (Figure 1). Dynamic dimension is the horizontal dimension, which includes phases of the methodology: *initiation*, *blueprint*, and *construction*. Discipline dimension is the vertical dimension that shows the disciplines, which logically group the steps, activities, and artifacts.

DIMMA has three sequential phases that each of them has several steps (Figure 2). In each step, we define several activities, which must be done to complete the steps. These phases are as follows: *initiation*, in which the problem in hand must be understood precisely, and the goal of designing metaheuristic must be clearly defined. The next phase is *blueprint*, the most important goals of this phase are selecting metaheuristic solution method, defining performance measures, and designing algorithm for our solution strategy. The last phase is *construction* in which implementing the designed algorithm, parameters tuning (parameter setting), analyzing its performance, and

Figure 1. Two dimensions of DIMMA and level of effort in each discipline during the phases

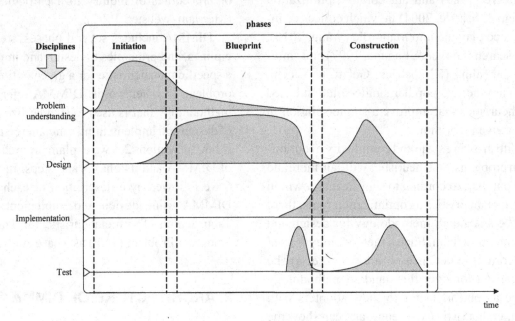

finally documentation of results must be done. In some steps, it is necessary to review pervious steps to justify and improve decisions and algorithm. For example, it is common for the algorithm to be modified after the performance evaluations. These backward movements are illustrated in Figure 2.

3. INITIATION PHASE

Step 1.1: State the Problem

Stating the problem is the step 1.1 in DIMMA that is helpful in narrowing the problem down and make it more manageable. To state the problem, one can write simple statement that includes one or more objectives, inputs, outputs, and assumptions of problem. In this step, a mathematical model can be provided for clarity. However, in some cases, it is difficult to formulate the problem with an unambiguous analytical mathematical notation.

The structure of problem such as multi-objective approaches, dynamic aspects, continuous or

discrete modeling which is defined here can have significant effects on the next steps including defining goals, selecting solution strategy, and defining performance measures.

Step 1.2: Define Goals

In the step 1.2 of DIMMA, the goals of developing the metaheuristic must be defined clearly. All the experiments, performance analysis measures, and statistical analysis will depend on these goals. In addition, goal definition can be helpful in selecting solution strategy.

Some goals of designing the metaheuristic are: (1) reducing search time in comparison with exact methods or another metaheuristics, (2) improving quality of solutions, (3) robustness in terms of the instances, (4) solving large-scale problems, (5) easiness of implementation, (6) easiness to combine with other algorithms to improve performance, (7) flexibility to solve other problems or optimization models, and (8) providing a tight approximation to the problem. Selecting instances and solution method, and defining performance

Figure 2. Steps in each phases of DIMMA

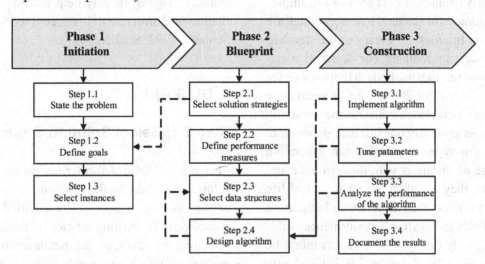

measures must be done according to selected goals. For example, if you want to reduce the search time, you must select time measurements in step 2.2, and you must select instances which can be comparable to another research works.

Step 1.3 Select Instances

In the step 1.3 of DIMMA, we must select input instances carefully to perform the evaluation of the algorithm. The chosen instances must be representative of the problem that one is trying to solve. The selected structure of input instances may influence the performance of metaheuristics significantly. To obtain interesting result and to allow the generalization of the conclusions, the selected instances must be diverse in terms of size of the instances, their complexity, and their structure (Alba & Lugue, 2005; Talbi, 2009; Silberholz & Golden, 2010). Keep in mind that according to No Free Lunch (NFL) theorem (Wolpert & Macready, 1997), no optimization algorithm is better than any other on all possible optimization problems; it means that, if algorithm *A* performs better than *B* for a given problem, there is no proof that *A* is always better than *B* and there is always another problem where *B* performs better than *A*.

Therefore, the aim of designing an algorithm must be for a class of problems (Talbi, 2009).

Instances which are used for implementing and analyzing metaheuristics can be divided into *real-life* and *constructed* instances. Real-life instances are taken from real world applications. *Pure real-life* and *random real-life* instances are the two types of real life instances. Pure real-life instances are the practical instances of real world applications. If available, they are the good tools for evaluating the performance of a metaheuristic. Obtaining pure real-life instances is difficult, because those data aren't public, and collecting such data may be time consuming or expensive (Talbi, 2009; Silberholz & Golden, 2010). Random real-life instances are an alternative of real-life instances which use random real instances. In this type of instances, the structure of the real-life problem is preserved, but details are randomly changed to produce new instances (Alba & Lugue, 2005; Fischetti, Gonzalez, & Toth, 1997).

Standard instances and *pure random instances* are the two types of constructed instances. Standard instances are the instances that are widely used in experimentations, and because of that, became standard in literature. OR-Library (Beasley, 1990), MIPLIB (Achterberg, Koch, & Martin, 2003), and TSPLIB (Reinelt, 1991) are three examples of public libraries of standard instances which are available on Internet. By means of the standard instances we can compare our designed metaheuristic with another methods in literature (Alba & Lugue, 2005; Talbi, 2009). Finally, when none of the above instances are available, the remaining alternative is pure random instance generation. Although this type of instances can generate a wide range of instances with different size and complexity, they are often too far from real-life problems to reflect their structure and important characteristics and as a result, performance evaluation using only this type of instances might be controversial (Alba & Lugue, 2005; Gendreau, Laporte, & Semet, 1998).

After selecting instances, the selected instances must be divided into two subsets; one for tuning the metaheuristic parameters and the second for evaluating the algorithm performance with tuned parameters. Tuning instances should be representative of the whole class of instances that the algorithm will eventually encounter. Therefore, since tuning instances are representative of another, the performance of algorithm on these two subsets of instances must be similar to each other. Also the instances which are used for tuning parameters must not be applied in performance evaluation because this may lead to controversial results that the parameters are just suitable for these problems (Biratteri, 2009).

In addition, after selecting instances, classifying them might be useful. Classify instances means categorizing them into classes according to some important factors such as size and complexity. Performance analysis of constructed metaheuristic algorithm must be done on each class of this problem instances (Silberholz & Golden, 2010). This kind of approach can be found in Hartmann and Kolisch (2000) in which three factors such as network complexity, resource factor, and resource strength are used to classify instances for project scheduling problem. Sometimes it is useful to use *fitness landscape analysis* for classifying the instance. This work may help to know the difficulties and structure of instances (see Stadler & Schnabl, 1992; Stadler, 1995).

4. BLUEPRINT PHASE

Step 2.1: Select Solution Strategy

In step 2.1 of DIMMA, after reviewing existing solution methods for the problem, the necessity of using metaheuristics must be specified. Indeed, according to the existing solution methods, it must be distinguished if applying metaheuristic for the problem is necessary or not. If a metaheuristic approach is selected as a solution method, one can go to the next step; otherwise we must stop in this point.

According to the situation, we can select one of the solution strategies such as exact algorithm, heuristic algorithm, metaheuristic algorithm, *hybrid method*, *parallel algorithm*, and *cooperative algorithm*.

For selecting metaheuristic or exact methods as a solution strategy, we must keep in mind four main factors. First, one is the *complexity* of a problem. Complexity can be seen as an indication of hardness of the problem. The second important factor is the *size* of input instances. In the case of small instances, the problem may be solved by an exact approach, even if the problem is NP-hard. The *structure* of the instances is another important factor. Some of the problems with specific structure by medium or even large dimensions may be solved optimally by exact algorithms. The last factor is the *required search time* to solve a given problem which must take into account. If we have real-time constraint (depend on problem, can be some seconds to some months), even if the complexity of problem is polynomial, the using of metaheuristic can be justified. If for a given problem, there is an exact or other state of the art algorithm in literature, selecting metaheuristic, as a solution strategy is not rational (Talbi, 2009).

In addition to above factors, ease of use of certain metaheuristic over certain problem can play an important role. For example, ACO is very intuitive for TSP, but may be difficult to adapt to continuous problems. Also, in some cases, the direct use of a generic metaheuristic would not lead to good results and sometimes there is a need to adapt it for the problem with the use of specialized heuristics.

Hybrid algorithms are one of the approaches to use metaheuristics as optimization tools. A hybrid algorithm is a combination of complete (exact) or approximate algorithms (or both) used to solve the problem in hand (El-Abd & Kamel, 2005). These methods are used when we want the specific advantages of different approaches.

The central goal of parallel computing is to speed up computation by dividing the workload among several processors. From the view point of algorithm design, *pure* parallel computing strategies exploit the partial order of algorithms (i.e., the sets of operations that may be executed concurrently in time without modifying the solution method and the final solution obtained) and thus correspond to the *natural parallelism* present in the algorithm (Crainic & Toulouse, 2003). Cooperative algorithms are a category of parallel algorithms, in which several search algorithms are run in parallel in order to solve the optimization problem in hand. The search algorithms (run in parallel) may be different, that is why a cooperative search technique may be also viewed as a hybrid algorithm (El-Abd & Kamel, 2005).

After selecting solution strategy, we must specify algorithm components for our problem. This specification can be helpful in the step of selecting data structure and designing the algorithm.

Step 2.2: Define Performance Measures

In this step, the performance measures are selected for the step of performance analysis. We must select the appropriate measures according to the selected goals of using metaheuristics. For exact solution methods, in which the global optimality is guaranteed, search time is the main indicator to evaluate the performances of the algorithms. But, in the case of metaheuristics which try to find near optimal solution in reasonable time, both solution quality and computational time are the two main indicators of performance (Alba & Lugue, 2005; Talbi, 2009). In metaheuristic search methods, the indicators to evaluate the effectiveness include *quality of solutions*, *computational effort*, and *robustness* (Barr et al., 1995).

Quality of solutions is based on measuring the distance to one of the following solutions (Figure 3): *global optimal solution, lower (upper) bound solution, best known solution*, and *requirements or actual implemented solution*. For constructed instances, the global optimal is known. In this case, the percentage of runs in which the result is equivalent to global optimal (success rate), can be the best indicator. However, usually this global optimal is not available, so the lower or upper bound can be used for minimization and maximization problems, respectively. Several relaxation methods such as Lagrangian relaxation can be used to find lower and upper bound solution. For some standard and popular problems, the best known solution is available in the literature which can be used as an indicator to evaluating the quality of solutions. For real world application, there might be predefined goal that can be as a quality measurement (Talbi, 2009).

Computational effort is the worst-case or average-case complexity and CPU time that can be used for theoretical and empirical analysis of algorithm efficiency. For theoretical analysis, one can use complexity theory to calculate the complexity of an algorithm. However, it is not always sufficient to analyze the computation effort theoretically. CPU time is a measurement to analyze the computational effort empirically. One of the disadvantages of CPU time is that it depends on computer characteristics and compiler in which the algorithm is compiled (Talbi, 2009; Silberholz

Figure 3. Performance assessment of the quality of the solutions in a minimization problem. (Adapted from Talbi, 2009)

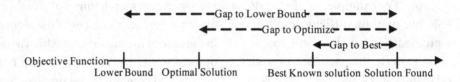

& Golden, 2010). Therefore, many researchers use the number of objective function evaluations as a measurement of the computational effort, since it eliminates the effects of these characteristics (Talbi, 2009). However, number of evaluations of objective function is not also the best metric for computation time, because it may not be the part that takes the most of computation time.

As we mentioned, another metric for performance evaluation is robustness. If the results of algorithm have no or small changes by deviating in the input instances, the algorithm is robust (Montgomery, 2005). Once the experimental results are obtained, standard deviation of solution quality must be considered as a measurement of robustness.

Performance measures for multiobjective optimization (measures for convergence of metaheuristics towards the Pareto frontier) can be found in Collette and Siarry (2005). Moreover, performance measures for parallel optimization can be found in Crainic & Tolouse (1998). In addition, performance metrics for comparison of metaheuristics, such as run time and quality of solution, is well discussed in Silberholz and Golden (2010). It must be stated here that statistical analysis which must be done to evaluate performance of algorithm is discussed in section 3.3.

Step 2.3: Select Data Structure

Before designing the algorithm, it is necessary to select a proper data structure in step 2.3 of DIMMA. Data structure is a scheme for organiz-

ing information in memory, for better algorithm efficiency (MacAllister, 2009; Puntambekar, 2009). Array, files, lists, trees, and tables are the important types of data structures. For instance, for TSP, as we will mention in section 6.2, for representing a solution, one can use an array with the length of number of cities.

Selecting the right data structure can make an enormous difference in the complexity of the resulting implementation. Pick the right data representation can make the programming easier. If we select wrong data structure for an algorithm, implementing it might be too time consuming (Cormen et al., 2002; Skiena & Revilla, 2003).

Step 2.4 Design Algorithm

In the step 2.4 of DIMMA, overall structure of algorithm must be specified. There are various ways for specifying an algorithm (Puntambekar, 2009). Using *natural language* is the simplest way for specifying an algorithm. In this case, we specify the algorithm simply with natural language. Although such a specification is very simple, it is not usually clear enough to implement. *Pseudocode* is another way of specifying an algorithm that is a combination of natural and programming language. Using pseudocode, one can specify algorithm more precisely than a natural language. Instead of two previous ways for specifying an algorithm, one can use *flowchart*. Flowchart is a graphical specification of an algorithm. After specifying the overall structure of algorithm, the correctness of it must be checked. This work can be done by using one small instance of valid input.

In addition to the above tools of description of an algorithm, the dynamic behaviours of metaheuristics can be described by means of some concepts from RUP, such as system sequence diagram (SSD) in the UML (Unified Modeling Language) (Siau & Halpin, 2001). A sequence diagram in UML is a kind of interaction diagram that shows how processes operate with one another and in what order. It is a construct of a Message Sequence Chart.

The algorithm must also be analyzed according to four factors including *complexity*, *space efficiency*, *simplicity* and *generality*. The number of steps of pseudocode needed to specify the algorithm can be the metrics for complexity. However, these metrics depend on programming language and style of pseudocode (Silberholz & Golden, 2010). Space efficiency is space or memory usage of an algorithm. Simplicity is an important factor, because the simpler the algorithm is, the easier it can be programmed and debugged. Finally, generality is applicability of an algorithm to a wide range of inputs (Puntambekar, 2009).

5. CONSTRUCTION PHASE

Step 3.1 Implement Algorithm

The implementation of an algorithm is done by suitable programming language in step 3.1 of DIMMA. For example, if an algorithm consists of objects and related methods then it will be better to implement such algorithm using one of the object oriented programming language such as C++, C# or Java.

In this step, in order to speed out programming and reducing development costs, one can use many free software frameworks. Software frameworks are reusable programming codes and components for metaheuristics. One can use frameworks to implement a metaheuristic without in-depth knowledge of programming. Some of the software frameworks which have been proposed for single-objective problems are EasyLocal++ (Gaspero & Schaerf, 2001), Localizer++ (Michel & Van 2001), GAlib (Wall, 1996), MAFRA (Krasnogor & Smith, 2000), Hotframe (Fink, Voss, & Woodruff, 1999), iOpt (Voudouris et al., 2001), DREAM (Arenas et al. 2002), MALLBA (Alba et al., 2002), ECJ (Wilson, 2004), and CIlib (Cloete, Engelbrecht, & Pampar, 2008). EasyLocal++ and Localizer++ have been designed for local search algorithms, while GAlib is the framework for genetic algorithm. MAFRA is a framework for genetic local search algorithm (memtic algorithm). Hotframe is for evolutionary algorithms and metaheuristics which use single solution instead of population of solutions. Some of these frameworks including MALLBA, and ECJ are just for evolutionary algorithms. iOpt is a framework for genetic algorithm that can handle hybrid approaches. CIlib is a framework for swarm intelligence and evolutionary computing algorithms. Many frameworks, and reusable codes for Particle Swarm Intelligence (PSO) can be found in Particle Swarm Central[1]. There are also frameworks for several metaheuristics in MetaYourHeuristic (Yin, 2010) that can be used for new adopters in the field of metaheuristics.

In the case of multi-objective optimization some of software frameworks including PISA (Bleuler et al., 2003) and ParadiseEO[2] have been developed. However, ParadiseEO can also handle single-objective problems. There are also several genetic algorithm source codes for single and multi-objective problems in Kanpur Genetic Algorithms Laboratory website[3].

Step 3.2: Tune Parameters

Parameters are the configurable components of a metaheuristic algorithm. Metaheuristics are sensitive to the value of their parameters. Therefore, in step 3.2 of DIMMA, parameter tuning, also known as parameter setting, should be done. To do this, several number of numerical and/or categorical parameters, has to be tuned, and to do this scientific method and statistical analysis could and should be employed (Biratteri, 2009; Talbi, 2009; Barr et al., 1995).

In the most of research papers in the field of metaheuristics, parameters are tuned by hand in a trial-and-error procedure. This approach has several disadvantages such as: time-consuming, labor-intensive, and it need practitioner with special skills (Biratteri, 2009).

The proper values for the parameters depend on three main factors: the problem at hand, the instance of the problem, and the required search time. There are two different strategies for parameter tuning including *off-line* and *on-line* strategies.

In off-line tuning strategy, the parameters are set before the execution of metaheuristics and don't update during the execution. In this strategy one-by-one parameter tuning doesn't guarantee the optimality of parameters values, because there is no interaction between parameters. To overcome this problem, *Design of Experiments* (DoE) can be used (Fisher, 1935; Montgomery, 2005; Frigon, 1997; Antony, 2003; Box, 2005). In DoE approaches, there are some factors (parameters) that each of them has different levels (potential values of parameters). With a full factorial design, the best level of each factor can be obtained, but this work takes high computational time. However, there are several DoE approaches which reduce the number of experiments (Montgomery, 2005). DOE refers to the process of planning the experiment so that appropriate data that can be analyzed by statistical methods will be collected, resulting in valid and objective conclusions (Biratteri, 2009).

The three basic principles of DoE are replication, randomization, and blocking. Replication means a repetition of the basic experiment. Replication has two important properties. First, it allows the experimenter to obtain an estimate of the experimental error. Second, if the sample mean is used to estimate the effect of a factor in the experiment, replication permits the experimenter to obtain a more precise estimate of this effect. Randomization means that both the allocation of

the experimental material and the order in which the individual runs or trials of the experiment are determined randomly. Randomization usually makes this assumption valid. Blocking is a design technique used to improve the precision with which comparisons among the factors of interest are made. Often blocking is used to reduce or eliminate the variability transmitted from nuisance factors; that is, factors that may influence the experimental response but in which we are not directly interested (Montgomery, 2005). The important parameters in DoE approach are response variable, factor, level, treatment and effect. The response variable is the measured variable of interest. In the analysis of metaheuristics, the typically measures are the solution quality and computation time (Adenso-Díaz & laguna, 2006). A factor is an independent variable manipulated in an experiment because it is thought to affect one or more of the response variables. The various values at which the factor is set are known as its levels. In metaheuristic performance analysis, the factors include both the metaheuristic tuning parameters and the most important problem characteristics (Biratteri, 2009). A treatment is a specific combination of factor levels. The particular treatments will depend on the particular experiment design and on the ranges over which factors are varied. An effect is a change in the response variable due to a change in one or more factors (Ridge, 2007). Design of experiments is a tool that can be used to determine important parameters and interactions between them. Four-stages of DoE consist of screening and diagnosis of important factors, modeling, optimization and assessment. This methodology is called sequential experimentation, which is used to set the parameters in the DoE approach and has been used in this paper for the proposed algorithm in the case study section (Montgomery, 2005).

Another approach in off-line parameter tuning, is to formulate tuning of parameters of a metaheuristic as an optimization problem (Talbi, 2009). This problem can be seen as an independent problem that by optimizing it, the best values of parameters are obtained. In the case of off-line parameter tuning, Coy et al. (2000) proposed a procedure, based on statistical design of experiments and gradient descent that finds effective settings for parameters found in heuristics. Adenso-Diaz and Laguna (2006) proposed a procedure for parameter tuning by means of fractional design of experiments and local search. Hutter et al. (2009) proposed An Automatic Algorithm Configuration Framework (ParamILS) as a procedure for automatic parameter tuning. Another approach for off-line tuning parameters is machine learning that can be found in Biratteri (2009).

At different time of the search, different values for parameters are optimal. Because of this, an important drawback of off-line strategies is that the value or parameters are fixed and can't change during the search. Therefore, online approaches that update parameters dynamically (a random or deterministic update of the parameter values without take into account the search process) or adaptively (changes the values according to the search progress using the memory of the search) during the search must be designed. In adaptive approaches, the parameters are encoded into the representation of solutions and as a result by changing solution the value of the parameters are also changed.

Resent works on tuning parameters for metaheuristic algorithms can be found in Birattari et al. (2002), Bartz-Beielstein (2006), Fukunaga (2008), and Hutter, Hoos, and Stützle (2007).

Step 3.3: Analyze the Performance of Algorithm

In step 3.3 of DIMMA, we must obtain the experimental results for different indicators to analyze performance of metaheuristic algorithms with statistical tests, such as *t-test*, and ANOVA models for a comparison of more than two algorithms (Cohen, 1995). To use these tests, we must obtain some aggregation number that summarizes the average and deviation tendencies. These statistical tests are used to determine whether obtained conclusion is due to a sampling error or not. The selection of a given statistical hypothesis-testing tool is performed according to the characteristics of the data (Montgomery, 2005). Generally, it is not sufficient to analyze an algorithm based only on theoretical approach, so that empirical performance analysis is a necessary task to perform and must be done on a fair basis (Bartz-Beielstein, 2006; Rardin & Uzsoy, 2001; Dean & Voss, 1999). Many trials (at least 10, more than 100 if possible) must be carried out to derive significant statistical results. From this set of trials, many measures may be computed (Talbi, 2009) such as mean, median, minimum, maximum, standard deviation, the success rate that the reference solution (e.g., global optimum, best known, given goal) has been attained, and so on.

Step 3.4: Document the Results

In this step of DIMMA, the documentation must be done. The interpretation of the results must be explicit and driven using the defined goals and considered performance measures. Generally, graphical tools are more understandable than presenting the large amount of data results using tables. Some popular graphical tools include interaction plots, scatter plots, and box plots (Talbi, 2009).

Interaction plots represent the interaction between different factors and their effect on the obtained response (performance measure). Scatter plot is a tool to illustrate the compromise between various performance indicators. For instance, the plots display quality of solutions versus time, or time versus robustness, or robustness versus quality. Box plot illustrate the distribution of the results through their five-number summaries: the smallest value, lower quartile (Q1), median (Q2), upper quartile (Q3), and largest value. Box plot is useful in detecting outliers and indicating the dispersion of the output data without any assumptions on the statistical distribution of the data. In addition, scatter plot is useful to illustrate compromise between different performance indicators (Tufte, 2001).

6. A CASE STUDY

In this section, we design and implement tabu search metaheuristic for travelling salesman problem as a case study to illustrate applicability DIMMA. The reason of choosing TS and TSP is that they are well known in the literature.

Initiation Phase

In Step 1.1, we state the TSP problem. Given a list of m cities and their pairwise distances (or costs), the problem is to find a minimum tour that visits each city exactly once. In the other word, we want to find a minimum Hamiltonian tour between a set of cities. According to the direction of arcs between cities, the TSP problem is divided into two categories: *symmetric* and *asymmetric*. In symmetric TSP, the arcs are undirected; while in the asymmetric TSP, the arcs are directed and the costs are depend on the directions. In this section, the symmetric TSP is chosen as a case study.

For clarity, here a mathematical formulation is presented for the symmetric TSP. Let $x_j \in \{0,1\}$ *be the de*cision variable where j runs through all arcs A of the undirected graph and c_j is the cost of traveling that arc. To find a tour in this graph, one must select a subset of arcs such that every city is contained in exactly two of the arcs selected. The problem can therefore be formulated as:

$$\min \frac{1}{2} \sum_{j=1}^{m} \sum_{k \in J(j)} c_k x_k \qquad (1)$$

Subject to:

$$\sum_{k \in J(j)} x_k = 2 \quad \forall j = 1, \dots, m \qquad (2)$$

$$\sum_{j \in A(K)} x_j \le |K| - 1 \quad \forall K \subset \{1, \dots, m\} \qquad (3)$$

$$x_j = 0 \, or \, 1 \quad \forall j \in A \qquad (4)$$

where $J(j)$ is the set of all undirected arcs connected to city j and $A(K)$ is the subset of all undirected arcs connecting the cities in any proper, nonempty subset K of all cities. The objective function (1) is to minimize the tour length. Constraint (2) ensures that every city is contained in exactly two of the selected arc. Indeed, this constraint ensures that the selected arcs construct a tour. Constraint (3) is a sub-tour elimination constraint that prevents construction of sub-tours.

In the next step, the goal of solving TSP should be defined. Finding a minimum tour in acceptable time is the goal of this case study.

In step 1.3, the TSP instances are selected. We choose instances from TSPLIB (Reinelt, 1991) that is one of the popular sources for TSP instances (Table 1). Selected instances must have enough diversity in terms of size. Therefore, we select 12 instances from TSPLIB with different sizes.

Blueprint Phase

In the first step of blueprint phase, solution strategy should be selected. Because the TSP is an NP-hard problem (Garey & Johnson, 1979), so that we use approximate a metaheuristic algorithm to solve it. In this example, to illustrate DIMMA, we use tabu search (Glover & Laguna, 1997; Gendreau, 2003) as a solution method for TSP. It should be noted that, according to the structure of TSP, some other metaheuristic could be used to solve it.

The main components of TS are *representation of solution, neighborhood structure (move), tabu list, tabu tenure, aspiration criteria, termination*

Table 1. Problem instances for TSP from TSPLIB

#	Problem name	Number of cities	Global optima	#	Problem name	Number of cities	Global optima
1	ulysses16	16	6859	7	gr202	202	40160
2	ulysses22	22	7013	8	a280	280	2579
3	eil51	51	426	9	pcb442	442	50778
4	berlin52	52	7542	10	gr666	666	294358
5	kroA100	100	21282	11	pr1002	1002	259045
6	rd100	100	7910	12	u1060	1060	224094

condition, *intensification*, and *diversification strategies*.

In step 2.2 the performance measures for solving TSP with TS is defined. The defined goal is to find a good solution in a reasonable time. Therefore, as a case study, performance measures which are used for this example are solution quality and CPU time. The global optima are known for the selected instances (Table 1). Therefore, for solution quality measure we use error rate from global optima.

In step 2.3, data structure is selected. To solve TSP with tabu search, one can use an integer array for representation of individuals, which shows the permutation of the cities (Figure 4). To store this array and its length, *currentTour*[] and *currentTourLength* are considered in data structure, respectively.

To construct initial solution we use nearest neighborhood heuristic method (Dorigo & Stützle, 2004). Therefore, we need an array and a variable to store them. Integer array *nearestNeighborArray*[] and integer variable *nearestNeighborTourLength* are used for this purpose. For calculating tour length, we need distances between cities, so that, two dimensional integer array *distancesMatrix*[][] is used to store distances.

A neighborhood solution can be obtained by swapping two positions of cities in representation array (Figure 4). Therefore, neighborhood of a solution is all of the solutions that can be obtained by one swap.

The characteristics that must be saved in tabu list are the pair of cities that recently swapped. In this problem, the tabu list is a two dimensional array, *tabuList*[][]. In this array, the tabu tenure of swapping two cities i and j are stored in i^{th} raw

Figure 4. Neighborhood structure for TS to solve TSP

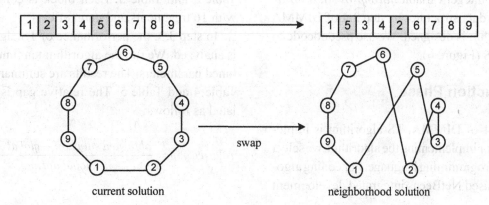

current solution   swap   neighborhood solution

Figure 5. (a) Tabu list for TS to solve TSP, (b) frequency based memory for diversification

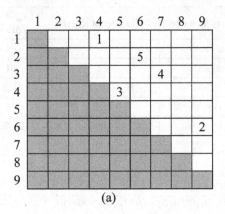

(b)

	1	2	3	4	5	6	7	8	9
1		0	2	3	3	0	1	1	4
2			2	1	3	1	1	0	1
3				2	3	3	4	0	0
4					1	1	2	1	4
5						4	2	1	3
6							3	1	2
7								6	0
8									6
9									

(a)

	1	2	3	4	5	6	7	8	9
1				1					
2						5			
3							4		
4					3				
5									
6									2
7									
8									
9									

and j^{th} column (Figure 5a). For example, the value in 6th raw and 9th column in Figure 5a shows the tabu tenure for swapping 6th and 9th cities. It means cities 6 and 9 cannot swap for 2 next iterations.

In this example, aspiration criteria is that if the result of a tabu move is better than that of the current best-known solution, then this move is allowed. For diversification we use *frequency based memory* (Glover, 1997), in this memory the information of swapping frequencies are stored (Figure 5b). For example, the value in 6th raw and 9th column in Figure 5b shows the frequency of swapping cities 6 and 9 in 70 iteration. According to these frequencies, one can assign penalty to swap pair cities. The more frequency is the more penalties are assigned. Therefore, the search can do swaps that are rarely done. Finally, for termination condition a number of iteration is chosen. To do this, integer variable *notImproveBestSoFar* is used in data structure. In step 2.4 of DIMMA TS algorithm is designed. We use pseudocode to specify TS (Figure 6).

Construction Phase

In step 3.1 of DIMMA, TS algorithm is implemented. For implementing the algorithm, we select Java as a programming language. For coding algorithm we used NetBeens integrated development environment. We construct 2 classes (TSPByTS and Execution) and 20 methods for our algorithm.

In step 3.2, parameters of the TS algorithm are tuned. In this example, we use a DoE approach and Design-Expert statistical software (Vaughn et al., 2000) to obtain optimal values for parameters.

To tune parameters for the TS algorithm we classified instances into two classes, according to the number of cities. The instances that have less than or equal to 100 cities are categorized in class 1, and the other instances are classified into class 2. For the first class, instances kroA100 and eil51 and for the second-class a280 and pr1002 are chosen as representatives for parameter tuning. In the TS algorithm, solution quality and CPU time are considered as the response variables. Factors, their levels, and the final obtained values for classes 1 and 2 instances are summarized in Table 2 and Table 3. Each block is considered with 16 treatments and main effects.

In step 3.3, the performance of TS algorithm is analyzed. We run the algorithm ten times with tuned parameters. The results are summarized in Table 4 and Table 5. The relative gap is calculated as follows:

$$relative\ gap = \frac{obtained\ solution - global\ optima}{global\ optima}$$

Figure 6. The TS pseudocode for TSP

```
Start
/* generate initial feasible solution by nearest neighbor algorithm*/
Set currentTour[]= generate InitialSolution();
Set currentTourLength = computeTourLength(currentTour[]);
Set bestTourLength = currentTourLength;
Initialize tabuList and frequency based memory;
While (termination condition not met)
    Set currentTour[] = move (currentTour[]);
    Set currentTourLength = computeTourLength(currentTour[]);
    If (currentTour[] < bestTourLength), then bestTourLength = currentTourLength;
        /* save the best so far solution */
    If (iteration criterion met), then do diversification
    update tabuList and frequency based memory;
End While;
Output bestTourLength;
End.
```

Table 2. Factors, their levels, and the final obtained values for instances of class 1

Parameter	Lowest value	Highest value	Final Value
Tabu tenure	5	15	10
Termination Condition*	5000	40000	30000
Diversification condition*	1000	10000	3000

* The number of iteration that the best so far solution is not improved

Table 3. Initial, ranges, and final values for instances of class 2

Parameter	Initial value	Range of change	Final Value
Tabu tenure	5	15	14
Termination Condition*	1000	5000	3000
Diversification condition*	1000	5000	2000

* The number of iteration that the best so far solution is not improved

Table 4. Result of instance of class 1

Test problem	Global optimal	Average tour length	Average relative gap	Average CPU time (ms)	Best solution	Relative gap
ulysses16	6859	6859.00	0.0000	191.5	6859.0	0.0000
ulysses22	7013	7013.00	0.0000	449.6	7013.0	0.0000
berlin52	7542	7744.05	0.0267	5039.2	7544.3	0.0003
kroA100	21282	22170.47	0.0417	40847.1	22104.1	0.0492
rd100	7910	8232.51	0.0408	9111.1	8217.6	0.0389
Average			0.0218			0.0177

Table 5. Result of instance of class 2

Test problem	Global optimal	Average tour length	Average relative gap	Average CPU time (ms)	Best solution	Relative gap
gr202	40160	43304.29	0.0783	9419.4	41787.7	0.0405
pcb442	50778	58197.84	0.1461	60771.5	57386.2	0.1301
gr666	294358	338786.10	0.1509	99886.7	336833.6	0.1443
u1060	224094	256958.92	0.1467	159526.2	252441.6	0.1265
Average			0.1305			0.1104

Figure 7. Convergence of proposed TS for TSP during the time for eil51 problem

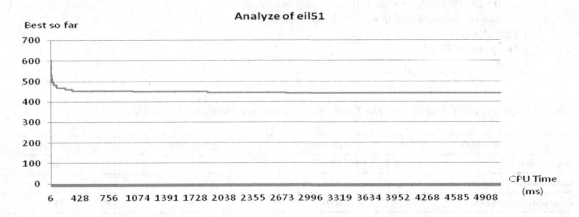

Figure 8. global optimum and obtained solutions in each instances of class 2

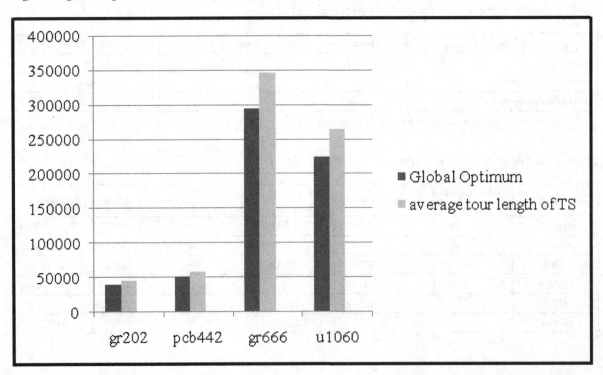

The step 3.4 of DIMMA is documentation that can be done by means of graphical tools. Figure 7 shows a sample to illustrate the performance of TS for TSP during the time for problem eil51. Figure 8 also compares the obtained solutions with global optimal in each instance. The figure illustrates that the algorithm can reach to near optimal.

CONCLUSION

According to significant growth in using metaheuristics as optimization tools, there must be a standard methodology for implementing them. Such a methodology is used for recording experience and allows projects to be replicated. Moreover, this standard process can be a comfort factor for new adopters with little metaheuristic background.

We have proposed the *DIMMA* as a methodology to design and implement metaheuristic algorithms. The proposed methodology includes series of phases, activities, disciplines, and principles to design and implement a specific metaheuristic for a given optimization problem. In the other word, the DIMMA refers to the methodology that is used to standardize process of design and implementing a metaheuristic.

We hope the proposed methodological approach to design and implementation of metaheuristics will draw more researchers to standardization of developing metaheuristics.

REFERENCES

Achterberg, T., Koch, T., & Martin, A. (2003). *The mixed integer programming library: Miplib.* Retrieved from http://miplib.zib.de

Adenso-Díaz, B., & laguna, M. (2006). Fine-tuning of algorithms using fractional experimental design and local search. *Operations Research, 54*(1), 99–114. doi:10.1287/opre.1050.0243

Alba, E., Almeida, F., Blesa, M., Cotta, C., D'ıaz, M., Dorta, I., et al. Le'on, C., Moreno, L., Petit, J., Roda, J., Rojas, A., & Xhafa, F. (2002). MALLBA: A library of skeletons for combinatorial optimization. In B. Monien & R. Feldman (Eds.), *Euro-Par 2002 Parallel Processing Conference* (LNCS 2400, pp. 927-932). Berlin: Springer.

Alba, E., & Lugue, G. (2005). Measuring the performance of parallel metaheuristics. In Alba, E. (Ed.), *Parallel metaheuristics: A new class of algorithm* (pp. 43–60). New York: John Wiley & Sons.

Antony, J. (2003). *Design of experiments for engineers and scientists.* Barlington, UK: Butterworth-Heinemann.

Arenas, M. G., Collet, P., Eiben, A. E., Jelasity, M., Merelo, J. J., Paechter, B., et al. (2002). A framework for distributed evolutionary algorithms. In *Parallel Problem Solving from Nature Conference (PPSN VII)* (LNCS 2439, pp. 665-675). Berlin: Springer.

Barr, R. S., Golden, B. L., Kelly, J. P., Resende, M. G. C., & Stewart, W. R. (1995). Designing and reporting computational experiments with heuristic methods. *Journal of Heuristics, 1*(1), 9–32. doi:10.1007/BF02430363

Bartz-Beielstein, T. (2006). *Experimental research in evolutionary computation.* New York: Springer.

Beasley, J. E. (1990). OR-Library: distributing test problems by electronic mail. *The Journal of the Operational Research Society, 41*(11), 1069–1072.

Birattari, M., Stuetzle, T., Paquete, L., & Varrentrapp, K. (2002). A racing algorithm for configuring metaheuristics. In W. B. Langdon et al. (Eds.), *Proceedings of the Genetic and Evolutionary Computation Conference (GECCO 2002)* (pp. 11-18). San Francisco: Morgan Kaufmann Publishers.

Biratteri, M. (2009). *Tuning Metaheuristics: A machine learning perspective*. Heidelberg, Germany: Springer.

Bleuler, S., Laumanns, M., Thiele, L., & Zitzler, E. (2003). PISA: A platform and programming language independent interface for search algorithms. In *Proceedings of the Conference on Evolutionary Multi-Criterion optimization (EMO'03)*, Faro, Portugal (pp. 494-508).

Box, G., Hunter, J. S., & Hunter, W. G. (2005). *Statistics for experimenters: design, innovation, and discovery*. New York: Wiley.

Cloete, T., Engelbrecht, A. P., & Pampar, G. (2008). *CIlib: A collaborative framework for computational intelligence algorithms – part I*. Retrieved from http://www.cilib.net/

Cohen, P. R. (1995). *Empirical methods for artificial intelligence*. Cambridge, UK: MIT Press.

Collette, Y., & Siarry, P. (2005). Three new metrics to measure the convergence of metaheuristics towards the Pareto frontier and the aesthetic of a set of solutions in biobjective optimization. *Computers & Operations Research, 32*, 773–792. doi:10.1016/j.cor.2003.08.017

Cormen, T. H., Leiserson, C. E., Rivest, R. L., & Stein, C. (2002). *Introduction to algorithms*. London: MIT Press.

Coy, S., Golden, B. L., Runger, G. C., & Wasil, E. A. (2000). Using experimental design to find effective parameter settings for heuristics. *Journal of Heuristics, 7*, 77–97. doi:10.1023/A:1026569813391

Crainic, T. G., & Tolouse, M. (1998). Parallel metaheuristic. In Crainic, T. G., & Laporte, G. (Eds.), *Fleet management And logistic* (pp. 205–235). Norwell, MA: Kluwer Academic publishers.

Crainic, T. G., & Tolouse, M. (2003). Parallel Strategies FOR Meta-heuristics. In Glover, F., & Kochenberger, G. (Eds.), *Handbook of metaheuristics* (pp. 475–514). Norwell, MA: Kluwer Academic Publishers.

Doreo, J., Siarry, E., Petrowski, A., & Taillard, E. (2006). *Metaheuristics for hard optimization*. Heidelberg, Germany: Springer.

Dorigo, M., & Stützle, T. (2004). *Ant colony optimization*. Cambridge, UK: MIT Press.

El-Abd, M., & Kamel, M. (2005). A taxonomy of cooprative search algorithms. In Blesa, M. J., Blume, C., Roli, A., & Samples, M. (Eds.), *Hybrid metaheuristic* (pp. 32–42). Heidelberg, Germany: Springer. doi:10.1007/11546245_4

Fink, A., Voss, S., & Woodruff, D. L. (1999). Building reusable software components for heuristic search. In Kall, P., & Luthi, H. J. (Eds.), *Operations Research Proceedings* (pp. 210–219). Heidelberg, Germany: Springer.

Fischetti, M., Salazar Gonzalez, J. J., & Toth, P. (1997). A branch-and-cut algorithm for the symmetric generalized traveling salesman problem. *Operations Research, 45*(3), 378–394. doi:10.1287/opre.45.3.378

Fisher, W. (1935). *The Design of Experiments*. Edinburgh, UK: Oliver and Boyd.

Frigon, N. L., & Mathews, D. (1997). *Practical guide to experimental design*. New York: Wiley.

Fukunaga, A. (2008). Automated discovery of local search heuristics for satisfiability testing. *Evolutionary Computation, 16*(1), 31–61. doi:10.1162/evco.2008.16.1.31

Garey, M. R., & Johnson, D. S. (1979). *Computers and intractability*. San Francisco: Freeman and Co.

Gaspero, L. Di, & Schaerf, A. (2001). EasyLocal++: An object-oriented framework for the design of local search algorithms and metaheuristics. In *Proceedings of the MIC'2001 4th Metaheuristics International Conference*, Porto, Portugal (pp. 287-292).

Gendreau, M. (2003). An introduction to tabu search. In Glover, F., & Kochenberger, G. A. (Eds.), *Handbook of metaheuristics* (pp. 37–54). Norwell, MA: Kluwer Academic publishers.

Gendreau, M., Laporte, G., & Semet, F. (1998). A tabu search heuristic for the undirected selective travelling salesman problem. *European Journal of Operational Research, 106*(2-3), 539–545. doi:10.1016/S0377-2217(97)00289-0

Glover, F., & Laguna, M. (1997). *Tabu search.* Dordrecht, The Netherlands: Kluwer Academic Publishers.

Goldberg, D. E. (1989). *Genetic algorithms in search, optimization and machine learning.* Reading, MA: Addison Wesley.

Hartmann, S., & Kolisch, R. (2000). Experimental evaluation of state-of-the-art heuristics for the resource-constrained project scheduling problem. *European Journal of Operational Research, 127*(2), 394–407. doi:10.1016/S0377-2217(99)00485-3

Hutter, F., Hoos, H. H., Leyton-Brown, K., & Stützle, T. (2009). ParamILS: An automatic algorithm configuration framework. *Journal of Artificial Intelligence Research, 36,* 267–306.

Hutter, F., Hoos, H. H., & Stützle, T. (2007). Automatic algorithm configuration based on local search. *AAAI,* 1152-1157.

Kirkpatrick, S., Gelatt, C., & Vecchi, M. (1983). Optimization by simulated annealing. *Science, 220,* 671–680. doi:10.1126/science.220.4598.671

Krasnogor, N., & Smith, J. (2000). MAFRA: A Java memetic algorithms framework. In Freitas, A. A., Hart, W., Krasnogor, N., & Smith, J. (Eds.), *Data Mining with Evolutionary Algorithms* (pp. 125–131). Las Vega, NV.

Kroll, P., & Krutchten, P. (2003). *The Rational unified process Made Easy.* Reading, MA: Addison-Wesley.

MacAllister, W. (2009). *Data Structures and algorithms using java.* New York: Jones & Bartlett publishers.

Merriam-Webster. (1997). *Merriam-Websters's Collegiate Dictionary.* Merriam-Websters.

Michel, L., & Van, P. (2001). *Hentenryck. Localizer++: An open library for local search* (Tech. Rep. No. CS-01-02). Providence, RI: Department of Computer Science, Brown University.

Montgomery, D. (2005). *Design and analysis of experiments.* New York: Wiley.

Morago, R. J., DePuy, G. W., & Whitehouse, G. E. (2006). A solution methodology for optimization problems. In A. B. Badiru (Ed.), *Metaheuristics* (pp. 1-10, 13). New York: Taylor & Francis Group.

Puntambekar, A. A. (2009). *Analysis of algorithm and design.* New York: technical publications pune.

Rardin, R. L., & Uzsoy, R. (2001). Experimental evaluation of heuristic optimization. *Journal of Heuristics, 7*(3), 261–304. doi:10.1023/A:1011319115230

Reinelt, G. (1991). TSPLIB: a traveling salesman problem library. *ORSA Journal on Computing, 3,* 376-384. Retrieved from http://softl ib.rice.edu/softlib/tsplib/

Ridge, E. (2007). *Design of experiments for the tuning of optimization algorithms.* Unpublished doctoral dissertation, Department of Computer Science, University of York, UK.

Siau, K., & Halpin, T. (2001). *Unified Modeling Language: system analysis, design and development issues.* Hershey, PA: IGI Global.

Silberholz, J., & Golden, B. (2010). Comparison of metaheuristics. In Gendreau, M., & Potvin, J.-V. (Eds.), *Handbook of metaheuristics*. Heidelberg, Germany: Springer. doi:10.1007/978-1-4419-1665-5_21

Skiena, S. S., & Revilla, M. A. (2003). *Programming challenges: The programming contest training manual*. New York: Springer.

Stadler, P., & Schnabl, W. (1992). The landscape of the traveling salesman problem. *Physics Letters. [Part A]*, *161*, 337–344. doi:10.1016/0375-9601(92)90557-3

Stadler, P. F. (1995). Towards a theory of landscapes. In R. Lop'ez-Pe˜na, R. Capovilla, R. Garc'ıa- Pelayo, H. Waelbroeck, & F. Zertuche (Eds.), *Complex Systems and Binary Networks* (Vol. 461, pp. 77-163). Berlin: Springer.

Talbi, E. (2006). *Parallel combinatorial optimization*. Hoboken, NJ: John Wily & Sons. doi:10.1002/0470053925

Talbi, E. (2009). *Metaheuristics: from design to implementation*. Hoboken, NJ: John Wiley & sons.

Thierens, D. (2008). From Multi-start Local Search to Genetic Local Search: a Practitioner's Guide. In *Proceedings of the 2nd International Conference on Metaheuristics and Nature Inspired Computing (META'08)*. Tunisia: Hammamet.

Tufte, E. R. (2001). *The Visual Display of Quantitative Information* (2nd ed.). Cheshire, CN: Graphics Press.

Vaughn, N., Polnaszek, C., Smith, B., & Helseth, T. (2000). *Design-Expert 6 User's Guide*. Stat-Ease Inc.

Voss, S., & Woodruff, D. L. (2002). *Optimization software class libraries*. Norwell, MA: Kluwer.

Voudouris, C., Dorne, R., Lesaint, D., & Liret, A. (2001). iOpt: A software toolkit for heuristic search methods. In *Proceedings of the International Conference on Principles and Practice of Constraint Programming* (LNCS 2239, pp. 716-729). Berlin: Springer.

Wall, M. (1996). *GAlib: A C++ library of genetic algorithm components (Tech. Rep.)*. Mechanical Engineering Department, Massachusetts Institute of Technology.

Wang, Y. (2010). A Sociopsychological Perspective on Collective Intelligence in Metaheuristic Computing. *International Journal of Applied Metaheuristic Computing*, *1*(1), 110–128.

Wilson, G. C., McIntyre, A., & Heywood, M. I. (2004). Resource review: Three open source systems for evolving programs—Lilgp, ECJ and grammatical evolution. *Genetic Programming and Evolvable Machines*, *5*(19), 103–105. doi:10.1023/B:GENP.0000017053.10351.dc

Wolpert, D. W., & Macready, W. G. (1997). No free lunch theorems for optimization. *IEEE Transactions on Evolutionary Computation*, *1*(1), 67–82. doi:10.1109/4235.585893

Yin, P. Y. (2010). *MetaYourHeuristic V. 1.3, Intelligence Computing Laboratory, National Chi Nan University, Taiwan*. Retrieved from http://intelligence.im.ncnu.edu.tw

ENDNOTES

[1] http://www.particleswarm.info/Programs.html
[2] http://paradiseo.gforge.inria.fr
[3] http://www.iitk.ac.in/kangal/codes.shtml

This work was previously published in International Journal of Applied Metaheuristic Computing, Volume 1, Issue 4, edited by Peng-Yeng Yin, pp. 58-75, copyright 2010 by IGI Publishing (an imprint of IGI Global).

Chapter 8
Movement Strategies for Multi-Objective Particle Swarm Optimization

S. Nguyen
Asian Institute of Technology, Thailand

V. Kachitvichyanukul
Asian Institute of Technology, Thailand

ABSTRACT

Particle Swarm Optimization (PSO) is one of the most effective metaheuristics algorithms, with many successful real-world applications. The reason for the success of PSO is the movement behavior, which allows the swarm to effectively explore the search space. Unfortunately, the original PSO algorithm is only suitable for single objective optimization problems. In this paper, three movement strategies are discussed for multi-objective PSO (MOPSO) and popular test problems are used to confirm their effectiveness. In addition, these algorithms are also applied to solve the engineering design and portfolio optimization problems. Results show that the algorithms are effective with both direct and indirect encoding schemes.

1. INTRODUCTION

Many real-world problems contain multiple conflicting objectives and multi-objective optimization (MO) is gaining increasing attention from both practitioners and researchers. Aggregated objective function was often used to convert the multi-objective problems to single objec-

tive problems which can be solved by standard algorithms. However, the aggregated objective function required a set of weights based on the prior preference of the decision makers, which can only be applied subjectively because the decision makers have only little or no knowledge about the range of each objective functions. Besides, the fact that only single solution is found provides the decision makers with very little information about potential trade-offs. In order to solve this

DOI: 10.4018/978-1-4666-0270-0.ch008

problem, the algorithm needs to be run several times with different set of weights and the cost of this approach is the high computational time. As a result, weight-free methods such as multi-objective Evolutionary Algorithm (EA) are preferred by researchers in this field because of their ability to find various non-dominated solutions on the Pareto front.

Srinivas and Deb (1994) introduced the Non-dominated Sorting Genetic Algorithm (NSGA), which can be considered as one of the first EA methods to deal with multi-objective optimization problems. The basic idea was to measure the fitness of each solution based on their dominance (with respect to all objective functions) in the population rather than a single objective value in traditional EA methods. The drawbacks of this method are the high computational complexity and the use of the pre-determined sharing parameter. Deb et al. (2002) introduced NSGA-II which could eliminate the problems with the old version by adopting an elitism structure and a measurement of the crowdedness. This algorithm had outperformed other MOEAs such as Pareto-archived evolutionary strategy (PAES) and strength-Pareto EA (SPEA) on many test problems.

Similar to the GA research community, the group of researchers interested in PSO have also developed new algorithms for multi-objective optimization. The most popular technique is to use an external archive to store the non-dominated solutions via the search of the swarm and to perform a selection procedure to choose the candidates to guide the search of each particle. Coello el al. (2002) proposed the idea to store flying experience in an external archive which is then updated by using geographically-based system. In their algorithm, the search area in the objective-space is divided into hypercubes. Each hypercube is assigned a fitness based on the number of particles it covers. Roulette-wheel selection is applied to choose the hypercube and a random particle from that hypercube is selected as the leader or global guidance for a particle in the swarm in each itera-

tion. The disadvantage of this algorithm is that its complexity increases with the number of objective functions to be minimized. Fieldsend el al. (2002) improved this work by using a tree data structure to maintain unconstrained archive. More recently, Raquel et al. (2005) adopted the idea of crowding distance (CD) proposed in NSGA-II in their PSO algorithm as a criterion for selection of leader from the particles. In this method, when preparing to move, a particle will select its global leader from the top particles in the external archive which are sorted in decreasing order of CD. The same mechanism was also adopted by Li (2003) where two parameter-free niching techniques (niche count and crowding distance) are used to promote solution diversity. Other algorithms which were not based on non-dominance concept have been also proposed. Parsopoulos and Vrahatis (2002) introduced three types of aggregate functions which included a conventional linear aggregate function; a dynamic aggregate function and the bang-bang weighted aggregation approach aiming at generate concave portions of the Pareto front. Hu and Eberhart (2002) proposed a PSO algorithm for multi-objective problem in which only one objective is optimized at a time using a scheme similar to lexicographic ordering. The drawback of this algorithm is that it depends on the number of objective functions to be optimized.

It is noted that one of the most challenges tasks when using PSO to solve multi-objective optimization problems is the selection of the suitable guidance for the swarm among a set of potential non-dominated solutions. Moreover, the traditional movement behaviour of PSO also needs not be strictly followed when the single global best and local best experience do not exist in the case of multi-objective optimization. This paper focuses on the movement strategies of PSO in order to obtain high quality Pareto front. Three multi-objective PSO (MOPSO) algorithms are introduced and their performances are tested with a set of well-known benchmarking problems. Also, the effectiveness of these algorithms are confirmed when they are used to solve two real-world applications.

In the next section, the related background on multi-objective optimization, the basic PSO algorithm and the PSO framework for the multi-objective optimization are given. Section 3 discusses the concepts of movement strategies and their implementations. The performances of three proposed PSO algorithms on test problems are discussed in section 4. In section 5, the formulations of two real-world applications are given and the PSO based solutions are compared with other results in literature. Finally, a conclusion is given in section 6.

2. BACKGROUND INFORMATION

This section provides a necessary background to appreciate the work presented in this paper. The multi-objective optimization, specially the Pareto optimality concept is briefly introduced in section 2.1. The basic PSO algorithm is introduced and their extended framework for multi-objective optimization is presented in sections 2.2 and 2.3.

2.1 Multi-Objective Optimization

Multi-objective Optimization is a complex optimization problem with various conflicting objective functions. Without any loss of generality, the mathematical formulation for a minimization problem with multiple objective functions is given as follow:

Minimize

$$\vec{f}\left(\vec{x}\right) = \left[f_1\left(\vec{x}\right), f_2\left(\vec{x}\right), \dots, f_K\left(\vec{x}\right)\right] \qquad (1)$$

Subject to:

$$g_i\left(\vec{x}\right) \leq 0 \quad i = 1, 2, \dots m \qquad (2)$$

$$h_i\left(\vec{x}\right) = 0 \quad i = 1, 2, \dots l \qquad (3)$$

where $\vec{x}$ is the vector of decision variables, $f_i\left(\vec{x}\right)$ is a function of $\vec{x}$, K is the number of objective function to be minimized, $g_i\left(\vec{x}\right)$ and $h_i\left(\vec{x}\right)$ are the constraint functions of the problem.

Given two decision vectors $\vec{x}, \vec{y} \in R^D$, the vector $\vec{x}$ is considered to dominate vector $\vec{y}\sqrt{a^2 + b^2}$ (denote $\vec{x} \prec \vec{y}$), if $f_i\left(\vec{x}\right) \leq f_i\left(\vec{y}\right)$ for $\forall i = 1, 2, \dots, K$ and $\exists j = 1, 2, \dots K \mid f_j\left(\vec{x}\right) < f_j\left(\vec{y}\right)$.

Different from single objective optimization, the quality of a solution in MO are explain in term of "trade-offs". As shown in Figure 1, for the cases that neither $\vec{x} \prec \vec{y}$ nor $\vec{y} \prec \vec{x}$, $\vec{x}$ and $\vec{y}$ are called non-dominated solutions or trade-off solutions. A non-dominated front $\mathcal{N}$ is defined as a set of non-dominated solutions if $\forall x \in \mathcal{N}$, $\nexists y \in \mathcal{N} \mid \vec{y} \prec \vec{x}$. A Pareto Optimal front $\mathcal{P}$ is a non-dominated front which includes any solution $\vec{x}$ is non-dominated by any other $\vec{y} \in \mathcal{F}, \vec{y} \neq \vec{x}$ where $\mathcal{F} \in R^D$ is the feasible region.

2.2 Particle Swarm Optimization

Particle Swarm Optimization (PSO) is a population based random search method that imitates the physical movements of the individuals in the

Figure 1. for the case with two objectives

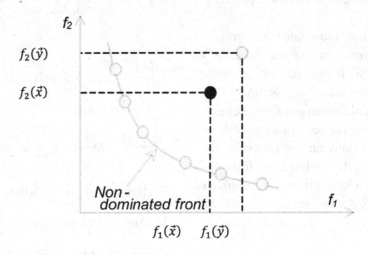

swarm as a searching mechanism. The first PSO algorithm was proposed by Kennedy and Eberhart (1995). The key concept of PSO is to learn from the cognitive knowledge of each particle and the social knowledge of the swarm to guide particles to better positions. In the PSO algorithm, a solution of a specific problem is represented by an n-dimensional position of a particle. A swarm of fixed number of particles is generated and each particle is initialized with a random position in a multidimensional search space. Each particle flies through the multidimensional search space with a velocity. In each step of the iteration the velocity of each particle is adjusted based on three components: current velocity of the particle which represents the inertia term or momentum of the particle, the position corresponds to the best solution achieved so far by the particle normally referred to as personal best and the position corresponds to the best solution achieved so far by all the particles, i.e., the global best. The basic velocity updating formula of PSO is:

$$\omega_{id}\left(t\right) = w\omega_{id}\left(t-1\right) + c_{p}u\left(\psi_{id}^{p} - \theta_{id}\right) + c_{g}u\left(\psi_{id}^{g} - \theta_{id}\right) \qquad (4)$$

Where $\omega_{id}(t)$ and Θ_{ID} are the velocity and position of the dth dimension for the particle i at in the tth iteration respectively. In this formula, $\psi_{id}^{p}, \psi_{id}^{g}$, represent the dth dimension of the personal best of particle i and the global best of the swarm respectively. The inertia weight is w and c_{p} and c_{g} are the acceleration constants to control the movement of particle toward its personal best and the global best position. u is a uniform random number in the interval [0,1].

The velocity is then used to guide a particle to the new position. The new position of particle i can be obtained as follow:

$$\theta_{id} = \theta_{id} + \omega_{id}\left(t\right) \qquad (5)$$

One of the drawbacks of the basic PSO algorithm is that the particles in a swarm tend to cluster quickly toward the global best particle and the swarm is frequently trapped in a local optimum and can no longer moved. To deal with the tendency to converge prematurely to a local optimum, a popular approach was proposed by Veeramachaneni et al. (2003) to divide the swarm into subgroups and to replace the global best with local best or near neighbour best particle.

Pongchairerks and Kachitvichyanukul (2005, 2009) introduced the used of multiple social learning terms and extend the concept of the standard PSO in GLNPSO. Instead of using just the global best particle, GLNPSO also incorporates the local best and near-neighbour best (Veeramachaneni et al., 2003) as additional social learning factors. In GLNPSO, the updating formula for particle velocity is:

$$\omega_{id}(t) = w\omega_{id}(t-1) + c_p u\left(\psi_{id}^p - \theta_{id}\right) + c_g u\left(\psi_{id}^g - \theta_{id}\right)$$
$$+ c_l u\left(\psi_{id}^l - \theta_{id}\right) + c_n u\left(\psi_{id}^n - \theta_{id}\right)$$

$$(6)$$

ψ_{id}^l, and ψ_{id}^n represent the dth dimension of the local best and the near neighbour best of particle i.

2.3 Framework for MOPSO

In this study, the multi-objective optimization PSO framework is proposed as shown in Figure 2. In this framework, the swarm experience is stored in an external archive as a set of non-dominated solutions. After each movement, the objective values corresponding to the position of each particle are re-evaluated and the non-dominated sorting procedure is used to identify the group of new non-dominated solutions. Again, the non-dominated sorting procedure is applied to the group of new solutions and current solutions in the external archive and only the non-dominated solutions via the trajectories of all particles are stored in the external archive similar to the Elitist structure of NSGA-II.

Similar to the traditional PSO algorithm, the learning terms must be determined. However, it is not trivial in this case because of the existence of multiple global non-dominated positions in the external archive. One of the most common methods is to choose the candidate guidance located in the less crowded areas to improve the spread as well as the distribution of the near Pareto optimal front. The first attempt to measure the crowdedness is introduced in NSGA with the support of sharing parameter. However, this approach is criticized for its complexity. A parameter-free method is proposed in NSGA-II which measure the crowding distance (CD) for each member in the population. This approach estimates the density of solutions surrounding a specific solution by calculating the average distance of two points on either side of this point along each of the objective (see Deb et al., 2002 for more details).

Coello el al. (2002) proposed a PSO algorithm with a geographically-based system to locate crowded regions. They divided the objective space into a number of hypercubes and then each member in the Elite archive is assigned to one of these hypercubes. After the archive is classified, a hypercube with smallest density is considered and one of its members is randomly selected to be used as the global guidance.

It is worth noting that in the multi-objective cases, a particle has many more options on which direction it should move in each iteration and the quality of the final solutions will be influenced strongly by the movement strategies adopted by the swarm. In the next section, three typical movement strategies are discussed.

3. MOVEMENT STRATEGIES

As mentioned in previous section, the external archive stores the important information about the Pareto front which can be used to guide particle in the swarm. In this paper, three typical movement strategies to utilize the information provided by the Elite group in the external archive are discussed.

Figure 2. Framework for MOPSO

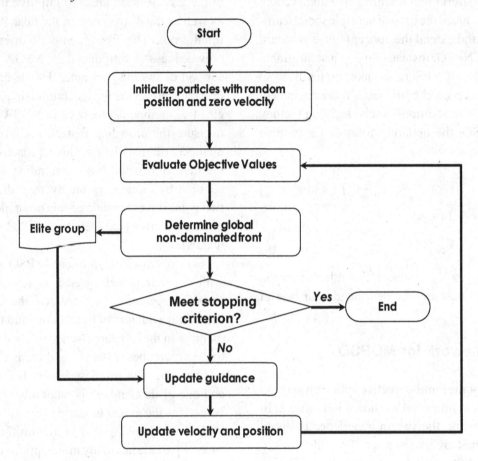

3.1 Ms1: Pick a Global Guidance Located In the Least Crowded Areas

The key idea of this movement strategy is to guide the swarm toward the less crowded areas in the current non-dominated front as shown in Figure 3 as proposed by Raquel et al. (2005) and Li (2002). In order to measure the crowdedness of a particle in the non-dominated front, the crowding distance (CD) in NSGA-II is applied. In this movement strategy, after the Elite group is updated, CD value of each particle in this group is calculated. Particles with higher CDs are located in less crowded area and they are considered to be better candidates for global guidance in this movement strategy. The pseudo code for Ms1 are

shown in Algorithm A1 where $\mathcal{E}$ is the Elite archive.

A1. Algorithm for Ms1

i.   *Calculate_crowding_distance* $(\mathcal{E})$
ii. *Sort* $\mathcal{E}$ by decreasing order of crowding distance (CD) values
iii. *Randomly select a particle g from top t% of* $\mathcal{E}$
iv. Update global term in particle i movement by $c_g u \ [(E_{1,d} - \theta_{i,d}) + r * (E_{1,d} - E_{2,d})]$ for all dimension *d with u ~ U(0,1)*

Figure 3. Movement strategy Ms1 in bi-objective space

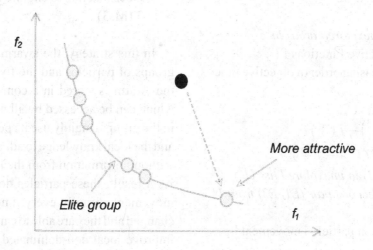

3.2 Ms2: Explore the Unexplored Space in the Non-Dominated Front

Different from movement strategy Ms1, strategy Ms2 is aimed at filling the gap in the non-dominated front and hence improving the distribution of the solutions in the front. Figure 4 shows how the movement direction of a particle when a gap is identified.

The first step of this strategy is to identify the potential gap in the Elite group. For each objective function fk(.), the Elite is sorted in the decreasing order of fk(.) and the difference of two consecutive particles are computed. If the difference is bigger than x% of the current range of the non-dominated front constructed by the Elite group, it is considered as a gap and the two corresponding particles are stored as a pair in an unexplored set. When updating the velocity, a pair of particle is randomly selected from the unexplored set to guide particles in the swarm to new positions. Algorithm A2 shows the implementation of Ms2.

Figure 4. Movement strategy Ms2 in bi-objective space

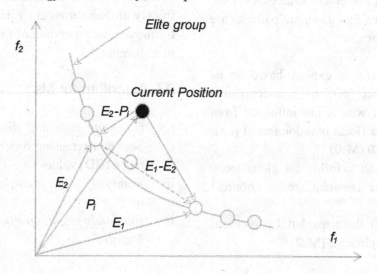

A2. Algorithm for Ms2

i. *Identify the unexplored areas in $\mathcal{E}$*
   For each objective functions $f_k(.)$
   Sort $\mathcal{E}$ in increasing order of objective function $f_k(.)$
   For $i=1$ to $|\mathcal{E}|-1$
   $Gap = f_k(\tilde{\,}_{i+1}) - f_k(\tilde{\,}_i)$
   If $Gap > x\% * (f_k^{max} - f_k^{min})$:
   add pair $(i,i+1)$ in unexplored list $\mathcal{U}$
ii. *Randomly select one pair $(E1, E2)$ from $\mathcal{U}$*

Update global term in particle i movement by

$$c_g u \ [(E_{1,d} - \theta_{i,d}) + r * (E_{1,d} - E_{2,d})]$$

for all dimension d with u, r $\sim$ U(0,1)

3.3 Ms*: Explore Solution Space with Mixed Particles

Because each movement strategy has its own advantages and different path to reach the Pareto optimal front, it is expected that the swarm with combination of different particles can effectively employ these advantages to increase the quality of the non-dominated front. For this reason, a heterogeneous swarm with a mixture of particles following different movement strategies is used in this strategy. Here, four groups of particles are included in a swarm:

- Ones that prefer to explore based on its own experience (personal non-dominated position) and with some influence from its neighbours (local non-dominated position)– Group 0 (Ms0)
- Ones that prefer to follow the global trend but avoid the crowded areas– Group 1 (Ms1)
- Ones that fill the gaps left by previous movements– Group 2 (Ms2)
- Ones that like to explore new areas– Group 3 (Ms3)

In this strategy, the swarm will include four groups of particles and the flying experience of the swarm is stored in a common Elite archive which can be accessed by all members. Particles in the group 0 mainly use its personal experience and the local knowledge to adjust their movement without information from the Elite group (Ms0). As a result, these particles do not change their movement abruptly every time the global trend changed and they are able to carefully explore and improve local non-dominated solutions. Different from the first group, the remaining groups of particles depend on the global information from Elite group to move to new positions. Since the movement strategy Ms1 guide particles to less crowded areas of the non-dominated front, the movement of particles in group 1 will depend on how the solutions are distributed in the current Elite archive. It is noted that even when the multiple movement strategies are adopted, the gaps in the non-dominated are unavoidable because of the premature convergence. The task of particles in group 2 (following Ms2) is to move to fill these gaps so that the final front can have a better distribution. Particles in group 3 (flowing Ms3), on the other hand, focus on exploring border to increase the spread of non-dominated fronts with their perturbation ability. The algorithm for movement procedure of this group is shown in Algorithm A3.

A3. Algorithm for Ms3

i. *Calculate_crowding_distance $(\mathcal{E})$*
ii. Sort by decreasing order of crowding distance (CD) values
iii. *Randomly select a particle R_1 from top $t\%$ of $\mathcal{E}$*
iv. *Randomly select a particle R_2 from bottom $b\%$ of $\mathcal{E}$*

Update global term in particle i movement by

$$c_g u \left(\Psi_{R1,d} - \Psi_{R2,d} \right)$$

for all dimension d with u ~ U(0,1)

4. EXPERIMENTS

Five popular test problems introduced by Deb et al. (2002) for evaluating multi-objective optimization algorithms are used in this section to measure the performance of the three movement strategies. These results are compared with those from NSGA-II and the self adaptive NSGA-II reported by Zeng et al (2010). The test problems are defined in Table 1. Two benchmark metrics, Inverted Generational Distance (IGD) and SPREAD are employed to measure the performance. The true Pareto front is needed to calculate the distance of each of the solution points with respect to the front as follow:

$$IGD = \frac{\sqrt{\sum_{i=1}^{n} d_i^2}}{n} \qquad (7)$$

where d_i is the Euclidian distance between the solution points and the nearest member of the true Pareto front and n is the number of solution points in the true Pareto front. IGD is smaller when the non-dominated solutions obtained are close to the true Pareto front. The second measure is SPREAD which indicates the extent of spread among the solutions obtained and it can be measured as:

$$Spread = \frac{d_f + d_l + \sum_{i=1}^{n-1} \left| d_i - \overline{d} \right|}{d_f + d_l + (n-1)\overline{d}} \qquad (8)$$

where d_f and d_l are the Euclidian distance between the boundary of obtained solution and the extreme points of the true Pareto front and $\overline{d}$ is

the average of all distances d_i which is the Euclidian distance between consecutive solutions in the obtained non-dominated set of solutions.

General PSO parameters used for the experiments are presented in Table 2. In Ms*, the ratio of numbers of particles in each group is 1:1:1:1 respectively. In order to prevent the swarm from being trapped in local Pareto front, the position of a particle will be reinitialized if the velocity at that position remains zero for 50 iterations. Ten replications are performed for each experiment. In the proposed algorithm, a fixed external archive (Elite group) is used. When the number of new non-dominated solutions found by the swarm exceeds the upper limit of this archive, the solutions with lower crowding distance will be removed.

The experimental results for these test problems are summarized in Table 2. The results of the three PSO algorithms are compared to those of NSGA-II and the NSGA-II with self adaptive mechanism (SAM) reported by Zeng et al. (2010).

Movement strategy Ms* achieves lower means for both IDG and SPREAD in all test problems with reasonably small standard deviations compared to NSGA-II and NSGA-II+SAM. However, it is noted that Pareto fronts provided by movement strategy Ms2 show very good performances and have the best SPREAD among all algorithms in all test problems. These results confirms that the swarms following movement strategy Ms2 are most suitable for filling gaps in the Pareto front, and as a result, the solutions can be well distributed on the non-dominated front obtained. Movement strategy Ms1 shows good performance for easy test problems like ZDT1, ZDT2, and ZDT3 but it is not very effective in difficult problems like ZDT4 and ZDT6.

The experiments in this sections show that the quality of the non-dominated solutions obtained depends significantly on the movement strategy adopted by the swarm. Fortunately, the advantages of movement strategies can be easily combined in the PSO framework by simply changing the

Table 1. Test problems (all objectives are to be minimized)

Problem	#. Var.	Variable bound	Objective function
ZDT1	30	[0,1]	$f_1(x) = x_1$ $f_2(x) = g(x)\left[1 - \sqrt{x_1 / g(x)}\right]$ $g(x) = 1 + 9\left(\sum_{i=2}^{n} x_i\right) / (n-1)$
ZDT2	30	[0,1]	$f_1(x) = x_1$ $f_2(x) = g(x)\left[1 - \left(x_1 / g(x)\right)^2\right]$ $g(x) = 1 + 9\left(\sum_{i=2}^{n} x_i\right) / (n-1)$
ZDT3	30	[0,1]	$f_1(x) = x_1$ $f_2(x) = g(x)\left[1 - \sqrt{x_1 / g(x)} - \dfrac{x_1}{g(x)} \sin\left(10\pi x_1\right)\right]$ $g(x) = 1 + 9\left(\sum_{i=2}^{n} x_i\right) / (n-1)$
ZDT4	10	$x_1 \in [0,1]$ $x_i \in [-5,5],$ $i = 2,..,10$	$f_1(x) = x_1$ $f_2(x) = g(x)\left[1 - \sqrt{x_1 / g(x)}\right]$ $g(x) = 1 + 10(n-1) + \sum_{i=2}^{n}\left[x_i^2 - 10\cos(4\pi x_i)\right]$
ZDT6	10	[0,1]	$f_1(x) = 1 - \exp\left(-4x_1\right)\sin^2(6\pi x_1)$ $f_2(x) = g(x)\left[1 - \left(f_1(x) / g(x)\right)^2\right]$ $g(x) = 1 + 9\left[\left(\sum_{i=2}^{n} x_i\right) / (n-1)\right]^{0.25}$

Table 2. Parameters of PSO

Inertia	Linearly reduced from 0.9 to 0.2
Constant acceleration	$c_p=c_g=c_l=c_n=1$
Swarm size	50 particles
Upper limit of Elite group	100 particles
% top members	5% (Ms1, Ms*)
% bottom members	20% (Ms*)
Potential gap	4% (Ms2, Ms*)
Number of iterations	2000

Table 3. Experimental results for test problems

Test Problem	Strategy	IDG		SPREAD	
		Mean	Standard Deviation	Mean	Standard Deviation
ZDT1	PSO-Ms1	1.76E-04	6.39E-06	3.37E-01	1.71E-02
	PSO-Ms2	**1.48E-04**	3.89E-06	**1.97E-01**	2.21E-02
	PSO-Ms*	1.68E-04	1.02E-05	3.08E-01	2.51E-02
	NSGA-II + SAM	1.74E-04	5.10E-06	2.92E-01	3.25E-02
	NSGA-II	1.91E-04	1.08E-05	3.83E-01	3.14E-02
ZDT2	PSO-Ms1	2.02E-04	1.86E-05	3.53E-01	2.39E-02
	PSO-Ms2	**1.51E-04**	4.19E-06	**1.87E-01**	2.05E-02
	PSO-Ms*	1.74E-04	9.06E-06	2.96E-01	2.40E-02
	NSGA-II + SAM	1.79E-04	5.64E-06	3.15E-01	2.01E-02
	NSGA-II	1.88E-04	8.36E-06	3.52E-01	7.25E-02
ZDT3	PSO-Ms1	1.99E-04	1.14E-05	5.31E-01	2.80E-02
	PSO-Ms2	2.08E-04	8.18E-06	**5.00E-01**	1.02E-02
	PSO-Ms*	**1.98E-04**	1.16E-05	5.16E-01	1.66E-02
	NSGA-II + SAM	2.46E-04	7.74E-06	7.31E-01	1.20E-02
	NSGA-II	2.59E-04	1.16E-05	7.49E-01	1.49E-02
ZDT4	PSO-Ms1	1.54E-01	5.08E-03	9.63E-01	1.04E-03
	PSO-Ms2	1.71E-04	4.93E-11	**3.01E-01**	5.74E-04
	PSO-Ms*	**1.65E-04**	6.49E-06	3.22E-01	2.51E-02
	NSGA-II + SAM	1.67E-04	8.02E-06	3.27E-01	2.71E-02
	NSGA-II	1.84E-04	9.86E-06	3.96E-01	2.94E-02
ZDT6	PSO-Ms1	3.43E-04	1.71E-04	8.97E-01	1.61E-01
	PSO-Ms2	1.79E-04	5.25E-05	**4.04E-01**	4.43E-02
	PSO-Ms*	**1.28E-04**	2.82E-05	4.52E-01	3.26E-01
	NSGA-II + SAM	1.51E-04	1.06E-05	4.73E-01	2.98E-02
	NSGA-II	1.59E-04	1.24E-05	4.80E-01	4.49E-02

*The best performance for each test case is marked in bold

global guidance and velocity updating formula. In Table 3, the PSO algorithm which adopts multiple movement strategies shows good convergence behaviour to the true Pareto front.

The proposed MOPSO algorithms emphasize on improving the movement behaviour of PSO by utilizing the information of the Elite group which is different from other MOPSO algorithms found in literature that mainly used traditional selection scheme borrowed from NSGA. It is noted that the use of multiple global best solutions to guide particles can improve the performance of PSO algorithms and separate MOPSO from other evolutionary approaches. Also, since the proposed algorithms do not depend on the number of objective functions to be minimized like that of Coello el al. (2002), it can be easily adapted to solve more complex problems without significant deterioration in the performance. In the next section, the proposed PSO algorithms are used to solve two practical applications.

5. REAL-WORLD APPLICATIONS

Although several multi-objective PSO algorithms have been proposed in the literature, only a limited number of cases where these algorithms are used to solve practical applications. In this section, the performances of the proposed PSO algorithm are tested on two real-world problems. The first problem is used to test the ability of the algorithms to solve constrained problems. The second problem is used to confirm the performance of the algorithms with high dimensional problems and with indirect encoding.

5.1 Engineering Design Problem

This is a non-linear design problem to find the dimension of an I-beam as shown in Figure 5, which must satisfy the geometric and strength constraints and minimize following objective functions:

Figure 5. I-Beam design problem

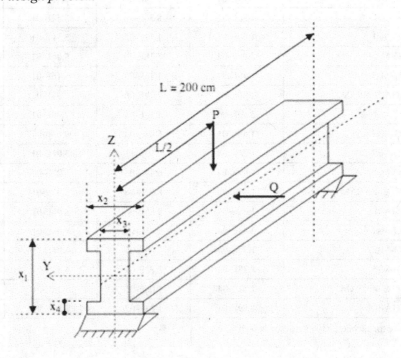

Figure 6. Pareto front for I-Beam design problem

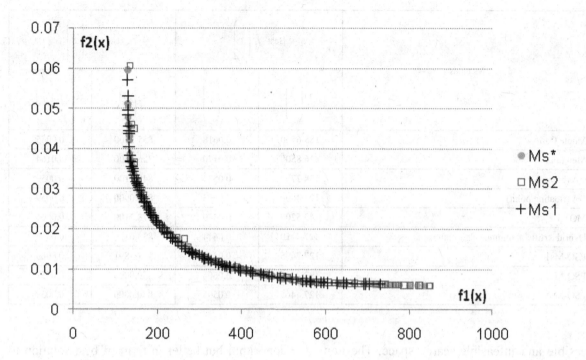

- Cross section area of beam
- Static deflection of the beam under a certain force

The mathematical model of this problem by Coello and Christiansen (1999) are given as follows:

$$f_1\left(\vec{x}\right) = 2x_2x_4 + x_3\left(x_1 - 2x_4\right) \quad (cm)$$

$$f_2\left(\vec{x}\right) = \frac{60000}{x_3(x_1 - 2x_4)^3 + 2x_2x_4\left[4x_4^2 + 3x_1\left(x_1 - 2x_4\right)\right]}$$

subject to:

$$g\left(\vec{x}\right) = 16 - \frac{180000x_1}{x_3\left(x_1 - 2x_4\right)^3 + 2x_2x_4\left[4x_4^2 + 3x_1\left(x_1 - 2x_4\right)\right]}$$

$$-\frac{15000x_2}{(x_1 - 2x_4)^3 x_3^3 + 2x_4x_2^3} \geq 0$$

$$10 \leq x_1 \leq 80,$$
$$10 \leq x_2 \leq 50, \ 0.9 \leq x_3 \leq 5,$$
$$0.9 \leq x_4 \leq 5$$

Since the objective functions of this problem are very well-defined, the values of particle's position can be directly used to represent the decision vector $\vec{x}$. Therefore, the dimension of particle is 4 and each dimension will have the upper and lower bounds corresponding to those defined in the mathematical model. For this problem, the number of violated constraints is treated as an objective function. The difference is that the solutions which satisfy the constraint are preferred in the updating process of the Elite group. The advantage of this method is that the true Pareto front can be approached from both the

Table 4. Comparison of results for I-Beam design problem

Methods	Best $f_1\left(\vec{x}\right)$		Best $f_2\left(\vec{x}\right)$	
	$f_1\left(\vec{x}\right)$	$f_2\left(\vec{x}\right)$	$f_1\left(\vec{x}\right)$	$f_2\left(\vec{x}\right)$
Monte Carlo	188.6500	0.0618	555.2200	0.0085
Min–max	316.8500	0.0170	326.4900	0.0164
GA (binary)	128.2700	0.0524	848.4100	0.0059
GA (floating point)	127.4600	0.0603	850.0000	0.0059
MOTS	143.5200	0.0370	678.2100	0.0066
Hybrid Artificial immune algorithm	127.4110	0.0614	833.0390	0.0060
PSO-Ms1	127.7695	0.0571	731.5891	0.0063
PSO-Ms2	133.3537	0.0606	850.0000	0.0059
PSO-Ms*	127.4465	0.0595	850.0000	0.0059

feasible and infeasible search space. The non-dominated solutions found by the three PSO algorithms are shown in Figure 6 and the comparison of these algorithms with GA and other algorithms are shown in Table 4.

The PSO parameters to solve this problem are similar to those in section 4. However, in order to make a fair comparison, only 60 iterations are performed to maintain the number of objective function evaluations of 3000 as used by Yildiz (2009). Table 4 shows the objective values at extreme points because only these points are reported in literature. It is interesting to note that the proposed algorithms have found very good extremes points although they are basically designed to generate Pareto front. Algorithm PSO-Ms* are very competitive with other popular algorithms and the extreme points obtained from this algorithm are better than those found by Genetic Algorithm. The best solution to minimize $f_1\left(\vec{x}\right)$ from Ms* is just slightly greater than best known solution found by Hybrid Artificial immune

algorithm but better in term of best solution to minimize $f_2\left(\vec{x}\right)$.

5.2 Portfolio Optimization

Portfolio Optimization (PO) is a critical problem in finance aiming at finding an optimal way to distribute a given budget on a set of available assets. Although many investment decisions are normally made on qualitative basis, there are an increasing number of quantitative approaches adopted.

The most seminal mathematical model was initiated by Markowitz (1952) more than 50 years ago and there have been many extensions of his models since then. The classical mean-variance portfolio selection problem proposed by Markowitz can be given as:

Minimizing the variance of the portfolio
$$\sum_{i=1}^{N}\sum_{j=1}^{N} w_i w_j \sigma_{ij}$$

Maximizing the expected return of the portfolio $\sum_{i=1}^{N} w_i \mu_i$

Subject to:

$$\sum_{i=1}^{N} w_i = 1$$

$$0 \le w_i \le 1 \, for \, \forall i = 1 \ldots N$$

The basic assumption in this model is that asset returns follow multivariate normal distribution. The decision variable w_i is the proportion of the budget which is distributed to asset i. Parameter $\frac{1}{4}_i$ and $\tilde{A}_{ij}$ are the expected return of asset i and the covariance between asset i and j. Because it is difficult to weigh the two criteria before the alternatives are known, the popular approach in this case is to search for the whole efficient frontier.

Though the mean-variance model above play an important role in portfolio theory, some constraints need to be added to make it more realistic. A popular extension of Markowitz model is the Limited Assets Markowitz (LAM) model, which considers the limit of number of assets to be held in the efficient portfolio and buy-in assets must follow threshold constraints. This model is referred as cardinality constrained portfolio optimization and has been receiving serious attention from both researchers and practitioners due to its practical relevance.

While the classical model can be solved in polynomial time, the presence of cardinality and threshold constraints poses a much higher complexity issues. The fact is that the real world problems of this type with less than one hundred of assets have not yet been solve to optimality. The LAM model has been classified into the class of NP-Hard problems. The cardinality constrained portfolio optimization can be formulated as follow:

Minimizing the variance of the portfolio

$$\sum_{i=1}^{N}\sum_{j=1}^{N} w_i w_j \sigma_{ij}$$

Maximizing the expected return of the portfolio $\sum_{i=1}^{N} w_i \mu_i$

Subject to:

$$\sum_{i=1}^{N} w_i = 1$$

$$\sum_{i=1}^{N} \rho_i \le K$$

$$\rho_i l_i \le w_i \le \rho_i u_i \, for \, \forall i = 1 \ldots N$$

$$0 \le w_i \le 1 \, for \, \forall i = 1 \ldots N$$

$$\rho_i = \begin{cases} 1 \, if \, w_i \ge 0 \\ 0 \, otherwise \end{cases}$$

The decision variable ρ_i is 1 if asset i is included in the portfolio and the number of assets in the portfolio must not greater than K. l_i and u_i are the lower bound and upper bound of asset i respectively in case that asset i is included in the portfolio. In this problem the decision variable w_i can be modeled as the particle position ranging from 0 to 1. However, because the sum of all values of w_i must be equal to 1, positions of particles cannot guarantee to provide feasible solutions. Fortunately, an infeasible solution can be easily repaired to become a feasible one. To illustrate the encoding/decoding scheme, a simple example with 4 assets is used. The data for this problem is provided in Table 5. The encoding/decoding scheme for the portfolio optimization problem is shown in Figure 7.

To handle the cardinality and threshold constraints, a simple repair mechanism is applied. In the decoding process, assets are sorted in the decreasing order of weights represented by the

Table 5. Four asset example

Asset	Expected Return	Std. Deviation	Correlation Matrix			
			1	2	3	4
1	0.004798	0.046351	1	0.118368	0.143822	0.252213
2	0.000659	0.030586		1	0.164589	0.099763
3	0.003174	0.030474			1	0.083122
4	0.001377	0.035770				1

particle's position. The top K (cardinality constraints) assets with the weights smaller than their lower bound will be set to zero like other assets which are not in the top K candidate assets. The weights are then normalized as the procedure given in Figure 7. If the normalized weights are greater than upper bounds, their surplus will be moved to the next assets in the group of the top K candidate assets.

The benchmark data sets from OR-Library (Beasley, 2006) is used in this study to compare the efficiency of the proposed algorithms, and the quality of the non-dominated solutions found to those obtained via the use of heuristics and CPLEX. The data sets include covariance matrices and expected return vectors obtained from price data from March 1992 to September 1997 for Hang Seng, DAX, FTSE 100, S&P 100, and Nikkei capital market indices. Besides three large test cases including S&P 500, Russell 2000, and Russell 3000 indices are also solved to check scalability of the PSO algorithms. The quality of non-dominated solutions obtained is compared to the optimal solutions and shown in Table 6 and Table 7. Table 8 and Table 9 show the computational time of the PSO algorithms and CPLEX and Increasing Set Algorithm (Cesarone et al., 2008). Each data set is solved with K = 5 and 10 and the lower bounds of 0.01 and the upper bound of 1 for all assets as used in most experiments in literature.

Figure 7. Decoding scheme for classical portfolio optimization problem

	1	2	3	4	Sum
Particle's position	0.4	0.2	0.8	0.6	2

Normalization: $w_i = w_i/\text{Sum}$

	1	2	3	4
Decision variables	0.2	0.1	0.4	0.3

$$\text{The variance of the portfolio } \sum_{i=1}^{N}\sum_{j=1}^{N} w_i w_j \sigma_{ij} = 0.0004889$$

$$\text{The expected return of the portfolio } \sum_{i=1}^{N} w_i \mu_i = 0.0027082$$

Table 6. Performance of PSO algorithms with K=5

Test Problem	Strategy	IGD		Spread	
		Mean	Standard Deviation	Mean	Standard Deviation
Hang Seng	PSO-Ms1	3.76E-06	1.76E-06	**3.27E-01**	3.52E-02
	PSO-Ms2	7.34E-06	2.08E-06	5.05E-01	4.49E-02
	PSO-Ms*	**3.54E-06**	1.98E-06	3.32E-01	3.03E-02
DAX	PSO-Ms1	4.97E-06	2.58E-06	**4.39E-01**	2.44E-02
	PSO-Ms2	7.55E-06	1.68E-06	7.66E-01	1.05E-01
	PSO-Ms*	**4.79E-06**	3.05E-06	4.50E-01	3.56E-02
FTSE	PSO-Ms1	5.72E-06	2.27E-06	**4.36E-01**	1.93E-02
	PSO-Ms2	9.13E-06	5.85E-06	7.65E-01	6.37E-02
	PSO-Ms*	**5.43E-06**	2.85E-06	4.46E-01	3.55E-02
S&P 100	PSO-Ms1	3.28E-06	1.25E-06	**3.97E-01**	3.26E-02
	PSO-Ms2	7.89E-06	1.08E-06	6.85E-01	6.16E-02
	PSO-Ms*	**3.03E-06**	6.01E-07	4.01E-01	1.80E-02
Nikkei	PSO-Ms1	2.18E-06	1.03E-06	4.35E-01	3.07E-02
	PSO-Ms2	6.63E-06	2.47E-06	9.55E-01	1.11E-01
	PSO-Ms*	**1.11E-06**	2.63E-07	**4.17E-01**	4.14E-02
S&P 500	PSO-Ms1	4.5E-06	1.23E-06	3.42E-01	7.15E-02
	PSO-Ms2	2.72E-05	4.22E-06	9.57E-01	8.75E-02
	PSO-Ms*	**5.93E-06**	1.51E-06	**3.21E-01**	1.89E-02
Russell 2000	PSO-Ms1	1.62E-05	5.81E-06	5.57E-01	1.21E-01
	PSO-Ms2	4.93E-05	1.26E-05	1.18E+00	7.66E-02
	PSO-Ms*	**1.49E-05**	5.69E-06	**5.33E-01**	1.05E-01
Russell 3000	PSO-Ms1	1.21E-05	9.14E-06	**5.05E-01**	2.90E-02
	PSO-Ms2	5.16E-05	1.68E-05	1.21E+00	7.63E-02
	PSO-Ms*	**1.18E-05**	2.08E-06	5.15E-01	2.41E-02

*The best performance for each test case is marked in bold

The same PSO parameters in section 4 are used. In the first 4 problems, the PSO algorithms are run for 500 iterations. The last 4 problems are solved in 2000 iterations, which is equivalent to 100000 objective function evaluations. All the experiments are performed on a computer with Intel Core2 Duo CPU (T8100, 2.1 GHz, 2 Gb RAM) under Windows Vista.

The performances in Table 6 and Table 7 show that the non-dominated portfolios found by PSO algorithms are very close to the optimal efficient frontiers. Movement strategy Ms1 and movement strategy Ms* are very effective even when the dimension significantly increases and indirect encoding/decoding procedure is employed. On the other hand, the performance of movement strategy Ms2 deteriorates when more assets are considered. An example of non-dominated solution found by PSO-Ms* algorithms is shown in Figure 8.

Figure 8 shows that the non-dominated solutions obtained from PSO-Ms* algorithm successfully converges to the true optimal Pareto front. Moreover, the solutions are distributed very well

Table 7. Performance of PSO algorithms with K=10

Test Problem	Strategy	IGD		Spread	
		Mean	Standard Deviation	Mean	Standard Deviation
Hang Seng	PSO-Ms1	2.24E-06	5.25E-07	3.26E-01	2.97E-02
	PSO-Ms2	8.1E-06	2.43E-06	4.96E-01	4.45E-02
	PSO-Ms*	**1.99E-06**	2.95E-07	**3.15E-01**	1.83E-02
DAX	PSO-Ms1	8.04E-06	2.99E-06	**4.18E-01**	2.29E-02
	PSO-Ms2	7.63E-06	1.27E-06	7.44E-01	8.32E-02
	PSO-Ms*	**6.83E-06**	2.77E-06	4.27E-01	2.79E-02
FTSE	PSO-Ms1	6.32E-06	2.14E-06	**4.42E-01**	2.32E-02
	PSO-Ms2	6.75E-06	1.10E-06	7.61E-01	4.00E-02
	PSO-Ms*	**3.76E-06**	1.66E-06	4.50E-01	1.42E-02
S&P 100	PSO-Ms1	6.28E-06	2.53E-06	**3.92E-01**	2.64E-02
	PSO-Ms2	8.55E-06	6.69E-07	6.51E-01	5.10E-02
	PSO-Ms*	**5.43E-06**	2.23E-06	3.97E-01	2.34E-02
Nikkei	PSO-Ms1	4.91E-06	2.00E-06	**4.27E-01**	2.92E-02
	PSO-Ms2	8.79E-06	4.61E-06	9.22E-01	1.08E-01
	PSO-Ms*	**3.77E-06**	1.72E-06	4.47E-01	3.17E-02
S&P 500	PSO-Ms1	8.33E-06	1.50E-06	3.40E-01	2.18E-02
	PSO-Ms2	3.12E-05	4.73E-06	9.61E-01	8.18E-02
	PSO-Ms*	**6.36E-06**	2.65E-06	**3.16E-01**	1.79E-02
Russell 2000	PSO-Ms1	2.81E-05	5.63E-06	**4.88E-01**	3.21E-02
	PSO-Ms2	5.79E-05	7.03E-06	1.18E+00	6.47E-02
	PSO-Ms*	**2.33E-05**	7.53E-06	6.19E-01	1.50E-01
Russell 3000	PSO-Ms1	1.96E-05	6.26E-06	5.69E-01	9.27E-02
	PSO-Ms2	5.14E-05	1.39E-05	1.23E+00	9.58E-02
	PSO-Ms*	**1.86E-05**	2.91E-06	**5.29E-01**	2.16E-02

*The best performance for each test case is marked in bold

Table 8. Computational time (in seconds) with K=5

Data Set	Number Assets	K=5				
		CPLEX	INC. SET	PSO-Ms1	PSO-Ms2	PSO-Ms*
Hang Seng	31	12	39	3	2	2
DAX 100	85	906	363	3	2	3
FTSE 100	89	3190	638	3	2	3
S&P 100	98	12055	1363	3	2	3
Nikkei	225	186	389	18	16	18
S&P 500	457	-	2625	31	26	26
Russell 2000	1318	-	14819	73	72	74
Russell 3000	2151	-	47964	120	117	121

Figure 8. Efficient frontier found by PSO-Ms*– S&P 500 (457 assets)

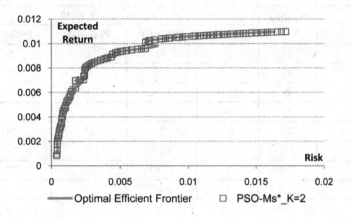

(a) *K=2*

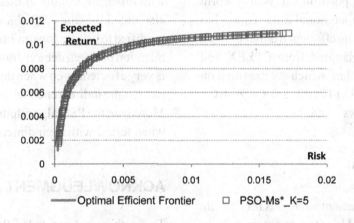

(b) *K=5*

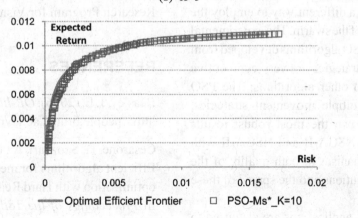

(c) *K=10*

Table 9. Computational time (in seconds) with K=10

Data Set	Number Assets	K=10				
		CPLEX	INC. SET	PSO-Ms1	PSO-Ms2	PSO-Ms*
Hang Seng	31	10	58	3	2	2
DAX 100	85	135	811	3	2	3
FTSE 100	89	1414	2155	3	2	3
S&P 100	98	39600	4844	3	2	3
Nikkei	225	83	724	18	14	18
S&P 500	457	-	4127	33	27	32
Russell 2000	1318	-	15763	73	77	78
Russell 3000	2151	-	56499	123	115	123

which totally outline the efficient front and reveal all potential trade-off portfolios. It is also worth noticing that the computational time required to obtain such approximate efficient frontier is much smaller than those obtained from CPLEX and Increasing Set Algorithm, which are executed on Intel Core2 Duo CPU (T7500, 2.2 GHz, 4 Gb RAM) under Windows Vista.

6. CONCLUSION

In this study, the movement strategies for Particle Swarm Optimization Algorithm to obtain the near optimal Pareto front are discussed. Each movement strategy uses a different way to employ the search experience of the swarm. The experimental results show that PSO algorithms developed from these movement strategies are very competitive when compared to other algorithms. The PSO algorithm with multiple movement strategies, PSO-Ms*, has shown the most robust results and outperformed NSGA-II and NSGA-II with self adaptive mechanism in both quality of the non-dominated solutions and the spread of these solutions.

Two real-world applications are also used to confirm the effectiveness of multi-objective PSO algorithms. In the engineering design problem, the solutions found by PSO-Ms* are very competitive with other algorithms in literature. Besides, it is also noted that the PSO algorithms can be easily modified to handle constraints. The portfolio optimization problem demonstrated that the algorithm is very efficient even when dealing with problems that require indirect encoding/decoding procedure. Moreover, the PSO algorithms are also very robust when tested with high dimensional problems.

ACKNOWLEDGMENT

The authors acknowledge the financial support from the 2008 Royal Thai Government Joint Research Program for Visiting Scholars.

REFERENCES

Beasley, J. E. (2006). *OR-library*. Retrieved from http://people.brunel.ac.uk/mastjjb/jeb/info.html

Cesarone, F., Scozzari, A., & Tardella, F. (2008). Efficient algorithms for mean-variance portfolio optimization with Hard Real -World Constraints. In *Proceedings of the 18th International AFIR Colloquium*, Rome, Italy.

Coello Coello, C. A., & Christiansen, A. D. (1999). MOSES: a multiple objective optimization tool for engineering design. *Journal of Engineering Optimization, 31*(3), 337–368. doi:10.1080/03052159908941377

Coello Coello, C. A., & Lechuga, M. S. (2002). MOPSO: A proposal for multiple objective particle swarm optimization, Evolutionary Computation. In *Proceedings of the 2002 Congress on Evolutionary Computation* (Vol. 2, pp. 1051-1056).

Deb, K., Pratap, A., Agarwal, S., & Meyarivan, T. (2002). A fast and elitist multiobjective genetic algorithm: NSGA-ii. *Evolutionary Computation, 6*(2), 182–197. doi:10.1109/4235.996017

Fieldsend, J., & Singh, S. (2002). A multi-objective algorithm based upon article swarm optimisation, an efficient data structure and turbulence. In *Proceedings of the 2002 U.K. Workshop on Computational Intelligence*, Birmingham, UK (pp. 37-44).

Hu, X., & Eberhart, H. (2002). Multiobjective optimization using dynamic Neighborhood Particle Swarm Optimization. In *Proceedings of the Congress on Evolutionary* Computation *(CEC' 2002)*, Picataway, NJ (Vol. 2, pp. 1677-1681). Washington, DC: IEEE.

Kennedy, J., & Eberhart, R. (1995). Particle swarm optimization. In *Proceedings, IEEE International Conference on Neural Networks* (Vol. 4, pp. 1942-1948).

Li, X. (2003). A non-dominated sorting particle swarm optimizer for multiobjective optimization. In *Proceedings of the 2003 international conference on Genetic and evolutionary computation*: Part I, Chicago (pp. 37-48).

Markowitz, H. M. (1952). Portfolio selection. *The Journal of Finance, 7*, 77–91. doi:10.2307/2975974

Parsopoulos, K. E., & Vrahatis, M. N. (2002). Particle swarm optimization method in multi-objective problems. In *Proceeding of the 2002 ACM Symposium on Applied Computing (SAC' 2002)*, Madrid, Spain (pp. 603-607). New York: ACM Press.

Pongchairerks, P., & Kachitvichyanukul, V. (2005). Non-homogenous particle swarm optimization with multiple social structures. In V. Kachitvichyanukul, U. Purintrapiban, & P. Utayopas (Eds.), In *Proceedings of the Simulation and Modeling: Integrating Sciences and Technology for Effective Resource Management, the international conference on simulation and modeling*, Asian Institute of Technology, Bangkok, Thailand.

Pongchairerks, P., & Kachitvichyanukul, V. (2009). Particle swarm optimization algorithm with multiple social learning structures. *International Journal of Operational Research, 6*(2), 176–194. doi:10.1504/IJOR.2009.026534

Raquel, C., Prospero, C., & Naval, Jr. (2005). An effective use of crowding distance in multiobjective particle swarm optimization. In *Proceedings of the 2005 conference on Genetic and evolutionary computation*, Washington, DC.

Shi, Y., & Eberhart, R. (1998). A modified particle swarm optimizer. In Proceedings of the Evolutionary Computation *World Congress on Computational Intelligence* (pp. 69-73). Washington, DC: IEEE.

Srinivas, N., & Deb, K. (1994). Multiobjective optimization using nondominated sorting in genetic algorithms. *Evolutionary Computation, 2*(3), 221–248. doi:10.1162/evco.1994.2.3.221

Veeramachaneni, K., Peram, T., Mohan, C., & Osadciw, L. A. (2003). *Optimization Using Particle Swarms with Near Neighbour Interactions* (LNCS 2723). New York: Springer. ISBN:0302-9743

Yıldız, A. R. (2009). A novel hybrid immune algorithm for global optimization in design and manufacturing. *Robotics and Computer-integrated Manufacturing, 25*, 261–270. doi:10.1016/j.rcim.2007.08.002

Zeng, F., Low, M. Y. H., Decraene, J., Zhou, S., & Cai, W. (2010). Self-Adaptive Mechanism for Multi-objective Evolutionary Algorithms. In *Proceedings of the 2010 IAENG International Conference on Artificial Intelligence and Applications.*

Zitzler, E., Deb, K., & Thiele, L. (2000). Comparison of multi-objective evolutionary algorithms: Empirical results. *Evolutionary Computation, 8*(2), 173–195. doi:10.1162/106365600568202

Chapter 9
A New Multiagent Algorithm for Dynamic Continuous Optimization

Julien Lepagnot
Université de Paris 12, France

Amir Nakib
Université de Paris 12, France

Hamouche Oulhadj
Université de Paris 12, France

Patrick Siarry
Université de Paris 12, France

ABSTRACT

Many real-world problems are dynamic and require an optimization algorithm that is able to continuously track a changing optimum over time. In this paper, a new multiagent algorithm is proposed to solve dynamic problems. This algorithm is based on multiple trajectory searches and saving the optima found to use them when a change is detected in the environment. The proposed algorithm is analyzed using the Moving Peaks Benchmark, and its performances are compared to competing dynamic optimization algorithms on several instances of this benchmark. The obtained results show the efficiency of the proposed algorithm, even in multimodal environments.

1. INTRODUCTION

Recently, optimization in dynamic environments has attracted a growing interest, due to its practical relevance. Many real-world problems are dynamic optimization problems (DOPs), i.e. their objective function changes over time: typical examples are in vehicle routing (Larsen, 2000), inventory management (Minner, 2003) and scheduling (Branke & Mattfeld, 2005). For dynamic environments, the goal is not only to locate the optimum, but to

DOI: 10.4018/978-1-4666-0270-0.ch009

follow it as closely as possible. A dynamic optimization problem can be expressed by:

$$
\begin{aligned}
max \quad & f(\vec{x}, t) \\
s.t. \quad & h_j(\vec{x}, t) = 0 \ for \ j = 1, 2, ..., p \\
& g_k(\vec{x}, t) \leq 0 \ for \ k = 1, 2, ..., l \\
& \vec{x} = \left[x_1, x_2, ..., x_n\right]
\end{aligned}
\tag{1}
$$

where $f(\vec{x}, t)$ is the objective function of the problem, $h_j(\vec{x}, t)$ denotes the jth equality constraint and $g_k(\vec{x}, t)$ denotes the kth inequality constraint. Both of them may change over time, denoted by t. In this paper, we focus on a dynamic optimization problem with time constant constraints.

The main approaches to deal with DOPs can be classified into the following five groups (Jin & Branke, 2005):

1. **Generated diversity after a change:** When a change in the environment is detected, explicit actions are taken to increase diversity and to facilitate the shift to the new optimum.

2. **Maintained diversity throughout the run:** Convergence is avoided all the time and it is hoped that a spread-out population can adapt to change more efficiently.

3. **Memory-based approaches:** These methods are supplied with a memory to be able to recall useful information from the past. In practice, they store good solutions in order to reuse them when a change is detected.

4. **Multipopulation approaches:** Dividing up the population into several subpopulations, distributed on different optima, allows tracking of multiple optima simultaneously and increases the probability to find new ones.

5. **Future prediction:** Recently, another kind of methods, trying to predict future changes, has attracted much attention (Rossi, Abderrahim, & Diaz, 2008), (Rossi, Barrientos, & Cerro, 2007), (Simoes & Costa, 2008). This approach is based on the fact that in a real problem, changes can follow some pattern that could be learned.

We focus on population-based metaheuristics, which are global search, generally bio-inspired, algorithms. We can roughly classify them in four categories: evolutionary algorithms (EAs), particle swarm optimization (PSO), ant colony optimization (ACO) and hybrid methods. We will now describe dynamic metaheuristics that have been proposed in the literature in each of these categories.

A lot of existing dynamic optimization methods are EAs. EAs can be indeed well suited for optimization in changing environments, since they are inspired by the principles of natural evolution, and natural evolution deals very well with environmental changes. In (Rossi, Abderrahim, & Diaz, 2008), the algorithm incorporates a motion prediction technique based on Kalman filter, in order to improve the speed of optimum tracking. This kind of prediction could be suited for many problems, but it increases the complexity of the algorithm and the number of parameters. In (Tinos & Yang, 2007), the authors propose to maintain diversity in a genetic algorithm (GA) by replacing the worst individual and some others with randomly generated individuals, and maintaining their offspring in a subpopulation. However, this method is only designed for discrete problems (DDOPs). Another GA is described in (Yang, 2006), that is based on immune system and also devoted to DDOPs. In (Huang & Rocha, 2005), an agent-based coevolutionary GA is proposed. This algorithm makes coevolve the way the genotype of an agent is read along with its genotype. Thus, the chromosomes are transcribed into their "edited" counterparts, using the "editors" which coevolve with them, then crossed-over and mutated. In (Mendes & Mohais, 2005), a multipopulation differential evolution (DE) algorithm is proposed, in which some techniques are added in order to increase diversity. DE is a population-based approach, its strategy consists in generating a new position for an individual according to the differences calculated between other randomly selected individuals. This algorithm is based on two main parameters, that must be correctly fitted. However in (Mendes & Mohais, 2005), these parameters are randomly generated in order to make DE easier to use.

Another widely used class of algorithms for dynamic optimization is PSO. PSO is a population-based approach, similar in some respects to EAs, except that potential solutions (particles) move, rather than evolve, throughout the search space (Blackwell & Branke, 2004). The move rules, or particle dynamics, are inspired by models of swarming and flocking (Kennedy & Eberhart, 1995). In this class of methods, we can cite (Blackwell & Branke, 2004), where the authors propose two multi-swarm algorithms based on an atomic model. The first algorithm uses multiple swarms, composed of a sub-swarm of mutually repelling particles, orbiting around another sub-swarm of neutral, or conventional PSO particles. The second algorithm is based on a quantum model of the atom, where the charged particles (electrons) will not follow a classical trajectory, but will be rather randomized within a ball centered on the swarm attractor. Both of these algorithms place their swarms on each of localized optima, thus letting each swarm track a different optimum. However, these methods have many parameters that must be suitably fitted. Moreover, the obtained results with these methods are not good enough. This approach of using charged particles is also used in (Blackwell & Branke, 2006) and (Li, Branke, & Blackwell, 2006), with other techniques to increase diversity and to track optima. Another PSO algorithm is proposed in (Du & Li, 2008), that uses two populations of particles. The first one is for diversification, and the second is for intensification.

Another class of algorithms, ACO, has been used for dynamic optimization. ACO is also a population-based approach using swarm intelli-

gence, inspired from the way ants find the shortest path between the nest and a source of food (Dorigo & Gambardella, 2002). In this class of methods, we can cite (Dréo & Siarry, 2006), that proposes to hybridize an ACO algorithm with the Nelder-Mead simplex method (Nelder & Mead, 1965) for local search. A modified Nelder-Mead simplex method is also developed in this paper for dynamic optimization. However, this method does not perform well on functions having a lot of local optima. In (Tfaili & Siarry, 2008), charged ants are used in order to maintain diversity. Moreover, the attribution of an electrostatic charge to each ant prevents them from converging to same local optima. The performances of this method are not good enough, according to the benchmark defined in (Dréo & Siarry, 2006).

In order to perform better on dynamic problems, some authors have tried hybrid methods, like in (Lung & Dumitrescu, 2007) and (Lung & Dumitrescu, 2008), that propose hybrid PSO/EAs algorithms. However, the results of those methods are not so different from PSO or EAs methods, described previously.

An algorithm proposed in (Moser & Hendtlass, 2007) is based on extremal optimization (EO). EO does not use a population of solutions, but improves a single solution using mutation. This algorithm uses a "stepwise" sampling scheme that samples every dimension of the search space in equal distances. Then, the algorithm takes the best candidate as the next solution, afterwards it proceeds to a hill-climbing phase, in order to fine-tune the solution. Then, the solution is stored in memory, and the method is applied again on another randomly generated solution. This algorithm is simple and efficient, and allows to obtain good results on a specific test called the "Moving Peaks Benchmark" (MPB) (Branke, 1999). However, this method is especially developed and fitted for this benchmark, and it seems not applicable in real world problems.

In this paper, a new method is proposed to solve dynamic optimization problems. Our algorithm, called "MADO", for "MultiAgent Dynamic Optimization", has been developed in order to be efficient for solving a wide range of DOPs. It is a multiagent method, that makes use of a population of agents to explore the search space. The proposed algorithm is based on the following considerations: when optimizing in a multimodal environment, we need to keep track of each local optimum, to overcome the case where the global optimum "jumps" from one of them to another. The found optima are archived in a memory. Then, this memory can be used when a change is detected.

It is common that real world problems have time costly evaluation of fitness functions. Hence, the computational cost of the proposed algorithm should be made as short as possible and expressed in terms of number of evaluations. The proposed algorithm makes use of the following inspirations:

- Keeping information about the previous positions allows to prevent wasting evaluations in unpromising zones of the search space;
- Using a sampling of candidate solutions that optimally cover the local landscape may reduce the number of evaluations per trajectory step, without decreasing performance. For this goal, we maximize the distances between all the candidate solutions, whereas keeping them constricted into the current local landscape. More precisely, it is done by evaluating the candidate solutions on the surface of an hypersphere centered on the current position;
- The sampling of candidate solutions is adaptable to the local landscape. This is done by using an adaptable radius for the above-mentioned hypersphere;
- An exclusion radius for the current solution of each search trajectory is used to avoid the case where some search trajectories explore the same area of the search space.

The rest of this paper is organized as follows. Section 2 presents test problems used in the literature and introduces the benchmark set that will be used here. Section 3 describes the proposed algorithm. Experimental results are discussed in Section 4. Conclusion and works in progress are in Section 5.

2. BENCHMARK SET FOR DYNAMIC OPTIMIZATION

Table 1 presents a summary of competing methods available in the literature and gives the test problems used by each one. The test problems gathered in the first column of Table 1 are those used by the competing methods. These competing methods are described in the references listed in the third column. From Table 1, one can remark that the most commonly used testbed is the Moving Peaks Benchmark (MPB) (Branke, 1999). This benchmark is becoming the standard for testing dynamic optimization algorithms, and is claimed to be representative of real world problems (Branke, 1999). To compare our algorithm to the competing ones, this testbed was adopted.

MPB consists of a number of peaks that vary their shape, position and height randomly upon time. At any time, one of the local optima becomes the new global optimum. MPB generates DOPs consisting of a set of peaks that periodically move in a random direction, by a fixed amount s (the change "severity"). The movements are autocorrelated by a coefficient $0 \leq \lambda \leq 1$, where 0 means uncorrelated and 1 means highly autocorrelated. The peaks change position every α iterations (function evaluations), and α is called time span. The fitness function for the landscape of MPB is formulated as follows:

$$F(\vec{x}, t) = max_{i=1,\dots,m} \left(H_i(t) - \left(W_i(t) \sqrt{\sum_{j=1}^{d} \left(x_j - X_{ij}(t) \right)^2} \right) \right)$$

(2)

Table 1. Summary of recent DOP algorithms

Test problems	Base algorithm	Authors
MPB[1] and the dynamic Rastrigin function	PSO[2]	Du & Li, 2008
various continuous dynamic problems (Dréo & Siarry, 2006)	ACO[3]	Tfaili & Siarry, 2008
a computer vision problem	EAs[4]	Rossi, Abderrahim, & Diaz, 2008
MPB	Hybrid PSO/ EAs	Lung & Dumitrescu, 2008 *(ESCA)*
MPB	Hybrid PSO/ EAs	Lung & Dumitrescu, 2007 *(CESO)*
MPB	EO[5]	Moser & Hendtlass, 2007
a set of discrete dynamic problems (Yang, 2003), (Yang & Yao, 2005)	GA[6]	Tinos & Yang, 2007
a set of discrete dynamic problems (Yang, 2003), (Yang & Yao, 2005)	GA	Yang, 2006
various continuous dynamic problems (Dréo & Siarry, 2006)	ACO	Dréo & Siarry, 2006
MPB	PSO	Li, Branke, & Blackwell, 2006
MPB	PSO	Blackwell & Branke, 2006 *(2nd version)*
MPB	DE[7]	Mendes & Mohais, 2005
a testbed proposed by the authors	EAs	Huang & Rocha, 2005
MPB	PSO	Blackwell & Branke, 2004 *(1st version)*

[1]The Moving Peaks Benchmark (Branke, 1999). [2]Particle Swarm Optimization. [3]Ant Colony Optimization. [4]Evolutionary Algorithms. [5]Extremal Optimization. [6]Genetic Algorithm. [7]Differential Evolution.

where m is the number of peaks, d is the number of dimensions, $H_i(t)$ is the height of the ith peak at the time t, $W_i(t)$ is the width of the ith peak at the time t and $\vec{X}_i(t)$ is the position of the ith peak at the time t.

Figure 1 illustrates an MPB landscape before and after a change (after one time span).

In order to evaluate the performance, the "offline error" is used. Offline error (*oe*) is defined as the average of the errors of the best points evaluated during each time span. It is defined by:

$$oe = \frac{1}{Nc} \sum_{j=1}^{Nc} \left(\frac{1}{Ne(j)} \sum_{i=1}^{Ne(j)} \left(f_j^* - f_{ji}^* \right) \right) \qquad (3)$$

where Nc is the total number of fitness landscape changes within a single experiment, $Ne(j)$ is the number of iterations performed for the jth state of the landscape, f_j^* is the value of the optimal solution for the jth landscape and f_{ji}^* is the current best fitness value found for the jth landscape.

We can remark that this measure has some weaknesses: it is sensitive to the overall height of the landscape, and to the number of peaks. It is important for an algorithm to find the global optimum quickly, to minimize the offline error. Hence, the most successful strategy is a multi-solution approach that keeps track of every local peak (Moser & Hendtlass, 2007).

Figure 1. An MPB landscape before and after a change

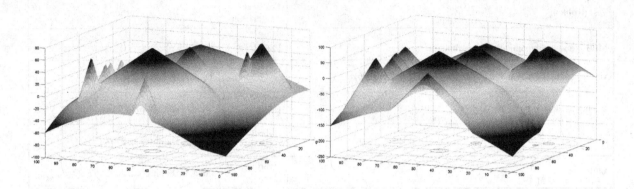

3. THE PROPOSED MADO ALGORITHM

3.1 Overall Scheme

MADO is a multiagent algorithm that consists in the following three modules:

1. **Memory module:** In case of a multimodal environment, a dynamic optimization method needs to keep track of each local optimum found, since one of them can become the new global optimum after a change. We propose to use a memory to archive the found optima.

2. **Agent manager:** It contains all the agents, and manages their execution, creation and deletion. Agents are nearsighted (they have only a local vision of the search space). More precisely, agents are only performing local search, they jump from their current position to a better one, in their neighborhood, until they cannot improve their current solution, reaching thus a local optimum.

3. **Coordinator:** It counterbalances the nearsightedness of the agents. The coordinator has indeed a global vision of the search performed by the agents, and it is able to

prevent them from searching in unpromising zones of the search space. The coordinator supervises the whole search, and manages the interactions between memory and agents modules.

In the following subsections, a detailed description of the overall scheme of the method is presented. Subsequently, the three modules that compose the MADO algorithm are described. Afterwards, the fitting of the parameters of the algorithm is presented, and their values, further used in the experimental section, are given.

The overall scheme of the MADO algorithm is illustrated in Figure 2. As it is shown, all the interactions between the memory manager and the agent manager are through the coordinator. Moreover, all global decisions are taken by the coordinator. The memory manager maintains the archive of local optima, that are provided by the coordinator. The agent manager informs the coordinator about the found optima, and receives its instructions for creating, deleting, and repositioning agents.

Before explaining in detail these modules, we need to describe how the distances are calculated in MADO. As we are considering an Euclidian space of d dimensions as the search space, the

Euclidian distance will be used. However, the search space may not have the same bounds on each dimension. Then, we will use a "normalized" basis. We denote by Δ_i the size of each interval that defines the search space, with $i \in [1, d]$. Then, the unit vectors $\vec{e}_i$ in the direction of each axis of the Cartesian coordinates system are "scaled" in order to produce modified unit vectors u_i, that make all the Δ_i equal to 1 in the basis defined by these modified unit vectors. This is done by using $\{\vec{u}_1 = \dfrac{\vec{e}_1}{\Delta_1}, \vec{u}_2 = \dfrac{\vec{e}_2}{\Delta_2}, ..., \vec{u}_d = \dfrac{\vec{e}_d}{\Delta_d}\}$ as the basis of the Euclidian space where the search space is defined. Consequently, when a hypersphere inside the search space is considered, it will correspond to an ellipsoid in the canonical basis.

3.2 Agent Management Module

3.2.1 The Exploration Strategy of the Agents

Agents explore the search space step-by-step, moving from their current position to a better one in their neighborhood, until they reach a local optimum. Hence, to precisely describe the behavior of the agents, we first explain the used kind of neighborhood, and how the agents make use of it. As agents are nearsighted, they can only test candidate solutions for their next move in a delimited zone of the search space, centered on their current position. This zone must be bounded. Without any information about the local landscape of an agent, a good choice is to make it isotropic. Then, the most adapted topology is a ball. To keep small the number of fitness function evaluations, we need a sampling that optimally covers the local landscape. Afterwards, we maximize the distances

Figure 2. Overall scheme of MADO algorithm

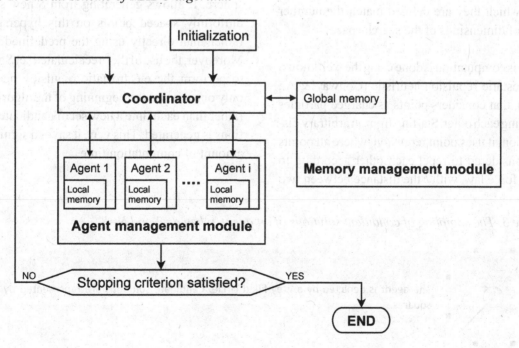

between all candidate solutions inside this ball. It leads to sample them on the boundary of the ball (on a hypersphere centered on the current solution of an agent). This delimited zone of the search space must be adaptive to the local landscape, to increase the efficiency of the agents. It is done by using an adaptive radius for the ball that defines this zone. From all these considerations, we define the neighborhood of the agents as a set of N candidate solutions placed on the hypersphere of radius R centered on the current position of an agent (N is a parameter of the algorithm). Figure 3 illustrates this neighborhood in dimension 2. Another set of N points are generated and stored at the beginning of the MADO algorithm. These points are calculated in order to meet the following constraints:

- The smallest distance between them is maximized;
- The distances between them and the origin of the space (the point $(0,0,\ldots0)$) are equal to 1;
- The number of dimensions of the space in which they are defined match the number of dimensions of the search space.

This computation is done using the well known electrostatic repulsion heuristic (Conway & A., 1998), that considers points as charged particles repelling each other. Starting from an arbitrary distribution, it uses point repulsion, where all points are considered to repel each other according to a $1/r^2$ force law, with r the distance between two

points, and dynamics are simulated. The algorithm runs until the satisfaction of a stopping criterion, and the resulting set of points is returned. We use a stopping criterion that is satisfied when no point can be moved by a distance greater than ε, typically equal to 10^{-4}. Then, this set of points is used by agents to get the positions of the candidate solutions of their current neighborhood. The procedure used to get the exact positions of candidate solutions is presented in Algorithm 1.

Where S' is the computed set of an agent's candidate solutions, d is the number of dimensions of the search space, S is the precalculated set of uniformly spaced N points on the unit hypersphere and $\vec{P}_c$ is the current position of the agent. We can note that, for $d=1$, the only possible set of points for S is $\{(-1),(1)\}$ and agents can only move forward or backward by steps of length equal to R. In this particular case, the generated unit vector $\vec{V}$ can only be (-1) or (1). The use of the Householder reflection (Householder, 1958) is required here in order to sample candidate solutions on the whole surface of the unit hypersphere. It allows generating from S new sets of uniformly spaced points on this hypersphere, rather than directly using the predefined set S. Moreover, the use of the precalculated set S allows to perform the electrostatic repulsion heuristic only one time (at the beginning of the algorithm), rather than each time a new set of candidate solutions is generated. This way, it saves a significant amount of computation time.

Figure 3. The sampling of candidate solutions of an agent, when d=2 and N=8

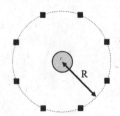

The agent is depicted by a grey-filled circle. Candidate solutions are represented by black squares.

Algorithm 1. Calculates the set of candidate solutions of an agent

$S' \leftarrow \varnothing$ $\vec{V} \leftarrow$ a random unit vector uniformly distributed on the hypersphere of radius 1, of d dimensions and centered on the origin

foreach point $\vec{P_i} \in S$ **do**

    $\vec{P_i^r} \leftarrow$ the Householder reflection of $\vec{P_i}$ which uses $\vec{V}$ as the Householder vector   *(to randomly reflect $\vec{P_i}$)*

    $\vec{P_i^{rs}} \leftarrow \vec{P_i^r} \cdot R$ *(to scale $\vec{P_i^r}$ by R)*

    $\vec{P_i^{rst}} \leftarrow \vec{P_i^{rs}} + \vec{P_c}$ *(to translate $\vec{P_i^{rs}}$ on the agent's local landscape hypersphere)*

    if $\vec{P_i^{rst}}$ is inside the search space **then**   *(if it is not beyond the boundary of the search space)*

        $S' \leftarrow S' \cup \{\vec{P_i^{rst}}\}$

    end

end

return S'

3.2.2 The Step Size Adaptation Strategy

The adaptation of the radius R makes use of trajectory information gathered along the steps of an agent. We propose to use the "cumulative path length control" described in (Hansen & Ostermeier, 2001), with much simpler calculations. The Figure 4 illustrates the two possible kinds of "bad" trajectories that an agent may follow. When one of these cases is detected, an increase or a

decrease of the step size R is performed. The first case (Figure 4 (a)) may mean that the agent is turning around an optimum, without being able to reach it directly. This is due to a too large step size, leading to back and forth displacements, which cancel each other out. Thus, in this first case, a decrease in R is needed. On the contrary, the displacements on Figure 4 (b) are oriented in the same direction, which may mean that the agent is hill climbing a large peak (a peak is considered to be large when, climbed by an agent, the state-

Figure 4. The two kinds of trajectories that lead to a step size adaptation

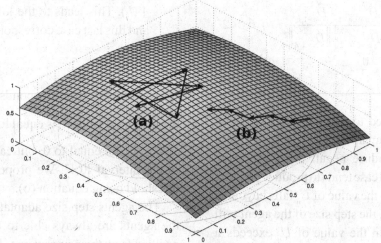

(*a*) Agent turning around an optimum. (*b*) Agent hill climbing a large peak.

ment $U_n > s_u$ becomes true (see equation (5) and Algorithm 2)). Then, to avoid too slow moves to the top of this peak, an increase in R is performed.

Information about the successive moves of an agent is collected by using a "cumulative dot product" of old successive displacement vectors. It is done using the following formula:

$$U_n = \begin{cases} \sum_{i=1}^{n-2} \left((c_u)^{n-i-2} \dfrac{\vec{D}_{i,i+1} \cdot \vec{D}_{i+1,i+2}}{\left\| \vec{D}_{i,i+1} \right\| \left\| \vec{D}_{i+1,i+2} \right\|} \right) & if\ n > 2 \\ 0 & otherwise \end{cases}$$

(4)

Where U_n is the cumulative dot product of an agent's search trajectory, n is the number of successive positions of this trajectory, $\vec{D}_{i,i+1}$ is the displacement vector from the ith position to the $(i+1)^{th}$ position in this trajectory, and c_u is a constant in $[0,1]$, where 0 gives no weight to displacements before the last one, whereas 1 applies the same weight to the last displacement and to its previous ones. In practice, U_n is computed using a recurrence relation on U_{n-1} and on the two last displacements (see equation (5)). There is no need to record all the displacement vectors of the agents, but only their two last ones.

$$U_n = \begin{cases} c_u\ U_{n-1} + \dfrac{\vec{D}_{n-2,n-1} \cdot \vec{D}_{n-1,n}}{\left\| \vec{D}_{n-2,n-1} \right\| \left\| \vec{D}_{n-1,n} \right\|} & if\ n > 2 \\ 0 & otherwise \end{cases}$$

(5)

Then, U_n is used to determine the decision for the step size adaptation. The first case Figure 4 (a) tends to produce negative dot products, whereas the second case tends to produce positive ones. Hence, when the value of U_n falls beyond a negative threshold, the step size of the agent will decrease, and when the value of U_n exceeds a positive threshold, the step size of the agent will increase (Algorithm 2).

Where c_r is constant in $]0.1]$, and s_u is a constant threshold, calculated as follows:

$$s_u = cos(\frac{\pi}{3})\,(1 + c_u)$$

(6)

This formula can be explained by the following considerations. In the case of $c_u = 0$, the value of U_n (see equation (5)) will be equal to the cosinus of the angle, denoted a, between the last two displacement vectors of an agent. As a can take any value in $[0, \pi]$, this interval has been uniformly partitioned and linked to the three following cases:

1. The agent follows a trajectory as in Figure 4 (*a*). This case produces the highest values of a, and is associated to the interval $[\frac{2\pi}{3}, \pi]$;

2. The temporary situation, where we cannot take a decision about the agent. Hence, no step size adaptation is made in this case. It produces values of a around $\frac{\pi}{2}$, and it is related to the interval $[\frac{\pi}{3}, \frac{2\pi}{3}]$;

3. The agent follows a trajectory as in Figure 4 (*b*). This leads to the lowest values of a, and this last case corresponds to the interval $[0, \frac{\pi}{3}]$.

This case ($c_u = 0$) corresponds to the case where the threshold value s_u is equal to $cos(\frac{\pi}{3})$. Generally, c_u is not equal to 0, but can take any value in the interval $]0,1]$. We propose to adjust this threshold using equation (6).

The agents step size adaptation assumes that the agents are always able to move to a better position from their current one. This is a condition

Algorithm 2. Adaptation of the step size using the cumulative dot product

if $U_n < -s_u$ then

$\qquad R \leftarrow c_r\, R$

$\qquad U_n \leftarrow 0$

else if $U_n > s_u$ then

$\qquad R \leftarrow \dfrac{1}{c_r}\, R$

$\qquad U_n \leftarrow 0$

end

to be able to compute U_n from U_{n-1} and the last displacement. If an agent cannot find a better solution in its local landscape, the agent stays on its current position. Then, a second adaptation method is proposed in this particular case. This method is based on the following assumption: if the agent cannot find a better solution in its local landscape, then, it has probably finished hill climbing a peak, and an optimum may lay at a distance lower than the current radius of its neighborhood (the hypersphere of radius R). Then, reducing this radius may let the agent continue its search towards the nearby optimum. Briefly, the second adaptation method consists in decreasing R in order to let the agent converge to the found optimum ($R \leftarrow c_r\, R$).

3.2.3 The Convergence Process and the Stagnation Criterion

We consider that an agent converged to a local optimum, when none of its last δ_t steps improved significantly the fitness value of its current solution (if $\left| f_n - f_{n-1} \right| \le \delta_p$ *for* $n = 1, 2, \ldots, \delta_t$, where f_n is the fitness of the solution found by the agent n trajectory steps ago). This is a well known stagnation criterion for stopping a local search. We use the parameter δ_t to prevent unnecessary fitness evaluations. An adaptation method for the

number of neighbor solutions, that have to be evaluated in order to find the new position of an agent, is based on the following considerations. When an agent is close to a local optimum, it has a lower probability to get out of this local optimum than an agent that is still exploring the landscape. The agent will not be likely to escape from the basin of attraction (the region of the search space, around an optimum, that leads to trajectories towards this optimum) it has converged to, even if it performs a lot of fitness evaluations. However, for an agent that is still exploring the landscape, it is important to maintain a good trajectory, in order to hill climb towards a high quality solution. The convergence level of an agent can be expressed by the number of its last d_t steps that did not improve its fitness more than δ_p. The Algorithm 3 summarizes the procedure to find the next position of an agent.

Where v_c is the current fitness of the agent, $\vec{P}_c$ is its current position, S' is the set of all neighbor candidate solutions of the agent, $\vec{P}_i^{rst}$ is a reflected scaled translated position of a given solution, $rand(\delta_t)$ generates a uniform random number in $[0, \delta_t]$, d_t is the number of steps that the agent has made without improving its fitness more than δ_p, and $\vec{P}_{best}$ and v are the new solution of the agent in its search trajectory and its new fitness value, respectively.

When an agent has finally found a local optimum, the agent manager sends this optimum to the coordinator, that will transmit it to the memory manager. Then, the coordinator shows to the agent manager where this agent will be repositioned, in order to perform a new trajectory search. A new value is given to the step size (R) of this agent. The way the new step size value is calculated is described in subsection 3.4. One can remark that in a flat landscape, agents will not move from their initial position (their trajectory will consist in a succession of the same initial point), and stop their local search after δ_t steps. Thus, in a flat

Algorithm 3. The search for a better solution among the neighboring ones

$$v \leftarrow v_c$$
$$\vec{P}_{best} \leftarrow \vec{P}_c$$
foreach point $\vec{P}_i^{rst} \in S'$ **do**
    $v_i \leftarrow evaluate\ \vec{P}_i^{rst}$
    if $v_i > v$ **then**
        $v \leftarrow v_i$
        $\vec{P}_{best} \leftarrow \vec{P}_i^{rst}$
        if $rand(\delta_t) < d_t$ **then**
            return $(\vec{P}_{best}, v)$
        end
    end
end
return $(\vec{P}_{best}, v)$

landscape, the local optima transmitted to the memory manager will be always the initial positions of the agents. In this particular case, the only adaptation of the step size of an agent is a decrease in R, since no displacement vectors can be computed (the agent does not move).

3.2.4 The Diversity Maintaining Strategy

To prevent several agents from exploring the same zone of the search space, and to prevent them from converging to the same local optimum, an exclusion radius r_e is attributed to each agent. Hence, when an agent detects one or several other agents at a distance lower than r_e, only the agent with the best fitness, among the detected agents and the agent having detected them, is allowed to continue its search. All the other agents have to start a new search elsewhere (see subsection 3.4 to see how they are repositioned). The value of r_e is dynamically adjusted each time a new local optimum is memorized, and its new value is calculated by the memory manager. To prevent that r_e becomes too small, a given radius r_l needs to be introduced. This radius will be used

as a lower bound for r_e. It is required, in order to avoid the use of near zero values for r_e and as initial step size. Too small values for these radius will slow the adaptation processes. The update process of r_e is administrated by the coordinator, and executed by the memory manager.

3.2.5 The Flowchart of an Agent

Agents perform their search by running their local search algorithm independently of each other. The flowchart of the agents search algorithm is illustrated in Figure 5. One can remark that a special state named "SYNCHRONIZATION" appears two times in this flowchart. This state marks the end of one "loop" of the algorithm of an agent. Hence, when this state is reached, the agent manager halts the execution of this agent until all other agents have reached a SYNCHRONIZATION state. Then, the execution of the agents is resumed at the SYNCHRONIZATION state they previously halted on (not at another SYNCHRONIZATION state). This special state allows then the parallel execution of the agents.

3.3 Memory Management Module

3.3.1 Local Optima Archiving Strategy

The memory manager maintains the archive of local optima found by the agents. This archive must be bounded, its size is fixed by a predefined number n_m of entries. Thus, all the found optima cannot be included into this archive, only the n_m best ones will be stored. When the archive is full, we propose the following condition to update the archive:

- If the new optimum is better than the worst optimum of the archive, or its fitness value is at least equal to the one of this worst optimum, then this worst optimum is replaced by the new one;

Figure 5. The main algorithm flowchart of a MADO agent

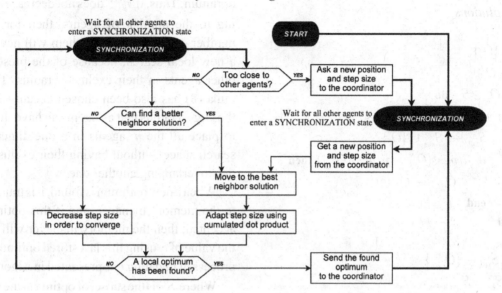

- If there is one or several other optima in the archive that are "too close" to the new optimum, then it is possible that all these optima close to each other are in fact scattered around the top of one peak. Thus, this subset of solutions is replaced by the best optimum among them. Hence, if there are other optima in the archive that are "too close" to the newly found one, this new optimum will replace them, only if it is better, or if its fitness is at least equal to the fitness of the best one. The process of detecting possible "too close" optima is presented in Algorithm 4.

Where O_c is the newly found optimum, S_m is the archive of stored optima, $dist(O_i, O_c)$ computes the distance between O_i and O_c, $fitness(O_i)$ is the fitness value of O_i and r_o is a threshold that defines the boundary of the suboptimal zone around an optimum, where there is not any other optimum.

r_o does not need to be lower than the lowest initial step size r_l of an agent, because even if there was another optimum O' at a distance from O_{best} lower than r_l, an agent starting a new search from O_{best} would detect O'. This is due to the fact that O' will lie in the local landscape of the agent (inside the hypersphere of radius R with $R \geq r_l$). Then, an agent starting a new search from O_{best} would be able to sample candidate solutions around O'. Moreover, r_o must be high enough in order, for most stored suboptimal solutions, to be detected and removed. One can remark that, in the case where the landscape has thin peaks close to each other, a high value of r_o will remove some of them. The value of r_e is adjusted in order to prevent agents from hill climbing a same peak, and this value should be indeed a good upper bound for r_o. From these considerations, a good choice for the value of r_o appeared to be the geometric average of r_l and r_e. The value of r_o is thus calculated according to (7).

$$r_o = \sqrt{r_l \, r_e} \tag{7}$$

Algorithm 4. The replacement of suboptimal stored solutions

$S_{sub} \leftarrow \{O_c\}$

$O_{best} \leftarrow O_c$

foreach $O_i \in S_m$ **do**

    if $dist(O_i, O_c) \leq r_o$ **then**

        $S_{sub} \leftarrow S_{sub} \cup \{O_i\}$

        if $fitness(O_i) > fitness(O_{best})$ **then**

            $O_{best} \leftarrow O_i$

        end

    end

end

$S_{sub} \leftarrow S_{sub} - \{O_{best}\}$

$S_m \leftarrow S_m - S_{sub}$

$S_m \leftarrow S_m \cup \{O_{best}\}$

3.3.2 The Computation of the Exclusion Radius

Another task assigned to the memory manager is updating the value of r_e. At the beginning, an initial value of r_e, denoted by r_e^{max}, is calculated according to (8).

$$r_e^{max} = \frac{1}{2\,n_a} \quad (8)$$

where n_a is the predefined number of agents created in the search space at the beginning of the MADO algorithm. As it will be shown in subsection 3.4, the number of agents may vary temporarily, but the average number of agents along the whole search process tends to be equal to n_a. According to (8), when n_a increases, r_e^{max} decreases. We have to take into account that the increase in the number of agents will increase the probability to have several agents converging to the same

optimum. Thus, if r_e^{max} does not decrease according to the number of agents, then for a high number of agents, most of them will never start a new local search, because of the presence of other agents in their exclusion radius. The formula (8) has also been chosen because it gives the largest radius that an agent can have. It allows to place all the n_a agents in a one-dimensional search space, without having their exclusion radius overlapping another one.

When a new optimum is found, it is transmitted to the memory manager, and if this optimum is accepted, then the memory manager will update the value of r_e using this last stored optimum. The process of updating r_e is presented in Algorithm 5.

Where S_m' is the subset of optima in the archive without the last stored optimum, S_m is the set of stored optima, O_c is the last stored optimum, $dist(O_i, O_c)$ computes the distance between O_i and O_c and $card(S_m')$ is the number of optima in the set S_m'. To update r_e, we compute the average value of the lowest distances from each stored optimum to the others, denoted by δ_{mean}. This is done using (9).

$$\delta_{mean} = \frac{\sum_{O_i \in S_m} \left(min_{O_j \in S_m - \{O_i\}} dist(O_j, O_i) \right)}{card(S_m)} \quad (9)$$

Assuming that r_e tends to be equal to the average value of the lowest distances from each optimum of S_m' to the others, then we can replace the sum of these lowest distances in (9) by $2\,card(S_m')\,r_e$. This leads to the formula (10).

$$\delta_{mean} \approx \frac{2\,card(S_m - \{O_c\})\,r_e + min_{O_j \in S_m - \{O_c\}} dist(O_j, O_c)}{card(S_m)} \quad (10)$$

Algorithm 5. The updating of the exclusion radius

$$S'_m \leftarrow S_m - \{O_c\}$$

if $card(S'_m) > 0$ **then**   (since we need to compute distances, there must be at least two optima in the archive)

$\quad \delta_{min} \leftarrow \infty$

$\quad$ **foreach** $O_i \in S'_m$ **do**   (computes the lowest distance between the new optimum and the previously stored ones)

$\quad\quad \delta_i \leftarrow dist(O_i, O_c)$

$\quad\quad$ **if** $\delta_i < \delta_{min}$ **then**

$\quad\quad\quad \delta_{min} \leftarrow \delta_i$

$\quad\quad$ **end**

$\quad$ **end**

(since a too high r_e might prevent the convergence to optima close to each other,

$\quad$ **if** $\dfrac{\delta_{min}}{2} < r_e^{max}$ **then** r_e^{max} is used as an upper bound for $\dfrac{\delta_{min}}{2}$)

$$r_{mean} \leftarrow \frac{card(S'_m)\, r_e + \dfrac{\delta_{min}}{2}}{card(S'_m) + 1}$$

$$r_e^{new} \leftarrow \frac{card(S'_m)\, r_{mean} + \left(n_m - card(S'_m)\right) r_e}{n_m}$$

$$r_e \leftarrow r_e^{new}$$

$\quad$ **end**

end

Since the exclusion radius r_e should match the average "radius" of the attractive zone of a peak, it is estimated by half the average lowest distance between the top of two peaks. This value, denoted by r_{mean}, is calculated from δ_{mean} using (11):

$$r_{mean} = \frac{\delta_{mean}}{2} \qquad (11)$$

When S_m is nearly empty, the updating process does not have enough optima to estimate a fitted average lowest distance between peaks. Then, it should not modify the value of r_e so much. However, when S_m will be filled out, this estimation will be adapted to the search space landscape, and r_e will be made close to r_{mean}. This is the idea behind the expression of r_e^{new} in Algorithm 5.

3.4 Coordinator

The coordinator administrates all the main operations of the search process, by giving instructions to memory and agent management modules, and receiving information from them. It is in charge of the creation of the agents at the beginning of the algorithm. The number of agents to be created is given by the parameter n_a. The locations of these agents at the start of the search process are not randomly generated, but are computed in order to maximize distances between them. This is done by using the electrostatic repulsion heuristic described in section 3.2.1. Rather than constraining the repulsing points to stay on the surface of the unit hypersphere, they are constrained to stay inside the hyperrectangle, denoted by T, that is centered in the search space

(Figure 6). As illustrated in Figure 6, T is the Cartesian product of intervals $T_i = [r_e^{max}, 1 - r_e^{max}]$ with $i = 1, 2, ..., d$. Thus, at the end of this heuristic, we get a set of initial positions for the initial set of agents, which are optimally covering the search space, i.e. the lowest distance between two of them is maximized inside T.

The instruction to create the initial set of agents is given to the agent management module, then the MADO algorithm can start the search process. The exploration of the search space is done by the agents, using trajectory local searches. Once an agent has found an optimum, this optimum is transmitted to the coordinator, that transmits it to the memory management module. Afterwards, the coordinator transmits a new location and a new step size to the agent. This new location is randomly generated and uniformly distributed in the search space, under the constraint that the lowest distance between this new location and the current position of any agent is greater or equal to the exclusion radius r_e. After five attempts to generate a new location at a random position outside the exclusion radii of agents without success, the coordinator sends a delete instruction to the agent manager. We did so because of the high probability that the search space is satured with

existing agents. If a random position satisfying the constraint is found, it is given as the new position of the agent, and its new step size is calculated as in (12):

$$R = max\left(r_e, rand(1)\right) \qquad (12)$$

where $rand(1)$ generates a uniform random number in [0,1].

The coordinator detects also the changes in the environment. This detection is performed when all the agents have finished one loop in their search algorithm, i.e. when all the agents have moved one step ahead in their trajectory and/or performed one adaptation of their step size.

Changes in the environment are detected by re-evaluating the fitness of the best optimum of the archive. When any optimum has been found yet, we re-evaluate the current fitness of an agent randomly chosen, and compare it to its previous value. If these values are different, a change is supposed to have occurred, and a tracking of the stored optima is performed (Algorithm 6).

Where S_a is the set of all agents, S_m is the archive of stored optima and r_l is the lowest possible initial step size of an agent, i.e. the lowest

Figure 6. Computation of an initial set of 5 agents in a two-dimensional search space

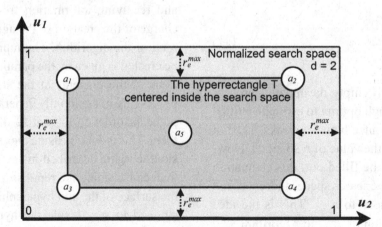

Agents are depicted by white-filled circles denoted by a_i with $i \in \{1, 2, ..., 5\}$

Algorithm 6. The tracking of stored optima after a change

foreach $a_i \in S_a$ **do**
    Re-evaluate the fitness of a_i
end
foreach $O_i \in S_m$ **do**
    Re-evaluate the fitness of O_i
    Create an agent located on O_i and with an initial step size of r_l
end
$S_m \leftarrow \varnothing$

allowed value for r_e. The use of such a low initial step size for these new agents is needed in order to track the optima, i.e. to hill climb the peaks of the previously stored optima to find their new position. A large initial step size allows these agents to leave the peaks of the tracked optima. Thus, they will explore other zones of the search space rather than staying on the peaks they have to hill climb. Hence, the best value for r_l is the value that takes into account the move of the peaks through the search space.

As we can see, the number of agents varies along the search process, and can be lower or greater than the initial number n_a. However, to prevent the number of agents to increase more and more at every detection of a change in the environment, the coordinator will send a delete instruction if the number of agents is higher than n_a, rather than letting an agent start a new search, when its trajectory search is finished. This way, the number of agents will be temporarily higher than n_a (after a change has been detected), and will decrease to n_a, because the excess agents will just track the previously stored optima and send back their new positions.

3.5 Parameter Setting of MADO

Table 2 summarizes the eight parameters of MADO that the user has to define. In this table, the values given are suitable for MPB and they were

fixed experimentally. These values will be used to perform the experiments reported in Section 4.

We fixed the number of agents equal to 4, because the convergence needs to be fast. Having too many agents exploring the search space will slow down the individual convergence of each agent and lead to a waste of fitness function evaluations. The precision parameter δ_p and the lowest step size r_l need to be correctly adapted to the change severity and to the change frequency of the environment. A low value for δ_p makes the agents unable to track optima in a fast changing environment, since they will spend too many iterations on fine-tuning their current solution, and might never be able to send it to the coordinator for archiving, before a new change in the environment occurs. Hence, the lower is the number of iterations between two changes, the higher should be the value of δ_p. This means that the precision of the found optima in fast changing environments might be worse than in slow changing ones.

The value of r_l needs also to be well suited to the severity of the changes, since a low value of r_l in a fast changing environment requires a lot of adaptations of the step size, and a waste of many fitness function evaluations. On the opposite, a high value of r_l may make the tracking agent leave the peak of the optimum it has to track, and make it begin exploring the search space

Table 2. MADO parameter setting

Name	Interval	Default value	Short description
n_a	N	4	initial (and average) number of agents
n_m	N	10	capacity of the archive of found optima
N	N	$round(0.28\,d + 2)$	number of candidate solutions per agent's move, where *round(v)* gives the nearest integer to v
c_u	[0,1]	0.5	coefficient which defines the weight of the cumulative dot product in the step size adaptation process
c_r	]0,1]	0.8	coefficient which specifies how much the step size is decreased (or increased) during its adaptation
r_l	]0,1]	0.0025	lowest possible step size (should match the change severity of the search space)
δ_t	N	8	maximum number of moves an agent can make without improving its fitness more that δ_p
δ_p	R	0.005	the precision parameter of the stagnation criterion of the agents trajectory searches

elsewhere. The other parameters of the algorithm are much less critical, and might be left at their default values (given in Table 2).

4. RESULTS AND DISCUSSION

We used the Moving Peaks Benchmark in order to test the MADO algorithm. In (Branke, 1999), three sets of parameters, called scenarios, were proposed. These scenarios are given as a set of standard settings, that can be used in order to produce comparable results. Authors have to specify the scenario they used to test their methods, preventing the use of custom settings that may differ from one paper to another. It appears that the most commonly used set of parameters for MPB is scenario 2 (see Table 3), hence, it will be used in this paper. In this scenario, the correlation coefficient λ is equal to 0, which means that when a change occurs, the peaks move in random directions that are not correlated to their previous moves. Hence, the direction of the peaks' moves cannot be predicted from the direction of their previous

moves. This leads to a harder scenario than if we used a value of λ strictly greater than 0. The rest of this section is organized as follows. Firstly, an experimental analysis of the MADO algorithm is made, justifying the use of each component of the algorithm. This analysis is followed by a comparison to other methods on scenario 2, for various numbers of peaks and dimensions.

Table 3. MPB parameters in scenario 2

Parameter	Scenario 2
Number of peaks	10
Dimensions	5
Peak heights	[30,70]
Peak widths	[1,12]
Change cycle	5000
Change severity	1
Height severity	7
Width severity	1
Correlation coefficient λ	0

4.1 Empirical Analysis of the MADO Algorithm

An evaluation of all the different components of the MADO algorithm is made, in order to justify their requirement for obtaining quality results. This evaluation is performed on scenario 2 of MPB, and the resulting offline errors and standard deviations averaged on 100 runs are summarized in Table 4, for different variants of MADO algorithm. The maximum number of iterations is fixed to $5 \cdot 10^5$, that corresponds to 100 changes occurred in the environment during each run.

As one can see, the standard MADO is better than all the simpler variants tested here. Among these variants, we can note that $MADO\underset{r_e}{-}$ does

not perform a detection of other agents inside the exclusion radius r_e of an agent, i.e. an agent has not to start a new search elsewhere when it is too close to another agent, and the coordinator has not to generate a new starting position, for an agent outside the exclusion radius of the other agents. Thus, all agents can explore the same zone of the search space. However, r_e is still used in $MADO\underset{r_e}{-}$ for the other procedures, as in equation (12) and in Algorithm 4. In $MADO\dfrac{}{r_e^{adapt}}$, the only difference with the standard version is that r_e is constant and equal to r_e^{max}, i.e. the Algorithm 5 is not performed. In $MADO\dfrac{}{S_a^{max}}$, the electrostatic repulsion heuristic is not used to

Table 4. Offline error on MPB for each simplified variant of the MADO algorithm

Variant	Offline error	Short description
$MADO$	0.80±0.19	the standard MADO algorithm
$MADO_{n_a=1}$	1.26±0.48	with only one exploring agent
$MADO_{n_m=0}$	5.96±0.37	without archiving local optima
$MADO\underset{r_e}{-}$	1.23±0.38	no exclusion radius for the agents
$MADO\dfrac{}{r_e^{adapt}}$	0.82±0.24	no adaptation of the exclusion radius
$MADO\dfrac{}{S_a^{max}}$	0.84±0.26	no lowest distance maximization for the initial set of agents
$MADO\dfrac{}{S}$	3.78±0.48	no lowest distance maximization for candidate solutions
$MADO\dfrac{}{CDPA}$	1.06±0.33	no cumulative dot product adaptation of the step size of the agents
$MADO\dfrac{}{R^{min}}$	0.91±0.33	using r_l instead of r_e as lower bound of the initial step size of an agent (see (12))
$MADO\dfrac{}{r_l^{track}}$	2.82±0.24	without using r_l as initial step size for agents created in place of stored optima

Table 5. Comparison with competing algorithms on MPB (scenario 2)

Algorithm	number of runs	offline error ± standard deviation
Moser & Hendtlass, 2007	100	0.66±0.20
MADO	100 50	0.80±0.19 0.78±0.22
Lung & Dumitrescu, 2007	50	1.38±0.02
Lung & Dumitrescu, 2008	50	1.53±0.01
Blackwell & Branke, 2006	50	1.72±0.06
Mendes & Mohais, 2005	50	1.75±0.03
Li, Branke, & Blackwell, 2006	50	1.93±0.06
Blackwell & Branke, 2004	50	2.16±0.06
Du & Li, 2008	50	4.02±0.56

produce the initial set of agents, since their positions are randomly generated inside the search space and outside the exclusion radius of existing agents. In $MADO\frac{}{S}$, the electrostatic repulsion heuristic is not used to produce the set S of candidate solutions of an agent, and the candidate solutions are randomly generated and uniformly distributed inside the hypersphere of radius R centered on the agent's current position. In $MADO\frac{}{CDPA}$, the cumulative dot product adaptation of the step size is not used, and the only adaptation process used is the reduction of R (when no better candidate solution can be found in the local landscape of an agent). Finally, we can also note that in $MADO\frac{}{r_l^{track}}$, the initial step size of an agent, created by the coordinator when a change is detected in the environment (on the location of a previously found optimum), is generated using equation (12).

From Table 4, one can conclude that the most important components of the MADO algorithm, in order to obtain good results, are the archiving of found local optima, the use of maximally spaced candidate solutions on the surface of the local landscape hypersphere of agents, and the use of r_l as initial step size of the agents created (in place of stored optima, when a change is detected).

To give an idea about the computational cost of the MADO algorithm, the average time on 100 runs needed to compute $5 \cdot 10^5$ fitness function evaluations on the scenario 2 of MPB, using a 2.26 GHz Intel Core 2 Duo P8400 processor, is equal to 363 milliseconds, including the time of evaluation of the fitness function of MPB.

4.2 Comparison with Competing Methods

The comparison, on MPB, of MADO with the other leading optimization algorithms in dynamic environments is summarized in Table 5.

Table 6. Offline error of MADO and MMEO on several instances of MPB

Algorithm	on 100 peaks	in 7 dimensions
MADO	1.12±0.08	1.61±0.13
MMEO	1.47*	1.73±0.55

The offline errors and the standard deviations are given, and the algorithms are sorted from the best to the worst. Results are averaged on 100 runs or 50 runs of the tested algorithms, and the maximum number of fitness evaluations per run is fixed to $5 \cdot 10^5$, i.e. 100 changes per run.

Results gathered in Table 5 for competing algorithms are those given in the references listed in the first column. As we can see, MADO is the second best algorithm in this classification, and its confidence interval overlaps the confidence interval of the best rated algorithm. Although MADO is rated behind MMEO (Moser & Hendtlass, 2007) on scenario 2 of MPB, MMEO produces worse results than MADO on some other instances of MPB, i.e. those with a higher number of peaks or dimensions. An extended comparison, averaged on 100 runs with 100 changes per run, between MMEO and MADO, is given in Table 6. Scenario 2 is still used, with a modified value of one parameter in each column, and the offline error is also used, with its standard deviation.

This comparison shows that MADO is more robust and can be applied to highly multimodal DOPs and DOPs with high dimensionality.

5. CONCLUSION

A new multiagent algorithm has been designed for continuous dynamic optimization problems. In this algorithm, a multiple trajectory local search strategy with an adaptive step size has been implemented. These local searches are conducted by the agents of the algorithm, and a memory was added for archiving the found optima. This way, when a change is detected in the environment, the archived optima can be re-used in order to track them through the search space. The agents and the memory are also encapsulated in two different modules, that are themselves coordinated by a third module. This third module, named the coordinator, takes all the global decisions and actions over the whole search process, like deleting or creating agents, and detecting changes in the environment. This implementation has been specifically designed for dynamic continuous optimization, and proved its efficiency on the Moving Peaks Benchmark. This algorithm can also be expected to produce good results, when solving static objective functions.

The major drawback of MADO is that its critical parameters are not automatically adjusted along with the search process, and need to be fine-tuned by the user. In works in progress, we would like to make these critical parameters adaptive. We will also attempt to make this algorithm simpler and lighter. Some of its components may be subject to replacement or deletion, and the number of parameters may be reduced. Finally, as a lot of real world DOPs are multi-objective, or have a lot of constraints that can be dynamic, the proposed algorithm may also be modified to make it multi-objective and able to handle hard and dynamic constraints.

REFERENCES

Blackwell, T., & Branke, J. (2004). Multi-swarm optimization in dynamic environments (LNCS 3005, pp. 489-500).

Blackwell, T., & Branke, J. (2006). Multi-swarms, exclusion and anti-convergence in dynamic environments. *IEEE Transactions on Evolutionary Computation, 10*, 459–472. doi:10.1109/TEVC.2005.857074

Branke, J. (1999). Memory enhanced evolutionary algorithms for changing optimization problems. In *Proceedings of the IEEE Congress on Evolutionary Computation (CEC 1999)* (pp. 1875-1882). Washington, DC: IEEE Computer Society.

Branke, J. (1999). *The moving peaks benchmark.* Retrieved from http://www.aifb.uni-karlsruhe.de/~jbr/MovPeaks

Branke, J., & Mattfeld, D. (2005). Anticipation and flexibility in dynamic scheduling. *International Journal of Production Research, 43,* 3103–3129. doi:10.1080/00207540500077140

Conway, J. H., & Alexander, N. J. (1998). *Sphere packings, lattices and groups* (3rd ed.). New York: Springer.

Dorigo, M., & Gambardella, L. M. (2002). Guest editorial special on ant colony optimization. *IEEE Transactions on Evolutionary Computation, 6,* 317–319. doi:10.1109/TEVC.2002.802446

Dréo, J., & Siarry, P. (2006). An ant colony algorithm aimed at dynamic continuous optimization. *Applied Mathematics and Computation, 181,* 457–467. doi:10.1016/j.amc.2005.12.051

Du, W., & Li, B. (2008). Multi-strategy ensemble particle swarm optimization for dynamic optimization. *Information Sciences, 178,* 3096–3109. doi:10.1016/j.ins.2008.01.020

Hansen, N., & Ostermeier, A. (2001). Completely derandomized self-adaptation in evolution strategies. *Evolutionary Computation, 9,* 159–195. doi:10.1162/106365601750190398

Householder, A. (1958). Unitary triangularization of a nonsymmetric matrix. *Journal of the ACM, 5,* 339–342. doi:10.1145/320941.320947

Huang, C.-F., & Rocha, L. M. (2005). Tracking extrema in dynamic environments using a coevolutionary agent-based model of genotype edition. In *Proceedings of the 2005 Conference on Genetic and Evolutionary Computation* (pp. 545-552). ACM Publishing.

Jin, Y., & Branke, J. (2005). Evolutionary optimization in uncertain environments - a survey. *IEEE Transactions on Evolutionary Computation, 9,* 303–317. doi:10.1109/TEVC.2005.846356

Kennedy, J., & Eberhart, R. C. (1995). Particle swarm optimization. In *Proceedings of the IEEE International Conference on Neural Networks* (pp. 1942-1948). Washington, DC: IEEE Computer Society.

Larsen, A. (2000). *The dynamic vehicle routing problem.* Copenhagen, Demark: Technical University of Denmark.

Li, X., Branke, J., & Blackwell, T. (2006). Particle swarm with speciation and adaptation in a dynamic environment. In *Proceedings of the 8th Annual Conference on Genetic and Evolutionary Computation* (pp. 51-58). ACM Publishing.

Lung, R. I., & Dumitrescu, D. (2007). Collaborative evolutionary swarm optimization with a Gauss Chaotic Sequence Generator. *Innovations in Hybrid Intelligent Systems, 44,* 207–214. doi:10.1007/978-3-540-74972-1_28

Lung, R. I., & Dumitrescu, D. (2008). ESCA: A new evolutionary-swarm cooperative algorithm. *Studies in Computational Intelligence, 129,* 105–114. doi:10.1007/978-3-540-78987-1_10

Mendes, R., & Mohais, A. (2005). DynDE: A differential evolution for dynamic optimization problems. In *Proceedings of the 2005 IEEE Congress on Evolutionary Computation* (pp. 2808-2815). Washington, DC: IEEE Computer Society.

Minner, S. (2003). Multiple-supplier inventory models in supply chain management: A review. *International Journal of Production Economics, 81,* 265–279. doi:10.1016/S0925-5273(02)00288-8

Moser, I., & Hendtlass, T. (2007). A simple and efficient multi-component algorithm for solving dynamic function optimisation problems. In *Proceedings of the 2005 IEEE Congress on Evolutionary Computation* (pp. 252-259). Washington, DC: IEEE Computer Society.

Nelder, J., & Mead, R. (1965). A simplex method for function minimization. *The Computer Journal*, *7*, 308–313.

Rossi, C., Abderrahim, M., & Diaz, J. C. (2008). Tracking moving optima using Kalman-based predictions. *Evolutionary Computation*, *16*, 1–30. doi:10.1162/evco.2008.16.1.1

Rossi, C., Barrientos, A., & Cerro, J. D. (2007). Two adaptive mutation operators for optima tracking in dynamic optimization problems with evolution strategies. In *Proceedings of the 9th Annual Conference on Genetic and Evolutionary Computation* (pp. 697-704). ACM Publishing.

Simoes, A., & Costa, E. (2008). Evolutionary algorithms for dynamic environments: Prediction using linear regression and Markov chains. In *Parallel problem solving from nature* (pp. 306-315). Springer.

Tfaili, W., & Siarry, P. (2008). A new charged ant colony algorithm for continuous dynamic optimization. *Applied Mathematics and Computation*, *197*, 604–613. doi:10.1016/j.amc.2007.08.087

Tinos, R., & Yang, S. (2007). A self-organizing random immigrants genetic algorithm for dynamic optimization problems. *Genetic Programming and Evolvable Machines*, *8*, 255–286. doi:10.1007/s10710-007-9024-z

Yang, S. (2003). Non-stationary problem optimization using the primal-dual genetic algorithm. In *Proceedings of the 2003 IEEE Congress on Evolutionary Computation* (pp. 2246-2253). Washington, DC: IEEE Computer Society.

Yang, S. (2006). A comparative study of immune system based genetic algorithms in dynamic environments. In *Proceedings of the 8th Annual Conference on Genetic and Evolutionary Computation* (pp. 1377-1384). ACM Publishing.

Yang, S., & Yao, X. (2005). Experimental study on population-based incremental learning algorithms for dynamic optimization problems. *Soft Computing - A Fusion of Foundations. Methodologies and Applications*, *9*, 815–834.

This work was previously published in International Journal of Applied Metaheuristic Computing, Volume 1, Issue 1, edited by Peng-Yeng Yin, pp. 17-39, copyright 2010 by IGI Publishing (an imprint of IGI Global).

Chapter 10

Improving Switched Current Sigma Delta Modulators' Performances via the Particle Swarm Optimization Technique

M. Fakhfakh
University of Sfax, Tunisia

S. Masmoudi
University of Sfax, Tunisia

Y. Cooren
University of Paris, France

M. Loulou
University of Sfax, Tunisia

P. Siarry
University of Paris, France

ABSTRACT

This paper presents the optimal design of a switched current sigma delta modulator. The Multi-objective Particle Swarm Optimization technique is adopted to optimize performances of the embryonic cell forming the modulator, that is, a class AB grounded gate switched current memory cell. The embryonic cell was optimized regarding to its main performances such as sampling frequency and signal to noise ratio. The optimized memory cell was used to design the switched current modulator which operates at a 100 MHz sampling frequency and the output signal spectrum presents a 45.75 dB signal to noise ratio.

DOI: 10.4018/978-1-4666-0270-0.ch010

INTRODUCTION

Oversampled analog-to-digital (A/D) converters are in good compatibility with digital VLSI technology. They become very popular and widely used in analog-to-digital conversion. In fact, this is mainly due to the following advantages (Medeiro, Perez-Verdu, & Rodriguez-Vasquez, 1999; Del-Rio, Medeiro, Perez-Verdu, Dela-Rosa, & Rodriguez-Vasquez, 2006):

- Oversampling and noise shaping techniques allow achieving accuracy that exceeds that of integrated circuit components;
- They relax requirements for anti-aliasing filters; they can be implemented with low order filters.

In addition, by cascading oversampled modulators, A/D converters can achieve large resolution, robust operation and low sensitivity to non-ideal effects. An oversampling $\Sigma\Delta$ converter (Medeiro, Perez-Verdu, & Rodriguez-Vasquez, 1999; Del-Rio, Medeiro, Perez-Verdu, Dela-Rosa, & Rodriguez-Vasquez, 2006) (Figure 1) encompasses an anti-aliasing filter, a modulator and a decimator. Among the converter blocks, the modulator is the hardest to design (Norsworthly, Schreier, & Themes, 1997). Indeed, anti-aliasing filters can be simplified up to a simple RC low-pass filter, thanks to oversampling. The decimator is a digital block that can be optimally designed by means of widely available CAD tools (Del-Rio, Medeiro, Perez-Verdu, Dela-Rosa, & Rodriguez-Vasquez, 2006;

Medeiro, Perez-Verdu, & Rodriguez-Vasquez, 1999; Norsworthly, Schreier, & Themes, 1997).

The modulator comprises many error mechanisms (Medeiro, Perez-Verdu, & Rodriguez-Vasquez, 1999), and performances of the converter highly depend on those of the modulator. Switched capacitor (SC) and switched current (SI) techniques have already been adopted for the design of such A/D converters (Del-Rio, Medeiro, Perez-Verdu, Dela-Rosa, & Rodriguez-Vasquez, 2006; Fakhfakh, Masmoudi, Tlelo-Cuautle, & Loulou, 2008; Loulou, Dallet, & Marchegay, 2000; Loulou, Dallet, Masmoudi, Marchegay, & Kamoun, 2004; Masmoudi, Fakhfakh, Loulou, Masmoudi, & Loumeau, 2007; Norsworthly, Schreier, & Themes, 1997; Oliaei, Loumeau, & Aboushady, 1997; Tan, 1997). Even though SI technique is not mature enough to cope with SC technique, advantages of the SI approach over those of SC make this technique very promising (Hughes, Worapishet, & Toumazou, 2000). Consequently, SI $\Sigma\Delta$ converters are excellent alternatives where much remains to be made (Fakhfakh, Masmoudi, Tlelo-Cuautle, & Loulou, 2008; Tan, 1997).

In this work we deal with designing high performance SI $\Sigma\Delta$ modulators. The main block of a modulator is the integrator. Performances of the later highly depend on those of the embryonic delay cell (z^{-1}) (Medeiro, Perez-Verdu, & Rodriguez-Vasquez, 1999; Del-Rio, Medeiro, Perez-Verdu, Dela-Rosa, & Rodriguez-Vasquez, 2006). Since a SI cell performs a half delay operation ($z^{-1/2}$), cascading two SI cells performs the full

Figure 1. Block diagram of a sigma delta A/D converter

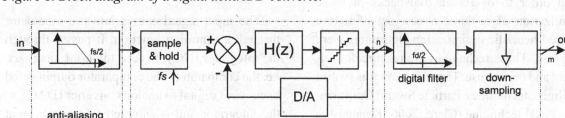

delay (z^{-1}). Thus, we mainly focus on optimizing performances of the SI memory cell regarding to its operating frequency and its precision (i.e. signal to noise ratio (SNR)). These performances are in conflict, i.e., maximizing one objective leads to the degradation of the other. Consequently, each performance has an individual optimal solution different from the other performance, then, a trade-off set of optimal solutions has to be found.

When dealing with "hard optimization" problems, analog designers make generally appeal to statistic-based approaches (Graeb, Zizala, Eckmueller, & Antreich, 2001; Medeiro, Rodríguez-Macías, Fernández, Domínguez-Astro, Huertas & Rodríguez-Vázquez, 1994). Performances of these approaches mainly rely on the experience of the designer, since the later fixes the operating point coordinates. These statistic-based approaches are time consuming and do not guarantee the convergence to the global optimum solution (Talbi, 2002).

Simulated annealing (Courat, Raynaud, Mrad, & Siarry, 1994; Kirkpatrick, Gelatt, & Vecchi, 1983; Siarry, Berthiau, Durbin, & Haussy, 1997) and genetic algorithms (Dinger, 1998; Grimbleby, 2000; Marseguerra & Zio, 2000; Tlelo-Cuautle & Duarte-Villaseñor, 2008) are examples of heuristic-based mathematical approaches adopted to deal with hard optimization problems. However, these techniques do not offer general solution strategies that can be applied to problem formulations where different types of variables, objectives and constraint functions are handled. In addition, their efficiency is also highly dependent on the algorithm parameters, the dimension of the solution space, the convexity of the solution space, and the number of variables.

In order to overcome drawbacks of these optimization algorithms, a new set of nature inspired heuristic optimization algorithms were proposed. These techniques are resourceful, efficient and easy to use. They are known as swarm intelligent techniques. Particle Swarm Optimization (PSO) technique (Clerc, 2006; Kennedy & Eberhart, 1995) is one of these swarm intelligent

techniques. PSO became popular due to the fact that the algorithm is relatively straightforward, and that it is easy to be implemented to deal with mono-objective and multi-objective problems, as well. Thus, in this paper, a multi-objective particle swarm optimization (MO-PSO) (Coello-Coello & Lechuga, 2002; Cooren, Fakhfakh, Loulou, & Siarry, 2007; Raquel & Naval, 2005; Reyes-Sierra & Coello-Coello, 2006) technique is adopted to optimize performances of the embryonic half delay SI cell.

The remainder of the paper is structured as follows. In section II, basic concepts of oversampling and $\Sigma\Delta$ modulation are reviewed. In section III, the SI technique is briefly introduced. Section IV puts the stress on the MO-PSO algorithm. In section V, optimization results of the SI cell and those of the $\Sigma\Delta$ modulator are presented. Finally, section VI gives some concluding remarks.

BASIC CONCEPTS OF OVERSAMPLED $\Sigma\Delta$ MODULATORS

Figure 1 presents the block diagram of an oversampling $\Sigma\Delta$ A/D converter. It includes:

- An anti-aliasing filter, which eliminates the spectral components higher than half of the sampling frequency,
- A modulator that samples, quantizes and modulates the signal,
- A decimator, which is a digital block that filters the quantization error and decimates data to take back the sampling frequency up to the *Nyquist* frequency.

The input signal comes into the modulator through a summing junction. It passes through the integrator ($H(z)$) to feed the n-bit quantizer, i.e. the comparator. The comparator output is fed back, via a digital to analog converter (DAC), to the integrator and is subtracted from the input signal (Luh, Choma, & Draper, 1998; Medeiro,

Figure 2. The quantizer acts like an added noise source

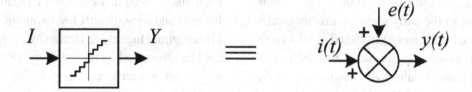

Perez-Verdu, & Rodriguez-Vasquez, 1999; Wang & Harjani, 1997).

The quantizer acts as an added noise source $e(t)$, as it is illustrated by Figure 2.

The modulator can be viewed as a two input block. In the z domain, we have:

$$Y(z)=STF(z)\ X(z) + NTF(z)\ E(z) \tag{1}$$

where $Y(z)$, $X(z)$ and $E(z)$ are z-transforms of the output signal, the input signal and the quantization noise, respectively. $STF(z)$ and $NTF(z)$ are transfer functions of the input signal and quantization noise, respectively.

Ideally, $\|STF(z)\|$ is constant and $NTF(z)$ tends to zero when z tends to 1. According to the scheme of Figure 2 and to the structure of the $\Sigma\Delta$ modulator presented in Figure 1, we have:

$$Y(z) = \frac{H(z)}{1 + H(z)} X(z) + \frac{1}{1 + H(z)} E(z) \tag{2}$$

The simplest block achieving the desired characteristics is the integrator $H(z)=(z^{-1})/(1\text{-}z^{-1})$, this yields to the modulator output:

$$Y(z) = z^{-1}X(z) + (1 - z^{-1})E(z) \tag{3}$$

In time domain, we have:

$$y(n) = \left[x(n-1)\right] + \left[e(n) - e(n-1)\right] \tag{4}$$

The quantization error power decreases in the low frequency range, where the difference from sample to sample is smaller.

A more effective cancellation of the quantization error can be performed by increasing the order of the filter $H(z)$ (Del-Rio, Medeiro, Perez-Verdu, Dela-Rosa, & Rodriguez-Vasquez, 2006). This leads to increase the order of the noise transfer function $NTF(z)$. Figure 3 shows the classical architecture of a second order $\Sigma\Delta$ modulator.

The SI Technique

Switched current technique (SI) is a new analogue sampled data technique that overcomes problems associated with its counterpart, i.e., the switched capacitor technique (SC) (Hughes, Macbeth, & Pattullo, 1990; Oliaei & Loumeau, 1996; Toumazou, Hughes, & Buttersby, 1993). SI cells are implemented in full CMOS technology, whereas

Figure 3. Architecture of a second order $\Sigma\Delta$ modulator

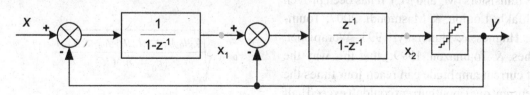

SC cells require additional capacitors (Hughes, Worapishet, & Toumazou, 2000). Since their introduction in the early eighties, memory cells have evolved and many published works have contributed to the improvement of such SI cells (e.g., Fakhfakh, Loulou, & Masmoudi, 2007; O'Connor & Kaiser, 2000; Worapishet, Hughes, & Toumazou, 1999; Worapishet, Hughes, & Toumazou, 2000).

SI technique principle exploits the ability of the intrinsic gate to source capacitance of a MOS transistor to hold on a voltage corresponding to the drain to source current reached at the end of the memory phase. This forces the MOS transistor to be driven by the corresponding current. Expression (5) presents the current square law linking the drain current (I_D) to the gate voltage (Toumazou, Hughes, & Buttersby, 1993):

$$I_D = \frac{1}{2}\mu C_{ox}\frac{W}{L}\left(V_{GS}-V_T\right)^2\left(1+\lambda\ V_{DS}\right)$$

(5)

W and L are the MOS transistor channel width and length, respectively. V_{GS} and V_{DS} denote grid to source and drain to source voltages, respectively. μ, C_{ox}, λ and V_T are technology parameters.

The conventional second generation SI cell (Figure 4-a) has been improved regarding to the input signal swing range and to input to output conductance ratio error (Fakhfakh, Loulou, & Masmoudi, 2007; Toumazou, Hughes, & Buttersby, 1993; Worapishet, Hughes, & Toumazou, 1999). The class AB cell and then the class AB grounded gate memory cell, presented by Figures 4-b and 4-c, were proposed. In the class AB topology, current is memorized thanks to the gate to source capacitances of two complementary MOS transistors (M_N and M_P). It has been proven (Fakhfakh, Loulou, & Masmoudi, 2007; Toumazou, Hughes, & Buttersby, 1993; Worapishet, Hughes, & Toumazou, 1999;) that this way the input current amplitude can reach four times the bias current one (input current couldn't exceed half

the bias current in the class A topologies). It has been also proven that class AB lie insures better linearity and consequently less harmonic distortion (Toumazou, Hughes, & Buttersby, 1993).

The grounded gate topology (Figure 4-c) comprises a translinear loop which role is to control the input/output node voltage, thus annihilating the input to output conductance error. Thus, we choose the grounded gate class AB SI memory cell to design the SI ΣΔ modulator.

As it was introduced in section I, two major characteristics have to be taken into consideration to optimize performances of the SI half delay cell (Fakhfakh, Loulou, & Masmoudi, 2007):

- The settling characteristic: SI technique is based on the principle of charging the gate to source capacitance of a saturated MOS transistor and the ability of this device to hold on this charge, even when its gate is at the floating state. It has been proven in (Fakhfakh, Loulou, & Masmoudi, 2007) that the class AB cell response is equivalent to a second order system one. Expression (6) gives the current transfer function i_{mem}/i_{in}, where i_{mem} refers to the memorized current.

$$\frac{i_{mem}}{i_{in}} = \frac{1}{\left[1+\dfrac{1}{2\xi}\dfrac{s}{\omega_0}+\dfrac{s^2}{\omega_0^2}\right]}$$

(6)

where:

$$\xi = \frac{1}{2}\frac{[(g_{0g}+g_{mg})(g_0+g_s)+g_0 g_s]C+g_{0g}(g_0+g_s)C_g}{\sqrt{[g_0 g_{0g}g_s+g_m g_s(g_{0g}+g_{mg})](g_0+g_s)CC_g}}$$

(7)

$$\omega_0 = \sqrt{\frac{g_0 g_{0g}g_s+g_m g_s(g_{0g}+g_{mg})}{(g_0+g_s)CC_g}}$$

(8)

Figure 4. (a) The conventional second generation class A SI cell, (b) The class AB SI cell, (c) The grounded gate class AB SI cell. (Φ_1 and Φ_2 are two non overlapping clocks)

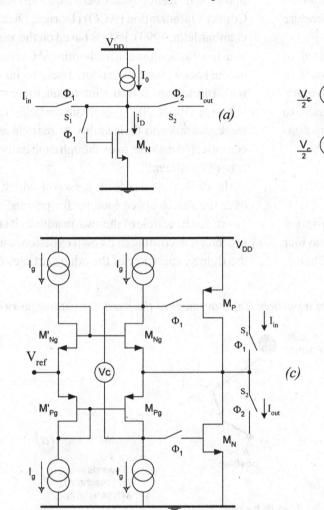

(a)

(b)

(c)

ξ and ω_0 are the dumping factor and the proper pulsation, respectively. g_0, g_{0g} and g_s denote conductances of the memory transistors, the grounded gate transistors and the voltage switch, respectively. gm and gmg are transconductances of the corresponding transistors. C and C_g refer to grid to source parasitic capacitances of the memory and the grounded gate transistors, respectively.

Accordingly, reduced time response of the cell can be minimized by fixing the maximum value (ε), $\left| \xi - \sqrt{2}/2 \right| < \varepsilon$, and maximizing ω_0.

- Signal to noise ratio: all transistors forming the SI memory cell are noise sources, mainly the memory and grounded gate transistors. Expression of the signal to noise ratio is given by (9).

$$SNR = 10 \log \left[16 \left(V_{DD} - V_{TN} - \left| V_{TP} \right| - V_C \right)^4 \right]$$
$$+ 10 \log \left[3C \left(g_m + \frac{g_0 g_{0g}}{g_{mg}} \right)^2 \right] - 10 \log \left[4KT g_m{}^4 \right]$$

$$(9)$$

V_{DD} is the supply voltage, V_{TN} and $|V_{TP}|$ are the threshold voltages of NMOS and PMOS transistors, respectively. T is the absolute temperature and K is the *Boltzmann* constant.

Reduced time response (*rtr*) and signal to noise ratio (*SNR*) are the main performances of the SI cell. They show conflicting behaviours. A multi-objective PSO algorithm was used to generate the front (*rtr vs. SNR*) comprising non-dominated solutions.

Particle Swarm Optimization

At the beginning of the nineties, new optimization techniques based on analogies of swarm behaviour of natural creatures have been proposed (Chan &

Tiwari, 2007), such as Particle Swarm Optimization (PSO) (Kennedy & Eberhart, 1995) and Ant Colony Optimization (ACO) (Dorigo, Dicaro, & Gambardella, 1999). PSO is based on the analogy with bird flocking and fish schooling. ACO is based on the social insect metaphor. These techniques, which are known as swarm intelligence techniques (Chan & Tiwari, 2007), simulate the behaviour of these swarms and their ability to react in a very complicated manner, even though each individual is not "intelligent".

In PSO, particles form a swarm which flies over the search space looking for promising regions. Each particle of the swarm adjusts its flight trajectory, according to its own experience and to the flying experience of the other particles of the

Figure 5. (a) Principle of the movement of a particle, (b) movement of the particles within the swarm

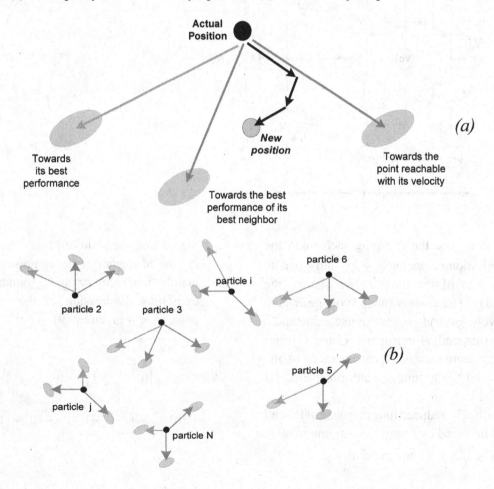

Figure 6. Pseudo code of the general PSO algorithm

```
Begin
    Initialize the swarm
    Initialize the leaders
    Number_iteration=0
    Do
       For each particle
             Update velocity
             Update position
             Evaluate fitness
             Update Pi
       End For
       Update leader
       Number_iteration++
    While Number_iteration < Number_iteration_MAX
End
```

Figure 7. Pseudo code of the MO-PSO algorithm

```
Begin
    Initialize the Swarm
    Evaluate fitness of each particle
    Initialize archives
    Number_iteration=0
    Do
      For each particle
            Update velocity
            Update position

            Mutation
            Evaluate fitness
            Update Pi
      End For
      Update leader
      Update archives
      Number_iteration++

    While Number_iteration < Number_iteration_MAX
End
```

Figure 8. Archive's update.

```
For i=1..N
    If particle[i] dominates some elements of the archive
        Delete dominated elements
    End If
    If particle[i] is nondominated
        If the archive is not full
            Add particle[i] to the archive
        Else
            Compute the crowding distances
            Sort the element of the archive by crowding distance
            Replace the particle with the lower crowding distance by particle[i]
        End If
    End If
End For
```

Figure 9. Pareto fronts for different constraints on power

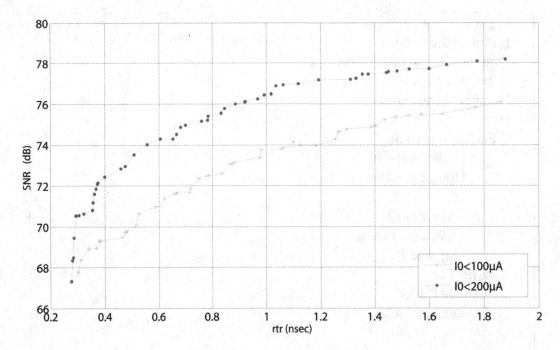

Table 1. The PSO algorithm parameters

Swarm size	Number of iterations	w	c_1	c_2
20	1000	linearly decreased from 0.9 to 0.4	2.1	2.1

Table 2. Optimal parameters (minimum rtr)

$L_N = 2.12\ \mu m$	$W_N = 22.97\ \mu m$	$L_P = 0.77\ \mu m$	$W_P = 37.85\ \mu m$	$I_0 = 68.87\ \mu A$
$L_{Ng} = 1.65\ \mu m$	$W_{Ng} = 6.03\ \mu m$	$L_{Pg} = 1.00\ \mu m$	$W_{Pg} = 9.95\ \mu m$	

Table 3. Simulation conditions

Sampling frequency	Number of points of the Fast Fourier Transform	Oversampling ratio	Input current
100 MHz	16384	64	480 μA / 410 kHz

Figure 10. Comparison between PSO (dots) and NSGA II (solid line) Pareto fronts, for $I_0 < 200\mu A$

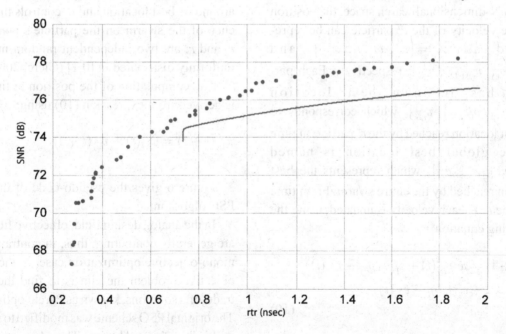

Figure 11. Output power spectral density of the class AB grounded gate SI cell sampled at 100 MHz

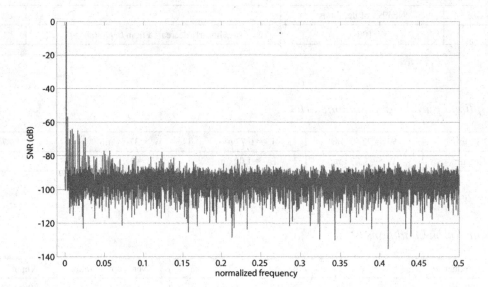

swarm, as well (Clerc, 2006; Fakhfakh, Cooren, Loulou, & Siarry, 2008). Figure 5 illustrates the principle of the movement of the particles.

In a N-dimensional search space, the position and the velocity of the ith particle can be represented as $X_i = [x_{i,1}, x_{i,2}, ..., x_{i,N}]$ and $V_i = [v_{i,1}, v_{i,2}, ..., v_{i,N}]$, respectively. Each particle has its own best location $P_i = [p_{i,1}, p_{i,2}, ..., p_{i,N}]$, which corresponds to the best location reached by the ith particle at time t. The global best location is named $g = [g_1, g_2, ..., g_N]$, which represents the best location reached by the entire swarm. From time t to time $t+1$, each velocity is updated, using the following equation:

$$v_{i,j}(t+1) = w \, v_{i,j}(t) + c_1 \, r_1(p_{i,j} - v_{i,j}(t)) \\ + c_2 \, r_2(g_i - v_{i,j}(t))$$

$$(10)$$

where w is a constant called inertia factor. It controls the impact of the previous velocity on the current one, so it ensures the diversity of the swarm, which is the main mean to avoid the stagnation of particles at local optima. c_1 and c_2 are constants called acceleration coefficients. c_1 controls the attitude of the particle of searching around its best location and c_2 controls the influence of the swarm on the particle's behaviour. r_1 and r_2 are two independent random numbers uniformly distributed in [0,1] (Clerc, 2006).

The computation of the position at time $t+1$ is derived from expression (10) using:

$$x_{i,j}(t+1) = x_{i,j}(t) + v_{i,j}(t+1)$$

$$(11)$$

Figure 6 gives the pseudo-code of the basic PSO algorithm.

In the analog design field, objective functions are generally competing; thus, in contrast to the mono-objective optimization case, in the multi-objective problem the aim is to find the set of trade-offs solutions, known as Pareto optimal set. The original PSO scheme was modified to support multi-objective problems. The idea consists of the use of an external memory, called archive, in which each particle deposits its flight experience at each step. The archive is a depository where non-dominated solutions found during the opti-

Figure 12. (a) Output power spectral density of the second order ΣΔ modulator,(b) Zoom on the output spectrum of the second order ΣΔ modulator

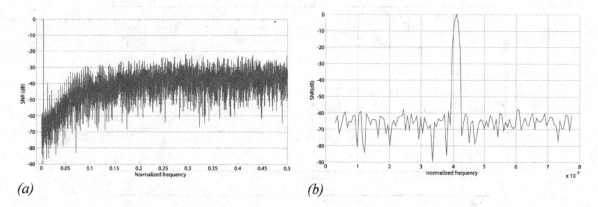

(a)   *(b)*

mization process are stored. Solutions contained in the archive are used as leaders to update positions of the particles. Moreover, the contents of the external archive are reported as the Pareto set at the end of the running cycles. Figure 7 gives the pseudo code of the MO-PSO algorithm.

A quality measure (Kennedy & Eberhart, 1995) is applied in order to select one leader for each particle. A mutation operator is applied after each flight. It allows escaping from local minima. Then,

fitness of each particle is evaluated and the corresponding Pi is updated, and consequently, the set of leaders. Finally, it is to be highlighted that the archive tends to be bounded. Thus, in order to avoid excessive growing of this archive, an update mechanism is integrated in the algorithm. This algorithm uses the crowding distance as a diversity criterion. The crowding distance estimates the size of the largest cuboid enclosing the particle, without including any other particle of

Figure 13. Outputs (x_1 vs. x_2) of the integrators

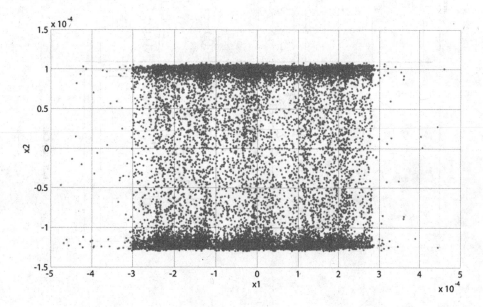

Figure 14. The SI second order ΣΔ modulator

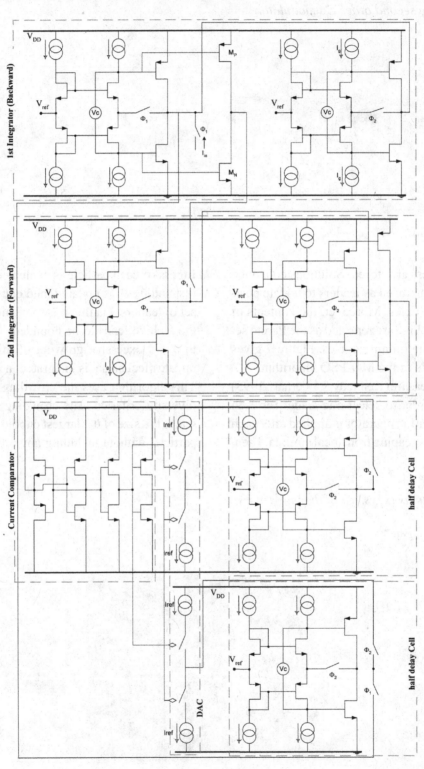

the swarm. This is performed to obtain a Pareto front as uniformly spread as possible. Figure 8 gives the archive's update pseudo code.

OPTIMIZATION AND SIMULATION RESULTS

As it was introduced above, the half delay cell is the embryo that forms the SI integrator, and thus the modulator. The SI class AB grounded gate memory cell, presented in Figure 4-c, was optimized regarding to its reduced time response (*rtr*) and the signal to noise ratio (*SNR*).

PSO technique was used to generate the Pareto front (minimize *rtr*, maximize *SNR*). Classical PSO parameters were adopted; they are given in Table 1 (Clerc, 2006). The swarm topology was randomly changed at each iteration (Clerc & Kennedy, 2002). Figure 9 shows this trade-off set. Optimal parameters values correspond to the edge of the Pareto front (minimum *rtr*). Table 2 gives the corresponding scaling.

For comparison reasons and in order to highlight potentialities of PSO technique, the Pareto front (*rtr*, *SNR*) was also generated using NSGA II algorithm (Seshadri, 2009). Figure 10 shows a comparison between fronts obtained using PSO (dots) and using NSGA II (solid line). The NSGA II Pareto front was obtained for a 600 population size and for 1000 generations. Results obtained using PSO are much better than those of NSGA II. This is mainly due to the fact that PSO handles constraints better than its counterpart.

Figure 11 presents an example of the output current power spectral density. Simulations were performed using Spice software. AMS 0.35 μm technology was used, and the voltage power supply equals 3.3 V. (V_C = 1.31 V, Vref = 1.65 V).

The second order modulator, presented in Figure 14, was designed using the 'optimized' SI memory cell. Figure 12.a shows the output spectral density of the modulator corresponding to the simulation conditions given in Table 3. Figure 12.b presents a zoom, from Figure 12.a, on the band [0 - 0.8 MHz]. SNR equals 45.75 dB and the SNR peak is higher than 60 dB. Finally, Figure 13 shows that both integrators forming the SI $\Sigma\Delta$ modulator operate out of saturation.

CONCLUSION

This paper details the MO-PSO and its application to optimize performances of mixed circuits. A switched current class AB grounded gate memory cell was optimized regarding to its signal to noise ratio and its reduced time response. The optimized SI cell, which performs a half delay cell and forms the basic block forming the integrator, was used to design a $\Sigma\Delta$ SI modulator. Spice simulation results were given to show reached high performances. Best reached performances can be summarized as follows: the embryonic cell can be sampled up to 100 MHz and performs 70 dB at this sampling frequency. The $\Sigma\Delta$ SI modulator performs 45.75 dB for an oversampling ratio that equals 64 and a sampling frequency that equals 100 MHz.

REFERENCES

Chan, F. T. S., & Tiwari, M. K. (2007). *Swarm intelligence: focus on ant and particle swarm optimization*. Gaborone, Botswana: I-Tech Publications.

Clerc, M. (2006). Particle swarm optimization. *International scientific and technical encyclopaedia*

Clerc, M., & Kennedy, J. (2002). The particle swarm: explosion, stability, and convergence in multi-dimensional complex space. *IEEE Transactions on Evolutionary Computation, 6*(1), 58–73. doi:10.1109/4235.985692

Coello-Coello, C. A., & Lechuga, M. S. (2002). MOPSO: a proposal for multiple objective particle swarm optimization. *The congress on evolutionary computation* (pp. 1051-1056)

Cooren, Y., Fakhfakh, M., Loulou, M., & Siarry, P. (2007). Optimizing second generation current conveyors using particle swarm optimization. In *Proceedings of the IEEE international conference on microelectronics* (pp. 378-381)

Courat, J. P., Raynaud, G., Mrad, I., & Siarry, P. (1994). Electronic component model minimization based on log simulated annealing. *IEEE Transactions on Circuits and Systems, 41*(12), 790–795. doi:10.1109/81.340841

Del-Rio, R., Medeiro, F., Perez-Verdu, B., Dela-Rosa, J. M., & Rodriguez-Vasquez, A. (2006). *CMOS cascade sigma-delta modulators for sensors and telecom.* New York: Springer.

Dinger, R. H. (1998). Engineering design optimization with genetic algorithm. In *Proceedings of the IEEE northcon conference* (pp. 114-119).

Dorigo, M., Dicaro, G., & Gambardella, L. M. (1999). Ant algorithms for discrete optimization. *Artificial life journal, 5*(2), 137-172.

Fakhfakh, M., Cooren, Y., Loulou, M., & Siarry, P. (2008). A particle swarm optimization technique used for the improvement of analog circuit performances. In Lazinica, A. (Ed.), *Particle Swarm Optimization* (pp. 169–182). Gaborone, Botswana: I-Tech Publications.

Fakhfakh, M., Loulou, M., & Masmoudi, N. (2007). Optimizing performances of switched current memory cells through a heuristic. *Analog Integrated Circuits and Signal Processing, 50*(2), 115–126. doi:10.1007/s10470-006-9009-5

Fakhfakh, M., Masmoudi, S., Tlelo-Cuautle, E., & Loulou, M. (2008). Synthesis of switched current memory cells using the nullor approach and application to the design of high performance SI sigma delta modulators. *WSEAS Transactions on electronics, 5*(6), 265-273

Graeb, H., Zizala, S., Eckmueller, J., & Antreich, K. (2001). The sizing rules method for analog integrated circuit design. In *Proceedings of the IEEE/ACM international conference on computer-aided design*

Grimbleby, J. B. (2000). Automatic analogue circuit synthesis using genetic algorithms. *The IEE Circuits. Devices and Systems, 147*(6), 319–323. doi:10.1049/ip-cds:20000770

Hughes, J. B., Macbeth, I. C., & Pattullo, D. M. (1990). Second generation switched current signal processing. In *Proceedings of the IEEE international symposium on circuits and system* (pp. 2805-2808).

Hughes, J. B., Worapishet, A., & Toumazou, C. (2000). Switched capacitors versus switched-currents: a theoretical comparison. In *Proceedings of the IEEE international symposium on circuits and systems* (pp. 409-412).

Kennedy, J., & Eberhart, R. C. (1995). Particle swarm optimization. In *Proceedings of the IEEE international conference on neural networks* (pp. 1942-1948)

Kirkpatrick, S., Gelatt, C. D., & Vecchi, M. P. (1983). Optimization by simulated annealing. *Journal of Science, 220*(4598), 671–680. doi:10.1126/science.220.4598.671

Loulou, M., Dallet, D., & Marchegay, P. (2000). A 3.3V switched-current second order sigma-delta modulator for audio applications. In *Proceedings of the IEEE international symposium on circuits and systems* (pp. 409-412).

Loulou, M., Dallet, D., Masmoudi, N., Marchegay, P., & Kamoun, L. (2004). A 3.3V, 10 bits, switched-current second order sigma-delta modulator. *Journal of analog integrated circuits and signal processing, 39*(1), 81-87

Luh, L., Choma, J. J., & Draper, J. (1998). A 50-MHz continuous-time switched-current $\Sigma\Delta$ modulator. In *Proceedings of the IEEE international symposium on circuits and systems* (pp. 579-582)

Marseguerra, M., & Zio, E. (2000). System design optimization by genetic algorithms. In *Proceedings of the IEEE reliability and maintainability symposium* (pp. 222-227)

Masmoudi, S., Fakhfakh, M., Loulou, M., Masmoudi, N., & Loumeau, P. (2007). A CMOS 80 MHz low-pass switched-current fourth order sigma-delta modulator. In *Proceedings of the international multi-conference on systems, signals and devices. Conference on sensors, circuits and instrumentation systems.*

Medeiro, F., Perez-Verdu, B., & Rodriguez-Vasquez, A. (1999). *Top-down design of high-performance sigma-delta modulators.* Dordrecht, The Netherlands: Kluwer.

Medeiro, F., Rodríguez-Macías, R., Fernández, F. V., Domínguez-Astro, R., Huertas, J. L., & Rodríguez-Vázquez, A. (1994). Global design of analog cells using statistical optimization techniques. *Analog Integrated Circuits and Signal Processing, 6*(3), 179–195. doi:10.1007/BF01238887

Norsworthly, S. R., Schreier, R., & Themes, G. C. (1997). *Delta sigma data converters: theory, design and simulation.* Washington, DC: IEEE Press.

O'Connor, I., & Kaiser, A. (2000). Automated synthesis of current memory cells. *IEEE Transactions on Computer-Aided Design of Integrated Circuits and Systems, 19*(4), 413–424. doi:10.1109/43.838991

Oliaei, O., & Loumeau, P. (1996). Current mode class AB design using floating voltage-source. *Electronics Letters, 32*(17), 1526–1527. doi:10.1049/el:19961065

Oliaei, O., Loumeau, P., & Aboushady, H. (1997). A switched current class AB delta-sigma modulators. In *Proceedings of the IEEE international symposium on circuits and systems* (pp. 393-396)

Raquel, C. R., & Naval, P. C. (2005). An Effective use of distance in multi-objective particle swarm optimization. In *Proceedings of the genetic and evolutionary computation conference* (pp. 257-364).

Reyes-Sierra, M., & Coello-Coello, C. A. (2006). Multi-objective particle swarm optimizers: a survey of the state-of-the-art. *International journal of computational intelligence research, 2*(3), 287-308.

Seshadri, A. (2009). *Multi-Objective Optimization using Evolutionary Algorithm.* Retrieved from http://www.mathworks.com/matlabcentral/fileexchange/10351

Siarry, P., Berthiau, G., Durbin, F., & Haussy, J. (1997). Enhanced simulated annealing for globally minimizing functions of many-continuous variables. *ACM Transactions on Mathematical Software, 23*(2), 209–228. doi:10.1145/264029.264043

Talbi, E. G. (2002). A taxonomy of hybrid meta-heuristics. *Journal of Heuristics, 5*(8), 541–564. doi:10.1023/A:1016540724870

Tan, N. (1997). *Switched-current design and implementation of oversampling A/D converters.* Berlin: Springer Verlag.

Tlelo-Cuautle, E., & Duarte-Villaseñor, M. A. (2008). Evolutionary electronics: automatic synthesis of analog circuits by GAs. In Ang, Y., Yin, S., & Bui, L. T. (Eds.), *Success in Evolutionary Computation* (pp. 165–187). Berlin: Springer Verlag. doi:10.1007/978-3-540-76286-7_8

Toumazou, C., Hughes, J. B., & Buttersby, N. C. (1993). *Switched currents an analogue technique for digital technology*. London: Peter Peregrinus.

Wang, F., & Harjani, R. (1997). *Design of modulators for oversampled converters*. New York: Springer.

Worapishet, A., Hughes, J. B., & Toumazou, C. (1999). Class AB technique for high performance switched-current memory cells. In *Proceedings of the IEEE international symposium on circuits and systems* (pp. 456-459)

Worapishet, A., Hughes, J. B., & Toumazou, C. (2000). Low-voltage class AB two-step sampling switched-currents. In *Proceedings of the IEEE international symposium on circuits and systems* (pp. 413-416).

This work was previously published in International Journal of Applied Metaheuristic Computing, Volume 1, Issue 2, edited by Peng-Yeng Yin, pp. 18-28, copyright 2010 by IGI Publishing (an imprint of IGI Global).

Chapter 11
A Reinforced Tabu Search Approach for 2D Strip Packing

Giglia Gómez-Villouta
Université d'Angers, France

Jean-Philippe Hamiez
Université d'Angers, France

Jin-Kao Hao
Université d'Angers, France

ABSTRACT

This paper discusses a particular "packing" problem, namely the two dimensional strip packing problem, where a finite set of objects have to be located in a strip of fixed width and infinite height. The variant studied considers regular items, rectangular to be precise, that must be packed without overlap, not allowing rotations. The objective is to minimize the height of the resulting packing. In this regard, the authors present a local search algorithm based on the well-known tabu search metaheuristic. Two important components of the presented tabu search strategy are reinforced in attempting to include problem knowledge. The fitness function incorporates a measure related to the empty spaces, while the diversification relies on a set of historically "frozen" objects. The resulting reinforced tabu search approach is evaluated on a set of well-known hard benchmark instances and compared with state-of-the-art algorithms.

INTRODUCTION

In packing problems, "small" items (also called "boxes", "modules", "objects", or "pieces" e.g.) of various shapes (regular or not) and dimensions have to be packed (i.e., located) without overlap, with rotation and "guillotine" cuts (see Figure 1)

DOI: 10.4018/978-1-4666-0270-0.ch011

allowed or not, in other "larger" items of regular forms or not[1]. These larger objects are usually called "containers" or "pallets" for the three-dimensional cases (3D, all dimensions fixed or infinite height) and "bins", "plates", or "(stock) sheets" (all dimensions fixed) or "strips" (only width fixed, infinite height) in 2D.

Objectives are, for instance, to minimize the number of containers or to maximize the mate-

Figure 1. The guillotine constraint imposes a pattern where the items can be extracted by a sequence of "edge-to-edge" cuts, i.e., the cutting tool cannot change of direction within the same cutting step (dark zones map wasted areas)

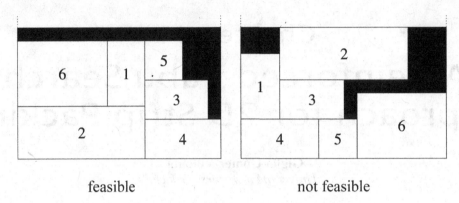

feasible   not feasible

rial used (hence to minimize the "trim loss", i.e. the wasted area). A huge number of practical or industrial applications are concerned, such as truck loading, cardboard packing, facilities, fashion, plant, machine, newspaper, or web page layout design, VLSI macro-cell placement, glass, cloth, metal, paper, or wood industries, dynamic memory allocation, meta-computing, multi-processor or publicity scheduling for instance. This may explain why (commercial) software packages exist, sometimes for a long time. See (Dowsland & Dowsland, 1992; Lodi et al., 2002; Wäscher et al., 2007) just to mention a few surveys.

These problems are usually generalizations or restrictions of the well-known NP-hard (or NP-complete for decision variants) quadratic assignment, bin packing, knapsack, or quadratic set covering problems. Packing problems are thus optimization or satisfaction problems (sometimes with multiple objectives) that are NP-hard or NP-complete in the general case (Fowler et al., 1981; Garey & Johnson, 1979).

This paper is dedicated to the NP-hard 2D Strip Packing Problem (2D-SPP) which can be informally stated as follows: Given a finite set of objects, pack all of them without overlap in one strip of an infinite height and fixed width (also called "basis") while minimizing the height of the resulting packing. The guillotine constraint is not considered here. Furthermore, all objects are regular (rectangular to be more precise) and cannot be rotated, i.e., they have a fixed orientation (Figure 1).

In this paper, we introduce CTS (for "Consistent Tabu Search"); a reinforced tabu search algorithm dedicated to the 2D-SPP. Compared with previous algorithms for the 2D-SPP, our CTS has several notable features. First, it handles a *consistent* neighborhood. Second, CTS evaluates packings, possibly partial, using *problem knowledge*. Finally, our algorithm includes a *diversification* mechanism relying on a set of historically "frozen" rectangles. Computational results suggest that CTS may be of great interest to solve the 2D-SPP.

In the two next sections, the 2D-SPP is formally stated and a brief description of various existing methods is given. Section 4 is devoted to the detailed presentation of our dedicated tabu search algorithm for the 2D-SPP. Experimental results are finally shown in Section 5 on a set of well-known benchmarks and compared with previous attempts including best performing state-of-the-art algorithms.

Figure 2. A strip with basic notations

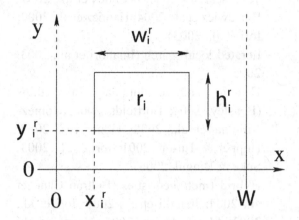

1. PROBLEM FORMULATION

A "strip" is a 2D vertical space with fixed width W and infinite height, see Figure 2. The bottom-left (BL) corner of the strip stands for the $(0, 0)$ point of a xy-plane where the x-axis (respectively y-axis) is the direction of the width (resp. height).

The set of $n \geq 2$ *Rectangles* to be positioned in the strip is $R = \{r_1,..., r_n\}$ where the weight (resp. height) of each object $r_{1 \leq i \leq n}$ is $0 < w_i^r \leq W$ (resp. $h_i^r > 0$).

According to these notations, the 2D-SPP is then to determine the (x_i^r, y_i^r) coordinates of the BL corner of all rectangles (i.e., the location of each $r_i \in R$ in the strip) so as to minimize the height of the resulting packing. This can be formally stated as follows:

Minimize f:

$$\max_{1 \leq i \leq n}\{y_i^r + h_i^r\} \tag{1}$$

Subject to:

$$0 \leq x_i^r \leq W - w_i^r \wedge y_i^r \geq 0 \tag{2}$$

$$\wedge(x_i^r \geq x_j^r + w_j^r \vee x_i^r + w_i^r \leq x_j^r \tag{3}$$

$$\vee y_i^r \geq y_j^r + h_j^r \vee y_i^r + h_i^r \leq y_j^r) \tag{4}$$

where (2) forces each rectangle r_i to be inside the strip and (3–4) specify that any two r_i and $r_{j \neq i}$ objects must not overlap horizontally or vertically.

2. LITERATURE REVIEW

Only a few *exact* methods are available for 2D-SPP or closely related problems (see Section 3.1), while a wide range of *approximate* heuristics has been reported (Section 3.2). Among these strategies, the *greedy randomized adaptive search procedure* from Alvarez-Valdes et al. (2008) and the hybrid *hyperheuristic + intensification / diversification walk* strategy from Neveu et al. (2008) are probably the best performing ones for 2D-SPP (these two effective methods are briefly summarized in Sect. 3.2).

2.1. Exact Methods

These approaches are often based on implicit enumeration of the search space. They are thus usually limited to **small** instances. However, given sufficient time, they can in theory either find a solution (optimal for optimization problems) or prove that none exists (for satisfaction problems).

The *branch-and-bound* algorithm presented by Martello et al. (2003) relies on a 2D-SPP relaxation (basically, cutting each object $r_i \in R$ into items of height lower than h_i^r) that can be solved as a particular NP-hard one-dimensional bin-packing problem (with "side" constraints). This leads to a lower bound on f_{OPT}, the *OPT*imum value of (1), better than those previously proposed.

Recently, two *branch-and-bound* approaches faster than those from Martello et al. (2003) were designed by Kenmochi et al. (2009). Including many components, dynamic programming cuts for instance, the 2D-SPP *optimization* problem (as formally defined in Section 2) is reduced here to the "perfect packing problem" which is a *satisfaction* problem (determine if a packing without wasted space exists), sometimes by adding new objects.

Other (recent) exact methods related to 2D-SPP, or bounds, can be found, e.g., in (Belov et al., 2009; Clautiaux et al., 2008; Soh et al., 2008).

2.2. Approximate Heuristics

These approaches include, e.g., "greedy" constructive strategies or "(meta) heuristics". While they loss the completeness of exact methods, they can handle **large** instances and usually obtain good quality solutions in reasonable time. In this section, we review two best-performing algorithms and discuss about other representative heuristics related to 2D-SPP.

Alvarez-Valdes et al. (2008) proposed a *Greedy Randomized Adaptive Search Procedure* (GRASP) for 2D-SPP. It is a multi-start scheme that iteratively builds a feasible solution in a greedy way following various dynamic pseudo-random selection rules. This solution is then modified to try to correct previous wrong random choices, for use in the next greedy step, by different "simple local search" algorithms.

Neveu et al. (2008) developed a hybrid approach combining a *hyperheuristic* (HH) with the *intensification / diversification walk* strategy (IDW). It starts (HH phase) with a greedy packing, where the selection rule possibly alternates between different criteria, e.g., in a round robin manner. This solution is then perturbed (IDW phase) by iteratively moving an object at the top of the strip below its current location. If such a perturbation generates overlaps, they are repaired using a greedy heuristic (possibly randomly chosen).

Other representative approaches for 2D-SPP (or closely related variants) include, for instance:

- Simulated annealing (Burke et al., 2009; Hopper & Turton, 2001; Soke & Bingul, 2006).

- Tabu search (Alvarez-Valdes et al., 2007; Błażewicz et al., 2004; Hamiez et al., 2009; Iori et al., 2003).

- Iterated local search (Imahori et al., 2003, 2005).

- Genetic and evolutionary algorithms (Beasley, 2004; Bortfeldt, 2006; Gómez-Villouta et al., 2008; Gonçalves, 2007; Hopper & Turton, 2001; Iori et al., 2003; Soke & Bingul, 2006).

- Hybrid (meta)heuristics (Beltrán Cano et al., 2004; Ibaraki et al., 2008; Iori et al., 2003; Mir & Imam, 2001; Neveu et al., 2008; Yeung & Tang, 2004).

- Hyperheuristics (Araya et al., 2008; Garrido & Riff, 2007; Terashima-Marín et al., 2005).

Note that *polynomial-time approximation schemes* with (asymptotic or absolute) performance guarantee are also available for these problems (Harren & van Stee, 2009; Jansen & van Stee, 2005).

3. CTS: A CONSISTENT TABU SEARCH FOR 2D-SPP

We first recall here the fundamentals of tabu search (Section 4.1) and how the problem is addressed (Section 4.2). Next sections (4.3–4.8) describe then the problem-specific components of our CTS, where all p variables (with subscripts) are *parameters* whose values will be given in the experimentation part (Section 5.1). The general CTS procedure is finally summarized in Sect. 0.

3.1. A Brief Review of Tabu Search

Tabu search is an advanced metaheuristic designed for tackling hard combinatorial optimization or satisfaction problems (Glover & Laguna, 1997). It relies on a neighborhood relation as well as some forms of memory and learning strategies to explore effectively a search space. Let (S, f) be our search problem where S and f are respectively the search space and the optimization objective.

A "neighborhood" N over S is any function that associates to each individual $s \in S$ some solutions $N(s) \subset S$. Any solution $s' \in N(s)$ is called a neighboring solution or simply a neighbor of s. For a given neighborhood N, a solution s is a "local optimum" with respect to N if s is the best among the solutions in $N(s)$. The notion of neighborhood can be explained in terms of the "move" operator. Typically applying a move μ to a solution s changes slightly s and leads to a neighboring solution s'. This transition from a solution to a neighbor is denoted by $s' = s \oplus \mu$. Let $\Gamma(s)$ be the set of all possible moves which can be applied to solution s, then the neighborhood $N(s)$ of s can be defined by: $N(s) = \{s \oplus \mu : \mu \in \Gamma(s)\}$.

A typical tabu search algorithm begins with an initial configuration in S and proceeds iteratively to visit a series of locally best configurations following the neighborhood. At each iteration, a *best* neighbor $s' \in N(s)$ is sought to replace the current configuration s even if s' does not improve s in terms of the cost function.

To avoid the problem of possible cycling and to allow the search to go beyond local optima, tabu search introduces the notion of "tabu list", one of the most important components of the method. A tabu list τ is a special short term memory that maintains a selective history composed of previously encountered solutions or, more generally, pertinent attributes (or moves) of such solutions. A simple strategy based on this short term memory consists in preventing previously visited solutions from being reconsidered for the next p_τ iterations (p_τ, called "tabu tenure", is problem dependent). Now, at each iteration, tabu search searches for a best neighbor from this dynamically modified neighborhood.

3.2. Solving Scheme

Let 2D-SPP$_{k>0}$ be the following *satisfaction* problem: Is there a solution s to 2D-SPP such that $f(s) \leq k$? Obviously, 2D-SPP is equivalent to find the lowest k such that 2D-SPP$_k$ holds.

CTS treats the 2D-SPP *optimization* problem (minimizing the height f) as successive 2D-SPP$_k$. Starting from a complete packing s_0 of height $f(s_0)$, e.g. obtained with a greedy method (see Section 4.4), CTS tackles 2D-SPP$_k$ with decreasing values of $f(s_0)$ for k. To be more precise, if CTS finds a solution s to 2D-SPP$_k$, it then tries to solve 2D-SPP$_{f(s)-pf}$ ($p_f > 0$, for decrement of the height).

3.3. Search Space: A Direct Representation

Some approaches for 2D-SPP, or closely related variants, consider a (quite natural or, at least, intuitive) search space S composed of the set of (all) permutations of the objects, see (Gómez-Villouta et al., 2008; Iori et al., 2003; Soke & Bingul, 2006; Yeung & Tang, 2004) for instance.

More precisely, for a given n-set R of objects to be packed, a permutation $s \in S$ of $[1,\ldots, n]$ is built (statically or dynamically) using a *selection heuristic* σ^2 which is followed by a given *placement heuristic* ϕ (or "decoder"). In other words, given a selection operator σ and a ϕ decoder, one can locate all the objects using ϕ and according to the order imposed by σ, see Algorithm 1 where s_ρ is the element at rank ρ in permutation s. The problem is then to find a particular permutation $s_* \in S$ (from the $n!$ available) such that the resulting packing is optimal, i.e. $f(s_*) = f_{OPT}$.

Note that many (usually greedy) selection / placement heuristics have been investigated according to various criteria (Alvarez-Valdes et al., 2007, 2008; Aşik & Özcan, 2009; Burke et al., 2009).

CTS does not code packings with permutations but adopts a *direct representation* where a 2D-SPP$_k$ packing $s \in S$ (optimal or not, possibly partial) is a $\{L, E\}$ set[3]:

- $L \subseteq R$ is the set of rectangles properly Located in the strip, i.e. r_i verifies (2) with $y_i^r + h_i^r \leq k \; \forall \; r_i \in L$ and (r_i, r_j) verifies (3–4) $\forall \, (r_i, r_{j \neq i}) \in L \times L$. Let the set of "free" objects, i.e., rectangles not (yet) located in the strip, be $\overline{L} = R \setminus L$.

- E is a set of rectangular *E*mpty spaces in the strip. Each empty space $e_i \in E$ is characterized by the coordinates (x_i^e, y_i^e) of its BL corner, a width $0 < w_i^e \leq W$, and a height $0 < h_i^e \leq k$, with $0 \leq x_i^e \leq W - w_i^e$ and $0 \leq y_i^e \leq k - h_i^e$.

Each empty space $e_i \in E$ is a maximal rectangle[4], i.e. e_i is not included in another empty space e_j: $\forall \, (e_i, e_{j \neq i}) \in E \times E$, $x_i^e < x_j^e \; \vee$ $x_i^e + w_i^e > x_j^e + w_j^e$ $\vee$ $y_i^e < y_j^e$ $\vee$ $y_i^e + h_i^e > y_j^e + h_j^e$.

3.4. Initial Configuration

Tabu search needs an initial configuration s_0 that specifies where the search begins in the search space S. CTS uses Algorithm 1 to construct s_0, where the ϕ placement heuristic is the "Bottom Left Fill" procedure (BLF) from Baker et al. (1980) and

Algorithm 1. The simplest greedy algorithm for 2D-SPP

Require: A selection operator σ and a placement heuristic ϕ
$R' \leftarrow R$
for $\rho = 1$ **to** n **do**
Select a rectangle $r_i \in R'$ according to σ
$R' \leftarrow R' \setminus \{r_i\}$
$s_\rho \leftarrow i$
Locate the r_i object in the strip according to ϕ
end for
return $f(s)$ and s

the σ selection operator orders all rectangles $r_i \in R$ first by decreasing width, secondly by decreasing height (when two objects r_i and $r_{j \neq i}$ have the same width), randomly last if necessary (r_i and $r_{j \neq i}$ have the same width and height).

BLF is capable of filling enclosed wasted areas; see Figure 3 where rectangle r_5 has to be packed. Notice that, according to the way BLF is implemented, its worst time complexity goes from $O(n^3)$ (Hopper & Turton, 2001) to $O(n^2)$ (Chazelle, 1983) for a permutation of n objects. We employed this decoder / order since some previous experiments (Hopper & Turton, 2001; Imahori et al., 2007) suggested that the BLF placement algorithm usually outperforms other decoders[5].

Note that the initial packing s_0 is a solution to 2D-SPP$_k$ $\forall \, k \geq f(s_0)$. So, s_0 provides a trivial upper bound for 2D-SPP: $f_{OPT} \leq f(s_0)$.

3.5. Cost Function

This measure, also called "evaluation" or "fitness" function, is a key component of tabu search because it guides the choices of the algorithm at each iteration.

Let the *M*aximum *w*idth and *h*eight of free rectangles be respectively $M_w = \max_{r_i \in \overline{L}} \{w_i^r\}$ and $M_h = \max_{r_i \in \overline{L}} \{h_i^r\}$, the number of free objects with width M_w be $\alpha = \left| \{r_i \in \overline{L} : w_i^r = M_w \} \right|$, the "density" of a 2D-SPP$_k$ packing be $\delta = \sum_{e_j \in E} (W - x_j^e)(k - y_j^e)$[6], and the *M*aximum *a*rea of empty spaces be $M_a = \max_{e_j \in E} \{w_j^e \cdot h_j^e\}$. CTS uses the c function (for "*c*ost", to be minimized) formally defined by (5) to evaluate a (possibly partial) 2D-SPP$_k$ packing $s \in S$, see also Figure 4 for a numerical example.

Figure 3. Basically, BLF places each object at the left-most and lowest possible free area

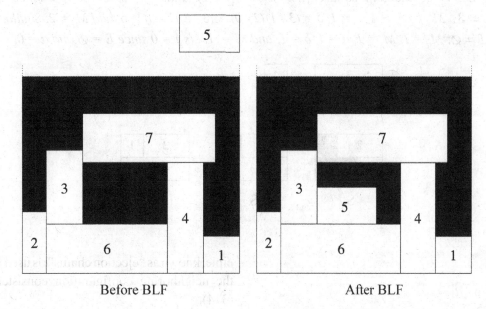

Before BLF   After BLF

$$c(s) = \begin{cases} \alpha M_w M_h & \text{if } E = \theta \\ \dfrac{\alpha \delta M_w M_h / M_a}{M_a} & \text{otherwise} \end{cases}$$

(5)

Roughly speaking, the value $c(s)$ measures the quality of solution s with respect to 2D-SPPk, the current satisfaction problem considered:

- $c(s) = 0$ signifies that s is a solution to 2D-SPP$_k$. Furthermore, s is usually called a "perfect" packing if it does not include an empty space ($E = \emptyset$). In this case, s is an *optimal* solution to 2D-SPP (i.e., 2D-SPP$_k$, admits no solution $\forall\, k' < k$): $f_{OPT} = k$.

- $c(s) > 0$ indicates a *partial* packing. Here, $E = \emptyset$ (no empty space) means that 2D-SPP$_k$, has no solution $\forall\, k' \leq k$ and that a trivial *lower bound* has been found for 2D-SPP: $f_{OPT} > k$.

The cost and objective functions, c (5) and f (1) respectively, are used to compare any two

packings s_1 and s_2 (possibly partial): With respect to 2D-SPP$_k$, s_1 is said to be "better" than s_2 if the evaluation of s_1 is lower than that of s_2, formally $c(s_1) < c(s_2)$. However, note that the c fitness function is inadequate when s_1 and s_2 are both solutions to 2D-SPP$_k$, i.e. when $c(s_1) = c(s_2) = 0$. In this case, s_1 is better than s_2 if $f(s_1) < f(s_2)$.

Other evaluation functions have been proposed for 2D-SPP. Neveu et al. (2007) consider the number u of "*u*nits filled by rectangles on the highest line of the strip" to define $c_N(s) = (f(s) - 1) W + u$. Hamiez et al. (2009) proposed a similar fitness function, relying on the set $\lceil R \rceil \subseteq R$ of rectangles at the top of the strip, formally defined by (6) where $\lceil R \rceil = \{ r_i \in R : y_i^r + h_i^r > H_* - p_H \}$ p_H is an integer parameter, and H_* is the best height found, initially the height $f(s_0)$ of the starting solution s_0. One can observe that c_N and c_H compute a measure solely based on rectangles at the top of the strip and do not consider what happens below these rectangles. Our c cost function seems thus more relevant since it precisely includes a measure (the δ component) related to this useful information.

Figure 4. Let r_1 be the unit square (i.e. $w_1^r = h_1^r = 1$) and $k = 2$. $c(s_1) = 9$ since $E \neq \varnothing$, $M_w = w_3^r = 3$, $M_h = h_3^r = 1$, $\alpha = 1$, $\delta = (3 - 1)(2 - 0) + (3 - 2)(2 - 0) = 6$, and $M_a = 2$. Similarly, $c(s_2) = 1$ since $E \neq \varnothing$, $M_w = 1$, $M_h = 1$, $\alpha = 1$, $\delta = 1$, and $M_a = 1$. $c(s_3) = 0$ since $E = \varnothing$ and $\alpha = 0$.

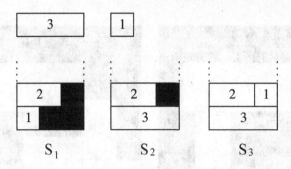

$$S_1 \qquad S_2 \qquad S_3$$

$$c_H(s) = \begin{cases} 0 \text{ if } \lceil R \rceil = \varnothing \\ \sum_{r_i \in \lceil R \rceil} w_i^r * (y_i^r + h_i^r - H_* + p_H) & \text{otherwise} \end{cases}$$

$$(6)$$

3.6. Neighborhood

The neighborhood N is another key element of tabu search. It defines a structure of the search space S and determines the paths the algorithm will follow to explore S.

The main goal of the CTS neighborhood is to empty the set of free objects, i.e., the set $\bar{L}$ of rectangles not yet placed in the strip. Basically, it tries to locate a free rectangle r_i in the strip (r_i moves then from $\bar{L}$ to L), at the BL corner either of an empty space (defining a sub-neighborhood N_E, described in Section 4.6.1) or of another placed object (defining N_L, Section 4.6.2).

This location for object r_i may generate overlaps with a set $L_i \subseteq L$ of other rectangles already in the strip:

$$L_i = \begin{cases} r_{j \neq i} \in L : x_i^r < x_j^r + w_j^r \wedge x_i^r + \\ w_i^r > x_j^r \wedge y_i^r < y_j^r + h_j^r \wedge y_i^r + h_i^r > y_j^r \end{cases}$$

. All objects overlapping with the r_i rectangle are thus removed from the strip to repair these overlaps ($\forall r_j \in L_i$, r_j moves from L to $\bar{L}$). This prin-

ciple, known as "ejection chains", is used to make the neighboring configuration consistent with (3–4).

Finally, notice that locating a rectangle in the strip and the possible ejection of all overlapping objects imply updates of the set of empty spaces (E). This is done using the efficient "incremental" procedures detailed in (Neveu et al., 2008).

3.6.1 Neighborhood N_E: Consider the Empty Spaces

CTS examines two cases here, with two different objectives: To reduce the number of free rectangles, i.e. to minimize $|\bar{L}|$ (defining $N_E^{|\bar{L}|}$), or to make the packing *Denser* (N_E^D).

The case of $N_E^{|\bar{L}|}$. E. All free objects $r_i \in \bar{L}$ are tried to be located in the strip to the BL corner of all empty spaces $e_j \in E$ such that r_i fits entirely in e_j. More formally, r_i and e_j must verify $x_j^e + w_i^r \leq W \wedge y_j^e + h_i^r \leq k \wedge w_j^e \geq w_i^r \wedge h_j^r \geq h_i^r$. This generates $|\bar{L}|$ sets $N_E^{|\bar{L}|}(s, i)$ of neighbors for configuration s (some possibly empty), $N_E^{|\bar{L}|}(s)$ being the union of these sets: $N_E^{|\bar{L}|}(s) = \bigcup_{r_i \in \bar{L}} N_E^{|\bar{L}|}(s, i)$.

Note that $N_E^{|\bar{L}|}(s) \neq \emptyset$ means that there is at least one free rectangle $r_i \in \bar{L}$ and one empty space $e_j \in E$ such that r_i fits in e_j, i.e., that the number of free objects can be reduced. Furthermore, in this case, locating r_i will generate no overlap ($L_i = \emptyset$), hence no repairing is needed.

The case of N_E^D. Here again, all free rectangles $r_i \in \bar{L}$ are tried to be located to the BL corner of all empty spaces $e_j \in E$ but the previous condition on e_j and r_i is relaxed to allow overlaps. More formally, r_i and e_j must only verify $x_j^e + w_i^r \leq W \wedge y_j^e + h_i^r \leq k$.

Note that $N_E^D(s) = \emptyset$ means either, $\forall\,(r_i, e_j) \in \bar{L} \times E$, that the empty space e_j is located rather to the right (top, respectively) of the strip and placing the r_i rectangle in e_j will violate (2) since $x_j^e + w_i^r > W$ (resp. will not follow the definition of 2D-SPP$_k$ since $y_j^e + h_i^r > k$) or that it is forbidden to remove at least one rectangle overlapping with the r_i object (this is due to some restrictions described in Sect. 0).

3.6.2 Neighborhood N_L: Consider All Rectangles Already Packed

From the current configuration s, all free objects $r_i \in \bar{L}$ are tried to be located to the BL corner of all already packed rectangles $r_j \in L$ such that r_i and r_j have different sizes, locating r_i will respect (2), and the resulting packings will follow the definition of 2D-SPP$_k$. More formally, r_i and r_j must verify
$$\left(w_i^r \neq w_j^r \vee h_i^r \neq h_j^r\right) \wedge x_j^r + w_i^r \leq W \wedge y_j^r + h_i^r \leq k$$

This generates $|\bar{L}|$ sets $N_L(s, i)$ of neighbors for the configuration s with $0 \leq |N_L(s, i)| \leq |L|$: $N_L(s)$ is the union of these sets. Similarly to N_E^D, note that $N_L(s) = \emptyset$ means that all overlapping objects cannot be removed from the strip (see Sect. 0).

3.6.3 Search strategy

Our neighborhood N is composed of the three sub-neighborhoods described above: $N_E^{|\bar{L}|}$ and N_E^D (Section 4.6.1), and N_L (Section 4.6.2). They are explored by CTS in a hierarchical way: $N_E^{|\bar{L}|}$ is always tried the first, then N_E^D is used only if $N_E^{|\bar{L}|}$ is not applicable (i.e., empty), N_L being (possibly) considered the last. This scheme is more formally detailed in Algorithm 2.

Note that if configuration s has no neighbor, i.e. $N(s) = N_E^{|\bar{L}|}(s) = N_E^D(s) = N_L(s) = \emptyset$, no move is performed and diversification is invoked (see Sect. 4.8).

3.7. Tabu List

At current iteration m, since a CTS move from solution s to a neighbor $s' \in N(s)$ consists in locating one free rectangle $r_i \in \bar{L}$ in the strip, it seems quite natural to forbid object r_i leaving the strip from configuration s'. This "reverse" move will then be stored in the tabu list τ for a duration $0 < p_\tau \leq n$ (integer) to indicate that r_i cannot be removed from the strip at least up to iteration $m + p_\tau$.

Note that the tabu list τ is made empty at the beginning of the search or when CTS finds a solution to the current satisfaction problem considered (2D-SPP$_k$), i.e., if there is no free rectangle at all ($\bar{L} = \emptyset$).

3.8. Diversification

Let s_* be the overall best complete packing, according to (1), found by CTS at iteration m_* (initially s_* is the initial configuration s_0 introduced in Sect. 4.4 with $m_* = 0$).

When a solution s has no neighbor (i.e., $N(s) = \emptyset$) or s_* keeps unchanged for a number $p_* > 0$ of iterations, CTS first resets the tabu list τ and reloads s_* in s ($s \leftarrow s_*$, $\tau \leftarrow \emptyset$). This new current

Algorithm 2. The neighborhood is explored in a hierarchical way

---

Require: A configuration $s = \{L, E\}$

if $N_E^{|L|}(s) \neq \emptyset$ then return $N_E^{|L|}(s)$

else if $N_E^D(s) \neq \emptyset$ then return $N_E^D(s)$

  else if $N_L(s) \neq \emptyset$ then return $N_L(s)$

    else return $\emptyset$

end if

---

complete packing s is then perturbed according to two different *Diversification* schemes called D_I (for "*I*nterchange", performed with probability p_D) and D_T (for "*T*etris-like", probability $1 - p_D$). After perturbation, p_* supplementary moves are given to CTS to update the overall best complete packing s_*.

3.8.1 D_I: A Basic Perturbation

L and $\bar{L}$ are first modified according to 2D-SPP$_k$ with $k = f(s_*) - p_f$: $L \leftarrow \{r_i \in R : y_i^r + h_i^r \leq k\}$, $\bar{L} \leftarrow R \setminus L$. Diversification D_I considers then all $(r_i, r_j) \in L \times \bar{L}$ such that the r_i packed rectangle and the r_j free object have different sizes, more formally r_i and r_j verify $\left(w_i^r \neq w_j^r \vee h_i^r \neq h_j^r \right) \wedge x_i^r + w_j^r \leq W \wedge y_i^r + h_j^r \leq k$. It simply interchanges two such elements (randomly selected) and makes r_j tabu.

Note that locating the free object r_j at the place of r_i (i.e., swapping r_j from $\bar{L}$ to L and r_i from L to $\bar{L}$) may cause overlaps. In this case, repairing is done like in Section 4.6.

3.8.2 D_T: A perturbation based on the history

During the overall search process, CTS keeps for each rectangle $r_i \in R$ the number F_i (for "Frequency") of times r_i leaved the strip, i.e. the number of times r_i swaps from L to $\bar{L}$ [7].

The D_T diversification scheme considers a π_F permutation that orders all objects $r_i \in R$ first by increasing frequencies, secondly by decreasing widths (when $F_i = F_{j \neq i}$), then by decreasing heights ($w_i^r = w_{j \neq i}^r$), randomly last if necessary ($h_i^r = h_{j \neq i}^r$). Let the set $\lfloor F \rfloor$ be composed of the first p_τ elements of π_F.

All rectangles $r_i \in \lfloor F \rfloor$ are first temporarily removed from the strip and their frequencies are updated[8]. Then, the partial packing is pushed down to the basis of the strip, like in the famous Tetris game. Finally, all objects $r_i \in \lfloor F \rfloor$ are sorted like in Section 4.4 and relocated in the strip with BLF, see Figure 5.

CTS deals now with 2D-SPP$_k$ with $k = f(s) - p_f$: $L \leftarrow \{r_i \in R : y_i^r + h_i^r \leq k\}$, $\bar{L} \leftarrow R \setminus L$. This means that CTS possibly considers 2D-SPP$_k$ problems with $k \geq f(s_0) \geq f(s_*)$.

3.9. CTS: The General Procedure

The CTS procedure is summarized in Algorithm 3. It requires an initial complete packing (Section 4.4). Then CTS proceeds iteratively to solve a series of 2D-SPP$_k$ satisfaction problems. If it finds a solution s to 2D-SPP$_k$ (i.e., $\bar{L} = \emptyset$), it then tries to solve the next 2D-SPP$_{f(s)-pf}$ problem (see lines 3–6). Note that $f(s) = f(s_*)$ (line 4) may occur only after diversification D_T (see Section 4.8) or at the beginning of the search process.

While it is not mentioned here for simplicity, note that CTS can also end before reaching the $p_M \geq 0$ *M*aximum number of allowed moves (line 2). This may occur each time the overall best complete packing s_* is updated (lines 1 and 4) whenever the optimum height f_{OPT} (or an upper bound) is known and $f(s_*) \leq f_{OPT}$.

Figure 5. The D_T diversification. Surprisingly, experiments showed that almost all rectangles with lowest frequency (F) were located close to the bottom of the strip.

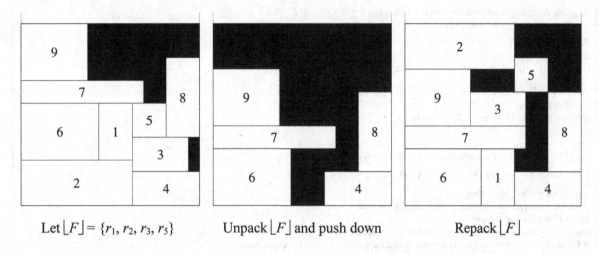

Let $\lfloor F \rfloor = \{r_1, r_2, r_3, r_5\}$ Unpack $\lfloor F \rfloor$ and push down   Repack $\lfloor F \rfloor$

4. EXPERIMENTATIONS

We use the complete set of the 21 well-known (perfect) instances defined in (Hopper & Turton, 2001)[9] to assess the performance of our CTS algorithm. These instances (or a subset of them) are largely studied in the literature. The main characteristics of these instances, including their known optimal height f_{OPT}, are given in Figure 6.

Notice that the instances of categories C4–C7 are very difficult because, to our knowledge, none algorithm is known to be able to optimally solve them. Indeed, some studies don't even report computational results for them, perhaps due to the (very) large size of these instances. Further-more, the difficulty sometimes also holds for small size instances from categories C1–C3. In par-ticular, various studies report more computa-tional effort for C1P2, C2P2, or C3P2 or never reach (or are more distant from) an optimal solu-tion for these three specific instances compared to the other similar instances within the same categories.

4.1. Experimentation Conditions

CTS is coded in the C programming language ("gcc" compiler). All computational results were obtained running CTS on a computer equipped with a 2.83 Ghz quad-core Intel® Xeon® E5440 processor and 8 Gb RAM[10]. The values of the CTS parameters are:

- $p_f = 1$. To build the starting configuration of 2D-SPP$_k$, the current satisfaction problem considered.
- $p_\approx \in [0.4, …, 0.8]$. Probability that a com-plete packing s replaces the overall best complete packing s_*, according to (1), whenever $f(s) = f(s_*)$.
- $p_\tau \in [2, …, 6]$. Tabu tenure.
- $p_* \in [200, …, 500]$. Maximum number of moves to update s_*.
- $p_D \in [0.7, …, 1]$. Probability to apply di-versification D_T.
- $p_M \in [1\,000\,000, …, 20\,000\,000]$. Maximum number of allowed moves per run.

Algorithm 3. An overview of CTS

Require: A starting configuration $s = \{L, E\}$ such that $L = R$ // Hence $\overline{L} = \varnothing$
$m \leftarrow 0$, $s_* \leftarrow s$, $m_* \leftarrow 0$ // Initialization
while $m \leq p_M$ **do**
if $\overline{L} = \varnothing$ **then**
if $f(s) < f(s_*)$ **or** ($f(s) = f(s_*)$ **and** some probability p_* is verified) **then** $s_* \leftarrow s$, $m_* \leftarrow m$
$L \leftarrow \left\{ r_i \in R : y_i^r + h_i^r \leq f(s) - p_f \right\}$, $\overline{L} \leftarrow R \setminus L$
$\tau \leftarrow \varnothing$ // Tabu list
if $N(s) = \varnothing$ **then** $Div \leftarrow$ true // To *Diversify*
else
$m \leftarrow m + 1$
Let $\lfloor N(s) \rfloor$ be the set of the *best evaluated* neighbors s' of s according to (5):
$$\lfloor N(s) \rfloor = \left\{ s_1' \in N(s) : \forall s_2' \in N(s), c(s_1') \leq c(s_2') \right\}$$
if $c(s') > 0 \; \forall \, s' \in \lfloor N(s) \rfloor$ **then**
if $(m - m_*)$ mod $p_* = 0$ **then** $Div \leftarrow$ true **else** $Div \leftarrow$ false
Select $s' \in \lfloor N(s) \rfloor$ at random
else $Div \leftarrow$ false, select $s' \in \lfloor N(s) \rfloor$ minimizing (1) at random
if Div **then** $s \leftarrow s_*$, $\tau \leftarrow \varnothing$, modify s using D_I or D_T according to p_D // Diversification
else $s \leftarrow s'$, update τ
return $f(s_*)$ and s_*

The comparison is based on the percentage gap γ of a solution s from the optimum or its best bound (f_{OPT}): $\gamma(s) = 100(1 - f_{OPT} / f(s))$. The lower is $\gamma(s)$, the better is the solution s. For CTS, mean gap $\overline{\gamma}$ (resp. best gap γ_*) is averaged over 5 runs (resp. over best runs only).

4.2. Computational Results

CTS is compared in Figure 7 with five state-of-the-art algorithms that deal with the whole set of instances, or at least categories C1–C6.

We consider two Tabu Search procedures, denoted as TS1 (Iori et al., 2003)[11] and TS2 (Hamiez et al., 2009), one of the most effective Genetic Algorithm (GA) from Bortfeldt (2006), and two best performing state-of-the-art ap-

Figure 6. Main characteristics of the test problems defined in (Hopper & Turton, 2001). These instances are grouped by "categories" according to the f_{OPT} value.

Category	Instances	W	n	f_{OPT}
C1	C1P1, C1P2, C1P3	20	16, 17, 16	20
C2	C2P1, C2P2, C2P3	40	25	15
C3	C3P1, C3P2, C3P3	60	28, 29, 28	30
C4	C4P1, C4P2, C4P3	60	49	60
C5	C5P1, C5P2, C5P3	60	73	90
C6	C6P1, C6P2, C6P3	80	97	120
C7	C7P1, C7P2, C7P3	160	196, 197, 196	240

Figure 7. Mean and best percentage gaps ($\bar{\gamma}$ and γ_* resp.) on instances from Hopper & Turton (2001)

Instances	CTS		TS1	TS2		GA		GRASP		HH+IDW	
	$\bar{\gamma}$	γ_*	γ_*	$\bar{\gamma}$	γ_*	$\bar{\gamma}$	γ_*	$\bar{\gamma}$	γ_*	$\bar{\gamma}$	γ_*
C1P1	0.00	0.00	9.09	0.00	0.00	–	–	0.00	0.00	–	–
C1P2	0.00	0.00	9.09	4.76	0.00	–	–	0.00	0.00	–	–
C1P3	0.00	0.00	4.76	0.00	0.00	–	–	0.00	0.00	–	–
Mean C1	0.00	0.00	7.65	1.59	0.00	1.59	1.59	0.00	0.00	0.48	0.00
C2P1	0.00	0.00	0.00	0.00	0.00	–	–	0.00	0.00	–	–
C2P2	0.00	0.00	6.25	0.00	0.00	–	–	0.00	0.00	–	–
C2P3	0.00	0.00	0.00	0.00	0.00	–	–	0.00	0.00	–	–
Mean C2	0.00	0.00	2.08	0.00	0.00	3.33	2.08	0.00	0.00	1.87	0.00
C3P1	0.00	0.00	3.23	0.00	0.00	–	–	0.00	0.00	–	–
C3P2	2.60	0.00	9.09	3.23	3.23	–	–	3.23	3.23	–	–
C3P3	0.00	0.00	9.09	0.00	0.00	–	–	0.00	0.00	–	–
Mean C3	0.87	0.00	7.14	1.08	1.08	3.16	3.16	1.08	1.08	2.58	1.08
C4P1	1.64	1.64	6.25	1.64	1.64	–	–	1.64	1.64	–	–
C4P2	1.64	1.64	4.76	1.64	1.64	–	–	1.64	1.64	–	–
C4P3	1.64	1.64	3.23	1.64	1.64	–	–	1.64	1.64	–	–
Mean C4	1.64	1.64	4.75	1.64	1.64	3.52	2.70	1.64	1.64	2.43	1.64
C5P1	2.17	2.17	5.26	1.10	1.10	–	–	1.10	1.10	–	–
C5P2	1.96	1.10	3.23	1.10	1.10	–	–	1.10	1.10	–	–
C5P3	1.10	1.10	6.25	1.10	1.10	–	–	1.10	1.10	–	–
Mean C5	1.74	1.46	4.91	1.10	1.10	2.03	1.46	1.10	1.10	1.78	1.10
C6P1	1.80	1.64	4.76	1.64	0.83	–	–	1.56	0.83	–	–
C6P2	2.44	2.44	3.23	0.83	0.83	–	–	1.56	0.83	–	–
C6P3	2.28	1.64	3.23	1.64	0.83	–	–	1.56	0.83	–	–
Mean C6	2.17	1.91	3.74	1.37	0.83	1.72	1.64	1.56	0.83	1.75	1.10
C7P1	2.20	2.04	–	1.23	1.23	–	–	1.64	1.64	–	–
C7P2	2.04	2.04	–	1.23	1.23	–	–	1.19	0.83	–	–
C7P3	2.20	2.04	–	1.23	1.23	–	–	1.23	1.23	–	–
Mean C7	2.15	2.04	–	1.23	1.23	1.52	1.23	1.36	1.23	1.42	1.10
C1–C2	0.00	0.00	4.86	0.79	0.00	2.46	1.84	0.00	0.00	1.18	0.00
C1–C3	0.29	0.00	5.62	0.89	0.36	2.69	2.28	0.36	0.36	1.64	0.36
C1–C4	0.63	0.41	5.40	1.08	0.68	2.90	2.38	0.68	0.68	1.84	0.68
C1–C5	0.85	0.62	5.31	1.08	0.76	2.73	2.20	0.76	0.76	1.83	0.76
C1–C6	1.07	0.83	5.04	1.13	0.77	2.57	2.11	0.90	0.77	1.82	0.82
C1–C7	1.22	1.01	–	1.14	0.84	2.41	1.98	0.96	0.84	1.76	0.86
#f_{OPT}/21	9		2	8		–		8		8	

proaches: The *Greedy Randomized Adaptive Search Procedure* (GRASP) from Alvarez-Valdes et al. (2008) and the hybrid *HyperHeuristic + Intensification / Diversification Walk* strategy (HH+IDW) from Neveu et al. (2008).

In Figure 7, "–" marks (for HH+IDW, GA, or TS1) mean either that $\bar{\gamma}$ or γ_* cannot be computed or that we did not found the information in (Bortfeldt, 2006; Iori et al., 2003; Neveu et al., 2008). "Mean Ci" are averaged values on cate-

gory Ci. The "C1–Cj" aggregated lines, reporting averaged values for all instances in categories C1 to Cj, can be used to identify up to which problem size a particular approach may be effective. The last line shows the number of instances optimally solved.

According to Figure 7, TS1 is the worst performing (tabu search) approach for the benchmark tried. Indeed, $\gamma_* = 0$ only for C2P1 and C2P3 while the other methods (possibly except GA) always solved at least 8 instances. Almost all other approaches (except TS1 and GA) solved the C1 and C2 instances, see line "C1–C2" where $\gamma_* = 0.00$ or $\bar{\gamma} = 0.00$.

To our knowledge, the only approaches solving all the 9 instances C1P1–C3P3 are the tabu search from Alvarez-Valdes et al. (2007) and the recent exact procedures described in (Kenmochi et al., 2009; Soh et al., 2008). In Figure 7, CTS is the only method reaching the same qualitative results, see line "C1–C3" where $\gamma_* = 0.00$ just for CTS. Furthermore, note that CTS achieves here the lowest $\bar{\gamma}$ value ($0.29 < 0.36 < 0.89 < 1.64 < 2.69$).

Aggregated results show that CTS compares also well with the competitors if one considers instances up to C5. Indeed, line "C1–C4" indicates better CTS values for γ_* ($0.41 < 0.68 \leq 0.68 \leq 0.68 < 2.38 < 5.40$) and $\bar{\gamma}$ ($0.63 < 0.68 < 1.08 < 1.84 < 2.90$). The same observation holds in line "C1–C5" only for γ_* ($0.62 < 0.76 \leq 0.76 \leq 0.76 < 2.20 < 5.31$) but the difference is sharp between the best $\bar{\gamma}$ (0.76 for GRASP) and that of CTS (0.85).

CTS obtains worst γ_* or $\bar{\gamma}$ values than those of the two best-known state-of-the-art approaches considered here (GRASP and HH+IDW) only when adding the largest two categories of instances. For C1–C6, note, however, that the difference is still reasonable considering γ_* ($0.83 - 0.77 = 0.06$).

5. CONCLUSION

In this paper, we presented CTS, a Consistent Tabu Search algorithm for the 2D Strip Packing Problem (2D-SPP). CTS includes some components already used by (or, at least, similar to) other approaches, such as the direct representation of the problem or the neighborhood mentioned, e.g., in (Hamiez et al., 2009). Apart from these traditional components, our CTS approach was reinforced mainly by introducing two novel elements that, to our knowledge, were never tried for 2D-SPP:

- A fitness function including a measure related to the empty spaces. This was motivated by the fact that most of the previous studies on 2D-SPP usually employ evaluation functions solely based on the rectangles. This is the case, for instance, in (Hamiez et al., 2009; Neveu et al., 2008). Such an additional criterion may be helpful to guide more efficiently the search process.
- A diversification scheme based on a frequency measure (D_T). The motivation behind this component of the *generic* tabu search strategy, which can help to escape from local optima, e.g., originates from running profile observations. Indeed, preliminary tests (without diversification D_T) shown that some rectangles were almost always in the strip and, so, their location changed rarely. D_T was thus designed to force these "frozen" objects, that may be considered as problematic (since, perhaps, they are not positioned there in optimal solutions), to leave the strip and to be packed at other locations.

These components proved to be quite useful for the effectiveness of the CTS algorithm. We believe that the basic ideas behind these components could be applicable to other optimization problems.

ACKNOWLEDGMENT

We would like to thank the reviewers of the paper for their comments. This work was partially supported by three grants from the French "Pays de la Loire" region (MILES, RadaPop, and LigeRO projects). The first author is supported by a Chilean CONICIT scholarship.

REFERENCES

Alvarez-Valdes, R., Parreño, F., & Tamarit, J. (2007). A tabu search algorithm for a two-dimensional non-guillotine cutting problem. *European Journal of Operational Research, 183,* 1167–1182. doi:10.1016/j.ejor.2005.11.068

Alvarez-Valdes, R., Parreño, F., & Tamarit, J. (2008). Reactive GRASP for the strip-packing problem. *Computers & Operations Research, 35,* 1065–1083. doi:10.1016/j.cor.2006.07.004

Araya, I., Neveu, B., & Riff, M.-C. (2008). An efficient hyperheuristic for strip-packing problems. In Cotta, C., Sevaux, M., & Sörensen, K. (Eds.), *Adaptive and Multilevel Metaheuristics (Vol. 136,* pp. 61–76). Berlin: Springer. doi:10.1007/978-3-540-79438-7_3

Aşik, O., & Özcan, E. (2009). Bidirectional best-fit heuristic for orthogonal rectangular strip packing. *Annals of Operations Research, 172,* 405–427. doi:10.1007/s10479-009-0642-0

Baker, B., Brown, D., & Katseff, H. (1981). A 5/4 algorithm for two-dimensional packing. *Journal of Algorithms, 2,* 348–368. doi:10.1016/0196-6774(81)90034-1

Baker, B. Jr, & Rivest, R. (1980). Orthogonal packings in two dimensions. *SIAM Journal on Computing, 9,* 846–855. doi:10.1137/0209064

Beasley, J. (2004). A population heuristic for constrained two-dimensional non-guillotine cutting. *European Journal of Operational Research, 156,* 601–627. doi:10.1016/S0377-2217(03)00139-5

Belov, G., Kartak, V., Rohling, H., & Scheithauer, G. (2009). One-dimensional relaxations and LP bounds for orthogonal packing. *International Transactions in Operational Research, 16,* 745–766. doi:10.1111/j.1475-3995.2009.00713.x

Beltrán Cano, J., Calderón, J., Cabrera, R., Moreno Pérez, J., & Moreno-Vega, J. (2004). GRASP / VNS hybrid for the strip packing problem. In C. Blum, A. Roli, & M. Sampels (Eds.), *First International Workshop on Hybrid Metaheuristics* (pp. 79-90).

Błażewicz, J., Moret-Salvador, A., & Walkowiak, R. (2004). Parallel tabu search approaches for two-dimensional cutting. *Parallel Processing Letters, 14,* 23–32. doi:10.1142/S0129626404001684

Bortfeldt, A. (2006). A genetic algorithm for the two-dimensional strip packing problem with rectangular pieces. *European Journal of Operational Research, 172,* 814–837. doi:10.1016/j.ejor.2004.11.016

Burke, E., Kendall, G., & Whitwell, G. (2009). A simulated annealing enhancement of the best-fit heuristic for the orthogonal stock cutting problem. *INFORMS Journal on Computing, 21,* 505–516. doi:10.1287/ijoc.1080.0306

Chazelle, B. (1983). The bottom-left bin-packing heuristic: An efficient implementation. *IEEE Transactions on Computers, 32,* 697–707. doi:10.1109/TC.1983.1676307

Clautiaux, F., Jouglet, A., Carlier, J., & Moukrim, A. (2008). A new constraint programming approach for the orthogonal packing problem. *Computers & Operations Research, 35,* 944–959. doi:10.1016/j.cor.2006.05.012

Coffman, E. Jr, Garey, M., Johnson, D., & Tarjan, R. (1980). Performance bounds for level-oriented two-dimensional packing algorithms. *SIAM Journal on Computing, 9,* 808–826. doi:10.1137/0209062

Dowsland, K., & Dowsland, W. (1992). Packing problems. *European Journal of Operational Research, 56,* 2–14. doi:10.1016/0377-2217(92)90288-K

El Hayek, J., Moukrim, A., & Negre, S. (2008). New resolution algorithm and pretreatments for the two-dimensional bin-packing problem. *Computers & Operations Research, 35*, 3184–3201. doi:10.1016/j.cor.2007.02.013

Fowler, R., Paterson, M., & Tanimoto, S. (1981). Optimal packing and covering in the plane are NP-complete. *Information Processing Letters, 12*, 133–137. doi:10.1016/0020-0190(81)90111-3

Garey, M. R., & Johnson, D. S. (1979). *Computers and Intractability: A Guide to the Theory of NP-Completeness*. San Francisco, CA: W. H. Freeman and Company.

Garrido, P., & Riff, M.-C. (2007). Collaboration between hyperheuristics to solve strip-packing problems. In P. Melin, O. Castillo, L. Aguilar, J. Kacprzyk, & W. Pedrycz (Eds.), *Twelfth International Fuzzy Systems Association World Congress* (LNCS 4529, pp. 698-707). Berlin: Springer.

Glover, F. W., & Laguna, M. (1997). *Tabu Search*. Dordrecht, The Netherlands: Kluwer.

Gómez-Villouta, G., Hamiez, J.-P., & Hao, J.-K. (2008). A dedicated genetic algorithm for two-dimensional non-guillotine strip packing. In *Proceedings of the Sixth Mexican International Conference on Artificial Intelligence, Special Session* (pp. 264-274). Washington, DC: IEEE Computer Society.

Gonçalves, J. (2007). A hybrid genetic algorithm-heuristic for a two-dimensional orthogonal packing problem. *European Journal of Operational Research, 183*, 1212–1229. doi:10.1016/j.ejor.2005.11.062

Hamiez, J.-P., Robet, J., & Hao, J.-K. (2009). A tabu search algorithm with direct representation for strip packing. In C. Cotta & P. Cowling (Eds.), *Proceedings of the Ninth European Conference on Evolutionary Computation in Combinatorial Optimization* (LNCS 5482, pp. 61-72). Berlin: Springer.

Harren, R., & van Stee, R. (2009). Improved absolute approximation ratios for two-dimensional packing problems. In I. Dinur, K. Jansen, J. Naor, & J. Rolim (Eds.), *Approximation, Randomization, and Combinatorial Optimization* (LNCS 5687, pp. 177-189). Berlin: Springer.

Hopper, E., & Turton, B. (2001). An empirical investigation of meta-heuristic and heuristic algorithms for a 2D packing problem. *European Journal of Operational Research, 128*, 34–57. doi:10.1016/S0377-2217(99)00357-4

Ibaraki, T., Imahori, S., & Yagiura, M. (2008). Hybrid metaheuristics for packing problems. In C. Blum, M. B. Aguilera, A. Roli, & M. Sampels (Eds.), *Hybrid Metaheuristics: An Emerging Approach to Optimization* (Vol. 114 of Studies in Computational Intelligence, pp. 185-219). Berlin: Springer.

Imahori, S., Yagiura, M., & Ibaraki, T. (2003). Local search algorithms for the rectangle packing problem with general spatial costs. *Mathematical Programming, 97*, 543–569. doi:10.1007/s10107-003-0427-1

Imahori, S., Yagiura, M., & Ibaraki, T. (2005). Improved local search algorithms for the rectangle packing problem with general spatial costs. *European Journal of Operational Research, 167*, 48–67. doi:10.1016/j.ejor.2004.02.020

Imahori, S., Yagiura, M., & Nagamochi, H. (2007). Practical algorithms for two-dimensional packing. In Gonzalez, T. (Ed.), *Handbook of Approximation Algorithms and Metaheuristics (Vol. 13)*. London: CRC Press.

Iori, M., Martello, S., & Monaci, M. (2003). Metaheuristic algorithms for the strip packing problem. In Pardalos, P., & Korotkikh, V. (Eds.), *Optimization and Industry: New Frontiers (Vol. 78*, pp. 159–179). Berlin: Springer.

Jansen, K., & van Stee, R. (2005). On strip packing with rotations. In H. Gabow & R. Fagin (Eds.), *Proceedings of the Thirty-Seventh annual ACM symposium on Theory of computing* (pp. 755-761). New York: ACM Press.

Kenmochi, M., Imamichi, T., Nonobe, K., Yagiura, M., & Nagamochi, H. (2009). Exact algorithms for the two-dimensional strip packing problem with and without rotations. *European Journal of Operational Research, 198*, 73–83. doi:10.1016/j.ejor.2008.08.020

Lodi, A., Martello, S., & Monaci, M. (2002). Two-dimensional packing problems: A survey. *European Journal of Operational Research, 141*, 241–252. doi:10.1016/S0377-2217(02)00123-6

Martello, S., Monaci, M., & Vigo, D. (2003). An exact approach to the strip packing problem. *INFORMS Journal on Computing, 15*, 310–319. doi:10.1287/ijoc.15.3.310.16082

Mir, M., & Imam, M. (2001). A hybrid optimization approach for layout design of unequal-area facilities. *Computers & Industrial Engineering, 39*, 49–63. doi:10.1016/S0360-8352(00)00065-6

Neveu, B., Trombettoni, G., & Araya, I. (2007). Incremental move for strip-packing. In N. Avouris, N. Bourbakis, & I. Hatzilygeroudis (Eds.), *Proceedings of the Nineteenth IEEE International Conference on Tools with Artificial Intelligence* (Vol. 2, pp. 489-496). Washington, DC: IEEE Computer Society.

Neveu, B., Trombettoni, G., Araya, I., & Riff, M.-C. (2008). A strip packing solving method using an incremental move based on maximal holes. *International Journal of Artificial Intelligence Tools, 17*, 881–901. doi:10.1142/S0218213008004205

Schiermeyer, I. (1994). Reverse-Fit: A 2-optimal algorithm for packing rectangles. In J. van Leeuwen (Ed.), *Proceedings of the Second Annual European Symposium on Algorithms* (LNCS 855, pp. 290-299). Berlin: Springer.

Soh, T., Inoue, K., Tamura, N., Banbara, M., & Nabeshima, H. (2008). A SAT-based method for solving the two-dimensional strip packing problem. In M. Gavanelli & T. Mancini (Eds.), *Proceedings of the Fifteenth International RCRA Workshop on Experimental Evaluation of Algorithms for Solving Problems with Combinatorial Explosion*. Aachen, Germany: RWTH Aachen University.

Soke, A., & Bingul, Z. (2006). Hybrid genetic algorithm and simulated annealing for two-dimensional non-guillotine rectangular packing problems. *Engineering Applications of Artificial Intelligence, 19*, 557–567. doi:10.1016/j.engappai.2005.12.003

Terashima-Marín, H., Flores-Álvarez, E., & Ross, P. (2005). Hyper-heuristics and classifier systems for solving 2D-regular cutting stock problems. In *Proceedings of the 2005 Conference on Genetic and Evolutionary Computation* (Vol. 2, pp. 637-643). New York: ACM Press.

Wäscher, G., Haußner, H., & Schumann, H. (2007). An improved typology of cutting and packing problems. *European Journal of Operational Research, 183*, 1109–1130. doi:10.1016/j.ejor.2005.12.047

Yeung, L., & Tang, W. (2004). Strip-packing using hybrid genetic approach. *Engineering Applications of Artificial Intelligence, 17*, 169–177. doi:10.1016/j.engappai.2004.02.003

ENDNOTES

[1] Expressions like "(pallet) loading", "containment", "marker making", "nesting", "(layout) design", "placement", "(resource) allocation", or "(stock) cutting", e.g., are also sometimes employed to refer to this type of problems.

[2] σ introduces then an order for all the objects.

3 Other approaches that do not use permutations to model the problem, or closely related variants, can also be found, e.g., in (Bortfeldt, 2006; Hamiez et al., 2009; Soh et al., 2008).

4 The notion of "maximal rectangular empty space" seems to have been independently introduced in (El Hayek et al., 2008) (where it is called "maximal area") and (Neveu et al., 2008) ("maximal hole"). $|E|$ is at most (i.e. in the worst case) in $O(n^2)$ according to El Hayek et al. (2008).

5 However, note that while BLF has an asymptotic performance of $3f_{OPT}$, other heuristics achieved better (asymptotic or absolute) performance ratio: 2.7 (Coffman Jr. et al., 1980), 2 (Schiermeyer, 1994), $1 + \varepsilon$ (Baker et al., 1981).

6 A "small" δ value indicates that (almost) all empty spaces are concentrated close to the top-right corner of the strip.

7 $F_{1 \leq i \leq n} = 0$ at the beginning of the search.

8 $F_i \leftarrow 2F_i$ is used here to avoid considering (almost) the same $\lfloor F \rfloor$ set in next applications of diversification D_T while $F_i \leftarrow F_i + 1$ is applied when performing a move.

9 They are available from the "PackLib2" benchmarks library, e.g., see http://www.ibr.cs.tu-bs.de/alg/packlib/xml/ht-eimhh-01-xml.shtml.

10 For indicative purpose, the mean running time of CTS ranges from a few seconds (for the smallest instances) to about 33 hours (for the largest instances).

11 TS1 is perhaps the first tabu search approach for 2D-SPP.

Chapter 12
A Study of Tabu Search for Coloring Random 3–Colorable Graphs Around the Phase Transition

Jean-Philippe Hamiez
Université d'Angers/LERIA, France

Jin-Kao Hao
Université d'Angers, France

Fred W. Glover
OptTek Systems Inc., USA

ABSTRACT

The authors present an experimental investigation of tabu search (TS) to solve the 3-coloring problem (3-COL). Computational results reveal that a basic TS algorithm is able to find proper 3-colorings for random 3-colorable graphs with up to 11000 vertices and beyond when instances follow the uniform or equipartite well-known models, and up to 1500 vertices for the hardest class of flat graphs. This study also validates and reinforces some existing phase transition thresholds for 3-COL.

INTRODUCTION

Given a simple undirected graph $G = (V(G), E(G))$, where $V(G) = \{v_1, v_2, ..., v_n\}$ is a set of n vertices (n is usually called the "order" of G) and $E(G) \subset V(G) \times V(G)$ a set of m edges, and a set $C = \{c_1, c_2, ..., c_k\}$ of k colors, a k-coloring of G is any assignment of one of the k available colors

from C to every vertex in $V(G)$. More formally, a k-coloring of G is a mapping $c: V(G) \rightarrow C$. The k-coloring problem (k-COL) is to find such a mapping (or prove that none exists) such that adjacent vertices receive different colors (called "proper" k-coloring). More formally, a proper k-coloring of G verifies $\{v_i, v_j\} \in E(G) \rightarrow c(v_i) \neq c(v_j)$. The tightly related optimization version of k-COL is the graph coloring problem (COL): Determine a

DOI: 10.4018/978-1-4666-0270-0.ch012

proper k-coloring of G with k minimum, i.e. the *chromatic number* $\chi(G)$.

k-COL is known to be *NP-complete* when $k \geq 3$ for general graphs (Garey & Johnson, 1979; Karp, 1972). It remains NP-complete even for *particular* classes of graphs, including, for instance, triangle-free graphs with maximum degree 4 (Maffray & Preissmann, 1996). Classes of graphs for which 3-COL can be decided in polynomial time are discussed, for instance, in (Alekseev et al., 2007; Kochol et al., 2003).

Another way to express the difficulty of a combinatorial search problem is to consider the *phase transition* phenomenon which refers to the "easy-hard-easy" transition regions where a problem goes from easy to hard, and conversely (Cheeseman et al., 1991; Dubois et al., 2001; Gent et al., 1996; Hartmann & Weigt, 2005; Hogg et al., 1996; Monasson et al., 1999), see also (Barbosa & Ferreira, 2004; Krzakała et al., 2004; Zdeborová & Krzakała, 2007) for k-COL. Various phase transition thresholds (noted τ hereafter) have been identified for some classes of random graphs. For 3-COL, τ seems to occur when the edge probability p is such that $2pn/3 \approx 16/3$ according to Petford & Welsh (1989) (referred as τ_w in the rest of the paper), when the mean connection degree $2m/n \approx 5.4$ (τ_c from Cheeseman et al. (1991)), when $7/n \leq p \leq 8/n$ (τ_h from Eiben, van der Hauw, & van Hemert, 1998), when $2m/n \approx 4.6$ (τ_g from Culberson & Gent, 2001), or when $p \approx 3/n + 3(n - 3)(1 - 1/6^{2/n})/2n$ (τ_e from Erben (2001)). Note that τ_e and τ_w are similar to the upper bound of τ_h ($8/n$). τ_c and τ_g are also similar but τ_c holds only for graphs that are first transformed (before solving) using three "particular reduction operators" (Cheeseman et al., 1991). Additionally, τ_e was characterized just for equipartite graphs and τ_w only for equipartite and uniform graphs. Henceforth, we use the terminology *outside* of τ_h (or τ_c or τ_g, etc.) to indicate parameter values outside of the indicated τ setting.

This paper focuses on an experimental study of finding solution for 3-colorable random graphs

around and outside of phase transitions. We are particularly interested in two questions. First, are graphs around phase transitions really difficult to color from a practical solution point of view? Effectively, the different thresholds for phase transition have been established either theoretically or empirically. In both cases, it would be interesting to verify these thresholds by large scale computational experimentation. Notice that, except (Eiben et al., 1998), most experimental studies (see e.g., Cheeseman et al., 1991; Hogg et al., 1996) are based only on systematic backtracking search algorithms and small graphs (with no more than 200 vertices). Little is known about the behavior of a (metaheuristic-based) search algorithm on solving large and very large 3-colorable graphs.

Closely related to this first question is another interesting point: Given the phase transition phenomenon, what are the largest sizes of the graphs that can be colored in practice? Actually, the phase transition thresholds distinguish the relative hardness of instances around and outside of the thresholds. They don't tell much about whether such instances can be solved easily with a practical solution algorithm (such as tabu search) and for which problem sizes a solution is possible.

In this study, we aim to investigate these issues by studying a large range of random graphs generated according to three well-known distributions: Uniform, equipartite, and flat (see next section for more details). For the solution algorithm, we employ a simple tabu search (TS) algorithm (Glover & Laguna, 1997) which can be considered as a baseline reference for the class of metaheuristic (k-) coloring algorithms.

We report computational results on graphs with up to 11000 vertices, leading to two main findings. First, the variation of solution difficulty of random graphs around and outside of phase transition thresholds are clearly confirmed throughout the experiments: Graphs around the phase transition thresholds are actually more difficult to color than those outside of the thresholds. Second, for the three classes of graphs (uniform, equipartie and flat), the TS algorithm is able to find solutions for graphs with up to at least 11000 vertices if the graphs are outside of the phase transitions. For graphs around the phase transitions, the TS algorithm always manages to find solutions for uniform and equipartie graphs with up to at least 11000 vertices, but for flat graphs, the performance seems limited to graphs of 1500 vertices.

The next section presents the three classes of 3-colorable random graphs studied in this paper. The TS 3-coloring algorithm is then described followed by computational results before concluding.

RANDOM GRAPHS

While many classes of random graphs exist (Bollobás, 2001; Krivelevich & Sudakov, 2006), we focus our study on three well-known classes of 3-colorable graphs: Uniform, equipartite, and flat.

There are several reasons for this choice. These random graphs have been object of a number of theoretical (and sometimes practical) studies and analyses, see e.g., (Bollobás, 2001; Braunstein et al., 2003; Culberson & Gent, 2001; Erben, 2001; Fleurent & Ferland, 1996a; Krzakała et al., 2004; Zdeborová & Krzakała, 2007). There is a publicly available generator from http://web.cs.ualberta.ca/~joe/Coloring/Generators/generate.html (newer version). The work reported in (Eiben et al., 1998), the only paper that we are aware of on practical solution of the 3-coloring problem, is based on random graphs generated by the same generator, making it possible to use the results of Eiben et al. (1998) as a reference for reporting the 3-coloring results of our TS algorithm.

Uniform. Vertices are first randomly assigned to one of the 3 colors uniformly and independently. Then, each edge $\{v_i, v_j\}$ verifying $c(v_i) \neq c(v_j)$ appears with probability p. We will refer to these graphs with the $U_{n,p}$ notation (or U, for short). Specify 3 at "K-coloring schemes", 3 at "partition number", 0 at "variability", and 1 at "graph type" prompts when running the generator.

Equipartite. In $E_{n,p}$ graphs, $V(G)$ is first split into 3 subsets $V_{ci \in C}$ ($C = \{c_1, c_2, c_3\}$ since $k = 3$) such that $|V_{ci}| = \lfloor n/3 \rfloor$ or $|V_{ci}| = \lceil n/3 \rceil$ $\forall$ $c_i \in C$ (i.e., all V_{ci} are nearly equal in size, the smallest subset having one less member than the largest), $v_j \in V_{ci}$ meaning $c(v_j) = c_i$. Then, edges appear as in U graphs. Specify 2 at "K-coloring schemes", 3 at "partition number", and 1 at "graph type" prompts.

Flat. Based on E graphs, the $F_{n,p}$ graphs have an additional property related to the variation of the expected degree of the vertices. Specify 6 at "K-coloring schemes", 3 at "partition number", and 0 at "flatness" prompts.

TC: A TABU SEARCH ALGORITHM FOR 3-COL

In this section, we describe the components and overall scheme of our tabu search 3-coloring algorithm (called TC) used for our 3-COL experiments. TC is an application to 3-COL of the TS metaheuristic (Glover & Laguna, 1997). Its implementation is based on the TS (k-)coloring algorithms given in (Dorne & Hao, 1998; Fleurent & Ferland, 1996a), which themselves are improved variants of TABUCOL, the first TS algorithm for general (k-)COL introduced in (Hertz & de Werra, 1987)[1].

Starting state. The well known greedy DSATUR algorithm (Brélaz, 1979) is used to build a starting 3-coloring (proper or not) while restricting the number of available colors to 3. Vertices that cannot be assigned any of the 3 colors without generating conflicts are (temporarily) removed from the graph with their incident edges. After running DSATUR, these free vertices are finally randomly assigned one of the 3 authorized colors.

Fitness function. Let C be the set of all 3-colorings (proper or not) of G and $\tilde{E}(c)$ be the set of conflicting edges (i.e., with endpoints colored the same) of $c \in$ C: $\tilde{E}(c) = \{\{v_i, v_j\} \in E(G): c(v_i) = c(v_j)\}$. Any 3-coloring c is evaluated according to the following fitness function to be minimized: $f(c) = |\tilde{E}(c)|$ (f: C $\rightarrow \{0, 1, …, m\}$). Note that c is a proper 3-coloring if $f(c) = 0$.

Move operator. A move m maps a 3-coloring c to another 3-coloring c' (i.e., m: C $\rightarrow$ C) by changing the color of exactly one vertex v_j to $c'(v_j) \neq c(v_j)$, noted $c' = m_c(v_j, c'(v_j))$. Let $M(c)$ be the set of all potential moves available from c: $M(c) = \{(v_j, c'(v_j)): c'(v_j) \neq c(v_j)\}$.

Neighborhood. The set of 3-colorings c' reachable from c by applying all potential moves defines the neighborhood $N(c)$ of c. More formally, $N(c) = \{c' = m_c(v_j, c'(v_j)): (v_j, c'(v_j)) \in M(c)\}$.

Tabu list. When a move m is performed from a 3-coloring c to $c' \in N(c)$, the reverse move $m_{c'}^{-1}\left(v_j, c\left(v_j\right)\right) = c$ (i.e. assigning to v_j its previous color) is "tabu" (forbidden) for the next

$$TT = \min\left\{(k-1)f(c), \alpha\left|\tilde{V}(c)\right| + rand(\gamma)\right\}$$

iterations[2], where α is a TC parameter, $rand(\gamma)$ is a random integer from $\{1, 2, …, \gamma\}$ (the role of γ is just to introduce a few stochastic noise), and $\tilde{V}(c) \subseteq V(G)$ is the set of conflicting vertices of c ($\tilde{V}(c) = \{v_i: \{v_i, v_j\} \in E(G) \rightarrow c'(v_i) = c(v_j)\}$).

Stopping criterion. TC halts whenever $f(c) = 0$ (a proper 3-coloring c has been found) or after a maximum allowed number of moves.

Given the previous components of TC, the core procedure (see the subsequent algorithm) searches for a 3-coloring $c^* \in$ C (proper or not) with a minimum number of conflicting edges (with $f(c^*) = 0$ ideally, meaning that TC halts since it has found a proper 3-coloring c^*). To do so, TC iteratively moves from a 3-coloring $c \in$ C to a c'

$\in N(c)$. Let $M_*(c) \subset M(c)$ be the set of **best** moves (according to f) available from c and involving a conflicting vertex such that, $\forall m \in M_*(c)$, m is not tabu or m leads to a neighbor better than the best 3-coloring c^* found so far (aspiration criterion). If $M_*(c) \neq \emptyset$, m is chosen at random from $M_*(c)$ according to some probability π. Otherwise, i.e., with probability $1 - \pi$ or when $M_*(c) = \emptyset$, m is chosen at random from $M(c)$. Note that c^* is updated each time $f(c') < f(c^*)$.

TC ALGORITHM

Require: A 3-colorable graph $G = (V(G), E(G))$ and a set $C = \{c_1, c_2, c_3\}$ of three colors

Require: A starting 3-coloring $c \in$ C of G // Proper or not

1. $c^* \leftarrow c$ // Best 3-coloring found so far
2. $TL(j, i) \leftarrow 0 \; \forall \; (v_j, c_i) \in V(G) \times C$ // Make the tabu list TL empty
3. $\mu \leftarrow 0$ // Current number of moves
4. **while** stopping criterion not met **do**
5. $\quad \mu \leftarrow \mu + 1$
6. $\quad$ Let $M(c) = \{(v_j, c'(v_j)): c' \in N(c)\}$
7. $\quad$ Let $M_*(c) = \{(v_j, c'(v_j)) \in M(c):$
     $v_j \in \tilde{V}(c)$ **and** $\forall (v_i, c''(v_i)) \in M(c), f(c') \leq f(c'')$ **and** $(TL(j, c'(v_j)) < \mu$ **or** $f(c') < f(c^*))\}$
8. $\quad$ Let r be a random real number in $[0, 1]$
9. $\quad$ **if** $M_*(c) = \emptyset$ **or** $r > \pi$ **then**
10. $\quad$ Randomly select a move $(v_j, c'(v_j))$ from $M(c)$
11. $\quad$ **else**
12. $\quad$ Randomly select a move $(v_j, c'(v_j)) \in M_*(c)$
13. $\quad$ $TL(j, c(v_j)) \leftarrow \mu + TT$ // Forbid the reverse move m^{-1} at least up to iterations $\mu + TT$
14. $\quad$ $c(v_j) \leftarrow c'(v_j)$ // Do the selected move
15. $\quad$ **if** $f(c) < f(c^*)$ **then**
16. $\quad$ $c^* \leftarrow c$
17. **return** c^*

Note that selecting (lines 10 and 12 in the TC algorithm) or doing (line 14) a move in TC can be achieved efficiently, i.e., within small time complexity, using a particular data structure inspired by a technique from Fleurent & Ferland (1996b) and usually called "δ figure" in the wide tabu search literature. Basically, δ is a $n \times k$ matrix where $\delta_c(j, c'(v_j))$ stores the fitness variation (between $c \in C$ and $c' \in N(c)$) when the color assigned to $v_j \in V(G)$ changes from $c(v_j)$ to $c'(v_j)$: $\delta_c(j, c'(v_j))$ = $f(c') - f(c)$. δ is initialized once at the beginning of the search (before line 4, in time $O(nk)$) and updated each time a move is performed (after line 14, in time $O(nk)$ in the worst case but, in practice, only a subset of δ is updated). While selecting a move from the $M(c)$ set (line 10) takes $O(1)$ time, the evaluation of all "best" moves from the $M_*(c)$ set (line 12) is almost *incremental*: It can be achieved in $O(|\tilde{V}(c)|k)$ time in the worst case thanks to δ. Thus, each iteration takes $O(2nk)$ time at most since $|\tilde{V}(c)| \leq n$ for any 3-coloring c.

COMPUTATIONAL RESULTS

The computational experiments reported are based on the following general protocol.

Benchmark set. A collection consisting of 263 different instances is built. Recall that all these graphs are 3-colorable by construction. Their order ranges from 200 to 11000. Note that the generator requires an integer seed for randomization initialization: We always use 5 as in (Eiben et al., 1998) to deal exactly with the same instances. Additionally, Eiben et al. (1998) noted that this parameter seems to have no great influence on results.

Reference algorithm. For reporting computational results of TC, we use the SAW evolutionary algorithm (Eiben et al., 1998) as a reference. Indeed, according to Eiben et al. (1998), SAW is effective in 3-coloring random 3-col-

orable graphs of large order (up to 1500 vertices). Moreover, the authors clearly describe the graph generator employed and the seed for randomization initializations, making it possible to make direct comparisons. In all our figures shown later in the paper, "–" signals unavailable or inapplicable entries and results reported for SAW are approximated from figures in (Eiben et al., 1998). No information is given for SAW in some of our figures since it cannot be retrieved from (Eiben et al., 1998).

Performance criteria. The solution performance is assessed according to the well-known "Success Rate" measure (*SR*): It is the percentage of successful runs, i.e., in which a proper 3-coloring is found, over a given number of runs. To give an idea of the TC computational effort, we also report the mean number of moves required by TC to find a proper 3-coloring (*AMS*, for "*Average number of Moves to Solution*") and its standard deviation (σ_{AMS}). Eiben et al. (1998) used a slightly different measure, namely the mean number of fitness evaluations (*AES*, for "*Average number of Evaluations to Solution*"). Note that *AMS* and *AES* are implementation and hardware independent measures. The mean computation time T and its standard deviation σ_T (in seconds) are also reported for successful runs of TC.

Phase transition. In some figures, the cases the closest to τ_c, τ_e, τ_g, τ_h, and τ_w are identified with the appropriate "*c*", "*e*", "*g*", "*h*", and "*w*" letters in the τ columns. The bold entries in Figure 1, Figure 2, Figure 3, Figure 4, Figure 5, Figure 6, Figure 7, Figure 8, Figure 9, Figure 10, Figure 11, Figure 12, Figure 13, Figure 14, Figure 15, Figure 16, Figure 17 and Figure 18 indicates which τ is the closest to the hardest cases (minimum *SR*, or maximum *AMS* or *AES*), i.e., it suggests which τ seems to be best suited to locate the phase transition.

Figure 1. Small-order U graphs (n = 200): Influence of the edge probability p (100 runs)

p	τ	TC (300 000 moves)					SAW	
		SR	AMS	σ_{AMS}	T (s)	σ_T (s)	SR	AES
0.015		1	0.0	0.0	< 1	< 1	1	0
0.02		1	0.6	2.6	< 1	< 1	1	0
0.025		1	124.2	264.6	< 1	< 1	1	0
0.03		1	3 376.5	2 982.0	< 1	< 1	1	10 000
0.035	**g,h**	**1**	**14 423.6**	**13 371.8**	**< 1**	**< 1**	**0.90**	**75 000**
0.04	c,e,h,w	1	2 851.6	2 140.5	< 1	< 1	1	10 000
0.045		1	840.9	618.1	< 1	< 1	1	4 000
0.05		1	1 150.6	661.3	< 1	< 1	1	4 000
0.055		1	869.2	520.2	< 1	< 1	1	2 000
0.06		1	1 242.1	1 390.7	< 1	< 1	1	2 000
0.065		1	731.5	611.3	< 1	< 1	1	1 000
0.07		1	720.6	405.2	< 1	< 1	1	1 000
0.075		1	519.3	309.8	< 1	< 1	1	500

Figure 2. Small-order E graphs (n = 200): Influence of the edge probability p (100 runs)

p	τ	TC (300 000 moves)					SAW	
		SR	AMS	σ_{AMS}	T (s)	σ_T (s)	SR	AES
0.015		1	0.0	0.0	< 1	< 1	1	0
0.02		1	0.5	2.8	< 1	< 1	1	0
0.025		1	65.3	103.9	< 1	< 1	1	0
0.03		1	4 540.7	3 984.8	< 1	< 1	1	13 000
0.035	**g,h**	**1**	**11 865.1**	**9 946.7**	**< 1**	**< 1**	**0.85**	**68 000**
0.04	c,e,h,w	1	3 699.8	2 993.3	< 1	< 1	1	68 000
0.045		1	998.3	709.6	< 1	< 1	1	9 000
0.05		1	766.3	398.3	< 1	< 1	1	9 000
0.055		1	1 019.4	858.6	< 1	< 1	1	4 500
0.06		1	1 786.9	1 418.6	< 1	< 1	1	4 500
0.065		1	971.5	1 440.8	< 1	< 1	1	2 000
0.07		1	510.4	291.5	< 1	< 1	1	2 000
0.075		1	248.9	221.0	< 1	< 1	1	1 000

Figure 3. Small-order F graphs (n = 200): Influence of the edge probability p (100 runs)

p	τ	TC (300 000 moves)					SAW	
		SR	AMS	σ_{AMS}	T (s)	σ_T (s)	SR	AES
0.015		1	0.0	0.0	< 1	< 1	1	0
0.02		1	0.0	0.0	< 1	< 1	1	0
0.025		1	6.7	25.0	< 1	< 1	1	0
0.03		1	720.5	718.2	< 1	< 1	1	8 000
0.035	**g, h**	1	**58 636.4**	**47 428.0**	**< 1**	**< 1**	**0.37**	**110 000**
0.04	c, e, h, w	1	14 226.4	13 675.2	< 1	< 1	0.65	75 000
0.045		1	2 749.3	1 779.0	< 1	< 1	1	13 500
0.05		1	1 053.1	960.2	< 1	< 1	1	12 500
0.055		1	1 146.8	652.6	< 1	< 1	1	6 000
0.06		1	2 785.1	2 929.8	< 1	< 1	1	6 000
0.065		1	941.1	748.7	< 1	< 1	1	3 000
0.07		1	931.8	774.2	< 1	< 1	1	3 000
0.075		1	398.2	280.2	< 1	< 1	1	3 000

Figure 4. Medium-order U graphs (n = 500): Influence of the edge probability p (50 runs)

p	τ	TC (300 000 moves)					SAW	
		SR	AMS	σ_{AMS}	T (s)	σ_T (s)	SR	AES
0.006		1	0.0	0.0	< 1	< 1	1	0
0.01		1	286.9	381.9	< 1	< 1	1	8 000
0.014	**c, g, h, w**	**0.9**	**98 080.4**	**74 802.3**	**1.6**	**1.1**	**0.1**	**90 000**
0.018	e, w	1	4 754.1	2 405.9	< 1	< 1	1	25 000
0.022		1	5 113.1	2 852.4	< 1	< 1	1	8 000
0.026		1	5 235.8	3 378.6	< 1	< 1	1	8 000
0.03		1	1 769.5	744.1	< 1	< 1	1	8 000
0.034		1	2 504.7	1 937.4	< 1	< 1	1	8 000
0.038		1	956.8	796.2	< 1	< 1	1	8 000
0.042		1	935.4	480.5	< 1	< 1	1	8 000
0.046		1	1 380.1	4 739.4	< 1	< 1	1	8 000
0.05		1	874.7	556.0	< 1	< 1	1	8 000

Figure 5. Medium-order E graphs (n = 500): Influence of the edge probability p (50 runs)

p	τ	TC (300 000 moves)					SAW	
		SR	AMS	σ_{AMS}	T (s)	σ_T (s)	SR	AES
0.006		1	0.0	0.0	< 1	< 1	1	0
0.01		1	263.7	252.2	< 1	< 1	1	8 000
0.014	*c, g, h, w*	**0.56**	**180 950.9**	**63 173.1**	**2.8**	**< 1**	**0**	**–**
0.018	*e, w*	1	6 913.4	7 106.6	< 1	< 1	1	30 000
0.022		1	4 678.5	2 060.6	< 1	< 1	1	20 000
0.026		1	9 008.2	19 218.4	< 1	< 1	1	12 500
0.03		1	1 855.7	1 363.8	< 1	< 1	1	12 500
0.034		1	1 205.9	1 628.4	< 1	< 1	1	12 500
0.038		1	2 021.1	1 149.9	< 1	< 1	1	8 000
0.042		1	1 415.1	4 915.3	< 1	< 1	1	8 000
0.046		1	5 756.4	27 617.0	< 1	< 1	1	8 000
0.05		1	469.4	609.2	< 1	< 1	1	8 000

Figure 6. Medium-order F graphs (n = 500): Influence of the edge probability p (50 runs)

p	τ	TC (300 000 moves)					SAW	
		SR	AMS	σ_{AMS}	T (s)	σ_T (s)	SR	AES
0.006		1	0.0	0.0	< 1	< 1	1	0
0.01		1	26.7	60.2	< 1	< 1	1	500
0.014	*g, h, w*	**0.72**	**133 391.3**	**69 861.7**	**2.1**	**1.1**	**0.08**	**115 000**
0.018	*c, e, w*	1	26 981.2	28 508.1	< 1	< 1	0.54	85 000
0.022		1	7 931.2	4 684.5	< 1	< 1	0.94	55 000
0.026		1	17 668.1	30 915.4	< 1	< 1	1	16 500
0.03		1	1 732.8	962.6	< 1	< 1	1	12 500
0.034		1	3 757.1	1 727.3	< 1	< 1	1	4 000
0.038		1	2 247.9	1 975.9	< 1	< 1	1	4 000
0.042		1	288.5	250.8	< 1	< 1	1	4 000
0.046		1	1 289.3	1 001.6	< 1	< 1	1	4 000
0.05		1	1 019.7	856.1	< 1	< 1	1	4 000

Implementation. Our TC algorithm is coded in the C programming language ("gcc" compiler). All TC computational results were obtained on a Sun Fire V880 server with 8 Gb RAM (UltraSPARC III CPU 750 MHz).

The values of the main TC parameters were empirically determined during a few preliminary computational experiments (not shown here): $\alpha = 0.5$, $\gamma = 2$, and $k = 3$ (to compute the tabu tenure TT), and $\pi = 0.85$ (probability to select a move in M_*).

Figure 7. Large-order U graphs (n = 1000): Influence of the edge probability p (25 runs)

p	τ	TC (300 000 moves)					SAW	
		SR	AMS	σ_{AMS}	T (s)	σ_T (s)	SR	AES
0.002		1	0.0	0.0	< 1	< 1	1	0
0.004		1	82.9	203.7	< 1	< 1	1	4 000
0.006	g	1	113 985.8	78 314.6	3.6	2.4	1	95 000
0.008	**c, e, h, w**	**1**	**117 190.8**	**73 166.9**	**5.7**	**3.6**	**0.04**	**135 000**
0.01		1	13 928.6	5 770.6	< 1	< 1	1	60 000
0.012		1	35 546.6	32 219.9	1.4	1.1	1	35 000
0.014		1	4 972.1	2 014.5	< 1	< 1	1	20 000
0.016		1	11 020.4	6 874.4	< 1	< 1	1	20 000
0.018		1	8 920.1	4 135.9	< 1	< 1	1	20 000
0.02		1	3 220.8	1 130.9	< 1	< 1	1	10 000
0.022		1	4 874.2	3 029.0	< 1	< 1	1	10 000
0.024		1	4 685.3	1 895.9	< 1	< 1	1	10 000
0.026		1	1 652.3	711.4	< 1	< 1	1	10 000

Figure 8. Large-order E graphs (n = 1000): Influence of the edge probability p (25 runs)

p	τ	TC (300 000 moves)					SAW	
		SR	AMS	σ_{AMS}	T (s)	σ_T (s)	SR	AES
0.002		1	0.0	0.0	< 1	< 1	1	0
0.004		1	82.9	203.7	< 1	< 1	1	4 000
0.006	g	1	113 985.8	78 314.6	3.6	2.4	1	95 000
0.008	**c, e, h, w**	**1**	**117 190.8**	**73 166.9**	**5.7**	**3.6**	**0.04**	**135 000**
0.01		1	13 928.6	5 770.6	< 1	< 1	1	60 000
0.012		1	35 546.6	32 219.9	1.4	1.1	1	35 000
0.014		1	4 972.1	2 014.5	< 1	< 1	1	20 000
0.016		1	11 020.4	6 874.4	< 1	< 1	1	20 000
0.018		1	8 920.1	4 135.9	< 1	< 1	1	20 000
0.02		1	3 220.8	1 130.9	< 1	< 1	1	10 000
0.022		1	4 874.2	3 029.0	< 1	< 1	1	10 000
0.024		1	4 685.3	1 895.9	< 1	< 1	1	10 000
0.026		1	1 652.3	711.4	< 1	< 1	1	10 000

Figure 9. Large-order F graphs (n = 1000): Influence of the edge probability p (25 runs)

p	τ	TC (300 000 moves)					SAW	
		SR	*AMS*	σ_{AMS}	T (s)	σ_T (s)	*SR*	*AES*
0.002		1	0.0	0.0	< 1	< 1	1	0
0.004		1	0.0	0.0	< 1	< 1	1	0
0.006	g	1	22 952.4	14 409.0	< 1	< 1	1	50 000
0.008	c,e,h,w	**0.04**	**102 504.0**	**0.0**	**5.7**	**0.0**	**0**	**–**
0.01		1	38 349.3	30 597.6	3.1	2.5	0.48	132 500
0.012		1	83 314.1	55 334.2	3.0	1.9	0.88	100 000
0.014		1	19 289.2	12 835.6	1.2	< 1	1	50 000
0.016		1	10 703.1	3 251.3	< 1	< 1	1	22 500
0.018		1	9 633.8	4 490.6	< 1	< 1	1	22 500
0.02		1	5 937.3	2 540.5	< 1	< 1	1	10 000
0.022		1	6 327.8	2 685.7	< 1	< 1	1	10 000
0.024		1	4 107.8	2 385.4	< 1	< 1	1	10 000
0.026		1	3 523.8	1 568.8	< 1	< 1	1	10 000

Figure 10. Small-order U graphs (n = 200): Deeper experiments with TC around τ (100 runs, 300000 moves)

p	τ	*SR*	*AMS*	σ_{AMS}	T (s)	σ_T (s)
0.03		1	3 376.5	2 982.0	< 1	< 1
0.0325	g	1	8 256.4	6 963.3	< 1	< 1
0.035	h	**1**	**14 423.6**	**13 371.8**	**< 1**	**< 1**
0.0375	c,h	1	5 849.7	3 597.3	< 1	< 1
0.04	c,e,h,w	1	2 851.6	2 140.5	< 1	< 1
0.0425		1	1 916.3	1 436.7	< 1	< 1

Figure 11. Small-order E graphs (n = 200): Deeper experiments with TC around τ (100 runs, 300000 moves)

p	τ	*SR*	*AMS*	σ_{AMS}	T (s)	σ_T (s)
0.03		1	4 540.7	3 984.8	< 1	< 1
0.0325	g	**1**	**16 016.6**	**12 633.1**	**< 1**	**< 1**
0.035	h	1	11 865.1	9 946.7	< 1	< 1
0.0375	c,h	1	5 518.3	5 319.6	< 1	< 1
0.04	e,h,w	1	3 699.8	2 993.3	< 1	< 1
0.0425		1	1 399.6	1 279.6	< 1	< 1

Figure 12. Small-order F graphs (n = 200): Deeper experiments with TC around τ (100 runs, 300000 moves)

p	τ	SR	AMS	σ_{AMS}	T (s)	σ_T (s)
0.03		1	720.5	718.2	< 1	< 1
0.0325		1	6 018.3	5 727.3	< 1	< 1
0.035	g,h	1	58 636.4	47 428.0	< 1	< 1
0.0375	**h**	**0.82**	**78 110.1**	**76 498.8**	**< 1**	**< 1**
0.04	c,e,h,w	1	14 226.4	13 675.2	< 1	< 1
0.0425		1	14 091.3	12 096.2	< 1	< 1

Figure 13. Medium-order U graphs (n = 500): Deeper experiments with TC around τ (50 runs, 300000 moves)

p	τ	SR	AMS	σ_{AMS}	T (s)	σ_T (s)
0.012		1	12 126.5	9 510.6	< 1	< 1
0.014	**g,h**	**0.9**	**98 080.4**	**74 802.4**	**1.6**	**1.1**
0.016	c,e,h,w	1	16 411.1	14 708.0	< 1	< 1
0.018		1	4 754.1	2 405.9	< 1	< 1

Figure 14. Medium-order E graphs (n = 500): Deeper experiments with TC around τ (50 runs, 300000 moves)

p	τ	SR	AMS	σ_{AMS}	T (s)	σ_T (s)
0.012		1	7 852.9	4 524.5	< 1	< 1
0.014	**c,g,h**	**0.56**	**180 950.9**	**63 173.1**	**2.8**	**< 1**
0.016	e,h,w	1	24 717.1	20 670.7	< 1	< 1
0.018		1	6 913.4	7 106.6	< 1	< 1

INFLUENCE OF THE EDGE PROBABILITY *P* ON THE PROBLEM DIFFICULTY

Almost similarly to Eiben et al. (1998), we first limit the maximum allowed number of moves of the TC algorithm to 300000 and vary p from 0.015 to 0.075 for $n = 200$ (step 0.005, 100 runs per p value and per graph, a total of 39 graphs), 0.006 to 0.05 for $n = 500$ (step 0.004, 50 runs, 36 instances), and 0.002 to 0.026 for $n = 1000$ (step 0.002, 25 runs, 45 graphs). Note that three instances were generated per p value since we consider three types of graphs (U, E, and F). Re-

Figure 15. Medium-order F graphs (n = 500): Deeper experiments with TC around τ (50 runs, 300000 moves)

p	τ	SR	AMS	σ_{AMS}	T (s)	σ_T (s)
0.012		1	2 735.7	1 780.9	< 1	< 1
0.014	g, h	0.72	133 391.3	69 861.7	2.1	1.1
0.016	$\boldsymbol{c, e, h, w}$	**0.64**	**148 273.7**	**76 569.5**	**3.3**	**1.7**
0.018		1	26 981.2	28 508.1	< 1	< 1

Figure 16. Large-order U graphs (n = 1000): Deeper experiments with TC around τ (25 runs, 300000 moves)

p	τ	SR	AMS	σ_{AMS}	T (s)	σ_T (s)
0.006		1	113 985.8	78 314.6	3.6	2.4
0.007	$\boldsymbol{g, h}$	**0.04**	**236 891.0**	**0.0**	**8.3**	**0.0**
0.008	c, e, h, w	1	117 190.8	73 166.9	5.7	3.6
0.009		1	23 644.5	6 916.5	1.5	< 1

sults are reported in Figure 1, Figure 2, Figure 3, Figure 4, Figure 5, Figure 6, Figure 7, Figure 8, and Figure 9 where the two lines associated with τ (between the two dashed lines) correspond to graphs around (i.e. the closest to) the indicated phase transition thresholds while the other lines concern graphs outside of (i.e. more distant from) these thresholds.

On the set of small-order instances ($n = 200$, see Figure 1, Figure 2 and Figure 3), TC always succeeds in all runs (*SR* is always 1) for all the graphs within the time limit of 300000 moves, but needs more moves to find a solution for a graph at the phase transitions (when $p = 0.035$) than outside of the thresholds. Note that the initialization procedure DSATUR alone always finds a proper 3-coloring whenever $p = 0.015$ and for

Figure 17. Large-order E graphs (n = 1000): Deeper experiments with TC around τ (25 runs, 300000 moves)

p	τ	SR	AMS	σ_{AMS}	T (s)	σ_T (s)
0.006		1	132 932.7	74 624.1	4.2	2.3
0.007	$\boldsymbol{g, h}$	**0.08**	**215 655.5**	**31 855.5**	**8.1**	**1.0**
0.008	c, e, h, w	1	102 510.7	73 566.2	5.1	3.8
0.009		1	26 270.6	14 541.4	1.7	< 1

Figure 18. Large-order F graphs (n = 1000): Deeper experiments with TC around τ (25 runs, 300000 moves)

p	τ	SR	AMS	σ_{AMS}	T (s)	σ_T (s)
0.006		1	22 952.4	14 409.0	< 1	< 1
0.007	*g, h*	**0**	–	–	–	–
0.008	*c, e, h, w*	**0.04**	**102 504.0**	**0.0**	**5.7**	**0.0**
0.009		0.48	139 301.5	86 264.1	9.5	5.8

Figure 19. Which τ measure is the best to identify hard 3-COL instances?

n	Graph class			Best		Worst
	U	E	F			
200	h	g	h	h	g	c, e, w
500	g, h	c, g, h	c, e, h, w	h	c, g	e, w
1 000	g, h	g, h	c, e, g, h, w	g, h		c, e, w
Best	h	g	h			
	g	c, h	c, e, w			
Worst	c, e, w	e, w	g			

Figure 20. E graphs: Influence of the problem size outside of τ_h (p = 10/n, 50 runs)

n	TC (500 000 moves)					SAW	
	SR	AMS	σ_{AMS}	T (s)	σ_T (s)	SR	AES
250	1	1 487.3	862.1	< 1	< 1	1	12 500
500	1	3 568.5	2 091.2	< 1	< 1	1	37 500
750	1	5 932.9	2 500.8	< 1	< 1	1	57 000
1 000	1	10 239.2	5 300.0	1.5	< 1	1	100 000
1 250	1	13 254.8	6 376.8	2.3	1.1	0.9	150 000
1 500	1	21 103.1	9 217.5	4.4	1.8	0.9	185 500

Figure 21. U and F graphs: Influence of the problem size on TC outside of τ_h (p = 10/n, 50 runs, 500000 moves)

n	U					F				
	SR	AMS	σ_{AMS}	T (s)	σ_T (s)	SR	AMS	σ_{AMS}	T (s)	σ_T (s)
250	1	1 186.9	612.5	< 1	< 1	1	2 238.3	1 272.3	< 1	< 1
500	1	2 885.5	1 357.3	< 1	< 1	1	7 915.5	5 158.7	< 1	< 1
750	1	8 110.6	4 363.4	< 1	< 1	1	17 802.9	13 352.0	1.8	1.3
1 000	1	9 727.2	4 187.5	1.4	< 1	1	33 667.9	25 020.5	4.9	3.6
1 250	1	9 696.3	4 253.2	1.7	< 1	1	68 762.2	65 591.5	2.1	2.0
1 500	1	19 528.4	9 281.9	3.9	1.9	1	70 217.6	48 963.0	2.6	1.8

Figure 22. E graphs: Influence of the problem size around τ_h (p = 8/n, 25 runs)

n	TC (1 000 000 moves)					SAW	
	SR	AMS	σ_{AMS}	T (s)	σ_T (s)	SR	AES
250	1	5 256.3	3 524.6	< 1	< 1	1	28 500
500	1	20 774.4	13 021.1	< 1	< 1	0.88	200 000
750	1	44 542.8	34 333.0	3.2	2.4	0.52	300 000
1 000	1	102 510.7	73 566.2	5.1	3.8	0.16	418 500
1 250	1	130 037.1	184 316.4	15.4	21.3	0.20	400 000
1 500	1	172 020.7	154 432.5	25.2	22.5	0.08	771 900

the $F_{200, 0.02}$ graph (*AMS* = 0.0 means that TC performs no move at all). DSATUR also obtains proper 3-colorings in some runs for $p \in \{0.02, 0.025\}$ in each class.

At $n = 500$ (Figure 4, Figure 5, and Figure 6), while more computational effort (*AMS*) is sometimes needed by TC, the problem is still easy for TC outside of τ_g (*SR* is always 1). At τ_g, TC is always competitive in terms of *SR*, especially on the U graph where *SR* = 0.9 (see Figure 4). However, the problem is here slightly harder than the $n = 200$ cases for TC. This is particularly true on the F and E graphs where the *SR* achieved by TC at τ_g falls, respectively, to 0.72 and 0.56 (see Figure 5 and Figure 6). DSATUR continues to produce

proper 3-colorings for $n = 500$ in each class, in all runs when $p = 0.006$ and sometimes for $F_{500, 0.01}$.

On large-order graphs ($n = 1000$, Figure 7, Figure 8, and Figure 9), TC finds proper 3-colorings in all the 25 runs for each class whenever p is outside of τ_h. In these cases, mean computing times are still short. At τ_h, TC succeeds in all runs, but only on U and E graphs, see Figure 7 and Figure 8 respectively. Indeed, it achieves *SR* = 0.04 for the F instance (Figure 9). Here again, the DSATUR algorithm directly identifies proper 3-colorings in all runs whenever $p = 0.002$ and for $E_{1000, 0.004}$ and $F_{1000, 0.004}$, and in some runs for $U_{1000, 0.004}$.

Now, we turn our attention to the performance of the reference algorithm SAW. At $n = 200$, SAW

Figure 23. U graphs: Influence of the problem size on TC around τ_h (p = 8/n, 25 runs, 1000000 moves)

n	SR	AMS	σ_{AMS}	T (s)	σ_T (s)
250	1	2 432.7	1 376.1	< 1	< 1
500	1	17 637.4	17 818.6	< 1	< 1
750	1	51 467.3	34 610.7	3.6	2.4
1 000	1	117 190.8	73 166.9	5.7	3.6
1 250	1	118 455.1	88 368.2	13.9	10.4
1 500	1	177 317.3	179 939.3	3.4	3.4

Figure 24. F graphs: Influence of the problem size on TC around τ_h (p = 8/n, 25 runs, 1000000 moves)

n	SR	AMS	σ_{AMS}	T (s)	σ_T (s)
250	1	321 279.1	241 163.2	6.2	4.7
500	1	306 117.2	234 178.1	2.2	1.7
750	0.24	219 788.5	171 377.6	2.1	1.7
1 000	0.04	102 504.0	0.0	5.7	0.0
1 250	0	–	–	–	–
1 500	0	–	–	–	–

obtained interesting SR values on U and E graphs, see Figure 1 and Figure 2 where SR is always 1 except when $p = 0.035$ ($SR \approx 0.9$ and $SR \approx 0.85$, respectively). For F graphs (Figure 3), while SAW still verifies $SR = 1$ outside of τ, it achieves a lower SR around τ: $SR \approx 0.65$ for $p = 0.04$ and $SR \approx 0.37$ when $p = 0.035$. This confirms the well known fact that F graphs may be harder than U and E instances, even on small-order graphs. For medium-order graphs (see Figures 4–6), the SR of SAW is always 1 outside of τ_g except on $F_{500, 0.022}$ ($SR \approx 0{:}94$) and $F_{500, 0.018}$ ($SR \approx 0.54$). SAW starts to have (great) difficulties in finding proper 3-colorings at τ_g when $n = 500$. Indeed, $SR \approx 0.1$ on the U graph and $SR \approx 0.08$ for the F instance. Furthermore, it seems to fail on the E instance ($SR \approx 0$). At $n = 1000$ (Figures 7–9),

SAW always finds proper 3-colorings whenever p is outside of τ_h except on two E graphs ($SR \approx 0.96$ for $p \in \{0.006, 0.01\}$) and two F graphs ($SR \approx 0.88$ for $p = 0.012$ and $SR \approx 0.48$ for $p = 0.01$). SAW dramatically fails at τ_h: $SR \approx 0.04$ for the U instance and SAW seems to never solve E and F graphs ($SR \approx 0$). Consequently, one can conclude that TC reaches always the same or higher success rate than SAW on all the graphs.

DEEPER EXPERIMENTS AROUND THE PHASE TRANSITIONS

Figure 1, Figure 2, Figure 3, Figure 4, Figure 5, Figure 6, Figure 7, Figure 8 and Figure 9 disclose that 3-COL is typically harder at τ_h than at τ_c, τ_e,

Figure 25. Long TC runs on the hardest instances from Figures 12–18 where SR < 1 (25 runs, 1000000 moves)

Graph	τ	SR_s	SR_l	AMS_l	σ_{AMS_l}	T_l (s)	σ_{T_l} (s)
$F_{200,0.0375}$	h	0.82	1	147 017.4	171 001.0	1.7	2.0
$U_{500,0.014}$	g,h	0.90	1	196 277.7	156 315.5	3.0	2.3
$E_{500,0.014}$	c,g,h	0.56	0.96	304 047.6	235 099.6	4.7	3.6
$F_{500,0.014}$	g,h	0.72	1	293 927.9	171 530.3	4.5	2.6
$F_{500,0.016}$	c,e,h,w	0.64	0.96	329 983.9	270 385.5	7.1	5.8
$U_{1000,0.007}$	g,h	0.04	0.28	601 305.1	130 523.4	21.9	4.5
$E_{1000,0.007}$	g,h	0.08	0.60	619 195.7	254 241.8	22.0	9.0
$F_{1000,0.007}$	g,h	0	0.40	470 637.1	320 741.1	3.7	2.4
$F_{1000,0.008}$	c,e,h,w	0.04	0.04	102 504.0	0.0	5.7	0.0
$F_{1000,0.009}$		0.48	0.72	410 530.3	254 225.0	12.1	7.2

τ_g, or τ_w, i.e., that τ_h may be more effective at identifying the hardest instances. To try to verify this observation, we report deeper experiments with TC in Figure 10, Talbe 11, Figure 12, Figure 13, Figure 14, Figure 15, Figure 16, Figure 17, and Figure 18 for more detailed p values around τ. Note that this section includes 21 new graphs not considered (they appear in italic typeface).

Small-order graphs ($n = 200$) are still easy, even at τ, see Figure 10, Figure 11 and Figure 12.

Indeed, SR is always 1 except on $F_{200,0.0375}$ where $SR = 0.82$. Furthermore, mean computing time of TC is always smaller than a second. Medium-order graphs ($n = 500$, Figures 13–15) also seem to be quite easy for TC, even at τ. Indeed, SR is always 1 except on $U_{500,0.014}$ (0.9), $E_{500,0.014}$ (0.56), $F_{500,0.014}$ (0.72), and $F_{500,0.016}$ (0.64). Some large-order graphs ($n = 1000$, Figure 16, Figure 17 and Figure 18) are especially difficult for TC within the time limit of 300000 moves. This is particu-

Figure 26. Achieving SR = 1 with TC on the hardest instances from Figure 25 where SR_l <1 (5 runs, without time limit)

Graph	τ	SR_l	SR_∞	AMS_∞	σ_{AMS_∞}	T_∞ (s)	σ_{T_∞} (s)
$E_{500,0.014}$	c,g,h	0.96	1	693 830.4	641 679.3	2.2	2.1
$F_{500,0.016}$	c,e,h,w	0.96	1	450 009.4	430 902.2	3.4	3.2
$U_{1000,0.007}$	g,h	0.28	1	2 904 052.2	3 138 476.6	28.5	31.0
$E_{1000,0.007}$	g,h	0.60	1	1 161 061.6	1 209 402.4	11.6	11.7
$F_{1000,0.007}$	g,h	0.40	1	1 888 195.4	1 413 201.3	11.2	8.2
$F_{1000,0.008}$	c,e,h,w	0.04	1	298 129 024.1	165 232 840.6	3 983.7	2 205.2
$F_{1000,0.009}$		0.72	1	633 880.2	523 436.4	11.6	9.5

Figure 27. Achieving SR = 1 with TC around τ_h (p = 8/n) on the hardest F instances from Figure 24 where SR_l < 1 (5 runs, without time limit)

n	SR_l	SR_∞	AMS_∞	σ_{AMS_∞}	T_∞ (s)	σ_{T_∞} (s)
750	0.24	1	11 933 517.1	9 686 691.4	114.5	92.3
1 000	0.04	1	298 129 024.1	165 232 840.6	3 983.7	2 205.2
1 250	0	1	MAXINT	–	> 3 674.4	–
1 500	0	1	MAXINT	–	> 454 662.9	–

Figure 28. U graphs: The limits of TC outside of τ_h (p = 10/n, 50 runs, 500000 moves)

n	SR	AMS	σ_{AMS}	T (s)	σ_T (s)
2 000	1	28 506.6	12 760.3	1.3	< 1
2 500	1	26 098.0	9 887.6	1.6	< 1
3 000	1	43 744.6	13 434.0	3.2	< 1
3 500	1	60 434.0	23 081.1	2.0	< 1
4 000	1	69 174.7	25 391.7	2.8	1.0
4 500	1	67 340.3	26 422.2	3.3	1.3
5 000	1	82 123.8	29 815.0	4.5	1.5
5 500	1	88 009.3	26 729.8	4.6	1.4
6 000	1	104 856.0	32 455.8	6.9	2.1
6 500	1	122 111.1	42 108.0	8.3	2.8
7 000	1	123 161.9	41 666.6	8.4	2.8
7 500	1	167 213.7	57 518.7	13.1	4.5
8 000	1	168 917.2	56 505.6	13.2	4.4
8 500	1	170 589.2	46 071.5	13.9	3.5
9 000	1	216 444.0	70 894.6	19.3	6.2
9 500	1	221 415.8	71 346.4	22.0	6.8
10 000	1	199 860.9	69 193.1	19.5	6.7
10 500	1	223 878.2	68 928.2	22.8	6.9
11 000	1	264 433.7	78 143.3	28.5	8.3

Figure 29. E graphs: The limits of TC outside of τ_h (p = 10/n, 50 runs, 500000 moves)

n	SR	AMS	σ_{AMS}	T (s)	σ_T (s)
2 000	1	31 544.8	17 327.4	1.5	< 1
2 500	1	37 282.5	17 758.8	2.2	1.1
3 000	1	41 050.8	16 714.3	2.8	1.2
3 500	1	59 544.4	19 657.7	2.4	< 1
4 000	1	66 063.5	26 473.9	2.6	< 1
4 500	1	69 276.8	25 403.4	3.2	1.1
5 000	1	101 027.9	34 619.6	5.4	1.8
5 500	1	99 081.7	33 051.4	5.5	1.8
6 000	1	109 455.7	44 881.8	6.6	2.6
6 500	1	121 805.9	36 992.5	7.7	2.2
7 000	1	123 962.3	43 498.6	8.6	2.9
7 500	1	123 982.2	45 346.8	9.1	3.1
8 000	1	145 698.6	45 759.8	11.8	3.6
8 500	1	172 399.4	54 661.4	14.7	4.5
9 000	1	185 468.3	53 877.2	16.9	4.8
9 500	1	215 814.2	69 888.2	20.7	6.3
10 000	1	211 838.6	71 073.1	21.5	7.0
10 500	1	218 459.6	59 538.2	22.1	6.1
11 000	1	268 026.0	95 549.2	29.8	10.3

larly true at τ_g for all the instances (since $SR \leq$ 0.08) and outside of τ_g for one F graph ($SR = 0.04$ when $p = 0.008$). Furthermore, the difficulty also holds outside of τ in one case, when $p = 0.009$ for the F instance ($SR = 0.48$).

Figure 19 recalls the most effective τ measure from Figure 10, Figure 11, Figure 12, Figure 13, Figure 14, Figure 15, Figure 16, Figure 17 and Figure 18 depending on n and the class of graphs. The last three columns (respectively lines) also propose a ranking of τ_c, τ_e, τ_g, τ_h, and τ_w for a particular n value (respectively for a particular graph class). For instance, τ_h is classified as "Best"

when $n = 200$ since "h" appears more than the other thresholds on the "$n = 200$" line. Similarly, τ_c, τ_e, and τ_w are categorized as "Worst" for $n = 200$ since they are missing on the "$n = 200$" line.

From Figure 19, one can observe that τ_h is (almost) always the most effective τ measure whatever the value of n or the graph class. Indeed, if we define the overall score Σ (for all n values and all graphs) of a τ measure as the number of times it appears in the inner figure (intersection of lines 3–5 and columns U–F), we obtain $\Sigma_h > \Sigma_g > \Sigma_c > \Sigma_{e,w}$ (since $8 > 6 > 3 > 2$). One can then establish the following overall τ ranking: $\tau_h >_\Sigma \tau_g$

Figure 30. F graphs: The limits of TC outside of τ_h (p = 10/n, 50 runs, 500000 moves)

n	SR	AMS	σ_{AMS}	T (s)	σ_T (s)
2 000	1	144 239.7	89 756.7	11.2	6.9
2 500	1	155 953.6	91 872.9	15.2	8.9
3 000	0.68	270 358.6	129 986.0	7.7	3.7
3 500	0.28	262 949.6	110 083.5	9.2	3.8
4 000	0.28	311 626.9	89 354.3	11.3	3.2
4 500	0.30	312 356.9	106 744.1	15.8	5.4
5 000	0.22	326 451.3	111 325.0	16.8	5.4
5 500	0.28	340 731.7	112 833.7	20.0	6.6
6 000	0.20	388 958.3	83 763.7	24.1	5.1
6 500	0.04	359 221.5	90 857.5	25.0	5.8
7 000	0.04	375 040.5	25 217.5	24.6	1.4
7 500	0.04	456 035.5	24 982.5	36.0	1.9
8 000	0.06	439 747.3	56 787.3	35.6	4.4
8 500	0.04	334 201.0	78 082.0	27.6	6.4
9 000	0	–	–	–	–
9 500	0	–	–	–	–
10 000	0	–	–	–	–
10 500	0	–	–	–	–
11 000	0	–	–	–	–

$>_\Sigma \tau_c >_\Sigma \tau_{e,\,w}$, where "$>_\Sigma$" means "more effective than". Consequently, we will mainly use τ_h as the phase transition threshold in the rest of the paper.

INFLUENCE OF THE PROBLEM SIZE *n* ON THE PROBLEM DIFFICULTY

The scalability of TC, i.e., how its performance changes with growing problem size, can be observed in Figure 20, Figure 21, Figure 22, Figure 23 and Figure 24 (27 new instances), on graphs respectively outside of τ_h (within 500000 moves for TC) and around τ_h (1000000 moves), for various *n* values in [250, 1500] (see also where we

use much larger graph with *n* up to 11000 to test the limit of TC).

Figure 20 and Figure 21 show that graphs of these sizes outside of τ_h are really easy for TC since *SR* is always 1. Around τ_h (Figure 22, Figure 23 and Figure 24), the U and E graphs are still easy for TC (*SR* = 1) but the F instances become harder when $n \geq 1000$ ($SR \leq 0.04$).

SAW was checked for scalability only on E graphs in (Eiben et al., 1998). While it reached good *SR* values outside of τ_h (see Figure 20), its performance dramatically falls around τ_h when $n \geq 1000$ (Figure 22).

Figure 31. Long TC runs outside of τ_h (p = 10/n) on the hardest F instances from Figure 30 where SR < 1 (25 runs, 1000000 moves)

n	SR_s	SR_l	AMS_l	σ_{AMS_l}	T_l (s)	σ_{T_l} (s)
3 000	0.68	1	395 950.3	272 423.2	31.6	21.7
3 500	0.28	0.44	425 406.7	241 345.6	14.9	8.3
4 000	0.28	0.44	568 688.4	269 936.2	23.7	11.2
4 500	0.30	0.80	518 964.3	174 691.5	24.7	8.3
5 000	0.22	0.48	589 879.2	266 224.1	31.2	14.1
5 500	0.28	0.48	606 378.3	217 482.9	34.0	12.1
6 000	0.20	0.52	623 241.4	194 497.9	38.3	12.1
6 500	0.04	0.12	630 536.3	139 949.1	40.6	8.8
7 000	0.04	0.24	789 536.0	159 775.2	55.1	10.8
7 500	0.04	0.12	623 690.0	189 473.5	45.3	13.7
8 000	0.06	0.24	612 446.7	214 622.9	48.1	16.8
8 500	0.04	0.16	703 282.3	133 815.8	59.1	11.0
9 000	0	0.08	684 127.5	216 838.5	64.5	20.5
9 500	0	0	–	–	–	–
10 000	0	0	–	–	–	–
10 500	0	0.04	787 970.0	0.0	81.7	0.0
11 000	0	0	–	–	–	–

IMPACT OF LONGER RUNS ON THE SOLUTION PERFORMANCE

We just observed that, in some or all runs, TC fails to find a proper 3-coloring for some graphs within 300000 moves (see Figure 12, Figure 13, Figure 14, Figure 15, Figure 16, Figure 17 and Figure 18) or 1000000 moves (Figure 24). We study here the effect of giving more search time to TC, i.e. if longer runs can increase its success rates for solving these instances. So, we first extend the maximum number of moves per run to 1000000 for graphs and rerun TC whenever SR < 1 for TC in Figures 12–18. In Figure 25, SR_s again lists the SR achieved by TC in Figure 12, Figure 13, Figure 14, Figure 15, Figure 16, Figure 17 and Figure 18 (*short* runs with 300000 moves). Similarly, SR_l, AMS_l, and T_l are for 25 *long* runs (i.e., within 1000000 moves).

Figure 25 confirms that small and medium-order graphs ($n \leq 500$) are easily solved now by TC, even around τ_h ($SR_l \geq 0.96$). Significant improvements can also be observed on large-order U and E graphs ($n = 1000$). Nevertheless, the U instance is still quite challenging ($SR_l = 0.28$). The large-order F graphs remain difficult to color, even if some improvements are sometimes observed. Indeed, no improvement at all was possible when $p = 0.008$ ($SR_l = SR_s$).

Note that Eiben et al. (1998) reported one similar experiment using only one graph ($E_{1000, 0.008}$): The SR of SAW increased from 0 within 300000

Figure 32. Achieving SR = 1 with TC on the hardest F instances from Figure 31 where $SR_l < 1$ (5 runs, without time limit)

n	SR_l	SR_∞	AMS_∞	σ_{AMS_∞}	T_∞ (s)	σ_{T_∞} (s)
3 500	0.44	1	1 423 879.8	672 368.9	52.1	24.5
4 000	0.44	1	1 161 122.8	801 233.9	46.0	31.8
4 500	0.8	1	700 484.6	380 628.5	35.2	19.1
5 000	0.48	1	1 315 440.6	766 691.4	65.5	37.9
5 500	0.48	1	1 011 681.4	933 814.3	55.7	49.8
6 000	0.52	1	1 468 846.8	759 937.0	90.0	46.6
6 500	0.12	1	4 705 684.0	2 950 583.4	291.6	182.9
7 000	0.24	1	3 781 609.5	1 832 451.7	259.3	125.5
7 500	0.12	1	7 628 363.0	8 251 686.1	583.0	630.0
8 000	0.24	1	1 522 375.0	721 937.9	122.0	58.1
8 500	0.16	1	2 118 416.3	1 432 638.0	182.6	123.1
9 000	0.08	1	3 428 184.8	2 060 651.2	301.4	179.8
9 500	0	1	12 454 689.0	4 959 205.0	1 160.5	461.9
10 000	0	1	59 920 576.0	50 207 203.5	5 870.1	4 909.1
10 500	0.04	1	6 780 762.5	875 675.5	690.2	90.5
11 000	0	1	10 497 934.0	5 181 142.3	1 103.2	546.2

evaluations to 0.44 within 1000000 evaluations (AES = 407 283)[3].

Since TC still fails to reach $SR = 1$ within 1000000 moves for 10 instances (4 in Figure 24 and 7 in Figure 25, but $F_{1000, 0.008}$ is considered in both figures), we remove this limit and allow TC to run until it finds a proper 3-coloring. Results are summarized in Figures 26–27[4]. "MAXINT" entries in Figure 27 indicate values larger than the maximal integer authorized by the system (i.e. 4 294 967 295). In these cases, T_∞ indicates the minimum time needed to reach a proper 3-coloring.

Two main observations can be made from Figure 26 and Figure 27. First, all graphs are quite easy for TC whenever $p \neq 8/n$, see Figure 26 where $AMS_\infty \leq 2904052$ in this case. Second, only the large-order F instances constitute a real challenge for TC whenever $p = 8/n$, see Figure 27 where $AMS_\infty \geq 298\,129024$ for $n \geq 1000$.

HOW FAR CAN WE GO WITH TC?

The scalability of TC was studied for graphs with up to 1500 vertices as in (Eiben et al., 1998) for SAW. In this section, we report additional results for TC in Figure 28, Figure 29, Figure 30, Figure 31, Figure 32, Figure 33, Figure 34, Figure 35 and Figure 36 for some n values in [2000, 11000][5] around and outside of the threshold τ_h to try to determine the limits of TC (95 new graphs).

Figure 28, Figure 29 and Figure 30 show computational results outside of the phase transition with a time limit of 500000 moves. All U and E instances, and F graphs where $n \leq 2500$, are really easy for TC (since $SR = 1$ in this cases). Note that TC also performs well for $F_{2000, 10/n}$ since $SR = 0.68$. The problem becomes harder only on F instances from n = 3500 since the best SR achieved by TC when n $\geq$ 3500 falls to 0.30. So,

Figure 33. U graphs: The limits of TC around τ_h (p = 8/n, 25 runs, 1000000 moves)

n	SR	AMS	σ_{AMS}	T (s)	σ_T (s)
2 000	1	312 539.2	160 692.6	8.0	3.9
2 500	1	474 737.1	204 351.5	24.0	9.9
3 000	1	328 232.3	137 527.3	12.8	5.2
3 500	0.72	556 514.9	230 236.4	11.2	4.7
4 000	0.68	689 607.9	182 578.8	16.3	4.2
4 500	0.6	610 822.6	205 490.8	17.6	6.0
5 000	0.52	680 168.1	244 471.0	23.6	8.5
5 500	0.68	604 993.5	200 738.5	18.8	6.2
6 000	0.36	739 870.9	120 713.8	28.3	4.6
6 500	0.28	854 454.0	104 911.0	30.4	4.0
7 000	0.12	762 356.7	152 977.1	30.0	5.9
7 500	0.04	947 253.0	0.0	37.7	0.0
8 000	0.08	897 777.0	2 250.0	44.3	< 1
8 500	0.32	811 344.4	152 395.1	41.5	8.0
9 000	0.08	858 772.5	70 563.5	45.1	3.1
9 500	0.04	872 204.0	0.0	50.8	0.0
10 000	0.04	790 561.0	0.0	44.1	0.0
10 500	0.04	915 827.0	0.0	54.3	0.0
11 000	0	–	–	–	–

Figure 30 clearly confirms that F graphs are harder than U and E instances, even outside of τ.

Figure 31 and Figure 32 shows results for "longer" runs, with a time limit of 1000000 moves (Figure 31) or without time limit (Figure 32), to achieve $SR = 1$ on the hardest F instances from Figure 30. One observes that a solution is always found but, contrary to U and E instances, the computation effort required for 3-coloring large F graphs properly can be very high (up to more than 59 million moves in average).

Figure 33 and Figure 34 show computational results around the phase transition for U and E instances within a time limit of 1000000 moves. Note that no result is reported here (i.e., around τ_h) for the F graphs since, as already showed in Figure 24, TC cannot solve such instances once $n \geq 1\,250$ within the time limit of 1000000 moves. Indeed, Figure 27 indicates that TC needs more than 4 billion moves (about 126 hours) to solve $F_{1500, 8/n}$. This seems to indicate that, for F graphs around τ_h, $F_{1500, 8/n}$ would be the largest graph that can be colored by TC.

Figure 34. E graphs: The limits of TC around τ_h (p = 8/n, 25 runs, 1000000 moves)

n	SR	AMS	σ_{AMS}	T (s)	σ_T (s)
2 000	0.96	504 763.3	212 903.3	12.2	5.2
2 500	0.92	426 471.0	203 155.8	12.9	6.3
3 000	0.80	493 869.6	212 989.6	10.1	4.4
3 500	0.56	626 114.4	214 233.8	15.4	5.2
4 000	0.60	540 508.9	169 444.7	15.1	5.0
4 500	0.64	569 527.4	187 684.6	18.1	5.7
5 000	0.28	638 217.7	206 569.0	22.7	7.6
5 500	0.64	584 719.5	169 439.6	18.8	5.5
6 000	0.36	755 428.4	179 760.4	26.7	6.1
6 500	0.16	759 410.3	38 527.2	27.8	1.5
7 000	0.16	764 425.5	170 939.2	30.1	7.0
7 500	0.16	689 463.3	78 321.7	27.3	4.0
8 000	0.16	840 018.0	154 616.0	39.5	7.9
8 500	0.08	884 325.0	10 851.0	43.2	< 1
9 000	0.12	761 693.7	155 293.8	45.2	6.9
9 500	0.04	947 668.0	0.0	46.7	0.0
10 000	0.04	857 340.0	0.0	49.0	0.0
10 500	0	—	—	—	—
11 000	0	—	—	—	—

According to Figure 33, TC still always solves easily U graphs around τ_h up to $n = 3000$ since $SR = 1$ in these cases. Furthermore, TC also performs quite well on larger U instances since $SR \geq 0.52$ for n up to 5 500. E graphs (see Figure 34) start here to be a little bit harder than U instances since TC never reached $SR = 1$ but it performs well up to $n = 5\,500$ ($SR \geq 0.56$ except for $E_{5000, 8/n}$). The performance of TC falls below 0.5 only for the largest graphs ($n \geq 6000$ and for $E_{5000, 8/n}$).

Figure 35 and Figure 36 show results for runs without time limit on the graphs from Figure 33 and Figure 34 where $SR < 1$. One observes that a solution is always found for each run of TC, even for the largest instances with 11000 vertices. This indicates that TC is probably able to color U and E graphs with much larger n, even around the phase transition.

Figure 35. Achieving SR = 1 with TC around τ_h (p = 8/n) on the hardest U instances from Figure 33 (5 runs, without time limit)

n	SR_l	SR_∞	AMS_∞	σ_{AMS_∞}	T_∞ (s)	σ_{T_∞} (s)
3 500	0.72	1	674 481.0	524 132.0	16.3	12.5
4 000	0.68	1	718 282.2	577 635.5	17.4	13.0
4 500	0.60	1	735 476.4	395 813.7	20.3	10.9
5 000	0.52	1	1 299 003.3	1 050 951.6	29.2	17.2
5 500	0.68	1	1 377 980.4	406 716.0	40.5	12.1
6 000	0.36	1	1 639 610.8	554 939.4	55.5	21.0
6 500	0.28	1	1 887 605.3	929 657.3	69.1	32.7
7 000	0.12	1	1 958 313.0	753 376.6	73.4	27.1
7 500	0.04	1	3 541 162.0	2 309 180.9	126.6	71.1
8 000	0.08	1	2 359 020.8	1 947 452.6	101.0	78.0
8 500	0.32	1	2 543 023.5	1 329 579.5	124.8	63.8
9 000	0.08	1	2 937 435.0	1 129 824.7	149.7	59.1
9 500	0.04	1	2 407 969.5	975 149.0	129.9	53.7
10 000	0.04	1	2 969 634.0	1 495 455.2	180.6	91.7
10 500	0.04	1	4 426 329.0	3 903 536.4	246.4	207.3
11 000	0	1	4 877 196.0	2 224 861.0	295.1	130.7

CONCLUSION

We present an experimental investigation of a simple tabu search algorithm for coloring random 3-colorable graphs, studying three well-known classes of graphs (Uniform, Equipartite, and Flat) outside of or around the phase transition thresholds. The main findings of this study can be summarized as follows.

OUTSIDE OF THE PHASE TRANSITION THRESHOLDS

The simple tabu search algorithm can color any graph (U, E, F) with $200 \leq n \leq 11000$ vertices at each run. Moreover, as already observed in other studies, F graphs are more difficult to color than U and E graphs. More precisely:

- For the U and E classes, any graph with up to 11000 vertices can very easily be colored within 500000 moves (less than 30 seconds in average). This suggests that TC is probably able to color much larger ($n \gg$ 11000) U and E graphs within reasonable time.
- For the F class, a solution can always be found for graphs with $n \leq 3000$ in average within 1 million moves (less than 60 seconds). Larger graphs with $3500 \leq n \leq$ 11000 can also always be colored if more computing time is allowed. Typically this can be achieved in average with 60 millions of moves (about 1.5 hours).

Figure 36. Achieving SR = 1 with TC around τ_h (p = 8/n) on the hardest E instances from Figure 34 (5 runs, without time limit)

n	SR_l	SR_∞	AMS_∞	$\sigma_{AMS\infty}$	T_∞ (s)	$\sigma_{T\infty}$ (s)
2 000	0.96	1	511 059.2	277 824.1	13.2	6.9
2 500	0.92	1	464 184.2	343 839.3	14.8	10.8
3 000	0.80	1	687 144.4	310 374.7	27.1	12.0
3 500	0.56	1	1 032 754.4	823 348.6	25.3	19.6
4 000	0.60	1	868 927.4	378 278.6	25.2	10.9
4 500	0.64	1	844 836.2	481 748.7	26.3	14.5
5 000	0.28	1	2 097 527.5	1 047 561.4	72.5	36.1
5 500	0.64	1	2 100 852.5	894 367.8	57.0	22.7
6 000	0.36	1	1 144 047.0	245 704.9	40.1	9.1
6 500	0.16	1	2 123 158.3	1 409 654.3	84.1	56.6
7 000	0.16	1	1 969 999.4	1 149 751.0	81.9	46.0
7 500	0.16	1	2 247 856.3	763 401.7	91.9	30.0
8 000	0.16	1	1 997 386.0	1 203 102.3	86.5	52.9
8 500	0.08	1	3 118 057.0	1 693 211.6	151.4	81.2
9 000	0.12	1	3 243 706.3	3 819 214.4	175.5	204.6
9 500	0.04	1	3 269 792.5	527 271.4	165.7	24.3
10 000	0.04	1	3 582 580.8	1 845 239.8	196.5	98.6
10 500	0	1	4 844 833.0	1 346 013.9	299.5	82.8
11 000	0	1	4 904 942.0	1 222 402.3	294.1	80.7

AROUND THE PHASE TRANSITION THRESHOLDS

The simple tabu search algorithm can color any U and E graph with $200 \leq n \leq 11000$ vertices at each run. E graphs are a little more difficult to color than U graphs. It is very difficult to color F graphs with more than 1500 vertices. More precisely:

- For the U and E classes, any graph with up to 11000 vertices can be colored in average within 5 million moves (less than 5 minutes). This suggests that TC is probably able to color still larger ($n \gg 11000$) U and E graphs within reasonable time.

- For the F class, with a time limit of 1 million moves (a few seconds), a proper 3-coloring can always be found for graphs with up to 500 vertices, a solution can occasionally be found for graphs with $500 < n \leq 1000$. F graphs with up to 1500 vertices can also always be colored if no time limit is imposed. However, this may require up to more than 4 billion moves (about 126 hours). This suggests that F graphs larger than 1500 vertices around the phase transition thresholds constitute a real challenge for TC, but very probably for many (k-) coloring algorithms.

PHASE TRANSITION THRESHOLDS

Finally, concerning the different phase transition thresholds reported in the literature, the experimental results coincide globally well with what is predicted by these thresholds as to the relative hardness of a given graph. Nevertheless, it is observed that the threshold τ_h proposed in (Eiben, van der Hauw, & van Hemert, 1998) is better suited to locate the phase transitions compared with other τ measures. To be more precise, the lower bound of τ_h ($7/n$) seems more adequate for U and E instances while the whole interval ($7/n \leq p \leq 8/n$) remains valid for (sufficiently large) F graphs. Moreover, a ranking among these thresholds is proposed based on the computational observations.

ACKNOWLEDGMENTS

We would like to thank the reviewers of the paper for their useful comments. This work was partially supported by the French "Pays de la Loire" region (MILES and RadaPop projects, Chair of Excellence), the French Research Ministry, and the French "Centre National de la Recherche Scientifique" (CNRS, GdR RO project).

REFERENCES

Alekseev, V. E., Boliac, R., Korobitsyn, D. V., & Lozin, V. V. (2007). NP-hard graph problems and boundary classes of graphs. *Theoretical Computer Science, 389*(1-2), 219–236. doi:10.1016/j.tcs.2007.09.013

Barbosa, V. C., & Ferreira, R. G. (2004). On the phase transitions of graph coloring and independent sets. *Physica A: Statistical Mechanics and its Applications, 343*, 401-423.

Braunstein, A., Mulet, R., Pagnani, A., Weigt, M., & Zecchina, R. (2003). Polynomial iterative algorithms for coloring and analyzing random graphs. *Physical Review E: Statistical, Nonlinear, and Soft Matter Physics.* doi:10.1103/PhysRevE.68.036702

Brélaz, D. (1979). New methods to color the vertices of a graph. *Communications of the ACM, 22*(4), 251–256. doi:10.1145/359094.359101

Cheeseman, P., Kanefsky, B., & Taylor, W. M. (1991). Where the really hard problems are. In J. Mylopoulos & R. Reiter (Eds.), *Twelfth International Joint Conference on Artificial Intelligence* (Vol. 1, pp. 331-337). San Francisco: Morgan Kaufmann.

Culberson, J. C., & Gent, I. P. (2001). Frozen development in graph coloring. *Theoretical Computer Science, 265*(1-2), 227–264. doi:10.1016/S0304-3975(01)00164-5

Dorne, R., & Hao, J. K. (1998). Tabu search for graph coloring, T-colorings and set T-colorings. In Voss, S., Martello, S., Osman, I. H., & Roucairol, C. (Eds.), *Meta-Heuristics: Advances and Trends in Local Search Paradigms for Optimization* (pp. 77–92). Dordrecht, The Netherlands: Kluwer.

Dubois, O., Monasson, R., Selman, B., & Zecchina, R. (Eds.). (2001)... *Theoretical Computer Science, 265*(1-2).

Eiben, A. E., van der Hauw, J. K., & van Hemert, J. I. (1998). Graph coloring with adaptive evolutionary algorithms. *Journal of Heuristics, 4*(1), 24–46. doi:10.1023/A:1009638304510

Erben, W. (2001). A grouping genetic algorithm for graph colouring and exam timetabling. In E. Burke & W. Erben (Eds.), *Practice and Theory of Automated Timetabling III* (LNCS 2079, pp. 132-156). Berlin: Springer.

Fleurent, C., & Ferland, J. (1996a). Genetic and hybrid algorithms for graph coloring. *Annals of Operations Research, 6*(3), 437–461. doi:10.1007/BF02125407

Fleurent, C., & Ferland, J. (1996b). Object-oriented implementation of heuristic search methods for graph coloring, maximum clique, and satisfiability. In D. S. Johnson & M. A. Trick (Eds.), *Cliques, Coloring, and Satisfiability* (Volume 26 of DIMACS Series in Discrete Mathematics and Theoretical Computer Science, pp. 619-652). New Providence, NJ: American Mathematical Society.

Garey, M. R., & Johnson, D. S. (1979). *Computers and Intractability: A Guide to the Theory of NP-Completness*. San Francisco: W. H. Freeman and Company.

Gent, I. P., MacIntyre, E., Prosser, P., & Walsh, T. (1996). The constrainedness of search. In W. J. Clancey, D. Weld, H. E. Shrobe, & T. E. Senator (Eds.), *Thirteenth National Conference on Artificial Intelligence* (Vol. 1, pp. 246-252). Menlo Park, CA: AAAI Press.

Glover, F. W., & Laguna, M. (1997). *Tabu Search*. Dordrecht, The Netherladns: Kluwer.

Hartmann, A. K., & Weigt, M. (2005). *Phase Transitions in Combinatorial Optimization Problems: Basics, Algorithms and Statistical Mechanics*. New York: Wiley. doi:10.1002/3527606734

Hertz, A., & de Werra, D. (1987). Using tabu search techniques for graph coloring. *Computing, 39*(4), 345–351. doi:10.1007/BF02239976

Hogg, T., Huberman, B. A., & Williams, C. P. (Eds.). (1996)... *Artificial Intelligence, 81*(1-2).

Karp, R. M. (1972). Reducibility among combinatorial problems. In Miller, R. E., & Thatcher, J. W. (Eds.), *Complexity of Computer Computations* (pp. 85–103). New York: Plenum.

Kochol, M., Lozin, V., & Randerath, B. (2003). The 3-colorability problem on graphs with maximum degree four. *SIAM Journal on Computing, 32*(5), 1128–1139. doi:10.1137/S0097539702418759

Krivelevich, M., & Sudakov, B. (2006). Pseudo-random graphs. In Gyori, E., Katona, G. O. H., & Lovász, L. (Eds.), *More sets, graphs and numbers* (*Vol. 15*, pp. 199–262). Berlin: Springer. doi:10.1007/978-3-540-32439-3_10

Krzakała, F., Pagnani, A., & Weigt, M. (2004). Threshold values, stability analysis, and high-q asymptotics for the coloring problem on random graphs. *Physical Review E: Statistical, Nonlinear, and Soft Matter Physics*. doi:10.1103/PhysRevE.70.046705

Maffray, F., & Preissmann, M. (1996). On the NP-completeness of the k-colorability problem for triangle-free graphs. *Discrete Mathematics, 162*(1-3), 313–317. doi:10.1016/S0012-365X(97)89267-9

Monasson, R., Zecchina, R., Kirkpatrick, S., Selman, B., & Troyansky, L. (1999). Determining computational complexity from characteristic 'phase transitions'. *Nature, 400*, 133–137. doi:10.1038/22055

Petford, A. D., & Welsh, D. J. A. (1989). A randomized 3-colouring algorithm. *Discrete Mathematics, 74*(1-2), 253–261. doi:10.1016/0012-365X(89)90214-8

(2001). Random graphs. InBollobás, B. (Ed.), *Cambridge Studies in Advanced Mathematics* (2nd ed., *Vol. 78*). Cambridge, UK: Cambridge University Press.

Zdeborová, L., & Krzakała, F. (2007). Phase transitions in the coloring of random graphs. *Physical Review E.*

ENDNOTES

[1] A C++ source code implementing TABU-COL is available e.g. from www.imada.sdu.dk/~marco/gcp-study.

[2] *TT* is called the "tabu tenure". We used the same dynamic *TT* formula than that in (Dorne & Hao, 1998) since this approach achieved effective results.

[3] However, note that "0.44" is contradictory with Fig. 14 in (Eiben et al., 1998). Indeed, the plot rather suggests 0.16 as already indicated in Figure 22.

[4] For runs without time limit, we only report (mean) values based on 5 executions since no significant differences were observed (on easy instances) with a larger number of runs.

[5] The graph generator employed to build the graphs is restricted to $n \leq 5000$. So, we just modified two constants of the generator to generate instances with $n > 5000$.

This work was previously published in International Journal of Applied Metaheuristic Computing, Volume 1, Issue 4, edited by Peng-Yeng Yin, pp. 1-24, copyright 2010 by IGI Publishing (an imprint of IGI Global).

Chapter 13
A Metaheuristic Approach to the Graceful Labeling Problem

Houra Mahmoudzadeh
Sharif University of Technology, Iran

Kourosh Eshghi
Sharif University of Technology, Iran

ABSTRACT

In graph theory, a graceful labeling of a graph G = (V, E) with n vertices and m edges is a labeling of its vertices with distinct integers between 0 and m inclusive, such that each edge is uniquely identified by the absolute difference between its endpoints. In this paper, the well-known graceful labeling problem of graphs is represented as an optimization problem, and an algorithm based on Ant Colony Optimization metaheuristic is proposed for finding its solutions. In this regard, the proposed algorithm is applied to different classes of graphs and the results are compared with the few existing methods inside of different literature.

GRACEFUL LABELING PROBLEM

In graph theory, a graceful labeling of a graph $G = (V, E)$ with n vertices and m edges is a labeling of its vertices with distinct integers between 0 and m inclusive, such that each edge is uniquely identified by the absolute difference between its endpoints. To be more precise, if we assume $G = (V, E)$ to be an undirected graph without loops or double connections between vertices, a grace-

ful labeling of G, with n vertices and edges, is a one-to-one mapping f of the vertex set V into the set $\{0, 1, 2, ..., m\}$, so that if we assign an edge label $| f(x) - f(y) |$ to any edge (x, y), each edge receives a distinct positive integer label. A graph that can be gracefully labeled is called a graceful graph (Rosa, 1967). A sample graceful graph is shown in Figure 1. Vertex labels are shown inside the vertex circles, and edge labels are shown in red near the related edges.

The name "graceful labeling" is due to Solomon W. Golomb; however, this class of labelings was

DOI: 10.4018/978-1-4666-0270-0.ch013

Figure 1. An example of graceful labeling of a graph

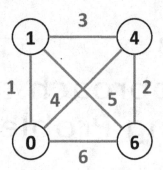

originally given the name β-labelings by Alex Rosa in a 1967 paper on graph labeling (Rosa, 1967). The computational complexity of the graceful labeling problem is not known, but a related problem called harmonious labeling was shown to be NP-complete (Gallian, 2009). In fact, the graceful labeling problem is rather a well-known example of the problems in NP, which are not known to be NP-complete, and neither known to be in P (Johnson, 2005). Many variations of graph labeling have been introduced in recent years by researchers. Various classes of graphs have been proven mathematically to be graceful or non-graceful. A detailed survey of graph labeling problems and the related results are shown in a survey by Gallian (2009). There is an unproved conjecture that all trees are graceful. Although, it is shown that trees with up to 27 vertices are graceful. It is shown that all cycles C_n are graceful if and only if $n \equiv 0$ or $3 \pmod 4$. All wheels W_n, Helms H_n, and Crowns R_n are graceful. The complete graphs K_n are graceful if and only if $n \leq 4$. The necessary condition for a windmill $K_n^{(m)}$ ($n \geq 3$) to be graceful is that $n \leq 5$; a windmill $K_n^{(m)}$ consists of m complete graphs K_n with one common vertex (Gallian, 2009). An example for each class of the graphs mentioned above and their graceful labelings are shown in Figure 2.

The graceful labeling problem is to find out whether a given graph is graceful or not, and if it is, how to label the vertices. The process of grace-

fully labeling a graph is a very tedious and difficult task for many classes of graphs (Eshghi & Azimi, 2004).

In the problem literature, many methods are presented for proving gracefulness of different classes of graphs theoretically, but most of them did not use a general method for finding the graceful labeling of the graphs to be studied. These theoretical methods focus on finding out whether the given graph is graceful or not, rather than finding its exact labeling. Therefore, the problem of finding a graceful labeling for a given graph, even when we know theoretically that the graph is graceful, is not yet targeted by many researchers. There exist only two mathematical programming methods for finding graceful labeling of graphs. The first one is a constraint programming approach (Redl, 2003), and the second one is a branch and bound (B&B) algorithm based on mathematical programming (Eshghi & Azimi, 2004). It is shown that the B&B method generates better solutions than the constraint programming method for graceful labeling problem (Eshghi & Azimi, 2004).

In this paper, a new general method for gracefully labeling any type of graphs is presented. Since this method inputs only the adjacency matrix of the graph, it is very easy to use; finally, it outputs the graceful labeling of the given graph, if any. In this approach, the graceful labeling problem is represented as an assignment-type problem with the aim of finding a feasible solution, and a metaheuristic approach based on Ant Colony Optimization (ACO) for gracefully labeling graphs is presented.

The rest of this paper is organized as follows: In the next section, Ant Colony Optimization is briefly introduced. Afterwards, a new representation of graceful labeling problem in a briefly modified framework of ACO, and the proposed metaheuristic algorithm are introduced. The final section shows the obtained results and compares them with those of the existing methods in the literature.

Figure 2. Examples for some classes of graceful graphs and their graceful labelings: (a) a cycle C_7, (b) a tree T_{10}, (c) a wheel W_4, (d) a helm H_5, (e) a crown R_5, (f) a windmill $K_3^{(4)}$

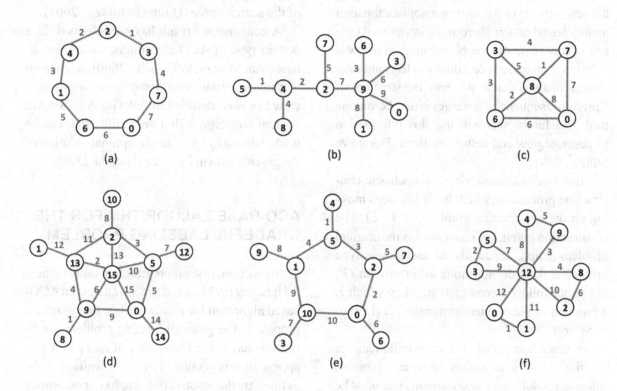

(a)   (b)   (c)

(d)   (e)   (f)

ANT COLONY OPTIMIZATION

Many problems of practical importance can be modeled as combinatorial optimization problems. It is known that the majority of these problems cannot be solved by a polynomial time algorithm, if $NP \neq P$. For this reason, heuristics have been invented to find solutions for these problems in a reasonable amount of time. Some of these heuristic algorithms are not restricted to specific problem types, and these "general-purpose" algorithms are called *metaheuristics*.

Recently, one of the most successful metaheuristics is Ant Colony Optimization (ACO), which was first introduced by Marco Dorigo (Dorigo & Stützle, 2004). Many ACO based algorithms have been proposed to solve different types of combinatorial optimization problems such as symmetric and asymmetric traveling salesman

problems (Dorigo & Gambardella, 1997), the graph coloring problem (Costa & Hertz, 1997), the knight's tour problem in graphs (Hingston & Kendall, 2004) and the adaptive routing in packet-switched communications networks (Di Caro & Dorigo, 1998).

Ants deposit chemicals, called *pheromone*, on the ground while searching for food. The collective pheromone-laying / pheromone-following behavior whereby an ant is influenced by the chemical trail left by other ants was the inspiring source of Ant Colony Optimization (Dorigo & Stützle, 2004).

In ACO, artificial ants make walks on a graph, and lay artificial pheromone trails on the vertices and/or edges of the graph. This artificial pheromone is accumulated at run-time through a learning mechanism that gives reward to good problem solutions. Artificial ants start from random vertices: next, according to the problem specifications, each ant chooses probabilistically the new vertex to visit using a probabilistic function mainly based on the pheromone intensity. At the end of any iteration, the pheromone on the best solution is increased according to a learning rule. The rationale is that in this way the structure of ''preferred sequences'' emerges in the pheromone trail, and future ants will use this information to generate new and better solutions (Dorigo & Stützle, 2001).

Ants can be characterized as stochastic construction procedures which build solutions moving on the construction graph $G' = (C, L)$. The construction graph, G', is not always the original problem graph, especially in assignment-type problems. Ants do not move arbitrarily on G', but rather follow a construction policy which is a function of the problem constraints Ω (Dorigo & Stützle, 2004).

In general, artificial ants try to build feasible solutions, but, if necessary, they can generate infeasible solutions. The constraints that must be satisfied necessarily are called *hard constraints*, and others that may be ignored when not possible to be satisfied are called *soft constraints* (Dorigo & Stützle, 2004). Components $c_i \in C$ and connections $l_{ij} \in L$ can receive a pheromone trail π (π_i if associated to components, π_{ij} if associated to connections) encoding a long-term memory about the whole ant search process that is updated by the ants themselves, and a heuristic value η (η_i and η_{ij}, respectively) representing a priori information about the problem instance definition or run-time information provided by a source different from the ants. In many cases heuristic information are used to make the ants satisfy the problem constraints. These values are used by the ants' heuristic rule to make probabilistic decisions on how to move on the graph (Dorigo & Stützle, 2004).

After the ants complete their solutions at each iteration, a procedure called *pheromone evaporation* occurs. This procedure is designed to avoid a too rapid convergence of the algorithm towards a sub-optimal region. It implements a useful form of *forgetting*, favoring the exploration of new areas of the search space (Dorigo & Stützle, 2001).

A convergence result has been derived for a certain type of ACO algorithms, called Graph-based Ant System, by Gutjahr (2000). It is shown that under certain conditions, the solutions generated in each iteration of this Graph-based Ant System converge with a probability that can be made arbitrarily close to the optimal solution of the given problem instance (Gutjahr, 2000).

ACO-BASED ALGORITHM FOR THE GRACEFUL LABELING PROBLEM

In this section, first a representation for the graceful labeling problem is defined and next an ACO-based algorithm for gracefully labeling graphs is proposed. The graceful labeling problem can be represented in the framework of ACO as it will appear in this section. The main features to be defined are the construction graph G', pheromone trails and their update rules, heuristic information and the probabilistic decision rule. Remember that unlike most combinatorial optimization problems, the goal in the graceful labeling problem is just to find a *feasible* solution among all possibilities.

Construction Graph

The goal in assignment-type problems is to assign a set of items to a given number of objects or resources subject to some constraints. A solution which satisfies the constraints is said to be a feasible solution (Costa & Hertz, 1997).

In this paper, graceful labeling problem is defined as an assignment-type problem in which a set of numbers are assigned to the vertices of a graph. In the framework of ACO, the construction graph for this problem is defined to be a complete bipartite graph, $G' = (C, L)$, where $C = V \bigcup \{0, 1, ..., m\}$. This means that the set of components, C, consists of two parts: the first part is V, the set of vertices of graph G, and the second is the set $\{0, 1, \ldots, m\}$.

The goal of the new problem is to find a feasible assignment of the labels $\{0, 1, \ldots, m\}$ to the set of vertices, V, so that the vertex labels in the original problem are distinct, and the corresponding edge labels in the original problem are also distinct. We consider the constraint of distinct vertex label as a hard constraint, and we try to minimize the number of the resulting repeated edge labels in the objective function. Therefore, for a solution to be the optimum solution of the original problem, the number of repeated edge labels in the represented problem should be equal to zero.

The degree of infeasibility is defined to be the number of repeated edge labels produced in the original problem, thus the optimum solution will have a degree of infeasibility equal to zero. We may say that if solution A produces fewer repeated edge labels in the original problem than solution B, then solution A is a better solution than B, and has a better *solution quality*. Further in this paper, we will use the term *solution quality* to show the desirability of a solution, based on the number of repeated edge labels it produces in the original graph problem.

Depending on the *solution quality*, at any iteration ants update pheromone trails on the connections L which fully connect the two parts of C. The amount of pheromone on each connection (i, j), where $i \in V$ and $j \in \{0, 1, \ldots, m\}$, shows the desirability of assigning label j to vertex i. The connections which are part of a *good* solution previously made, receive more and more pheromone, and pheromones on *bad* solution connections decrease by evaporation. After some iterations, the feasible solution will have the most desirability to be chosen by ants. As an example, the construction graph for the complete graph K_3 and its pheromone accumulation are shown in Figure 3.

Definitions of Pheromones, Accumulation, and Evaporation

Different types of pheromones, their update rules, the corresponding decision probabilities, and the pheromone evaporation procedure are defined in this section.

Definitions of different types of pheromones. Three types of artificial pheromones are defined to be used by foraging ants to make probabilistic decisions for making solutions. Each pheromone $\pi_k(v, j)$ shows the desirability of assigning label j to vertex i according to pheromone type k. The difference among them is the definition of a desirable assignment and the corresponding update rule. The pheromone values are updated after each iteration, and help the ants generate new solutions based on the knowledge gained during previous steps.

Pheromone type I. The first pheromone, $\pi_1(v, j)$, shows the desirability of assigning label j to vertex i, considering the number of repeated edge labels produced in the neighborhood of vertex v by making such an assignment in the previous iterations.

After a solution is completed, the artificial ant checks every vertex to see whether there are repeated edge labels produced in the edges adjacent to it. Whenever a repeated edge label is recognized, the amount of pheromone type I for the corresponding assignment on G' is decreased, otherwise some additional pheromone is deposited on the connection related to the assignment on the construction graph G'. Let θ be the *pheromone evaporation rate* and $ph1(v, j)$ be the amount of pheromone type I on the edge connecting vertex v and label j on the construction graph G'. The algorithmic structure will be similar to Figure 4.

Figure 3. The construction graph and its pheromone accumulation for the complete graph K_3

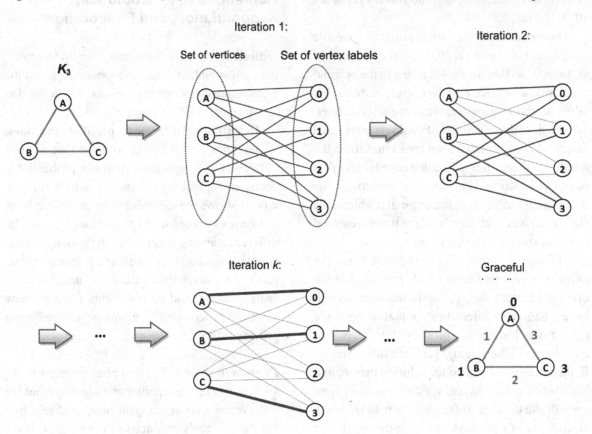

Pheromone type II. Pheromone type II enables us to make undesirable edge labels, in the previous iterations, more attractive. In the process of deciding which label should be assigned to a vertex, the edge labels in the neighborhood of the vertex play an important role. If a specific edge label is not produced in the neighborhood of the vertex, in previous iterations, it will have more probability to be assigned by the artificial ants in this iteration. Thus, if we assume $ph2(v, j)$ in the algorithm the second type pheromone, $\pi_2(v, j)$, it is updated during each step of the solution construction as it is shown in Figure 5.

Pheromone type III. The third type of pheromones, $\pi_3(v, j)$, checks the role of assigning label j to vertex v in increasing the total infeasibility of solutions found in the previous iterations. After completing a solution,

the artificial ant checks the partial role of the edge labels adjacent to every vertex in increasing the total infeasibility. If all the edge labels adjacent to a vertex are not repeated in the graph, the amount of the third pheromone for the corresponding assignment is increased, otherwise, the labels in the neighborhood of vertex v are repeated somewhere in the graph, and the pheromone on the edge connecting label j to vertex v on the construction graph is decreased by the negative effect of pheromone accumulation rate.

Like before, $ph3(v, j)$ is set to be the third type pheromone on the construction graph for assigning label j to vertex v and a general procedure for the update rule of pheromone type III is shown in Figure 6.

Pheromone probability. The pheromone probability of assigning label j to vertex v for pheromone type i, $\mathrm{pr}_i(v, j)$, is calculated by equation (1), where $\pi_i(v, j)$ is the amount of pheromone type i on the edge connecting vertex v and label j on the construction graph G', and m is the number of edges in the original graph G.

$$\mathrm{pr}_i(v,j) = \frac{\pi_i(v, j)}{\sum\limits_{j=0}^{m} \pi_i(v, j)} \qquad i = 1, 2, 3 \qquad (1)$$

Each of these pheromone probabilities affects the final probability of assigning label j to vertex v at each step of labeling.

Pheromone evaporation. It is shown previously that whenever a solution is desirable, the amount of pheromone on the corresponding edges on the construction graph is increased, otherwise, it is decreased. Therefore, in the proposed algorithm the definition of evaporation is different from the classic version of ACO, because it should avoid accumulation of the both positive and negative effect of pheromones. Pheromone evaporation occurs after each iteration, but it doesn't always decrease the amount of pheromones; instead,

Figure 4. Algorithmic structure for the update rule of pheromone type I

```
count(v,j)= average number of repeated edge labels in the neighborhood of vertex v,
while having label j in the previous iterations;
if count(v,j)>0
    ph1(v,j)=(ph1(v,j))*(1-θ);
else
    ph1(v,j)=(ph1(v,j))/(1-θ);
end
```

Figure 5. Algorithmic structure for the update rule of pheromone type II

```
point (j)= assignment of label j to vertex v in the previous iterations in
comparison with other labels
if point (j)>1
    ph2(v,j)=ph2(v,j)*(1-θ);
end
if point2(j)<1
    ph2(v,j)=ph2(v,j)/(1-θ);
end
```

Figure 6. Algorithmic structure for the update rule of pheromone type III

```
count(v,j)= average times that the labels in the neighborhood of vertex v were
repeated in a final solution where label j was assigned to vertex v in past
iterations;
if count(v,j)>1
    ph3(v,j)=ph3(v,j)/(1-θ)
else
    ph3(v,j)=ph3(v,j)*(1-θ)
end
```

whenever the amount of pheromone on a connection is more than 1 (the initial value of pheromone on all connections is set to be 1), evaporation occurs by a rate of σ, which means the amount of pheromone is decreased by being multiplied to $(1 - \sigma)$; on the other hand, if the amount of pheromone on a connection is less than 1, its value will be divided by $(1 - \sigma)$ an d so it will be increased. As we can see later, the evaporation procedure is modified to avoid a too rapid convergence to suboptimal regions, and also to implement a useful form of forgetting to avoid the complete elimination of the search areas which have not resulted in good solutions in the previous iterations.

Heuristic Information

Heuristic information are used to help ants implement the problem constraints, and therefore, these values are reset after each iteration. Four types of heuristic information are defined to be used by artificial ants in their probabilistic decision making at each iteration. This information is defined according to the special characteristics of the graceful labeling problem, and calculated at each step of the algorithm. Heuristics help ants avoid making infeasible assignments in the early steps of the algorithm. The two first heuristic information values are used to satisfy the problem constraints, and the next two help the ants to make better decisions. First heuristic information includes a *hard constraint* which must be satisfied in all solutions made by ants, but the other three are *soft constraints* which may be ignored if they cannot be satisfied with the hard constraint simultaneously in solution steps.

Heuristic value type 1. The first heuristic information value is defined to implement a hard constraint. This constraint says that all *vertex* labels must be distinct. This type of information is related to assigning label

j to vertex v, denoted by $\eta_1(v, j)$, and set to be zero if label j is already used for another vertex in this iteration. Otherwise, for all labels that are not yet used in this iteration, it is set equal to 1.

$$\eta_1(v, j) = \begin{cases} 0 & \text{if label } j \text{ is already used in this partial solution} \\ 1 & \text{otherwise} \end{cases}$$

Heuristic value type 2. The constraint of *edge* labels to be distinct is considered in the second heuristic value. This information, denoted by $\eta_2(v, j)$, is set to be zero if the edge labels produced by such an assignment are used before in this iteration. Since this type of heuristic information implements a soft constraint, at each step, if the remaining vertex labels (according to the hard constraint) can not satisfy this constraint, this heuristic value is ignored and ants can build infeasible solutions. Thus, $\eta_2(v, j)$ is defined as follows at the first step:

$$\eta_2(v, j) = \begin{cases} 0 & \text{if any of the resulting edge labels are already produced in this partial solution} \\ 1 & \text{otherwise} \end{cases}$$

After calculating $\eta_2(v, j)$ for all j in the algorithm steps, since η_2 represents a soft constraint, if for all j we have $\eta_1(v, j) \cdot \eta_2(v, j) = 0$, it means that it is impossible to satisfy the second heuristic information while maintaining the first one. In this case, we set $\eta_2(v, j) = 1$ for all which means $\eta_2(v, j)$ is equal for all labels, and its effect is ignored.

Heuristic value type 3. This heuristic value makes the ants prefer to produce the edge label 'm', if possible in any step. To explain the necessity of this heuristic value, let us consider a graph $G = (V, E)$ with m edges and n vertices. For G to be graceful, all the edge labels '1', '2', ..., 'm' must be assigned to the edges of G. Therefore, for a solution made by artificial ants in the metaheuristic algorithm, all the edge labels '1', '2', ..., 'm' must be produced. The remarkable point is that the edge label '1' can be produced in m different ways: by assigning one of the following pairs of vertex labels to adjacent vertices:

$$(0, 1), (1, 2), ..., (m-1, m)$$

Similarly, the edge label '2' can be produced in m-1 different ways by assigning one of the following pairs of vertex labels to adjacent vertices:

$$(0, 2), (1, 3), ..., (m-2, m)$$

Unfortunately, there is only *one* way for edge label 'm' to be produced: by assigning vertex labels '0' and 'm' to adjacent vertices. Therefore, heuristic value 3 is defined to help the ants make better solutions by necessarily assigning labels '0' and 'm' to adjacent vertices. If at a step of solution construction, edge label 'm' is not yet produced and can be produced at this step by a certain assignment, and by losing this opportunity, the edge label 'm' cannot be produced anywhere else in the graph, the ants prefer to produce it.

For example, when label 'm' is not yet produced, if a neighbor vertex is labeled '0', and its other neighbors are all labeled before, vertex v should certainly be labeled 'm'. In this case:

$$\begin{cases} \eta_3(v, j) = 1 & j \neq m \\ \eta_3(v, j) = 0 & j = m \end{cases}$$

Since η_3 is also a soft constraint, like η_2, after calculating $\eta_3(v, j)$ for all j in the algorithm steps, if for all j we have $\eta_1(v, j) \cdot \eta_2(v, j) \cdot \eta_3(v, j) = 0$, it means that it is impossible to satisfy the third heuristic information while maintaining the other

two. Therefore, in this criterion we set $\eta_3(v, j) = 1$ for all j, and η_3 is ignored, and does not affect the decision.

Heuristic value type 4. Similar to heuristic value type 3, the fourth heuristic value is defined for edge label 'm-1' to be preferred. Edge label 'm-1' can be produced by assigning one of the two pairs $(0, m-1)$ or $(1, m)$ of vertex labels to adjacent vertices. Heuristic value 4 works exactly like heuristic value 3 except that it prefers making edge label 'm-1'. Experimental results show that in many iterations, the cause of infeasibility was that edge label 'm-1' could not be produced. By adding this heuristic value, the results were noticeably improved as it can be seen in section 4. Again, since η_4 is also a soft constraint, it will be ignored if it cannot be satisfied simultaneously with the other three.

Probabilistic Decision Rule

The probability distribution function for choosing a label for a vertex depends on pheromone and heuristic information values for the corresponding assignment on the construction graph. Equation (2) shows the probability for assigning label 'l' to vertex 'v' in any step.

$$\Pr(v, l) = \frac{\prod_{t=1}^{3}(pr_t(v, l))^{b_t} \times \prod_{k=1}^{4}\eta_k(v, l)}{\sum_{j=0}^{m}(\prod_{t=1}^{3}(pr_t(v, j))^{b_t} \times \prod_{k=1}^{4}(\eta_k(v, j)))} \tag{2}$$

The weights b_t are considered for controlling the effect of each type of pheromones. For different classes of graphs, some certain pheromone type may be more effective than the others, and therefore, different values for these weights may prove more efficiency as it will be shown in the computational results.

Stopping Criteria

The algorithm stops when one of the following criteria is met:

1. If the degree of infeasibility of a solution is zero, the solution will be the output of the algorithm (The degree of infeasibility of a solution is determined by the number of repeated edge labels which should finally be zero in a feasible solution).
2. The number of iterations reaches a maximum limit. If no feasible solution is found during a certain number of iterations, the best solution found yet will be the output of the algorithm, mentioning that the result shows that no graceful labeling is found in a certain number of iterations.

Algorithmic Structure

The main steps of the proposed algorithm are the following:

Step 0. Start

Step 1. Input: The adjacency matrix of graph G.

Step 2. Check if the adjacency matrix is correct and corresponds to an undirected graph without loops. If the adjacency matrix is not correct, repeat Step 1.

Step 3. Calculate the number of vertices (n) and edges (m) according to the adjacency matrix.

Step 4. Initialize pheromone values according to the adjacency matrix.

Step 5. Initialize heuristic information values.

Step 6. Choose next vertex (v) to be labeled probabilistically

Step 7. Calculate heuristic values $\eta_k(v, j)$ for every label j to be assigned to vertex v for $k = 1, 2, 3, 4$ and $j = 0, 1, 2, \ldots, m$.

Step 8. Calculate pheromone probabilities $pr_t(v, l)$ for every label j to be assigned to vertex v for $t = 1, 2, 3$ and $j = 0, 1, 2, \ldots, m$.

Step 9. Calculate total probability for assigning any label j to vertex v, according to equation (2).

Step 10. Choose a label for vertex v probabilistically according to the values of $pr_t(v, l)$.

Step 11. Save the partial solution found so far.

Step 12. Check the solution to find out whether it is complete or not:
  a. If all the vertices are labeled, go to step 13 to calculate the objective value.
  b. Otherwise, in the incomplete solution if the objective value is already worse than the best solution ever found, skip the rest of this solution and go to step 15, else go to step 6 to continue labeling the remaining vertices.

Step 13. Calculate the objective function (number of repeated edge labels) of the completed solution, and update the best solution found if a better solution is resulted.

Step 14. Check the stopping criteria:
  a. If any of the stopping criteria are met, go to step 16.
  b. Otherwise, go to step 15.

Step 15. Update pheromones according to the specifications of the current solution, and start a new solution restarting heuristic values in step 5.

Step 16. Output: feasible solution or best solution found.

Step 17. End

COMPUTATIONAL RESULTS

As described before, heuristic values are information which help the ants complete a solution during the algorithm steps in one iteration. On the other hand, pheromones are values which are saved for future use in ongoing iterations and help the ants find the optimum solution of the problem. Since the heuristic and pheromone values are treated in different ways during the algorithm, they do not affect each other at all. In this section, first the effects of heuristic information are discussed, and then the effect of each type of pheromones is studied. Finally, the results obtained for different classes of graphs are presented and compared with those of the existing methods.

The Effect of Heuristic Values

As mentioned in section 3, the first two heuristic values are defined for implementing the problem constraints, but the third and fourth heuristics help the algorithm find solutions faster. This latter effect is illustrated here by testing the algorithm with and without the use of these information. The test is made on three different classes of graphs, and some parameters are compared in two cases in which heuristic information number 3 and 4 are either used or not. These parameters include number of iterations, running time, and the percentage of iterations in which infeasible solutions are made because edge labels '*m*' or '*m*-1' were not produced.

Although the procedure of calculating heuristic values 3 and 4 at each step of the algorithm takes running time, but it remarkably decreases the average number of iterations before finding the feasible solution and the total running time. Table

1 and Table 2 summarize these results for 30 runs of the algorithm on three classes of graphs. Table 1 shows the decrease in number of iterations and running time by using heuristic information 3 and 4. Table 2 compares percentage of iterations in which infeasible solutions are made because edge labels '*m*' or '*m*-1' were not produced with and without the use of heuristic information 3 and 4.

The Effect of Pheromones

The effect of each type of pheromones has been studied for different classes of graphs. We saw by experimental design that for certain classes of graphs, a specific setting for pheromone weights gives better results. One may obtain better results by modifying the weights for other special classes of graphs. We studied three classes of graphs to check the effect of pheromones. These classes include cycle-related graphs, trees and combined complete graphs. The best parameter settings found for each class of graphs are summarized in Table 3. One may contribute better parameter settings for specific classes of graphs which may result in decreased algorithm time for that special class.

Table 1. Improvement of the algorithm by using heuristic information type 3 and 4

	Decrease in running time	Decrease in number of iterations
Cycles	75.2%	72.3%
Trees	40.1%	65.2%
Windmills	35.2%	25.1%

*Table 2. Percentage of iterations in which edge label '*m*' or '*m*-1' is missed*

	Without heuristic values 3&4	With heuristic values 3&4
Cycles	83.7%	34.4%
Trees	81.2%	42.1%
Windmills	73.4%	60.2%

Table 3. Best parameter settings found for each class of graphs

Graph class	Parameter settings		
Cycle-related graphs	$b_1=5$	$b_2=10$	$b_3=5$
Trees	$b_1=5$	$b_2=5$	$b_3=5$
Windmills	$b_1=2$	$b_2=2$	$b_3=10$

Figure 7. Decrease in the number of repeated edge labels when the proposed algorithm was run on samples from different classes of graphs chosen randomly (a. a Windmill with n=11, m=15 ; b. a Cycle with n=8, m=7; c. a Helm with n=25, m=36; d. a Wheel with n=11, m =20; e. Petersen graph with n=10, m=15; f. a Tree with n=10, m=9; g. A Windmill with n=10, m=12 ; h. a Tree with n=14, m=13; i. a Crown with n=11, m=15.)

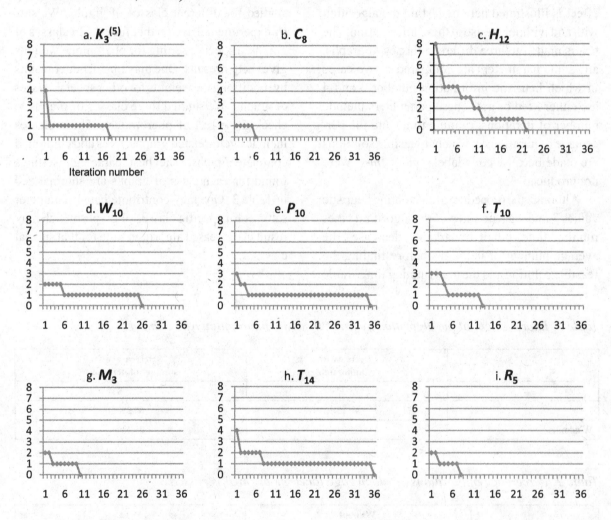

Table 4. Average run times of the algorithm for different classes of graphs

Graph type	Graph name	Number of vertices	Number of edges	Average running time (seconds)
Cycles	C_8	8	7	0.00
	C_{10}	10	9	4.18
	C_{15}	15	14	89.37
Complete graphs	K_3	3	3	0.00
	K_4	4	6	0.00
Windmills	$K_3^{(4)}$	9	12	0.25
	$K_3^{(5)}$	11	15	2.23
Wheels	W_4	5	8	0.10
	W_5	6	10	0.24
	W_8	9	16	2.54
	W_{10}	11	20	9.76
	W_{15}	16	30	128.73
	W_{20}	21	40	1034.52
Helms	H_5	11	15	0.81
	H_8	17	24	21.36
	H_{10}	21	30	38.45
	H_{12}	25	36	112.22
	H_{15}	31	45	736.78
Crowns	R_5	6	10	0.68
	R_8	9	16	2.96
	R_{10}	11	20	21.43
	R_{15}	16	30	235.54
Trees	T_5	5	4	0.00
	T_{10}	10	9	0.05
	T_{15}	15	14	120.64
	T_{20}	20	19	186.24
	T_{25}	25	24	1038.42

We saw during algorithm runs that by increasing any parameter more or less than the proposed settings, the algorithm performance decreases. If the effect of each type of pheromone is increased drastically, the algorithm may fail to find the graceful labeling, because it stays in suboptimal regions, and continues searching within the initial 'good' but still 'infeasible' solutions.

As you see in Table 3, for cycle-related graphs like simple cycles, wheels, helms, etc. by partially increasing the effect of the second pheromone, better results are obtained. The reason comes from this fact that the second pheromone does not insist on the absolute position of labels, but it rather provides information for searching the unexplored solution space. This ability, for cycle graphs which are completely symmetric, and the absolute position of labels is not important, is very useful. On the other hand, for other classes like combined complete graphs, there exist some

Table 5. Comparison of the proposed algorithm with other models

Graph type	Graph name	Number of vertices	Number of edges	Average run time (seconds)	
				Proposed ACO algorithm	Branch and Bound method
Wheels	W_{10}	11	20	**9.76**	55.50
	W_{15}	16	30	**128.73**	3358.11
	W_{20}	21	40	**1034.52**	- *
Helms	H_8	9	24	**21.36**	1585.44
	H_{10}	11	30	**38.45**	3471.22
	H_{12}	13	36	**112.22**	-
	H_{15}	16	30	**736.78**	-
Cycles	C_{10}	10	9	4.18	**0.00**
	C_{15}	15	14	89.37	**0.65**
Trees	T_{20}	20	19	186.24	**149.12**
	T_{25}	25	24	**1038.42**	2898.14

* A dash means that the results for the mentioned graphs are not obtained by the B&B method

vertices that always get a certain label in a graceful labeling (like the common middle vertex). This causes the third pheromone to be useful more than the others for this class of graphs. The third pheromone pays extra attention to the absolute position of each label. However, for the class of trees, all three types of pheromone seem to be equally efficient.

The proposed algorithm tries to decrease the number of repeated edge labels in the ongoing iterations. If, during an iteration, a solution made is worse than the best solution found yet, the algorithm does not continue making the solution and starts a new iteration. By using this feature and also pheromones, the algorithm always continues to find better solutions. Figure 7 shows the performance of the algorithm runs on a sample of different classes of graphs chosen randomly. The vertical axes correspond to the number of repeated edge labels and the horizontal axes show the number of iterations. Each bolded dot with coordination (x, y) represents a point at which in iteration x of algorithm, the number of repeated edge labels was equal to y. The lines show the iterative improvement in solutions during the algorithm run time.

Although these samples had up to 40 edges, it can be seen that in the worst case, the starting solution had at most 8 repeated edge labels and the degree of infeasibility decreased with use of pheromones when the iterations continue. The maximum number of iterations in which the graceful solution was found for these instances of graphs was 36 iterations, and the graceful labeling was found in all cases.

Computational Results

The proposed algorithm code was written in MATLAB 7.4 software, and ran on an Intel Core 2 Duo CPU with a 2.2 GHz processor, and 2046 MB of RAM. The program receives the adjacency matrix of a given graph, and outputs the graceful labeling of its vertices in a row vector where the i-th component shows the label of the i-th vertex according to the adjacency matrix. The average time of 20 runs of the algorithm for instances from different classes of graphs are shown in Table 4. The graceful labeling is found in all mentioned cases.

An advantage of the proposed graph labeling software is that it is very easy to use, and can be applied for gracefully labeling different types of graphs with entering only its adjacency matrix. As it can be seen from Table 4, the ACO-based algorithm for graceful labeling provides solutions in a reasonable run time for different graph types.

The existing exact method for graceful labeling of different types of graphs is a mathematical programming model which is solved by a branch and bound (B&B) method (Eshghi and Azimi, 2004). This method is very efficient for the classes of trees and cycles, but for more complex graphs like wheels, helms and windmills, etc. where the ratio of the number of edges to the number of vertices (m/n) increases, our algorithm performs much better than the (B&B) method.

The results of our algorithm are compared with those of the B&B method (Eshghi and Azimi, 2004) in Table 5. The shorter running time in each case is indicated by bold letters. Table 5 shows that the results of our metaheuristic algorithm are comparable with those of the B&B method which is based on mathematical programming. In some classes of graphs, like wheels and helms, the comparison shows that our algorithm finds the solution very faster than the B&B algorithm.

For the largest wheel tested in the B&B method, our algorithm performs about 25 times faster than the exact method, and for the largest helm it is about 90 times faster. The largest wheel that is tested by the exact algorithm has 10 vertices and the largest helm has 15 vertices, therefore, comparison was not possible for larger graphs on these classes.

FUTURE RESEARCH DIRECTIONS

As it can be seen in Table 5, the only class of graphs where the branch and bound method outperforms the proposed ACO algorithm is the class of cycles which are completely symmetric graphs. Finding symmetry breaking methods in gracefully labeling graphs may be a suitable research area, and will increase the effectiveness of the proposed ant based algorithm for gracefully labeling symmetric graphs. Also one may propose an ACO algorithm for a certain class of graphs by defining additional heuristic information considering their special characteristics in order to increase algorithm efficiency. Another research area may be applying other metaheuristic methods like Genetic Algorithm, Simulated Annealing and Neural Networks, etc. to the graceful labeling problem and comparing the results with the ant-based algorithm. Furthermore, ACO will probably be efficient when applied to other types of graph labeling problems like harmonious or magic labeling of graphs.

CONCLUSION

The graceful labeling problem is one of the best known labeling methods in graphs. Despite the large number of papers published on this subject, there are few techniques for finding a graceful labeling of a given graph. In this paper an ACO-based algorithm is proposed for gracefully labeling the vertices of a graph. The proposed algorithm was tested on a set of randomly generated graphs from different classes of graphs. The computational results showed that ACO metaheuristic was a powerful tool for finding solutions for the graceful labeling problem of graphs and outperforms the other existing methods in some certain classes of graphs.

ACKNOWLEDGMENT

We would like to thank the anonymous reviewers for their valuable comments.

REFERENCES

Costa, D., & Hertz, A. (1997). Ants can colour graphs. *The Journal of the Operational Research Society, 48*, 295–305.

Di Caro, G., & Dorigo, M. (1998). AntNet: Distributed stigmergetic control for communications networks. *Journal of Artificial Intelligence Research, 9*, 317–365.

Dorigo, M., & Gambardella, L. M. (1997). Ant colonies for the traveling salesman problem. *Biosystem, 43*, 73–81. doi:10.1016/S0303-2647(97)01708-5

Dorigo, M., & Stützle, T. (2001). *Ant Colony Optimization: algorithms, applications and advances. Metaheuristics Handbook, International Series in Operations Research and Management Science.* Dordrecht, The Netherlands: Kluwer.

Dorigo, M., & Stützle, T. (2004). *Ant Colony Optimization.* Cambridge, MA: MIT press.

Eshghi, K., & Azimi, P. (2004). Application of mathematical programming in graceful labeling problem of graphs. *Journal of Applied Mathematics, 1*, 1–8. doi:10.1155/S1110757X04310065

Gallian, J. A. (2009). A Dynamic survey of graph labeling. *Electronic Journal of Combinatorics, 16*, 1–216.

Gutjahr, W. J. (2000). graph-based Ant System and its convergence. *Future Generation Computer Systems, 16*, 873–888. doi:10.1016/S0167-739X(00)00044-3

Hingston, Ph., & Kendall, G. (2004). *Ant colonies discover knight tours.* Berlin: Springer Verlag.

Johnson, D. S. (2005). The NP-Completeness Column. *ACM Transactions on Algorithms, 1*(1), 160–176. doi:10.1145/1077464.1077476

Redl, T. A. (2003). *Graceful graphs and graceful labelings: two mathematical programming formulations and some other new results* (Tech. Rep. No. TR03-01). Houston, Texas: Rice University, Department of Computational and Applied Mathematics.

Rosa, A. (1967). On certain valuation of the vertices of a graph. In *Theory of Graphs, International Symposium*, Rome (pp. 349-355). New York: Gordon and Breach.

This work was previously published in International Journal of Applied Metaheuristic Computing, Volume 1, Issue 4, edited by Peng-Yeng Yin, pp. 43-57, copyright 2010 by IGI Publishing (an imprint of IGI Global).

Chapter 14
A Survey on Evolutionary Instance Selection and Generation

Joaquín Derrac
University of Granada, Spain

Salvador García
University of Jaén, Spain

Francisco Herrera
University of Granada, Spain

ABSTRACT

The use of Evolutionary Algorithms to perform data reduction tasks has become an effective approach to improve the performance of data mining algorithms. Many proposals in the literature have shown that Evolutionary Algorithms obtain excellent results in their application as Instance Selection and Instance Generation procedures. The purpose of this paper is to present a survey on the application of Evolutionary Algorithms to Instance Selection and Generation process. It will cover approaches applied to the enhancement of the nearest neighbor rule, as well as other approaches focused on the improvement of the models extracted by some well-known data mining algorithms. Furthermore, some proposals developed to tackle two emerging problems in data mining, Scaling Up and Imbalance Data Sets, also are reviewed.

1. INTRODUCTION

Data reduction (Pyle, 1999) is one of the data preprocessing tasks which can be applied in a data mining process. The main objective in data reduction is to reduce the original data by select-ing its most representative information. This way, it is possible to avoid excessive storage and time complexity, improving the results obtained by any data mining application, ranging from predictive processes (classification, regression) to descriptive processes (clustering, extraction of association rules, subgroup discovery).

DOI: 10.4018/978-1-4666-0270-0.ch014

Data reduction processes can be performed in many ways, some of the more remarkable being:

- Selecting features (Liu & Motoda, 2007), reducing the number of columns in a data set. This process is known as Feature Selection.
- Making the feature values discrete (Liu et al., 2002), reducing the number of possible values of features. This process is known as attribute Discretization.
- Generating new features (Guyon et al., 2006) which describe the data in a more suitable way. This process is known as Feature Extraction.
- Selecting instances (Liu & Motoda, 2001; Liu & Motoda, 2002), reducing the number of rows in a data set. This process is known as Instance Selection (IS)
- Generating new instances (Bezdek & Kuncheva, 2001; Lozano et al., 2006), which describes the initial data set by generating artificial examples. This process is known as Instance Generation (IG).

This paper discusses a wide number of IS and IG proposals. They can be divided into two types of techniques depending on the goal followed by the reduction. If the set of selected or replaced instances will be used as the reference data to instance-based classification, then we refer to Prototype Selection (PS) and Prototype Generation (PG). On the other hand, if the set of instances obtained will be used as input or training set of any data mining algorithm for building a model, then we refer to Training Set Selection (TSS)

In spite of the differences between PS and PG (the first one finds suitable prototypes, while the second one generates them), both have been mainly employed to improve the same classifier, the Nearest Neighbor rule (Cover & Hart, 1967; see also Papadopoulos & Manolopoulos, 2004; Shakhnarovich et al., 2006). This predicts the class of a new prototype by computing a similarity measure (Cunningham, in press) between it and all prototypes from the training set. In the k-Nearest Neighbors classifier, k nearest prototypes vote to decide the class of the new instance to classify. This algorithm is the baseline of the instance based learning field (Aha et al., 1991).

On the other hand, TSS consists of the selection of reduced training sets to improve the efficiency and the results obtained by any data mining algorithm. It has been mainly applied to improve the performance of decision trees, neural networks and subgroup discovery techniques. Although there exists a wide number of TSS approaches, no IG work on TSS has been reported yet, until our knowledge.

In recent years, the data mining community has identified some challenging problems in the area (Yang & Wu, 2006). Two of these are the *Scaling Up Problem* and the *Imbalance Data Sets Problem*. They are closely related to the data reduction field.

The *Scaling Up Problem* (Provost & Kolluri, 1999; Domingo et al., 2002) appears when an overwhelming amount of data must be processed, overcoming the capabilities of the traditional data mining algorithms. The *Imbalance Data Sets Problem* (Chawla et al., 2004; Batista et al., 2004) appears when the distribution of the class in the training data is not balanced, thus the number of instances of some classes is too low. This distribution can cause several problems in the classification of examples which belong to the minority classes.

Evolutionary Algorithms (Eiben & Smith, 2003) are general-purpose search algorithms that use principles inspired by natural genetic populations to evolve solutions to problems. The basic idea is to maintain a population of chromosomes which represent plausible solutions to the problem and evolve over time through a process of competition and controlled variation.

Evolutionary Algorithms have been successfully used in different data mining (Freitas, 2002; Ghosh & Jain, 2005; Abraham et al., 2006) and data reduction (Cano et al., 2003; Oh et al., 2004) problems. Given that the IS problem can be defined as a combinatorial problem, Evolutionary Algorithms have been used to solve it with promising results (Ho et al., 2002; García et al., 2008); these applications of Evolutionary Algorithms to tackle IS problems are usually called EIS (Evolutionary Instance Selection) methods. Furthermore, Evolutionary Algorithms have shown interesting behavior in their application to IG due to it can be defined as a parameter optimization problem (Fernández & Isasi, 2004; Nanni & Lumini, 2008).

The aim of this paper is to present a review on the use of Evolutionary Algorithms for PS, PG and TSS algorithms, called EIS-PS, EPG and EIS-TSS, respectively, giving their description and main characteristics. Several evolutionary proposals developed to tackle the *Scaling Up Problem* and the *Imbalance Data Sets Problem* will be included in the review.

This paper is organized as follows: Section 2 presents the definitions of the techniques and problems which will be reviewed in the rest of the paper. Section 3 presents an overall analysis of several EIS-PS methods. Section 4 reviews the EPG contributions presented in recent years. Section 5 deals with EIS-TSS methods and their application to tackle different data mining problems. Section 6, concludes the survey.

2. PRELIMINARIES

This section provides some preliminary concepts and definitions about the techniques and problems shown in the rest of this paper. Firstly, we describe the main characteristics of IS and IG. Secondly, we present the *Scaling Up Problem* and the *Imbalance Data Sets Problem* for classification, with reference to their relevance to data reduction. Finally, we briefly review some common features of the Evolutionary Algorithms approaches applied to tackle these problems.

Instance Selection and Generation

IS is one of the main data reduction techniques. In IS, the aim is to isolate the smallest set of instances which enable a data mining algorithm to predict the class of a query instance with the same quality as the initial data set (Liu & Motoda, 2001). By minimizing the data set size, it is possible to reduce the space complexity and decrease the computational cost of the data mining algorithms that will be applied later, improving their generalization capabilities through the elimination of noise.

More specifically, IS can be defined as follows: Let X_p be an instance where $X_p = (X_{p1}, X_{p2}, ..., X_{pm}, X_{pc})$, with X_p belonging to a class c given by X_{pc} and a m-dimensional space in which X_{pi} is the value of the i-th feature of the p-th sample. Then, let us assume that there is a training set TR which consists of N instances X_p and a test set TS composed by t instances X_p. Let $S \subset TR$ be the subset of selected samples that resulted from the execution of a IS algorithm, then we classify a new pattern from TS by a data mining algorithm acting over S. The whole data set is noted as D and it is composed of the union of TR and TS.

IS methods can be classified in two categories: PS methods and TSS methods. PS methods (Liu & Motoda, 2002) are IS methods which expect to find training sets offering best classification accuracy and reduction rates by using instance based classifiers which consider a certain similarity or distance measure. Recently, PS methods have increased in popularity within the data reduction field. Various approaches to PS algorithms have been proposed in the literature (see (Wilson & Martinez, 2000; Grochowski & Jankowski, 2004) for review). Figure 1 shows the basic steps of the PS process.

TSS methods are defined in a similar way. They are known as the application of IS methods over the training set used to build any predictive model (e.g. decision trees, neural networks ...) Thus, TSS can be employed as a way to improve the behavior of predictive models, precision and

Figure 1. Prototype selection process

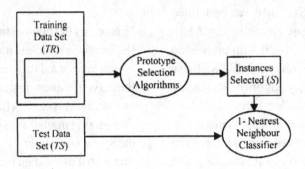

interpretability (Riquelme et al., 2003). Figure 2 shows the basic steps of processing a decision tree (C4.5) on the TSS.

IG is another important technique in data reduction. It has been mainly applied to instance-based classifiers, thus we can focus on describing PG in depth. PG can be defined as the application of instance construction algorithms (Liu & Motoda, 2001) over a data set to improve the classification accuracy of a nearest neighbor classifier.

More specifically, PG can be defined as follows: Let X_p be an instance where $X_p = (X_{p1}, X_{p2}, ..., X_{pm}, X_{pc})$, with X_p belonging to a class c given by X_{pc} and a m-dimensional space in which X_{pi} is the value of the i-th feature of the p-th sample. Then, let us assume that there is a training set *TR* which consists of N instances X_p and a test set *TS*

composed by t instances X_p. The purpose of PG is to obtain a prototype generate set, which consists of r, $r < n$, prototypes, which are either selected or generated from the examples of X_p. The prototypes of the generated set are determined to represent efficiently the distributions of the classes and to discriminate well when used to classify the training objects. Their cardinality should be sufficiently small to reduce both the storage and evaluation time spent by a nearest neighbor classifier.

A wide number of PG methods have been designed in the specialized literature, ranging from traditional ones (Chang, 1974; Kohonen, 1990), to more modern approaches (Lozano et al., 2006). It is important to point out the fact that the research on the EPG field has started recently, being (Fernandez & Isasi, 2004) the first proposal in applying Evolutionary Algorithms

Figure 2. Training set selection process

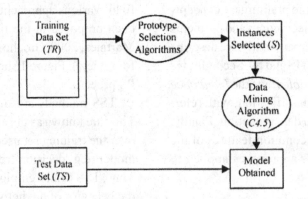

to perform a PG task, in contrast to the research in evolutionary IS, where the first proposal was made in (Kuncheva, 1995).

The Scaling Up and the Imbalance Data Sets Problems

IS methods are considered a useful tool to perform data reduction tasks, obtaining interesting results. They have also been employed successfully to tackle two emergent challenges in data mining, the *Scaling Up Problem* and the *Imbalance Data SetsProblem* (Yang & Wu, 2006).

The *Scaling Up Problem* appears when the number of training samples increases beyond the capacity of the traditional data mining algorithms, harming their effectiveness and efficiency. Due to large size data sets, it produces excessive storage requirement, increases times complexity and affects to generalization accuracy. Usually, when the input data set size affects the execution of the algorithms, it is possible to face this situation with two different strategies:

- **Scaling up the algorithm:** Proposing faster and lower consumption algorithms that can face large size data sets. (Provost & Kolluri, 1999)
- **Scaling down the data set:** In this case, the attention is directed toward the data set. The idea consists of modifying the data set by means of reductions to make it adequate to the original algorithm (Liu & Motoda, 2002).

This problem has been recently addressed by many authors. An interesting example can be found in (Haro-García & García-Pedrajas, 2009), where a divide-and-conquer recursive approach to the problem is applied to very large problems, being able to match in accuracy and even improve on storage reduction the results of well-known standard IS algorithms with a very significant reduction in execution time. Another proposal, mainly adapted

for use on evolutionary algorithms, is presented in (Cano et al., 2005), it will be described in the EIS-PS Section of this survey.

The *Imbalance Data Sets Problem* appears when the data contains many more examples of one class than the other and the less representative class represents the most interesting concept from the point of view of learning (Chawla et al., 2004). Imbalance in class distribution is pervasive in a variety of real-world applications, including but not limited to telecommunications (Tajbakhsh et al., 2009}, web services, finance, ecology (Kubat et al., 1998), biology and medicine (Freitas et al., 2007}.

Usually, in imbalanced classification problems, the instances are grouped into two types of classes: the majority or negative class, and the minority or positive class. The minority or positive class has more interest and it is also accompanied with a higher cost of misclassification. A standard classifier might ignore the importance of the minority class because its representation inside the data set is not strong enough. As a classic example, if the ratio of imbalance presented in the data is 1:100 (that is, there is one positive instance versus one hundred negatives), the error of ignoring this class is only 1%, so many classifiers could ignore it or not make any effort to learn an effective model for it.

Many approaches have been proposed to deal with the *Imbalance Data Sets Problem*. They can be divided into algorithmic approaches and data approaches. The first ones assume modifications in the operation of the algorithms, making them cost sensitive towards the minority class (Grzymala-Busse et al., 2005; Tajbakhsh et al., 2009). The data approaches modify the data distribution, conditioned on an evaluation function. Re-sampling of data could be done by means of under-sampling, by removing instances from the data (a process similar to IS) (Kubat & Matwin, 1997; Batista et al., 2004; Estabrooks et al., 2004), and over-sampling, by replicating or generating new minority examples (Chawla et al., 2002, Fernández et al., 2008).

Basic Ideas on Evolutionary Algorithms for Instance Selection and Generation

A wide number of proposals presented on the use of Evolutionary Algorithms in IS and IG share some common characteristics regarding the two key concepts of any evolutionary algorithm: The representation of the population and the fitness function employed.

Representation: In most of the evolutionary IS algorithms, every member of the population encodes information about all the instances which are currently selected at each step of the search process.

This scheme is often used both in EIS-PS and EIS-TSS proposals. A binary representation is employed. Typically, every individual is defined as a binary string of length N, where each bit represents the current state of each instance of the training set (marked as '1' if the corresponding instance is currently selected, or '0' if not). Figure 3 shows a typical individual of an evolutionary IS algorithm.

On the other hand, in evolutionary IG algorithms every member of the population encodes information describing a new instance (or a new set of instances) to be generated. The concrete representation employed will vary depending on the codification of the problem data, although real coding is mostly preferred.

Fitness function: The majority of the evolutionary IS algorithms define a fitness function where two quality measures are employed: The accuracy of the results obtained by the subsequent data mining algorithm (e.g., a classifier), and the reduction rate achieved between the selected instances and the whole data set. Depending on the concrete method, this reduction rate can be computed by counting the number of instances selected, or employing more sophisticated methods, e.g. valuating the reduction as a measure of the interpretability of the tree obtained, when the evolutionary IS method is applied to improve the results of a decision tree algorithm.

In contrast, in evolutionary IG algorithms the only quality measure employed to define the fitness function is the accuracy obtained by employing the actual set of instances generated (typically, the accuracy obtained with a k-Nearest Neighbors classifier). The reduction rate is not usually employed because the number of instances generated is always small (usually it is fixed to a concrete value), thus every solution is expected to achieve a high reduction rate, and the search process can be focused only on the goal of increasing the accuracy of the classification process.

3. EVOLUTIONARY PROTOTYPE SELECTION

In this section, we will present the main contributions of EIS-PS appeared in the literature in recent years. Firstly, we give a snapshot on the *state of the art* in EIS-PS. Secondly, we describe in depth the characteristics of the most representative EIS-PS methods appeared. Thirdly, we show some EIS-PS proposals dealing with the *Scaling Up* and the *Imbalance Data Sets* problems. Finally, we conclude this section presenting some EIS-PS mixed approaches.

Figure 3. A typical individual of an evolutionary IS algorithm

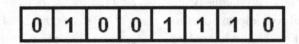

A Snapshot on Evolutionary Prototype Selection

The necessity of the Evolutionary Algorithms in PS is discussed in (Cano et al., 2003) where the authors differentiate between the selection based in heuristics (which appears in classic non-evolutionary PS algorithms, like for example CNN, IB3 or DROP described in (Wilson & Martinez, 2000)) and the selection developed by EIS-PS algorithms. EIS-PS presents a strategy that combines inner and boundary points. It does not tend to select instances depending on their a priori position in the search space (inner class or limit ones). EIS-PS selects the instances that increase the accuracy rates independently of their a priori position.

We will review the main contributions that have included or proposed an EIS-PS model in recent years. The first appearance of the application of an evolutionary algorithm to the PS problem can be found in (Kuncheva, 1995). Kuncheva applied a genetic algorithm to select a reference set for the k- Nearest Neighbors rule. Her genetic algorithm maps the training set onto a chromosome structure composed by genes, each one with two possible states (binary representation). The computed fitness function measures the error rate by application of the k- Nearest Neighbors rule. This genetic algorithm was improved in (Kuncheva & Bezdek, 1998; Ishibuchi & Nakashima, 1999)

At this point, all EIS-PS algorithms considered above adapt a classical genetic algorithm model to the PS problem. Later, a development of EIS-PS algorithms more conditioned to the problem is made. The first example of this can be found in (Sierra et al., 2001). In this paper, an Estimation of Distribution Algorithm is used. Another example can be found in (Ho et al., 2002), where a genetic algorithm design for obtaining an optimal nearest neighbor classifier based on orthogonal arrays is proposed.

The technical term EIS-PS has been adopted by Cano et al. (2003), in which they analyze the behavior of different evolutionary algorithms, generational genetic algorithms (GGAs), steady-state genetic algorithms (SSGAs), the CHC model (Eshelman, 1990) and Population Based Incremental Learning (PBIL) (Baluja, 1994) (which can be considered one of the basic Estimation of Distribution Algorithms). The fitness function used in these models combines two values: classification rate *clasRat* by using a 1-NN classifier and percentage reduction of prototypes of *S* with regards to *TR percRed*:

$$Fitness(S) = \alpha \cdot clasRat + (1 - \alpha) \cdot perc\,Red$$

Where α is a weighting factor usually set to 0.5, and *perc_red* is defined as:

$$perc\,Red = 100 \cdot (|TR| - |S| / |TR|)$$

One of the newest approaches to EIS-PS employs memetic algorithms (Ong et al., 2007). These are heuristic searches in optimization problems that combine a population-based algorithm with a local search. The memetic algorithm employed by (García et al., 2008) incorporates an *ad hoc* local search specifically designed for optimizing the search in prototype selection problem with the aim of tackling the scaling up problem. Another recent proposal (Gil-Pita & Yao, 2008), is focused in the enhancing of the fitness function and the mutation and crossover operators when applied to PS problems.

Later research has gone further, focusing its interest on other topics apart from improving the design of EIS-PS algorithms. Several efforts have been focused on developing methods which will be able to tackle new challenges in data mining. A representative example can be found in (Cano et al., 2005), where an evolutionary method to tackle the *Scaling Up Problem* on the PS process is proposed. Another challenging problem addressed recently by using EIS-PS algorithms is the *Imbalanced Data Sets Problem* (García & Herrera, 2009).

A brief review will be done regarding mixed evolutionary approaches to IS with another data preprocessing technique, e.g. Feature Selection and Feature Weighting. Two different proposals will be reviewed, (Ros et al. 2008) being the first one. In this paper, a hybrid genetic algorithm is applied to perform PS and Feature Selection simultaneously, trying to achieve three objectives simultaneously: Increasing the accuracy of the subsequent classification process, minimizing the dimensionality of the data (the number of features selected), and maximizing the number of instances selected.

The second proposal is an approach of data preprocessing with genetic algorithms in Case-Based Reasoning, which is described by the authors as an instance-based learning procedure (they also employ the k- Nearest Neighbors classifier). A basic genetic algorithm is conducted over a population of chromosomes which performs PS and Feature Weighting (which can be seen as a generalization of Feature Selection, where the weights are real valued between 0 and 1) simultaneously. This approach has been applied to two different scenarios: Customer classification and bankruptcy prediction modeling (Ahn et al., 2006; Ahn et al. 2009).

Overview on the EIS-PS Algorithms

In this subsection, we will describe in depth the characteristics of the most representative EIS-PS methods.

Generational Genetic Algorithm

Its basic idea is to maintain a population of chromosomes, which represent plausible solutions to the particular problem that evolves over successive iterations (generations) through a process of competition and controlled variation. Each chromosome in the population has an associated

fitness to determine which chromosomes are to be used to form new ones in the competition process. The new chromosomes are created using genetic operators such as crossover and mutation.

In GGA, the selection mechanism produces a new population $P(t)$ with copies of chromosomes in the old population $P(t-1)$. The number of copies received for each chromosome depends on its fitness; chromosomes with higher fitness have a greater chance of contributing copies to $P(t)$. Then, the crossover and mutation operators are applied to $P(t)$.

Algorithm 1 (See Figure 4) shows a basic pseudocode of GGA:

The GGA was the first scheme developed to perform EIS-PS processes. Although its results have been overcome by most of the subsequent proposals, it is still an important milestone in the field of PS.

Steady-State Genetic Algorithm

SSGA was firstly employed as an EIS-PS method in (Cano et al., 2003) In the SSGA usually one or two offspring are produced in each generation. Parents are selected to produce offspring and then a decision is made as to which individuals in the population will be selected for deletion in order to make room for the new offspring.

Algorithm 2 (See Figure 5) shows a basic pseudocode of SSGA:

In the construction of the SSGA, it is possible to select the replacement strategy (e.g., replacement of the worst, the oldest, or a randomly chosen individual) and the replacement condition (e.g., replacement if the new individual is better or unconditional replacement). A widely used combination is to replace the worst individual only if the new individual is better. Moreover, in (Goldberg & Deb, 1991), it is suggested that the deletion of the worst individuals can induce a high selective pressure, even when the parents are selected randomly.

Figure 4. Algorithm 1: Pseudocode of the GGA

Algorithm 1: GGA basic structure.

Input: A population.
Output: An optimized population.

1: Initialize population;
2: **While** *Termination Criterion not satisfied* **do**
3:     Evaluation of individual fitness;
4:     Formation of a gene pool (intermediate population) through selection mechanism;
5:     Recombination through crossover;
6:     Mutation operator;
7:     Replacement of the population;
8: **end**

This high selective pressure can help SSGA to improve the results of GGA in the performance of PS process. However, SSGA has been beaten also by most of the new proposals presented in recent years.

Population-Based Incremental Learning

PBIL (Baluja, 1994) is a specific Estimation of Distributions algorithm designed for binary search spaces. It attempts to explicitly maintain statistics about the search space to decide where to sample next.

The objective of the algorithm is to create a real valued probability vector V_p, which, when sampled, reveals high quality solution vectors with high probability. Initially, the values of V_p are set at 0.5. Sampling from this vector yields random solution vectors because the probability of generating a 1 or 0 for each gene is equal. As the search progresses, the values of V_p gradually shift to represent better solution vectors through the search process.

Algorithm 3 (See Figure 6) shows a basic pseudocode of PBIL algorithm:

Figure 5. Algorithm 2: Pseudocode of the SSGA

Algorithm 2: SSGA basic structure.

Input: A population.
Output: An optimized population.

1: Initialize population;
2: **While** *Termination Criterion not satisfied* **do**
3:     Select two parents from the population;
4:     Create one/two offspring using crossover and mutation;
5:     Evaluate the offspring with the Fitness function;
6:     Select one/two individuals in the population, which may be replaced by the offspring;
7:     Decide if this/these individuals will be replaced;
8: **end**

The two basic search moves are performed in steps 6 and 8. In step 6, V_p is pushed toward S_{Best}. *LR* is the learning rate, which specifies how close the movement to S_{Best} is. In step 8, V_p is pushed far away from S_{Worse}. LR_{neg} is the negative learning rate, which specifies how far away the steps are from the worst solution.

PBIL can be seen as one of the most representative evolutionary proposals for performing PS process, because it is almost the only example of EIS-PS method which its search process is not based in a genetic algorithm. In general, it obtained good results when compared with genetic-based methods in the study carried in (Cano et al., 2003).

The Evolutionary Model CHC

CHC algorithm (Eshelman, 1990) is a binary-coded genetic algorithm which involves the combination of a selection strategy with a very high selective pressure, and several components inducing a strong diversity. CHC is a robust evolutionary algorithm, which should often offer promising results in several search problems.

The four main components of the algorithm are:

- **An elitist selection:** To compose a new generation, the best individuals among parents and offspring are selected.

- **A highly disruptive crossover:** HUX, which crosses over exactly half of the non-matching alleles.

- **An incest prevention mechanism**, which only allows to cross over those pairs of individuals which has a Hamming distance higher than a difference threshold. This threshold is decreased, as time goes by, to help the population to converge.

- **A restart process**, which is applied when the population has converged (when the threshold has dropped to zero). It generates a new population by randomly flipping a percentage (usually a 35%) of the bits of the old population individuals.

Algorithm 4 (See Figure 7) shows a basic pseudocode of CHC algorithm:

In the study carried out by (Cano et al., 2003), the CHC algorithm was selected as the best EIS-PS strategy, being able to outperform all the remaining methods of the study (the evolutionary and the non-evolutionary ones).

An interesting conclusion derived from that study was that the key feature of the CHC algorithm is its ability to select the most representative instances independently of their position in the search space, satisfying both the objectives of high accuracy and reduction rates. Due to this fact, CHC has been widely used as a baseline method to perform many evolutionary IS tasks. Some examples are shown in the next sections of this survey.

Intelligent Genetic Algorithm

Ho et al. (2002) propose the Intelligent Genetic Algorithm (IGA) based on Orthogonal experimental design used for PS and Feature Selection. Besides its initial definition, it can also be applied as a PS method only, without changing its initial objectives of increasing accuracy and reduction rates on the training data.

IGA is a GGA that incorporates an Intelligent Crossover operator. It builds an orthogonal array from two parents of chromosomes and searches within the array for the two best individuals according to the fitness function. It takes about $2^{\log_2(y-1)}$ fitness evaluations to perform an Intelligent Crossover operation, where γ is the number of bits that differ between both parents. Note that the application of Intelligent Crossover operator to large-size chromosomes (resulting chromosomes from large size data sets) could consume a high number of evaluations.

Figure 6. Algorithm 3: Pseudocode of the PBIL algorithm

Algorithm 3: PBIL algorithm basic structure.

Input: V_p.

Output: Optimized V_p.

1: Initialize V_p;

2: **While** *Termination Criterion not satisfied* **do**

3:     Generate a fixed number of samples based upon the probabilities specified in V_p;

4:     Select the best sample, S_{Best}, and the worst sample, S_{Worst};

5:     **Foreach** I in V_p **do**

6:         $V_p[i] = V_p[i] * (1\text{-}LR) + S_{Best}[i] * LR$;

7:         **If** $S_{Best}[i] \mathrel{!=} S_{Worst}[i]$ **then**

8:             $V_p[i] = V_p[i] * (1\text{-}LR_{neg}) + S_{Best}[i] * LR_{neg}$;

9:         **end**

10:     **end**

11: **end**

Algorithm 5 (See Figure 8) shows a basic pseudocode of IGA:

As their authors concluded, the employment of the Intelligent Crossover operator allows IGA to be superior to conventional genetic algorithms when applied to problems where the solution space is large and complex, e.g. when it is composed of high dimensional overlapping patterns.

Thus, it is a good EIS-PS method to apply when facing medium and large sized data sets.

Steady-State Memetic Algorithm

The steady-state memetic algorithm (SSMA) was proposed in (García et al., 2008) to cover a drawback of the conventional EIS-PS methods that

Figure 7. Algorithm 4: Pseudocode of the CHC algorithm

Algorithm 4: CHC algorithm basic structure.

Input: A population.

Output: An optimized population.

1: Initialize population;

2: **While** *Termination Criterion not satisfied* **do**

3:     Select candidates from the population;

4:     Generate offspring by crossing parents;

5:     Evaluate the offspring with the fitness function;

6:     Select the individuals of the new population

7:     **If** population not changed **then**

8:         Decrease threshold;

9:     **end**

10:     **If** threshold<0 **then**

11:         Restart population and reinitialize threshold;

12:     **end**

13: **end**

Figure 8. Algorithm 5. Pseudocode of the IGA

Algorithm 5: IGA basic structure.

Input: A population.
Output: An optimized population.

1: Initialize population;
2: **While** *Termination Criterion not satisfied* **do**
3:     Evaluate all individuals using the fitness function;
4:     Use rank selection to select individuals to make a new population;
5:     Randomly cross some individuals by employing IC crossover;
6:     Select one/two individuals in the population, which may be replaced by the offspring;
7:     Apply the conventional bit inverse mutation operator to the population;
8: **end**

---

had appeared before: their lack of convergence when facing large problems.

SSMA makes use of a local search or meme specifically developed for this prototype selection problem. This interweaving of the global and local search phases allows the two to influence each other; i.e. SSGA chooses good starting points, and local search provides an accurate representation of that region of the domain. This local search scheme assigns a probability value to each chromosome generated by crossover and mutation, C_{new}:

$$P_{LS} = \begin{cases} 1 & \text{if } Fitness(C_{new}) \text{ is better than } Fitness(C_{worst}) \\ 0.625 & otherwise \end{cases}$$

Algorithm 6 (See Figure 9) shows a basic pseudocode of the SSMA:

Figure 9. Algorithm 6: Pseudocode of the SSMA

Algorithm 6: SSMA basic structure.

Input: A population.
Output: An optimized population.

1: Initialize population;
2: **While** *Termination Criterion not satisfied* **do**
3:     Use binary tournament to select two parents;
4:     Apply crossover operator to create offspring (Off$_1$, Off$_2$);
5:     Evaluate Off$_1$ and Off$_2$;
6:     **Foreach** Off$_i$ **do**
7:         Invoke *Adaptive-PLS-mechanism* to obtain PLS$_i$
8:         **If** u(0,1) < PLS$_i$ **then**
9:             Perform meme optimization for Off$_i$;
10:         **end**
11:     **end**
12:     Employ standard replacement for Off$_1$ and Off$_2$;
13: **end**

Where u(0,1) is a value in a uniform distribution u[0,1] and the standard replacement means that a the worst individual is replaced only if the new individual is better.

The *Adaptive-PLS-mechanism* is an adaptive fitness-based method. A description of the *Adaptive-PLS-mechanism* and the meme specifically developed for the prototype selection task can be found in (García et al., 2008).

The meme optimization mechanism is a local search specifically designed for the PS problem. It tries to improve the initial chromosome by generating its neighbors by unselecting one of its current selected prototypes. These neighbors are evaluated by a special fitness function which is able to consume only partial evaluations, saving computational resources for the whole evolutionary process.

The objective of the meme optimization mechanism is adjusted dynamically in the execution of the SSMA. Every time a certain number of evaluations have been spent, the accuracy and reduction rates achieved by the best chromosome of the population are registered. If the classification accuracy has not increased, then the meme optimization starts an *improving accuracy* stage, where only better results in accuracy are accepted through the local search. On the other hand, if the reduction rate has not increased, then the meme optimization starts an *Avoiding premature convergence* stage, where the local search accepts worse solutions in order to improve the diversity of the population.

As their authors concluded, the SSMA presents a good reduction rate and computational time. In fact, it is able to outperform the classical PS algorithms, when the accuracy and reduction rates are considered. When compared to other EIS-PS methods, SSMA is able to outperform or equal them, being particularly useful as the size of the databases increases.

Genetic Algorithm Based on Mean Square Error, Clustered Crossover and Fast Smart Mutation

A new genetic algorithm (concretely a GGA model) was proposed in (Gil-Pita & Yao, 2008) as an EIS-PS model. This algorithm (no name was provided by their authors) included the definition of a novel mean square error based fitness function, a novel clustered crossover technique, and a fast smart mutation scheme.

The fitness function employed was based on a mean square error measure:

$$F = \frac{1}{NC} \sum_{n=1}^{N} \sum_{i=1}^{C} (\frac{K_n[i]}{K} - d_n[i])^2$$

Where N is the number of training patterns, C is the number of classes, K is the number of nearest neighbors employed, K_n is the number of K nearest neighbors belonging to class *i*, and d_n is 1 when the desired output for the instance n is the class I, and 0 when not. As their authors stated, the error surface defined by this function is smoother than those obtained using counting estimator based functions, making easier the obtaining of its local minimum.

The clustering crossover operator firstly performs a k-means clustering process over the chromosomes, extracting the centroids of all the clusters found (the number of clusters is established randomly). Then, the centroids are employed with a classical random point cross operator to generate the individuals of the new generation.

The fast smart mutation procedure computes the effect of the change of one bit of the chromosome over its fitness value, testing all the possibilities. The change which produces the better fitness value is accepted as the result of the mutation operator. It is applied to every individual of the population. At the end of its application, the fit-

Figure 10. Algorithm 7: Pseudocode of the genetic algorithm based on mean square error, clustering crossover and fast smart mutation

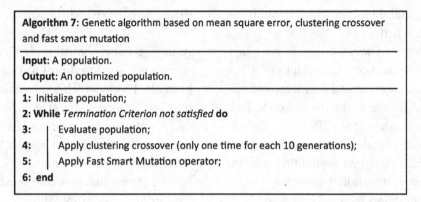

Algorithm 7: Genetic algorithm based on mean square error, clustering crossover and fast smart mutation

Input: A population.
Output: An optimized population.

1: Initialize population;
2: **While** *Termination Criterion not satisfied* **do**
3:     Evaluate population;
4:     Apply clustering crossover (only one time for each 10 generations);
5:     Apply Fast Smart Mutation operator;
6: **end**

ness value of the individuals is actualized, starting then a new generation of the evolutionary process.

Algorithm 7 (See Figure 10) shows a basic pseudocode of the algorithm:

The results obtained by the authors in the experimental study which was carried out suggested that the joint use of the three proposed methods could be quite interesting in the case of not very large training sets.

EIS-PS Proposals for the Scaling Up and Imbalanced Data Problems

In this subsection, we will analyze some EIS-PS proposals dealing with the *Scaling Up* and the *Imbalance Data Sets* problems.

Figure 11. Structure of the stratification process in EIS-PS

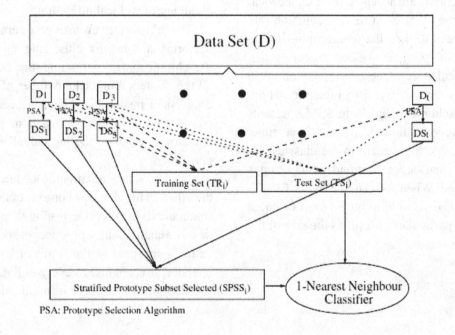

Stratification of EIS-PS to Tackle the Scaling Up Problem

Cano et al. (2005) proposed a method to tackle the *Scaling Up Problem* in EIS-PS. The method presented consists of a stratified strategy which divides the initial data set into disjoint strata with equal class distribution. The number of strata chosen will determine their size, depending on the size of the data set. Using the proper number of strata the stratified method is able to significantly reduce the training set, avoiding the drawbacks of the *Scaling Up Problem*.

Figure 11 shows the basic steps of the process.

Following the stratified strategy, the initial data set D is divided into t disjoint sets D_j, strata of equal size, D_1, D_2, ..., D_t maintaining class distribution within each subset. Then, PS algorithms will be applied to each D_j obtaining a selected subset DS_j. In this way, the subsets TR and TS will be obtained as follows:

$$TR = \bigcup_{j \in J} D_j, J \subset \{1, 2, .., t\} \quad TS = D - TR$$

And the Stratified Prototype Subset Selected (SPSS) is defined as:

$$SPSS = \bigcup_{j \in J} DS_j, J \subset \{1, 2, .., t\}$$

The nearest neighbor classifier is then evaluated using as training data the *SPSS* set, and the *TS* set as test data. Thus the classification process can be performed on higher size data sets, avoiding the usual drawbacks and still achieving acceptable results.

The concluding remarks of the study were that a proper choice in the number of strata makes it possible to decrease significantly execution time and resources consumption, maintaining the EIS-PS algorithm's behavior in accuracy and reduction rates. Also, the CHC was selected as the best EIS-PS algorithm when employed within the evolutionary stratified PS process.

EIS-PS Algorithms on Imbalanced Data Problems

In (García & Herrera, in press), a complete study of EUS (Evolutionary Under-Sampling) algorithms is carried out. A set of EUS methods is proposed, which take into consideration the nature of the problem and use different fitness functions to obtain a good trade-off between balance of distribution of classes and performance.

Eight different algorithms compose the set of methods proposed in the study. Furthermore every method shares the same basic structure, which is developed by using the CHC algorithms as an evolutionary model. There are three characteristics that differentiate them:

- The objective that they pursue.
  - Aiming for an optimal balancing of data without loss of effectiveness in classification accuracy. EUS models that follow this tendency will be called Evolutionary Balancing Under-Sampling.
  - Aiming for an optimal power of classification without taking into account the balancing of data, considering the latter as a sub-objective that may be an implicit process. EUS models that follow this tendency will be called Evolutionary Under-Sampling guided by Classification Measures.
- The way that they do the selection of instances.
  - If the selection scheme proceeds over any kind of instance, then it is called Global Selection. That is, the chromosome contains the state of all instances belonging to the training data

set and removals of minority class instances (those belonging to positive class) are allowed.

- ○ If the selection scheme only proceeds over majority class instances then it is called Majority Selection. In this case, the chromosome saves the state of instances that belong to the negative class and a removal of a positive or minority class instance is not allowed.

- The accuracy measure used for its fitness function.

- Geometric Mean methods, if the geometric mean is used as accuracy measure. Geometric mean was first employed in (Barandela et al., 2003} and is defined as:

$$S = K \cdot M$$

Where a^+ denotes accuracy in examples belonging to the minority class and a^- denotes accuracy in examples belonging to the majority class.

- Area Under the ROC Curve methods, if the Area Under the Curve measure is used instead the geometric mean. Area Under the ROC Curve (Bradley, 1997) can measure the efficacy of various classifiers simultaneously, employing the True Positive and False Positive rates of a classification process.

The eight methods were tested with several imbalanced datasets, and the results obtained were contrasted by using non-parametric statistical procedures. The main conclusions drawn from the study were:

- PS algorithms must not be used for handling imbalanced problems. They are prone to gain global performance by eliminating examples belonging to the minority class considered as noisy examples.

- During the evolutionary under-sampling process, the employment of a majority selection mechanism helps to obtain more accurate subsets of instances than the use of global selection. However, the latter mechanism is necessary to achieve the highest reduction rates.

- Data sets with a low imbalance ratio should be faced with Evolutionary Under-Sampling guided by Classification Measures models, and should use in particular the model with a global mechanism of selection and evaluation through the geometric mean measure.

- Data sets with a high imbalance ratio should be faced with Evolutionary Balancing Under-Sampling models, and should use in particular the model with a majority selection mechanism and evaluation through the geometric mean measure.

Mixed EIS-PS Approaches

In recent years, some proposals have appeared performing not only the PS process with evolutionary algorithms, but also performing another data preparation process simultaneously. This subsection will review two of the most remarkable approaches.

Ros et al. (2008) proposed a hybrid genetic algorithm (HGA) which performs IS and Feature Selection simultaneously. Its objectives are to increase the accuracy of the k- Nearest Neighbors over the reference set, to minimize the number of features selected (reducing the reference data) and to maximize the number of instances selected (to retain the most information possible without harming the classification accuracy).

The HGA is divided into three phases:

- A genetic algorithm is applied in the first phase. It includes a sophisticated selection scheme and some mechanisms to manage diversity and elitism (including an archive population and a dynamic analysis of the diversity of the population).

- By employing a histogram of the frequency with which each feature has been selected, a feature selection process is carried out, in order to simplify the problem.
- The genetic algorithm is applied again over the population. Also, some of the children generated by each generation are tuned by using local search procedures.

Despite the contradictory objectives in the number of instances and features selected, HGA is able to perform a dual IS and FS process with success, being a suitable evolutionary method to perform data reduction tasks.

A second mixed approach, GOCBR (Global Optimization of feature weighting and instance selection using genetic algorithms for Case Based Reasoning) was proposed in (Ahn et al., 2006; Ahn et al., 2009). This proposal performs a simultaneous IS and Feature Weighting process in the framework of a Case Based Reasoning system.

The search process of GOCBR consists of the application of a genetic algorithm with the common genetic operators (selection, crossover and mutation). Their individuals employ a binary representation, encoding the weights of the features by employing 14 bits to each one, and encoding the IS information in the second part of the chromosome by employing the usual binary scheme. Its fitness function measures only the accuracy obtained by employing the reference set defined by the chromosome to classify the train data in a k- Nearest Neighbors classifier.

GOCBR system has been applied successfully by the authors to various problems, such as customer classification or bankruptcy prediction modeling. Also, it is remarkable that is the only evolutionary method known of which performs a simultaneous IS and Feature Weighting process, until our knowledge.

4. EVOLUTIONARY PROTOTYPE GENERATION

In this section, we will present the main contributions of EPG appeared in the literature in recent years. In the first subsection, we give a snapshot on the *state of the art* in EPG. In the last subsection, we describe in depth the characteristics of the most representative EPG methods appeared.

A Snapshot on Evolutionary Prototype Generation

In recent years, the research efforts in the design of new PG techniques based on Evolutionary Algorithms have started to offer some interesting approaches. All of them still employ the NN rule as a reference classifier to measure the classification accuracy of the prototypes generated.

Usually, the prototypes are encoding as members of the population of the evolutionary algorithm employed to carry out the evolutionary process. A real codification scheme is used to represent them; each of its components has a concrete value for a concrete feature of the problem.

In this section, we will review the main contributions that have proposed an EPG model. The first contribution is (Fernandez & Isasi, 2004), where an evolutionary algorithm based on a two-dimensional grid is proposed, named Evolutionary Nearest Prototype Classifier. It defines a traditional evolutionary process to prepare the prototypes for its use on a 1-NN classifier, by employing a wide number of evolutionary operators.

The next two proposals are based on the Particle Swarm Optimization (PSO) Scheme (Kennedy et al., 2001). This technique is based on a set of potential solutions (particles) which evolves to find the global optimum of a real-valued function (fitness function) defined in a given space (search space). Particles represent the complete solution to the problem and move in the search space using both local information (the particle memory) and neighbor information (the knowledge of neighbor particles).

In (Nanni & Lumini, 2008) a PSO based PG method is proposed (no name is provided for the algorithm). It can be seen as a Pittsburgh-based model, because all the components of the solution (in this case, the prototypes generated) are encoded in a single particle. The method performs a PSO search process where a reduced set of prototypes is generated to finally perform a 1-NN classification process.

In (Cervantes et al., 2007; Cervantes et al, in press), inspired by the results of (Cervantes et al., 2005), an Adaptive Michigan PSO model for PG is proposed. This model is described as a Michigan approach because every particle contains only a component of the solution, thus the complete solution is built by joining the selected particles of the swarm. This approach also improves the traditional PSO scheme, because the online generation and destruction of particles is allowed in the search process.

Finally, the last proposal which will be reviewed, (Garain, 2008), is based on the Clonar Selection Algorithm (Castro & Zuben, 2002), a representation of an Artificial Immune System model (Dasgupta, 1998). Clonar Selection Algorithms are inspired by the behavior of the immune system when performing an immune response to an antigenic stimulus. It advocates the idea that only those cells that recognize the antigens proliferate, thus being selected against those which do not. This idea is employed to develop a PG system which is able to generate suitable prototypes to perform a 1-NN classification process.

Overview on the EIG Algorithms

In this subsection, we will describe in depth the characteristics of the most representative EIG methods.

Evolutionary Nearest Prototype Classifier

In (Fernandez & Isasi, 2004), an EPG method is proposed. It employs as a basic structure a two-dimensional matrix, where each row is associated with a prototype of the whole classifier, and each column is associated with a class to define regions where the prototypes are mapped.

On its initialization, the algorithm only defines one prototype. Then a whole evolutionary process starts: It carries out sequentially a set of evolutionary operations with the aim of generating a robust set of prototypes which will be able to correctly generalize the instances of the train set. The evolutionary operators defined are:

- **Mutation:** This operator is used to label each prototype with the most heavily populated class in each of its own regions.
- **Reproduction:** The reproduction operator function is to introduce new prototypes into the classifier, splitting the instances assigned to a prototype into two sets, where the second set is assigned to a new prototype.
- **Fight:** This operator allows prototypes to exchange their assigned instances. The fight can be performed in a cooperative or a competitive way, and it is ruled by the quality of the prototypes involved.
- **Movement:** The movement operator reallocates a prototype on the centroid of its assigned instances.
- **Die:** The current prototypes have a chance of being erased from the matrix, which is inversely proportional to its quality.

In the whole process, the quality of each prototype is defined by the number of prototypes which it has currently assigned and its classification accuracy. When the evolutionary process is finished, the generated set of prototypes is employed to classify the tests set, by means of the 1-NN classifier.

Algorithm 8 (See Figure 12) shows a basic pseudocode of Evolutionary Nearest Prototype Classifier algorithm:

The Evolutionary Nearest Prototype Classifier algorithm has shown good overall results, when compared against well-known classical methods in PG. Moreover, the results obtained when employing the prototypes generated with a 1-NN classifier were very competitive when compared with many classical instance-based classifiers as C4.5, Naïve Bayes or PART.

Particle Swarm Optimization for Prototype Generation

In (Nanni & Lumini, 2008) a PG method based on PSO is presented. This method defines the particles of the swarm as sets of a fixed number of prototypes, which are modified as the particle is moved in the search space.

The usual operators of PSO are employed by this proposal. The representation of each particle consists of a vector of length $S = K \cdot M$ given by the concatenation of K prototypes (dealing with M-dimensional data). The fitness function employed is defined as the classification error of the set of K prototypes over the training data.

Several runs (N) of the PSO process are carried out before finishing the PG stage (the authors recommend N=5). Each execution gives as result a reference set of K prototypes, being the result of the PG stage a collection of N reference sets. To classify a test instance, it is evaluated by each of the N reference sets, obtaining the final output as the result of a majority vote above all the reference sets. Thus, the proposed model can be seen as an ensemble of PSO-based classifiers.

Algorithm 9 (See Figure 13) shows a basic pseudocode of PSO-based PG algorithm:

The employment of the ensemble structure allows this proposal to obtain high accuracy rates. Furthermore, the authors suggested some ways to improve the model (like the employment of feature weighting methods). This proposal confirms that PSO is a very suitable model to perform PG processes.

An Adaptive Michigan Approach PSO for nearest Prototype Classification

In (Cervantes et al., 2007; Cervantes et al., in press), an Adaptive Michigan Approach PSO is proposed. Its particles encode a prototype, each one being the generated train data represented as the whole particle swarm. This method does not have a fixed number of particles. On the contrary,

Figure 12. Algorithm 8: Pseudocode of the Evolutionary Nearest Prototype Classifier algorithm

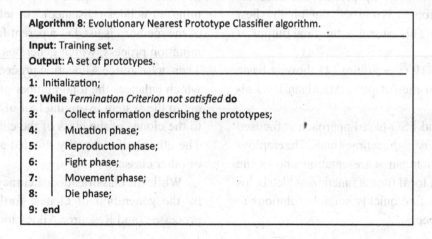

Algorithm 8: Evolutionary Nearest Prototype Classifier algorithm.

Input: Training set.
Output: A set of prototypes.

1: Initialization;
2: **While** *Termination Criterion not satisfied* **do**
3:      Collect information describing the prototypes;
4:      Mutation phase;
5:      Reproduction phase;
6:      Fight phase;
7:      Movement phase;
8:      Die phase;
9: **end**

Figure 13. Algorithm 9: Pseudocode of the PSO-Based PG algorithm

---

Algorithm 9: PSO-based PG algorithm.

Input: Training set and test set.
Output: Classification output for the test set.

1: Initialization;
2: **For** j=1:N **do**
3: $\quad$ | $\quad$ PG(j)= PSO-PG(Train set$_j$);
4: **end**
5: **Foreach** x$_i$ in test set **do**
6: $\quad$ | $\quad$ **For** j=1:N **do**
7: $\quad$ | $\quad$ | $\quad$ PartialOutput(j)= Classify(x$_i$, PG(j))
8: $\quad$ | $\quad$ **end**
9: $\quad$ | $\quad$ Output(x$_i$)= VoteRule(PartialOutput);
10: **end**

---

some new operations are defined to allow the PSO search procedure to increase or decrease dynamically the number of particles.

The algorithm employs two different fitness functions: The global fitness function, defined by the standard classification accuracy on a 1-NN classifier, which is used to find the best swarm over the whole PSO procedure; and a local fitness function valued in each particle, defined by using the number of prototypes correctly classified and misclassified by itself. This secondary fitness function is used to evaluate the quality of each particle, in order to judge if it must be erased from the swarm, or if it can be employed as a parent of a new particle.

When the whole PSO process has finished, a cleaning process is carried out on the best swarm found. This swarm is the final output of the algorithm.

Algorithm 10 (See Figure 14) shows a basic pseudocode of the Adaptive Michigan PSO algorithm:

This second PSO-based approach is focused in obtaining very high accuracy rates. The employment of a Michigan representation allows the definition of a local fitness function, which helps the method to find quickly suitable solutions in the search space.

Prototype Reduction Using an Artificial Immune Model

In (Garain, 2008), a PG based on a Clonar Selection algorithm is proposed. This model is composed of an immune memory which stores in its cells the best antigens found in the search process.

The Clonar Selection algorithm is initialized by representing the training instances as antigens, and choosing one antigen from each class to fill the immune memory. Then the search process starts. The first stage consists of a Hyper-mutation process. For each antigen on the training set, the most stimulating antigen in the immune memory is selected. The measure of stimulation is based on how close both antigens are (by means of Hamming or Euclidean Distance). The selected antigen of the memory is used as a parent for the Hyper-mutation process, which generates its offspring. Then, a Resource Allocation procedure is called, which balances the total number of clones present in the system by giving half of the resources to the clones of the class of the current antigen. The other half is equally divided among clones of other classes.

While the classification accuracy is improved by the generation of clones, further Mutation processes (and Resource Allocation procedures)

Figure 14. Algorithm 10: Pseudocode of the AMPSO algorithm

Algorithm 10: Adaptive Michigan PSO algorithm.

Input: Training set.
Output: A set of prototypes (best swarm).

1: Initialize swarm. Dimension of particles equals number of attributes;
2: Insert N particles of each class into the training patterns;
3: **While** *iterations < MAX and accuracyRate < 100%* **do**
4:     Check for particle reproduction and deletion;
5:     **Foreach** particle **do**
6:         Calculate local fitness;
7:         Calculate its next position;
8:     **End**
9:     Move the particles;
10:     Assign classes to the training patterns using the nearest particle;
11:     Evaluate the swarm classification accuracy;
12: **End**
13: Delete, from the best swarm found so far, the particles that can be removed without a reduction in the classification accuracy.

---

are carried out on the surviving clones. This Mutation produces a lower number of clones which depends on the stimulation value of each parent clone. When no improvement is achieved, the best clone found is inserted into the immune memory, performing a replacement with the worst antigen present. Then a new generation starts.

Finally, when the algorithm meets a global termination criterion, the antigens contained in the immune memory are employed as the training set to classify the test instances, by using the 1-NN classifier.

Algorithm 11 (See Figure 15) shows a basic pseudocode of PG-Clonar Selection algorithm:

The Clonar Selection Algorithm is a new method for PG based on a field of the Evolutionary Computation which has started to grown recently: The immune systems. Although it has high

Figure 15. Algorithm 11. Pseudocode of the PG-Clonar Selection algorithm

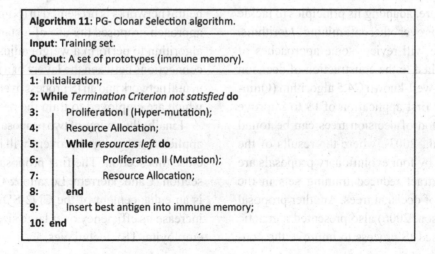

Algorithm 11: PG- Clonar Selection algorithm.

Input: Training set.
Output: A set of prototypes (immune memory).

1: Initialization;
2: **While** *Termination Criterion not satisfied* **do**
3:     Proliferation I (Hyper-mutation);
4:     Resource Allocation;
5:     **While** *resources left* **do**
6:         Proliferation II (Mutation);
7:         Resource Allocation;
8:     end
9:     Insert best antigen into immune memory;
10: end

---

storage requirements to allocate the clones generated, it is a first example of a new technique which can obtain promising results with further research.

5. EVOLUTIONARY TRAINING SET SELECTION

In this section, we will present the main contributions of EIS-TSS appeared in the literature in recent years. In the first subsection, we give a snapshot on the *state of the art* in EIS-TSS. The next subsections will analyze the main approaches of EIS-TSS in decision trees, neural networks and subgroup discovery, respectively.

A Snapshot on Evolutionary Training Set Selection

The advances in EIS-TSS in recent years have been directed towards improving the results of some well-known data mining algorithms, being principally focused on the enhancement of the performance of decision trees, neural networks and subgroup discovery.

A wide range of these proposals have been inspired by the good results obtained by EIS-PS in the task of improving the performance of instance-based classifiers. Thus, some of the EIS-TSS methods which will be presented in this section will share some components with EIS-PS proposed before, adapting its principles to tackle the IS problems over other data mining algorithms.

Firstly, we will review some approaches of EIS-TSS applied to the construction of decision trees with the well-known C4.5 algorithm (Quinlan, 1993). A first application of IS to improve the construction of decision trees can be found in (Cano et al., 2003), where the results of the IS conducted by four evolutionary proposals are applied to extract reduced training sets in the construction of decision trees. Another proposal (Wu & Olaffson, 2006) also presented a genetic algorithm based IS process to improve the con-

struction of decision trees, but they focused its effort on improving, not only the accuracy of the model and the reduction of the number of instances in the training set, but also in the interpretability and size of the trees obtained.

Later, Cano et al. (2007) presented two proposals of stratification to further improve the trees extracted by the C4.5 algorithm. The aim of both proposals was to improve the accuracy and interpretability of the trees extracted by means of stratification of the training data, trying to maintain a good trade-off between both quality measures.

As a last application of EIS-TSS in decision trees, we will review a proposal to improve the performance of C4.5 over imbalanced data sets (i.e. dealing with the *Imbalance Data Sets Problem* in the construction of decision trees) (García & Herrera, 2008). In this contribution it is shown how an evolutionary undersampling method is able to increase the accuracy of the decision tress in the classification of both majority and minority classes, employing the geometric mean accuracy measure.

Two approaches of EIS-TSS applied to neural networks will be analyzed. The first approach is (Ishibuchi et al., 2001), where a basic genetic algorithm is applied to perform both IS and Feature Selection processes to improve the results of standard three layered neural networks in classification.

A second approach to perform EIS-TSS on neural networks is presented in (Kim, 2006). This approach proposes the use of a standard genetic algorithm to perform a weight adjustment on the connections between the layers of a feed-forward neural network and an IS process over the instances which are employed to train the net.

Finally, the review of two proposals of EIS-TSS applied to subgroup discovery will be covered to close this section. The first proposal of this subsection (Cano, Herrera, Lozano & García, 2008) is an enhancement of the CN2-SD algorithm to increase its efficiency over large size datasets, by employing TSS techniques.

The second proposal (Cano et al., 2008) presents two stratification strategies to increase the presence of examples from minority classes in large size data sets with imbalanced data. The benefits shown in this study from the application of stratification includes the enhancement of Apriori-SD in its application to large size problems, and the improvement in the quality of the groups discovered over the minority classes of the problem analyzed.

EIS-TSS in Decision Trees

Cano et al. (2003) performed a complete study of the use of Evolutionary Algorithms to perform IS tasks. Although this work has been analyzed above, due to the number of EIS-PS which were presented in the study, it is important to note that a second experimental study was carried out employing the same IS algorithms as EIS-TSS methods to improve the trees built by C4.5.

The results obtained in the TSS part of the study were similar to the ones reached in the PS part: Evolutionary Algorithms based IS method were able to equal or outperform non-evolutionary methods, maintaining or increasing the accuracy of the trees obtained and increasing the reduction rates obtained by measuring the number of instances selected.

Wu & Olaffson (2006) performed a wide analysis of the application of IS to the induction of decision tress. They proposed a genetic algorithm to conduct the IS process, employing an integer codification in its chromosomes. Each individual is composed of a set of integer values, where each one represents one instance of the training set. Thus the selected instances of each individual are those whose integer identifier forms part of the chromosome.

The genetic algorithm search process employs a set of usual genetic operators: roulette wheel selection, crossover operator (which interchanges members of each set of instances defined by the parents) and mutation operator (which randomly replaces an instance by another one not selected).

The fitness function is a measure of the accuracy of the tree which can be induced by the chromosome, S, and its size. It is defined as follows:

$$Fitness(S) = -\log(e(\psi(S))) - a \cdot \log(\frac{size(\psi(S))}{K}), a > 1$$

Where e is an estimator of the error rate of the decision tree $\psi(S)$, K is an upper bound on the size of the tree, and a is a weighting factor.

The final tree is obtained by merging the instances selected at least one time with a fixed number of the best chromosomes in the population. Then the tree can be employed to classify new test instances.

In addition, a study of some relevant parameters is presented along with the results of the algorithm. A discussion of two additional measures, the Average Leaf Ratio (a measure of the number of instances in each leaf node of the tree), and the Instance Entropy of the training data, show some interesting conclusions, the most remarkable being:

- Genetic algorithm based IS is able to reduce the tree sizes with minimal loss in prediction accuracy.
- The best results are obtained when the Average Leaf Ratio of the final model is higher
- Genetic algorithm based IS works better on low entropy data sets. Higher values of entropy make the construction of more complex decision trees necessary.
- IS can be employed as a replacement for the traditional tree pruning techniques because it is able to outperform them when they are compared in terms of accuracy and tree size.

A third remarkable proposal of EIS-TSS can be found in (Cano et al., 2007), where the use of stratification is proposed to tackle the *Scaling Up* problem on the induction of decision trees. The aim of the study was to perform the extraction of classification rules from large size data by keeping a good tradeoff between the precision and the interpretability of the model generated. To accomplish its objective, the authors present a stratified strategy (similar as the employed in (Cano et al., 2005).

To conduct the EIS-TSS process, the CHC algorithm is used. Moreover, two different fitness functions are employed; they are based on the usual fitness function used for EIS-PS:

$$Fitness(TSS) = \alpha \cdot clasPer + (1 - \alpha) \cdot redPer$$

Where *clasPer* denotes the percentage of correctly classified objects from TR using only TSS to find the nearest neighbor or to extract a C4.5 model, depending on the concrete fitness function used. *redPer* denotes the reduction rate between TR and TSS.

- **Reduction-precision fitness function:** This fitness function uses the 1-Nearest Neighbor classifier for measuring the classification rate.
- **Interpretability-precision fitness function:** This fitness function extracts a model with C4.5 to compute the classification performance of TSS.

The two fitness definitions were tested with CHC and the stratification strategy. Several TSS methods were included in the experimental framework, to compare the performance of the proposed models against them. Finally, the results obtained were contrasted by using non-parametric statistical procedures.

The main conclusions reached in the study were as follows:

- The evolutionary stratified IS offers the best model size, maintaining an acceptable accuracy. It produces the smallest set of rules, with the minimal number of rules and the smallest number of antecedents per rule.
- The stratified CHC model with Interpretability-Precision fitness function allows us to obtain models with high test accuracy rates, similar to C4.5, but with the advantage that the size of the models are reduced considerably.
- The predictive model extraction by means of evolutionary stratified training set selection (with the CHC model and any of the fitness function presented) presents a good tradeoff between accuracy and interpretability. Thus, a very good scaling up behavior is observed, which allows us to obtain good results when the size of data set grows.

The last EIS-TSS proposal to improve the construction of decision trees which will be reviewed in this survey deals with the *Imbalance Data Sets* problem.

In (García & Herrera, in press) a new method is presented to deal with imbalanced data by performing the TSS process. The aim of the method is to improve the classification accuracy obtained by C4.5 when it is used on imbalanced data sets.

The proposed approach uses the same representation as the basic EIS-TSS methods. C4.5 is used to extract a model in order to compute the accuracy of the training set selected. The accuracy rates obtained by employing this model to classify the examples of the majority and minority classes are used to compute the geometric mean metric, which is used as fitness function.

Figure 16 shows the basic stages of the EUS process in EIS-TSS.

Although C4.5, in its standard definition, incorporates a pruning mechanism to avoid overfitting, the inclusion of the induction tree process

Figure 16. The EUS process in EIS-TSS

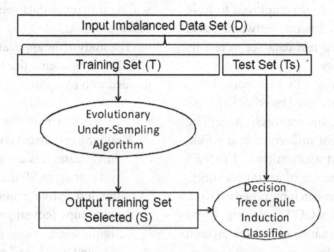

within an evolutionary cycle can direct the resulting tree to an optimal model for training data, losing the generalization ability. To avoid this drawback, a simple and effective mechanism is incorporated. It consists of providing a higher weight for the classification costs of the instances that are not included in TSS than to the instances that are. Therefore, the reduction ability of the selected subset is encouraged, allowing the proposed approach to avoid overfitting in the construction of the models.

To test the performance of the proposal, it was compared to a wide number of well-known re-sampling algorithms, including OSS (Kubat & Matwin, 1997), NCL (Laurikkala, 2001) and SMOTE (Chawla et al., 2002), among others. The results obtained were contrasted by using non-parametric statistical procedures, finally showing that the proposed approach is able to outperform, or, at least, to behave similarly to every method in the comparison with respect to the accuracy of the models obtained, it obtains very accurate trees with a low number of rules or leafs. Thus, the proposed approach is confirmed as a very accurate method, which is able to increase the interpretability of the models obtained.

EIS-TSS in Neural Networks

A first application of the use of EIS-TSS on neural networks can be found in (Ishibuchi et al., 2001). The aim of this proposal was to find an optimal subset of instances and features by employing a GGA.

The GGA designed to carry out the TSS task employed the usual representation of the solutions (binary coded, employing the first part of the chromosome to code the instances which are currently selected, and the second part to code the features), and a standard set of genetic operators: Random selection of parents, uniform crossover and bit flipping mutation (biased to decrease the number of instances selected). The fitness function defined by this proposal was:

$$Fitness = W_{Perf} \cdot Perf - W_f |F| - W_P \cdot |P|$$

Where *Perf* is a measure of the accuracy of a NN classifier when applied to the training data by using as a reference set the current subset selected by the chromosome, F and P are respectively the number of features and instances selected, and W_{Perf}, W_F and W_P are user-defined weights.

When the evolutionary process was finished, the final subset selected was employed to train a standard three layered neural network, being finally validated with a test data set to test its generalization capability.

Although the concrete EIS-TSS method employed has been outperformed by other EIS-TSS and EIS-PS proposals, this approach can still be considered an important milestone in the field because it was the first application of EIS-TSS to improve the performance of neural networks.

A more modern approach is proposed in (Kim, 2006). In this proposal, a GGA is also employed to optimize the performance of a three layered neural network, in the framework of an application for financial forecasting. The individuals of the genetic algorithm encode information about the instances selected and about the adjustment of the weights of the neural network, employing binary coding in both cases. Although an EIS-TSS process is performed, the genetic algorithm does not have as its objective the maintenance of a good reduction rate. Instead, the fitness function is defined as the classification accuracy of the neural network defined by the chromosome, instead of the usual application of the neural network as a baseline classifier.

The experimental study carried out concluded that, in the context of the financial forecasting problem selected, the application of IS to improve the performance of neural networks outperformed the classical proposals of weights adjustment with genetic algorithms, highlighting the benefits of using EIS-TSS to improve the quality of the training process of neural networks.

EIS-TSS in Subgroup Discovery

In (Cano, Herrera, Lozano & García, 2008), a proposal to improve the performance of the CN2-SD algorithm for subgroup discovery in the evaluation of large size data sets is presented. Although CN2-SD is based on a divide and conquer strategy, it has to face the *Scaling Up* problem. To

avoid it, the use of TSS algorithms is proposed for scaling down the data sets before the subgroup discovery task.

The study of the application of TSS algorithms, and the experiments that were carried out, was divided into two parts:

- In the first part, the effect of TSS on the subgroups discovered with CN2-SD in small data sets is studied. The objective is to analyze if the TSS process affects the descriptive qualitative measures of the subgroups (coverage, support, confidence, significance, unusualness, completeness, size and number of antecedents).

The basic IS methods applied to the TSS process were CNN (Hart, 1968), IB2, IB3 (Kibbler & Aha, 1987), DROP3 (Wilson & Martinez, 1997) ICF (Brightom & Mellish, 2002) and EIS-CHC. These methods were applied by using the stratification proposed in (Cano et al., 2005).

The results of this first part of the study were contrasted to a complete set of parametrical and non-parametrical statistical tests. Their application revealed that the use of TSS did not negatively affect the quality indexes of the subgroup discovered. Also the measures on size and number of antecedents were improved, showing that TSS algorithms were able to discover smaller and more interpretable sets of subgroups.

- In the second part, a TSS process is combined with CN2-SD to test its behavior in large size data sets. As basic IS methods, IB2 and EIS-CHC were selected because they were the IS algorithms with the smallest subsets selected in their application to the large size data sets.

The main conclusion of this part was that the combination of the highest reduction rates of IB2 and EIS-CHC with CN2-SD makes it possible to perform a SD task on large size data sets. In particular, EIS-CHC is recommended because it shows very good results in most of the qualitative measures tested, when employed in combination with CN2-SD.

As a final conclusion of the study, the authors stated that, thanks to the application of TSS methods, CN2-SD can be executed on large data set sizes pre-processed, maintaining and improving the quality of the subgroups discovered.

A second application of EIS-TSS for subgroup discovery can be found in (Cano et al., 2008). There, a different application of the stratified strategy presented in (Cano et al., 2005) was proposed: The employment of two modified strategies of stratification to increase the presence of minority classes. The aim of the proposal was to allow a subgroup discovery algorithm, Apriori-SD (Kavsek & Lavrac, 2006), to avoid the *Scalability problem* and to face a large data set without harming its accuracy due to a poor treatment of imbalanced data.

The data set used on the experiment was the KDD Cup'99. Firstly, it is shown that the Apriori-SD could not handle the KDD Cup'99 problem because of its expensive computational cost in time. Then the TSS methods are applied to tackle the problem. ENN (Hart, 1968), IB3 (Kibbler & Aha, 1987), and EIS-CHC (Cano et al., 2005) were proposed as baseline IS methods to be used.

To preserve the number of instances of the minority classes, two different strategies of stratification were proposed:

- **Instance selection in all classes:** The instances of the majority classes are assigned randomly over the strata created. Then the whole minority classes are added to each strata. After the IS process is carried out, the subsets selected are reunited, removing duplicities.

The employment of this strategy showed a severe drawback: Its application to every TSS subset obtained after the reunion of the instances selected from the strata decreased significantly the number of instances present from the minority classes. Thus, the minority classes were not sufficiently represented for a proper subgroup discovery task, due to use of the stratified IS.

- **Instance selection in majority classes:** The selection process is applied without the minority ones, just to the majority classes. The instances which belong to the minority classes were added to the TSS subset after the reunion of the subsets selected, and then the subgroup discovery tasks were carried out.

In this case, the instances which appear in the TSS selected were the most representative of the majority classes and all the instances belonging to the minority ones. Thus the IS process was able to reduce the initial data set without affecting the presence of instances from the minority classes, making the subgroup discovery process possible in those classes.

Both strategies were tested in combination with the selected IS methods, using confidence and support as qualitative measures. The conclusions of the experiment were that the combination of the TSS algorithms with stratification allows us to extract subgroups for most of the classes, including most of the minority ones, with high levels of confidence and support measures. Furthermore, the use of the *instance selection in majority classes* strategy of stratification was recommended to perform this task.

6. CONCLUSION

This paper presents a review of PS, TSS and PG techniques performed by evolutionary algorithms. A wide number of algorithms and proposals of the *state-of-the-art* have been discussed, showing that the research in these fields have produced numerous advances in recent years to improve the quality of Instance Selection and Generation techniques in Data Mining.

Furthermore, this survey has considered the use of Evolutionary Algorithms to tackle two important issues in Data Mining: *The Scaling up Problem* and the *Imbalance Data Sets Problem*. These proposals have provided a way to improve the results obtained over large sized and imbalanced data in such fields as supervised classification and subgroup discovery, being a clear example of how Evolutionary Algorithms can be a useful tool in order to overcome these challenging problems.

ACKNOWLEDGMENT

This work was supported by TIN2008-06681-C06-01.

REFERENCES

Abraham, A., Grosan, C., & Ramos, V. (Eds.). (2006). *Swarm intelligence in data mining.* Berlin, Germany: Springer-Verlag.

Aha, D. W., Kibler, D., & Albert, M. K. (1991). Instance-based learning algorithms. *Machine Learning, 6*, 37–66.

Ahn, H., & Kim, K. (2009). Bankruptcy prediction modeling with hybrid case-based reasoning and genetic algorithms approach. *Applied Soft Computing, 9*, 599–607. doi:10.1016/j.asoc.2008.08.002

Ahn, H., Kim, K., & Han, I. (2006). Hybrid genetic algorithms and case-based reasoning systems for customer classification. *Expert Systems: International Journal of Knowledge Engineering and Neural Networks, 23*(3), 127–144. doi:10.1111/j.1468-0394.2006.00329.x

Baluja, S. (1994). *Population-based incremental learning: A method for integrating genetic search based function optimization and competitive learning* (Tech. Rep. CMU-CS-94-163). Pittsburgh, PA: Carnegie Mellon University.

Barandela, R., Sánchez, J. S., García, V., & Rangel, E. (2003). Strategies for learning in class imbalance problems. *Pattern Recognition, 36*(3), 849–851. doi:10.1016/S0031-3203(02)00257-1

Batista, G. E. A. P. A., Prati, R. C., & Monard, M. C. (2004). A study of the behavior of several methods for balancing machine learning training data. *ACM Special Interest Group on Knowledge Discovery and Data Mining. SIGKDD Explorations, 6*(1), 20–29. doi:10.1145/1007730.1007735

Bezdek, J. C., & Kuncheva, L. I. (2001). Nearest prototype classifier designs: An experimental study. *International Journal of Intelligent Systems, 16*(12), 1445–1473. doi:10.1002/int.1068

Bradley, A. P. (1997). The use of the area under the ROC curve in the evaluation of machine learning algorithms. *Pattern Recognition, 30*(7), 1145–1159. doi:10.1016/S0031-3203(96)00142-2

Brightom, H., & Mellish, C. (2002). Advances in instance selection for instance based learning algorithms. *Data Mining and Knowledge Discovery, 6*, 153–172. doi:10.1023/A:1014043630878

Cano, J. R., García, S., & Herrera, F. (2008). Subgroup discovery in large size data sets preprocessed using stratified instance selection for increasing the presence of minority classes. *Pattern Recognition Letters, 29*, 2156–2164. doi:10.1016/j.patrec.2008.08.001

Cano, J. R., Herrera, F., & Lozano, M. (2003). Using evolutionary algorithms as instance selection for data reduction in KDD: An experimental study. *IEEE Transactions on Evolutionary Computation, 7*, 561–575. doi:10.1109/TEVC.2003.819265

Cano, J. R., Herrera, F., & Lozano, M. (2005). Stratification for scaling up evolutionary prototype selection. *Pattern Recognition Letters, 26*, 953–963. doi:10.1016/j.patrec.2004.09.043

Cano, J. R., Herrera, F., & Lozano, M. (2007). Evolutionary stratified training set selection for extracting classification rules with trade-off precision-interpretability. *Data & Knowledge Engineering, 60*, 90–100. doi:10.1016/j.datak.2006.01.008

Cano, J. R., Herrera, F., Lozano, M., & García, S. (2008). Making CN2-SD subgroup discovery algorithm scalable to large size data sets using instance selection. *Expert Systems with Applications, 35*, 1949–1965. doi:10.1016/j.eswa.2007.08.083

Castro, L. N., & Zuben, F. V. J. (2002). Learning and optimization using the clonal selection principle. *IEEE Transactions on Evolutionary Computation, 6*, 239–251. doi:10.1109/TEVC.2002.1011539

Cervantes, A., Galván, I., & Isasi, P. (2007). An adaptive michigan approach PSO for nearest prototype classification. In *Nature Inspired Problem-Solving Methods in Knowledge Engineering* (LNCS 4528, pp. 287-296).

Cervantes, A., Galván, I., & Isasi, P. (in press). AMPSO: A new particle swarm method for nearest neighborhood classification. *IEEE Transactions on Systems, Man and Cybernetics, part B*.

Cervantes, A., Isasi, P., & Galván, I. (2005). A comparison between the pittsburgh and michigan approaches for the binary pso algorithm. In *Proceedings of the 2005 IEEE Congress on Evolucionary Computation*, Munchen, Germany (pp. 290-297).

Chang, C.-L. (1974). Finding prototypes for nearest neighbor classifiers. *IEEE Transactions on Computers, 23*(11), 1179–1184. doi:10.1109/T-C.1974.223827

Chawla, N. V., Bowyer, K. W., Hall, L. O., & Kegelmeyer, W. P. (2002). SMOTE: Synthetic minority over-sampling technique. *Journal of Artificial Intelligence Research, 16*, 321–357.

Chawla, N. V., Japkowicz, N., & Kotcz, A. (2004). Editorial: Special issue on learning from imbalanced data sets. *ACM Special Interest Group on Knowledge Discovery and Data Mining. SIGKDD Explorations, 6*(1), 1–6. doi:10.1145/1007730.1007733

Cover, T. M., & Hart, P. E. (1967). Nearest neighbor pattern classification. *IEEE Transactions on Information Theory, 13*, 21–27. doi:10.1109/TIT.1967.1053964

Cunningham, P. (in press). A taxonomy of similarity mechanisms for case-based reasoning. *IEEE Transactions on Knowledge and Data Engineering*.

Dasgupta, D. (Ed.). (1998). *Artificial immune systems and their applications*. Berlin, Germany: Springer Verlag.

Domingo, C., Gavalda, R., & Watanabe, O. (2002). Adaptive sampling methods for scaling up knowledge discovery algorithms. *Data Mining and Knowledge Discovery, 6*(2), 131–152. doi:10.1023/A:1014091514039

Eiben, A. E., & Smith, J. E. (2003). *Introduction to evolutionary computing*. Berlin, Germany: Springer Verlag.

Eshelman, L. J. (1991). The CHC adaptive search algorithm: How to have safe search when engaging in nontraditional genetic recombination. In G. Rawlins (Ed.), *Foundations of genetic algorithms and classifier systems* (pp. 265-283). San Mateo, CA: Morgan Kaufmann.

Estabrooks, A., Jo, T., & Japkowicz, N. (2004). A multiple resampling method for learning from imbalanced data sets. *Computational Intelligence*, *20*(1), 18–36. doi:10.1111/j.0824-7935.2004.t01-1-00228.x

Fernández, A., García, S., del Jesus, M. J., & Herrera, F. (2008). A study of the behaviour of linguistic fuzzy rule based classification systems in the framework of imbalanced data-sets. *Fuzzy Sets and Systems*, *159*(18), 2378–2398. doi:10.1016/j.fss.2007.12.023

Fernández, F., & Isasi, P. (2004). Evolutionary design of nearest prototype classifiers. *Journal of Heuristics*, *10*, 431–454. doi:10.1023/B:HEUR.0000034715.70386.5b

Freitas, A. A. (2002). *Data mining and knowledge discovery with evolutionary algorithms*. New York: Springer-Verlag.

Freitas, A. A., da Costa Pereira, A., & Brazdil, P. (2007). Cost-sensitive decision trees applied to medical data. In *Data Warehousing and Knowledge Discovery* (LNCS 4654, pp. 303-312).

Garain, U. (2008). Prototype reduction using an artificial immune model. *Pattern Analysis & Applications*, *11*, 353–363. doi:10.1007/s10044-008-0106-1

García, S., Cano, J. R., & Herrera, F. (2008). A memetic algorithm for evolutionary prototype selection: A scaling up approach. *Pattern Recognition*, *41*(8), 2693–2709. doi:10.1016/j.patcog.2008.02.006

García, S., & Herrera, F. (in press). Evolutionary under-sampling for classification with imbalanced data sets: Proposals and taxonomy. *Evolutionary Computation*.

Ghosh, A., & Jain, L. C. (Eds.). (2005). *Evolutionary computation in data mining*. Berlin, Germany: Springer Verlag.

Ghosh, A., & Jain, L. C. (Eds.). (2005). *Evolutionary computation in data mining*. Berlin, Germany: Springer Verlag.

Gil-Pita, R., & Yao, X. (2008). Evolving edited k-nearest neighbor classifiers. *International Journal of Neural Systems*, *18*(6), 1–9. doi:10.1142/S0129065708001725

Goldberg, D. E., & Deb, K. (1991). A comparative analysis of selection schemes used in genetic algorithms. In G. Rawlins (Ed.), *Foundations of genetic algorithms and classifier systems* (pp. 69-93). San Mateo, CA: Morgan Kaufmann.

Gómez-Ballester, E., Micó, L., & Oncina, J. (2006). Some approaches to improve tree-based nearest neighbour search algorithms. *Pattern Recognition*, *39*(2), 171–179. doi:10.1016/j.patcog.2005.06.007

Grochowski, M., & Jankowski, N. (2004). Comparison of instance selection algorithms II. Results and comments. In *Proceedings of Artificial Intelligence and Soft Computing - ICAISC 2004* (LNCS 3070, pp. 580-585).

Grzymala-Busse, J. W., Stefanowski, J., & Wilk, S. (2005). A comparison of two approaches to data mining from imbalanced data. *Journal of Intelligent Manufacturing*, *16*, 565–573. doi:10.1007/s10845-005-4362-2

Guyon, I., Gunn, S., Nikravesh, M., & Zadeh, L. (Eds.). (2006). *Feature extraction*. Heidelberg, Germany: Springer.

Haro-García, A., & García-Pedrajas, N. (2009). A divide-and-conquer recursive approach for scaling up instance selection algorithms. *Data Mining and Knowledge Discovery*, *18*, 392–418. doi:10.1007/s10618-008-0121-2

Hart, P. E. (1968). The condesed nearest neighbour rule. *IEEE Transactions on Information Theory*, *18*(3), 431–433.

Ho, S.-Y., Liu, C. C., & Liu, S. (2002). Design of an optimal nearest neighbor classifier using an intelligent genetic algorithm. *Pattern Recognition Letters*, *23*(13), 1495–1503. doi:10.1016/S0167-8655(02)00109-5

Ishibuchi, H., & Nakashima, T. (1999). Evolution of reference sets in nearest neighbor classification. In *Selected papers from the Second Asia-Pacific Conference on Simulated Evolution and Learning on Simulated Evolution and Learning* (LNCS 1585, pp. 82-89).

Ishibuchi, H., Nakashima, T., & Nii, M. (2001). Learning of neural networks with GA-based instance selection. In *Proceedings of the 20th North American Fuzzy Information Processing Society International Conference,* Vancouver, Canada (Vol. 4, pp. 2102-2107).

Kavsek, B., & Lavrac, N. (2006). APRIORI-SD: Adapting association rule learning to subgroup discovery. *Applied Artificial Intelligence*, *20*(7), 543–583. doi:10.1080/08839510600779688

Kennedy, J., Eberhart, R. C., & Shi, Y. (2001). *Swarm intelligence*. San Francisco: Morgan Kaufmann Publishers.

Kibbler, D., & Aha, D. W. (1987). Learning representative exemplars of concepts: An initial case of study. In *Proceedings of the 4th International Workshop on Machine Learning,* Irvine, CA (pp. 24-30).

Kim, K. (2006). Artificial neural networks with evolutionary instance selection for financial forecasting. *Expert Systems with Applications*, *30*, 519–526. doi:10.1016/j.eswa.2005.10.007

Kohonen, T. (1990). The self-organizing map. *Proceedings of the IEEE*, *78*, 1464–1480. doi:10.1109/5.58325

Kubat, M., Holte, R. C., & Matwin, S. (1998). Machine learning for the detection of oil spills in satellite radar images. *Machine Learning*, *30*(2-3), 195–215. doi:10.1023/A:1007452223027

Kubat, M., & Matwin, S. (1997). Addressing the course of imbalanced training sets: One-sided selection. In *Proceedings of the 14th International Conference on Machine Learning,* Nashville, TN (pp. 179-186).

Kuncheva, L. I. (1995). Editing for the k-nearest neighbors rule by a genetic algorithm. *Pattern Recognition Letters*, *16*, 809–814. doi:10.1016/0167-8655(95)00047-K

Kuncheva, L. I., & Bezdek, J. C. (1998). Nearest prototype classification: Clustering, genetic algorithms, or random search? *IEEE Transactions on Systems, Man, and Cybernetics*, *28*(1), 160–164. doi:10.1109/5326.661099

Laurikkala, J. (2001). Improving identification of difficult small classes by balancing class distribution. In *Proceedings of the 8th Conference on Artificial Intelligence in Medicine in Europe,* Cascais, Portugal (pp. 63-66).

Lavrac, N., Kavsek, B., Flach, P., & Todorovski, L. (2004). Subgroup discovery with CN2-SD. *Journal of Machine Learning Research*, *5*, 153–188.

Liu, H., Hussain, F., Lim, C., & Dash, M. (2002). Discretization: An enabling technique. *Data Mining and Knowledge Discovery*, *6*(4), 393–423. doi:10.1023/A:1016304305535

Liu, H., & Motoda, H. (Eds.). (2001). *Instance selection and construction for data mining*. New York: Springer.

Liu, H., & Motoda, H. (2002). On issues of instance selection. *Data Mining and Knowledge Discovery*, *6*(2), 115–130. doi:10.1023/A:1014056429969

Liu, H., & Motoda, H. (Eds.). (2007). *Computational methods of feature selection*. New York: Chapman & Hall.

Lozano, M., Sotoca, J. M., Sánchez, J. S., Pla, F., Pekalska, E., & Duin, R. P. W. (2006). Experimental study on prototype optimisation algorithms for prototype-based classification in vector spaces. *Pattern Recognition, 39*(10), 1827–1838. doi:10.1016/j.patcog.2006.04.005

Nanni, L., & Lumini, A. (2008). Particle swarm optimization for prototype reduction. *Neurocomputing, 72*, 1092–1097. doi:10.1016/j.neucom.2008.03.008

Newman, D. J., Hettich, S., Blake, C. L., & Merz, C. J. (1998). *UCI repository of machine learning databases*. Irvine, CA: University of California, Irvine, Department of Information and Computer Sciences. Retrieved from http://www.ics.uci.edu/~mlearn/MLRepository.html

Oh, I., Lee, J., & Moon, B. (2004). Hybrid genetic algorithms for feature selection. *IEEE Transactions on Pattern Analysis and Machine Intelligence, 26*(11), 1424–1437. doi:10.1109/TPAMI.2004.105

Ong, Y. S., Krasnogor, N., & Ishibuchi, H. (2007). Special issue on memetic algorithms. *IEEE Transactions on Systems, Man and Cybernetics. Part B, 37*(1), 2–5.

Papadopoulos, A. N., & Manolopoulos, Y. (2004). *Nearest neighbor search: A database perspective*. Berlin, Germany: Springer-Verlag.

Paredes, R., & Vidal, E. (2006). Learning prototypes and distances: A prototype reduction technique based on nearest neighbor error minimization. *Pattern Recognition, 39*(2), 180–188. doi:10.1016/j.patcog.2005.06.001

Provost, F. J., & Kolluri, V. (1999). A survey of methods for scaling up inductive learning algorithms. *Data Mining and Knowledge Discovery, 2*, 131–169. doi:10.1023/A:1009876119989

Pyle, D. (1999). *Data preparation for data mining*. San Francisco: Morgan Kaufmann.

Quinlan, J. R. (1993). *C4.5: Programs for machine learning*. San Francisco: Morgan Kaufmann.

Riquelme, J. C., Aguilar, J. S., & Toro, M. (2003). Finding representative patterns with ordered projections. *Pattern Recognition, 36*(4), 1009–1018. doi:10.1016/S0031-3203(02)00119-X

Ros, F., Guillaume, S., Pintore, M., & Chretien, J. R. (2008). Hybrid genetic algorithm for dual selection. *Pattern Analysis & Applications, 11*, 179–198. doi:10.1007/s10044-007-0089-3

Sanchez, J. S., Barandela, R., Marques, A. I., Alejo, R., & Badenas, J. (2003). Analysis of new techniques to obtain quaylity training sets. *Pattern Recognition Letters, 24*, 1015–1022. doi:10.1016/S0167-8655(02)00225-8

Sebban, M., Nock, R., Chauchat, J. H., & Rakotomalala, R. (2000). Impact of learning set quality and size on decision tree performances. *International Journal of Computers. Systems and Signals, 1*(1), 85–105.

Shakhnarovich, G., Darrel, T., & Indyk, P. (Eds.). (2006). *Nearest-neighbor methods in learning and vision: Theory and practice*. Cambridge, MA: MIT Press.

Sierra, B., Lazkano, E., Inza, I., Merino, M., Larrañaga, P., & Quiroga, J. (2001). Prototype selection and feature subset selection by estimation of distribution algorithms. A case study in the survival of cirrhotic patients treated with TIPS. *Artificial Intelligence in Medicine* (LNAI 2101, pp. 20-29).

Tajbakhsh, A., Rahmati, M., & Mirzaei, A. (2009). Intrusion detection using fuzzy association rules. *Applied Soft Computing, 9*(2), 462–469. doi:10.1016/j.asoc.2008.06.001

Wilson, D. R., & Martinez, T. R. (1997). Instance pruning techniques. In *Proceedings of the 14th International Conference on Machine Learning*, Nashville, TN (pp. 403-411).

Wilson, D. R., & Martinez, T. R. (2000). Reduction techniques for instance-based learning algorithms. *Machine Learning, 38*, 257–286. doi:10.1023/A:1007626913721

Wu, S., & Olafsson, S. (2006). *Optimal instance selection for improved decision tree induction.* Paper presented at the 2006 IIE Annual Conference and Exhibition, Orlando, FL.

Yang, Q., & Wu, X. (2006). 10 challenging problems in data mining research. *International Journal of Information Technology and Decision Making, 5*(4), 597–604. doi:10.1142/S0219622006002258

APPENDIX: ACRONYMS TABLE

In this appendix, a table with all the acronyms employed on the text is provided (Table 1). For each acronym, it is shown its meaning and the page where it was defined:

Acronym	Meaning	Page
EIS	Evolutionary Instance Selection	4
EIS-PS	Evolutionary Instance Selection – Prototype Selection	4
EIS-TSS	Evolutionary Instance Selection – Training Set Selection	4
EUS	Evolutionary Under Sampling	23
EPG	Evolutionary Prototype Generation	4
GGA	Generational Genetic Algorithm	10
GOCBR	Global Optimization of feature weighting and instance selection using genetic algorithms for Case Based Reasoning	26
HGA	Hybrid Genetic Algorithm	26
IG	Instance Generation	3
IGA	Intelligent Genetic Algorithm	18
IS	Instance Selection	3
PBIL	Population Based Incremental Learning	10
PG	Prototype Generation	3
PS	Prototype Selection	3
PSO	Particle Swarm Optimization	28
SSGA	Steady State Genetic Algorithm	10
SSMA	Steady State Memetic Algorithm	18
TSS	Training Set Selection	3

This work was previously published in International Journal of Applied Metaheuristic Computing, Volume 1, Issue 1, edited by Peng-Yeng Yin, pp. 61-92, copyright 2010 by IGI Publishing (an imprint of IGI Global).

Chapter 15
A Sociopsychological Perspective on Collective Intelligence in Metaheuristic Computing

Yingxu Wang
University of Calgary, Canada

ABSTRACT

In studies of genetic algorithms, evolutionary computing, and ant colony mechanisms, it is recognized that the higher-order forms of collective intelligence play an important role in metaheuristic comput- ing and computational intelligence. Collective intelligence is an integration of collective behaviors of individuals in social groups or collective functions of components in computational intelligent systems. This paper presents the properties of collective intelligence and their applications in metaheuristic computing. A social psychological perspective on collected intelligence is elaborated toward the stud- ies on the structure, organization, operation, and development of collective intelligence. The collective behaviors underpinning collective intelligence in groups and societies are analyzed via the fundamental phenomenon of the basic human needs. A key question on how collective intelligence is constrained by social environment and group settings is explained by a formal motivation/attitude-driven behavioral model. Then, a metaheuristic computational model for a generic cognitive process of human problem solving is developed. This work helps to explain the cognitive and collective intelligent foundations of metaheuristic computing and its engineering applications.

INTRODUCTION

Metaheuristic computing is an emerging comput- ing methodology and technology (Geem et al., 2001; Blum & Roli; 2003; Glover & Gary; 2003; Talbi, 2009) developed in the field of genetic,

DOI: 10.4018/978-1-4666-0270-0.ch015

evolutional, autonomous, and search-based com- puting (Holland, 1975; Goldberg, 1989; Wang, 2008a, 2009c). The advances of metaheuristic computing are "higher-level problem solving without the hassle to design problem-specific operations each time a new application appears" (Yin, 2010).

In order to rigorously convey the concept of metaheuristic computing, the fundamental terms in metaheuristic computing are analyzed below.

Definition 1. A *heuristic* is a reasoning methodology in problem solving that enables a solution to a problem is derived by trial-and-error and/or rule of thumb.

Definition 2. A *metaheuristic* is a generic or higher-level heuristics that is more general in problem solving.

Definition 3. *Computing* in a narrow sense is an application of computers to solve a given problem by imperative instructions; while in a broad sense, it is a process to implement the instructive intelligence by a system that transfers a set of given information or instructions into expected intelligent behaviors.

On the basis of Definitions 1 through 3, the concept of metaheuristic computing can be described as follows.

Definition 4. *Metaheuristic computing* is an adaptive and/or autonomous methodology for computing that applies general heuristic rules, algorithms, and processes in solving a category of computational problems.

It is recognized in abstract intelligence (αI) (Wang, 2009a) and cognitive informatics (Wang, 2002a, 2003, 2007b, 2009b; Wang et al., 2009; Wang, Zadeh & Yao, 2009), there are three categories of intelligent behaviors known as the *imperative, autonomic (adaptive),* and *cognitive* intelligent behaviors. In a certain extent, metaheuristic computing intends to implement autonomic/adaptive intelligent behaviors beyond those of imperative ones in computational intelligence.

In order to explain the cognitive and sociopsychological properties of metaheuristic computing and it engineering applications, a transdisciplinary study between metaheuristic computing and collective intelligence are presented in this paper.

Parallel with studies in genetic algorithms, evolutionary computing, and ant colony mechanisms in metaheuristic computing and computational intelligence, the higher-order forms of collective intelligence are human groups and societies. This work turns the attention to the collective intelligence of human societies and its applications in metaheuristic computing. This paper presents a rigorous treatment of human social mechanisms in the context of collective intelligence. Collective behaviors in groups and societies underpinning collective intelligence are explored via analyses of the basic human needs. The constraints of collective intelligence are explained by social environment and group settings by a formal motivation/attitude-driven behavioral model. Then, the cognitive process of generic problem solving is formally described as a metaheuristic computing model for cognitive computing and computational intelligence.

COMPUTATIONAL INTELLIGENCE FOUNDATIONS OF METAHEURISTIC COMPUTING

As a preparation, the concept of metaheuristic computing is modeled using concept algebra. A formal model of genetic algorithms for metaheuristic computing is described via Real-Time Process Algebra (RTPA). A computational intelligence perspective on metaheuristic computing is presented, which synergizes metaheuristic computing with studies in collective intelligence.

The Concept Algebra Model of Metaheuristic Computing

Major metaheuristic computing concepts and techniques, according to Wikipedia, are such as genetic algorithms, evolutional algorithms, random optimizations, local search, reactive search, greedy algorithm, hill-climbing, best-first search, simulated annealing, ant colony optimization, stochastic diffusion search, harmony search, and variable neighborhood search (Wikipedia, 2009). Therefore, the intension of metaheuristic computing is a set of generic and meta algorithms, processes, and rules of computational problem solving. The extension of metaheuristic computing is a set of adaptive/autonomic, trial-and-error, and heuristic computing methodologies.

According to concept algebra (Wang, 2008b), a formal definition of metaheuristic computing based on Definition 4 can be rigorously described as follows.

Definition 5. *Metaheuristic computing*, MHC, is formally defined as a 5-tuple, i.e.:

$$MHC \triangleq (O, A, R^c, R^i, R^o) \qquad (1)$$

where

- O is a finite nonempty set of objects, i.e., a set of MHC methodologies, $O = \{meta$-*heuristic, adaptive, autonomic, trial-and-error, cognitive*$\}$;
- A is a finite nonempty set of attributes, i.e., a set of generic algorithms, processes, and rules, where $A = \{genetic$ *algorithms, evolutional algorithms, random optimizations, local search, reactive search, greedy algorithm, hill-climbing, best-first search, simulated annealing, ant colony optimization, stochastic diffusion search, harmony search, variable neighborhood search*$\}$;
- $R^c = O \times A$ is a set of internal relations;
- $R^i \subseteq A' \times A$, $A' \sqsubseteq C' \wedge A \sqsubseteq c$, is a set of input relations, where C' is a set of external concepts, $C' \subseteq \Theta$ known as the concept environment. For convenience, $R^i = A' \times A$ may be simply denoted as $R^i = C' \times c$.
- $R^o \subseteq c \times C'$ is a set of output relations.

The algebraic model of the concept of metahueristic computing, MHC, provides an abstract mathematical structure for the formal treatment of MHC and its algebraic relations, operations, and associations (Wang, 2008d).

The Formal Model of Genetic Algorithms for Metaheuristic Computing

Genetic algorithms are proposed by John Holland in 1975 based on studies of cellular automata (Holland, 1975). It is extended by work of Goldberg (1989), Davis (1991), and Buckles and Petry (1992).

Definition 6. A *genetic algorithm* is a recursive-search-based process that adopts adaptive selection in each generation of the recursive computation via crossovers and mutations.

A mathematical model of genetic algorithm can be formally described as follows using RTPA (Wang, 2002b, 2007a, 2008c). (See Figure 1)

The natural-evolutionary-mechanism inspired methodology of genetic algorithm provides a new approach to design and implement adaptive and autonomic systems in computing and computational intelligence. Two technologies known as *crossover* and *mutation* play a central role in the genetic algorithm. The former is a means that allows a new generation of computing entity and its mechanism to be inherently different based on the combinatory properties of the population pool. The latter is a dynamics that creates a new generation of computing entity and its algorithm with extended new features and properties beyond its earlier generations based on heuristic selections. Genetic algorithms form the most important metaheuristic model for evolutionary and metaheuristic computing.

Figure 1. The formal model of genetic algorithms

$$
\begin{aligned}
&\textbf{GeneticAlgorithm}(\langle I:: (\ )\rangle; \langle O:: (\ )\rangle; \langle UDM:: (G(\textit{t}\textbf{N})\textbf{ST})\rangle)\textbf{PC} \triangleq \\
&\{\ \textit{t}\textbf{N} := 0 \\
&\quad \rightarrow \text{Generate}\textbf{PC}\ (G(\textit{t}\textbf{N})\textbf{ST}) \\
&\quad \rightarrow \text{SolutionFound}\textbf{BL} := \textbf{F} \\
&\quad \rightarrow \underset{\text{SolutionFound}\textbf{BL}=\textbf{F}}{\overset{\textbf{T}}{R}}\ (\ \textit{t}\textbf{N} := \textit{t}\textbf{N} + 1 \\
&\qquad\qquad\qquad \rightarrow \text{Generate}\textbf{PC}\ (G(\textit{t}\textbf{N})\textbf{ST}) \\
&\qquad\qquad\qquad \rightarrow \text{Evaluate}\textbf{PC}((G(\textit{t}\textbf{N})\textbf{ST}) \\
&\qquad\qquad\qquad \rightarrow (\ \blacklozenge\ \text{Fitness}\textbf{N}((G(\textit{t}\textbf{N})\textbf{ST}) = \text{Satisfied} \\
&\qquad\qquad\qquad\qquad \rightarrow \text{SolutionFound}\textbf{BL} := \textbf{T} \\
&\qquad\qquad\qquad |\ \blacklozenge \sim \\
&\qquad\qquad\qquad\qquad \rightarrow \text{SolutionFound}\textbf{BL} := \textbf{F} \\
&\qquad\qquad\qquad\qquad \rightarrow \text{Crossover}\textbf{PC}((G(\textit{t}\textbf{N})\textbf{ST}) \\
&\qquad\qquad\qquad\qquad \rightarrow \text{Mutation}\textbf{PC}((G(\textit{t}\textbf{N})\textbf{ST}) \\
&\qquad\qquad\qquad) \\
&\qquad\qquad) \\
&\}
\end{aligned}
$$

Computational Intelligence Perspectives on Metaheuristic Computing

Intelligence is a driving force or an ability to acquire and use knowledge and skills, or to reason in problem solving. Therefore, computational intelligence is a paradigm of the generic intelligence kwon as *abstract intelligence* (αI), which is the universal mathematical form of intelligence that transfers information into knowledge and behaviors (Wang, 2009a). Wang's theory of αI states there are four types of intelligence known as the *reflective, perspective, instructive,* and *cognitive* intelligence. It is also recognized in αI that there are three categories of intelligent behaviors known as the *imperative, autonomic (adaptive),* and *cognitive* intelligent behaviors (Wang, 2009a; Wang, Kinsner & Zhang, 2009).

Parallel with studies in ant colony mechanisms in metaheuristic computing and computational intelligence, the higher-order forms of collective intelligence, i.e., the human groups and societies, are recognized. Collective intelligence is a special phenomenon in sociology that natural or machine intelligence may coordinately work together in a formal or contingent structure toward a common goal by group intelligence. It is recognized that a new approach may be taken to study the mechanisms of metaheuristic computing focusing on collective intelligence of human societies and its interactive and cumulative properties. This approach creates synergies between metaheuristic computing and collective intelligence in sociology. As a system science at the most complicated level of human social organizations (Wang, 2007a). Sociology studies structures and behaviors of human societies and how a human society may be organized efficiently and effectively on certain constraints of resources and environments (Macionis et al., 1997). In which, social psychology studies social interactions and their effects on human behaviors in collective intelligence (Wiggins et al., 1994).

Definition 7. *Collective intelligence* is an integration of collective behaviors of individuals in social groups or collective functions of components in computational intelligent systems.

A transdisciplinary study on metaheuristic computing and social psychology may explain a set of key mechanisms of collected intelligence. In this context, a society is a huge organized human system in which people are grouped, coordinated, interconnected, and interacted by a variety of organizations in order to form and enable collective intelligence. A society as a whole consists of individuals, groups, organizations, and sectors from the bottom up. Because the basic objects under study in sociology are individual human beings and their interactions, social psychology is the key to understand a wide range of complicated social phenomena and collective intelligence, as well as the driving forces underpinning them.

In collective intelligence, a group is the basic social unit formed by two or more persons working toward a particular purpose. Groups are needed because of the *interdependency* among members when a given work cannot be carried out by a single individual limited by the scarcity of physical or intelligent capabilities and resources. The study on organizational psychology and collective social behaviors within groups and organizations helps to explain how structures of groups and organizations may impact people's behaviors, productivity, and performance in collective intelligence.

COLLECTIVE BEHAVIORS OF COLLECTIVE INTELLIGENCE

From a sociological point of view, collective intelligence is an integration of collective behaviors of individuals in a group or society. This section explores the fundamental human traits and the basic needs of individuals in a society in order to understand the natural drives and constraints of human collective behaviors.

The Hierarchical Model of Basic Human Needs

As an individual, the bottom-level basic biological need of humans is a stable inner environment regulated by a mechanism known as homeostasis.

Definition 8. *Homeostasis* is an adaptive biological mechanism of the human body that maintains a relatively constant state in order to live and function.

In psychology, Sigmund Freud perceived that humans are motivated by internal tension states known as drives that build up until they are released. The basic drives that Freud identified are self-preservation, sex, and aggression. However, he focused only on the last two drives later in his theory (Freud, 1895; Leahey, 1997). Clark Hull proposed a drive-reduction theory that states motivation stems from a combination of drive and reinforcement of unfulfilled needs (Hull, 1943). The primary drives are innate drives such as hunger, thirst, and sex; the secondary drives are acquired drives such as studying, socializing, and earning money.

The hierarchical nature of human needs is identified by Abraham Maslow at five levels known as the needs of physiological, safety, social, esteem, and self-actualization from the bottom up (Maslow, 1962, 1970). The five basic levels of human needs are described in Table 1. Except those at Level 5, most needs identified by Maslow are deficiency needs, which are a need generated by a lack of something. The Level 5 needs for self-actualization can be classified as growth needs.

Table 1. Maslow's Hierarchy of Needs

Level	Category	Needs	Description
1	Lower order needs	Physiological	Needs for biological maintenance such as food, water, sex, sleep etc.
2		Safety	Needs for physical and social security, protection, and stability such as shelter
3		Belongingness	Needs for love, affection, socialization
4	Higher order needs	Esteem	Needs for respect, prestige, recognition, and self-satisfaction
5		Self-actualization	Need to express oneself, grow, and to fulfill one's maximum potential toward success

On the basis of the needs taxonomies of Maslow, Hull, and Freud, a formal human needs hierarchy model is developed below.

Definition 9. The *Human Needs Hierarchy* (HNH) model is a hierarchical model that encompasses five-level fundamental human needs known from the bottom-up as N_0 – physiological needs, N_1 – psychological needs, N_2 – cognitive needs, N_3 – social needs, and N_4 – self-expressive needs.

The HNH model can be illustrated as shown in Figure 2. Detailed explanations of each of the basic needs are provided in Table 2.

Lemma 1. The lower the level of a need in the HNH hierarchy, the more concrete or material-oriented the need. In other words, the higher the level of a need, the more virtualized or perception-oriented the need.

Definition 10. The predominant need of an individual is the need at the lowest unsatisfied level of the HNH model.

Maslow suggests that human needs should be satisfied level by level. That is, the lower level needs should be satisfied before any higher level need comes into play (Maslow, 1970). This observation leads to the following principle.

Theorem 1. When multiple needs of a person are unsatisfied at a given time, satisfaction of the most predominant need is most pressing.

Understanding of the nature of basic human needs is not only useful in predicating motivations of human beings in collective intelligence, but also important in identifying the driving forces for the approach of group and society organization.

Table 2. The Human Needs Hierarchy (HNH) Model

Level	Basic Needs	Description
N_0	Physiological	Needs for maintaining homeostasis, such as food, water, clothes, sex, sleep, and shelter
N_1	Psychological	Needs for feeling safe, comfortable, and wellbeing
N_2	Cognitive	Needs for satisfaction of curiosity, knowledge, pleasure, and interaction with the environment
N_3	Social	Needs for work, socialization, respect, prestige, esteem, and recognition
N_4	Self-expressive	Need to express oneself, grow, and to fulfill one's maximum potential toward success

Figure 2. The Human Needs Hierarchy (HNH) model

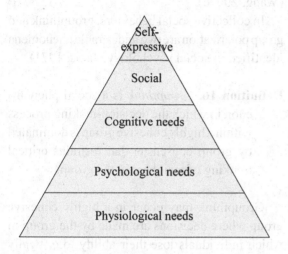

Collective Behaviors Underpinning Collective Intelligence

Studies on collective behaviors within groups and organizations may help to explain how structures of them impact people's behaviors, productivity, and performance, as well as the formation of collective intelligence. Psychological experiments indicate that individual's behavior may vary in a group influenced by the interactions with other members of the group, which is identified as collective behaviors (Zander, 1979; Wiggins et al., 1994).

Definition 11. A *collective behavior* is an integrated behavior of a group in which individuals' behaviors are influenced in different ways by the group.

Collective behaviors are one of the most important social properties of groups and organizations. It is perceived in sociology that any human social behavior may be compared and analyzed against the social norms, which forms a qualitative or quantitative standard for the behavior (Wiggins et al., 1994). Therefore, *individual behaviors* in

the social context are measurable and analytical in term of performance against the social norms.

A set of observable phenomena of collective behaviors is formally described below, such as social conformity, social synchronization, coaction, coordination, groupthink, group polarization, social dilemmas, and social loafing.

Individuals intend to adjust their behavior or actions, which reflect their thought, to the common goal and norms of a group that they involve and think belong to. This social phenomenon is called conformity.

Definition 12. *Social conformity* is a social phenomenon in which an individual's behavior is approached to a social norm or standard in forms of ethical values, role expectations, and laws.

Conformity may be explained by the principle of minimum energy consumption, especially when there is no obvious or intuitive best choice.

Individuals intend to set their behavior or actions to the timing of the group. This social phenomenon is called synchronization (Wang, 2007a).

Definition 13. *Social synchronization* is a social phenomenon in which an individual's behavior is timed to a social norm of a group.

Synchronization is a special type of social conformity. Synchronization may be explained by the principles of system synchronization and minimum energy consumption, because synchronization contributes to the maximum output of a group.

It is found that in temporary social situations and informal groups where no or little coordination is required, people still influence each other when their actions or tasks are identical or have similarity.

Definition 14. A *coaction* is a social phenomenon in which the identical or similar actions or tasks are carried out by different individuals with little interaction.

Coaction influences the performance of individuals because it puts the individual in a social context. The phenomena of coaction indicate there is a natural law, as described below, which constrains collective social behaviors of human beings even in a noncohesive social context and a highly temporary and random social relation.

Lemma 2. An *autonomous synchronization tendency* between individuals exists in any permanent or temporary social context where people automatically adjust to conjunctive goals and cooperative timing.

The coaction influences on individual's performance can be positive or negative. The former can be a higher expectation, an awareness of difference, and a learning of better practice; while the latter can be a distraction or disappointment.

Coaction discussed above is an *ad hoc* cooperation in an informal group where there is no common goal as well as predefined means of cooperation and communication. In contrary to coaction, coordination happens in a formal group where common goals as well as means of cooperation and communications exist.

Definition 15. A *coordination* is a social phenomenon in which the identical or similar action or task is carried out via intensive interactions between different individuals.

Coordination may influence the performance of individuals dramatically in a group context. Organizational theories of work coordination and efficiencies of group coordination have been extensively studied in engineering sciences, system science, and management science, respectively,

particularly the generic work coordination theory (Wang, 2007c).

In collective social behaviors, groupthink and group polarization are two undesirable phenomena identified in social psychology (Janis, 1971).

Definition 16. *Groupthink* is a social phenomenon in which the decision-making process within a highly cohesive group is dominated by group consensus that restrains critical thinking of members in the group.

Groupthink may occur in a highly cohesive group where decisions are made by the group in which individuals lose their ability to critically evaluate situations or information. Groupthink symptoms identified by Irving Janis in 1971 include illusion of invulnerability, illusion of morality, stereotypes of outsiders, pressure for conformity, self-censorship, and illusion of unanimity (Janis, 1971).

Groupthink acting as a filter of critical ideas may result in another social phenomenon known as group polarization that turns a group to a positive-feedback or instable system.

Definition 17. *Group polarization* is a social phenomenon in which group members intend to shift toward the extreme of an already preferred position of the group.

The tendency of group polarization is a powerful positive-feedback mechanism that may result in an instable state of a social unit or system. Behaviors of a positive-feedback system are sometime unpredictable even destructive. Therefore, the art of leadership for groups, to some extent, is to prevent the polarization situation in a group from happening.

Lemma 3. A weighting system that encourages and appreciates *negative or hesitant feedback* towards the current group's position is a stable system.

The rule of thumb is that, in a group polarization situation, the one who hesitates in the group is perhaps the wiser one. Therefore, Lemma 3 indicates that the negative-feedback mechanism is not only suitable for a natural system, but also applicable to social systems and collective intelligence.

Definition 18. The *social dilemma* is a social phenomenon in which members of a group face a conflict choice between the maximization of group's interests by cooperative actions and the maximization of own individual's interests by noncooperative actions.

The collective behaviors of social dilemmas have been identified by many sociologists and social psychologists since 1985 (Komorita & Barth, 1985; Coleman, 1990). If only egoism is adopted in a society, the social dilemma may exist forever. However, when altruism is recognized to balance egoism, social dilemmas may be resolved systematically.

The collective behavior known as social loafing was first identified in Max Ringelmann's experiments on rope-pulling before World War I (Kravits & Martin, 1986). The same experiment was replicated by Alan Ingham et al. in 1974. This collective phenomenon is then termed as social loafing by Latane and his colleagues in 1979 based on extended studies (Latane et al., 1979; Hardy & Latane, 1986).

Definition 19. *Social loafing* is a social phenomenon in which there exists the tendency for people to work less hard on a cooperative task in a group than they do individually.

Three independent experiments on the efficiency of coordinated group tasks as shown in Table 3 reveal similar patterns of efficiency decreasing when more persons are involved in collective group tasks. These are the main evidences of social loafing. However, it can also be scientifically explained by coordinate overhead and efficiency of systems according to Wang's abstract work coordination theory (Wang, 2007c).

A typical collective behavior of social loafing is the free-rider effect (Kerr, 1983).

Definition 20. The *free-rider effect* is a social phenomenon in which there exists the tendency for a member of a group to act noncooperatively based on the assumption that one's individual cooperative action may not be necessary because others will do for the interests of the group.

Another social loafing phenomenon is identified by Jackson and Harkins (1985) known as the sucker effect.

Definition 21. The *sucker effect* is a social phenomenon in which exists the tendency for a member of a group to act noncooperatively

Table 3. Experiments on efficiency of coordinated group work

Collective tasks		An individual	A group			
			2 persons	3 persons	2-6 persons	8 persons
Rope-pulling[1]	Force (lb.)	130		352		546
	Efficiency	100%		90.3%		52.5%
Rope-pulling[2]		100%	90%		85%	
Cheerleaders[3]		100%			92%	

Note: Experiment 1 is based on Max Ringelmann [Kravits and Martin, 1986]
Experiment 2 is based on Alan Ingham et al. in 1974.
Experiment 3 is based on Hardy and Latane in 1986.

based on the assumption that others may take advantage of one's individual cooperative contribution to the group.

Social loafing may happen in a group where tasks are parallel allocated and the sum of all parallel capacity is much larger than the workload of the group, for instance, a group of porters and a team of programmers. The studies on collective behaviors indicate that rational and suitable organizational forms may enable efficient coordinative work and reduce any negative effect.

COGNITIVE SOCIOPSYCHOLOGY OF COLLECTIVE INTELLIGENCE

On the basis of sociological foundations of collective intelligence, this section presents a rigorous treatment of human perceptual processes such as emotions, motivations, and attitudes, and their influences on human behaviors in collective intelligence. The interactions and relationships between motivation and attitude are formally described.

Emotions

Emotions are a set of states or results of perception that interprets the feelings of human beings on external stimuli or events in the binary categories of pleasant or unpleasant.

Definition 22. An *emotion* is a subjective feeling derived from one's current internal status, mood, circumstances, historical context, and external stimuli.

Emotions are closely related to desires and willingness. A desire is a personal feeling to possess an object, to conduct an interaction with the external world, or to prepare for an event to happen. A willingness is the faculty of conscious, deliberate, and voluntary choice of actions.

According to the study of Fischer and his colleagues (Fischer et al., 1990), the taxonomy of emotions can be described as shown in Table 4.

It can be observed that human emotions at the perceptual layer may be classified into only two opposite categories: pleasant and unpleasant. Various emotions in the two categories can be classified at five levels according to its strengths of subjective feelings as shown in Table 5, where each level encompasses a pair of positive/negative or pleasant/unpleasant emotions.

Definition 23. The *strength of emotion* $|E_m|$ is a normalized measure of how strong a person's emotion on a scale of 0 through 4, i.e.:

$$0 \leq |E_m| \leq 4 \qquad (2)$$

An organ known as the hypothalamus in the brain is supposed to interpret the properties or types of emotions in terms of pleasant or unpleasant (Smith, 1993; Leahey, 1997; Sternberg, 1998).

Definition 24. Letting T_e be a type of emotion, ES the external stimulus, IS the internal perceptual status, and BL the Boolean values true or false, the perceptual mechanism of hypothalamus can be described as a function, i.e.:

$$T_e: ES \times IS \rightarrow BL \qquad (3)$$

It is interesting that sometime the same event or stimulus ES may be explained in different types due to the difference of the real-time context of the perceptual status IS of the brain. For instance, walking from home to office may be interpreted as a pleasant activity for one who likes physical exercises, but the same walk due to a car breakdown will be interpreted as unpleasant.

Table 4. Taxonomy of emotions

Level	Description				
Supper level	Positive (pleasant)		Negative (unpleasant)		
Basic level	Joy	Love	Anger	Sadness	Fear
Sub-category level	Bliss, pride, contentment	Fondness, infatuation	Annoyance, hostility, contempt, jealousy	Agony, grief, guilt, loneliness	Horror, worry

Corollary 2. The *human emotional system* is a binary system that interprets or perceives an external stimulus and/or internal status as pleasant or unpleasant.

Although there are various emotional categories in different levels, the binary emotional system of the brain provides a set of pairwise universal solutions to express human feelings. For example, anger may be explained as a default solution or generic reaction for an emotional event when there was no better solution available; otherwise, delight will be the default emotional reaction.

Motivations

Motivation is an innate potential power of human beings that energizes behavior. It is motivation that transforms thought (information) into action (energy). In other words, human behaviors are the embodiment of motivations. Therefore, any cognitive behavior is driven by an individual motivation.

Definition 25. A *motivation* is a willingness or desire triggered by an emotion to pursue a goal or a reason for triggering an action.

As described in the LRMB model (Wang et al., 2006), motivation is a cognitive process of the brain at the perception layer that explains the initiation, persistence, and intensity of personal emotions and desires, which are the faculty of conscious, deliberate, and voluntary choices of actions.

Motivation is a psychological and social modulating and coordinating influence on the direction, vigor, and composition of behavior. This influence arises from a wide variety of internal, environmental, and social sources, and is manifested at many levels of behavioral and neural organizations.

Table 5. The hierarchy of emotions

Level (Positive/Negative)			Description
0	No emotion		-
1	Week emotion	Comfort	Safeness, contentment, fulfillment, trust
		Fear	Worry, horror, jealousy, frightening, threatening
2	Mediate emotion	Joy	Delight, fun, interest, pride
		Sadness	Anxiety, loneliness, regret, guilt, grief, sorrow, agony
3	Strong emotion	Pleasure	Happiness, bliss, excitement, ecstasy
		Anger	Annoyance, hostility, contempt, infuriated, enraged
4	Strongest emotion	Love	Intimacy, passion, amorousness, fondness, infatuation
		Hate	Disgust, detestation, abhorrence, bitter

The taxonomy of motives can be classified into two categories known as learned and unlearned (Wittig, 2001). The latter is the primary motives such as the *survival motives* (hunger, thirst, breathing, shelter, sleep, eliminating), and pain. The former is the secondary motives such as the need for achievement, friendship, affiliation, dominance of power, and relief from anxiety.

Definition 26. The *strength of motivation M* is a normalized measure of how strong a person's motivation is on a scale of 0 through 100, i.e.:

$$0 \leq M \leq 100 \tag{4}$$

where $M = 100$ is the strongest motivation and $M = 0$ is the weakest motivation.

It is observed that the strength of a motivation is determined by multiple factors (Westen, 1999; Wang, 2007d) such as:

a. The *absolute motivation* $|E_m|$: The strength of the emotion.
b. The *relative motivation E - S*: A relative difference or inequity between the expectancy of a person E for an object or an action towards a certain goal and the current status S of the person.
c. The *cost* to fulfill the motivation C: A subjective assessment of the effort needed to accomplish the expected goal.

Therefore, the strength of a motivation can be quantitatively analyzed and estimated by the subjective and objective motivations and their cost as described in the following theorem.

Theorem 2. The *strength of motivations* states that a motivation M is proportional to both the strength of emotion $|E_m|$ and the difference between the expectancy of desire E and the current status S, of a person, and is inversely proportional to the cost to accomplish the expected motivation C, i.e.:

$$M = \frac{2.5 \bullet |E_m| \bullet (E\text{-}S)}{C} \tag{5}$$

where $0 \leq |E_m| \leq 4$, $0 \leq (E,S) \leq 10$, and $1 \leq C \leq 10$.

In Theorem 2, the strength of a motivation is measured in the scope of [0 … 100], i.e., $0 \leq M \leq 100$. When $M > 1$, the motivation is considered being a desired motivation. The higher the value of M, the stronger the motivation.

It is noteworthy that motivation is only a potential mental power of human beings, and a strong motivation will not necessarily result in a behavior or action. The condition for transforming a motivation into a real behavior or action is dependent on multiple factors, such as values, social norms, expected difficulties, availability of resources, and the existence of alternative goals.

Attitudes

As described in the previous section, motivation is the potential power that may trigger an observable behavior or action. Before the behavior is performed, it is judged by an internal regulation system known as the attitude.

Attitudes are perceived in various ways in social psychology. Fazio describes an *attitude* as an association between an act or object and an evaluation (Fazio, 1986). Eagly and Chaiken define attitude as a tendency of a human to evaluate a person, concept, or group positively or negatively in a given context (1992). More recently, Arno Wittig describes attitude as a learned evaluative reaction to people, objects, events, and other stimuli (Wittig, 2001).

Definition 27. An *attitude* is a subjective tendency towards a motivation, an object, a goal, or an action based on an intuitive evaluation of its feasibility.

The modes of attitudes can be positive or negative, which can be quantitatively analyzed using the following definition.

Figure 3. The model of Motivation/Attitude-Driven Behavior (MADB) in collective intelligence

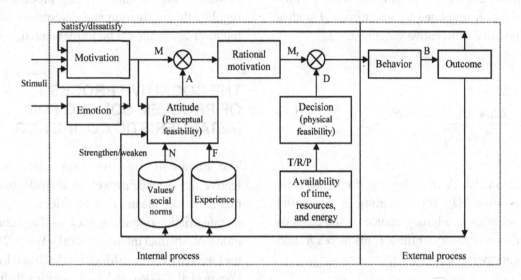

Definition 28. The *mode of an attitude A* is determined by both an *objective judgment* of its conformance to the social norm *N* and a *subjective judgment* of its empirical feasibility *F*, i.e.:

$$A = \begin{cases} 1, & N = \mathbf{T} \wedge F = \mathbf{T} \\ 0, & N = \mathbf{F} \vee F = \mathbf{F} \end{cases} \qquad (6)$$

where $A = 1$ indicates a positive attitude; otherwise, it indicates a negative attitude.

THE INTERACTIVE BEHAVIORAL MODEL OF COLLECTIVE INTELLIGENCE

Based on the preceding subsections, the relationship between a set of interlinked perceptual psychological processes such as emotions, motivations, attitudes, decisions, and behaviors can be integrated into a coherent framework. A motivation/attitude-driven behavioral model will be developed for formally describing the cognitive processes of motivation and attitude in collective intelligence.

It is observed that motivation and attitude have considerable impact on behavior and influence the way a person thinks and feels (Westen, 1999). A reasoned action model is proposed by Martin Fishbein and Icek Ajzen in 1975 that suggests human behavior is directly generated by behavioral intensions, which are controlled by the attitude and social norms (Fishbein & Ajzen, 1975). An initial motivation before the judgment by an attitude is only a temporal idea; with the judgment of the attitude, it becomes a rational motivation, also known as the behavioral intention.

The relationship between an emotion, motivation, attitude, and behavior can be formally and quantitatively described by the Motivation/Attitude-Driven Behavioral (MADB) model as illustrated in Figure 3. In the MADB model, motivation and attitude have been defined in Eqs. 5 and 6, respectively. It is noteworthy that, as shown in Figure 3, a motivation is triggered by an emotion or desire. The rational motivation, decision, and behavior can be quantitatively analyzed according to the following definitions.

Definition 29. A *rational motivation* M_r is a motivation regulated by an attitude A with a positive or negative judgment, i.e.:

$$M_r = M \cdot A$$
$$= \frac{2.5 \cdot |E_m| \cdot (E\text{-}S)}{C} \cdot A \qquad (7)$$

Definition 30. A *decision* for confirming an attitude, D_a, for executing a motivated behavior is a binary choice on the basis of the availability of time T, resources R, and energy P, i.e.:

$$D_a = \begin{cases} 1, & T \wedge R \wedge P = \text{T} \\ 0, & T \vee R \vee P = \text{F} \end{cases} \qquad (8)$$

Therefore, the formal model of MADB can be described as follows, where a behavior is determined by a product of the strength of motivation and the approval of the decision by a positive attitude.

Lemma 4. A *behavior* B driven by a motivation M_r and an attitude is a realized action initiated by a motivation M and supported by a positive attitude A and a positive decision D_a toward the action, i.e.:

$$B = \begin{cases} \text{T}, & M_r \cdot D_a = \frac{2.5 \cdot |E_m| \cdot (E\text{-}S)}{C} \cdot A \cdot D_a > 1 \\ \text{F}, & otherwise \end{cases}$$
$$\qquad (9)$$

The MADB model presented in Lemma 4 and Figure 3 provides a rigorous explanation of the mechanisms and relationship between motivation, attitude, and behavior. The model can be used to explain how the motivation process drives human behaviors and actions, and how the attitude as well as the decision making process help to regulate the motivation and determines whether the motivation should be implemented.

THE COGNITIVE PROCESS OF PROBLEM SOLVING FOR METAHUERISTIC COMPUTING

The studies in cognitive informatics and collective intelligence as well as their denotational mathematical means can be widely applied in metaheuristic computing such as the theoretical model of Abstract Intelligence (aI) (Wang, 2009a), the Layered Reference Model of the Brain (LRMB) (Wang et al., 2006), and the Cognitive Reference Model of Autonomous Agents (Wang, 2009c).

An interesting metaheuristic study in cognitive informatics and collective intelligence is the generic algorithm of problem solving as a fundamental cognitive process of the brain (Newell & Simon, 1972; Goldstein, 1978; Robertson, 2001; Wang & Chiew, 2009), which may be simulated and implemented by computational intelligence in metaheuristic computing.

Based on RTPA, concept algebra, and the Object-Attribute-Relation (OAR) model (Wang, 2007e) of internal knowledge representation in the brain, the cognitive process of problem solving can be formally elaborated in Figure 4, which can be divided into the following five steps:

a. **To define the problem:** This step describes the problem and its input layout X by identifying its object O_X and attributes A_X, in a sub-OAR model.

b. **To search the solution goals and paths:** In this step, the brain performs a parallel search for possible goals G and paths T for the solution. External memory and resources may be searched if there is no available or sufficient G or T in the internal knowledge of the problem solver.

Figure 4. Formal description of the cognitive process of problem solving in RTPA

The Problem Solving Process (PSP)

PSP_Process(I:: O**S**, OAR**ST**; O:: OAR'**ST**)**ST** $\triangleq$

{ // I. Define and represent the problem

$\hookrightarrow$ Identify (O**S**)   // Representation of the problem object

$\hookrightarrow$ Identify (A**ST**)   // Characteristics of the problem

$\hookrightarrow$ Identify (R(O**S**, A**ST**)**ST**)   // Representation of relations between O**S** and A**ST**

$\rightarrow$ X**ST** := (O**S**, A**ST**, R**ST**))**ST** // Representation of the problem

// II. Search solution goals and paths

$\overset{R}{\underset{\text{Satisfication\_of\_T = F}}{\longrightarrow}}$ ($\hookrightarrow$ Search (G**ST**)

$\hookrightarrow$ Quantify (G**ST**)

$\hookrightarrow$ Evaluate (G**ST**)

)

|| ($\hookrightarrow$ Search (T**ST**)

$\hookrightarrow$ Quantify (T**ST**)

$\hookrightarrow$ Evaluate (T**ST**)

)

}

// III. Generate solutions

$\rightarrow$ S**ST** := X**S** ×T**ST** ×G**ST**

// IV. Select solutions

$\hookrightarrow$ Evaluate (S**ST**)

$\rightarrow$ ($\blacklozenge$ρ(S**ST**) ≥ k   // k is a satisfaction threshold

$\rightarrow$ R**ST** := S(X**S**, T**ST**, G**ST**)**ST**   // Form a new relation on S**ST**

$\rightarrow$ ∅

| $\blacklozenge$ ~   // Otherwise

$\rightarrow$ ($\blacklozenge$ GiveUp**BL** = F

↻ PSP_Process(I:: O**S**; O::OAR(S**ST**)**ST**)**ST**

| $\blacklozenge$ ~

$\rightarrow$ ∅

)

)

// V. Represent problem solving result

$\rightarrow$ sOAR**ST** := (O**S**, A**ST**, R**ST**)**ST**   // Form a new sub-OAR**ST** model for S**ST**

$\rightarrow$ OAR'**ST** := OAR**ST** ⊎ sOAR**ST**   // Update OAR**ST**

$\hookrightarrow$ Memorize (OAR'**ST**)**ST**   // Memorize updated OAR**ST**

}

Figure 5. Interaction between problem solving and other cognitive processes in LRMB

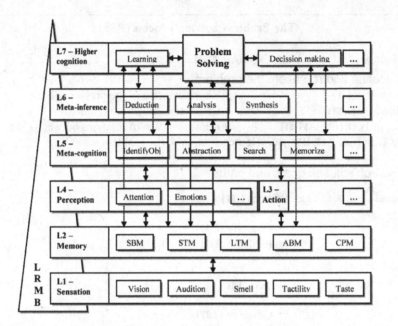

c. **To generate solutions:** This step forms a set of possible solutions by a Cartesian product $S = X \times T \times G$.

d. **To select suitable solutions:** This step evaluates each possible solutions $s \in S = X \times T \times G$ as obtained in Step (c). Recursive searching actions may be executed if the obtained solution(s) could not satisfy the problem solver's expectation.

e. **To represent the problem solving result:** This step incorporates and memorizes the solution(s), $s \in S$, as the result of problem solving into the entire OAR model in the long-term memory of the problem solver. Before memorization, the solution S is represented as a part of the relations, R, in the sub-OAR model.

It is noteworthy in Figure 4 that a number of lower layer cognitive processes, as represented by double-ended boxes, are adopted to carry out the problem solving process. The relationships and interactions between the problem solving process and other cognitive processes can be explained according to the LRMB model (Wang et al., 2006) as illustrated in Figure 5. As a top layer process of the conscious life functions of the brain in LRMB, the problem solving process interacts with other higher cognitive processes at Layer 7, such as the learning and comprehension processes, it also involves lower layer processes such as those of abstraction, search, and memorization

The generic cognitive process of problem solving provides a rigorous metaheuristic computing model for explaining a part of the functions of the natural intelligence from a social psychological point of view. On the basis of the metaheuristic model of problem solving, the cognitive process can be simulated by computational intelligence toward the mimic of the brain in metaheuristic computing.

CONCLUSION

A social psychological perspective on collected intelligence in metaheuristic computing has been presented toward the studies on the cognitive and social psychological foundations of metaheuristic computing. This paper has presented the properties of collective intelligence of human societies and its applications in metaheuristic computing. The fundamental human traits and collective behaviors have been described that form a foundation for explaining the human factors in collective intelligence. The fundamental problem on how collective intelligence is constrained by social environment and group settings has been explained with the formal motivation/attitude-driven behavioral model. The metaheuristic computational model of a generic cognitive process of problem solving has been developed. As a result, a coherent framework of sociological perspectives on collective intelligence has been established. A synergy between studies of genetic algorithms, evolutionary computing, and ant colony mechanisms in metaheuristic computing and the sociopsychological properties of collective intelligence has been created. Applications of collective intelligence in metaheuristic computing have identified in the studies of abstract intelligence, the denotational mathematical model of genetic algorithms, and the formal description of generic problem solving in natural and computational intelligence.

ACKNOWLEDGMENT

The author would like to acknowledge the Natural Science and Engineering Council of Canada (NSERC) for its partial support to this work. The author would like to thank Prof. Peng-Yeng Yin's support and the anonymous reviewers' comments and suggestions on this invited paper.

REFERENCES

Blum, C., & Roli, A. (2003). Metaheuristics in combinatorial optimization: Overview and conceptual comparison. *ACM Computing Surveys*, *35*(3), 268–308. doi:10.1145/937503.937505

Buckles, B. P., & Petry, F. E. (1992). *Genetic algorithms*. Los Alamitos, CA: IEEE CS Press.

Coleman, J. S. (1990). *Fundamentals of social theory*. Cambridge, MA: Belknap Press of Harvard Univ Press.

Davis, L. (Ed.). (1991). *Handbook of genetic algorithms*. Reinhold, NY: Van Nostrand.

Eagly, A. H., & Chaiken, S. (1992). *The psychology of attitudes*. San Diego, CA: Harcourt Brace.

Fazio, R. H. (1986). How do attitudes guide behavior? In R. M. Sorrentino & E. T. Higgins (Eds.), *The handbook of motivation and cognition: Foundations of social behavior*. New York: Guilford Press.

Fishbein, M., & Ajzen, I. (1975). *Belief, attitude, intention, and behavior: An introduction to theory and research*. Reading, MA: Addison-Wesley.

Freud, S. (1895). Project for a scientific psychology. In J. Strachey (Ed.), *The standard edition the complete psychological works of Sigmund Freud* (Vol. 1). London: Hogarth Press.

Geem, Z. W., Kim, J. H., & Loganathan, G. V. (2001). A new heuristic optimization algorithm: Harmony search. *Simulation*, *76*(2), 60–68. doi:10.1177/003754970107600201

Glover, F., & Gary, A. (Eds.). (2003). *Handbook of metaheuristics: International series in operations research & management science* (Vol. 57). New York: Springer.

Goldberg, D. E. (1989). *Genetic algorithms in search, optimization, and machine learning*. Reading, MA: Addison-Wesley.

Goldstein, I. (1978). *Developing a computational representation for problem solving skills* (AI Memo 495). Cambridge, MA: MIT.

Hardy, C., & Latane, B. (1986). Social loafing on a cheering task. *Social Science*, *71*, 165–172.

Holland, J. H. (1975). *Adaptation in natural and artificial systems*. Ann Arbor, MI: University of Michigan Press.

Hull, C. L. (1943). *Principles of behavior: An introduction to behavior theory*. New York: Oxford University Press.

Jackson, J. M., & Harkins, S. G. (1985). Equity in effort: An explanation of the social loafing effect. *Journal of Personality and Social Psychology, 49*, 1199–1206. doi:10.1037/0022-3514.49.5.1199

Janis, I. (1971). Groupthink. *Psychology Today,* 43-46.

Kerr, N. L. (1983). Motivation losses in small groups: A social dilemma analysis. *Journal of Personality and Social Psychology, 45*, 819–828. doi:10.1037/0022-3514.45.4.819

Komorita, S. S., & Barth, J. M. (1985). Components of reward in social bargaining. *Journal of Personality and Social Psychology, 48*, 364–373. doi:10.1037/0022-3514.48.2.364

Kravits, D. A., & Martin, B. (1986). Ringelmann Rediscovered: The Original Article. *Journal of Personality and Social Psychology, 50*, 936–941. doi:10.1037/0022-3514.50.5.936

Latane, B., Williams, K. D., & Harkins, S. G. (1979). Many hands make light the work: The cause and consequences of social loafing. *Journal of Personality and Social Psychology, 37*, 822–832. doi:10.1037/0022-3514.37.6.822

Leahey, T. H. (1997). *A history of psychology: Main currents in psychological thought* (4th ed.). Upper Saddle River, NJ: Prentice- Hall.

Macionis, J. J., Clarke, J. N., & Gerber, L. M. (1997). *Sociology* (2nd ed.). Scarborough, Ontario, Canada: Prentice Hall Allyn and Bacon.

Maslow, A. H. (1962). *Towards a psychology of being*. Princeton, NJ: Van Nostrand.

Maslow, A. H. (1970). *Motivation and personality* (2nd ed.). New York: Harper & Row.

Newell, A., & Simon, H. A. (1972). *Human problem solving*. Upper Saddle River, NJ: Prentice-Hall.

Robertson, I. (2001). *Problem solving*. Philadelphia: Psychology Press.

Smith, R. E. (1993). *Psychology*. St. Paul, MN: West Publishing Co.

Sternberg, R. J. (1998). *In search of the human mind* (2nd ed.). New York: Harcourt Brace.

Talbi, E.-G. (2009). *Metaheuristics: From design to implementation*. New York: Wiley & Sons.

Wang, Y. (2002a). Keynote: On cognitive informatics. In *Proceedings of the 1st IEEE International Conference on Cognitive Informatics (ICCI'02),* Calgary, Canada (pp. 34-42). Los Alamitos, CA: IEEE CS Press.

Wang, Y. (2002b). The real-time process algebra (RTPA). *Annals of Software Engineering, 14*, 235–274. doi:10.1023/A:1020561826073

Wang, Y. (2003). On cognitive informatics. *Brain and Mind: A Transdisciplinary Journal of Neuroscience and Neurophilosophy, 4*(3), 151-167.

Wang, Y. (2007a). *Software engineering foundations: A software science perspective*: CRC series in software engineering II. Boca Raton, FL: Auerbach Publications.

Wang, Y. (2007b). The theoretical framework of cognitive informatics. *International Journal of Cognitive Informatics and Natural Intelligence, 1*(1), 1–27.

Wang, Y. (2007c). On laws of work organization in human cooperation. *International Journal of Cognitive Informatics and Natural Intelligence, 1*(2), 1–15.

Wang, Y. (2007d). On the cognitive processes of perception with emotions, motivations, and attitudes. *International Journal of Cognitive Informatics and Natural Intelligence, 1*(4), 1–13.

Wang, Y. (2007e). The OAR model of neural informatics for internal knowledge representation in the brain. *International Journal of Cognitive Informatics and Natural Intelligence, 1*(3), 68–82.

Wang, Y. (2008a). On contemporary denotational mathematics for computational intelligence. *Transactions of Computational Science, 2,* 6–29. doi:10.1007/978-3-540-87563-5_2

Wang, Y. (2008b). On concept algebra: A denotational mathematical structure for knowledge and software modeling. *International Journal of Cognitive Informatics and Natural Intelligence, 2*(2), 1–19.

Wang, Y. (2008c). RTPA: A denotational mathematics for manipulating intelligent and computational behaviors. *International Journal of Cognitive Informatics and Natural Intelligence, 2*(2), 44–62.

Wang, Y. (2009a). On abstract intelligence: Toward a unified theory of natural, artificial, machinable, and computational intelligence. *International Journal of Software Science and Computational Intelligence, 1*(1), 1–17.

Wang, Y. (2009b). On cognitive computing. *International Journal of Software Science and Computational Intelligence, 1*(3), 1–15.

Wang, Y. (2009c). A cognitive informatics reference model of autonomous agent systems (AAS). *International Journal of Cognitive Informatics and Natural Intelligence, 3*(1), 1–16.

Wang, Y., & Chiew, V. (2009). On the cognitive process of human problem solving. *Cognitive Systems Research: An International Journal, 10*(4).

Wang, Y., Kinsner, W., Anderson, J. A., Zhang, D., Yao, Y., & Sheu, P. (2009). A doctrine of cognitive informatics. *Fundamenta Informaticae, 90*(3), 203–228.

Wang, Y., Kinsner, W., & Zhang, D. (2009). Contemporary cybernetics and its faces of cognitive informatics and computational intelligence. *IEEE Transactions on System, Man, and Cybernetics (B), 39*(4), 823–833. doi:10.1109/TSMCB.2009.2013721

Wang, Y., Wang, Y., Patel, S., & Patel, D. (2006). A layered reference model of the brain (LRMB). *IEEE Transactions on Systems, Man and Cybernetics. Part C, Applications and Reviews, 36*(2), 124–133. doi:10.1109/TSMCC.2006.871126

Wang, Y., Zadeh, L. A., & Yao, Y. (2009). On the system algebra foundations for granular computing. *International Journal of Software Science and Computational Intelligence, 1*(1), 64–86.

Westen, D. (1999). *Psychology: Mind, brain, and culture* (2nd ed.). New York: John Wiley & Sons.

Wiggins, J. A., Eiggins, B. B., & Zanden, J. V. (1994). *Social psychology* (5th ed.). New York: McGraw-Hill.

Wikipedia. (2009). *Metaheuristic.* Retrieved from http://en.wikipedia.org/wiki/Metaheuristic.

Wittig, A. F. (2001). *Schaum's outlines of theory and problems of introduction to psychology* (2nd ed.). New York: McGraw-Hill.

Yin, P.-Y. (2010). Editorial. *International Journal of Applied Metaheuristic Computing, 1*(1), 1.

Zander, A. (1979). The psychology of the group process. *Annual Review of Psychology,* 418.

This work was previously published in International Journal of Applied Metaheuristic Computing, Volume 1, Issue 1, edited by Peng-Yeng Yin, pp. 110-128, copyright 2010 by IGI Publishing (an imprint of IGI Global).

Chapter 16
Theorems Supporting r–flip Search for Pseudo–Boolean Optimization

Bahram Alidaee
University of Mississippi, USA

Gary Kochenberger
University of Colorado Denver, USA

Haibo Wang
Texas A&M International University, USA

ABSTRACT

Modern metaheuristic methodologies rely on well defined neighborhood structures and efficient means for evaluating potential moves within these structures. Move mechanisms range in complexity from simple 1-flip procedures where binary variables are "flipped" one at a time, to more expensive, but more powerful, r-flip approaches where "r" variables are simultaneously flipped. These multi-exchange neighborhood search strategies have proven to be effective approaches for solving a variety of combinatorial optimization problems. In this paper, we present a series of theorems based on partial derivatives that can be readily adopted to form the essential part of r-flip heuristic search methods for Pseudo-Boolean optimization. To illustrate the use of these results, we present preliminary results obtained from four simple heuristics designed to solve a set of Max 3-SAT problems.

INTRODUCTION

Pseudo Boolean formulations are widely known for their ability to represent a rich variety of important discrete problems. While special cases exist for which provably optimal solutions can be found in reasonable time, often the problems are NP-hard and heuristic methods must be employed to produce solutions in a reasonable amount of computer time. In their important early work (Hammer & Rudeanu, 1968), Hammer and Rudeanu discussed Pseudo-Boolean optimization and gave a dynamic programming procedure for solving certain problems. Furthermore, they gave

DOI: 10.4018/978-1-4666-0270-0.ch016

a definition of a *first-order derivative* and indicated its use in solving discrete Pseudo-Boolean optimization problems. Specifically they gave the necessary and sufficient results for any local optimal solution of the problem when one element of x is changed at a time (*1-flip* move, or *1-move*, defined later in the paper). More recently, excellent surveys of Pseudo-Boolean optimization are given by Boros and Hammer (2002) and Crama and Hammer (2007). These sources provide extensive discussions of key topics as well as comprehensive bibliographies.

In this paper we extend this notion of first order derivatives by defining *higher-order derivatives* for discrete Pseudo-Boolean optimization. Moreover, in the context of changing r elements of x at a time (the so-called *r-flip* moves for *r=2,3*), we present closed-form formulas that allow '*efficient*' implementation of such compound moves. Then, for the important special cases of quadratic and cubic optimization, we define a general *r-flip* move that allows efficient implementation of multi-exchange neighborhood search process for solving such problems. Finally, we illustrate the use of such moves by applying variants of simple search processes based on *r-flip* moves (with r = 1 and 2) to a test bed of max 3-sat problems. The paper then concludes with summary and a look ahead to future research.

We note that the use of simple exchange procedures such as *r-opt* for binary optimization have been reported by several authors (Ahuja, Ergun, Orlin, & Punnen, 2002; Ahuja, Orlin, Pallottino, Scaparra, & Scutellà, 2004; Deineko & Woeginger, 2000; Frangioni, Necciari, & Scutellà, 2004; Glover, 1996; Li & Alidaee, 2002; Magazine, Polak, & Sharma, 2002; Vredeveld & Lenstra, 2003; Yaguiura & Ibaraki, 1999; Yaguiura & Ibaraki, 2001). However, in all such applications the method presented are highly problem specific. The *r-flip* rules we present in this paper are quite general and can be applied to a variety of problem classes.

PSEUDO-BOOLEAN OPTIMIZATION

Let R be the set of reals, Z the set of integers, and $B = \{0,1\}$. For a positive integer n let $V = \{1, 2, \dots, n\}$. Let $x = (x_1, \dots, x_n) \in B^n$ be a binary vector and $\overline{x}_i = 1 - x_i$ complement of x_i for $i \in V$. Define the set of literals to be $L = \{x_1, \overline{x}_1, \dots, x_n, \overline{x}_n\}$. Mappings $f : B^n \to R$ are called *Pseudo-Boolean functions*. Since there is a one-to-one correspondence between subsets of V and the set of binary vectors B^n, these functions are *set functions*. All Pseudo-Boolean functions can be uniquely represented as multi-linear polynomials of the form given below (see (Boros & Hammer, 2002), for a comprehensive discussion) where q_s is a weight associated with the set $S \subseteq V$:

$$f(x_1, \dots, x_n) = \sum_{S \subseteq V} q_S \prod_{j \in S} x_j$$

The Pseudo-Boolean optimization problem can be stated as $\underset{x}{Max} \, f(x)$.

Definition 1: Hammer and Rudeanu (1968) defined the *first derivative* of f with respect to x_i as,

$$\Delta_i(x) = \frac{\partial f(x)}{\partial x_i} =$$
$$f(x_1, \dots, x_{i-1}, 1, x_{i+1}, \dots, x_n) -$$
$$f(x_1, \dots, x_{i-1}, 0, x_{i+1}, \dots, x_n), \quad \forall i \in V$$

Definition 2: For a given $x = (x_1, \dots, x_{i-1}, x_i, x_{i+1}, \dots, x_n)$, define $x' = (x_1, \dots, x_{i-1}, \overline{x}_i, x_{i+1}, \dots, x_n)$ to be 1-flip move with respect to the *ith* position of x.

Based on Definition 2 an *1-flip* local search process can be defined as follows:

Algorithm (1-flip Local Search):

Start with a solution x

Do

With some pre-specified order choose each
$i \in V$,

change x_i to $\bar{x}_i$ if it improves $f(x)$

UnDo

Stop if no *1-flip* move is possible.

Theorem 1. (Boros & Hammer, 2002): Given a Pseudo-Boolean function the first derivative is given by

$$\Delta_i(x) = \sum_{S \subseteq V \setminus \{i\}} q_{S \cup \{i\}} \prod_{j \in S} x_j$$

Furthermore, in any local optimal solution with respect to *1-flip* search we have

either $\quad (x_j = 0 \quad iff \quad \Delta_j(x) \geq 0)$

or $\quad (x_j = 1 \quad iff \quad \Delta_j(x) \leq 0), \quad$ for $j \in V$.

Since values for each variable is 0 or 1 we have $(x_i)^2 = x_i$ for $i \in V$. Thus, we assume in f all $(x_i)^2$ are presented as x_i. In the following we give a definition that applies to both first as well as higher order *derivatives*. The definitions and the results associated with them permit an efficient implementation of *r-flip* search strategies.

Definition 3: For a given solution x and given $S \subseteq V$ where $|S| = r$, let x' be a solution obtained from x by complementing all elements in S, i.e., x' is the same as x except that for all $i \in S$ where x_i is changed to $\bar{x}_i$. Such a move is called an *r-flip* move with respect to elements of S. Now, consider f in continuous form and let
$$f^{|T|}(x) = \Delta_T(x) = \frac{\partial^{|T|} f(x)}{\partial x_1 \partial x_2 \dots, \partial x_{|T|}}$$ be the

$|T|^{th}$ *partial derivative* of f with respect to x_i and $i \in T$, $T \subseteq S$. Thus, if $T = \{i_1, \dots, i_k\}$ and $|T| = k$, then we have

$$f^k(x) = \Delta_{i_1 i_2 i_3 \dots i_k}(x) = \frac{\partial^k f(x)}{\partial x_1 \partial x_2 \dots \partial x_k}$$

Now, restrict domain of function $\Delta_T(x)$ to binary vectors. We call this the *k^{th} partial derivative* of the Pseudo-Boolean function f with respect to elements of T. Note that the value of $\Delta_T(x)$ is independent of the order of partial derivative of elements in T. Also, note that the first derivative in this case is equal to the first derivative as shown in Theorem 1.

With respect to *1-flip local search*, Hammer and Rudeanu (1968) prove the following:

Theorem 2. For a Pseudo-Boolean optimization problem, given $x = (x_1, \dots, x_{i-1}, x_i, x_{i+1}, \dots, x_n)$ and $x' = (x_1, \dots, x_{i-1}, \bar{x}_i, x_{i+1}, \dots, x_n)$ we have

$$f(x') - f(\bar{x}) = (\bar{x}_i - x_i)\Delta_i(x),$$

Furthermore, in any local optimal solution with respect to *1-flip* search we have

either $\quad (x_j = 0 \quad iff \quad \Delta_j(x) \geq 0)$

or $\quad (x_j = 1 \quad iff \quad \Delta_j(x) \leq 0), \quad$ for $j \in V$.

Proof: Given $x = (x_1, \dots, x_{i-1}, x_i, x_{i+1}, \dots, x_n)$. By definition 3 we have

$$\Delta_i(x) = \sum_{S \subseteq V \setminus \{i\}} q_{S \cup \{i\}} \prod_{j \in S} x_j = q_{\{i\}} + \sum_{\substack{S \subseteq V \setminus \{i\} \\ S \neq \varnothing}} q_{S \cup \{i\}} \prod_{j \in S} x_j$$

Let $x^{'} = (x_1, \ldots, x_{i-1}, \overline{x}_i, x_{i+1}, \ldots, x_n)$.

We then have

$$f(x) = x_i \left[q_{\{i\}} + \sum_{\substack{S \subseteq V \setminus \{i\} \\ S \neq \varnothing}} q_{s \cup \{i\}} \prod_{j \in S} x_j \right] + \cdots$$

$$f(x) = x_i \left[\Delta_i(x) \right] + \cdots$$

$$f(x^{'}) = \overline{x}_i \left[\Delta_i(x) \right] + \cdots$$

$$f(x^{'}) - f(x) = (\overline{x}_i - x_i) \Delta_i(x)$$

From this, the necessary and sufficient condition of local optimality follows immediately.

Similar to the definition of an *1-flip* local search, using Definition 3 we define an *r-flip* local search process by:

Algorithm (r-flip Local Search):
Start with a solution x
Do
 With some pre-specified mechanism choose an
  $S \subseteq V$ and $|S| = r$,
 For all $i \in S$ change x_i to $\overline{x}_i$ if it improves $f(x)$
unDo
Stop if no *r-flip* move is possible.

With respect to *r-flip* search, Theorem 2 can easily be extended to address the cases when $r = 2$ and $r = 3$ as shown below in Theorem 3 (involving second derivatives) and Theorem 4 (involving third derivatives), respectively.

Theorem 3: (2-flip local search, 2nd derivatives).
For a Pseudo-Boolean optimization problem, given $x = (x_1, \ldots, x_i, \ldots, x_j, \ldots, x_n)$ and $x^{'} = (x_1, \ldots, \overline{x}_i, \ldots, \overline{x}_j, \ldots, x_n)$ we have

$$f(x^{'}) - f(x) = (\overline{x}_i - x_i) \Delta_i(x) + (\overline{x}_j - x_j) \Delta_j(x)$$
$$+ (\overline{x}_i - x_i)(\overline{x}_j - x_j) \Delta_{ij}(x)$$

Proof: (see appendix A)

Extending to 3-flip local search and third derivatives we have:

Theorem 4. (3-flip local search, 3rd derivatives):
For a Pseudo-Boolean optimization problem, given $x = (x_1, \ldots, x_i, \ldots, x_j, \ldots, x_k, \ldots, x_n)$ and $x^{'} = (x_1, \ldots, \overline{x}_i, \ldots, \overline{x}_j, \ldots, \overline{x}_k, \ldots, x_n)$ we have

$$f(x^{'}) - f(x) = (\overline{x}_i - x_i) \Delta_i(x) + (\overline{x}_j - x_j) \Delta_j(x)$$
$$+ (\overline{x}_k - x_k) \Delta_k(x) + (\overline{x}_i - x_i)(\overline{x}_j - x_j) \Delta_{ij}(x)$$
$$+ (\overline{x}_i - x_i)(\overline{x}_k - x_k) \Delta_{ik}(x)$$
$$+ (\overline{x}_j - x_j)(\overline{x}_k - x_k) \Delta_{jk}(x)$$
$$+ (\overline{x}_i - x_i)(\overline{x}_j - x_j)(\overline{x}_k - x_k) \Delta_{ijk}(x)$$

Proof: (*see appendix A*)

In the next section we will give a general *r-flip* search strategy for two special classes of Pseudo Boolean optimization models that have many important applications.

SPECIAL CASES

The application potential of quadratic and cubic Pseudo Boolean optimization is well known. This prominence leads us to single them out for special attention in light of theorems 3 and 4. These special cases are considered below:

Case 1: *Quadratic pseudo boolean optimization:*

Quadratic Unconstrained Binary Optimization (QUBO) can be stated as $\max_x f(x) = xQx$ where Q is a symmetric matrix. QUBO has numerous applications in optimization including binary linear program and maximum weighted 2-SAT. In fact any Pseudo-Boolean optimization can be transferred to QUBO (refer to (Kochenberger, Glover, Alidaee, & Rego, 2004), for a recent survey of applications of QUBO).

Glover, Kochenberger, Alidaee, and Amini (1999) used an efficient *1-flip* search implementation of QUBO and tested it in the context of Tabu Search and Scatter Search. We first give Glover's result and then extend it to the more general *r-flip* case for QUBO.

Definition 4: Let $x = (x_1,\ldots,x_i,\ldots,x_n)$ be a solution to QUBO and let $x' = (x_1,\ldots,\overline{x}_i,\ldots,x_n)$ be a solution obtained from x by complementing x_i. Since Q is upper triangular matrix then $(ij)th$ element, q_{ij}, is equal to the second de*rivative* of $f(x)$, i.e., $\Delta_{ij}(x) = q_{ij}$, with respect to x_i and x_j.

Theorem 5. (Glover, et al., 1999): For x and x' as given in Definition 4, the change in the value of the objective function is

$$f(x') - f(x) = (x_i' - x_i)\Delta_i(x).$$

Moreover, in any local optimal solution of the QUBO with respect to *1-flip* search we have

$$either \quad (x_i = 0 \;\; iff \;\; \Delta_i(x) \geq 0)$$
$$or \quad (x_i = 1 \;\; iff \;\; \Delta_i(x) \leq 0), \quad \forall\; i = 1,\ldots,n.$$

Furthermore, after changing x_i to $\overline{x}_i$ the update for all $\Delta_i(x)$ can be calculated as follows

$$\forall\; j < i,\; \Delta_j(x) = \Delta_j(x) + q_{ji}(x_i' - x_i),$$
$$\forall\; j > i,\; \Delta_j(x) = \Delta_j(x) + q_{ij}(x_i' - x_i),$$
$$j = i, \quad \Delta_j(x) = \Delta_i(x).$$

In Theorem 6, we extend the above result to general case for *r-flip* search for QUBO.

Theorem 6. Let x be a given solution of QUBO and x' obtained from x by an r-flip move where $S \subseteq V$, and $|S| = r$. Now, the change in the value of the objective function is

$$f(x') - f(x) = \sum_{i \in S}(\overline{x}_i - x_i)\Delta_i(x)$$
$$+ \sum_{\forall\; i,j \in S}(\overline{x}_i - x_i)(\overline{x}_j - x_j)\Delta_{ij}(x).$$

Furthermore, after changing x to x' the update for all $\Delta_i(x)$ can be calculated as follows,

$$\forall\; j \in V \setminus S \quad \Delta_j(x) = \Delta_j(x) +$$
$$\sum_{i \in S}(\overline{x}_i - x_i)\Delta_{ij}(x), \;\; and$$
$$\forall\; j \in S \quad \Delta_j(x) = \Delta_j(x) +$$
$$\sum_{i \in S \setminus \{j\}}(\overline{x}_i - x_i)\Delta_{ij}(x).$$

Proof: (see Appendix A)

Remarks: Theorem 6 extends theorem 3 to the case of r-flip search specialized for QUBO. As such, the theorem facilitates extensive neighborhood searches to be carried out when solving QUBO. Given a solution x, r-flip moves are made until no such move results to a better solution, yielding a local optimal solution with respect to the r-flip neighborhood. Such local search mechanisms can be embedded in a metaheuristic framework designed to escape the trap of local optimality and effectively search challenging solution spaces. From computational point of view the calculation of the impact of such an r-flip moves depends only on calculating first derivatives, $\Delta_i(x)$, for all $i \in V$ since $\Delta_{ij}(x) = q_{ij}$ is a constant. Thus, evaluation of change in the objective function can be done in $O(r^2)$ while the updating of $\Delta_i(x)$ can be done in O(r) for $i = 1,...,n$. Note also that depending on how $S \subseteq V$ is chosen, the operations indicated can be carried out in a parallel environment. Thus, appropriate implementation of theorem 6 can also result in a very strong parallel implementation.

Case 2: *Cubic pseudo boolean optimization:*

The Max 3-SAT problem, as well as other important problems, can be formulated as a cubic Pseudo-Boolean optimization problem. This case is taken up here where in Theorem 7 (below) we extend the previous result to the case when f(x) has up to cubic terms. Note that in this case for every two elements $\{i,j\} \subseteq V$ we have $\Delta_{ij}(x) = q_{ij} + \sum_{l \in V \setminus \{i,j\}} q_{ijl} x_l$ and for every three elements $\{i,j,k\} \subset V$ we have $\Delta_{ijk}(x) = q_{ijk}$ which is a constant. We use the following equations in our proof.

$$For\ i \in S, \quad \Delta_i(x) = q_i + \sum_{j \in S \setminus \{i\}} q_{ij} x_j + \sum_{j \notin S} q_{ij} x_j +$$
$$\sum_{\substack{j \in S \setminus \{i\} \\ k \notin S}} q_{ijk} x_j x_k + \sum_{j,k \in S \setminus \{i\}} q_{ijk} x_j x_k + \sum_{j,k \notin S} q_{ijk} x_j x_k$$

$$For\ i,j \in S, \quad \Delta_{ij}(x) = q_{ij} + \sum_{k \in S \setminus \{i,j\}} q_{ijk} x_k + \sum_{k \notin S} q_{ijk} x_k$$

Theorem 7. Let x be a given solution to a cubic Pseudo-Boolean function f(x) and x' obtained from x by an r-flip move where $S \subseteq V$ and $|S| = r$. The change to the value of the objective function is

$$f(x') - f(x) = \sum_{i \in S} (\overline{x}_i - x_i) \Delta_i(x)$$
$$+ \sum_{i,j \in S} (\overline{x}_i - x_i)(\overline{x}_j - x_j) \Delta_{ij}(x)$$
$$+ \sum_{i,j,k \in S} (\overline{x}_i - x_i)(\overline{x}_j - x_j)(\overline{x}_k - x_k) \Delta_{ijk}(x)$$

Furthermore, after changing x to x' the update for all $\Delta_i(x)$ can be calculated as follows,

$$\forall j \in V \setminus S \quad \Delta_j(x) = \Delta_j(x) +$$
$$\sum_{i \in S} (\overline{x}_i - x_i) q_{ij} + \sum_{i,k \in S} (\overline{x}_i \overline{x}_k - x_i x_k) q_{ijk}$$
$$\forall j \in S \quad \Delta_j(x) = \Delta_j(x) +$$
$$\sum_{i \in S \setminus \{j\}} (\overline{x}_i - x_i) q_{ij} + \sum_{i,k \in S \setminus \{j\}} (\overline{x}_i \overline{x}_k - x_i x_k) q_{ijk},$$

and the update for $\Delta_{ij}(x)$ for all i and j can be calculated as follows,

$$\forall i \notin S, j \notin S \quad \Delta_{ij}(x) = \Delta_{ij}(x) + \sum_{l \in S} (\overline{x}_l - x_l) q_{ijl},$$
$$\forall i \in S, j \in S \quad \Delta_{ij}(x) = \Delta_{ij}(x) + \sum_{l \in S \setminus \{i,j\}} (\overline{x}_l - x_l) q_{ijl},$$
$$\forall i \in S, j \notin S \quad \Delta_{ij}(x) = \Delta_{ij}(x) + \sum_{l \in S \setminus \{j\}} (\overline{x}_l - x_l) q_{ijl},$$

Proof: (see Appendix A)

Remarks: Theorem 7 extends theorem 4 to the case of r-flip search specialized for Cubic Pseudo Boolean optimization. As such it has significant implications for implementations aimed at solving cubic problems. Note that evaluating the r-flip change in the objective function can be done in $O(r^3)$ time. The calculation of each $\Delta_i(x)$ can be done in $O(r^2)$ while the update for all $\Delta_{ij}(x)$ and $i, j \in V$ can be done in $O(r)$.

The results of theorems 1-7 can be used to construct effective heuristic search processes for a variety of Pseudo Boolean optimization problems. In the computational section below we illustrate such use by solving some fairly large max 3-sat problems.

COMPUTATIONAL EXPERIENCE

It is well known (see, for instance, (Boros & Hammer, 2002; Hammer & Rudeanu, 1968; Hansen, Brunswick, & Jaumard, 1990)) that max 3-sat problems can be formulated as Pseudo Boolean optimization problems taking the form of minimizing a cubic pseudo Boolean function. The formulation procedure is as follows:

Denote the literals in a given clause by $u^\alpha = u$ if $\alpha = 1$ and $\bar{u}$ if $\alpha = 0$. Letting $\bar{\alpha} = 1 - \alpha$ and representing literals by binary variables, x_i, the max 3-Sat problem is equivalent to the unconstrained Pseudo Boolean optimization problem

$$Min \; f(x) = \sum_{j=1}^{m} \prod_{i \in I_j} x_i^{\bar{\alpha}_{ij}} \tag{1}$$

where m = the number of clauses in the problem and I_j is the index set denoting the variables in clause j. Denote by x* a solution to the above problem. If f(x*) = 0, x* satisfies all m clauses. Otherwise, x* is a solution to the max 3-sat problem and f(x*) is the number of clauses not satisfied by x*.

As an illustration, consider the 3-sat example with 12 clauses and 5 variables shown below:

1	$x_1 \vee x_2 \vee x_3$		7	$x_2 \vee x_4 \vee x_5$
2	$x_1 \vee \bar{x}_2 \vee x_3$		8	$\bar{x}_2 \vee x_3 \vee x_5$
3	$\bar{x}_1 \vee x_2 \vee \bar{x}_3$		9	$x_2 \vee \bar{x}_3 \vee x_5$
4	$x_2 \vee \bar{x}_3 \vee x_4$		10	$x_3 \vee x_4 \vee x_5$
5	$\bar{x}_2 \vee x_3 \vee x_4$		11	$x_3 \vee \bar{x}_4 \vee \bar{x}_5$
6	$\bar{x}_2 \vee \bar{x}_3 \vee \bar{x}_4$		12	$\bar{x}_3 \vee \bar{x}_4 \vee \bar{x}_5$

By the procedure given above, the corresponding optimization problem is:

$$\begin{aligned} Min \quad f(x) = \; & 3 - x_1 + x_2 - 2x_4 - 2x_5 + 2x_1x_3 - \\ & 4x_2x_3 + 3x_4x_5 - x_1x_2x_3 + 3x_2x_3x_4 - \\ & x_2x_4x_5 - x_3x_4x_5 + 2x_2x_3x_5 \end{aligned}$$

It is easy to see that $f(x^*) = 0$ for $x^* = (1,1,1,0,0)$ for this example implying that all 12 clauses are satisfied. More generally, any

max 3-sat problem can be solved by minimizing $f(x)$ defined by (1).

The results given in sections 2 and 3 of this paper were embedded in simple search strategies used to solve some fairly large instances of max 3-sat problems taken from the literature. In our computational experiments, we considered four simple variations of r-flip search applied to the test problems. To provide a benchmark for comparison, we also include in the results reported the performance of a standard metaheuristic method (GRASP) on these same problems. Below we give a brief overview of the methods tested followed by a table of results:

Method 1: (*1-flip*) A simple search process as described in Section 2.

In this method we start with all variables equal to zero and make simple *1-flip* moves. Several passes through the variables (taken in the order 1 through n) are made until additional moves fail to yield improvement.

Method 2: (*2-flip*) Here we used a simple implementation of *r-flip* local search, as described in section 2, for r = 2. In our implementation we used a double loop where one variable is flipped and temporarily fixed while a search over all other variables is made to identify the first improving flip to complete the *2-flip* move. The process continues until no improving *2-flip* move can be found.

Method 3: (*2-1-flip)* Here we implemented a slight extension of method 2 where the search process augments an initial *2-flip* search with an additional *1-flip* improvement procedure.

Our *2-flip* procedure of Method 2 was run until no further improvement was realized. Then, starting with the best solution at hand we applied the *1-flip* rule of Method 1.

Method 4: (F&F) Filtration and Sequential Fan (Glover, 1998) is a search process utilizing compound move strategies that have proven to be effective for a variety of combinatorial problems. Here we employ a simple version of F&F utilizing a combination of *r-flip* moves. In the paragraph below we give a brief overview of our implementation. Additional details are given in the appendix B of this paper.

F&F organizes an aggressive search process utilizing a variety of different *r-flip* moves. The version we tested here starts with a set of locally optimal solutions found using *1-flip* search. Then, for each solution in this set a second round of *1-flip* moves is executed. If an improving move is found we accept that move and initiate a complete new round of *1-flip* moves. If an improving second flip move can not be found, we initiate a series of *3-flip* moves starting with the best local optimal solutions found so far. This continues until a pre-set stopping criterion is satisfied or until no further improvement is realized.

Note that all four of the methods tested here are straightforward search procedures that make use of the theorems presented earlier in the paper.

Method 5: (GRASP) As a benchmark for comparison we used the well known GRASP implementation for solving max 3-sat problems as described in the papers (Resende, 1998; Resende & Feo, 1996). The code is available via http://www.research.att.com/~mgcr/.

All methods were coded in FORTRAN and all runs were made on a Cray Super Computer J916 at the University of Mississippi. The test problems considered here were taken from the DIMACS test bed of 3-sat problems. To illustrate performance across a range of problem sizes, we randomly chose instances ranging in size from 100 variables and 403 clauses up to 2000 variables and 8500 clauses. We note that the problems chosen are known to be satisfiable and thus optimal solutions are known to exist that satisfy all the clauses in each instance. The GRASP code was run utilizing all default parameters and our methods 1-4 were run until no further improvement was realized or a limit of 3600 seconds was reached. The results of our runs are shown in Table 1.

In Table 1, n denotes the number of variables and m denotes the number of clauses in a given problem. #Unsat gives the number of clauses not satisfied by the best solution found during the search process and "time in seconds" gives the total solution time. Note that for the F&F method and for GRASP, we list the "time to best" solution as well as the total time.

An examination of Table 1 clearly indicates that Method 4 (F&F) gives the best performance in terms of solution quality for these problems. F&F quickly found optimal solutions for all but the two largest problems and for these two it out performed GRASP, the second best performer, by a wide margin. The time performance of F&F is also greatly preferred to that of GRASP. While GRASP is competitive in terms of run time on the 100 variable problems, it degrades substantially in terms of run times on the larger problems. For all of the problems instances with 250 variables or more, GRASP produced inferior solutions in greatly inflated run times compared to F&F. The most extreme example of this is given by the last problem where GRASP took more than 40 hours to produce a solution with twice as many unsatisfied clauses as F&F found in 1 hour of search time.

As expected, our simple search methods improve in solution quality as we go from method 1 to method 4 (F&F). While methods 1-3 are very fast, the extra time spent in method 4 (F&F) pays considerable dividends in terms of solution quality. The problems considered here are known to be computationally challenging and thus it is not surprising that these simpler forms of search fall short of the more aggressive searches in term of solution quality.

Table 1. Max 3-Sat results from five different methods

n, m	Method 1: 1-flip		Method 2: 2-flip		Method 3: 2-1-flip		Method 4: F&F			GRASP		
	#Unsat	Time seconds	#Unsat	Time seconds	#Unsat	Time seconds	#Unsat	Time to Best seconds	Total Time Seconds	#Unsat	Time to Best seconds	Total Time seconds
100, 403	13	.01	7	.02	5	0.02	0	3.10	3.10	0	36.48	36.48
100, 403	12	.01	6	.02	4	0.02	0	195.10	195.10	0	641.89	641.89
100, 403	9	.02	9	.03	6	0.03	0	4.22	4.22	0	30.44	30.44
100, 403	7	.01	4	.02	5	0.02	0	11.01	11.01	0	10.75	10.75
250,1065	27	.60	14	1.74	14	1.74	0	161.25	161.25	4	2234.59	6227.66
250,1065	33	.59	20	1.58	18	1.58	0	189.34	189.34	8	342.32	4212.46
250,1065	28	.34	22	.99	13	0.99	0	119.12	119.12	5	5598.00	65605.40
250,1065	22	.32	16	1.01	15	1.01	0	385.32	385.32	8	1037.07	6483.66
250,1065	31	.31	21	1.04	11	1.04	0	184.82	184.82	5	1698.40	6386.63
600,2550	55	9.25	30	34.64	24	34.85	0	534.39	534.39	23	4467.11	27431.72
1000,4250	109	55.35	60	308.89	49	309.99	7	338.04	3600.00	49	35260.85	45359.88
2000,8500	202	259.02	126	649.38	107	661.44	49	982.21	3600.00	107	129157.39	159670.70

CONCLUSION

Organizing an effective search process requires an efficient assessment of the objective function response to a potential move. In this paper we presented derivative–based results for such assessment, intended to facilitate *r-flip* strategies for Pseudo–Boolean optimization. Closed form expressions for these derivatives were given permitting efficient implementation to a wide variety of combinatorial optimization problems. Four simple variations of *r-flip* search along with the well-known method, GRASP, were applied to a set of DIMACS 3-SAT test problems to illustrate the use of the ideas presented. Our results showed that the search processes organized by these methods could produce high quality solutions very quickly. Our method 4 in particular (F&F) was very successful giving better performance than the other methods, including GRASP, in terms of both solution quality and solution time.

In the testing undertaken here, we did not apply *r-flip* for $r > 3$. We intend to explore this as part of our on-going work. We also note the results of Theorems 6 and 7 are highly parallelizable opening the possibility for efficient implementation aimed at addressing large scale problems with very aggressive neighborhood search. These research avenues, along with more sophisticated versions of F&F, are part of our work in progress that we intend to report on in future papers.

REFERENCES

Ahuja, R., Ergun, O., Orlin, J., & Punnen, A. (2002). A survey of very large-scale neighborhood search techniques. *Discrete Applied Mathematics, 123*, 75–102. doi:10.1016/S0166-218X(01)00338-9

Ahuja, R., Orlin, J., Pallottino, S., Scaparra, M., & Scutellà, M. (2004). A multi-exchange heuristic for the single-source capacitated facility location problem. *Management Science, 50*, 749–760. doi:10.1287/mnsc.1030.0193

Boros, E., & Hammer, P. (2002). Pseudo-Boolean optimization. *Discrete Applied Mathematics, 123*(1-3), 155–225. doi:10.1016/S0166-218X(01)00336-5

Crama, Y., & Hammer, P. (2007). *Boolean functions: Theory, algorithms and applications.* Cambridge, UK: Cambridge University Press.

Deineko, V., & Woeginger, G. (2000). A study of exponential neighborhoods for the travelling salesman problem and for the quadratic assignment problem. *Mathematical Programming. Ser. A, 87*, 519–542.

Frangioni, A., Necciari, E., & Scutellà, M. (2004). A multi-exchange neighborhood for minimum makespan parallel machine scheduling problems. *Journal of Combinatorial Optimization, 8*, 195–220. doi:10.1023/B:JOCO.0000031420.05971.29

Glover, F. (1996). Finding the best traveling salesman 4-opt move in the same time as a best 2-opt move. *Journal of Heuristics, 2*, 169–179. doi:10.1007/BF00247211

Glover, F. (1998). A template for scatter search and path relinking. In J. K. Hao, E. Lutton, E. Ronald, M. Schoenauer, & D. Snyers (Eds.), *Artificial evolution* (Vol. 1363, pp. 13-54).

Glover, F., Kochenberger, G., Alidaee, B., & Amini, M. (1999). Tabu search with critical event memory: An enhanced application for binary quadratic programs. In S. M. S. Voss, I. Osman, & C. Roucairol (Eds.), *Meta-heuristics, Advances and trends in local search paradigms for optimization* (pp. 93-109). Dordrecht, The Netherlands, Kluwer Academic Publishers.

Hammer, P., & Rudeanu, S. (1968). *Boolean methods in operations research and related areas.* New York: Springer.

Hansen, P., Brunswick, N., & Jaumard, B. (1990). Algorithms for the maximum satisfiability problem. *Computing, 44,* 279–303. doi:10.1007/BF02241270

Kochenberger, G., Glover, F., Alidaee, B., & Rego, C. (2004). A unified modeling and solution framework for combinatorial optimization problems. *Operations Research Spectrum, 26*(2), 237–250.

Li, W., & Alidaee, B. (2002). Dynamics of local search heuristics for the traveling salesman problem. *IEEE Transactions on Systems, Man, and Cybernetics - Part A, 32,* 173-184.

Magazine, M., Polak, G., & Sharma, D. (2002). A multi-exchange neighborhood search for integrated clustering and machine setup model for PCB manufacturing. *Journal of Electronics Manufacturing, 11,* 107–119. doi:10.1142/S0960313102000448

Resende, M. G. C. (1998). Computing approximate solutions of the maximum covering problem using GRASP. *Journal of Heuristics, 4,* 161–171. doi:10.1023/A:1009677613792

Resende, M. G. C., & Feo, T. A. (Eds.). (1996). *A GRASP for satisfiability, cliques, coloring, and satisfiability: Second DIMACS implementation challenge* (Vol. 26). Providence, RI: American Mathematical Society.

Vredeveld, T., & Lenstra, J. (2003). On local search for the generalized graph coloring problem. *Operations Research Letters, 31,* 28–34. doi:10.1016/S0167-6377(02)00165-7

Yaguiura, M., & Ibaraki, T. (1999). Analyses on the 2 and 3-flip neighborhoods for the MAX SAT. *Journal of Combinatorial Optimization, 3,* 95–114. doi:10.1023/A:1009873324187

Yaguiura, M., & Ibaraki, T. (2001). Efficient 2 and 3-flip neighborhood search algorithms for the MAX SAT: Experimental evaluation. *Journal of Heuristics, 7,* 423–442. doi:10.1023/A:1011306011437

APPENDIX A: THEOREM PROOFS

Proof of Theorem 3:

For $x = (x_1, \ldots, x_i, \ldots, x_j, \ldots, x_n)$ and $x' = (x_1, \ldots, \overline{x}_i, \ldots, \overline{x}_j, \ldots, x_n)$ we have

$$f(x) = \quad x_i \left[q_{\{i\}} + \sum_{l \neq ij} q_{\{i,l\}} x_l + \sum_{lm \neq ij} q_{\{i,l,m\}} x_l x_m + \sum_{lmh \neq ij} q_{\{i,l,m,h\}} x_l x_m x_h + \ldots \right] +$$

$$x_j \left[q_{\{j\}} + \sum_{l \neq ij} q_{\{j,l\}} x_l + \sum_{lm \neq ij} q_{\{j,l,m\}} x_l x_m + \sum_{lmh \neq ij} q_{\{j,l,m,h\}} x_l x_m x_h + \ldots \right] +$$

$$x_i x_j (q_{\{i,j\}} + \sum_{l \neq ij} q_{\{i,j,l\}} x_l + \sum_{lm \neq ij} q_{\{i,j,l,m\}} x_l x_m + \sum_{lmh \neq ij} q_{\{i,j,l,m,h\}} x_l x_m x_h + \ldots) + \ldots$$

$$f(x') = \quad \overline{x}_i \left[q_{\{i\}} + \sum_{l \neq ij} q_{\{i,l\}} x_l + \sum_{lm \neq ij} q_{\{i,l,m\}} x_l x_m + \sum_{lmh \neq ij} q_{\{i,l,m,h\}} x_l x_m x_h + \ldots \right] +$$

$$\overline{x}_j \left[q_{\{j\}} + \sum_{l \neq ij} q_{\{j,l\}} x_l + \sum_{lm \neq ij} q_{\{j,l,m\}} x_l x_m + \sum_{lmh \neq ij} q_{\{j,l,m,h\}} x_l x_m x_h + \ldots \right] +$$

$$\overline{x}_i \overline{x}_j [q_{\{i,j\}} + \sum_{l \neq ij} q_{\{i,j,l\}} x_l + \sum_{lm \neq ij} q_{\{i,j,l,m\}} x_l x_m + \sum_{lmh \neq ij} q_{\{i,j,l,m,h\}} x_l x_m x_h + \ldots] + \ldots$$

For each bracket in $f(x)$ and $f(x')$ we can add and subtract appropriate terms to get the following:

$$f(x) = \quad x_i \left[\Delta_i(x) - x_j(q_{\{i,j\}} + \sum_{l \neq i,j} q_{\{i,j,l\}} x_l + \sum_{l,m \neq i,j} q_{\{i,j,l,m\}} x_l x_m + \ldots) \right] +$$

$$x_j \left[\Delta_j(x) - x_i(q_{\{i,j\}} + \sum_{l \neq i,j} q_{\{i,j,l\}} x_l + \sum_{l,m \neq i,j} q_{\{i,j,l,m\}} x_l x_m + \ldots) \right] +$$

$$x_i x_j \left[(q_{\{i,j\}} + \sum_{l \neq i,j} q_{\{i,j,l\}} x_l + \sum_{l,m \neq i,j} q_{\{i,j,l,m\}} x_l x_m + \ldots) \right] + \ldots$$

Which we can write as

$$f(x) = x_i \left[\Delta_i(x) - x_j \Delta_{ij}(x) \right] + x_j \left[\Delta_j(x) - x_i \Delta_{ij}(x) \right] + x_i x_j \left[\Delta_{ij}(x) \right] + \ldots$$

Likewise, we have

$$f(x^{'}) = \overline{x}_i \left[\Delta_i(x) - x_j(q_{\{i,j\}} + \sum_{l \neq i,j} q_{\{i,j,l\}} x_l + \sum_{l,m \neq i,j} q_{\{i,j,l,m\}} x_l x_m + ...) \right] +$$

$$\overline{x}_j \left[\Delta_j(x) - x_i(q_{\{i,j\}} + \sum_{l \neq i,j} q_{\{i,j,l\}} x_l + \sum_{l,m \neq i,j} q_{\{i,j,l,m\}} x_l x_m + ...) \right] +$$

$$\overline{x}_i \overline{x}_j \left[(q_{\{i,j\}} + \sum_{l \neq i,j} q_{\{i,j,l\}} x_l + \sum_{l,m \neq i,j} q_{\{i,j,l,m\}} x_l x_m + ...) \right] + ...$$

Which can be written as

$$f(x^{'}) = \overline{x}_i \left[\Delta_i(x) - x_j \Delta_{ij}(x) \right] + \overline{x}_j \left[\Delta_j(x) - x_i \Delta_{ij}(x) \right] + \overline{x}_i \overline{x}_j \left[\Delta_{ij}(x) \right] + ...$$

So that

$$f(x^{'}) - f(x) = (\overline{x}_i - x_i) \left[\Delta_i(x) - x_j \Delta_{ij}(x) \right] + (\overline{x}_j - x_j) \left[\Delta_j(x) - x_i \Delta_{ij}(x) \right] + (\overline{x}_i \overline{x}_j - x_i x_j) \Delta_{ij}(x)$$

or

$$f(x^{'}) - f(x) = (\overline{x}_i - x_i) \Delta_i(x) + (\overline{x}_j - x_j) \Delta_j(x) + (\overline{x}_i - x_i)(\overline{x}_j - x_j) \Delta_{ij}(x)$$

Proof of Theorem 4:

Let $x = (x_1, ..., x_i, ..., x_j, ..., x_k, ..., x_n)$ and $x^{'} = (x_1, ..., \overline{x}_i, ..., \overline{x}_j, ..., \overline{x}_k, ..., x_n)$ then we have

$$f(x) = x_i[q_i + \sum_{l \neq i,j,k} q_{il} x_l + \sum_{l,h \neq i,j,k} q_{ilh} x_l x_h + \sum_{\substack{T \subseteq V \setminus \{i,j,k\} \\ |T| \geq 3}} q_{iT} \prod_{t \in T} x_t] +$$

$$x_j[q_j + \sum_{l \neq i,j,k} q_{jl} x_l + \sum_{l,h \neq i,j,k} q_{jlh} x_l x_h + \sum_{\substack{T \subseteq V \setminus \{i,j,k\} \\ |T| \geq 3}} q_{jT} \prod_{t \in T} x_t] +$$

$$x_k[q_k + \sum_{l \neq i,j,k} q_{kl} x_l + \sum_{l,h \neq i,j,k} q_{klh} x_l x_h + \sum_{\substack{T \subseteq V \setminus \{i,j,k\} \\ |T| \geq 3}} q_{kT} \prod_{t \in T} x_t] +$$

$$x_i x_j \sum_{T \subseteq V \setminus \{i,j,k\}} q_{ijT} \prod_{t \in T} x_t + x_i x_k \sum_{T \subseteq V \setminus \{i,j,k\}} q_{ikT} \prod_{t \in T} x_t + x_j x_k \sum_{T \subseteq V \setminus \{i,j,k\}} q_{jkT} \prod_{t \in T} x_t +$$

$$x_i x_j x_k \sum_{T \subseteq V \setminus \{i,j,k\}} q_{ijkT} \prod_{t \in T} x_t + Terms\ not\ involving\ elements\ of\ S$$

Consider the first bracket of terms. By adding and subtracting appropriate terms we get:

$$x_i[q_i + \sum_{l \neq i,j,k} q_{il}x_l + \sum_{l,h \neq i,j,k} q_{ilh}x_l x_h + \sum_{\substack{T \subseteq V\setminus\{i,j,k\} \\ |T|\geq 3}} q_{iT}\prod_{t\in T}x_t +$$

$$x_j \sum_{T \subseteq V\setminus\{i,j,k\}} q_{ijT}\prod_{t\in T}x_t + x_k \sum_{T \subseteq V\setminus\{i,j,k\}} q_{ikT}\prod_{t\in T}x_t + x_j x_k \sum_{T \subseteq V\setminus\{i,j,k\}} q_{ijkT}\prod_{t\in T}x_t -$$

$$x_j \sum_{T \subseteq V\setminus\{i,j,k\}} q_{ijT}\prod_{t\in T}x_t - x_k \sum_{T \subseteq V\setminus\{i,j,k\}} q_{ikT}\prod_{t\in T}x_t - x_j x_k \sum_{T \subseteq V\setminus\{i,j,k\}} q_{ijkT}\prod_{t\in T}x_t] =$$

$$x_i[\Delta_i(x) - x_j \sum_{T \subseteq V\setminus\{i,j,k\}} q_{ijT}\prod_{t\in T}x_t - x_k \sum_{T \subseteq V\setminus\{i,j,k\}} q_{ikT}\prod_{t\in T}x_t - x_j x_k \sum_{T \subseteq V\setminus\{i,j,k\}} q_{ijkT}\prod_{t\in T}x_t] =$$

$$x_i[\Delta_i(x) - x_j \sum_{T \subseteq V\setminus\{i,j,k\}} q_{ijT}\prod_{t\in T}x_t - x_k \sum_{T \subseteq V\setminus\{i,j,k\}} q_{ikT}\prod_{t\in T}x_t - x_j x_k \sum_{T \subseteq V\setminus\{i,j,k\}} q_{ijkT}\prod_{t\in T}x_t$$

$$-x_j x_k \sum_{T \subseteq V\setminus\{i,j,k\}} q_{ijkT}\prod_{t\in T}x_t + x_j x_k \sum_{T \subseteq V\setminus\{i,j,k\}} q_{ijkT}\prod_{t\in T}x_t] =$$

$$x_i[\Delta_i(x) - x_j\Delta_{ij}(x) - x_k\Delta_{ik}(x) + x_j x_k \sum_{T \subseteq V\setminus\{i,j,k\}} q_{ijkT}\prod_{t\in T}x_t] =$$

$$x_i[\Delta_i(x) - x_j\Delta_{ij}(x) - x_k\Delta_{ik}(x) + x_j x_k \Delta_{ijk}(x)]$$

Similar pattern exists for each of the second and third brackets. Furthermore, the terms outside of the brackets can be written as:

$$x_i x_j \sum_{T \subseteq V\setminus\{i,j,k\}} q_{ijT}\prod_{t\in T}x_t + x_i x_k \sum_{T \subseteq V\setminus\{i,j,k\}} q_{ikT}\prod_{t\in T}x_t + x_j x_k \sum_{T \subseteq V\setminus\{i,j,k\}} q_{jkT}\prod_{t\in T}x_t +$$

$$x_i x_j x_k \sum_{T \subseteq V\setminus\{i,j,k\}} q_{ijkT}\prod_{t\in T}x_t + Terms\ not\ involving\ elements\ of\ S =$$

$$x_i x_j(\Delta_{ij}(x) - x_k\Delta_{ijk}(x)) + x_i x_k(\Delta_{ik}(x) - x_j\Delta_{ijk}(x)) + x_j x_k(\Delta_{jk}(x) - x_i\Delta_{ijk}(x)) +$$

$$x_i x_j x_k \Delta_{ijk}(x) + Terms\ not\ involving\ elements\ of\ S$$

Grouping and rearranging gives the result:

$$f(x) = \ x_i[\Delta_i(x) - x_j\Delta_{ij}(x) - x_k\Delta_{ik}(x) + x_j x_k\Delta_{ijk}(x)] +$$

$$x_j[\Delta_j(x) - x_i\Delta_{ij}(x) - x_k\Delta_{jk}(x) + x_i x_k\Delta_{ijk}(x)] +$$

$$x_k[\Delta_k(x) - x_i\Delta_{ik}(x) - x_j\Delta_{jk}(x) + x_i x_j\Delta_{ijk}(x)] +$$

$$x_i x_j(\Delta_{ij}(x) - x_k\Delta_{ijk}(x)) + x_i x_k(\Delta_{ik}(x) - x_j\Delta_{ijk}(x)) + x_j x_k(\Delta_{jk}(x) - x_i\Delta_{ijk}(x)) +$$

$$x_i x_j x_k\Delta_{ijk}(x) + Terms\ not\ involving\ elements\ of\ S$$

Similarly for $f(x')$ we get

$$f(x') = \overline{x}_i[\Delta_i(x) - x_j\Delta_{ij}(x) - x_k\Delta_{ik}(x) + x_jx_k\Delta_{ijk}(x)] +$$
$$\overline{x}_j[\Delta_j(x) - x_i\Delta_{ij}(x) - x_k\Delta_{jk}(x) + x_ix_k\Delta_{ijk}(x)] +$$
$$\overline{x}_k[\Delta_k(x) - x_i\Delta_{ik}(x) - x_j\Delta_{jk}(x) + x_ix_j\Delta_{ijk}(x)] +$$
$$\overline{x}_i\overline{x}_j(\Delta_{ij}(x) - x_k\Delta_{ijk}(x)) + \overline{x}_i\overline{x}_k(\Delta_{ik}(x) - x_j\Delta_{ijk}(x)) + \overline{x}_j\overline{x}_k(\Delta_{jk}(x) - x_i\Delta_{ijk}(x)) +$$
$$\overline{x}_i\overline{x}_j\overline{x}_k\Delta_{ijk}(x) + Terms\ not\ involving\ elements\ of\ S$$

Note that in $f(x')$ all elements in brackets and parentheses are related to the solution x . Using the above results we get

$$f(x') - f(x) = (\overline{x}_i - x_i)[\Delta_i(x) - x_j\Delta_{ij}(x) - x_k\Delta_{ik}(x) + x_jx_k\Delta_{ijk}(x)] +$$
$$(\overline{x}_j - x_j)[\Delta_j(x) - x_i\Delta_{ij}(x) - x_k\Delta_{jk}(x) + x_ix_k\Delta_{ijk}(x)] +$$
$$(\overline{x}_k - x_k)[\Delta_k(x) - x_i\Delta_{ik}(x) - x_j\Delta_{jk}(x) + x_ix_j\Delta_{ijk}(x)] +$$
$$(\overline{x}_i\overline{x}_j - x_ix_j)(\Delta_{ij}(x) - x_k\Delta_{ijk}(x)) +$$
$$(\overline{x}_i\overline{x}_k - x_ix_k)(\Delta_{ik}(x) - x_j\Delta_{ijk}(x)) +$$
$$(\overline{x}_j\overline{x}_k - x_jx_k)(\Delta_{jk}(x) - x_i\Delta_{ijk}(x)) +$$
$$(\overline{x}_i\overline{x}_j\overline{x}_k - x_ix_jx_k)\Delta_{ijk}(x).$$

Rearranging yields the desired result.

Proof of Theorem 6:

For two vectors x' and x where component x_i for all $i \in S$ are complemented we have $f(x)$ and $f(x')$ as follows:

$$f(x) = \sum_{i \in S} x_i[q_{ij} + \sum_{j \notin S} x_jq_{ij}] + \sum_{ij \in S} x_ix_jq_{ij} + \ldots$$
$$f(x) = \sum_{i \in S} x_i[\Delta_i(x) - \sum_{j \notin S \setminus \{i\}} x_jq_{ij}] + \sum_{ij \in S} x_ix_jq_{ij} + \ldots$$

$$f(x') = \sum_{i \in S} \overline{x}_i[q_{ij} + \sum_{j \notin S} x_jq_{ij}] + \sum_{ij \in S} \overline{x}_i\overline{x}_jq_{ij} + \ldots$$
$$f(x') = \sum_{i \in S} \overline{x}_i[\Delta_i(x) - \sum_{j \notin S \setminus \{i\}} x_jq_{ij}] + \sum_{ij \in S} \overline{x}_i\overline{x}_jq_{ij} + \ldots$$

$$f(x') - f(x) = \sum_{i \in S} (\overline{x}_i - x_i)[\Delta_i(x) - \sum_{j \notin S \setminus \{i\}} x_j q_{ij}] + \sum_{ij \in S} (\overline{x}_i \overline{x}_j - x_i x_j) q_{ij}$$

$$f(x') - f(x) = \sum_{i \in S} (\overline{x}_i - x_i)\Delta_i(x) - \sum_{i \in S} \sum_{j \notin S \setminus \{i\}} (\overline{x}_i - x_i) x_j q_{ij} + \sum_{ij \in S} (\overline{x}_i \overline{x}_j - x_i x_j) q_{ij}$$

For each pair of elements i, j in the second and the third terms we have

$$\overline{x}_i \overline{x}_j + x_i x_j - \overline{x}_i x_j - x_i \overline{x}_j = (\overline{x}_i - x_i)(\overline{x}_j - x_j)$$

$$f(x') - f(x) = \sum_{i \in S} (\overline{x}_i - x_i)\Delta_i(x) + \sum_{\forall\, i,j \in S} (\overline{x}_i - x_i)(\overline{x}_j - x_j)\Delta_{ij}(x)$$

When the elements of the set S are flipped we need to update elements of vector $\Delta(x) = (\Delta_1(x), \ldots, \Delta_n(x))$. Since each element of the vector, i.e., the jth element, is the first derivative of f with respect to the jth component, updating this vector after complementing elements of S only involves the addition or subtraction of q_{ij} depending on the present value of x_i. In fact we have

$$\forall\, j \notin S, \quad \Delta_j(x) = q_j + \sum_{i \notin S \setminus \{j\}} q_{ij} x_i + \sum_{i \in S} q_{ij} x_i \quad \text{and} \quad \Delta_j(x') = q_j + \sum_{i \notin S \setminus \{j\}} q_{ij} x_i + \sum_{i \in S} q_{ij} \overline{x}_i$$

$$\forall\, j \in S, \quad \Delta_j(x) = q_j + \sum_{i \notin S} q_{ij} x_i + \sum_{i \in S \setminus \{j\}} q_{ij} x_i \quad \text{and} \quad \Delta_j(x') = q_j + \sum_{i \notin S} q_{ij} x_i + \sum_{i \in S \setminus \{j\}} q_{ij} \overline{x}_i$$

Note that we can substitute $\Delta_{ij}(x)$ for q_{ij}. From this the desired result follows immediately.

Proof of theorem 7:

Given *x*, let x' be a solution obtained from *x* by complementing x_i for all $i \in S$ and $|S| = r$. Values of $f(x)$ and $f(x')$ can be calculated as follows,

$$f(x) = \sum_{i \in S} x_i [q_i + \sum_{j \notin S} q_{ij} x_j + \sum_{j,k \notin S} q_{ijk} x_j x_k] +$$

$$\sum_{i,j \in S} q_{ij} x_i x_j + \sum_{\substack{i,j \in S \\ k \notin S}} q_{ijk} x_i x_j x_k + \sum_{i,j,k \in S} q_{ijk} x_i x_j x_k +$$

Terms not involving elements of S

$$f(x) = \sum_{i \in S} x_i \left[\Delta_i(x) - \sum_{j \in S \setminus \{i\}} q_{ij} x_j - \sum_{\substack{j \in S \setminus \{i\} \\ k \notin S}} q_{ijk} x_j x_k - \sum_{j,k \in S \setminus \{i\}} q_{ijk} x_j x_k \right] +$$

$$\sum_{i,j \in S} x_i x_j \left(q_{ij} + \sum_{k \notin S} q_{ijk} x_k \right) + \sum_{i,j,k \in S} q_{ijk} x_i x_j x_k +$$

Terms not involving elements of S

$$f(x) = \sum_{i \in S} x_i \left[\Delta_i(x) - \sum_{j \in S \setminus \{i\}} \Delta_{ij}(x) x_j + \sum_{j,k \in S \setminus \{i\}} q_{ijk} x_j x_k \right] +$$

$$\sum_{i,j \in S} x_i x_j \left(\Delta_{ij}(x) - \sum_{k \in S \setminus \{i,j\}} q_{ijk} x_k \right) + \sum_{i,j,k \in S} q_{ijk} x_i x_j x_k +$$

Terms not involving elements of S

$$f(x) = \sum_{i \in S} x_i \left[\Delta_i(x) - \sum_{j \in S \setminus \{i\}} \Delta_{ij}(x) x_j + \sum_{j,k \in S \setminus \{i\}} \Delta_{ijk}(x) x_j x_k \right] +$$

$$\sum_{i,j \in S} x_i x_j \left(\Delta_{ij}(x) - \sum_{k \in S \setminus \{i,j\}} \Delta_{ijk}(x) x_k \right) + \sum_{i,j,k \in S} \Delta_{ijk}(x) x_i x_j x_k +$$

Terms not involving elements of S

Similarly, we can calculate $f(x^{'})$ as follows.

$$f(x^{'}) = \sum_{i \in S} \overline{x}_i \left[q_i + \sum_{j \notin S} q_{ij} x_j + \sum_{j,k \notin S} q_{ijk} x_j x_k \right] +$$

$$\sum_{i,j \in S} q_{ij} \overline{x}_i \overline{x}_j + \sum_{\substack{i,j \in S \\ k \notin S}} q_{ijk} \overline{x}_i \overline{x}_j x_k + \sum_{i,j \in S} q_{ijk} \overline{x}_i \overline{x}_j \overline{x}_k +$$

Terms not involving elements of S

$$f(x^{'}) = \sum_{i \in S} \overline{x}_i \left[\Delta_i(x) - \sum_{j \in S \setminus \{i\}} q_{ij} x_j - \sum_{\substack{j \in S \setminus \{i\} \\ k \notin S}} q_{ijk} x_j x_k - \sum_{j,k \in S \setminus \{i\}} q_{ijk} x_j x_k \right] +$$

$$\sum_{i,j \in S} \overline{x}_i \overline{x}_j \left(q_{ij} + \sum_{k \notin S} q_{ijk} x_k \right) + \sum_{i,j \in S} q_{ijk} \overline{x}_i \overline{x}_j \overline{x}_k +$$

Terms not involving elements of S

or,

$$f(x') = \sum_{i \in S} \overline{x}_i [\Delta_i(x) - \sum_{j \in S \setminus \{i\}} \Delta_{ij}(x) x_j + \sum_{j,k \in S \setminus \{i\}} \Delta_{ijk}(x) x_j x_k] +$$

$$\sum_{i,j \in S} \overline{x}_i \overline{x}_j (\Delta_{ij}(x) - \sum_{k \in S \setminus \{i,j\}} \Delta_{ijk}(x) x_k) + \sum_{i,j,k \in S} \Delta_{ijk}(x) \overline{x}_i \overline{x}_j \overline{x}_k +$$

Terms not involving elements of S

Given these expressions for f(x) and f(x') we then have

$$f(x') - f(x) = \sum_{i \in S} (\overline{x}_i - x_i)[\Delta_i(x) - \sum_{j \in S \setminus \{i\}} \Delta_{ij}(x) x_j + \sum_{j,k \in S \setminus \{i\}} \Delta_{ijk}(x) x_j x_k] +$$

$$\sum_{i,j \in S} (\overline{x}_i \overline{x}_j - x_i x_j)(\Delta_{ij}(x) - \sum_{k \in S \setminus \{i,j\}} \Delta_{ijk}(x) x_k) + \sum_{i,j,k \in S} \Delta_{ijk}(x)(\overline{x}_i \overline{x}_j \overline{x}_k - x_i x_j x_k)$$

$$-(\overline{x}_i - x_i)\Delta_{ij}(x) x_j - (\overline{x}_j - x_j)\Delta_{ij}(x) x_i + (\overline{x}_i \overline{x}_j - x_i x_j)\Delta_{ij}(x) =$$
$$\Delta_{ij}(x)(x_i x_j - \overline{x}_i x_j + x_i x_j - x_i \overline{x}_j + \overline{x}_i \overline{x}_j - x_i x_j) = (\overline{x}_i - x_i)(\overline{x}_j - x_j)\Delta_{ij}(x),$$

$$\big[(\overline{x}_i - x_i)x_j x_k + (\overline{x}_j - x_j)x_i x_k + (\overline{x}_k - x_k)x_i x_j$$
$$-(\overline{x}_i \overline{x}_j - x_i x_j)x_k - (\overline{x}_i \overline{x}_k - x_i x_k)x_j - (\overline{x}_j \overline{x}_k - x_j x_k)x_i$$
$$+\overline{x}_j \overline{x}_k x_i - x_i x_j x_k\big]\Delta_{ijk}(x) = (\overline{x}_i - x_i)(\overline{x}_j - x_j)(\overline{x}_k - x_k)\Delta_{ijk}(x)$$

Regrouping yields the desired result

$$f(x') - f(x) = \sum_{i \in S} (\overline{x}_i - x_i)\Delta_i(x) + \sum_{i,j \in S} (\overline{x}_i - x_i)(\overline{x}_j - x_j)\Delta_{ij}(x) +$$
$$\sum_{i,j,k \in S} (\overline{x}_i - x_i)(\overline{x}_j - x_j)(\overline{x}_k - x_k)\Delta_{ijk}(x)$$

Which completes the first part of the proof.

To prove the second part of the theorem we consider

$$\forall\, j \in V \setminus S \qquad \Delta_j(x) = q_j + \sum_{i \notin S \setminus \{j\}} q_{ij} x_i + \sum_{i,k \notin S \setminus \{j\}} q_{ijk} x_i x_k + \sum_{i \in S} q_{ij} x_i + \sum_{i,k \in S} q_{ijk} x_i x_k \quad \text{and}$$

$$\forall\, j \in S \qquad \Delta_j(x) = q_j + \sum_{i \notin S} q_{ij} x_i + \sum_{i,k \notin S} q_{ijk} x_i x_k + \sum_{i \in S \setminus \{j\}} q_{ij} x_i + \sum_{i,k \in S \setminus \{j\}} q_{ijk} x_i x_k.$$

$$\forall\, j \in V \setminus S \qquad \Delta_j(x') = q_j + \sum_{i \notin S \setminus \{j\}} q_{ij} x_i + \sum_{i,k \notin S \setminus \{j\}} q_{ijk} x_i x_k + \sum_{i \in S} q_{ij} \overline{x}_i + \sum_{i,k \in S} q_{ijk} \overline{x}_i \overline{x}_k \quad \text{and}$$

$$\forall\, j \in S \qquad \Delta_j(x') = q_j + \sum_{i \notin S} q_{ij} x_i + \sum_{i,k \notin S} q_{ijk} x_i x_k + \sum_{i \in S \setminus \{j\}} q_{ij} \overline{x}_i + \sum_{i,k \in S \setminus \{j\}} q_{ijk} \overline{x}_i \overline{x}_k.$$

Upon applying $\Delta_j(x') - \Delta_j(x)$ the desired result follows immediately.

To prove the third part of the theorem we consider

$$\forall\, i \notin S,\, j \notin S \qquad \Delta_{ij}(x) = q_{ij} + \sum_{l \in (V \setminus S \cup \{i,j\})} q_{ijl} x_l + \sum_{l \in S} q_{ijl} x_l, \quad \text{and}$$

$$\Delta_{ij}(x') = q_{ij} + \sum_{l \in (V \setminus S \cup \{i,j\})} q_{ijl} x_l + \sum_{l \in S} q_{ijl} \overline{x}_l$$

$$\forall\, i \in S,\, j \in S \qquad \Delta_{ij}(x) = q_{ij} + \sum_{l \in V \setminus S} q_{ijl} x_l + \sum_{l \in S \setminus \{i,j\}} q_{ijl} x_l, \quad \text{and}$$

$$\Delta_{ij}(x') = q_{ij} + \sum_{l \in V \setminus S} q_{ijl} x_l + \sum_{l \in S \setminus \{i,j\}} q_{ijl} \overline{x}_l$$

$$\forall\, i \in S,\, j \notin S \qquad \Delta_{ij}(x) = \Delta_{ij}(x) = q_{ij} + \sum_{l \in (V \setminus S \cup \{i\})} q_{ijl} x_l + \sum_{l \in S \setminus \{j\}} q_{ijl} x_l, \quad \text{and}$$

$$\Delta_{ij}(x') = q_{ij} + \sum_{l \in (V \setminus S \cup \{i\})} q_{ijl} x_l + \sum_{l \in S \setminus \{j\}} q_{ijl} \overline{x}_l.$$

Upon applying $\Delta_{ij}(x') - \Delta_{ij}(x)$ the desired result follows.

APPENDIX B: A FILTER AND FAN PROCEDURE

The Filter and Fan (F&F) method, originally proposed by Glover (1998) as an improvement method for Scatter Search, can be used as a standalone search method that organizes a search process that dynamically cycles through alternative neighborhoods depending on conditions encountered. This form of strategic oscillation, employing a variety of neighborhood structures and r-flip moves, is intended to produce a robust yet economical search of the solution space. While F&F is rather general and can be implemented in a variety of ways, our work here employs a basic version known as "Strict Improvement F&F." We summarize this method below as given by Glover (1998).

1. **Generate a candidate list of 1-moves for the current solution x:**
   a. If any of the 1-moves are improving: choose the best member from the list and execute it to create a new current solution x. (The best member may be the only member if the list terminates with the first improving move encountered.) Then return to the start of step 1.
   b. If none of the 1-moves is improving: Identify the set M of the n0 best 1-moves examined. Let M(1) be a subset of the n1 best moves from M, and let X(1) be the set of solutions produced by these moves. Set L=1 and proceed to step 2.
2. **For each L-move m in M(L):** Identify the associated set A(m) of the n2 best compatible moves m' derived from M, and evaluate each solution that results by applying move m' to the corresponding member of X(L). When fewer than n2 moves of M are compatible with move m, restrict consideration to this smaller set of moves in composing A(m).
   a. If an improving move is found during the foregoing process: Select the best such move generated (by the point where the process is elected to terminate), and execute the move to create a new current solution x. Then return to step 1.

If no improving move is found by the time all moves in M(L) are examined: Stop if L has reached a chosen upper limit MaxL. Otherwise, identify the set M(L+1) of the n1 best (L+1)-moves evaluated (and/or identify the associated set X(L+1)). (If fewer than n1 distinct (L+1)-moves in M(L+1).). Then set L=L+1 and return to the start of Step 2.

In Step 1(a) of the procedure, 1-flip (1-move) local search is applied to a starting solution to produce a local optimal solution. When the 1-move process fails to yield further improvement, a set of the best moves considered, M, is maintained and a subset of these moves, *M(1)*, is used to create a set of solutions *X(1)* in Step 1(b). The moves carried out here are called the Level-1 moves. Then in Step2, for each move m in *M(1)*, the set A(m) of compatible m' move(s) is constructed from M and compound moves are executed. During the process if an improving move is created the procedure goes to Step 1(a), i.e., to create a new local optimal solution.

When creating compound moves if no improving moves are found by the compound moves in step2(a), choose a set of high quality moves from the compound moves to create *M(2)* and an associated set of solutions *X(2)*. (Level-2 moves). Continue the process to even higher levels of moves until a stopping criteria, *MaxL* is reached. In our implementation we chose parameters as follows, *|M|=40, |M(L)|=4, |A(m)|=4*, and *MaxL=20*. We used simple short term Tabu implementation by making a tabu list for the set *M(L)* equal to $\min\{50, 0.25n\}$. (See Table 1)

This work was previously published in International Journal of Applied Metaheuristic Computing, Volume 1, Issue 1, edited by Peng-Yeng Yin, pp. 93-109, copyright 2010 by IGI Publishing (an imprint of IGI Global).

Chapter 17
Stochastic Learning for SAT– Encoded Graph Coloring Problems

Noureddine Bouhmala
Vestfold University College, Norway

Ole-Christoffer Granmo
University of Agder, Norway

ABSTRACT

The graph coloring problem (GCP) is a widely studied combinatorial optimization problem due to its numerous applications in many areas, including time tabling, frequency assignment, and register allocation. The need for more efficient algorithms has led to the development of several GC solvers. In this paper, the authors introduce a team of Finite Learning Automata, combined with the random walk algorithm, using Boolean satisfiability encoding for the GCP. The authors present an experimental analysis of the new algorithm's performance compared to the random walk technique, using a benchmark set containing SAT-encoding graph coloring test sets.

1. INTRODUCTION

In the graph coloring problem (GCP) an undirected graph $G(V, E)$ is given, where V is a set of vertices, and E is a set of pairs of vertices called edges. We call a k-coloring of G, a mapping $C : V \rightarrow \{1 \ldots k\}$ such that if $C(p) = C(q)$ then $(p, q) \notin E$. The set $\{1 \ldots k\}$ is the set of colors.

There exist two variants of this problem. In the *optimization* variant, the goal is to find the chromatic number $X(G)$, which is the minimal k for which there exists a k-coloring of G. In the *decision variant*, the question is to decide whether for a particular number of colors, a coloring of G exists. All these problems are known to be NP-complete, so it is unlikely that a polynomial-time algorithm exists that solves any of these problems.

DOI: 10.4018/978-1-4666-0270-0.ch017

In this paper the focus is on the decision variant of the GCP. Encoding the GCP as a Boolean satisfiability problem (SAT) and solving it using efficient SAT algorithms has caused considerable interest. The SAT problem, which is known to be NP-complete (Cook, 1971), can be defined as follows. A propositional formula $\Phi = \bigwedge_{j=1}^{m} C_j$ with m clauses and n Boolean variables is given. A Boolean variable is a variable that can take one of the two values, *True* or *False*. Each clause C_j, in turn, has the form:

$$C_j = \left(\bigvee_{k \in I_j} x_k \right) \vee \left(\bigvee_{l \in \overline{I}_j} \overline{x}_l \right),$$

where $I_j, \overline{I}_j \subseteq \{1, \ldots n\}, I_j \cap \overline{I}_j = \varnothing$, and $\overline{x}_i$ denotes the negation of x_i. The task is to determine whether the propositional formula Φ evaluates to *True*. Such an assignment, if it exists, is called a satisfying assignment for Φ, and Φ is called satisfiable. Otherwise, Φ is said to be unsatisfiable. Most SAT solvers use a Conjunctive Normal Form (CNF) representation of the propositional formula. In CNF, the formula is represented as a conjunction of clauses, where each clause is a disjunction of literals, and a literal is a Boolean variable or its negation. For example, $P \vee Q$ is a clause containing the two literals P and Q. This clause is satisfied if either P is *True* or Q is *True*. When each clause in Φ contains exactly k literals, the resulting SAT problem is called k-SAT.

The paper is organized as follows. In Section 2, we review various algorithms for solving GCP, as well as satisfiability algorithms for solving SAT-encoded GCP. Section 3 explains the basic concepts of Learning Automata (LA) and introduces our new LA based approach to graph coloring. In Section 4, we look at the results from testing the new approach and draw some conclusions. Finally, in Section 5 we present a summary of the work.

2. RELATED WORK

2.1 Graph Coloring Algorithms

The GCP is a well-known problem in combinatorial optimization. It is among the earliest problems proved to be NP-Complete (Karp, 1991). It has been extensively studied due to its simplicity and applicability. The simplicity of the problem coupled with its intractability makes it an ideal platform for exploring new algorithmic techniques. A number of exact approaches based on integer programming models have been proposed (Brown, 1972; Brelaz, 1979; Swell, 1996; Hansen, Labbe, & Schindl, 2005; Mendez-Diaz & Zabala, 2008). Still, compared to the variety of graph coloring methods proposed in the field as a whole, the number of such algorithms remains small. Other approaches were based on greedy constructive algorithms (Leighton, 1979; Culberson & Luo, 1996). These algorithms color the vertices of a graph in a sequential manner, adopting a chosen mechanism for selecting the next vertex to color and the color to use. The resulting algorithms are very fast, but not particularly efficient. Meta-heuristics methods such as Tabu Search (Hertz & de Werra, 1987), Simulated Annealing (Johnsen, Aragon, McGeoch, & Schevon, 1991), Evolutionary Algorithms (Galinier & Hao, 1999), Minimal-state processing search algorithm (Funabiki & Higashino, 2000), AMACOL (Galinier, Hertz, & Zufferey, 2008), Variable Search Space (Hertz, Plumettaz, & Zufferey, 2008) represent the last category of techniques widely used to solve the graph coloring problem. A recent survey for graph coloring algorithms is provided in (Enrico & Paolo, 2010).

2.2 SAT-Encoded Graph Coloring Approaches

The GCP has been extensively studied due to its simplicity and applicability. The simplicity of the problem coupled with its intractability makes it an ideal platform for exploring new algorithmic techniques. This has led to the development of stochastic local search algorithms for solving the graph coloring problem (Malaguti & Toth, 2010; Johnson, Mehrotra, & Trick, 2008; Chiarandini, Dumitrescu, & Sttzle, 2003; Galinier & Hertz, 2006). When transforming the GCP into SAT (Prestwich, 2004), a decision variant is encoded for which the goal is to find a feasible coloring for a given number of colors. This section aims at presenting a survey of methods used to solve the graph coloring problem via propositional satisfiability.

Due to their combinatorial explosive nature, large and complex SAT-encoded graph coloring problems are hard to solve using systematic algorithms. One way to overcome the combinatorial explosion is to give up completeness. Stochastic Local search algorithms (SLS) are techniques which use this strategy. SLS are based on what is perhaps the oldest optimization method – trial and error. Typically, they start with an initial assignment of values to variables randomly or heuristically generated. During each iteration, a new assignment is selected from the neighborhood of the current one by performing a move. Choosing a good neighborhood, and a method for searching it, is usually guided by intuition, because very little theory is available as a guide. Most SLS use a 1-flip neighbor-hood relation for which two truth value assignments are neighbors if they differ in the truth value of one variable. If the new truth assignments provide a better value in light of the objective function, the new assignment becomes the current one. The search terminates if no better truth assignment can be found in the neighborhood of the current assignment. Note that choosing a fruitful neighborhood, and a method for searching it, is usually guided by intuition – theoretical results that can be used as guidance are sparse.

One of the earliest local search algorithms for solving SAT is GSAT (Selman, Levesque, & Mitchell, 1992). Basically, GSAT begins with a random generated assignment of values to variables, and then iteratively uses the steepest descent heuristic to find a new truth value assignment (the one that decreases the numbers of unsatisfied clauses the most). After a fixed number of moves, the search is restarted from a new random assignment. The search continues until a solution is found or a fixed number of restarts have been performed.

The introduction of randomness (i.e., noise) into a local search method is common practice for improving its effectiveness through diversification (Blum & Roli, 2003). To this end, an extension of GSAT, referred to as random-walk (Selman & Kautz, 1993) has been realized with the purpose of escaping from local optima. In a random walk step, a randomly unsatisfied clause is selected. Then, one of the variables appearing in that clause is flipped, thus effectively forcing the selected clause to become satisfied. The main idea is to decide at each search step whether to perform a standard GSAT or a random-walk strategy with a probability called the walk probability. Another widely used variant of GSAT is the Walk-SAT algorithm, originally introduced in (Selman, Kautz, & Cohen, 1992). It first picks randomly an unsatisfied clause, and then, in a second step, one of the variables with the lowest break count, appearing in the selected clause, is randomly selected. The break count of a variable is defined as the number of clauses that would be unsatisfied by flipping the chosen variable. If there exists a variable with break count equal to zero, this variable is flipped; otherwise the variable with minimal break count is selected with a certain probability (noise probability). It turns out that the choice of unsatisfied clauses, combined with the randomness in the selection of variables, enable Walk-SAT to avoid local minima and to better explore the search space.

Extensive tests have led to the introduction of new variants of the WalkSAT algorithm referred to as Novelty and R-Novelty (McAllester & Selman, 1997). These two variants use a combination of two criteria when choosing a variable to flip from within an unsatisfied clause. Quite often, these two algorithms can get stuck in local minima and fail to get out. To this end, recent variants have been designed (Li & Huang, 2005; Li, Wei, & Zhang, 2007; Hoos, 2002) using a combination of search intensification and diversification mechanisms leading to good performance on a wide range of SAT instances. Other algorithms (Glover, 1993; Hansen, Labbe, & Schindl, 2005; Gent & Walsh, 1995; Gent & Walsh, 1993) used history-based variable selection strategies in order to avoid flipping the same variable.

In parallel to the development of more sophisticated versions of randomized improvement techniques, other methods based on the idea of modifying the evaluation function (Wu & Wah, 2000; Hutter, Tompkins, & Hoos, 2002; Thomton, Pham, Bain, & Ferreira, 2004; Schuumans & Southey, 2000; Schuumans, Southey, & Holte, 2000) in order to prevent the search from getting stuck in non-attractive areas of the underlying search space, have become increasingly popular in SAT solving. The key idea is to associate the clauses of the given CNF formula with weights. Although these clause weighting SLS algorithms differ in the way clause weights should be updated (probabilistic or deterministic), they all choose to increase the weights of all the unsatisfied clauses as soon as a local minimum is encountered. A new approach to clause weighting known as Divide and Distribute Fixed Weights (DDFW; Ishtaiwi, Thomton, Sattar, & Pham, 2005) exploits the transfer of weights from neighboring satisfied clauses to unsatisfied clauses in order to break out form local minima. Recently, a strategy based on assigning weights to variables (Prestwich, 2005) instead of clauses greatly enhances the performance of the Walk-SAT algorithm, leading to the best known results on some benchmarks.

Lacking theoretical guidelines, while being stochastic in nature, the deployment of several meta-heuristics involves extensive experimentation to find the optimal noise or walk probability settings. To avoid manual parameter tuning, new methods have been designed to automatically adapt parameter settings during the search (Li, Wei, & Zhang, 2007; Patterson & Krautz, 2001) and results have shown their effectiveness for a wide range of problems. The work conducted in (Granmo & Bouhmala, 2007) introduced Learning Automata (LA) as a mechanism for enhancing local search based SAT Solvers, thus laying the foundation for novel LA-based SAT solvers. Finally, a new approach based on an automatic procedure for integrating selected components from various existing solvers in order to build new efficient algorithms that draw the strengths of multiple algorithms, has been recently reported in (Xu, Hutter, Hoose, & Leyton-Brown, 2008; KhudaBukhsh, Xu, Hoos, & Leyton-Brown, 2009).

3. FINITE LEARNING AUTOMATA FOR SAT-ENCODED GCP

We base our work on the principles of Learning Automata (Narendra & Thathachar, 1989; Thathachar & Sastry, 2004). Learning Automata have been used to model biological systems (Tsetlin, 1973), and have attracted considerable interest because they can learn the optimal actions when operating in (or interacting with) unknown stochastic environments. Furthermore, they combine rapid and accurate convergence with low computational complexity. Although the SAT problem has not been addressed from a Learning Automata point of view before, Learning Automata solutions have recently been proposed for several other combinatorial optimization problems. In Oommen and Ma (1988) and Gale, Das, and Yu (1990), a so-called Object Migration Automaton is used for solving the classical equipartitioning problem. An order of magnitude faster convergence is reported compared to the best known algorithms at that time. A similar approach has also been discovered for the Graph Partitioning

Figure 1. A learning automaton interacting with an environment

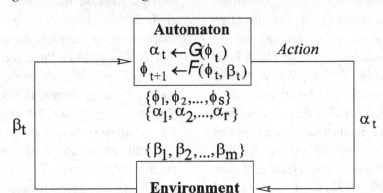

Problem (Oommen & St. Croix, 1988). Finally, the list organization problem has successfully been addressed by Learning Automata schemes and has been found to converge to the optimal arrangement with probability arbitrary close to unity (Oommen & Hansen, 1987). Learning Automata solutions have recently been proposed for several other combinatorial optimization problems (Granmo & Oommen, 2010; Oommen, Misra, & Granmo, 2007; Granmo, Oommen, Myrer, & Olsen, 1993) and inspired by the success of the above solution schemes, we will in the following propose a Learning Automata based solution scheme for the SAT-encoded GCPs.

3.1 A Learning SAT Automaton

Generally stated, a finite learning automaton performs a sequence of actions on an environment. The environment can be seen as a generic unknown medium that responds to each action with some sort of reward or penalty, perhaps stochastically. Based on the responses from the environment, the aim of the finite learning automaton is to find the action that minimizes the expected number of penalties received. Figure 1 illustrates the interaction between the finite learning automaton and the environment. Because we treat the environment as unknown, we will here only consider the definition of the finite learning automaton.

The finite learning automaton can be defined in terms of a quintuple (Narendra & Thathachar, 1989):

$$\{\underline{\Phi}, \underline{\alpha}, \underline{\beta}, F(\cdot, \cdot), G(\cdot, \cdot)\}.$$

$\underline{\Phi} = \{\phi_1, \phi_2, \ldots, \phi_s\}$ is the set of internal automaton states. $\underline{\alpha} = \{\alpha_1, \alpha_2, \ldots, \alpha_r\}$ is the set of automaton actions. And, $\underline{\beta} = \{\beta_1, \beta_2, \ldots, \beta_m\}$ is the set of inputs that can be given to the automaton. An output function $\alpha_t = G[\phi_t]$ determines the next action performed by the automaton given the current automaton state. Finally, a transition function $\phi_{t+1} = F[\phi_t, \beta_t]$ determines the new automaton state from: (1) the current automaton state and (2) the response of the environment to the action performed by the automaton. Based on the above generic framework, the crucial issue is to design automata that can learn the optimal action when interacting with the environment.

Several designs have been proposed in the literature, and the reader is referred to [31, 45] for an extensive treatment. In this paper we target the SAT problem, and our goal is to design a team of Learning Automata that seeks the solution of SAT problem instances. We build upon the work of Tsetlin and the linear two-action automaton

[31, 47]. Briefly stated, for each variable in the SAT problem instance that is to be solved, we construct an automaton with

- **States:**
$\Phi = \{-N, -(N-1), \ldots, -1, 0, \ldots, N-2, N-1\}$.
- **Actions:** $\underline{\alpha} = \{True, False\}$.
- **Inputs:** $\beta = \{reward, penalty\}$.

Figure 2 specifies the F and G matrices. The G matrix can be summarized as follows. If the automaton state is positive, then action True will be chosen by the automaton. If the state is negative, on the other hand, action False will be chosen. Note that since we initially do not know which action is optimal, we set the initial state of each Learning SAT Automaton randomly to either '-1' or '0'.

The state transition matrix F determines how learning proceeds. As seen from the finite automaton in the figure, providing a reward input to the automaton strengthens the currently chosen action, essentially by making it less likely that the other action will be chosen in the future. Correspondingly, a penalty input weakens the currently selected action by making it more likely that the other action will be chosen later on. In other words, the automaton attempts to incorporate past responses when deciding on a sequence of actions.

3.2 Learning Automata Random Walk (LARW)

Overview: In addition to the definition of the LA, we must define the environment that the LA interacts with. Simply put, the environment is a SAT-encoded GCP instance as defined in Section 1. Each variable x_i of the SAT problem instance is assigned a dedicated automaton LA_i, resulting in a team $\{LA_1, \ldots, LA_n\}$ of LA. The task of each LA_i is to determine the truth value of its corresponding variable x_i, with the aim of satisfying all of the clauses C_j where the variable appears. This means that when each automaton has reached its own goal, then the overall SAT problem at hand has also been solved and the corresponding coloring is found.

Pseudo-code: Figure 3 contains the complete pseudo-code for solving SAT-encoded GCP, using a team of LA. As seen from the figure, each LA is initially assigned either the state '0' or '-1'. According to the operation of each LA_i, specified in Figure 2, the corresponding variable x_i is then assigned either *True* or *False*. In the main loop, LARW switches between randomly selecting an unsatisfied clause and a satisfied clause. An unsatisfied clause C_j is selected first. Then a literal i from that clause is selected, again randomly. The corresponding LAi is given a penalty since it has failed to satisfy the clause C_j. The penalty is finally processed by the LA as specified by the state transitions in Figure 2.

Figure 2. The state transitions and actions of the Learning SAT Automaton

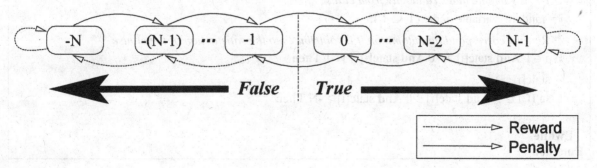

The other case is the selection of a satisfied clause C_j. Again a random literal i is selected from the clause, however, in this case, the corresponding LA_i is given a reward. Note that this reward is only given if the LA_i causes C_j to be satisfied, that is, the truth assignment selected by LA_i is sufficient for keeping the clause satisfied.

In the above sense, the LARW corresponds to an ordinary Random Walk (RW), however, both satisfied and unsatisfied clauses are used in the search. Furthermore, notice that the assignment of truth values to variables is indirect, governed by the states of the LA. Thus, at the core of the LARW is a punishment/rewarding scheme that

Figure 3. Learning automata random walk algorithm

```
Procedure learning_automata_random_walk()
Begin
  /* Initialization */
  For i = 1 To n Do
    /* The initial state of each automaton is set to either '-1' or '1' */
    state[i] = random_element({-1,0});
    /* And the respective variables are assigned corresponding truth values */
    If state[i] == -1 Then xᵢ = False Else xᵢ = True;
  /* Main loop */
  While Not stop() Do
    /* Draw unsatisfied clause randomly */
    Cⱼ = random_unsatisfied_clause();
    /* Draw variable index randomly from clause */
    i = random_variable_index( Iⱼ ∪ Ῑⱼ );

    /* The corresponding automaton is penalized for choosing the ``wrong'' action */
    If i ∈ Iⱼ Then

        state[i]++;
        /* Flip variable when automaton changes its action */
        If state[i] == 0 Then
          flip(xᵢ);
    Else If i ∈ Ῑⱼ Then

        state[i]- -;
        /* Flip variable when automaton changes its action */
        If state[i] == -1 Then
          flip(xᵢ);
    /* Draw satisfied clause randomly */
    Cⱼ = random_satisfied_clause();
    /* Draw variable index randomly from clause */
    i = random_variable_index( Iⱼ ∪ Ῑⱼ );

    /* Reward corresponding automaton if it contributes to the satisfaction of the clause */
    If i ∈ Iⱼ And state[i] >= 0 And state[i] < N-1 Then

        state[i]++;
    Else If i ∈ Ῑⱼ And state[i] < 0 And state[i] > -N Then

        state[i]- -;
  Ewhile
Emethod
```

guides the team of LA towards the optimal assignment. In the spirit of automata based learning, this scheme is incremental, and learning is performed gradually, in small steps.

Remark 1: Like a two-action Tsetlin Automaton, our proposed LA seeks to minimize the expected number of penalties it receives. In other words, it seeks finding the truth assignment that minimizes the number of unsatisfied clauses among the clauses where its variable appears.

Remark 2: Note that because multiple variables, and thereby multiple LA, may be involved in each clause, we are dealing with a game of LA (Narendra & Thathachar, 1989). That is, multiple LA interact with the same environment, and the response of the environment depends on the actions of several LA. In fact, because there may be conflicting goals among the LA involved in the LARW, the resulting game is competitive. The convergence properties of general competitive games of LA have not yet been successfully analyzed, however, results exist for certain classes of games, such as the Prisoner's Dilemma game (Narendra & Thathachar, 1989). In our case, the LA involved in the LARW is non-absorbing, i.e., every state can be reached from every other state with positive probability. This means that the probability of reaching the solution of the SAT problem instance at hand is equal to 1 when running the game infinitely. Also note that the solution of the SAT problem corresponds to a Nash equilibrium of the game.

Remark 3: In order to maximize speed of learning, we initialize each LA randomly to either the state '-1' or '0'. In this initial configuration, the variables will be flipped relatively quickly because only a single LA state transition is necessary for a flip. Accordingly, the joint state space of the LA is quickly explored in this configuration. However, as learning proceeds and the LA move towards their boundary states, i.e., states '-N' and 'N-1', the flipping of variables calms down. Accordingly, the search for a solution to the SAT problem instance at hand becomes increasingly focused.

4. EMPIRICAL RESULTS

4.1 Benchmark Instances

As a basis for the empirical evaluation of LARW, we selected a benchmark test suite of 1804 problem instances. The suite consists of 3-colorables SAT-encoded flat graphs, 5-colorables SAT-encoded morphed graphs, and finally 4 large SAT-encoded graph coloring problems. All the instances lie close to the so-called phase transition point (typically SLS are exponentially slower near this transition point than on either side).

As described on the SATLIB website (http://www.informatik.tu-darmstadt.de/AI/SATLIB), SAT-encoded morphed graphs are a class of Graph Coloring Problems obtained by morphing regular ring lattices with random graphs. The amount of structure in the problem is controlled by a morphing ratio p. The performance of an algorithm is dependent on the degree of structure and randomness of a problem, and thus, by varying p, the behavior of an algorithm can be studied.

Encoding GCP instances into SAT is accomplished by allowing each Boolean variable to represent the color assigned to a single vertex. Each coloring constraint (edge of the graph) is represented by a set of clauses ensuring that the corresponding vertices have different colors, and two additional sets of clauses ensure that valid SAT assignments assign exactly one color to each vertex. All instances are available from the SATLIB website. All the benchmark instances used in this experiment are satisfiable instances (i.e., colorable instances) and have been used widely in the literature. Due to the randomization of the algorithm, the number of flips required for solving a problem instance varies widely between different runs. Therefore, for each problem instance, we run LARW and RW 100 times with a cutoff parameter (maxflips) setting which is high enough (107)to guarantee a success rate close to 100%.

4.2 Search Pattern

The manner in which LA converges on a truth value assignment is crucial to a better understanding of LARW's behavior. In Figure 4, we show how the best and current assignment progresses during the search using two flat graphs taken from the SAT benchmark library. The two plots suggest that problem solving with LARW happens in two phases. In the first phase, which corresponds to the early part of the search (the first *5%* of the search), LARW behaves as a hill- climbing method. This phase which can be described as a short one, where up to *95%* of the clauses are satisfied. The best assignment climbs rapidly at first, and then flattens out as we mount the plateau, marking the start of the second phase. The plateau spans a region in the search space where flips typically leave the best assignment unchanged. The length of the plateaus becomes even more

pronounced as the number of flips increases, and occurs more specifically when LARW is trying to satisfy the last few remaining clauses. Finally, observe that the plots in Figure 4 show that the LA mechanism allows the acceptance of "bad" moves at any stage of the search, leading to efficient search diversification. This can be considered as an advantage compared to other meta-heuristics, such as the simulated annealing algorithm where the probability of accepting bad moves decreases as the search proceeds, forcing the algorithm to behave as a pure greedy local search.

To further investigate the behavior of LARW once on the plateau, we looked at the corresponding average state of the LA as the search progresses. The plot located on the left in Figure 5 shows the reported observations. The start of plateau search coincides in general with an increase in the average state. The longer the plateau, the higher the average state. An automaton with high average state needs to perform a series of actions before its current state changes to either -1 or 0, thereby making the flipping of the corresponding variable possible. The transition between each plateau corresponds to a change to the region where a small number of flips gradually improves

Figure 4. (Left) LARW's search pattern on a 150 variable problem with 545 clauses (flat50-115)). (Right) LARW's search pattern on a 600 variable problem with 2237 clauses (flat200-497). Along the horizontal axis we give the number of flips and along the vertical axis the percentage of the number of satisfied clauses.

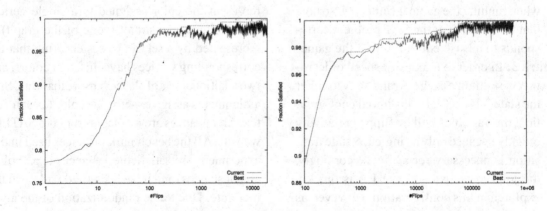

Figure 5. (Left) Average state of automaton. Horizontal axis gives the number of flips, and the vertical axis shows the average state of automaton for flat50-115. (Right) Success rate as a function of N for the morphed graph sw100-8-lp2 with 500 variables, 3100 clauses and a morphing ratio p=0.25.

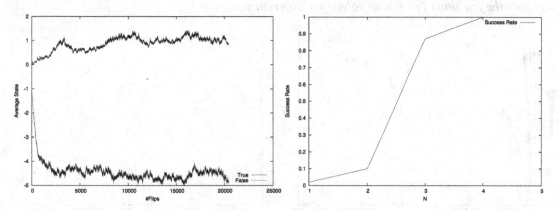

the score of the current solution ending with an improvement of the best assignment.

The above search pattern brings out an interesting difference between LARW and the standard use of SLS. In the latter, one generally stops the search as soon as no more improvements are found. This can be appropriate when looking for a close-to-optimal truth assignment. On the other hand, when searching for a global maximum (i.e., a satisfying assignment) stopping when no single flip yields an immediate improvement is a poor strategy.

An important part of the preliminary testing is to establish a good choice of parameters for the algorithm under consideration. An interesting aspect of the behavior of LARW is for which value of N (i.e., value of the boundary state) does it reaches the optimal success rate. The plot located on the right in Figure 5 shows the impact of N on the success rate of LARW. The performance of the algorithm varies significantly depending on the assigned value to N. For this particular example, the success rate is very low for $N = 1$ (i.e., typical random walk), but increases as N increases, until it reaches a success rate of 1 with $N = 5$. Notice that this is the only parameter that needs to be adjusted in a prepossessing phase before running the algorithm.

4.3 Run-Length-Distribution (RLDs)

As an indicator of the behavior of the algorithm on a single instance, we choose the median cost when trying to solve a given instance in *100* trials, and using an extremely high cutoff parameter setting of Max−steps = *107* in order to obtain a maximal number of successful tries. The reason behind choosing the median cost rather than the mean cost is due to the large variation in the number of flips required to find a solution.

To get an idea of the variability of the search cost, we analyzed the cumulative distribution of the number of search flips needed by both LARW and RW for solving single instances. Due to non-deterministic decisions involved in the algorithm (i.e., initial assignment, random moves), the number of flips needed by both algorithms to find a solution is a random variable that varies from run to run. More formally, let k denotes the total number of runs, and let $f'(j)$ denote the number of flips for the j-th successful run (i.e., run during which a solution is found) in a list of all successful runs, sorted according to increasing number of flips, then the cumulative empirical RLD is defined by $P[f'(j) \leq f] = \dfrac{\left| \{ j \mid f'(j) \leq f \} \right|}{k}$. For

Figure 6. LARW Vs RW - (Left) cumulative distributions for a 150-variables graph coloring problems with 545 clauses (flat50-115). (Right) cumulative distribution for a 225-variable graph coloring problem with 840 clauses (flat75-180). Along the horizontal axis we give the number of flips, and along the vertical axis the fraction of problems solved for different values of N.

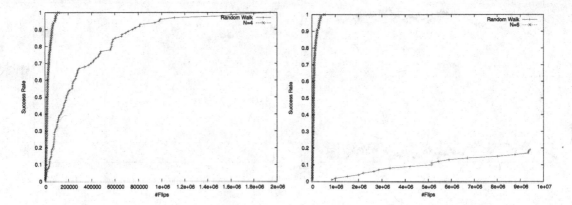

practical reasons we restrict our presentation here to the instances corresponding to small, medium, and large size from the underlying test-set.

Figures 6 show RLDs obtained by applying RW and LARW to individual SAT-encoded flat graph coloring problem instances. Several interesting observations can be drawn from the two plots. Figure 6 shows the only two instances RW was capable of solving. The performance of RW is rather unsatisfactory for flat75-180 and is getting

even far more dramatic for larger problems as the probability of finding a feasible solution within the required number of steps approaches *0*. The curves show no cross-over in their corresponding RLDs. This implies that for both short and long runs LARW dominates RW making it the clear winner as it gives consistently higher success probabilities regardless of the number of steps. The length of the different runs is furthermore consistently much higher with RW than with

Figure 7. LARW Vs RW - (Left) cumulative distributions for a 300-variables graph coloring problems with 1117 clauses (flat100-239). (Right) cumulative distribution for a 375-variable graph coloring problem with 1403 clauses (flat125-301). Along the horizontal axis we give the number of flips, and along the vertical axis the fraction of problems solved for different values of N.

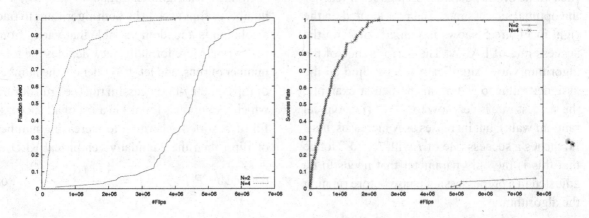

Figure 8. LARW Vs RW - (Left) cumulative distributions for a 450-variables graph coloring problems with 1680 clauses (flat150-360). (Right) cumulative distribution for a 600-variable graph coloring problem with 2237 clauses (flat200-479). Along the horizontal axis we give the number of flips, and along the vertical axis the fraction of problems solved for different values of N.

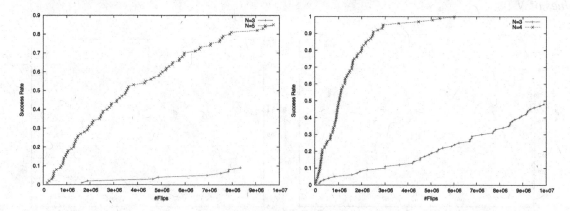

LARW. We also observe stagnation with a low asymptotic solution probability corresponding to a value around *20%* for flat75-180. The differences in performance is a factor of approximately *10* in the median for flat50-115 and far more dramatic for flat75-180 with a factor as high as *77*.

The plots in Figure 7 and Figure 8 show the lowest value of N leading to a success rate different from *0%* and the optimal value of N. Using the optimal setting of N, LARW was able to solve all flat graphs coloring problems with a success rate of *100%*, except for flat150-360 where the success rate was about *85%*.

The plots also report the existence of an initial phase below which the probability for LARW to find a solution is *0*. LARW starts the search from a randomly chosen assignment which typically violates many clauses. Consequently, LARW

Figure 9. LARW Vs RW - (Left) cumulative distributions for a 500-variables morphed graph coloring problems with 310 clauses (sw100-8-1p0-c5: p =1). (Right) cumulative distribution for a 500-variable morphed graph coloring problem with 3100 clauses (sw100-8-1p1-c5: p=0.5). Along the horizontal axis we give the number of flips, and along the vertical axis the fraction of problems solved for different values of N.

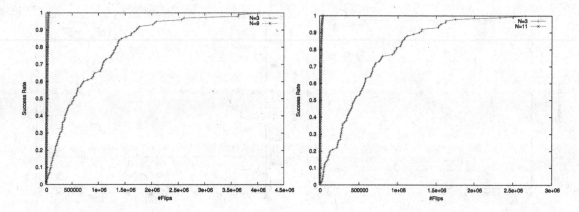

Figure 10. LARW Vs RW - (Left) cumulative distributions for a 500-variables morphed graph coloring problems with 310 clauses (sw100-8-1p2-c5: p=0.25). (Right) cumulative distribution for a 500-variable morphed graph coloring problem with 3100 clauses (sw100-8-1p3-c5: p=0.125). Along the horizontal axis we give the number of flips, and along the vertical axis the fraction of problems solved for different values of N.

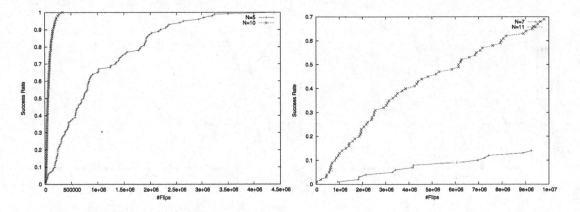

needs some time to reach the first local optimum which possibly could be a feasible solution. The value of the distance between the minimum and the maximum number of search steps needed for finding a feasible solution increases with the hardness of the problem.

Finally, the plots in Figure 9 and Figure 10 report the results for morphed graphs. First of all,

RW was again unable to solve a single morphed graph within the required number of steps. As can be seen from these two figures, there exists a rather small variability between the different runs when applied to problems with a morphing ratio $p \geq 0.25$. For a lower value of p such as the problem sw100-8-1p3-c5, this difference becomes much more obvious. We observe for this particu-

Figure 11. LARW Vs RW - (Left) percentage excess over the solution for a 500-variable morphed graph coloring problem with 3100 clauses (sw100-8-lp4-c5: $p=2.10^{-4}$). (Right) percentage excess for a 500-variable morphed graph coloring problem with 3100 clauses (sw100-8-1p5-c5: $p=2.10^{-5}$). Along the horizontal axis we give the number of trials and along the vertical axis the percentage excess over the solution.

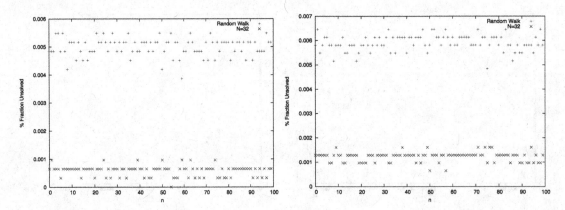

Figure 12. LARW Vs RW - (Left) percentage excess over the solution for a 500-variable morphed graph coloring problem with 3100 clauses (sw100-8-1p6-c5: p=2.10⁻⁶). (Right) percentage excess for a 500-variable morphed graph coloring problem with 3100 clauses (sw100-8-1p7-c5: p=2.10⁻⁷). Along the horizontal axis we give the number of trials and along the vertical axis the percentage excess over the solution.

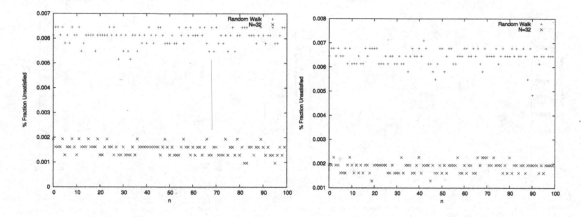

lar example that the distribution has a heavy tail, which indicate that the algorithm gets stuck in local minima for a relatively large number of runs.

4.4 Hard Problems

This section aims at comparing LARW against RW using hard SAT-encoded graph coloring problems where both algorithms have failed to find a solution within the required limit of steps. The two algorithms were executed to the allowed maximal number of steps and the percentage in excess of the solution was recorded. Figure 11, Figure 12 and Figure 13 report the results for SAT morphed graph coloring problems with a morphing ratio lower than *0.125*, while results for large SAT graph coloring problems are depicted in Figures 14 and 15. All the plots support the fact that the

Figure 13. LARW Vs RW - (Left) percentage excess over the solution for a 500-variables morphed graph coloring problem with 3100 clauses (sw100-8-1p8-c5: p=2.10⁻⁸). (Right) percentage excess for a 500-variable morphed graph coloring problem with 3100 clauses (sw100-8-p0-c5: p=0). Along the horizontal axis we give the number of trials and along the vertical axis the percentage excess over the solution.

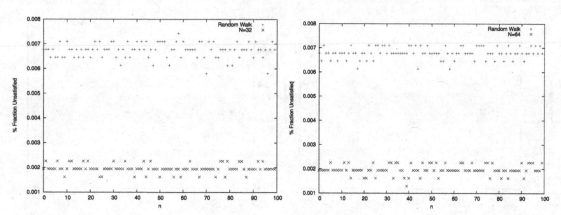

Figure 14. LARW Vs RW - (Left) percentage excess over the solution for a 2125-variable large SAT graph coloring problem with 70163 clauses (g125.18.cnf). (Right) percentage excess for a 2250-variable large SAT graph coloring problem with 70163 clauses (g125.18.cnf). Along the horizontal axis we give the number of trials and along the vertical axis the percentage excess over the solution.

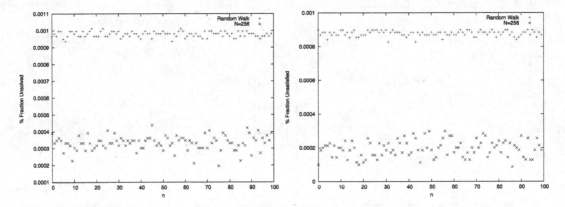

performance of LARW surpasses that of RW. The convergence behavior is quite conclusive. LARW appears to have a better asymptotic convergence up to *0.3%* compared to RW which can reaches up *0.8%*.

4.5 Mean Search Cost

In order to give an impression of variability of the hardness of the problem in- stances, we focus

on the behavior of the mean search cost for two algorithms. For each instance, the median search cost (i.e., mean number of local search steps) is measured and we analyze the distribution of the mean search cost over the instances. The curves shown on the different plots show the cumulative hardness distributions produced by *100* trials on *100* instances from a test set.

Several observations can be made from the plots in Figure 16, and Figure 17, which show

Figure 15. LARW Vs RW: (Left) percentage excess over the solution for a 3750-variable large SAT graph coloring problem with 233965 clauses (g250.15.cnf). (Right) percentage excess for a 7250-variable large SAT graph coloring problem with 454622 clauses (g250.29.cnf). Along the horizontal axis we give the number of trials and along the vertical axis the percentage excess over the solution.

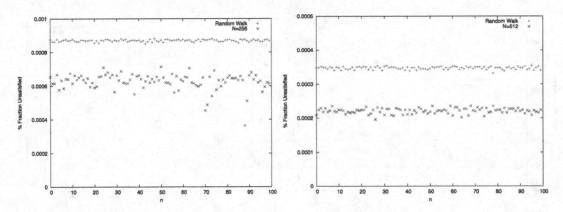

Figure 16. (Left) Hardness distribution across test-set flat100-239 (300 variables - 1117 clauses). (Right) Hardness distribution across test-set flat200-479 (600 variables - 2273 clauses). Along the horizontal axis we give the median number of flips per solution, and along the vertical axis the fraction of problems solved.

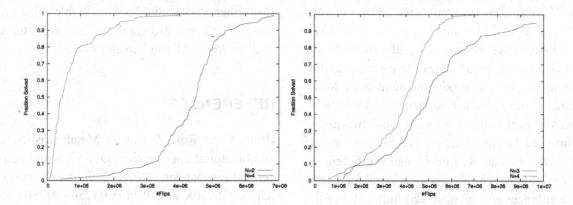

the hardness distributions of the two algorithms for SAT-encoded graph coloring problem instances. First of all, there exist no cross-overs in the plots of both figures which make LARW the clear winner. The RW shows a higher variability in search cost compared to LARW between the instances of each test set. The distributions of the two algorithms confirm the existence of instances which are harder to solve than others. In particular, as can be seen from the long tails of these distributions, a substantial part of problem

instances are dramatically harder to solve with RW than with LARW. The harder the instance, the more significant the difference between the average searches costs of two algorithms (a factor of approximately up to 50).

In brief, the LA mechanism employed in LARW arguably offers an efficient way to escape from highly attractive areas in the search space of hard instances leading to a higher probability success as well as reducing the average number of local search steps to find a solution. Overall,

Figure 17. (Left) Hardness distribution across test-set sw-8-4 (500 variables - 3100 clauses). (Right) Hardness distribution across test-set sw100-8-8 (500 variables - 3100 clauses). Along the horizontal axis we give the median number of flips per solution, and along the vertical axis the fraction of problems solved.

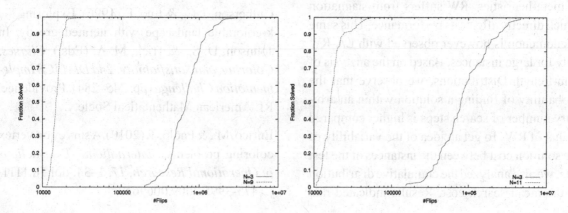

the empirical hardness distribution of SAT-encoded graph coloring problems in the respective figures show that it was rather easy for both algorithms to find a feasible solution in each trial, with LARW showing on average a lower search cost within a given probability compared to RW. For LARW, we observe a small variability in search cost indicated by the distance between the minimum and the maximum number of local search steps needed to find a solution. The differences in performance between these two algorithms can be characterized by a factor of about 10 in the median. The performance differences observed between the two algorithms for small size instances are still observed and very significant for medium size instances. This suggests that the LA mechanism of LARW is more effective for larger instances.

5. CONCLUSION

In this work, we have introduced a new approach based on combining learning automata (LA) with random walk (RW) for the graph coloring problem. Thus, in order to get a comprehensive picture of the new algorithm's performance, we used a set of problems of randomly generated SAT-encoded graph coloring instances. All the selected problem instances are located in the phase transition and have been widely used by different authors in the context of evaluating the performance of meta-heuristics. RW suffers from stagnation which directly affects its performance. This same phenomenon is however observed with LA-RW only for large instances. Based on the analysis of Run-Length-Distributions, we observe that the probability of finding a solution within an arbitrary number of search steps is higher compared to that of RW. To get an idea of the variability of the solution cost between the instances of the test sets, we also analyzed the cumulative distribution of the mean search cost. Results indicated that

the harder the instance, the higher the difference between the mean search costs of the two algorithms. The difference can be several orders of magnitude in favor of LARW. An obvious subject for further work would be the possible enhancement of SAT-encoded graph coloring algorithms such as WalkSAT and Novelty using LA.

REFERENCES

Blum, C., & Roli, A. (2003). Metaheuristics in combinatorial optimization: Overview and conceptual comparison. *ACM Computing Surveys*, *35*(3), 268–308. doi:10.1145/937503.937505

Brelaz, D. (1979). New methods to color the vertices of a graph. *Communications of the ACM*, *22*(4), 251–256. doi:10.1145/359094.359101

Brown, J. (1972). Chromatic scheduling and the chromatic number problem. *Management Science*, *19*(4), 456–463. doi:10.1287/mnsc.19.4.456

Chiarandini, M., Dumitrescu, I., & Sttzle, T. (2007). Stochastic local search algorithms for the graph colouring problem. In Gonzalez, T. F. (Ed.), *Handbook of Approximation Algorithms and Metaheuristics*. London: Chapman and Hall/CRC.

Cook, S. A. (1971). The complexity of theorem-proving procedures. In *Proceedings of the Third ACM Symposium on Theory of Computing* (pp. 151-158).

Culberson, J. C., & Luo, F. (1996). Exploring the k-colorable landscape with iterated greedy. In Johnson, D. S., & Trick, M. A. (Eds.), *Cliques, Coloring, and Satisfiability: 2nd DIMACS Implementation Challenge* (pp. 245–284). Providence, RI: American Mathematical Society.

Enrico, M., & Paolo, T. (2010). A survey on vertex coloring problems. *International Transactions in Operational Research*, *17*, 1–34. doi:10.1111/j.1475-3995.2009.00696.x

Funabiki, N., & Higashino, T. (2000). A minimal state processing search algorithm for graph coloring problems. *IEICE Transactions Fundamentals E, 83-A*(7), 1420–1430.

Gale, W., Das, S., & Yu, C. T. (1990). Improvements to an Algorithm for Equipartitioning. *IEEE Transactions on Computers, 39*(5), 706–710. doi:10.1109/12.53585

Galinier, P., & Hao, J. K. (1999). Hybrid evolutionary algorithms for graph coloring. *Journal of Combinatorial Optimization, 3*(4), 379–397. doi:10.1023/A:1009823419804

Galinier, P., & Hertz, A. (2006). A survey of local search methods for graph coloring. *Computers & Operations Research, 33*, 2547–2562. doi:10.1016/j.cor.2005.07.028

Galinier, P., Hertz, A., & Zufferey, N. (2008). An adaptive memory algorithm for the k-coloring problem. *Discrete Applied Mathematics, 156*, 267–279. doi:10.1016/j.dam.2006.07.017

Gent, L. P., & Walsh, T. (1993). Towards an Understanding of Hill-Climbing Procedures for SAT. In *Proceedings of AAAI, 93*, 28–33. Cambridge, MA: MIT Press.

Gent, L. P., & Walsh, T. (1995). Unsatisfied Variables in Local Search. In Hallam, J. (Ed.), *Hybrid Problems, Hybrid Solutions* (pp. 73–85). Amsterdam: IOS Press.

Glover, F. (1989). Tabu Search - Part 1. *ORSA Journal on Computing, 1*(3), 190–206.

Granmo, O.-C., & Bouhmala, N. (2007). Solving the Satisfiability Problem Using Finite Learning Automata. *International Journal of Computer Science and Applications, 4*(3), 15–29.

Granmo, O.-C., & Oommen, B. J. (2010). Solving Stochastic Nonlinear Resource Allocation Problems Using a Hierarchy of Twofold Resource Allocation Automata. *IEEE Transactions on Computers, 59*(4), 545–560. doi:10.1109/TC.2009.189

Granmo, O.-C., Oommen, B. J., Myrer, S. A., & Olsen, M. G. (2007). Learning Automata-Based Solutions to the Nonlinear Fractional Knapsack Problem with Applications to Optimal Resource Allocation. *IEEE Transactions on Systems, Man and Cybernetics, SMC-37(B)*, 166-175.

Hansen, P., Labbe, M., & Schindl, D. (2005). *Set covering and packing formulations of graph coloring: algorithms and first polyhedral results* (Tech. Rep. No. G-2005-76). GERARD, Universite de Montreal, Quebec, Canada.

Hertz, A., & de Werra, D. (1987). Using tabu search techniques for graph coloring. *Computing, 39*, 345–351. doi:10.1007/BF02239976

Hertz, A., Plumettaz, M., & Zufferey, N. (2008). Variable space search for graph coloring. *Discrete Applied Mathematics, 156*, 2551–2560. doi:10.1016/j.dam.2008.03.022

Hoos, H. (2002). An adaptive noise mechanism for Walk-SAT. In *Proceedings of the Eighteenth National Conference in Artificial Intelligence* (pp. 655-660).

Hutter, F., Tompkins, D., & Hoos, H. (2002). Scaling and probabilistic smoothing: Efficient dynamic local search for SAT. In *Proceedings of the Eight International Conference of the Principles and Practice of Constraint Programming* (pp. 233-248).

Ishtaiwi, A., Thornton, J., Sattar, A., & Pham, D. N. (2005). Neighborhood clause weight redistribution in local search for SAT. In *Proceedings of the Eleventh International Conference on Principles and Practice Programming* (LNCS 3709, pp. 772-776).

Johnson, D. E., Aragon, C. R., McGeoch, L. A., & Schevon, C. (1991). Optimization by simulated annealing: an experimental evaluation; Part II, graph coloring and number partitioning. *Operations Research, 39*, 378–406. doi:10.1287/opre.39.3.378

Johnson, D. S., Mehrotra, A., & Trick, M. A. (2008). Special issue on computational methods for graph coloring and its generalizations. *Discrete Applied Mathematics, 156*(2), 145–146. doi:10.1016/j.dam.2007.10.007

Karp, R. (1972). Reducibility among combinatorial problems. In Miller, R. E., & Thatcher, J. W. (Eds.), *Complexity of computer computations* (pp. 85–103). New York: Plenum Press.

KhudaBukhsh. A. R., Xu, L., Hoos, H., & Leyton-Brown, K. (2009). SATenstein: Automatically Building Local Search SAT Solvers from Components. In *Proceedings of the 25th International Joint Conference on Artificial Intelligence (IJCAI-09)*.

Leighton, F. T. (1979). A graph coloring algorithm for large scheduling problems. *Journal of Research of the National Bureau of Standards, 84*(6), 489–503.

Li, C. M., & Huang, W. Q. (2005). Diversification and determinism in local search for satisfiability. In *Proceedings of the Eight International Conference on Theory and Applications of Satisfiability Testing (SAT-05)* (LNCS 3569, pp. 158-172).

Li, C. M., Wei, W., & Zhang, H. (2007). Combining adaptive noise and look-ahead in local search for SAT. In *Proceedings of the Tenth International Conference on Theory and Applications of Satisfiability Testing* (LNCS 4501).

Li, C. M., Wei, W., & Zhang, H. (2007). Combining adaptive noise and look-ahead in local search for SAT. In *Proceedings of the Tenth International Conference on Theory and Applications of Satisfiability Testing (SAT-07)* (LNCS 4501, pp. 121-133).

Malaguti, E., & Toth, P. (2010). A survey on vertex coloring problems. *International Transactions in Operational Research, 17*(1), 1–34. doi:10.1111/j.1475-3995.2009.00696.x

McAllester, D., Selman, B., & Kautz, H. (1997). Evidence for Invariants in Local Search. In *Proceedings of AAAI, 97*, 321–326. Cambridge, MA: MIT Press.

Mendez-Diaz, I., & Zabala, P. (2008). A cutting plane algorithm for graph coloring. *Discrete Applied Mathematics, 156*, 159–179. doi:10.1016/j.dam.2006.07.010

Narendra, K. S., & Thathachar, M. A. L. (1989). *Learning Automata: An Introduction*. Upper Saddle River, NJ: Prentice Hall.

Oommen, B. J., & Hansen, E. R. (1987). List organizing strategies using stochastic move-to-front and stochastic move-to-rear operations. *SIAM Journal on Computing, 16*, 705–716. doi:10.1137/0216047

Oommen, B. J., & Ma, D. C. Y. (1988). Deterministic Learning Automata Solutions to the Equipartitioning Problem. *IEEE Transactions on Computers, 37*(1), 2–13. doi:10.1109/12.75146

Oommen, B. J., Misra, S., & Granmo, O.-C. (2007). Routing Bandwidth Guaranteed Paths in MPLS Traffic Engineering: A Multiple Race Track Learning Approach. *IEEE Transactions on Computers, 56*(7), 959–976. doi:10.1109/TC.2007.1045

Oommen, B. J., & St. Croix, E. V. (1996). Graph partitioning using learning automata. *IEEE Transactions on Computers, 45*(2), 195–208. doi:10.1109/12.485372

Patterson, D. J., & Kautz, H. (2001). Auto-Walksat: A Self-Tuning Implementation of Walk-sat. *Electronic Notes in Discrete Mathematics, 9*.

Prestwich, S. (2004). Local Search on SAT-encoded Colouring Problems. In *Theory and Applications of Satisfiability Testing* (LNCS 2919, pp. 105-119).

Prestwich, S. (2005). Random walk with continuously smoothed variable weights. In *Proceedings of the Eight International Conference on Theory and Applications of Satisfiability Testing (SAT-05)* (LNCS 3569, pp. 203-215).

Schuurmans, D., & Southey, F. (2000). Local search characteristics of incomplete SAT procedures. In *Proceedings, AAAI-2000*, 297–302. Menlo Park, CA: AAAI Press.

Schuurmans, D., Southey, F., & Holte, R. C. (2001). The exponentiated sub-gradient algorithm for heuristic Boolean programming. In *Proceedings, IJCAI-01*, 334–341. San Francisco, CA: Morgan Kaufman Publishers.

Selman, B., Kautz, H. A., & Cohen, B. (1994). Noise Strategies for Improving Local Search. In *Proceedings of AAAI*, 94, 337–343. Cambridge, MA: MIT Press.

Selman, B., & Kautz, K. A. (1993). Domain-Independent extensions to GSAT: Solving large structured satisfiability problems. In R. Bajcsy (Ed.), *Proceedings of the international Joint Conference on Artificial Intelligence* (Vol. 1, pp. 290-295). San Francisco, CA: Morgan Kaufmann Publishers Inc.

Selman, B., Levesque, H., & Mitchell, D. (1992). A New Method for Solving Hard Satisfiability Problems. In *Proceedings of AAA*, 92, 440–446. Cambridge, MA: MIT Press.

Swell, E. C. (1996). An improved algorithm for exact graph coloring. In Johnson, D. S., & Trick, M. A. (Eds.), *Cliques, Coloring, and Satisfiability: 2nd DIMACS Implementation Challenge* (pp. 359–373). Providence, RI: American Mathematical society.

Thathachar, M. A. L., & Sastry, P. S. (2004). *Network of Learning Automata: Techniques for On line Stochastic Optimization*. Dordrecht, The Netherlands: Kluwer Academic Publishers.

Thornton, J., Pham, D. N., Bain, S., & Ferreira, V., Jr. (2004). Additive versus multiplicative clause weighting for SAT. In *Proceedings of the Nineteenth National Conference of Artificial Intelligence* (pp. 191-196).

Tsetlin, M. L. (1973). *Automaton Theory and Modeling of Biological Systems*. New York: Academic Press.

Wu, Z., & Wah, B. (2000). An efficient global-search strategy in discrete Lagrangian methods for solving hard satisfiability problems. In *Proceedings of the Seventeenth National Conference on Artificial Intelligence* (pp. 310-315).

Xu, L., Hutter, F., Hoos, H., & Leyton-Brown, K. (2008). SATzilla: Portfolio-based Algorithm Selection for SAT. *Journal of Artificial Intelligence Research, 32*, 565–606.

This work was previously published in International Journal of Applied Metaheuristic Computing, Volume 1, Issue 3, edited by Peng-Yeng Yin, pp. 1-19, copyright 2010 by IGI Publishing (an imprint of IGI Global).

Chapter 18
Page Number and Graph Treewidth

Li Xianglu
Zhongyuan University of Technology, China

ABSTRACT

Book-embedding of graph G involves embedding its vertices along the spine of the book and assigning its edges to pages of the book such that no two edges cross on the same page. The pagenumber of G is the minimum number of pages in a book-embedding of G. In this paper, the authors also examine the treewidth TW(G), which is the minimum k such that G is a subgraph of a k-tree. The authors then study the relationship between pagenumber and treewidth. Results show that PN(G)≤TW(G), which proves a conjecture of Ganley and Heath showing that some known upper bounds for the pagenumber can be improved.

INTRODUCTION

The book-embedding problem for graph G is to embed its vertices onto a line along the spine of the book and to draw the edges on pages of the book such that no two edges on the same page cross, and the number of used pages is minimized.

The book-embedding problem has been motivated by several areas of computer science such as VLSL theory, multilayer printed circuit boards (PCB), sorting with parallel stacks and Turning-machine and the design of fault-tolerant processor arrays, etc (e.g., Chung et al., 1987). The DIOGENES approach to fault-tolerant processor arrays, proposed by Rosenberg (1986), is the most famous one. In the DIOGENES approach, the processing elements are laid out in a logical line, and some number of bundles of wires run in parallel with the line. The faulty elements are bypassed, and the fault-free ones are interconnected through the bundles. Here, the bundles work as queues and/ or stacks. If the bundles work as stacks, then the

DOI: 10.4018/978-1-4666-0270-0.ch018

realization of an interconnection network needs a book-embedding of the interconnection network. In this case, the number of pages corresponds to the number of bundles of the DIOGENES stack layout. Therefore, book-embeddings with few pages realize more hardware-efficient DIOGENES stacks layouts.

The book-embedding problem can be stated as a graph-labeling problem as follows. We shall follow the graph-theoretic terminology and notation used by Bondy and Murty (1976) and Golumbic (1980).

Given a simple connected graph $G=(V,E)$ with n vertices, a bijection $f: V \rightarrow \{1, 2, \cdots, n\}$ is called a *labeling* of G by Chung(1988), where $f(v) \in \{1, 2, \cdots, n\}$ represents the label of vertex $v \in V$. Let $u_i = f^{-1}(i)$ be the vertex with label i. Then the labeling f can also be regarded as an ordering $(u_1, u_2, \cdots u_n)$ on a line. For a labeling f, two edges $uv, xy \in E$ are said to be *crossing* if
$f(u) < f(x) < f(v) < f(y)$
or $f(x) < f(u) < f(y) < f(v)$.

With respect to a labeling f, a partition $\mathcal{C} = (E_1, \cdots, E_p)$ of the edge set $E(G)$ is called a *page partition* if no two edges in any subset E_i $(1 \leq i \leq p)$ are crossing. This page partition can be thought of as a coloring of $E(G)$ where the edges in E_i have color i and no two edges of the same color are crossing. Thus, a page partition C represents an assignment of edges of G to pages of the book. We call the minimum number of subsets in a page partition C the page number of G under labeling f, and denote it by $PN(G,f)$. The pagenumber of G is then defined as

$$PN(G) = \min_f PN(G, f)$$

where f is taken over all labelings of G.

Even for a given labeling f, determining the pagenumber $PN(G,f)$ is known to be NP-complete (e.g., Chung et al., 1987). In other words, this is a hard problem in general. So, most researchers now are interested in the polynomially solvable special cases and lower or upper bounds of the pagenumber (e.g., Chung et al., 1987; Ganley & Heath, 2001). Recently, Ganley and Heath (2001) proved that $PN(G) \leq k+1$ if G is a k-tree. In the present paper we present a better result that $PN(G) \leq TW(G)$ for any graph G, where $TW(G)$ stands for the treewidth of G. This upper bound is sharp; and by means of it, we can improve the relations between pagenumber and other graph-theoretic parameters (such as pathwidth, bandwidth, cutwidth). In particular, the result on k-trees can be improved as $PN(G) \leq k$, and thus the conjecture of Ganley and Heath (2001) that every k-tree has a k-page embedding is proved to be true.

1. PRELIMINARIES

Let us recall some definitions and results on chordal graphs and k-trees.

A graph G is called a chordal graph if every cycle of length greater than three has a chord. Here, a chord means an edge joining two nonconsecutive vertices of the cycle. There have been many results on the characterization of chordal graphs in the literature (e.g., Blair & Peyton, 1993; Bodlaender, 1993; Golumbic, 1980; Kloks, 1994). The following is known as the clique-intersection property of chordal graphs, in which the tree T is called the *clique-tree* of G (e.g., Blair & Peyton, 1993; Golumbic, 1980).

Lemma 1. Let $\mathcal{X} = \{X_1, X_2, \cdots, X_m\}$ be the set of all maximal cliques of G. Then G is chordal if and only if there exists a tree T with vertex set $\mathcal{X}$ such that for each vertex v of G, the subgraph of T induced by $\{X \in \mathcal{X} \mid v \in X\}$ is connected and thus is a subtree of T.

The above-mentioned condition can be equivalently stated as: if X_j is lying on the path connecting X_i and X_k in T, then $X_i \cap X_k \subseteq X_j$. This has been uesd to produce the notion of tree-decomposition by Bodlaender (1993), Kloks (1994) and Robertson and Seymour (1986).

The k-trees are special chordal graphs. They can be defined inductively as follows. A complete graph on $k+1$ vertices is a k-tree. If G is a k-tree and $v_1, v_2, \cdots, v_k$ are the vertices of a k-clique in G, then the graph obtained by adding a new vertex v to G together with edges from v to each of $v_1, v_2, \cdots, v_k$ is also a k-tree.

In the clique-tree T of a k-tree G, every vertex (maximal clique) is a $k+1$-clique and two adjacent cliques have exactly k vertices of G in common. For example, a 2-tree G and its clique-tree T (taken from Ganley & Heath, 2001) are shown in Figure 1.

The clique-tree T of a k-tree can be regarded as a rooted tree by choosing a certain vertex as the root and drawing the tree level by level downwards. The notion of rooted trees is widely used by Aho and Hopcroft and Ullman (1976) and Hu(1982) in graph algorithms.

First, we take an end-vertex of the diameter (the longest path) as the root of T (e.g., CDE in Figure 1b). In a rooted tree, the root forms level 0; and all children of the vertices at level i form level $i+1$ ($i=1,2,\cdots$). In a rooted tree, the *depth* of a vertex means the maximum distance for it to its descendants. As a convention, suppose that in the clique-tree T, all children of a vertex are arranged from left to right in a nondecreasing order of their depths (see Figure 1b). So, two siblings have the left-right order. Further, if a vertex u is on the left of a vertex v, then all descendants of u are specified to be on the left of the descendants of v. In this way, any two vertices have the left-right order unless they have the relation of ancestor and descendant. In particular, all leaves are ordered from left to right (regardless of their levels). So we can say the leftmost leaf, the rightmost leaf, and so on. In addition, due to the above convention, the diameter is lying on the right side of T. We may call this the *normal form* of the clique-tree T, which is precisely given in advance.

In this clique-tree T, we can order all vertices in the following way: repeatedly scan the leftmost leaf and then remove it, until reach the root. We call this the *backtrack ordering* of clique-tree T.

Figure 1. A 2-tree and its clique-tree

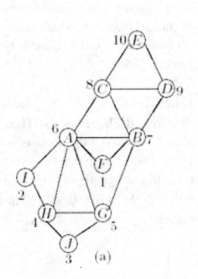

(a)

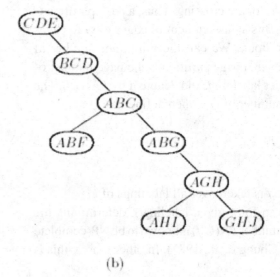

(b)

In fact, this is a reverse order of the depth-first search (e.g., Aho, Hopcroft, & Ullman, 1976; Hu, 1982). For example, in the clique-tree of Figure 1b, the backtrack ordering is *ABF,AHI,GHJ,A GH,ABG,ABC,BCD,CDE*. To avoid confusion, we will call the vertices of T the clique-vertices if necessary.

By means of the backtrack ordering of clique-tree T, we may define the *backtrack labeling* of k-tree G as follows:

1. Pick the leftmost X leaf of T and label the vertex of G which is only contained in X but not in its parent.
2. If X is the root of T, label the remaining vertices, stop.
3. Delete X from T and return to step (1).

The backtrack labeling of the 2-tree G in Figure 1a is shown by the labels $1,2,\cdots 10$ therein. Let $f\colon V \to \{1,2,\cdots,n\}$ be the backtrack labeling of k-tree G. Denote $u_i = f^{(-1)}(i)$, $i=1,2,\cdots,n$. Then this labeling f can be alternatively represented by the sequence $\sigma = (u_1, u_2, \cdots, u_n)$, which is called the *backtrack ordering* of G.

2. THE MAIN RESULTS

We are ready to show the main result.

Theorem 1. For any k-tree G, $PN(G) \leq k$.

Proof. Let T be the clique-tree of k-tree G in normal form and $\sigma = (u_1, u_2, \cdots, u_n)$ the backtrack ordering of G. It suffices to prove that for this ordering there exists a k-page partition of the edge set $E(G)$. As mentioned before, we consider the partition as a k color coloring C such that no two edges of the same color are crossing. Further, a coloring C is said to be *regular* if (i) for each vertex u_j, all edges $u_i u_j (i < j)$ leading

downwards from u_j have the same color, which will be called the color *represented* at u_j; (ii) In each clique-vertex of T, the colors represented at the last k vertices are distinct from each other. We proceed to prove the following

Claim. For the backtrack ordering $\sigma = (u_1, u_2, \cdots, u_n)$ of G, there exists a regular coloring C.

By induction on the order m of the clique-tree T. If $m=2$ namely, G is complete and $k=n-1$, then for each j $(1 \leq j \leq k)$, we may assign color i to the edges $u_i u_j$ with $1 \leq i < j$ and the claim follows. Suppose that the clique-tree T has $m \geq 2$ vertices and the claim holds for clique-trees of smaller order. Let $X = (u_1, u_{i_1}, u_{i_2}, \cdots, u_{i_k})$ be the leftmost leaf of T and Y the parent of X. Then $(u_{i_1}, u_{i_2}, \cdots, u_{i_k}) \subseteq Y$. So we may assume that is the only child of Y. Suppose that $Y = \{u_1, u_{i_1}, u_{i_2}, \cdots u_{i_k}, y\}$ with some vertex y in G. Let $G' = G - u_1$. Then G' is a k-tree with clique-tree $T' = T - X$ and T' is still in normal form. Moreover, $\sigma' = (u_2, u_3, \cdots, u_n)$ is the backtrack ordering of G'. Since T' has order $m-1$, it follows from the inductive hypothesis that there exists a regular coloring C' for the ordering σ' of G'. Note that u_1 is only adjacent to $u_{i_1}, u_{i_2}, \cdots, u_{i_k}$ in G. To obtain a coloring C for σ of G, we need only assign the color represented at u_{i_l} to the edge $u_1 u_{i_l} (l = 1, 2, \cdots k)$. Then, we can show that coloring C determines a page partition, namely, no two edges of the same color are crossing. Indeed, suppose that this is not the case. Then there would be an edge $u_p u_q$ crossing a mew edge $u_1 u_{i_l} (i < p < i_l < q)$ with the same color. Note that in the backtract labeling algorithm of G, the vertices in Y cannot be labeled before all vertices in the descendants (clique) of Y have been labeled. Let Ω be the set of vertices of G contained in Y and descendants of Y. In other words, Ω is the union of all clique-vertices of the subtree of T rooted at Y. By $p < i_l$ $(1 \leq l \leq k)$, we see that u_p is ordered before $u_{i_l} \in Y$ according to the σ of G. So we have $u_p \in \Omega$. Also, by $u_p u_q \in E(G)$, we see that u_q belongs to the clique-vertex of T which is eliminated when u_p is labeled. So, $u_q \in \Omega$. Further, since $i_l < q$, it follows that $u_q \in Y$. By the regularity of $\mathcal{C}^l$, the colors represented at u_{i_l} and u_q are different, and so $u_1 u_{i_l}$ and $u_p u_q$ are of different colors, which contradicts the assumption. In addition, by noting the color assignment for the edges incident to u_1, we can conclude that C is regular. Thus the claim is proved and the theorem follows.

This theorem shows the existence of regular colorings. So we have the following coloring (page-partition) algorithm.

Let $\sigma = (u_1, u_2, u_3, \cdots, u_n)$ be a backtrack ordering of the k-tree G. Denote by $c(u_i u_j) \in \{1, 2, \cdots k\}$ the color assigned to edge $u_i u_j$.

First, set $c(u_i u_j) = 1$ for all edges $u_i u_n \in E$. The color 1 is represented at vertex u_n. For $j < n$, a color c is said to be *forbidden* to u_j if c is represented at a vertex u_l with $l > j$ and there exist edges $u_h u_l$ and $u_i u_j$ being crossing $(i < h < j < l)$. Then we assign the color

$$c(u_i u_j) =$$
$$\min\{c \in \{1, 2, \cdots, k\} \mid c \text{ is not forbidden to } u_j\}$$

to all edges $u_i u_j \in E (i < j)$. This color is represented at u_j. This procedure is carried out until $j=2$.

For example, a 2-page partition of the 2-tree of Figure 1 is shown in Figure 2.

The result of Theorem 1 can be generalized to a general graph G.

There are several equivalent definitions of treewidth in the literature (e.g., Bodlaender, 1993; Kloks, 1994; Robertson & Seymour, 1986). For our purpose, the following suffices. The treewidth $TW(G)$ of graph G is the minimum integer k such that G is a subgraph of a k-tree.

Theorem 2. For any graph G, $PN(G) \leq TW(G)$.
Proof. Suppose that $TW(G) = k$. It follows from definition that there is a k-tree H such that G is a subgraph of H. Then, by Theorem 1, $PN(G) \leq PN(H) \leq k = TW(G)$. Thus the result follows.

The upper bound in this theorem is best possible, since the equality holds for trees (with treewidth 1) and series-parallel graphs (with treewidth 2).

Let $\omega(G)$ denote the clique size of G, i.e., the cardinality of a maximum clique of G. It is easy to see that a k-tree has clique size $\omega(G) = k + 1$. And for any chordal graph G, $TW(G) = \omega(G) - 1$.

Figure 2. A 2-page embedding of the 2-tree of Figure 1

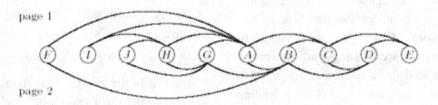

Hence we have the following consequence (the lower bound is due to the result for complete graphs).

Corollary 3. For chordal graph G, $\left\lfloor \frac{1}{2}\omega(G) \right\rfloor \leq PN(G) \leq \omega(G) - 1$.

In particular, for a k - tree, $\left\lfloor \frac{1}{2}(k+1) \right\rfloor \leq PN(G) \leq k$.

A perfect elimination ordering of a chordal graph can be found in linear time (e.g., Blair & Peyton, 1993; Golumbic, 1980). Hence, the treewidth of a chordal graph can be determined in quadratic time. Invoking Corollary 3, we conclude that a 2-approximation of the pagenumber of a chordal graph can be computed in quadratic time.

All these results reduce the corresponding upper bounds proposed by Ganley and Heath (2001) by one. And thus the conjecture of Ganley and Heath that every k-tree has a k-page book embedding is proved to be true.

CONCLUSION

The relation between pagenumber and treewidth is investigate in this paper, we show that $PN(G) \leq TW(G)$, this proves a conjecture of Ganley and Heath.

The pagenumber and the treewidth would have deeper relations in algorithmic aspects. A number of combinatorial optimization problems, including those formulated in monadic second order logic (e.g., Bodlaender, 1994; Courcelle, 1994), have been proved to be polynomial solvable for graphs with bounded treewidth. It is interesting to know whether the pagenumber problem has this property.

ACKNOWLEDGMENT

The present research work has been supported by Natural Science Foundation of Henan Province (No. 0411011400). The author would also like to thank the referees for their helpful comments on improving the representation of the paper.

REFERENCES

Aho, A. V., Hopcroft, J. E., & Ullman, J. D. (1976). *The Design and Analysis of Computer Algorithms.* Reading, MA: Addison-Wesley.

Blair, J. R. S., & Peyton, B. (1993). An introduction to chordal graphs and clique trees . In George, A., Glibert, J. R., & Liu, J. W. H. (Eds.), *Graph Theory and Sparse Matrix Computation* (pp. 1–29). New York: Springer Verlag.

Bodlaender, H. L. (1993). A tourist guide through treewidth. *Acta Cybernetica, 11,* 1–21.

Bodlaender, H. L. (1994). Improved self-reduction algorithms for graphs with bounded treewidth. *Discrete Applied Mathematics, 54,* 101–105. doi:10.1016/0166-218X(94)90018-3

Bondy, J. A., & Murty, U. S. R. (1976). *Graph Theory with Applications.* New York: Elsevier.

Chung, F. R. K. (1988). Labelings of graphs . In Beineke, L. W., & Wilson, R. J. (Eds.), *Selected Topics in Graph Theory* (*Vol. 3,* pp. 151–168).

Chung, F. R. K., Leighton, F. T., & Rosenberg, A. L. (1987). Embedding graphs in books: a layout problem with applications to VLSI design. *SIAM J. Algebraic Disc. Meth., 8,* 33–58. doi:10.1137/0608002

Courcelle, B. (1994). The monadic second order logic of graph VI: On several representations of graphs by relational structures. *Discrete Applied Mathematics, 54,* 117–149. doi:10.1016/0166-218X(94)90019-1

Ganley, J. L., & Heath, L. S. (2001). The pagenumber of k-trees is O(k). *Discrete Applied Mathematics*, *109*, 215–221. doi:10.1016/S0166-218X(00)00178-5

Golumbic, M. C. (1980). *Algorithmic Graph Theory and Perfect Graphs*. New York: Academic Press.

Hu, T. C. (1982). *Combinatorial Algorithms*. New York: Addison-Wesley.

Kloks, T. (1994). *Treewidth (LNCS)*. Berlin: Springer Verlag. doi:10.1007/BFb0045375

Robertson, N., & Seymour, P. D. (1986). Graph minors II: Algorithmic aspects of tree-width. *Journal of Algorithms*, *7*, 309–322. doi:10.1016/0196-6774(86)90023-4

Rosenberg, A. (1986). DIOGENES. In *Proceedings of the Aegean Workshop on Computing VLSI Algorithms and Architectures*, Loutraki, Greece (LNCS 227, pp. 96-107). Berlin: Springer.

This work was previously published in International Journal of Applied Metaheuristic Computing, Volume 1, Issue 3, edited by Peng-Yeng Yin, pp. 53-58, copyright 2010 by IGI Publishing (an imprint of IGI Global).

Chapter 19
The Analysis of Zero Inventory Drift Variants Based on Simple and General Order–Up–To Policies

Jianing He
South China Normal University, China

Haibo Wang
Texas A&M International University, USA

ABSTRACT

In this paper, simple and general Order-Up-To (OUT) models with Minimum Mean Square Error (MMSE) forecast for the AR(1) demand pattern are introduced in the control engineering perspective. Important insights about lead-time misidentification are derived from the analysis of variance discrepancy. By applying the Final Value Theorem (FVI), a final value offset (i.e., inventory drift) is proved to exist and can be measured even though the actual lead-time is known. In this regard, to eliminate the inherent offset and keep the system variances acceptable, two kinds of zero inventory drift variants based on the general OUT model are presented. The analysis of variance amplification suggests lead-times should always be estimated conservatively in variant models. The stability conditions for zero inventory drift variants are evaluated in succession and some valuable attributes of the new variants are illustrated via spreadsheet simulation under the assumption that lead-time misidentification is inevitable.

INTRODUCTION

The use of control engineering approaches to solve production and inventory problems has been well studied. Simon (1952) initiated this research stream using Laplace-transform in con-tinuous time scale. This approach was quickly translated into the newly favored z-transform because of the discrete nature of the practical problems. Many researchers, especially the professors from Linköping University and Cardiff University, tried to improve it thereafter. Coyle (1977) presented the Inventory and Order Based

DOI: 10.4018/978-1-4666-0270-0.ch019

Production Control System (IOBPCS) model, which laid the foundation of a generic family of production control systems. Disney and Towill (2005) reviewed the IOBPCS family of decision support systems. To formalize the decision making process by utilizing simple and robust algorithms, Sterman (1989) suggested that a decision making model should allow suitable consideration of the pipeline to lead to stable dynamic behavior. This approach is known as Automatic Pipeline, Variable Inventory and Order Based Production Control System (APVIOBPCS), which was examined by John et al. (1994) via mathematical and simulation analysis. The equivalence of APVIOBPCS model and Oder-Up-To (OUT) policy was subsequently established by Dejonckheere et al. (2003), who also proposed general OUT rule to decrease the bullwhip effect and to generate smoothing orders.

All the policies mentioned before are under the assumption of having accurate estimates of the production and delivery lead-times. It's readily shown that systems would suffer from inventory drift if the lead-time is misidentified (John et al., 1994). Inventory drift is used to describe the phenomena that inventory levels do not lock on target levels over time when a step change in the consumption rate has occurred (Disney & Towill, 2005). It affects the net stock level and thus definitely changes system dynamic. The most effective solution is monitoring actual lead-times continuously. However, this requires significant amount of management effort, and that no theoretical support on the stability.

2. LITERATURE REVIEW

After searching papers concerning inventory drift, much fewer were found than we expected. Two seminal papers, written by John et al. (1994) and Disney and Towill (2005) respectively, both worked on APVIOBPCS model or OUT policy with independent and identically distributed (i.i.d.) demand and exponential smoothing forecasting.

John et al. (1994) first examined the existence of inventory drift using the Final Value Theorem (FVT) when the lead-time estimation was not accurate. Then Disney and Towill (2005) presented a novel Estimated Pipeline Variable Inventory and Order Based Production Control System (EPVIOBPS) to eliminate the inventory drift instead of monitoring actual lead-times continuously. When facing different demand patterns or using different forecasting methods, sometimes the inventory deficit is inherent even though the accurate lead-time is known. Is the solution presented still effective? No clear answer has been found so far based on the literature. However, we prove the solution presented by Disney and Towill (2005) is not suitable for OUT policy with Minimum Mean Square Error (MMSE) forecast, which will be explained later in this article.

An outstanding order policy not just has zero inventory drift. As stated by Disney et al. (2006), inventory managers must balance two primary factors on making replenishments. One is the order variability measured by the bullwhip effect (i.e., the ratio of the variance of orders over the variance of demand). The other is the variance of the net stock measured by the net stock amplification (i.e., the ratio of net stock variance over the variance of demand). Trying to dampen the bullwhip effect may have a negative impact on net stock amplification and vice versa (Disney et al., 2006).

So the task of this paper is to analyze and design better replenishment policies, which concern factors in every respect. On one hand, new order policy should not arouse inventory drift and still keep the system stable. On the other hand, both variance amplifications from new order policy should be kept in an acceptable range, although it may never be totally avoided. In the ensuing paragraphs, we analyze the widely used OUT policy and point out its shortcomings. Then we present the new zero inventory drift model and report the simulation results compared to simple OUT policy. Finally, the paper concludes with a summary and a look ahead to future research.

Figure 1. Block diagram of the AR(1) demand generator

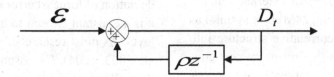

3. REPLENISHMENT POLICIES

We consider a single-stage supply chain including one retailer and one manufacturer. The sequence of events is assumed as follows: (1) incoming shipments from the upstream manufacturer are received and placed to the inventory; (2) incoming demands are observed and either filled or back-logged; and (3) the retailer places orders to the manufacturer based on the new inventory level. The first order Auto-Regressive (AR(1)) demand pattern is assumed and the demand D_t faced by the retailer in period t is shown in equation (1) (see Figure 1 for the block diagram).

$$D_t = \mu + \rho(D_{t-1} - \mu) + \varepsilon_t \qquad (1)$$

where μ is the mean of demand, ε_t is an i.i.d. normally distributed random error, and ρ is the first-order autocorrelation coefficient which is subjected to $|\rho| \prec 1$. When $\rho = 0$, the AR(1) pro-

cess will simplify to i.i.d. normally distributed demand pattern. According to block diagram Figure 2, the transfer function of AR(1) is obtained by using z-transform technique as follows.

$$\frac{D_t}{\varepsilon_t} = \frac{z}{z - \rho} \qquad (2)$$

It is common in the literature that assumes Exponential Smoothing (ES) or Moving Average (MA) forecasting method even though an AR(1) demand process is confronted (e.g., Xu et al., 2001; Kim & Ryan, 2003). It seems reasonable that ES and MA are widely used in the real business world for their ease of use, flexibility, and robustness in dealing with non-linear demand processes (Silver et al., 2000). However, they can lead to specification error for pre-specified demand processes (Badinelli, 1990). Zhang (2004) studies the role of forecasting in relation to the bullwhip effect. The Minimum Mean Square Error (MMSE)

Figure 2. Block diagram for simple OUT policy with MMSE forecast

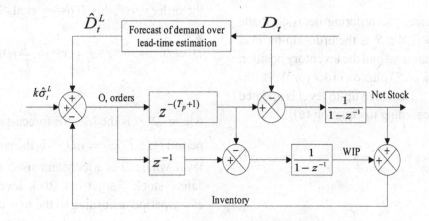

forecasting is the winner among the three methods including ES and MA. When external demand subjects to AR(1) process, MMSE is optimal as it explicitly takes the correlative structure into account and minimizes the inventory cost concerned (Zhang, 2004). The estimates of τ-period-ahead AR(1) demand and total lead-time demand forecasted by MMSE are given in equations (3)-(4).

$$\hat{D}_{t+\tau} = \mu + \rho^{\tau}(D_t - \mu) \tag{3}$$

$$\hat{D}_t^L = \sum_{\tau=1}^{L} \hat{D}_{t+\tau} = L\mu + \frac{\rho - \rho^{L+1}}{1-\rho}(D_t - \mu) \tag{4}$$

The total lead-time includes not just the physical production/distribution delay T_p, but also a nominal delay of events—the review period (+1). Thus, the total lead-time $L = T_p + 1$.

3.1 Simple OUT Policy

This paper assumes simple OUT replenishment policy as most related research dose (Sterman, 1989; John et al., 1994; Dejonckheere et al., 2003). The formation of simple OUT is given in equation (5).

$$O_t = S_t - inventory_t = S_t - WIP_t - NS_t \tag{5}$$

where O_t indicates the ordering decision made at the end of period t, S_t is the order-up-to level used in replenishments and the inventory position equals net stock (NS_t) plus on order (or Work-In-Progress, WIP_t). The order-up-to level is updated every period according to equation (6).

$$S_t = \hat{D}_t^L + k\hat{\sigma}_t^L \tag{6}$$

where $\hat{\sigma}_t^L$ indicates the estimate of the standard deviation of forecast error in total lead-time, and k is a constant chosen to meet a desired service level. As most researchers do (Dejonckheere et al., 2003, 2004), k is assumed to be 0. Applying the well-established techniques for block diagram (see Figure 2) reduction, we obtain the following transfer functions for simple OUT policy with MMSE forecast.

$$\frac{O_t}{D_t} = 1 + \frac{\rho(1-\rho^{T_p+1})(z-1)}{(1-\rho)z} \tag{7}$$

$$\frac{NS_t}{D_t} =$$
$$\frac{z^{-(T_p+1)}[\rho + \rho^{T_p+2}(z-1) - \rho \cdot z^{T_p+2} + z(z^{T_p+1}-1)]}{(\rho-1)(z-1)} \tag{8}$$

3.2 General OUT Policy

We state a special case of APVIOBPCS, which emphasizes the system stability by setting the smoothing parameters or the controllers of net stock and WIP loop to be equal (Deziel & Eilon, 1967). Dejonckheere et al. (2004) proved the equivalence of APVIOBPCS and general OUT (Dejonckheere et al., 2003), which is given in equation (9) and is well-known for its highly desirable ability to keep system robust and reduce the order variability (Disney et al., 2006).

$$O_t = \hat{D}_{t+L} + \frac{1}{T_n}(TNS_t - NS_t) + \frac{1}{T_n}(DWIP_t - WIP_t) \tag{9}$$

where $\hat{D}_{t+L}$ is the MMSE forecast of demand in period $t+L$. $TNS_t = a\hat{D}_{t+L}$ is the target net stock level where a is a constant used to adjust the safety stock. Target net stock level is updated every period according to the new demand forecast. $DWIP_t' = \sum_{i=1}^{T_p} \hat{D}_{t+i}$ is the desired WIP level, which is updated every period as well. T_n is the smoothing parameter or controller of the decision rule.

The policy indicated in equation (9) can be described as "ordering quantities are set equal to the sum of forecasted demand, an equal fraction of the discrepancy of finished goods net stock and on-order position discrepancy". The corresponding block diagram is given in Figure 3. Apparently the simple OUT is a special case of the general OUT when $a=0$ and $T_n = T_w = 1$. The key difference is that net stock and WIP discrepancies are included only fractionally in the latter.

4. THE SHORTCOMINGS OF REPLENISHMENT POLICIES

4.1 Lead-Time Misidentification

Since continuous monitoring is far away from easy, it is crucial to understand how misidentification of lead-time will affect the system performance in the form of variance amplification. If we replace the actual T_p by the misidentification T_p' in the estimation of order-up-to level (see

Figure 2), then the transfer functions turn to equation (9) and (10) correspondingly.

$$\frac{O_t'}{D_t} = 1 + \frac{\rho(1 - \rho^{T_p'+1})(z-1)}{(1-\rho)z} \tag{10}$$

$$\frac{NS_t'}{D_t} = $$
$$\frac{z^{-(T_p'+1)}[\rho + \rho^{T_p'+2}(z-1) - \rho \cdot z^{T_p'+2} + z(z^{T_p'+1} - 1)]}{(\rho-1)(z-1)} \tag{11}$$

Please note that the misidentification of lead-time doesn't affect the actual lag in production and delivery. So the actual delay T_p still exists in the recursion of net stock and WIP. We set $T_p = 3$ throughout this paper to quantify and compare variance amplification. Other values can be chosen and the same conclusion will be found after the following procedure.

There are some different ways to calculate the variance ratio based on transfer functions (John et al., 1994; Disney & Towill, 2003; Hosoda & Disney, 2006). Setting

$$r1 = (\text{var } O - \text{var } O') / \text{var } D$$

Figure 3. Block diagram for general OUT policy with MMSE forecast

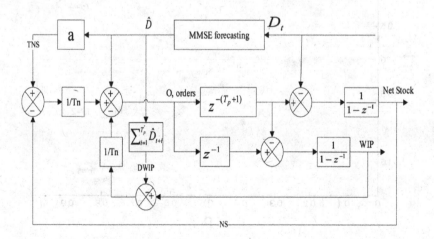

and $r2 = (\text{var } NS - \text{var } NS') / \text{var } D$,

we may plot the variance discrepancy of simple OUT with or without lead-time misidentification, which is shown in Figure 3 and Figure 4. As sales patterns of most products tend to be positively correlated, we analyze and observe variance amplification when $0 \prec \rho \prec 1$. Simple inspection of Figure 3 and Figure 4 shows that:

1. When ρ is relatively small, both r1 and r2 approximately equal to zero. This means the misidentification doesn't affect the system performance of simple OUT policy when demand pattern confronted is less correlated.

2. When ρ is relatively large, the misidentification does affect the system performance a lot in both order and net stock variance. The bigger the absolute misidentification is, the larger the variance discrepancies are.

Overall, order variance increases when the lead-time estimate is larger than the actual value and vice versa; however the net stock amplification increases whenever the misidentification of lead-time occurs. When ρ is relatively large, any lead-time misidentification within the simple OUT policy will change the variance amplification both in orders and net stocks. This will make the lead-time value used play an essential role in determining the system performance, which will chop and change fantasticality according to the accuracy of lead-time estimation. In other words, the simple OUT policy with MMSE forecast is not an ideal replenishment model to eliminate the disturbance of the lead-time misidentification. This is the one shortcoming we obtained in this paper.

4.2 Inventory Drift

In order to determine the behavioral boundary conditions for a stable system, the Initial and Final Value Theorems (IVT and FVT, respectively) are

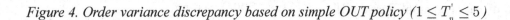

Figure 4. Order variance discrepancy based on simple OUT policy ($1 \leq T_p' \leq 5$)

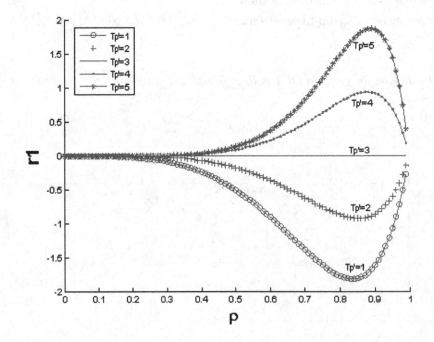

employed. This approach was first presented by John et al. (1994) in the form of continuous Laplace transform. Here they are restated in z-domain.

$$IVT: \quad \lim_{t \to 0}\left\{f(t)i(t)\right\} = \lim_{z \to 0}\left\{(1 - z^{-1})F(z)I(z)\right\} \tag{12}$$

$$FVT: \quad \lim_{t \to \infty}\left\{f(t)i(t)\right\} = \lim_{z \to 1}\left\{(1 - z^{-1})F(z)I(z)\right\} \tag{13}$$

where the unit step input $I(z) = 1/(1 - z^{-1})$ is used and F(z) represents the corresponding transfer functions. To apply IVT and FVT Theorems, normally i.i.d. random error ε_t is treated as the input of the whole system. The net stock transfer functions of the simple and the general OUT over ε_t are shown in equation (14) and (15) respectively (see Exhibit 1).

IVT and FVT have been applied to net stocks and the results are shown in Table 1. The Initial Value of infinity indicates that the responses of the variable input can match those of the previous unsteady state at period t=0. In other words, both OUT policies have the ability to deal with unstable initial net stock levels. Given parameters, the Final Value is always a constant, which shows that there might be a final value offset (i.e., inven-

tory drift) even though the estimate $T_p^{'}$ is equal to actual lead-time 3.

Keeping the inventory level stable is important because the inventory offset can make net stock variance dramatically large when the lead-time is variable and frequent estimations is inevitable. It is essential to develop a replenishment policy which can not only keep the system variances acceptable but also can eliminate the inherent inventory drift. Apparently the simple OUT policy with MMSE forecast can not address this issue. This is the other shortcoming we obtained in our research.

5. ZERO INVENTORY DRIFT VARIANTS

According to Table 1, given the value of $T_p^{'}$, the inventory drift of simple OUT is a constant. In this replenishment policy, there are not enough parameters to control or much room for further design. So we jump to general OUT to explain the deduction procedure of zero inventory drift variants.

Exhibit 1. Equations 14 and 15

$\dfrac{NS_t^{'}}{\varepsilon_t} = \dfrac{NS_t^{'}}{D_t} \times \dfrac{D_t}{\varepsilon_t} =$ $\dfrac{z^{-T_p}[\rho + \rho^{T_p^{'}+2}(z-1) - \rho \cdot z^{T_p^{'}+2} + z(z^{T_p^{'}+1} - 1)]}{(\rho - 1)(z - 1)(z - \rho)}$	(14)
$\dfrac{NS_t^{'}}{\varepsilon_t} =$ $\dfrac{-\rho^{1+T_p^{'}}(-1 + a + T_n) + \rho^{2+T_p^{'}}(a + T_n) + z(1 + z + z^2 + T_n z^3) - \rho(1 + z + z^2 + z^3 + T_n z^4)}{(-1 + \rho)(1 + T_n(-1 + z))(\rho - z)z^2}$	(15)

Table 1. Initial and final values of net stocks ($T_p = 3$)

Policies ⇓	Initial Value	Final Value
Simple OUT	$-\infty$	$\dfrac{5\rho - 4 - \rho^{T_p' + 2}}{(\rho - 1)^2}$
General OUT	∞	$\dfrac{-3 - T_n + \rho(4 + T_n) + \rho^{1+T_p'}(-1 + a + T_n) - \rho^{2+T_p'}(a + T_n)}{(-1 + \rho)^2}$
Single-loop OUT	0	$\dfrac{a\rho^{T_p'+1} + T_n(\rho^{T_p'+1} - 1)}{1 - \rho}$

5.1 General OUT Variant

According to Table 1, the final value of general OUT can be eliminated by apropriate parameter setting. We set T_n as shown in equation (16) to gain the benefit of zero inventory drift in our new policy, which will be called General OUT variant thereafter.

$$FV_{NS} = 0 \Rightarrow T_n = \frac{-3 + 4\rho - \rho^{1+T_p'} + a\rho^{1+T_p'} - a\rho^{2+T_p'}}{(-1 + \rho)(-1 + \rho^{1+T_p'})} \quad (16)$$

The parameter a is not solely used to determine the desired net stock level. We treat it as a key parameter to ensure no inventory offset even though the lead-time is varying over time and misidentification occurred frequently.

The variance amplification of orders (i.e., bullwhip effect) and net stocks are quantified by using the frequency response technique (Dejonckheere et al., 2003). Simple inspection of Figure 4 and Figure 5 reveals that:

1. General OUT variant will arouse some instability issues when a is relatively small.

This will be discussed later in stability analysis section.

2. Both the order and the net stock variance amplification will lock on a constant level when a is big enough. But the smallest estimation of lead-time is the winner when a is relatively small but still can keep the system stable.

3. The misidentification of lead-time has no effect on the variance amplification when a is big enough. In other words, both the order and the net stock variance amplification will converge to a constant level respectively no matter what lead-time estimation is.

Thus we conclude that estimating the lead-time conservatively works well in general OUT variant. Besides the property of no inventory drift, another valuable attribute of general OUT variant is both variance amplification ratios decrease as a increases. This distinguishes our new variant from preceding replenishment policies mentioned. Usually bullwhip effect and net stock variance amplification are against to each other.

5.2 Single-Loop OUT Variant

John et al. (1994) proved the addition of WIP feedback improves the stability of the decision

Figure 5. Net stock variance discrepancy based on simple OUT policy ($1 \leq T_p' \leq 5$)

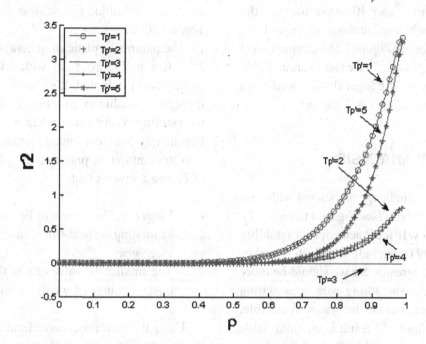

support system although this requires accurate (sometimes costly) visibility of the pipeline lead-time. He also declared WIP feedback term introduces a final value offset in the actual inventory which makes the risk of out-of-stock greater, though it does improve dynamic performance. When the lead-time misidentification occurs, the WIP discrepancy will become even worse and make both variances increase.

Next we will study the general OUT without the WIP feedback loop as shown in equation (17). The net stock transfer function over ε_t aroused by this single-loop policy is shown in equation (18).

$$O_t = \hat{D}_{t+L} + \frac{1}{T_n}(a\hat{D}_{t+L} - NS_t) \qquad (17)$$

$$\frac{NS_t}{\varepsilon_t} = \frac{z[T_n(z^{T_p+1} - \rho^{T_p'+1}) - a\rho^{T_p'+1}]}{(\rho - z)[1 + T_n(z-1)z^{T_p}]} \qquad (18)$$

Apply IVT and FVT to equation (18) and the results are shown in Table 1. The Initial Value 0 indicates the responses of variable inputs match those of previous steady states. Applying the same procedure as general OUT variant, we can obtain the appropriate setting of T_n, which will be called single-loop OUT variant thereafter.

$$FV_{NS} =$$
$$\frac{a\rho^{T_p'+1} + T_n(\rho^{T_p'+1} - 1)}{1 - \rho} = 0 \quad \Rightarrow \quad T_n = \frac{a\rho^{T_p'}}{(1 - \rho^{T_p'})} \qquad (19)$$

The variance amplification of orders and net stocks are shown in Figure 6 and Figure 7. Simple inspection reveals that single-loop OUT variant has almost the same attributes as general OUT variant. Comparing Figure 6 and Figure 7 to Figure 4 and Figure 5, we obtain almost the same curve shapes for both variants except only one difference, which is the convergence rate of general OUT variant is faster than that of single-loop OUT variant. For example, in Figure 5 the net stock variance amplification reaches the constant level when a increases to around 30. But in corresponding Figure 7, the constant level will be achieved when a increases to around 100. That is also why we use logarithmic coordinates in figures of single-loop OUT variant.

6. STABILITY ANALYSIS

The stability is a challenge associated with zero inventory drift variants (see Figure 4 to Figure 7). While including WIP feedback improves stability (John et al., 1994), excluding definitely makes the unstable risk greater. So we should be more cautions with the smoothing parameter setting of feedback loops. In case the system is instable, any change of input will result in uncontrollable oscillations of output and in the end the apparent chaos. In this section we will apply Tustin transformation combined with Routh-Hurwitz stability criterion to determine limiting conditions

for stability analysis. For more details of stability analyzing technique please refer to Disney and Towill (2002).

The parameter plane of general OUT variant is shown in Figure 8, in which logarithm Y-coordinates is adopted. It's clear that sometimes it might be unable to set a big enough to satisfy the stability requirement when ρ is very small. Fortunately less correlated demand pattern is also uncommon in practice. Simple inspection of Figure 8 reveals that:

1. Larger stable zone will be obtained when estimating the lead-time conservatively, and vice versa.
2. The smaller the value of ρ is, the bigger the unstable range of a will be, and vice versa.

Using the same procedure of stability analysis, we can obtain the parameter plane of single-loop OUT variant as shown in Figure 9. Almost the same conclusion can be obtained after simple comparison of Figure 8 and Figure 9.

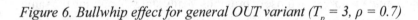

Figure 6. Bullwhip effect for general OUT variant ($T_p = 3$, $\rho = 0.7$)

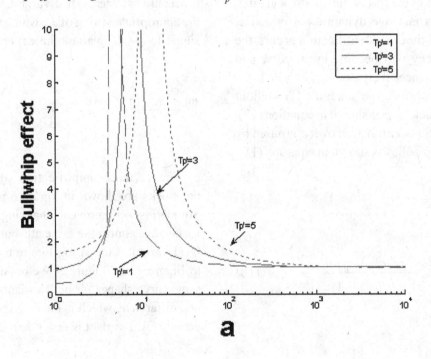

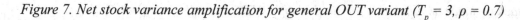

Figure 7. Net stock variance amplification for general OUT variant ($T_p = 3$, $\rho = 0.7$)

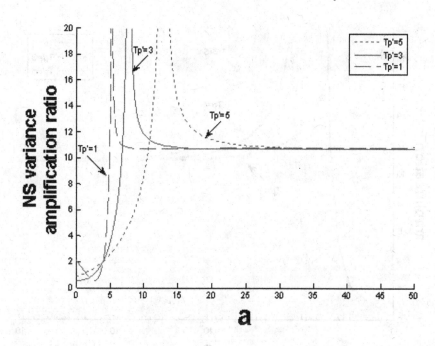

Figure 8. Bullwhip effect for single-loop OUT variant ($T_p = 3$, $\rho = 0.7$)

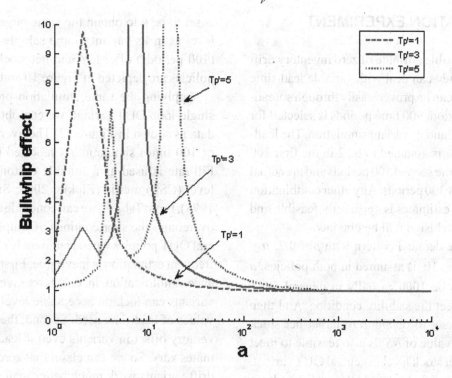

Figure 9. Net stock variance amplification for single-loop OUT variant ($T_p = 3$, $\rho = 0.7$)

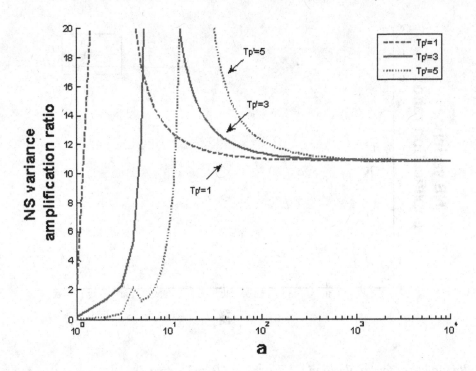

7. SIMULATION EXPERIMENT

Another valuable attribute of zero inventory drift variants is they can deal with variable lead-time estimates. It can be proved easily through spreadsheet simulation. 900 time periods is selected for general OUT and its variant simulation. The lead-time estimate is assumed to be 2 in the first 300 periods, 4 in the second 300 periods and the actual value 3 in last 300 periods. Any other combination of lead-time estimates is apparently feasible and the same conclusion will be obtained.

The same demand pattern with $\rho = 0.7$, $\mu = 100$ and $\sigma_\varepsilon^2 = 10$ is assumed in both policies. a is chosen to be 1000 casually in general OUT variant to meet the stability condition. And then $NS_0 = a\mu$ is set to obtain zero target net stock level. Other value of NS_0 is also feasible to meet a different net stock level in general OUT variant. $T_n = 4$ is assumed in general OUT policy to keep the bullwhip effect around 1. And the value of a

is set to be 0 to obtain the same target net stock level as in its variant. Some sample simulation (100 periods) of orders and net stocks for both policies are depicted in Figure 10 and Figure 11.

Applying the same simulation procedure to single-loop OUT variant, we can obtain sample data as shown in Figure 12. The average results of 100 times simulation is reported in Table 2. Fill-rate is used as a suitable customer service level (CSL) metric (Zipkin, 2000; Silver et al., 1998). From Table 2, we can conclude the variants overcomes the shortcomings of simple and general OUT policies when lead time is variable and frequent estimation is inevitable. First, both variance amplification in our zero inventory drift variants can lock on acceptable levels whatever values of lead-time used. Second, there is no inventory offset in variants even if lead-time estimates vary. So we can claim that zero inventory drift variants work much better than simple and general OUT policies in all facets concerned.

Figure 10. Parameter plane of stability based on general OUT variant ($T_p = 3$)

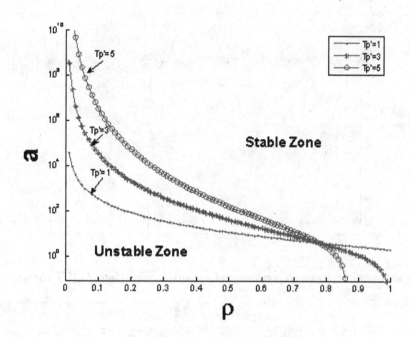

Figure 11. Parameter plane of stability based on single-loop OUT variant ($T_p = 3$)

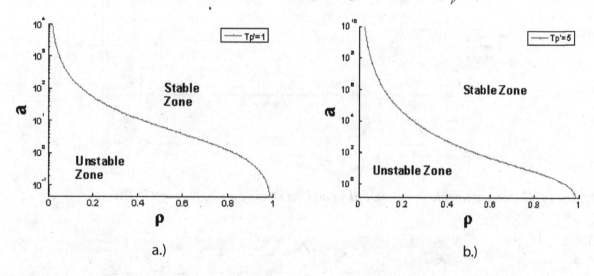

a.)   b.)

Table 2. Simulation results of general OUT policy and it's variant

Measures ⇓	Simple OUT policy	General OUT policy	General OUT variant	Single-loop OUT variant
Bullwhip	15.20	1.22	1.14	1.20
NS variance	1410.41	333.16	22.34	11.92
Fillrate	32.62%	65.80%	96.74%	96.67%

Figure 12. Generated sample demands, orders and net stocks for general OUT model

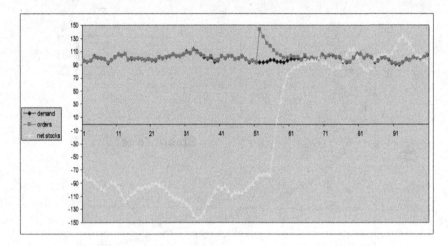

Figure 13. Generated sample demands, orders and net stocks for general OUT variant

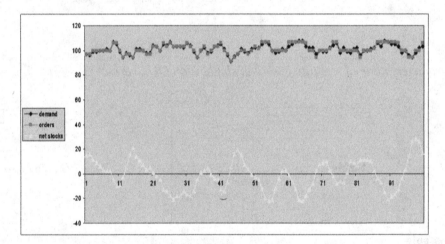

Figure 14. Generated sample demands, orders and net stocks for single-loop OUT variant

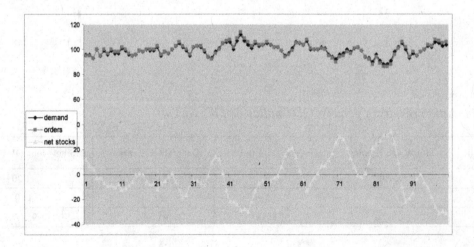

8. CONCLUSION

In this paper, the simple and general OUT models with MMSE forecast have first been introduced. The analysis of variance discrepancy suggests the lead-time should always be estimated conservatively in simple OUT policy. Applying the Final Value Theorem, we demonstrate that there must be a final value offset (i.e., inventory drift) in both simple and general OUT even though the actual lead-time is known. Thus we develop zero inventory drift variants to eliminate the inherent inventory drift and keep the system variances acceptable. The following variance analysis suggests lead-times should still be estimated conservatively in both zero inventory drift variants. And the stability conditions of our variants have been evaluated for further research.

Two most valuable attributes about zero inventory drift variants are stated. One is both order and net stock variances decrease as the value of *a* increases, which distinguish our new variants from simple and general OUT policies. The other is lead-time estimates can be treated as variables in variant policies, which can still work very well because of no inventory drift. These advantages are illustrated by spreadsheet simulation comparing to simple and general OUT models. We show clearly zero inventory drift variants work much better in all facets concerned.

Future work will focus on the analytical procedure to obtain desirable policies when different demand patterns and forecasting methods are involved. In addition, it would be of interest to analyze the system performance when loss or deterioration is occurred in production and delivery process (i.e., the WIP feedback loop), which is not included in our new replenishment variants in this paper.

REFERENCES

Badinelli, R. D. (1990). The inventory costs of common misspecification of demand-forecastingmodels. *International Journal of Production Research*, *28*(12), 2321–2340. doi:10.1080/00207549008942869

Coyle, R. G. (1977). *Management System Dynamics*. New York: John Wiley & Sons.

Dejonckheere, J., Disney, S. M., Lambrecht, M. R., & Towill, D. R. (2003). Measuring and avoiding the bullwhip effect: A control theoretic approach. *European Journal of Operational Research*, *147*(3), 567–590. doi:10.1016/S0377-2217(02)00369-7

Dejonckheere, J., Disney, S. M., Lambrecht, M. R., & Towill, D. R. (2004). The impact of information enrichment on the bullwhip effect in supply chains: A control engineering perspective. *European Journal of Operational Research*, *153*(3), 727–750. doi:10.1016/S0377-2217(02)00808-1

Deziel, D. P., & Eilon, S. (1967). A linear production-inventory control rule. *Production Engineering*, *43*, 93–104.

Disney, S. M., Farasyn, I., Lambrecht, M., Towill, D. R., & Velde, W. V. d. (2006). Taming the bullwhip effect whilst watching customer service in a single supply chain echelon. *European Journal of Operational Research*, *173*(1), 151–172. doi:10.1016/j.ejor.2005.01.026

Disney, S. M., & Towill, D. R. (2002). A discrete transfer function model to determine the dynamic stability of a vendor managed inventory supply chain. *International Journal of Production Research*, *40*(1), 179–204. doi:10.1080/00207540110072975

Disney, S. M., & Towill, D. R. (2003). On the bullwhip and inventory variance produced by an ordering policy. *Omega*, *31*(3), 157–167. doi:10.1016/S0305-0483(03)00028-8

Disney, S. M., & Towill, D. R. (2005). Eliminating drift in inventoryand order based production control systems. *International Journal of Production Economics, 93-94*, 331–344. doi:10.1016/j.ijpe.2004.06.031

Hosoda, T., & Disney, S. M. (2006). On variance amplification in a three-echelon supply chain with minimum mean square error forecasting. *Omega, 34*(4), 344–358. doi:10.1016/j.omega.2004.11.005

John, S., Naim, M. M., & Towill, D. R. (1994). Dynamic analysis of a WIP compensated decision support system. *International Journal of Manufacturing System Design, 1*(4), 283–297.

Kim, H., & Ryan, J. (2003). The cost impact of using simple forecasting techniques in a supply chain. *Naval Research Logistics, 50*(5), 388–411. doi:10.1002/nav.10065

Silver, E., Peterson, R., & Pyke, D. F. (2000). *Decision Systems for Inventory Management and Production*. New York: John Wiley & Sons.

Silver, E. A., Pyke, D. F., & Peterson, R. (1998). *Inventory Management and Production Planning and Scheduling*. New York: John Wiley & Sons.

Simon, H. A. (1952). On the application of servomechanism theory in the study of production control. *Econometrica, 20*(2), 247–268. doi:10.2307/1907849

Sterman, J. (1989). Modelling managerial behaviour: Misperceptions of feedback in a dynamic decision making experiment. *Management Science, 35*(3), 321–339. doi:10.1287/mnsc.35.3.321

Xu, K., Dong, Y., & Evers, P. (2001). Towards better coordination of the supply chain. *Transportation Research Part E, Logistics and Transportation Review, 37*(1), 35–54. doi:10.1016/S1366-5545(00)00010-7

Zhang, X. (2004). The impact of forecasting methods on the bullwhip effect. *International Journal of Production Economics, 88*(1), 15–27. doi:10.1016/S0925-5273(03)00128-2

Zipkin, P. H. (2000). *Foundations of Inventory Management*. New York: McGraw-Hill.

This work was previously published in International Journal of Applied Metaheuristic Computing, Volume 1, Issue 3, edited by Peng-Yeng Yin, pp. 37-52, copyright 2010 by IGI Publishing (an imprint of IGI Global).

Chapter 20
BDD–Based Synthesis of Reversible Logic

Robert Wille
University of Bremen, Germany

Rolf Drechsler
University of Bremen, Germany

ABSTRACT

Reversible logic became a promising alternative to traditional circuits because of its applications in emerging technologies such as quantum computing, low-power design, DNA computing, or nanotechnologies. As a result, synthesis of the respective circuits is an intensely studied topic. However, most synthesis methods are limited, because they rely on a truth table representation of the function to be synthesized. In this paper, the authors present a synthesis approach that is based on Binary Decision Diagrams (BDDs). The authors propose a technique to derive reversible or quantum circuits from BDDs by substituting all nodes of the BDD with a cascade of Toffoli or quantum gates, respectively. Boolean functions containing more than a hundred of variables can efficiently be synthesized. More precisely, a circuit can be obtained from a given BDD using an algorithm with linear worst case behavior regarding run-time and space requirements. Furthermore, using the proposed approach, theoretical results known from BDDs can be transferred to reversible circuits. Experiments show better results (with respect to the circuit cost) and a significantly better scalability in comparison to previous synthesis approaches.

1. INTRODUCTION

Reversible logic (Landauer, 1961; Bennett, 1973; Toffoli, 1980) realizes n-input n-output functions that map each possible input vector to a unique output vector (i.e., bijections). Although reversible logic significantly differs from traditional (irreversible) logic (e.g., fan-out and feedback are not allowed), it has become an intensely studied research area in recent years. In particular, this is caused by the fact that reversible logic is the basis for several emerging technologies, while traditional methods suffer from the increasing miniaturization and the exponential growth of

DOI: 10.4018/978-1-4666-0270-0.ch020

the number of transistors in integrated circuits. Researchers expect that in 10-20 years duplication of transistor density every 18 months (according to Moore's Law) is not possible any longer (Zhirnov, Cavin, Hutchby, & Bourianoff, 2003). Then, alternatives are needed. Reversible logic offers such alternatives as the following applications show:

- **Reversible Logic for Low-Power Design:** Power dissipation and therewith heat generation is a serious problem for today's computer chips. Landauer and Bennett showed (Landauer, 1961; Bennett, 1973) that (1) using traditional (irreversible) logic gates always leads to energy dissipation regardless of the underlying technology and (2) that circuits with zero power dissipation must be information-lossless. This holds for reversible logic, since data is bijectively transformed without losing any of the original information. Even if today energy dissipation is mainly caused by non-ideal behaviors of transistors and materials, the theoretically possible zero power dissipation makes reversible logic quite interesting for the future. Moreover, in 2002 first reversible circuits have been physically implemented (Desoete & De Vos, 2002) that exploit these observations in the sense that they are powered by their input signals only and did not need additional power supplies.

- **Reversible Logic as Basis for Quantum Computation:** Quantum circuits (Nielsen & Chuang, 2000) offer a new kind of computation. Here, qubits instead of traditional bits are used that allow to represent not only 0 and 1 but also a superposition of both. As a result, qubits can represent multiple states at the same time enabling enormous speed-ups in computations. Even if research in the domain of quantum circuits is still at the beginning, first quantum circuits have already been built. Reversible

logic is important in this area, because every quantum operation is inherently reversible. Thus, progress in the domain of reversible logic can directly be applied to quantum logic.

Further applications of reversible logic can be found in the domain of optical computing (Cuykendall & Andersen, 1987), DNA computing (Bennett, 1973), and nanotechnologies (Merkle, 1993).

However, currently the synthesis of reversible or quantum circuits, respectively, is limited. Exact (Hung, Song, Yang, Yang & Perkowski, 2006; Große, Wille, Dueck & Drechsler, 2009) as well as heuristic (Shende, Prasad, Markov & Hayes, 2003; Miller, Maslov & Dueck, 2003; Kerntopf, 2004; Maslov, Dueck & Miller, 2005, 2007; Gupta, Agrawal, & Jha, 2006) methods have been proposed. But both are applicable only for relatively small functions. Exact approaches reach their limits with functions containing more than 6 variables (Große, Wille, Dueck & Drechsler, 2009) while heuristic methods are able to synthesize functions with at most 30 variables (Gupta, Agrawal, & Jha, 2006). Moreover, often a significant amount of run-time is needed to achieve these results.

These limitations are caused by the underlying techniques. The existing synthesis approaches often rely on truth tables (or similar descriptions like permutations) of the function to be synthesized (Shende, Prasad, Markov & Hayes, 2003; Miller, Maslov & Dueck, 2003). But even if more compact data-structures like BDDs (Kerntopf, 2004), positive-polarity Reed-Muller expansion (Gupta, Agrawal, & Jha, 2006), or Reed-Muller spectra (Maslov, Dueck & Miller, 2007) are used, the same limitations can be observed since all these approaches apply similar strategies (namely selecting reversible gates so that the chosen function representation becomes the identity).

In this work, we introduce a synthesis method that can cope with significantly larger functions.

The basic idea is as follows: First, for the function to be synthesized a BDD (Bryant, 1986) is built. This can efficiently be done for large functions using existing well-developed techniques. Then, each node of the BDD is substituted by a cascade of reversible gates or quantum gates, respectively. Depending on the respective cases, this may require additional circuit lines.

BDD optimization techniques, for example complement edges (Brace, Rudell & Bryant, 1990) or reordering strategies like sifting (Rudell, 1993) thereby may affect the size of the resulting circuit. Thus, we describe how to support these techniques during synthesis and discuss possible improvements and drawbacks. In a case study, we evaluate the effect of these optimization methods on the resulting circuit sizes.

Overall, using the proposed approaches, circuits composed of Toffoli or quantum gates, respectively, are obtained in linear time and with memory linear to the size of the BDD. Moreover, the size of the resulting circuit is bounded by the BDD, so that theoretical results known from BDDs (Wegener, 2000; Drechsler & Sieling, 2001) can be transferred to reversible circuits.

Our experiments show significant improvements (with respect to the resulting circuit cost as well as to the run-time) in comparison to previous approaches. Furthermore, for the first time large functions with more than a hundred of variables can be synthesized at very low run-time.

The remainder of the paper is structured as follows: Section 2 provides the basics of reversible logic, quantum logic, and BDDs. Afterwards, in Section 3 the general idea and the resulting synthesis approach is introduced. How to exploit BDD optimization is shown in Section 4 while Section 5 briefly reviews some of the already known theoretical results from reversible logic synthesis and introduces bounds which follow from the new synthesis approach. Finally, in Section 6 experimental results are given and the paper is concluded in Section 7.

2. PRELIMINARIES

To keep the paper self-contained this section briefly reviews the concepts of reversible and quantum logic. We also describe the basics of BDDs which are used as the main data-structure in our synthesis approach.

Reversible and Quantum Logic

A logic function is reversible if it maps each input assignment to a unique output assignment. Such a function must have the same number of input and output variables $X := \{x_1, ..., x_n\}$. Since fanout and feedback are not allowed in reversible logic, a circuit realizing a reversible function is a cascade of reversible gates. A reversible gate has the form $g(C, T)$, where $C = \{x_{i1}, ..., x_{ik}\} \subset X$ is the set of control lines and $T = \{x_{j1}, ..., x_{jl}\} \subset X$ with $C \cap T = \emptyset$ is the set of target lines. C may be empty. The gate operation is applied to the target lines iff all control lines meet the required control conditions. Control lines and unconnected lines always pass through the gate unaltered.

In the literature, several types of reversible gates have been introduced. Besides the Fredkin gate (Fredkin & Toffoli, 1982) and the Peres gate (Peres, 1985), (multiple controlled) Toffoli gates (Toffoli, 1980) are widely used. Each Toffoli gate has one target line xj, which is inverted if all control lines are assigned to 1. That is, a multiple controlled Toffoli gate maps $(x_1, ..., x_j, ..., x_n)$ to $(x_1, ..., x_{i1} x_{i2} \cdots x_{ik} \oplus x_j, ..., x_n)$.

Example 1. Figure 1(a) shows a Toffoli gate realization of a full adder. Control lines are denoted by black circles while target lines are denoted by $\oplus$.

The cost of a reversible circuit is defined either by the number of gates or by so called quantum cost (Barenco et al., 1995; Maslov & Miller, 2007). The latter can be derived by substituting the re-

Figure 1. Two Circuits realizing a full adder

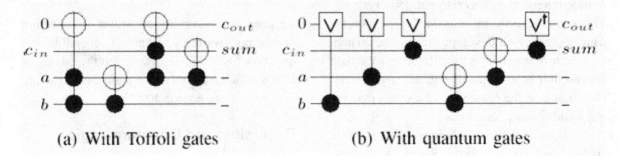

(a) With Toffoli gates   (b) With quantum gates

versible gates of a circuit by a cascade of quantum gates (Nielsen & Chuang, 2000).

Quantum gates realize quantum circuits that are inherently reversible and manipulate qubits rather than pure logic values. The state of a qubit for two pure logic states can be expressed as

$|\Psi = \alpha|0> + \beta|1>$, where $|0>$ and $|1>$ denote 0 and 1, respectively, and α and β are complex numbers such that $|\alpha>^2 + |\beta>^2 = 1$. Frequently used quantum gates are:

- **Inverter (NOT):** A single qubit is inverted.
- **Controlled inverter (CNOT):** The target qubit is inverted if the single control qubit is 1.
- **Controlled V gate:** The V operation is also known as the square root of NOT, since two consecutive V operations are equivalent to an inversion.
- **Contr. V+ gate:** The V+ gate performs the inverse operation of the V gate, i.e., $V+ = V^{-1}$.

Example 2. Figure 1(b) shows a quantum gate realization of a full adder. Again control lines are denoted by black circles. Depending on the type of the gate, the target line is denoted by a $\oplus$, a V-box, or a V+-box, respectively.

Since quantum circuits are reversible, to realize a non-reversible function (e.g., an n-input m-output function with $n>m$) it must be embedded into a reversible one (Maslov & Dueck, 2004). Therefore, it is often necessary to add circuit lines including constant inputs and/or garbage outputs. Garbage outputs are by definition don't cares and can be left unspecified.

Binary Decision Diagrams

Every Boolean function $f: B^n \rightarrow B$ can be represented by a graph-structure defined as follows:

Definition. A Binary Decision Diagram *(BDD) (Bryant, 1986) over Boolean variables X with terminals T={0, 1} is a directed acyclic graph G = (V, E) with the following properties:*
1. Each node $v \in V$ is either a terminal or a non-terminal.
2. Each terminal node $v \in V$ is labeled by a value $t \in T$ and has no outgoing edges.
3. Each non-terminal node $v \in V$ is labeled by a Boolean variable $x_i \in X$ and represents a Boolean function f.

In each non-terminal node (labeled by x_i), the Shannon decomposition (Shannon, 1938)

$$f = \sim x_i \, f_{xi=0} + x_i \, f_{xi=1}$$

is carried out, leading to two outgoing edges e ∈ E whose successors are denoted by low(f) (for f_{xi}=0) and high(f) (for f_{xi}=1), respectively.

The size of a BDD is defined by the number of its (non-terminal) nodes.

Example 3. Figure 2 shows a BDD representing the function $f = x_1 \oplus x_2 \cdot x_3$. Edges leading to a node f_{xi} =0 (f_{xi} =1) are marked by a 0 (1). This BDD has a size of 5.

A BDD is called free if each variable is encountered at most once on each path from the root to a terminal node. A BDD is called ordered if in addition all variables are encountered in the same order on all such paths. The respective order is defined by $\pi: \{1, ..., n\} \to \{1, ..., n\}$. Finally, a BDD is called reduced if it does neither contain isomorphic sub-graphs nor redundant nodes. To

Figure 2. BDD representing $f = x_1 \oplus x_2 \cdot x_3$

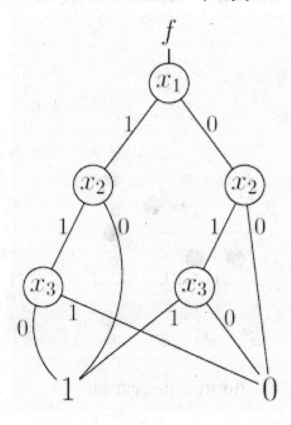

achieve reduced BDDs, reduction rules are applied (Bryant, 1986). Applying the reduction rules leads to shared nodes, i.e., nodes that have more than one predecessor.

In the following, reduced ordered binary decision diagrams are called BDDs for brevity. BDDs are canonical representations, i.e., for a given Boolean function and a fixed order, the BDD is unique (Bryant, 1986).

BDDs are very sensitive to the chosen variable order. It has been shown in Bollig and Wegener (1996) that proving the existence of a BDD with a lower number of nodes (i.e., proving that no other order leads to a smaller BDD size) is N P-complete. As a consequence, several heuristics to determine good orders have been proposed. In particular, sifting (Rudell, 1993) has been shown to be quite effective.

Further reductions of the BDD size can be achieved, if complement edges (Brace, Rudell & Bryant, 1990) are applied. They represent a function as well as its complement by one single node only. BDDs can also be used to represent multi-output functions. Then, all BDDs for the respective functions are shared, i.e., isomorphic sub-functions are represented by a single node as well.

3. GENERAL IDEA

In this section, the general idea of the BDD-based synthesis is proposed. The aim of the approach is to determine a circuit realization for a given Boolean function. It is well known that Boolean functions can be efficiently represented by BDDs. Given a BDD $G = (V, E)$, a reversible circuit can be derived by traversing the decision diagram and substituting each node $v \in V$ with a cascade of reversible gates. The concrete cascade of gates depends on whether the successors of the node v are terminals or not. For the general case (no terminals), the first rows of Figure 4 show a substitution with two Toffoli gates or five quantum gates, respectively. The following rows give the substitutions for the remaining cases. These cascades can be applied to derive a complete Toffoli circuit (or quantum circuit, respectively) from a BDD without shared nodes.

Example 4. Consider the BDD in Figure 3(a). Applying the substitutions given in Figure 4 to each node of the BDD, the Toffoli circuit depicted in Figure 3(b) results.

Remark. As shown in Figure 4, an additional (constant) line is necessary if one of the edges low(v) or high(v) leads to a terminal node. This is because of the reversibility which has to be ensured when synthesizing reversible logic. As an example consider a node v with high(v)=0 (second row of Figure 4). Without loss of generality, the first three lines of the corresponding truth table can be embedded with respect to reversibility as depicted in Figure 5(a). However, since f is 0 in the last line, no reversible embedding for the whole function is possible. Thus, an additional line is required to make the respective substitution reversible (see Figure 5(b)).

Based on these substitutions, a method for synthesizing Boolean functions in reversible or quantum logic can be formulated: First, a BDD for function f to be synthesized is created. This can be done efficiently using state-of-the-art BDD packages, for example CUDD (Somenzi, 2001). Next, the resulting BDD $G = (V, E)$ is processed by a depth-first traversal. For each node $v \in V$, cascades as depicted in Figure 4 are added to the circuit. As a result, circuits are synthesized that realize the given function f.

4. EXPLOITING BDD OPTIMIZATION

To build compact BDDs, current state-of-the-art BDD packages exploit several optimization techniques such as shared nodes (Bryant, 1986), complement edges (Brace, Rudell & Bryant, 1990), or reordering (Bryant, 1986; Rudell, 1993). In this section, it is shown how these techniques can be applied to the proposed BDD-based synthesis.

Figure 3. BDD and Tiffoli circuit for $f = x_1 \oplus x_2$

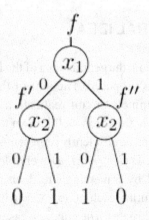

(a) BDD

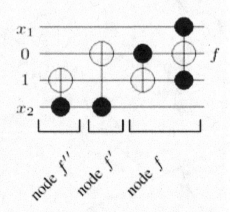

(b) Resulting circuit

Figure 4. Substitution of BDD nodes to reversible/quantum circuits

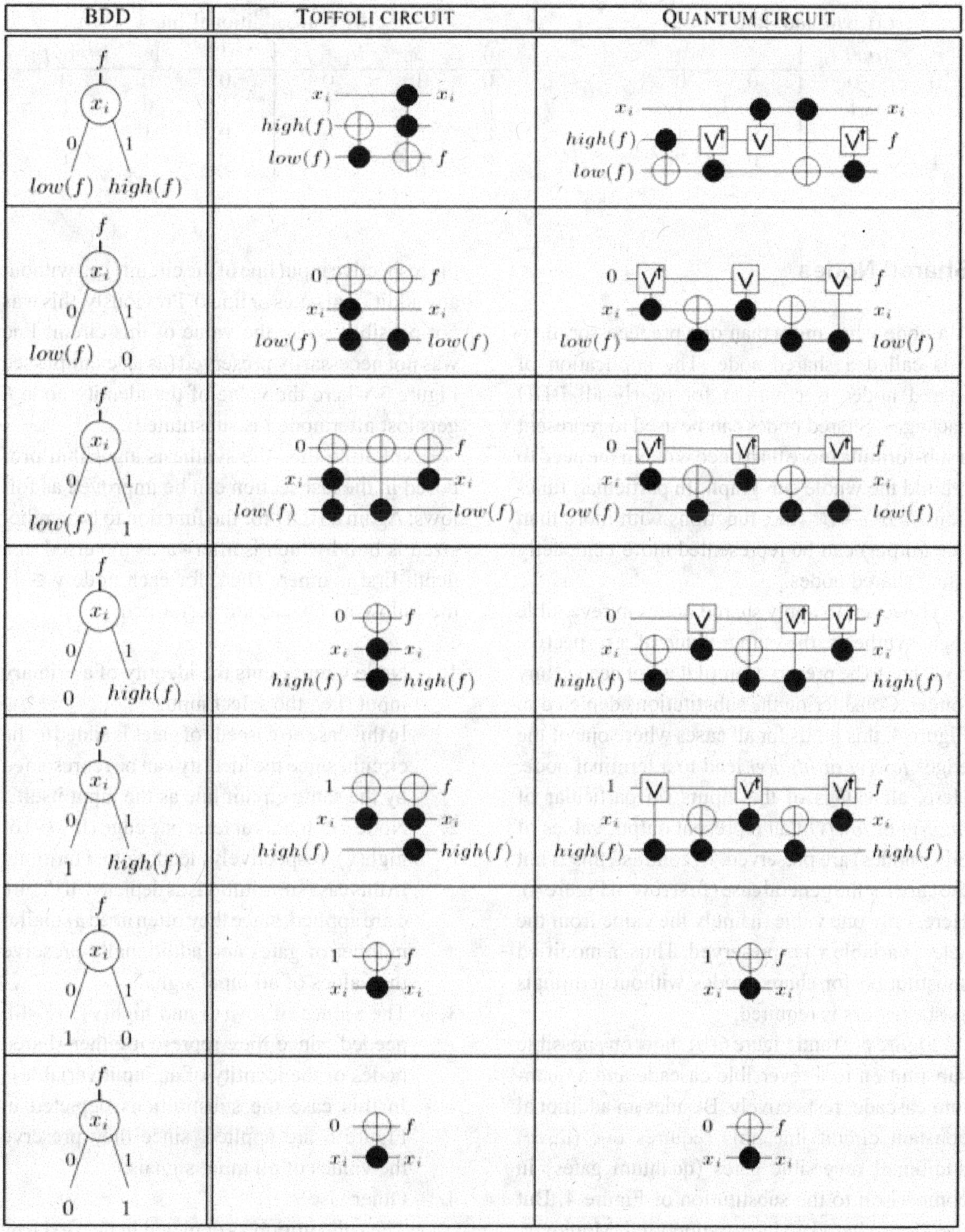

Figure 5. (Partial) truth tables for node v with high(v) = 0

(a) w/o add. line					(b) with additional line				
x_i	$low(f)$	f	–		0	x_i	$low(f)$	f	x_i	$low(f)$
0	0	0	0		0	0	0	0	0	0
0	1	1	1		0	0	1	1	0	1
1	0	0	1		0	1	0	0	1	0
1	1	0	?		0	1	1	0	1	1

Shared Nodes

If a node v has more than one predecessor, then v is called a shared node. The application of shared nodes is common for nearly all BDD packages. Shared nodes can be used to represent a sub-formula more than once without the need to rebuild the whole sub-graph. In particular, functions $f: B^n \to B^m$ (i.e., functions with more than one output) can be represented more compactly using shared nodes.

However, to apply shared nodes in reversible logic synthesis, the output value of a respective node has to be preserved until it is not needed any longer. Considering the substitutions depicted in Figure 4, this holds for all cases where one of the edges $low(v)$ or $high(v)$ lead to a terminal node. Here, all values of the inputs (in particular of $high(v)$ or $low(v)$ that represent output values of other nodes) are preserved. In contrast, this is not the case for the general case (first row of Figure 4). Here, only one value (namely the value from the select variable x_i) is preserved. Thus, a modified substitution for shared nodes without terminals as successors is required.

Figure 6(a) and Figure 6(b) show one possible substitution to a reversible cascade and a quantum cascade, respectively. Besides an additional constant circuit line, this requires one (three) additional reversible gates (quantum gates) in comparison to the substitution of Figure 4. But therefore, shared nodes are supported. Moreover, this substitution also allows to represent the identity of a select variable (last row of Figure 4) by the respective input line of the circuit (i.e., without any additional gates or lines). Previously, this was not possible, since the value of this circuit line was not necessarily preserved (as an example see Figure 3 where the value of the identity node f gets lost after node f is substituted).

Exploiting this, the synthesis algorithm proposed in the last section can be improved as follows: Again a BDD for the function to be synthesized is build which is afterwards traversed in a depth-first manner. Then, for each node $v \in V$, the following checks are performed:

1.   Node v represents the identity of a primary input (i.e., the select input)
     In this case no cascade of gates is added to the circuit, since the identity can be represented by the same circuit line as the input itself.
2.   Node v contains at least one edge (low(v) or high(v), respectively) leading to a terminal
     In this case substitutions as depicted in Figure 4 are applied, since they often need a smaller number of gates and additionally preserve the values of all input signals.
3.   The values of low(v) and high(v) are still needed, since they represent either shared nodes or the identity of an input variable
     In this case the substitutions depicted in Figure 6 are applied, since they preserve the values of all input signals.
4.   Otherwise
     The substitution as depicted in the first row of Figure 4 is applied, since no input values must be preserved or a terminal successor

Figure 6. Substitution for shard nodes without terminals as successors

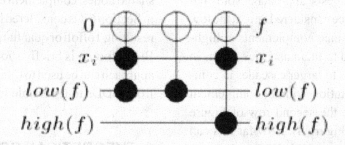

(a) Toffoli cascade

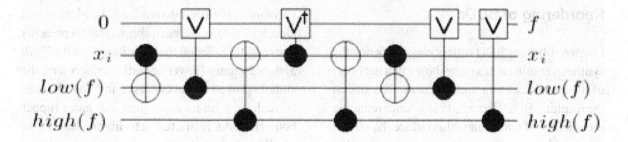

(b) Quantum gates cascade

occurs, respectively. In this case, the smaller cascades (with respect to both the number of additional lines and the number of gates) are preferred.

Example 5. In Figure 7(a) a partial BDD including a shared node f' is shown. Since the value of node f' is used twice (by nodes f_1 and f_2), an additional line (the second one in Figure 7(b)) and the cascade of gates as depicted in Figure 6 are applied to substitute node f_1. Then, the value of f' is still available such that the substitution of node f_2 can be applied. The resulting circuit is given in Figure 7(b).

Figure 7(c) shows the resulting circuit for low(f')=0 and high(f')=1, i.e., for f' representing

the identity of x_j. In this case no gates for f' are added. Instead, the fifth line is used to store the value for both, x_j and f. Besides that, the remaining substitutions are equal to the ones described above.

Complement Edges

Further reductions in BDD sizes can be achieved if complement edges (Brace, Rudell & Bryant, 1990) are applied. In particular, this allows to represent a function as well as its negation by a single node only. If there is a complement edge, e.g., between v and *low(v)*, then Shannon decomposition with an inverted value of *low(v)* is applied. To support complement edges in the proposed synthesis approach, adjusted substitutions have to be used that take the inversion of complemented edges into account.

Figure 8 shows the resulting cascades used in the proposed synthesis approach. Note that complements have to be considered only at the low edges of the nodes, since complements at high-edges can be mapped to them and vice versa. In some cases, this leads to larger cascades in comparison to the substitution without complement edges (e.g., compare the second row of Figure 8 to the first row of Figure 4). How far this can be compensated by the possible BDD reductions is discussed in the experimental evaluation in Section 6.

Reordering of BDDs

Finally, different BDD orders may influence the synthesis results. It has been shown that the order of the variables has a high impact to the size of the resulting BDD (Bryant, 1986). Since reducing the number of nodes may also reduce the size of the resulting circuits, reordering is considered in this section.

In the past, several approaches have been proposed to achieve good orders (Rudell, 1993) or to determine exact results (Drechsler, Drechsler & Günther, 2000) with respect to the number of nodes. All these techniques can be directly applied to the BDD-based synthesis approach and need no further adjustments of the already introduced substitutions.

Using these optimization techniques (i.e., shared nodes, complement edges, and reordering), in Section 6 it is considered how they influence the resulting Toffoli or quantum circuits, respectively. But before, it is briefly shown how the proposed approach can be used to transfer theoretical results from BDDs to reversible logic.

5. THEORETICAL CONSIDERATION

In the past, first lower and upper bounds for the synthesis of reversible functions containing n variables have been determined. In Maslov and Dueck (2004), it has been shown that there exists a reversible function that requires at least $(2^n / ln\ 3) + o(2^n)$ gates (lower bound). Furthermore, the authors proved that every reversible function can be realized with no more than $n \cdot 2^n$ gates (upper bound). For a restricted gate library leading to smaller quantum cost and thus only consisting of NOT, CNOT, and two-controlled Toffoli gates (the same as applied for the substitutions proposed here), functions can be synthesized with at most n NOT gates, n^2 CNOT gates, and $9 \cdot n \cdot 2^n + o(n \cdot 2^n)$ two-controlled Toffoli gates (Shende, Prasad, Markov & Hayes, 2003). A tighter upper bound of n NOT gates, $2 \cdot n^2 + o(n \cdot 2^n)$ CNOT gates, and $3 \cdot n \cdot 2^n + o(n \cdot 2^n)$ two-controlled Toffoli gates has been proved in Maslov, Dueck and Miller

Figure 7. Toffoli circuits for shared BDD

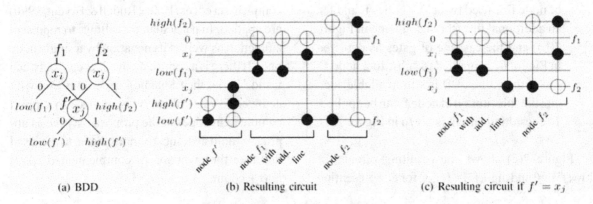

(a) BDD   (b) Resulting circuit   (c) Resulting circuit if $f' = x_j$

Figure 8. Substitution of BDD nodes with complement edge to reversible/quantum circuits

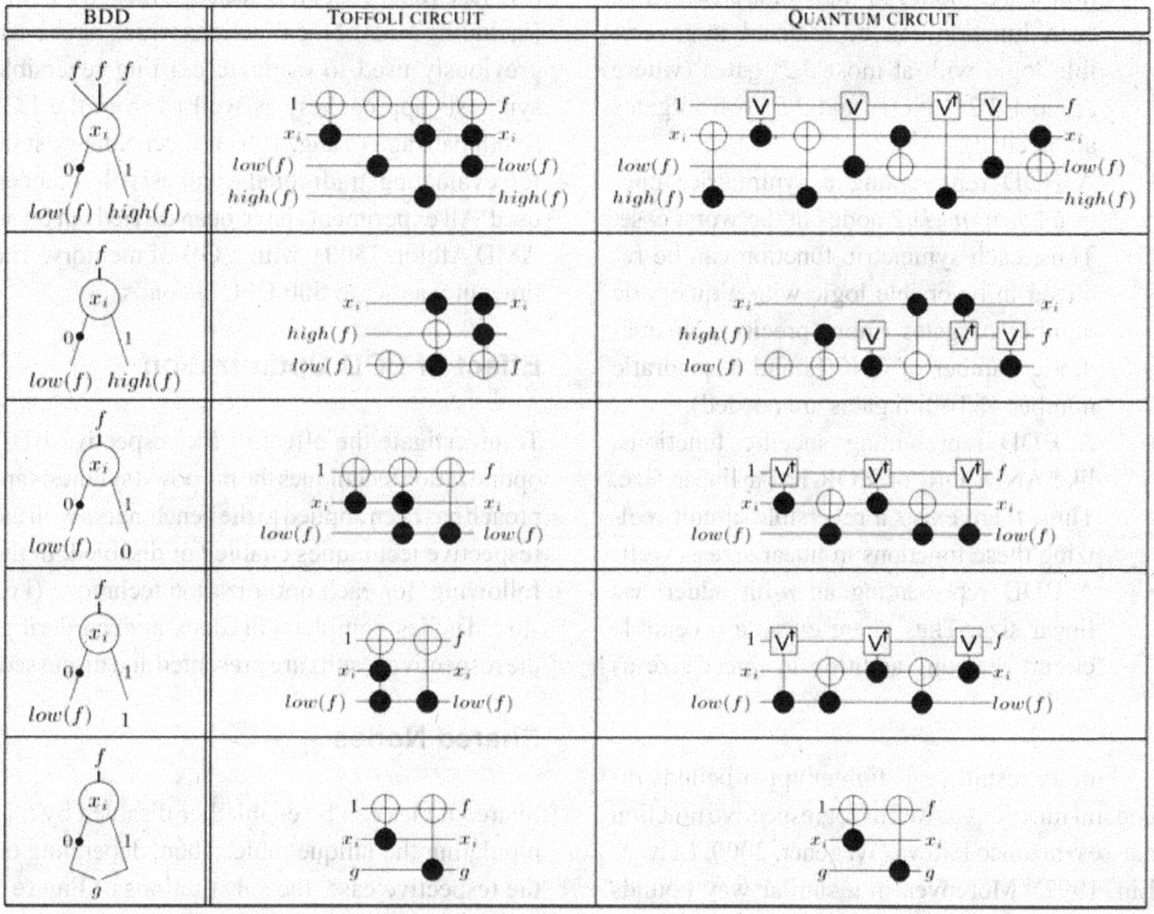

BDD	TOFFOLI CIRCUIT	QUANTUM CIRCUIT

(2007). In Patel Markov and Hayes (2008) it has been shown that linear reversible functions are synthesizable with CNOT gates only. Moreover, their algorithm never needs more than $\Theta(n^2 / \log n)$ CNOT gates for any linear function f with n variables.

Using the synthesis approach proposed in the last sections, reversible circuits for a function f with a size dependent on the number of nodes in the BDD can be constructed. More precisely, let f be a function with n primary inputs which is represented by a BDD containing k nodes. Then, the resulting Toffoli circuit consists of at most

- $k+n$ circuit lines (since besides the input lines, for each node at most one additional line is added) and
- $3 \cdot k$ gates (since for each node cascades of at most 3 gates are added according to the substitutions of Figure 4 and Figure 6, respectively).

Asymptotically, the resulting reversible circuits are bounded by the BDD size. Since for BDDs many theoretical results exist, using the proposed synthesis approach, these results can be transferred to reversible logic as well. In the following, some results obtained by this observation are sketched.

- A BDD representing a single-output function has 2^n nodes in the worst case. Thus, each function can be realized in reversible logic with at most $3 \cdot 2^n$ gates (where at most $2 \cdot 2^n$ CNOTs and $2 \cdot 2^n$ Toffoli gates are needed).
- A BDD representing a symmetric function has $n \cdot (n+1)/2$ nodes in the worst case. Thus, each symmetric function can be realized in reversible logic with a quadratic number of gates (more precisely, a quadratic number of CNOTs and a quadratic number of Toffoli gates are needed).
- A BDD representing specific functions, like AND, OR, or XOR has a linear size. Thus, there exists a reversible circuit realizing these functions in linear size as well.
- A BDD representing an n-bit adder has linear size. Thus, there exists a reversible circuit realizing addition in linear size as well.

Further results (e.g., tighter upper bounds for general functions as well as for respective function classes) are also known (Wegener, 2000; Liaw & Lin, 1992). Moreover, in a similar way bounds for quantum circuits can be obtained. However, a detailed analysis of the theoretical results that can be obtained by the BDD-based synthesis is left for future work.

6. EXPERIMENTAL RESULTS

The BDD-based synthesis method together with the suggested improvements has been implemented in C++ on top of the BDD package CUDD (Somenzi, 2001). In this section, first a case study is given evaluating the effect of the respective BDD optimization techniques on the resulting reversible or quantum circuits. Afterwards, the proposed approach is compared against two previously proposed synthesis methods.

Benchmarks functions provided by RevLib (Wille, Große, Teuber, Dueck & Drechsler, 2008) (including most of the functions which have been previously used to evaluate existing reversible synthesis approaches) as well as from the LG-Synth package (Yang, 1991) (a benchmark suite for evaluating traditional synthesis) have been used. All experiments have been carried out on an AMD Athlon 3500+ with 1 GB of memory. The timeout was set to 500 CPU seconds.

Effect of BDD Optimization

To investigate the effect of the respective BDD optimization techniques the proposed synthesis approach has been applied to the benchmarks with the respective techniques enabled or disabled. In the following, for each optimization technique (i.e., shared nodes, complement edges, and reordering) the respective results are presented and discussed.

Shared Nodes

Shared nodes can be enabled or disabled by manipulating the unique table. Then, depending on the respective case, the substitutions of Figure 4 or additionally of Figure 4 are applied.

The results are summarized in Figure 9. The first two columns give the name of the benchmark (FUNCTION) as well as the number of primary inputs and outputs (PI/PO). Then, the number of resulting circuit lines (n), Toffoli gates (d_{Tof}), or quantum gates (d_{Qua}), as well as the run-time of the synthesis approach (in CPU seconds) is given for the naive approach (denoted by W/O SHARED NODES) and the approach that exploits shared nodes (denoted by WITH SHARED NODES).

One can clearly conclude that the application of shared nodes leads to better realizations for reversible and quantum logic. Both, the number of lines and the number of gates can be significantly reduced. In particular, for the number of lines this might not be obvious, since additional lines are required to support shared nodes (see

Figure 9. Effect of shared nodes

FUNCTION	PI/PO	W/O SHARED NODES				WITH SHARED NODES			
		n	d_{Tof}	d_{Qua}	TIME	n	d_{Tof}	d_{Qua}	TIME
REVLIB FUNCTIONS									
decod24_10	2/4	7	7	21	<0.01	7	7	21	<0.01
4mod5_8	4/1	9	13	36	<0.01	9	13	36	<0.01
mini-alu_84	4/2	12	21	57	<0.01	11	20	52	<0.01
alu_9	5/1	15	30	73	<0.01	14	29	72	<0.01
rd53_68	5/3	31	85	212	<0.01	20	49	130	<0.01
hwb5_13	5/5	36	105	277	<0.01	32	91	238	<0.01
sym6_63	6/1	23	57	126	0.01	17	34	83	<0.01
hwb6_14	6/6	68	239	618	<0.01	53	167	437	<0.01
rd73_69	7/3	86	301	730	<0.01	38	105	272	<0.01
ham7_29	7/7	75	231	595	<0.01	36	88	224	<0.01
hwb7_15	7/7	136	526	1353	<0.01	84	284	744	<0.01
rd84_70	8/4	194	679	1650	0.01	52	140	373	<0.01
hwb8_64	8/8	277	1132	2903	0.02	129	456	1195	<0.01
sym9_71	9/1	104	325	724	<0.01	35	79	201	<0.01
LGSYNTH FUNCTIONS									
xor5	5/1	17	40	98	<0.01	10	19	48	<0.01
bw	5/28	125	381	935	0.01	97	286	747	<0.01
9sym	9/1	104	325	724	<0.01	35	79	201	<0.01

Section 4). But due to the fact that shared nodes also decrease the number of terminal nodes (which require additional lines as well), this effect is compensated.

Complement Edges

Complement edges are supported by the CUDD package and can easily be disabled and enabled.

For comparison, circuits from both, BDDs with and BDDs without complement edges (denoted by WITH COMPL. EDGES and W/O COMPL. E DGES, respectively), are synthesized. In the latter case, the substitutions shown in Figure 8 are applied whenever a successor is connected by a complement edge. Shared nodes are also applied, since they make complement edges more beneficial. The results are given in Figure 10. The columns are labeled as described above for Figure 9.

Even if the cascades representing nodes with complement edges are larger in some cases (see Section 4), improvements in the circuit sizes can be observed (e.g., rd84 70, 9sym, or cordic). But in particular for the LGSynth functions, sometimes better circuits result, when complement edges are disabled (e.g., spla). Here, the larger cascades obviously cannot be compensated by complement edge optimization. In contrast, for quantum circuits in nearly all cases better realizations are obtained with complement edges enabled. A reason for that is that the quantum cascades for nodes with complement edges have the same size as the respective cascades for nodes without complement

Figure 10. Effect of complement edges

FUNCTION	PI/PO	W/O COMPL. EDGES				WITH COMPL. EDGES			
		n	d_{Tof}	d_{Qua}	TIME	n	d_{Tof}	d_{Qua}	TIME
REVLIB FUNCTIONS									
decod24_10	2/4	7	**7**	**21**	<0.01	**6**	11	23	<0.01
4mod5_8	4/1	9	13	**36**	<0.01	**8**	**16**	37	<0.01
mini-alu_84	4/2	11	**20**	52	<0.01	**10**	22	**49**	<0.01
alu_9	5/1	14	29	72	<0.01	**11**	**25**	**53**	<0.01
rd53_68	5/3	20	49	130	<0.01	**13**	**34**	**75**	<0.01
hwb5_13	5/5	32	91	238	<0.01	**27**	**85**	**201**	<0.01
sym6_63	6/1	17	34	83	<0.01	**14**	**29**	**69**	<0.01
hwb6_14	6/6	53	167	437	<0.01	**46**	**157**	**377**	<0.01
rd73_69	7/3	38	105	272	<0.01	**25**	**73**	**162**	<0.01
ham7_29	7/7	36	88	224	<0.01	**18**	**50**	**82**	<0.01
*hwb7_15	7/7	84	284	744	<0.01	**74**	**276**	**665**	<0.01
rd84_70	8/4	52	140	373	<0.01	**34**	**104**	**229**	<0.01
hwb8_64	8/8	129	456	1195	<0.01	**116**	**442**	**1067**	<0.01
sym9_71	9/1	35	79	201	<0.01	**27**	**62**	**153**	<0.01
LGSYNTH FUNCTIONS									
xor5	5/1	10	19	48	<0.01	**6**	**8**	**8**	<0.01
bw	5/28	97	**286**	747	<0.01	**91**	317	**732**	<0.01
ex5p	8/63	276	**680**	1676	0.02	**233**	706	**1520**	0.02
9sym	9/1	35	79	201	<0.01	**27**	**62**	**153**	<0.01
pdc	16/40	648	**2074**	4844	0.12	**631**	2109	**4803**	0.12
spla	16/46	567	**1422**	**3753**	0.09	**559**	1728	3799	0.09
cordic	23/2	76	177	448	0.02	**53**	**109**	**265**	0.02

edges in nearly all cases (see Figure 4, Figure 6, and Figure 8, respectively). Thus, the advantage of complement edges (namely the possibility

to create smaller BDDs) can be fully exploited without the drawback that the respective gate substitutions become larger.

Reordering of BDDs

To evaluate the effect of reordering the BDD on the resulting circuit sizes, three techniques are considered: (1) An order given by the occurrences of the primary inputs in the function to be synthesized (denoted by ORIGINAL), (2)

an optimized order achieved by sifting (Rudell, 1993) (denoted by SIFTING), and (3) an exact order (Drechsler, Drechsler & Günther, 2000) which ensures the BDD to be minimal (denoted by EXACT). Again, all created BDDs exploit shared nodes. Furthermore, complement edges are enabled in this evaluation. After applying the synthesis approach, circuit sizes as summarized in Figure 11 result. Here again, the columns are labeled as described above.

The results show that the order has a significant effect on the circuit size. In particular for the LGSynth functions, the best results are achieved with the exact order. But as a drawback, this re-

Figure 11. Effect of variable ordering

FUNCTION	PI/PO	ORIGINAL				SIFTING				EXACT			
		n	d_{Tof}	d_{Qua}	TIME	n	d_{Tof}	d_{Qua}	TIME	n	d_{Tof}	d_{Qua}	TIME
REVLIB FUNCTIONS													
decod24_10	2/4	6	11	23	<0.01	6	11	23	<0.01	6	11	23	<0.01
4mod5_8	4/1	8	16	37	<0.01	7	8	18	<0.01	7	8	18	<0.01
mini-alu_84	4/2	10	22	49	<0.01	10	20	43	<0.01	10	20	43	<0.01
alu_9	5/1	11	25	53	<0.01	7	9	22	<0.01	7	9	22	<0.01
rd53_68	5/3	13	34	75	<0.01	13	34	75	<0.01	13	34	75	<0.01
hwb5_13	5/5	27	85	201	<0.01	28	88	205	0.01	28	88	205	0.01
sym6_63	6/1	14	29	69	<0.01	14	29	69	<0.01	14	29	69	<0.01
hwb6_14	6/6	46	157	377	<0.01	46	159	375	<0.01	46	159	375	0.01
rd73_69	7/3	25	73	162	<0.01	25	73	162	<0.01	25	73	162	<0.01
ham7_29	7/7	18	50	82	<0.01	21	61	107	<0.01	21	61	107	0.01
hwb7_15	7/7	74	276	665	<0.01	73	281	653	<0.01	76	278	658	0.01
rd84_70	8/4	34	104	229	<0.01	34	104	229	<0.01	34	104	229	<0.01
hwb8_64	8/8	116	442	1067	<0.01	112	449	1047	<0.01	114	440	1051	0.03
sym9_71	9/1	27	62	153	<0.01	27	62	153	<0.01	27	62	153	<0.01
LGSYNTH FUNCTIONS													
xor5	5/1	6	8	8	<0.01	6	8	8	<0.01	6	8	8	<0.01
bw	5/28	91	317	732	<0.01	87	307	693	<0.01	84	306	667	<0.01
ex5p	8/63	233	706	1520	0.02	206	647	1388	0.02	206	647	1388	0.06
9sym	9/1	27	62	153	<0.01	27	62	153	<0.01	27	62	153	0.01
pdc	16/40	631	2109	4803	0.12	619	2080	4781	0.13	619	2087	4850	66.38
spla	16/46	559	1728	3799	0.09	489	1709	4372	0.09	483	1687	4322	86.92
cordic	23/2	53	109	265	0.02	52	101	247	0.03	50	95	237	6.90

quires a longer run-time. Besides that, also in this evaluation, examples can be found, showing that optimization for BDDs not always leads to smaller circuits. Altogether, particularly for larger functions reordering is beneficial. In most of the cases it is thereby sufficient to perform sifting instead of exact reordering, since this lead to results of similar quality but without a notable increase in run-time. For the following evaluations, BDD-based synthesis with shared nodes, complement edges, and sifting has been applied.

Comparison to Previous Synthesis Approaches

In this section, circuits synthesized by the BDD-based approach are compared to the results generated by (1) the RMRLS approach (Gupta, Agrawal, & Jha, 2006) using version 0.2 in the default settings) and (2) the RMS approach (Maslov, Dueck & Miller, 2007) in its most recent version including improved handling of don't care conditions at the output. Since previous approaches (i.e., RMRLS and RMS) require reversible functions

as input, non-reversible functions are embedded into reversible ones (Maslov & Dueck, 2004). For BDD-based synthesis, the original function description has been used which automatically leads to an embedding.

The results are summarized in Figure 12. The first columns give the name as well as the number of the primary inputs (PI) and primary outputs (PO) of the original function. In the following columns, the number of lines (n), the gate count (d_{Tof}), the quantum cost (QC), and the synthesis time (TIME) for the respective approaches (i.e., RMRLS, RMS, and the BDD- BASED SYNTHESIS) are reported. For BDD-based synthesis, additionally the resulting number of gates (and thus the quantum cost) when directly synthesizing quantum gate circuits is given in the column denoted by d_{Qua}. Furthermore, a "~" denotes that an embedding needed by the previous synthesis approaches could not be created within the given timeout. Finally, the last two columns (ΔQC) give the absolute difference of the quantum cost for the resulting circuits obtained by the BDD-based

Figure 12. Comparison of BDD-based synthesis to previous methods

FUNCTION	PI/PO		PREVIOUS APPROACHES						BDD-BASED SYNTHESIS					Δ QC (RMRLS)	Δ QC (RMS)
			RMRLS [16]			RMS [17]									
		n	d_{Tof}	QC	TIME	d_{Tof}	QC	TIME	n	d_{Tof}	QC	d_{Qua}	TIME		
REVLIB FUNCTIONS															
decod24_10	2/4	4	11	55	497.51	7	19	<0.01	6	11	27	23	<0.01	-32	4
4mod5_8	4/1	5	9	25	0.86	5	9	<0.01	7	8	24	18	<0.01	-7	9
mini-alu_84	4/2	5	21	173	495.61	36	248	<0.01	10	20	60	43	<0.01	-130	-205
alu_9	5/1	5	9	49	122.48	9	25	0.01	7	9	29	22	0.01	-27	-3
rd53_68	5/3	7	–	–	>500.00	221	2646	0.14	13	34	98	75	<0.01	–	-2571
hwb5_13	5/5	5	–	–	>500.00	42	214	0.01	28	88	276	205	0.01	–	-9
sym6_63	6/1	7	36	777	485.47	15	119	0.13	14	29	93	69	<0.01	-708	-50
mod5adder_66	6/6	6	37	529	494.46	35	151	0.06	32	96	292	213	<0.01	-316	62
hwb6_14	6/6	6	–	–	>500.00	100	740	0.04	46	159	507	375	<0.01	–	-365
rd73_69	7/3	9	–	–	>500.00	1344	20779	1.93	13	73	217	162	<0.01	–	-20617
hwb7_15	7/7	7	–	–	>500.00	375	3378	0.18	73	281	909	653	<0.01	–	-2725
ham7_29	7/7	7	–	–	>500.00	26	90	0.09	21	61	141	107	<0.01	–	17
rd84_70	8/4	11	–	–	>500.00	124	8738	9.92	34	104	304	229	<0.01	–	-8509
hwb8_64	8/8	8	–	–	>500.00	229	3846	0.90	112	449	1461	1047	0.01	–	-2799
sym9_71	9/1	10	–	–	>500.00	27	201	3.98	27	62	206	153	<0.01	–	-48
hwb9_65	9/9	9	–	–	>500.00	2021	23311	1.45	170	699	2275	1620	0.02	–	-21691
cycle10_2_61	12/12	12	26	1435	491.87	41	1837	26.17	39	78	202	164	0.09	-1271	-1673
plus63mod4096_79	12/12	12	–	–	>500.00	24	4873	17.74	23	49	89	79	0.08	–	-4794
plus127mod8192_78	13/13	13	–	–	>500.00	25	9131	57.16	25	54	98	86	0.21	–	-9045
plus63mod8192_80	13/13	13	–	–	>500.00	28	9183	57.19	25	53	97	87	0.20	–	-9096
ham15_30	15/15	15	–	–	>500.00	–	–	>500.00	45	153	309	246	1.25	–	–
LGSYNTH FUNCTIONS															
xor5	5/1	6	27	387	484.11	8	68	0.01	6	8	8	8	<0.01	-379	-60
bw	5/28	~	~	~	~	~	~	~	87	307	943	693	<0.01	–	–
ex5p	8/63	~	~	~	~	~	~	~	206	647	1843	1388	0.02	–	–
9sym	9/1	10	–	–	>500.00	27	201	4.00	27	62	206	153	<0.01	–	-48
pdc	16/40	~	~	~	~	~	~	~	619	2080	6500	4781	0.14	–	–
spla	16/46	~	~	~	~	~	~	~	489	1709	5925	4372	0.10	–	–
cordic	23/2	~	~	~	~	~	~	~	52	101	325	247	0.02	–	–
cps	24/109	~	~	~	~	~	~	~	930	2676	8136	6301	0.10	–	–
apex2	39/3	~	~	~	~	~	~	~	498	1746	5922	4435	0.24	–	–
seq	41/35	~	~	~	~	~	~	~	1617	5990	19362	14259	1.14	–	–
c64	65/65	~	~	~	~	~	~	~	195	387	907	713	0.04	–	–
apex5	117/88	~	~	~	~	~	~	~	1147	3308	11292	8387	0.14	–	–
ex4p	128/28	~	~	~	~	~	~	~	510	1277	4009	3093	0.03	–	–

quantum circuit synthesis and the RMRLS and RMS approach, respectively.

As a first result, one can conclude that for large functions to be synthesized it is not always feasible to create a reversible embedding needed by the previous approaches. Moreover, even if this is possible, both RMRLS and RMS need a significant amount of run-time to synthesize a circuit from the embedding. As a consequence, for most of the LGSynth benchmarks no result can be generated within the given time-out. In contrast, the BDD-based approach is able to synthesize circuits for all given functions within a few CPU seconds.

Furthermore, although BDD-based synthesis often leads to larger circuits with respect to gate count and number of lines, the resulting quantum cost are significantly lower in most of the cases (except for decod24 10, 4mod5 8, mod5adder 66, and ham7 29). As an example, for plus63mod4096 79 the BDD-BASED SYNTHESIS synthesizes a circuit with twice the number of lines but with two orders of magnitude fewer quantum cost in comparison to RMS. In the best cases (e.g., hwb9 65) a reduction of several thousands in quantum cost is achieved. Note that quantum costs are more important than gate count, since they consider gates with more control lines to be more costly. Thus, even if the total number of circuit lines that have been added by the BDD- BASED SYNTHESIS is higher than by previous approaches, significant improvements in the quantum cost are obtained.

Furthermore, reversible logic for functions with more than 100 variables can be automatically synthesized.

7. CONCLUSION

In this paper, we introduced a synthesis approach which can cope with large functions. The basic idea is to create a Binary Decision Diagram for the function to be synthesized and afterwards substituting each node by a cascade of Toffoli or quantum gates, respectively. Since BDDs may include shared nodes causing fan-outs (which are not allowed in reversible logic), also substitutions including an additional circuit line are proposed.

While previous approaches are only able to handle functions with up to 30 variables at high run-time, our BDD-based approach can synthesize circuits for functions with more than one hundred variables in just a few CPU seconds. Furthermore, in most of the cases reductions in the resulting quantum cost have been observed.

ACKNOWLEDGMENT

This paper is an expanded work from Wille and Drechsler (2009) and Wille and Drechsler (2010).

REFERENCES

Barenco, A., Bennett, C. H., Cleve, R., DiVinchenzo, D. P., Margolus, N., & Shor, P. (1995). Elementary gates for quantum computation. *The American Physical Society, 52*, 3457–3467.

Bennett, C. H. (1973). Logical reversibility of computation. *IBM Journal of Research and Development, 17*(6), 525–532. doi:10.1147/rd.176.0525

Bollig, B., & Wegener, I. (1996). Improving the variable ordering of OBDDs is NP-complete. *IEEE Transactions on Computers, 45*(9), 993–1002. doi:10.1109/12.537122

Brace, K. S., Rudell, R. L., & Bryant, R. E. (1990). Efficient implementation of a BDD package. In *Proceedings of the Design Automation Conference* (pp. 40-45).

Bryant, R. E. (1986). Graph-based algorithms for Boolean function manipulation. *IEEE Transactions on Computers, 35*(8), 677–691. doi:10.1109/TC.1986.1676819

Cuykendall, R., & Andersen, D. R. (1987). Reversible optical computing circuits. *Optics Letters, 12*(7), 542–544. doi:10.1364/OL.12.000542

Desoete, B., & De Vos, A. (2002). A reversible carry-look-ahead adder using control gates. *Integration, the VLSI Journal, 33*(1-2), 89-104.

Drechsler, R., Drechsler, N., & Günther, W. (2000). Fast exact minimization of BDDs. *IEEE Transactions on Computer-Aided Design of Integrated Circuits and Systems, 19*(3), 384–389. doi:10.1109/43.833206

Drechsler, R., & Sieling, D. (2001). Binary decision diagrams in theory and practice. *Software Tools for Technology Transfer, 3*, 112–136.

Feinstein, D. Y., Thornton, M. A., & Miller, D. M. (2008). *Partially redundant logic detection using symbolic equivalence checking in reversible and irreversible logic circuits* (pp. 1378–1381). Design, Automation and Test in Europe.

Fredkin, E. F., & Toffoli, T. (1982). Conservative logic. *International Journal of Theoretical Physics, 21*(3-4), 219–253. doi:10.1007/BF01857727

Große, D., Wille, R., Dueck, G. W., & Drechsler, R. (2009). Exact multiple control Toffoli network synthesis with SAT techniques. *IEEE Trans. On CAD, 28*(5), 703–715.

Gupta, P., Agrawal, A., & Jha, N. K. (2006). An algorithm for synthesis of reversible logic circuits. *IEEE Transactions on Computer-Aided Design of Integrated Circuits and Systems*, 25(11), 2317–2330. doi:10.1109/TCAD.2006.871622

Hung, W. N. N., Song, X., Yang, G., Yang, J., & Perkowski, M. (2006). Optimal synthesis of multiple output Boolean functions using a set of quantum gates by symbolic reachability analysis. *IEEE Transactions on Computer-Aided Design of Integrated Circuits and Systems*, 25(9), 1652–1663. doi:10.1109/TCAD.2005.858352

Kerntopf, P. (2004). A new heuristic algorithm for reversible logic synthesis. In *Proceedings of the Design Automation Conference* (pp. 834-837).

Landauer, R. (1961). Irreversibility and heat generation in the computing process. *IBM Journal of Research and Development*, 5, 183. doi:10.1147/rd.53.0183

Liaw, H.-T., & Lin, C.-S. (1992). On the OBDD-representation of general Boolean functions. *IEEE Transactions on Computers*, 41, 661–664. doi:10.1109/12.144618

Maslov, D., & Dueck, G. W. (2004). Reversible cascades with minimal garbage. *IEEE Transactions on Computer-Aided Design of Integrated Circuits and Systems*, 23(11), 1497–1509. doi:10.1109/TCAD.2004.836735

Maslov, D., Dueck, G. W., & Miller, D. M. (2005). Toffoli network synthesis with templates. *IEEE Transactions on Computer-Aided Design of Integrated Circuits and Systems*, 24(6), 807–817. doi:10.1109/TCAD.2005.847911

Maslov, D., Dueck, G. W., & Miller, D. M. (2007). Techniques for the synthesis of reversible Toffoli networks. *ACM Transactions on Design Automation of Electronic Systems*, 12(4). doi:10.1145/1278349.1278355

Maslov, D., & Miller, D. M. (2007). Comparison of the cost metrics through investigation of the relation between optimal ncv and optimal nct 3-qubit reversible circuits. *IET Computers & Digital Techniques*, 1(2), 98–104. doi:10.1049/iet-cdt:20060070

Merkle, R. C. N. (1993). Reversible electronic logic using switches. *Nanotechnology*, 4, 21–40. doi:10.1088/0957-4484/4/1/002

Miller, D. M., Maslov, D., & Dueck, G. W. (2003). A transformation based algorithm for reversible logic synthesis. In *Proceedings of the Design Automation Conference* (pp. 318-323).

Nielsen, M., & Chuang, I. (2000). *Quantum Computation and Quantum Information*. Cambridge, UK: Cambridge University Press.

Patel, K., Markov, I., & Hayes, J. (2008). Optimal synthesis of linear reversible circuits. *Quantum Information and Computation*, 8(3-4), 282–294.

Peres, A. (1985). Reversible logic and quantum computers. *Physical Review A.*, 32(6), 3266–3276. doi:10.1103/PhysRevA.32.3266

Prasad, A. K., Shende, V. V., Markov, I. L., Hayes, J. P., & Patel, K. N. (2006). Data structures and algorithms for simplifying reversible circuits. *Journal on Emerging Technologies in Computing Systems*, 2(4), 277–293. doi:10.1145/1216396.1216399

Rudell, R. (1993). Dynamic variable ordering for ordered binary decision diagrams. In *Proceedings of the International Conference on CAD* (pp. 42-47).

Shannon, C. E. (1938). A symbolic analysis of relay and switching circuits. *Transactions of the AIEE*, 57, 713–723.

Shende, V. V., Prasad, A. K., Markov, I. L., & Hayes, J. P. (2003). Synthesis of reversible logic circuits. *IEEE Transactions on Computer-Aided Design of Integrated Circuits and Systems*, 22(6), 710–722. doi:10.1109/TCAD.2003.811448

Somenzi, F. (2001). *CUDD: CU Decision Diagram Package Release 2.3.1*. Boulder, CO: University of Colorado at Boulder.

Toffoli, T. (1980). Reversible computing . In de Bakker, W., & van Leeuwen, J. (Eds.), *Automata, Languages and Programming* (p. 632). New York: Springer.

Wegener, I. (2000). *Branching programs and binary decision diagrams: theory and applications*. Philadelphia: Society for Industrial and Applied Mathematics.

Wille, R., & Drechsler, R. (2009). BDD-based synthesis of reversible logic for large functions. In *Proceedings of the Design Automation Conference* (pp. 270-275).

Wille, R., & Drechsler, R. (2010). Effect of BDD Optimization on Synthesis of Reversible and Quantum Logic. *Electronic Notes in Theoretical Computer Science*, *253*(6), 57–70. doi:10.1016/j.entcs.2010.02.006

Wille, R., Große, D., Teuber, L., Dueck, G. W., & Drechsler, R. (2008). RevLib: an online resource for reversible functions and reversible circuits. In *Proceedings of the International Symposium on Multi-Valued Logic* (pp. 220-225). Retrieved from http://www.revlib.org

Yang, S. (1991). *Logic synthesis and optimization benchmarks user guide* (Tech. Rep. No. 1/95). Durham, NC: Microelectronic Center of North Carolina.

Zhirnov, V. V., Cavin, R. K., Hutchby, J. A., & Bourianoff, G. I. (2003). Limits to binary logic switch scaling – a gedanken model. *Proceedings of the IEEE*, *91*(11), 1934–1939. doi:10.1109/JPROC.2003.818324

Zhong, J., & Muzio, J. C. (2006). Using crosspoint faults in simplifying Toffoli networks. In *Proceedings of the IEEE Northeast Workshop on Circuits and Systems* (pp. 129-132).

This work was previously published in International Journal of Applied Metaheuristic Computing, Volume 1, Issue 4, edited by Peng-Yeng Yin, pp. 25-42, copyright 2010 by IGI Publishing (an imprint of IGI Global).

Compilation of References

(2001). Random graphs. In Bollobás, B. (Ed.), *Cambridge Studies in Advanced Mathematics* (2nd ed., *Vol. 78*). Cambridge, UK: Cambridge University Press.

Abdullah, S., Ahmadi, S., Burke, E. K., & Dror, M. (2007). Investigating Ahuja-Orlins large neighbourhood search for examination timetabling. *OR-Spektrum*, *29*(2), 351–372. doi:10.1007/s00291-006-0034-7

Abraham, A., Grosan, C., & Ramos, V. (Eds.). (2006). *Swarm intelligence in data mining*. Berlin, Germany: Springer-Verlag.

Achterberg, T., Koch, T., & Martin, A. (2003). *The mixed integer programming library: Miplib*. Retrieved from http://miplib.zib.de

Adenso-Díaz, B., & laguna, M. (2006). Fine-tuning of algorithms using fractional experimental design and local search. *Operations Research*, *54*(1), 99–114. doi:10.1287/opre.1050.0243

Aha, D. W., Kibler, D., & Albert, M. K. (1991). Instance-based learning algorithms. *Machine Learning*, *6*, 37–66.

Ahn, H., & Kim, K. (2009). Bankruptcy prediction modeling with hybrid case-based reasoning and genetic algorithms approach. *Applied Soft Computing*, *9*, 599–607. doi:10.1016/j.asoc.2008.08.002

Ahn, H., Kim, K., & Han, I. (2006). Hybrid genetic algorithms and case-based reasoning systems for customer classification. *Expert Systems: International Journal of Knowledge Engineering and Neural Networks*, *23*(3), 127–144. doi:10.1111/j.1468-0394.2006.00329.x

Aho, A. V., Hopcroft, J. E., & Ullman, J. D. (1976). *The Design and Analysis of Computer Algorithms*. Reading, MA: Addison-Wesley.

Ahuja, R., Ergun, O., Orlin, J., & Punnen, A. (2002). A survey of very large-scale neighborhood search techniques. *Discrete Applied Mathematics*, *123*, 75–102. doi:10.1016/S0166-218X(01)00338-9

Ahuja, R., Orlin, J., Pallottino, S., Scaparra, M., & Scutellà, M. (2004). A multi-exchange heuristic for the single-source capacitated facility location problem. *Management Science*, *50*, 749–760. doi:10.1287/mnsc.1030.0193

Alba, E., Almeida, F., Blesa, M., Cotta, C., D'ıaz, M., Dorta, I., et al. Le'on, C., Moreno, L., Petit, J., Roda, J., Rojas, A., & Xhafa, F. (2002). MALLBA: A library of skeletons for combinatorial optimization. In B. Monien & R. Feldman (Eds.), *Euro-Par 2002 Parallel Processing Conference* (LNCS 2400, pp. 927-932). Berlin: Springer.

Alba, E., & Lugue, G. (2005). Measuring the performance of parallel metaheuristics. In Alba, E. (Ed.), *Parallel metaheuristics: A new class of algorithm* (pp. 43–60). New York: John Wiley & Sons.

Al-Betar, M., Khader, A., & Gani, T. (2008). A harmony search algorithm for university course timetabling. In *Proceedings of the 7th International Conference on the Practice and Theory of Automated Timetabling (PATAT 2008)*, Montreal, Canada.

Alekseev, V. E., Boliac, R., Korobitsyn, D. V., & Lozin, V. V. (2007). NP-hard graph problems and boundary classes of graphs. *Theoretical Computer Science*, *389*(1-2), 219–236. doi:10.1016/j.tcs.2007.09.013

Alkan, A., & Özcan, E. (2003). Memetic algorithms for timetabling. In *Proceedings of 2003 IEEE Congress on Evolutionary Computation* (pp. 1796-1802).

Alvarez-Valdes, R., Parreño, F., & Tamarit, J. (2007). A tabu search algorithm for a two-dimensional non-guillotine cutting problem. *European Journal of Operational Research, 183*, 1167–1182. doi:10.1016/j.ejor.2005.11.068

Alvarez-Valdes, R., Parreño, F., & Tamarit, J. (2008). Reactive GRASP for the strip-packing problem. *Computers & Operations Research, 35*, 1065–1083. doi:10.1016/j.cor.2006.07.004

Alves, C., & Carvalhoa, J. M. V. (2007). Accelerating column generation for variable sized bin-packing problems. *European Journal of Operational Research, 183*(3), 1333–1352. doi:10.1016/j.ejor.2005.07.033

Anagnostopoulos, A., Michel, L., Hentenryck, P. V., & Vergados, Y. (2006). A simulated annealing approach to the traveling tournament problem. *Journal of Scheduling, 9*, 177–193. doi:10.1007/s10951-006-7187-8

Antony, J. (2003). *Design of experiments for engineers and scientists*. Barlington, UK: Butterworth-Heinemann.

Araya, I., Neveu, B., & Riff, M.-C. (2008). An efficient hyperheuristic for strip-packing problems. In Cotta, C., Sevaux, M., & Sörensen, K. (Eds.), *Adaptive and Multilevel Metaheuristics* (*Vol. 136*, pp. 61–76). Berlin: Springer. doi:10.1007/978-3-540-79438-7_3

Arenas, M. G., Collet, P., Eiben, A. E., Jelasity, M., Merelo, J. J., Paechter, B., et al. (2002). A framework for distributed evolutionary algorithms. In *Parallel Problem Solving from Nature Conference (PPSN VII)* (LNCS 2439, pp. 665-675). Berlin: Springer.

Aşik, O., & Özcan, E. (2009). Bidirectional best-fit heuristic for orthogonal rectangular strip packing. *Annals of Operations Research, 172*, 405–427. doi:10.1007/s10479-009-0642-0

Ayob, M., & Kendall, G. (2003). A monte carlo hyper-Heuristic to optimise component placement sequencing for multi head placement machine. In *Proceedings of the International Conference on Intelligent Technologies (InTech'03)* (pp. 132-141).

Azimi, Z. N. (2005). Hybrid heuristics for examination timetabling problem. *Applied Mathematics and Computation, 163*(2), 705–733. doi:10.1016/j.amc.2003.10.061

Bäck, T. (1992). Self-adaptation in genetic algorithms. In *Proceedings Toward a practice of autonomous systems: the First European Conference on Artificial Life* (pp. 263-271).

Bäck, T., Hoffmeister, F., & Schwefel, H. (1991). A survey of evolution strategies. In *Proceedings of the Fourth International Conference on Genetic Algorithms*.

Bäck, T., Rudolph, G., & Schwefel, H. (1993). Evolutionary programming and evolution strategies: Similarities and differences. In *Proceedings of the Second Annual Conference on Evolutionary Programming* (pp. 11-22).

Bäck, T., Fogel, D., & Michalewicz, Z. (2000a). [Bristol, UK: Institute of Physics Publishing.]. *Evolutionary Computation, 1*.

Bäck, T., Fogel, D., & Michalewicz, Z. (2000b). [*Advanced algorithms and operators*. Bristol, UK: Institute of Physics Publishing.]. *Evolutionary Computation, 2*.

Bäck, T., & Schwefel, H. (1993). An overview of evolutionary algorithms for parameter optimization. *Evolutionary Computation, 1*(1), 1–23. doi:10.1162/evco.1993.1.1.1

Badinelli, R. D. (1990). The inventory costs of common misspecification of demand-forecastingmodels. *International Journal of Production Research, 28*(12), 2321–2340. doi:10.1080/00207549008942869

Bai, R., & Kendall, G. (2003). An investigation of automated planograms using a simulated annealing based hyper-heuristics. In T. Ibaraki, K. Nonobe, & M. Yagiura (Ed.), *Meta-heuristics: Progress as Real Problem Solvers, selected papers from the 5th Metaheuristics International Conference (MIC'03)* (pp. 87-108). New York: Springer.

Bai, R., Blazewicz, J., Burke, E., Kendall, G., & McCollum, B. (2007a). *A simulated annealing hyper-heuristic methodology for flexible decision support* (Computer Science Tech. Rep. No. NOTTCS-TR-2007-8). Nottingham, UK: University of Nottingham.

Bai, R., Burke, E. K., Kendall, G., & McCollum, B. (2007b). Memory length in hyper-heuristics: an empirical study. In *Proceedings of 2007 IEEE Symposium on Computational Intelligence in Scheduling (CISched2007)* (pp. 173-178).

Baker, B., Brown, D., & Katseff, H. (1981). A 5/4 algorithm for two-dimensional packing. *Journal of Algorithms, 2,* 348–368. doi:10.1016/0196-6774(81)90034-1

Baker, B. Jr, & Rivest, R. (1980). Orthogonal packings in two dimensions. *SIAM Journal on Computing, 9,* 846–855. doi:10.1137/0209064

Balas, E., & Jeroslow, R. (1972). Canonical Cuts on the Unit Hypercube. *SIAM Journal on Applied Mathematics, 23*(1), 60–69. doi:10.1137/0123007

Baluja, S. (1994). *Population-based incremental learning: A method for integrating genetic search based function optimization and competitive learning* (Tech. Rep. CMU-CS-94-163). Pittsburgh, PA: Carnegie Mellon University.

Barandela, R., Sánchez, J. S., García, V., & Rangel, E. (2003). Strategies for learning in class imbalance problems. *Pattern Recognition, 36*(3), 849–851. doi:10.1016/S0031-3203(02)00257-1

Barbosa, V. C., & Ferreira, R. G. (2004). On the phase transitions of graph coloring and independent sets. *Physica A: Statistical Mechanics and its Applications, 343,* 401-423.

Barenco, A., Bennett, C. H., Cleve, R., DiVinchenzo, D. P., Margolus, N., & Shor, P. (1995). Elementary gates for quantum computation. *The American Physical Society, 52,* 3457–3467.

Barr, R., Golden, B., Kelly, J., Steward, W., & Resende, M. (2001). Guidelines for designing and reporting on computational experiments with heuristic methods. In *Proceedings of International Conference on Meta-heuristics for Optimization* (pp. 1-17). Dordrecht, The Netherlands: Kluwer.

Barr, R. S., Golden, B. L., Kelly, J. P., Resende, M. G. C., & Stewart, W. R. (1995). Designing and reporting computational experiments with heuristic methods. *Journal of Heuristics, 1*(1), 9–32. doi:10.1007/BF02430363

Bartz-Beielstein, T. (2006). *Experimental research in evolutionary computation.* New York: Springer.

Batista, G. E. A. P. A., Prati, R. C., & Monard, M. C. (2004). A study of the behavior of several methods for balancing machine learning training data. *ACM Special Interest Group on Knowledge Discovery and Data Mining. SIGKDD Explorations, 6*(1), 20–29. doi:10.1145/1007730.1007735

Beasley, J. E. (2006). *OR-library.* Retrieved from http://people.brunel.ac.uk/mastjjb/jeb/info.html

Beasley, J. (2004). A population heuristic for constrained two-dimensional non-guillotine cutting. *European Journal of Operational Research, 156,* 601–627. doi:10.1016/S0377-2217(03)00139-5

Beasley, J. E. (1990). OR-Library: distributing test problems by electronic mail. *The Journal of the Operational Research Society, 41*(11), 1069–1072.

Belov, G., Kartak, V., Rohling, H., & Scheithauer, G. (2009). One-dimensional relaxations and LP bounds for orthogonal packing. *International Transactions in Operational Research, 16,* 745–766. doi:10.1111/j.1475-3995.2009.00713.x

Beltrán Cano, J., Calderón, J., Cabrera, R., Moreno Pérez, J., & Moreno-Vega, J. (2004). GRASP / VNS hybrid for the strip packing problem. In C. Blum, A. Roli, & M. Sampels (Eds.), *First International Workshop on Hybrid Metaheuristics* (pp. 79-90).

Benati, S. (1997). An algorithm for a cutting stock problem on a strip. *The Journal of the Operational Research Society, 48,* 288–294.

Bennett, C. H. (1973). Logical reversibility of computation. *IBM Journal of Research and Development, 17*(6), 525–532. doi:10.1147/rd.176.0525

Berger, J., Salois, M., & Begin, R. (1998). *A hybrid genetic algorithm for the vehicle routing problem with time windows* (LNCS, *1418,* 114–127.

Beyer, H. (1998). *On the "explorative power" of ES/EP-like algorithms* (pp. 323–334). LNCS.

Beyer, H.-G., & Schwefel, H.-P. (2002). Evolution strategies: A comprehensive introduction. *Natural Computing, 1*(1), 3–52. doi:10.1023/A:1015059928466

Beyer, H., & Schwefel, H. (2002). Evolution strategies – A comprehensive introduction. *Natural Computing, 1*(1), 3–52. doi:10.1023/A:1015059928466

Bezdek, J. C., & Kuncheva, L. I. (2001). Nearest prototype classifier designs: An experimental study. *International Journal of Intelligent Systems, 16*(12), 1445–1473. doi:10.1002/int.1068

Bilgin, B., Özcan, E., & Korkmaz, E. E. (2007). An experimental study on hyper-heuristics and exam scheduling. In *Proceedings of the 6th International Conference on the Practice and Theory of Automated Timetabling (PATAT'06)* (LNCS 3867, pp. 394-412).

Birattari, M., Stuetzle, T., Paquete, L., & Varrentrapp, K. (2002). A racing algorithm for configuring metaheuristics. In W. B. Langdon et al. (Eds.), *Proceedings of the Genetic and Evolutionary Computation Conference (GECCO 2002)* (pp. 11-18). San Francisco: Morgan Kaufmann Publishers.

Biratteri, M. (2009). *Tuning Metaheuristics: A machine learning perspective*. Heidelberg, Germany: Springer.

Blackwell, T., & Branke, J. (2004). Multi-swarm optimization in dynamic environments (LNCS 3005, pp. 489-500).

Blackwell, T., & Branke, J. (2006). Multi-swarms, exclusion and anti-convergence in dynamic environments. *IEEE Transactions on Evolutionary Computation, 10*, 459–472. doi:10.1109/TEVC.2005.857074

Blair, J. R. S., & Peyton, B. (1993). An introduction to chordal graphs and clique trees. In George, A., Glibert, J. R., & Liu, J. W. H. (Eds.), *Graph Theory and Sparse Matrix Computation* (pp. 1–29). New York: Springer Verlag.

Błażewicz, J., Moret-Salvador, A., & Walkowiak, R. (2004). Parallel tabu search approaches for two-dimensional cutting. *Parallel Processing Letters, 14*, 23–32. doi:10.1142/S0129626404001684

Bleuler, S., Laumanns, M., Thiele, L., & Zitzler, E. (2003). PISA: A platform and programming language independent interface for search algorithms. In *Proceedings of the Conference on Evolutionary Multi-Criterion optimization (EMO'03)*, Faro, Portugal (pp. 494-508).

Blum, C., & Roli, A. (2003). Metaheuristics in combinatorial optimization: Overview and conceptual comparison. *ACM Computing Surveys, 35*(3), 268–308. doi:10.1145/937503.937505

Bodlaender, H. L. (1993). A tourist guide through treewidth. *Acta Cybernetica, 11*, 1–21.

Bodlaender, H. L. (1994). Improved self-reduction algorithms for graphs with bounded treewidth. *Discrete Applied Mathematics, 54*, 101–105. doi:10.1016/0166-218X(94)90018-3

Bollig, B., & Wegener, I. (1996). Improving the variable ordering of OBDDs is NP-complete. *IEEE Transactions on Computers, 45*(9), 993–1002. doi:10.1109/12.537122

Bondy, J. A., & Murty, U. S. R. (1976). *Graph Theory with Applications*. New York: Elsevier.

Boros, E., & Hammer, P. (2002). Pseudo-Boolean optimization. *Discrete Applied Mathematics, 123*(1-3), 155–225. doi:10.1016/S0166-218X(01)00336-5

Bortfeldt, A. (2006). A genetic algorithm for the two-dimensional strip packing problem with rectangular pieces. *European Journal of Operational Research, 172*, 814–837. doi:10.1016/j.ejor.2004.11.016

Box, G., Hunter, J. S., & Hunter, W. G. (2005). *Statistics for experimenters: design, innovation, and discovery*. New York: Wiley.

Brace, K. S., Rudell, R. L., & Bryant, R. E. (1990). Efficient implementation of a BDD package. In *Proceedings of the Design Automation Conference* (pp. 40-45).

Bradley, A. P. (1997). The use of the area under the ROC curve in the evaluation of machine learning algorithms. *Pattern Recognition, 30*(7), 1145–1159. doi:10.1016/S0031-3203(96)00142-2

Branke, J. (1999). Memory enhanced evolutionary algorithms for changing optimization problems. In *Proceedings of the IEEE Congress on Evolutionary Computation (CEC 1999)* (pp. 1875-1882). Washington, DC: IEEE Computer Society.

Branke, J. (1999). *The moving peaks benchmark*. Retrieved from http://www.aifb.uni-karlsruhe.de/ ~jbr/MovPeaks

Branke, J., & Mattfeld, D. (2005). Anticipation and flexibility in dynamic scheduling. *International Journal of Production Research*, 43, 3103–3129. doi:10.1080/00207540500077140

Braunstein, A., Mulet, R., Pagnani, A., Weigt, M., & Zecchina, R. (2003). Polynomial iterative algorithms for coloring and analyzing random graphs. *Physical Review E: Statistical, Nonlinear, and Soft Matter Physics*. doi:10.1103/PhysRevE.68.036702

Brelaz, D. (1979). New methods to color the vertices of a graph. *Communications of the ACM*, 22(4), 251–256. doi:10.1145/359094.359101

Brightom, H., & Mellish, C. (2002). Advances in instance selection for instance based learning algorithms. *Data Mining and Knowledge Discovery*, 6, 153–172. doi:10.1023/A:1014043630878

Broder, S. (1964). Final examination scheduling. *Communications of the ACM*, 7(8), 494–498. doi:10.1145/355586.364824

Brown, J. (1972). Chromatic scheduling and the chromatic number problem. *Management Science*, 19(4), 456–463. doi:10.1287/mnsc.19.4.456

Bryant, R. E. (1986). Graph-based algorithms for Boolean function manipulation. *IEEE Transactions on Computers*, 35(8), 677–691. doi:10.1109/TC.1986.1676819

Buckles, B. P., & Petry, F. E. (1992). *Genetic algorithms*. Los Alamitos, CA: IEEE CS Press.

Burke, E. K., Dror, M., Petrovic, S., & Qu, R. (2005). Hybrid graph heuristics within a hyper-heuristic approach to exam timetabling problems. In B. L. Golden, S. Raghavan, & E. A. Wasil (Ed.), *The next wave in computing, optimization, and decision technologies: Proceedings of the 9th Informs Computing Society Conference* (pp. 79-91). Springer.

Burke, E. K., Elliman, D. G., Ford, P. H., & Weare, R. F. (1996a). Examination timetabling in British universities - a survey. In E. K. Burke & P. Ross (Eds.), *Selected Papers from the 1st International Conference on the Practice and Theory of Automated Timetabling*, Edinburgh (LNCS 1153, pp.76-92).

Burke, E. K., Newall, J. P., & Weare, R. F. (1996b). A memetic algorithm for university exam timetabling. In E. K. Burke & P. Ross (Eds.), *Selected Papers from the 1st International Conference on the Practice and Theory of Automated Timetabling*, Edinburgh (LNCS 1153, pp. 241-250).

Burke, E., Hyde, M., Kendall, G., Ochoa, G., Özcan, E., & Rong, Q. (2009b). *A survey of hyper-heuristics* (Computer Science Tech. Rep. No. NOTTCS-TR-SUB-0906241418-2747). Nottingham, UK: University of Nottingham.

Burke, E., Hyde, M., Kendall, G., Ochoa, G., Özcan, E., & Woodward, J. R. (2009a). Exploring hyper-heuristic methodologies with genetic programming. In C. L. Mumford & L. C. Jain (Eds.), *Computational intelligence: Collaboration, fusion and emergence* (pp. 177-201). New York: Springer.

Burke, E., Hyde, M., Kendall, G., Ochoa, G., Özcan, E., & Woodward, J. R. (2009c). *A classification of hyper-heuristic appraoches* (Computer Science Tech. Rep. No. NOTTCS-TR-SUB-0907061259-5808). Nottingham, UK: University of Nottingham.

Burke, E., Kendall, G., Newall, J., Hart, E., Ross, P., & Schulenburg, S. (2003a). Hyper-heuristics: An emerging direction in modern search technology. In F. W. Glover & G. A. Kochenberger (Ed.), *Handbook of Metaheuristics* (Vol. 57, pp. 457-474). Dordrecht, The Netherlands: Kluwer International Publishing.

Burke, E. K., McCollum, B., Meisels, A., Petrovic, S., & Qu, R. (2007). A graph-based hyper-heuristic for educational timetabling problems. *European Journal of Operational Research*, 176(1), 177–192. doi:10.1016/j.ejor.2005.08.012

Burke, E. K., & Newall, J. P. (2004). Solving examination timetabling problems through adaption of heuristic orderings: Models and algorithms for planning and scheduling problems. *Annals of Operations Research*, 129, 107–134. doi:10.1023/B:ANOR.0000030684.30824.08

Burke, E. K., Petrovic, S., & Qu, R. (2006). Case based heuristic selection for timetabling problems. *Journal of Scheduling*, 9, 115–132. doi:10.1007/s10951-006-6775-y

Burke, E., Bykov, Y., Newall, J. P., & Petrovic, S. (2003). A time-predefined approach to course timetabling. [YU-JOR]. *Yugoslav Journal of Operations Research, 13*(2), 139–151. doi:10.2298/YJOR0302139B

Burke, E., Kendall, G., & Soubeiga, E. (2003b). A tabu-search hyper-heuristic for timetabling and rostering. *Journal of Heuristics, 9*, 451–470. doi:10.1023/B:HEUR.0000012446.94732.b6

Burke, E., Kendall, G., & Whitwell, G. (2009). A simulated annealing enhancement of the best-fit heuristic for the orthogonal stock cutting problem. *INFORMS Journal on Computing, 21*, 505–516. doi:10.1287/ijoc.1080.0306

Cano, J. R., García, S., & Herrera, F. (2008). Subgroup discovery in large size data sets preprocessed using stratified instance selection for increasing the presence of minority classes. *Pattern Recognition Letters, 29*, 2156–2164. doi:10.1016/j.patrec.2008.08.001

Cano, J. R., Herrera, F., & Lozano, M. (2003). Using evolutionary algorithms as instance selection for data reduction in KDD: An experimental study. *IEEE Transactions on Evolutionary Computation, 7*, 561–575. doi:10.1109/TEVC.2003.819265

Cano, J. R., Herrera, F., & Lozano, M. (2005). Stratification for scaling up evolutionary prototype selection. *Pattern Recognition Letters, 26*, 953–963. doi:10.1016/j.patrec.2004.09.043

Cano, J. R., Herrera, F., & Lozano, M. (2007). Evolutionary stratified training set selection for extracting classification rules with trade-off precision-interpretability. *Data & Knowledge Engineering, 60*, 90–100. doi:10.1016/j.datak.2006.01.008

Cano, J. R., Herrera, F., Lozano, M., & García, S. (2008). Making CN2-SD subgroup discovery algorithm scalable to large size data sets using instance selection. *Expert Systems with Applications, 35*, 1949–1965. doi:10.1016/j.eswa.2007.08.083

Caramia, M., DellOlmo, P., & Italiano, G. F. (2001). New algorithms for examination timetabling. In S. Naher & D. Wagner (Eds.), *Algorithm Engineering 4th International Workshop (WAE'00)* (LNCS 1982, pp. 230-241).

Caramia, M., & Dell'Olmo, P. (2007). Coupling stochastic and deterministic local search in examination timetabling. *Operations Research, 55*(2). doi:10.1287/opre.1060.0354

Carter, M. W., & Laporte, G. (1996a). Recent developments in practical examination timetabling. In E. K. Burke & P. Ross (Eds.), *Selected Papers from the 1st International Conference on the Practice and Theory of Automated Timetabling,* Edinburgh (LNCS 1153, pp. 3-21).

Carter, M. W. (1986). A survey of practical applications of examination timetabling algorithms. *Operations Research, 34*, 193–202. doi:10.1287/opre.34.2.193

Carter, M. W., Laporte, G., & Lee, S. (1996b). Examination timetabling: Algorithmic strategies and applications. *The Journal of the Operational Research Society, 47*(3), 373–383.

Casey, S., & Thompson, J. (2003). GRASPing the examination scheduling problem. In E. K. Burke & P. De Causmaecker (Eds.), *Practice and theory of automated timetabling: Selected Papers from the 4th International Conference* (LNCS 2740, pp. 232-244).

Castro, L. N., & Zuben, F. V. J. (2002). Learning and optimization using the clonal selection principle. *IEEE Transactions on Evolutionary Computation, 6*, 239–251. doi:10.1109/TEVC.2002.1011539

Cervantes, A., Galván, I., & Isasi, P. (2007). An adaptive michigan approach PSO for nearest prototype classification. In *Nature Inspired Problem-Solving Methods in Knowledge Engineering* (LNCS 4528, pp. 287-296).

Cervantes, A., Galván, I., & Isasi, P. (in press). AMPSO: A new particle swarm method for nearest neighborhood classification. *IEEE Transactions on Systems, Man and Cybernetics, part B.*

Cervantes, A., Isasi, P., & Galván, I. (2005). A comparison between the pittsburgh and michigan approaches for the binary pso algorithm. In *Proceedings of the 2005 IEEE Congress on Evolucionary Computation,* Munchen, Germany (pp. 290-297).

Cesarone, F., Scozzari, A., & Tardella, F. (2008). Efficient algorithms for mean-variance portfolio optimization with Hard Real-World Constraints. In *Proceedings of the 18th International AFIR Colloquium*, Rome, Italy.

Chakhlevitch, K., & Cowling, P. I. (2008). Hyperheuristics: Recent developments. In *Adaptive and Multilevel Metaheuristics* (pp. 3-29).

Chan, F. T. S., & Tiwari, M. K. (2007). *Swarm intelligence: focus on ant and particle swarm optimization*. Gaborone, Botswana: I-Tech Publications.

Chang, C.-L. (1974). Finding prototypes for nearest neighbor classifiers. *IEEE Transactions on Computers*, *23*(11), 1179–1184. doi:10.1109/T-C.1974.223827

Chawla, N. V., Bowyer, K. W., Hall, L. O., & Kegelmeyer, W. P. (2002). SMOTE: Synthetic minority over-sampling technique. *Journal of Artificial Intelligence Research*, *16*, 321–357.

Chawla, N. V., Japkowicz, N., & Kotcz, A. (2004). Editorial: Special issue on learning from imbalanced data sets. *ACM Special Interest Group on Knowledge Discovery and Data Mining. SIGKDD Explorations*, *6*(1), 1–6. doi:10.1145/1007730.1007733

Chazelle, B. (1983). The bottom-left bin-packing heuristic: An efficient implementation. *IEEE Transactions on Computers*, *32*, 697–707. doi:10.1109/TC.1983.1676307

Cheeseman, P., Kanefsky, B., & Taylor, W. M. (1991). Where the really hard problems are. In J. Mylopoulos & R. Reiter (Eds.), *Twelfth International Joint Conference on Artificial Intelligence* (Vol. 1, pp. 331-337). San Francisco: Morgan Kaufmann.

Chen, P.-C., Kendall, G., & Berghe, G. V. (2007). An ant based hyper-heuristic for the travelling tournament problem. In *Proceedings of IEEE Symposium of Computational Intelligence in Scheduling (CISched'07)* (pp. 19-26).

Cheong, C. Y., Tan, K. C., & Veeravalli, B. (2007). Solving the exam timetabling problem via a multi-objective evolutionary algorithm – a more general approach. In *Proceedings of the IEEE Symposium on Computational Intelligence in Scheduling (CI-Sched'07)* (pp. 165-172).

Chiarandini, M., Dumitrescu, I., & Sttzle, T. (2007). Stochastic local search algorithms for the graph colouring problem. In Gonzalez, T. F. (Ed.), *Handbook of Approximation Algorithms and Metaheuristics*. London: Chapman and Hall/CRC.

Chung, F. R. K. (1988). Labelings of graphs. In Beineke, L. W., & Wilson, R. J. (Eds.), *Selected Topics in Graph Theory* (*Vol. 3*, pp. 151–168).

Chung, F. R. K., Leighton, F. T., & Rosenberg, A. L. (1987). Embedding graphs in books: a layout problem with applications to VLSI design. *SIAM J. Algebraic Disc. Meth.*, *8*, 33–58. doi:10.1137/0608002

Clautiaux, F., Jouglet, A., Carlier, J., & Moukrim, A. (2008). A new constraint programming approach for the orthogonal packing problem. *Computers & Operations Research*, *35*, 944–959. doi:10.1016/j.cor.2006.05.012

Clerc, M. (2006). Particle swarm optimization. *International scientific and technical encyclopaedia*

Clerc, M., & Kennedy, J. (2002). The particle swarm: explosion, stability, and convergence in multi-dimensional complex space. *IEEE Transactions on Evolutionary Computation*, *6*(1), 58–73. doi:10.1109/4235.985692

Cloete, T., Engelbrecht, A. P., & Pampar, G. (2008). *CIlib: A collaborative framework for computational intelligence algorithms – part I*. Retrieved from http://www.cilib.net/

Coello Coello, C. A., & Lechuga, M. S. (2002). MOPSO: A proposal for multiple objective particle swarm optimization, Evolutionary Computation. In *Proceedings of the 2002 Congress on Evolutionary Computation* (Vol. 2, pp. 1051-1056).

Coello Coello, C. A., & Christiansen, A. D. (1999). MOSES: a multiple objective optimization tool for engineering design. *Journal of Engineering Optimization*, *31*(3), 337–368. doi:10.1080/03052159908941377

Coffman, E. Jr, Garey, M., Johnson, D., & Tarjan, R. (1980). Performance bounds for level-oriented two-dimensional packing algorithms. *SIAM Journal on Computing*, *9*, 808–826. doi:10.1137/0209062

Cohen, P. R. (1995). *Empirical methods for artificial intelligence*. Cambridge, UK: MIT Press.

Cole, A. J. (1964). The preparation of examination timetables using a small-store computer. *The Computer Journal*, *7*, 117–121. doi:10.1093/comjnl/7.2.117

Coleman, J. S. (1990). *Fundamentals of social theory*. Cambridge, MA: Belknap Press of Harvard Univ Press.

Collette, Y., & Siarry, P. (2005). Three new metrics to measure the convergence of metaheuristics towards the Pareto frontier and the aesthetic of a set of solutions in biobjective optimization. *Computers & Operations Research, 32*, 773–792. doi:10.1016/j.cor.2003.08.017

Conway, J. H., & Alexander, N. J. (1998). *Sphere packings, lattices and groups* (3rd ed.). New York: Springer.

Cook, S. A. (1971). The complexity of theorem-proving procedures. In *Proceedings of the Third ACM Symposium on Theory of Computing* (pp. 151-158).

Cooren, Y., Fakhfakh, M., Loulou, M., & Siarry, P. (2007). Optimizing second generation current conveyors using particle swarm optimization. In *Proceedings of the IEEE international conference on microelectronics* (pp. 378-381)

Cormen, T. H., Leiserson, C. E., Rivest, R. L., & Stein, C. (2002). *Introduction to algorithms*. London: MIT Press.

Corr, P. H., McCollum, B., McGreevy, M. A. J., & McMullan, P. (2006). A new neural network based construction heuristic for the examination timetabling problem. In T. P. Runarsson et al. (Eds.), *PPSN IX* (LNCS 4193, pp. 392-401).

Costa, D., & Hertz, A. (1997). Ants can colour graphs. *The Journal of the Operational Research Society, 48*, 295–305.

Courat, J. P., Raynaud, G., Mrad, I., & Siarry, P. (1994). Electronic component model minimization based on log simulated annealing. *IEEE Transactions on Circuits and Systems, 41*(12), 790–795. doi:10.1109/81.340841

Courcelle, B. (1994). The monadic second order logic of graph VI: On several representations of graphs by relational structures. *Discrete Applied Mathematics, 54*, 117–149. doi:10.1016/0166-218X(94)90019-1

Cover, T. M., & Hart, P. E. (1967). Nearest neighbor pattern classification. *IEEE Transactions on Information Theory, 13*, 21–27. doi:10.1109/TIT.1967.1053964

Cowling, P., & Chakhlevitch, K. (2003). Hyperheuristics for managing a large collection of low level heuristics to schedule personnel. In *Proceedings of the IEEE Congress on Evolutionary Computation (CEC'03)* (pp. 1214-1221).

Cowling, P., Kendall, G., & Han, L. (2002). An investigation of a hyperheuristic genetic algorithm applied to a trainer scheduling problem. In *Proceedings of the IEEE Congress on Evolutionary Computation (CEC'02)* (pp. 1185-1190).

Cowling, P., Kendall, G., & Soubeiga, E. (2001a). A hyperheuristic approach to scheduling a sales summit. In *Proceedings of the 3rd International Conference on Practice and Theory of Automated Timetabling (PATAT'00)* (pp. 176-190). Springer-Verlag.

Cowling, P., Kendall, G., & Soubeiga, E. (2001b). A parameter-free hyperheuristic for scheduling a sales summit. In *Proceedings of 4th Metaheuristics International Conference (MIC'01)* (pp. 127-131).

Coyle, R. G. (1977). *Management System Dynamics*. New York: John Wiley & Sons.

Coy, S., Golden, B. L., Runger, G. C., & Wasil, E. A. (2000). Using experimental design to find effective parameter settings for heuristics. *Journal of Heuristics, 7*, 77–97. doi:10.1023/A:1026569813391

Crainica, T. G., Perbolib, G., Pezzutob, M., & Tadeib, R. (2007). Computing the asymptotic worst-case of bin packing lower bounds. *European Journal of Operational Research, 183*(3), 1295–1303. doi:10.1016/j.ejor.2005.07.032

Crainic, T. G., & Tolouse, M. (1998). Parallel metaheuristic. In Crainic, T. G., & Laporte, G. (Eds.), *Fleet management And logistic* (pp. 205–235). Norwell, MA: Kluwer Academic publishers.

Crainic, T. G., & Toulouse, M. (2003). Parallel Strategies for Meta-Heuristics. In Kochenberger, G., & Glover, F. (Eds.), *Handbook of Metaheuristics*. Dordrecht, The Netherlands: Kluwer Academic Publishers.

Crama, Y., & Hammer, P. (2007). *Boolean functions: Theory, algorithms and applications*. Cambridge, UK: Cambridge University Press.

Cuesta-Canada, A., Garrido, L., & Terashima-Marin, H. (2005). Building hyper-heuristics through ant colony optimization for the 2d bin packing problem. In *Proceedings of the 9th International Conference on Knowledge-Based Intelligent Information and Engineering Systems (KES'05)* (LNCS 3684, pp. 654-660).

Culberson, J. C., & Gent, I. P. (2001). Frozen development in graph coloring. *Theoretical Computer Science, 265*(1-2), 227–264. doi:10.1016/S0304-3975(01)00164-5

Culberson, J. C., & Luo, F. (1996). Exploring the k-colorable landscape with iterated greedy. In Johnson, D. S., & Trick, M. A. (Eds.), *Cliques, Coloring, and Satisfiability: 2nd DIMACS Implementation Challenge* (pp. 245–284). Providence, RI: American Mathematical Society.

Cunningham, P. (in press). A taxonomy of similarity mechanisms for case-based reasoning. *IEEE Transactions on Knowledge and Data Engineering*.

Cuykendall, R., & Andersen, D. R. (1987). Reversible optical computing circuits. *Optics Letters, 12*(7), 542–544. doi:10.1364/OL.12.000542

Dantzig, G. (1963). *Linear Programming and Extensions*. Princeton, NJ: Princeton University Press.

Dasgupta, D. (Ed.). (1998). *Artificial immune systems and their applications*. Berlin, Germany: Springer Verlag.

Davis, L. (1990). Hybrid genetic algorithms for machine learning. In *Proceedings of IEE Colloquium on Machine Learning* (pp. 9).

Davis, L. (Ed.). (1991). *Handbook of genetic algorithms*. Reinhold, NY: Van Nostrand.

Davoine, T., Hammer, P. L., & Vizvári, B. (2003). A Heuristic for Boolean optimization problems. *Journal of Heuristics, 9*, 229–247. doi:10.1023/A:1023717307746

Deb, K., Pratap, A., Agarwal, S., & Meyarivan, T. (2002). A fast and elitist multiobjective genetic algorithm: NSGA-ii. *Evolutionary Computation, 6*(2), 182–197. doi:10.1109/4235.996017

Degertekin, S. (2008). Optimum design of steel frames using harmony search algorithm. *Structural and Multidisciplinary Optimization, 36*(4), 393–401. doi:10.1007/s00158-007-0177-4

Deineko, V., & Woeginger, G. (2000). A study of exponential neighborhoods for the travelling salesman problem and for the quadratic assignment problem. *Mathematical Programming. Ser. A, 87*, 519–542.

Dejonckheere, J., Disney, S. M., Lambrecht, M. R., & Towill, D. R. (2003). Measuring and avoiding the bullwhip effect: A control theoretic approach. *European Journal of Operational Research, 147*(3), 567–590. doi:10.1016/S0377-2217(02)00369-7

Dejonckheere, J., Disney, S. M., Lambrecht, M. R., & Towill, D. R. (2004). The impact of information enrichment on the bullwhip effect in supply chains: A control engineering perspective. *European Journal of Operational Research, 153*(3), 727–750. doi:10.1016/S0377-2217(02)00808-1

Del-Rio, R., Medeiro, F., Perez-Verdu, B., Dela-Rosa, J. M., & Rodriguez-Vasquez, A. (2006). *CMOS cascade sigma-delta modulators for sensors and telecom*. New York: Springer.

Denzinger, J., Fuchs, M., & Fuchs, M. (1997). High performance ATP systems by combining several ai methods. In *Proceedings of the Fifteenth International Joint Conference on Artificial Intelligence (IJCAI 97)* (pp. 102-107).

Desoete, B., & De Vos, A. (2002). A reversible carry-look-ahead adder using control gates. *Integration, the VLSI Journal, 33*(1-2), 89-104.

Deziel, D. P., & Eilon, S. (1967). A linear production-inventory control rule. *Production Engineering, 43*, 93–104.

Di Caro, G., & Dorigo, M. (1998). AntNet: Distributed stigmergetic control for communications networks. *Journal of Artificial Intelligence Research, 9*, 317–365.

Di Gaspero, L., & Schaerf, A. (2001). Tabu search techniques for examination timetabling. In E. K. Burke & W. Erben (Eds.), *Selected Papers from the 3rd International Conference on the Practice and Theory of Automated Timetabling (PATAT'00)* (LNCS 2079, pp. 104-117).

Dinger, R. H. (1998). Engineering design optimization with genetic algorithm. In *Proceedings of the IEEE northcon conference* (pp. 114-119).

Disney, S. M., Farasyn, I., Lambrecht, M., Towill, D. R., & Velde, W. V. d. (2006). Taming the bullwhip effect whilst watching customer service in a single supply chain echelon. *European Journal of Operational Research, 173*(1), 151–172. doi:10.1016/j.ejor.2005.01.026

Disney, S. M., & Towill, D. R. (2002). A discrete transfer function model to determine the dynamic stability of a vendor managed inventory supply chain. *International Journal of Production Research*, 40(1), 179–204. doi:10.1080/00207540110072975

Disney, S. M., & Towill, D. R. (2003). On the bullwhip and inventory variance produced by an ordering policy. *Omega*, 31(3), 157–167. doi:10.1016/S0305-0483(03)00028-8

Disney, S. M., & Towill, D. R. (2005). Eliminating drift in inventory and order based production control systems. *International Journal of Production Economics*, 93-94, 331–344. doi:10.1016/j.ijpe.2004.06.031

Domingo, C., Gavalda, R., & Watanabe, O. (2002). Adaptive sampling methods for scaling up knowledge discovery algorithms. *Data Mining and Knowledge Discovery*, 6(2), 131–152. doi:10.1023/A:1014091514039

Doreo, J., Siarry, E., Petrowski, A., & Taillard, E. (2006). *Metaheuristics for hard optimization*. Heidelberg, Germany: Springer.

Dorigo, M., Dicaro, G., & Gambardella, L. M. (1999). Ant algorithms for discrete optimization. *Artificial life journal*, 5(2), 137-172.

Dorigo, M., & Gambardella, L. M. (1997). Ant colonies for the traveling salesman problem. *Biosystem*, 43, 73–81. doi:10.1016/S0303-2647(97)01708-5

Dorigo, M., & Gambardella, L. M. (2002). Guest editorial special on ant colony optimization. *IEEE Transactions on Evolutionary Computation*, 6, 317–319. doi:10.1109/TEVC.2002.802446

Dorigo, M., & Stützle, T. (2001). *Ant Colony Optimization: algorithms, applications and advances. Metaheuristics Handbook, International Series in Operations Research and Management Science*. Dordrecht, The Netherlands: Kluwer.

Dorigo, M., & Stützle, T. (2004). *Ant Colony Optimization*. Cambridge, MA: MIT press.

Dorigo, M., & Stützle, T. (2004). *Ant colony optimization*. Cambridge, UK: MIT Press.

Dorne, R., & Hao, J. K. (1998). Tabu search for graph coloring, T-colorings and set T-colorings. In Voss, S., Martello, S., Osman, I. H., & Roucairol, C. (Eds.), *Meta-Heuristics: Advances and Trends in Local Search Paradigms for Optimization* (pp. 77–92). Dordrecht, The Netherlands: Kluwer.

Dowsland, K. A., Soubeiga, E., & Burke, E. (2007). A simulated annealing hyper-heuristic for determining shipper sizes. *European Journal of Operational Research*, 179(3), 759–774. doi:10.1016/j.ejor.2005.03.058

Dowsland, K., & Dowsland, W. (1992). Packing problems. *European Journal of Operational Research*, 56, 2–14. doi:10.1016/0377-2217(92)90288-K

Dowsland, K., & Thompson, J. (2005). Ant colony optimization for the examination scheduling problem. *The Journal of the Operational Research Society*, 56(4), 426–438. doi:10.1057/palgrave.jors.2601830

Drechsler, R., Drechsler, N., & Günther, W. (2000). Fast exact minimization of BDDs. *IEEE Transactions on Computer-Aided Design of Integrated Circuits and Systems*, 19(3), 384–389. doi:10.1109/43.833206

Drechsler, R., & Sieling, D. (2001). Binary decision diagrams in theory and practice. *Software Tools for Technology Transfer*, 3, 112–136.

Dréo, J., & Siarry, P. (2006). An ant colony algorithm aimed at dynamic continuous optimization. *Applied Mathematics and Computation*, 181, 457–467. doi:10.1016/j.amc.2005.12.051

Dubois, O., Monasson, R., Selman, B., & Zecchina, R. (Eds.). (2001)... *Theoretical Computer Science*, 265(1-2).

Dueck, G. (1993). New optimization heuristics: the great deluge algorithm and the record-to-record travel. *Journal of Computational Physics*, 104, 86–92. doi:10.1006/jcph.1993.1010

Du, W., & Li, B. (2008). Multi-strategy ensemble particle swarm optimization for dynamic optimization. *Information Sciences*, 178, 3096–3109. doi:10.1016/j.ins.2008.01.020

Dyckhoff, H. (1990). A typology of cutting and packing problems. *European Journal of Operational Research*, 44(2), 145–159. doi:10.1016/0377-2217(90)90350-K

Eagly, A. H., & Chaiken, S. (1992). *The psychology of attitudes*. San Diego, CA: Harcourt Brace.

Eberhart, R., & Kennedy, J. (1995). A new optimizer using particle swarm theory. In *Proceedings of the Sixth Symposium on Micro Machine and Human Science* (pp. 39-43).

Eiben, A. E., & Smith, J. E. (2003). *Introduction to evolutionary computing*. Berlin, Germany: Springer Verlag.

Eiben, A. E., van der Hauw, J. K., & van Hemert, J. I. (1998). Graph coloring with adaptive evolutionary algorithms. *Journal of Heuristics*, *4*(1), 24–46. doi:10.1023/A:1009638304510

El Hayek, J., Moukrim, A., & Negre, S. (2008). New resolution algorithm and pretreatments for the two-dimensional bin-packing problem. *Computers & Operations Research*, *35*, 3184–3201. doi:10.1016/j.cor.2007.02.013

El-Abd, M., & Kamel, M. (2005). A taxonomy of cooprative search algorithms. In Blesa, M. J., Blume, C., Roli, A., & Samples, M. (Eds.), *Hybrid metaheuristic* (pp. 32–42). Heidelberg, Germany: Springer. doi:10.1007/11546245_4

Enrico, M., & Paolo, T. (2010). A survey on vertex coloring problems. *International Transactions in Operational Research*, *17*, 1–34. doi:10.1111/j.1475-3995.2009.00696.x

Erben, W. (2001). A grouping genetic algorithm for graph colouring and exam timetabling. In K. Burke & W. Erben (Eds.), *Proceedings of the 3rd International Conference on the Practice and Theory of Automated Timetabling (PATAT'00)* (LNCS 2079, pp. 132-156).

Erdal, F., & Saka, M. (2006). Optimum design of grillage systems using harmony search algorithm. In *Proceedings of 8th International Conference on Computational Structures Technology (CST 2006)*, Las Palmas de Gran Canaria, Spain.

Erdal, F., & Saka, M. (2008). Effect of beam spacing in the harmony search based optimum design of grillages. [Building and Housing]. *Asian Journal of Civil Engineering*, *9*(3), 215–228.

Ergul, A. (1996). GA-based examination scheduling experience at Middle East Technical University. In E. K. Burke & P. Ross (Eds.), *Selected Papers from the 1st International Conference on the Practice and Theory of Automated Timetabling*, Edinburgh (LNCS 1153, pp. 212-226).

Ersoy, E., Özcan, E., & Uyar, S. (2007). Memetic algorithms and hyperhill-climbers. In *Proceedings of the 3rd Multidisciplinary International Scheduling Conference: Theory and Applications (MISTA'07)* (pp. 156-166).

Esbensen, H. (1992). Genetic algorithm for macro cell placement. In *Proceedings of the European Design Automation Conference (EUDO-VHDL)* (pp. 52-57).

Eshelman, L. J. (1991). The CHC adaptive search algorithm: How to have safe search when engaging in nontraditional genetic recombination. In G. Rawlins (Ed.), *Foundations of genetic algorithms and classifier systems* (pp. 265-283). San Mateo, CA: Morgan Kaufmann.

Eshghi, K., & Azimi, P. (2004). Application of mathematical programming in graceful labeling problem of graphs. *Journal of Applied Mathematics*, *1*, 1–8. doi:10.1155/S1110757X04310065

Estabrooks, A., Jo, T., & Japkowicz, N. (2004). A multiple resampling method for learning from imbalanced data sets. *Computational Intelligence*, *20*(1), 18–36. doi:10.1111/j.0824-7935.2004.t01-1-00228.x

Even, S., Itai, A., & Shamir, A. (1976). On the complexity of timetable and multicommodity Flow problems. *SIAM Journal on Computing*, *5*(4), 691–703. doi:10.1137/0205048

Fakhfakh, M., Masmoudi, S., Tlelo-Cuautle, E., & Loulou, M. (2008). Synthesis of switched current memory cells using the nullor approach and application to the design of high performance SI sigma delta modulators. *WSEAS Transactions on electronics*, *5*(6), 265-273

Fakhfakh, M., Cooren, Y., Loulou, M., & Siarry, P. (2008). A particle swarm optimization technique used for the improvement of analog circuit performances. In Lazinica, A. (Ed.), *Particle Swarm Optimization* (pp. 169–182). Gaborone, Botswana: I-Tech Publications.

Fakhfakh, M., Loulou, M., & Masmoudi, N. (2007). Optimizing performances of switched current memory cells through a heuristic. *Analog Integrated Circuits and Signal Processing*, *50*(2), 115–126. doi:10.1007/s10470-006-9009-5

Farley, A. (1988). Mathematical programming models for cutting stock problems in the clothing industry. *The Journal of the Operational Research Society*, *39*, 41–53.

Fazio, R. H. (1986). How do attitudes guide behavior? In R. M. Sorrentino & E. T. Higgins (Eds.), *The handbook of motivation and cognition: Foundations of social behavior.* New York: Guilford Press.

Feinstein, D. Y., Thornton, M. A., & Miller, D. M. (2008). *Partially redundant logic detection using symbolic equivalence checking in reversible and irreversible logic circuits* (pp. 1378–1381). Design, Automation and Test in Europe.

Fekete, S. P., Schepers, J., & Veen, J. C. V. D. (2007). An exact algorithm for higher-dimensional orthogonal packing. *Operations Research, 55,* 569–587. doi:10.1287/opre.1060.0369

Fernández, A., García, S., del Jesus, M. J., & Herrera, F. (2008). A study of the behaviour of linguistic fuzzy rule based classification systems in the framework of imbalanced data-sets. *Fuzzy Sets and Systems, 159*(18), 2378–2398. doi:10.1016/j.fss.2007.12.023

Fernández, F., & Isasi, P. (2004). Evolutionary design of nearest prototype classifiers. *Journal of Heuristics, 10,* 431–454. doi:10.1023/B:HEUR.0000034715.70386.5b

Fesanghary, M., Mahdavi, M., Minary-Jolandan, M., & Alizadeh, Y. (2008). Hybridizing harmony search algorithm with sequential quadratic programming for engineering optimization problems. *Computer Methods in Applied Mechanics and Engineering, 197*(33-40), 3080-3091.

Fieldsend, J., & Singh, S. (2002). A multi-objective algorithm based upon article swarm optimisation, an efficient data structure and turbulence. In *Proceedings of the 2002 U.K. Workshop on Computational Intelligence,* Birmingham, UK (pp. 37-44).

Fink, A., Voss, S., & Woodruff, D. L. (1999). Building reusable software components for heuristic search. In Kall, P., & Luthi, H. J. (Eds.), *Operations Research Proceedings* (pp. 210–219). Heidelberg, Germany: Springer.

Fischetti, M., Glover, F., Lodi, A., & Monaci, M. (2006). *Feasibility Net.*

Fischetti, M., Glover, F., & Lodi, A. (2005). Feasibility Pump. *Mathematical Programming - Series A, 104,* 91–104. doi:10.1007/s10107-004-0570-3

Fischetti, M., Salazar Gonzalez, J. J., & Toth, P. (1997). A branch-and-cut algorithm for the symmetric generalized traveling salesman problem. *Operations Research, 45*(3), 378–394. doi:10.1287/opre.45.3.378

Fishbein, M., & Ajzen, I. (1975). *Belief, attitude, intention, and behavior: An introduction to theory and research.* Reading, MA: Addison-Wesley.

Fisher, H., & Thompson, G. L. (1961). *Probabilistic learning combinations of local job-shop scheduling rules.* Paper presented at the *Factory Scheduling Conference,* Carnegie Institue of Technology.

Fisher, W. (1935). *The Design of Experiments.* Edinburgh, UK: Oliver and Boyd.

Fleurent, C., & Ferland, J. (1996b). Object-oriented implementation of heuristic search methods for graph coloring, maximum clique, and satisfiability. In D. S. Johnson & M. A. Trick (Eds.), *Cliques, Coloring, and Satisfiability* (Volume 26 of DIMACS Series in Discrete Mathematics and Theoretical Computer Science, pp. 619-652). New Providence, NJ: American Mathematical Society.

Fleurent, C., & Ferland, J. (1996a). Genetic and hybrid algorithms for graph coloring. *Annals of Operations Research, 6*(3), 437–461. doi:10.1007/BF02125407

Fogel, D. B. (1995). A Comparison of Evolutionary Programming and Genetic Algorithms on Selected Constrained Optimization Problems. *Simulation, 64*(6), 399–406. doi:10.1177/003754979506400605

Fogel, D., & Atmar, J. (1990). Comparing genetic operators with Gaussian mutations in simulated evolutionary processes using linear systems. *Biological Cybernetics, 63*(2), 111–114. doi:10.1007/BF00203032

Forsati, R., Mahdavi, M., Kangavari, M., & Safarkhani, B. (2008b). Web page clustering using harmony search optimization. In *Proceedings of Electrical and Computer Engineering (CCECE 2008)* (pp. 1601-1604).

Forsati, R., Haghighat, A., & Mahdavi, M. (2008a). *Harmony search based algorithms for bandwidth-delay-constrained least-cost multicast routing.* Computer Communications.

Fowler, R., Paterson, M., & Tanimoto, S. (1981). Optimal packing and covering in the plane are NP-complete. *Information Processing Letters, 12*, 133–137. doi:10.1016/0020-0190(81)90111-3

Frangioni, A., Necciari, E., & Scutellà, M. (2004). A multi-exchange neighborhood for minimum makespan parallel machine scheduling problems. *Journal of Combinatorial Optimization, 8*, 195–220. doi:10.1023/B:JOCO.0000031420.05971.29

Fredkin, E. F., & Toffoli, T. (1982). Conservative logic. *International Journal of Theoretical Physics, 21*(3-4), 219–253. doi:10.1007/BF01857727

Freitas, A. A. (2002). *Data mining and knowledge discovery with evolutionary algorithms*. New York: Springer-Verlag.

Freitas, A. A., da Costa Pereira, A., & Brazdil, P. (2007). Cost-sensitive decision trees applied to medical data. In *Data Warehousing and Knowledge Discovery* (LNCS 4654, pp. 303-312).

Freud, S. (1895). Project for a scientific psychology. In J. Strachey (Ed.), *The standard edition the complete psychological works of Sigmund Freud* (Vol. 1). London: Hogarth Press.

Frigon, N. L., & Mathews, D. (1997). *Practical guide to experimental design*. New York: Wiley.

Fukunaga, A. (2008). Automated discovery of local search heuristics for satisfiability testing. *Evolutionary Computation, 16*(1), 31–61. doi:10.1162/evco.2008.16.1.31

Funabiki, N., & Higashino, T. (2000). A minimal state processing search algorithm for graph coloring problems. *IEICE Transactions Fundamentals E, 83-A*(7), 1420–1430.

Gale, W., Das, S., & Yu, C. T. (1990). Improvements to an Algorithm for Equipartitioning. *IEEE Transactions on Computers, 39*(5), 706–710. doi:10.1109/12.53585

Galinier, P., & Hao, J. K. (1999). Hybrid evolutionary algorithms for graph coloring. *Journal of Combinatorial Optimization, 3*(4), 379–397. doi:10.1023/A:1009823419804

Galinier, P., & Hertz, A. (2006). A survey of local search methods for graph coloring. *Computers & Operations Research, 33*, 2547–2562. doi:10.1016/j.cor.2005.07.028

Galinier, P., Hertz, A., & Zufferey, N. (2008). An adaptive memory algorithm for the k-coloring problem. *Discrete Applied Mathematics, 156*, 267–279. doi:10.1016/j.dam.2006.07.017

Gallian, J. A. (2009). A Dynamic survey of graph labeling. *Electronic Journal of Combinatorics, 16*, 1–216.

Ganley, J. L., & Heath, L. S. (2001). The pagenumber of k-trees is O(k). *Discrete Applied Mathematics, 109*, 215–221. doi:10.1016/S0166-218X(00)00178-5

Garain, U. (2008). Prototype reduction using an artificial immune model. *Pattern Analysis & Applications, 11*, 353–363. doi:10.1007/s10044-008-0106-1

García, S., Cano, J. R., & Herrera, F. (2008). A memetic algorithm for evolutionary prototype selection: A scaling up approach. *Pattern Recognition, 41*(8), 2693–2709. doi:10.1016/j.patcog.2008.02.006

García, S., & Herrera, F. (in press). Evolutionary undersampling for classification with imbalanced data sets: Proposals and taxonomy. *Evolutionary Computation.*

Garey, M. R., & Johnson, D. S. (1979). *Computers and Intractability: A Guide to the Theory of NP-Completeness*. San Francisco, CA: W. H. Freeman and Company.

Garrido, P., & Riff, M.-C. (2007). Collaboration between hyperheuristics to solve strip-packing problems. In P. Melin, O. Castillo, L. Aguilar, J. Kacprzyk, & W. Pedrycz (Eds.), *Twelfth International Fuzzy Systems Association World Congress* (LNCS 4529, pp. 698-707). Berlin: Springer.

Gaspero, L. Di, & Schaerf, A. (2001). EasyLocal++: An object-oriented framework for the design of local search algorithms and metaheuristics. In *Proceedings of the MIC'2001 4th Metaheuristics International Conference*, Porto, Portugal (pp. 287-292).

Geem, Z. (2000). *Optimal design of water distribution networks using harmony search*. Unpublished doctoral dissertation, Korea University, Seoul, South Korea.

Geem, Z. (2005b). School bus routing using harmony search. In *Proceedings of the Genetic and Evolutionary Computation Conference (GECCO 2005)*, Washington, DC.

Geem, Z. (2007b). Harmony search algorithm for the optimal design of largescale water distribution network. In *Proceedings of the 7th International IWA Symposium on Systems Analysis and Integrated Assessment in Water Management (Watermatex 2007)*, Washington, DC.

Geem, Z. (2010). *Recent advances in harmony search algorithm*.

Geem, Z., & Hwangbo, H. (2006). Application of harmony search to multi-objective optimization for satellite heat pipe design. In *Proceedings of US-Korea Conference on Science, Technology, and Entrepreneurship (UKC 2006)*, Teaneck, NJ.

Geem, Z., Kim, J., & Yoon, Y. (2000). Optimal layout of pipe networks using harmony search. In *Proceedings of 4th International Conference on Hydro-Science and Engineering*, Seoul, South Korea.

Geem, Z., Lee, K., & Tseng, C. (2005b). Harmony search for structural design. In *Proceedings of the 2005 conference on Genetic and evolutionary computation* (pp. 651-652). New York: ACM.

Geem, Z., Tseng, C., & Park, Y. (2005c). *Harmony search for generalized orienteering problem: best touring in China* (LNCS 3612, p. 741).

Geem, Z. (2006a). *Comparison Harmony Search with Other Meta-Heuristics in Water Distribution Network Design*. Reston, VA: ASCE.

Geem, Z. (2006b). *Improved harmony search from ensemble of music players* (Lecture Notes in Computer Science, 4251:86. Geem, Z. (2007a). *Harmony search algorithm for solving Sudoku* (. LNCS, 4692, 371.

Geem, Z. (2008). *Harmony search optimisation to the pump-included water distribution network design*. Civil Engineering and Environmental Systems.

Geem, Z. W. (2005). Harmony Search in Water Pump Switching Problem. *Lecture Notes in Computer Science*, *3612*, 751–760. doi:10.1007/11539902_92

Geem, Z. W. (2007). Optimal Scheduling of Multiple Dam System Using Harmony Search Algorithm. *Lecture Notes in Computer Science*, *4507*, 316–323. doi:10.1007/978-3-540-73007-1_39

Geem, Z. W. (2008). Novel Derivative of Harmony Search Algorithm for Discrete Design Variables. *Applied Mathematics and Computation*, *199*(1), 223–230. doi:10.1016/j.amc.2007.09.049

Geem, Z. W. (2009). Particle-Swarm Harmony Search for Water Network Design. *Engineering Optimization*, *41*(4), 297–311. doi:10.1080/03052150802449227

Geem, Z. W., & Choi, J. Y. (2007). Music Composition Using Harmony Search Algorithm. *Lecture Notes in Computer Science*, *4448*, 593–600. doi:10.1007/978-3-540-71805-5_65

Geem, Z. W., Kim, J. H., & Loganathan, G. V. (2001). A New Heuristic Optimization Algorithm: Harmony Search. *Simulation*, *76*(2), 60–68. doi:10.1177/003754970107600201

Geem, Z. W., & Williams, J. C. (2007). Harmony Search and Ecological Optimization. *International Journal of Energy and Environment*, *1*(2), 150–154.

Geem, Z., & Choi, J. (2007). *Music composition using harmony search algorithm* (. LNCS, 4448, 593.

Geem, Z., & Kim, J. (2001). A new heuristic optimization algorithm: harmony search. *Simulation*, *76*(2), 60. doi:10.1177/003754970107600201

Geem, Z., Kim, J., & Loganathan, G. (2002). Harmony search optimization: Application to pipe network design. *International Journal of Modelling & Simulation*, *22*(2), 125–133.

Geem, Z., Lee, K., & Park, Y. (2005a). Application of harmony search to vehicle routing. *American Journal of Applied Sciences*, *2*(12), 1552–1557. doi:10.3844/ajassp.2005.1552.1557

Geem, Z., & Williams, J. (2007). Harmony search and ecological optimization. *International Journal of Energy and Environment*, *1*, 150–154.

Gendreau, M. (2003). An introduction to tabu search. In Glover, F., & Kochenberger, G. A. (Eds.), *Handbook of metaheuristics* (pp. 37–54). Norwell, MA: Kluwer Academic publishers.

Gendreau, M., Laporte, G., & Semet, F. (1998). A tabu search heuristic for the undirected selective travelling salesman problem. *European Journal of Operational Research*, *106*(2-3), 539–545. doi:10.1016/S0377-2217(97)00289-0

Gent, I. P., MacIntyre, E., Prosser, P., & Walsh, T. (1996). The constrainedness of search. In W. J. Clancey, D. Weld, H. E. Shrobe, & T. E. Senator (Eds.), *Thirteenth National Conference on Artificial Intelligence* (Vol. 1, pp. 246-252). Menlo Park, CA: AAAI Press.

Gent, L. P., & Walsh, T. (1993). Towards an Understanding of Hill-Climbing Procedures for SAT. In [Cambridge, MA: MIT Press.]. *Proceedings of AAAI*, *93*, 28–33.

Gent, L. P., & Walsh, T. (1995). Unsatisfied Variables in Local Search. In Hallam, J. (Ed.), *Hybrid Problems, Hybrid Solutions* (pp. 73–85). Amsterdam: IOS Press.

Ghosh, A., & Jain, L. C. (Eds.). (2005). *Evolutionary computation in data mining*. Berlin, Germany: Springer Verlag.

Gil-Pita, R., & Yao, X. (2008). Evolving edited k-nearest neighbor classifiers. *International Journal of Neural Systems*, *18*(6), 1–9. doi:10.1142/S0129065708001725

Glover, F. (1998). A template for scatter search and path relinking. In J. K. Hao, E. Lutton, E. Ronald, M. Schoenauer, & D. Snyers (Eds.), *Artificial evolution* (Vol. 1363, pp. 13-54).

Glover, F. (2005). Adaptive Memory Projection Methods for Integer Programming. In C. Rego & B. Alidaee (Eds.), *Metaheuristic Optimization Via Memory and Evolution: Tabu Search and Scatter Search* (pp. 425-440). Dordrecht, The Netherland: Kluwer Academic Publishers.

Glover, F. (2007). Infeasible/Feasible Search Trajectories and Directional Rounding in Integer Programming. *Journal of Heuristics*.

Glover, F. W., & Laguna, M. (1997). *Tabu Search*. Dordrecht, The Netherladns: Kluwer.

Glover, F., & Gary, A. (Eds.). (2003). *Handbook of metaheuristics: International series in operations research & management science* (Vol. 57). New York: Springer.

Glover, F., Kochenberger, G., Alidaee, B., & Amini, M. (1999). Tabu search with critical event memory: An enhanced application for binary quadratic programs. In S. M. S. Voss, I. Osman, & C. Roucairol (Eds.), *Metaheuristics, Advances and trends in local search paradigms for optimization* (pp. 93-109). Dordrecht, The Netherlands, Kluwer Academic Publishers.

Glover, F. (1978). Parametric branch and bound. *OMEGA. The International Journal of Management Science*, *6*(2), 145–152.

Glover, F. (1989). Tabu Search - Part 1. *ORSA Journal on Computing*, *1*(3), 190–206.

Glover, F. (1996). Finding the best traveling salesman 4-opt move in the same time as a best 2-opt move. *Journal of Heuristics*, *2*, 169–179. doi:10.1007/BF00247211

Glover, F. (2005). Adaptive memory projection methods for integer programming. In Rego, C., & Alidaee, B. (Eds.), *Metaheuristic optimization via memory and evolution: Tabu search and scatter search* (pp. 425–440). Dordecht, The Netherlands: Kluwer Academic Publishers. doi:10.1007/0-387-23667-8_19

Glover, F. (2006). Parametric Tabu Search for Mixed Integer Programs. *Computers & Operations Research*, *33*(9), 2449–2494. doi:10.1016/j.cor.2005.07.009

Glover, F. (2006a). *Satisfiability Data Mining for Binary Data Classification Problems (Tech. Rep.)*. Boulder, CO: University of Colorado, Boulder.

Glover, F. (2007). Infeasible/feasible search trajectories and directional rounding in integer programming. *Journal of Heuristics*, *13*(6), 505–542. doi:10.1007/s10732-007-9029-z

Glover, F. (2008). Inequalities and target objectives for metaheuristic search – part I: Mixed binary optimization. In Siarry, P., & Michalewicz, Z. (Eds.), *Advances in metaheuristics for hard optimization* (pp. 439–474). New York: Springer. doi:10.1007/978-3-540-72960-0_21

Glover, F. W., & Laguna, M. (1997). *Tabu Search*. Dordrecht, The Netherlands: Kluwer.

Glover, F., & Greenberg, H. (1989). New Approaches for Heuristic Search: A Bilateral Linkage with Artificial Intelligence. *European Journal of Operational Research*, *39*(2), 119–130. doi:10.1016/0377-2217(89)90185-9

Glover, F., & Hanafi, S. (2002). Tabu Search and Finite Convergence. *Discrete Applied Mathematics, 119*, 3–36. doi:10.1016/S0166-218X(01)00263-3

Glover, F., & Hanafi, S. (2010). Metaheuristic Search with Inequalities and Target Objectives for Mixed Binary Optimization Part I: Exploiting Proximity. *International Journal of Applied Metaheuristic Computing, 1*(1), 1–15.

Glover, F., & Laguna, M. (1997). *Tabu search*. Dordecht, The Netherlands: Kluwer Academic Publishers. doi:10.1007/978-1-4615-6089-0

Glover, F., & Sherali, H. D. (2003). Foundation-Penalty Cuts for Mixed-Integer Programs. *Operations Research Letters, 31*, 245–253. doi:10.1016/S0167-6377(03)00014-2

Goldberg, D. E. (1989). *Genetic algorithms in search, optimization, and machine learning*. Reading, MA: Addison-Wesley.

Goldberg, D. E., & Deb, K. (1991). A comparative analysis of selection schemes used in genetic algorithms. In G. Rawlins (Ed.), *Foundations of genetic algorithms and classifier systems* (pp. 69-93). San Mateo, CA: Morgan Kaufmann.

Goldstein, I. (1978). *Developing a computational representation for problem solving skills* (AI Memo 495). Cambridge, MA: MIT.

Golumbic, M. C. (1980). *Algorithmic Graph Theory and Perfect Graphs*. New York: Academic Press.

Gomez, A. (2000). Resolution of strip-packing problems with genetic algorithms. *The Journal of the Operational Research Society, 51*, 1289–1295.

Gómez-Ballester, E., Micó, L., & Oncina, J. (2006). Some approaches to improve tree-based nearest neighbour search algorithms. *Pattern Recognition, 39*(2), 171–179. doi:10.1016/j.patcog.2005.06.007

Gómez-Villouta, G., Hamiez, J.-P., & Hao, J.-K. (2008). A dedicated genetic algorithm for two-dimensional non-guillotine strip packing. In *Proceedings of the Sixth Mexican International Conference on Artificial Intelligence, Special Session* (pp. 264-274). Washington, DC: IEEE Computer Society.

Gonçalves, J. (2007). A hybrid genetic algorithm-heuristic for a two-dimensional orthogonal packing problem. *European Journal of Operational Research, 183*, 1212–1229. doi:10.1016/j.ejor.2005.11.062

Graeb, H., Zizala, S., Eckmueller, J., & Antreich, K. (2001). The sizing rules method for analog integrated circuit design. In *Proceedings of the IEEE/ACM international conference on computer-aided design*

Granmo, O.-C., Oommen, B. J., Myrer, S. A., & Olsen, M. G. (2007). Learning Automata-Based Solutions to the Nonlinear Fractional Knapsack Problem with Applications to Optimal Resource Allocation. *IEEE Transactions on Systems, Man and Cybernetics, SMC-37(B)*, 166-175.

Granmo, O.-C., & Bouhmala, N. (2007). Solving the Satisfiability Problem Using Finite Learning Automata. *International Journal of Computer Science and Applications, 4*(3), 15–29.

Granmo, O.-C., & Oommen, B. J. (2010). Solving Stochastic Nonlinear Resource Allocation Problems Using a Hierarchy of Twofold Resource Allocation Automata. *IEEE Transactions on Computers, 59*(4), 545–560. doi:10.1109/TC.2009.189

Grimbleby, J. B. (2000). Automatic analogue circuit synthesis using genetic algorithms. *The IEE Circuits. Devices and Systems, 147*(6), 319–323. doi:10.1049/ip-cds:20000770

Grochowski, M., & Jankowski, N. (2004). Comparison of instance selection algorithms II. Results and comments. In *Proceedings of Artificial Intelligence and Soft Computing - ICAISC 2004* (LNCS 3070, pp. 580-585).

Große, D., Wille, R., Dueck, G. W., & Drechsler, R. (2009). Exact multiple control Toffoli network synthesis with SAT techniques. *IEEE Trans. On CAD, 28*(5), 703–715.

Grzymala-Busse, J. W., Stefanowski, J., & Wilk, S. (2005). A comparison of two approaches to data mining from imbalanced data. *Journal of Intelligent Manufacturing, 16*, 565–573. doi:10.1007/s10845-005-4362-2

Guignard, M., & Spielberg, K. (2003). *Double Contraction, Double Probing, Short Starts and BB-Probing Cuts for Mixed (0,1) Programming (Tech. Rep.)*. Philadelphia, PA: University of Pennsylvania, Wharton School.

Gupta, P., Agrawal, A., & Jha, N. K. (2006). An algorithm for synthesis of reversible logic circuits. *IEEE Transactions on Computer-Aided Design of Integrated Circuits and Systems, 25*(11), 2317–2330. doi:10.1109/TCAD.2006.871622

Gutjahr, W. J. (2000). graph-based Ant System and its convergence. *Future Generation Computer Systems, 16*, 873–888. doi:10.1016/S0167-739X(00)00044-3

Guyon, I., Gunn, S., Nikravesh, M., & Zadeh, L. (Eds.). (2006). *Feature extraction*. Heidelberg, Germany: Springer.

Hamiez, J.-P., Robet, J., & Hao, J.-K. (2009). A tabu search algorithm with direct representation for strip packing. In C. Cotta & P. Cowling (Eds.), *Proceedings of the Ninth European Conference on Evolutionary Computation in Combinatorial Optimization* (LNCS 5482, pp. 61-72). Berlin: Springer.

Hammer, P., & Rudeanu, S. (1968). *Boolean methods in operations research and related areas*. New York: Springer.

Han, L., & Kendall, G. (2003). An investigation of a tabu assisted hyper-heuristic genetic algorithm. *Proceedings of the IEEE Congress on Evolutionary Computation (CEC'03), 3*, (pp. 2230-2237).

Hanafi, S., & Wilbaut, C. (2006). Improved Convergent Heuristic for 0-1 Mixed Integer Programming. *Annals of Operations Research*. doi:.doi:10.1007/s10479-009-0546-z

Hanafi, S., & Wilbaut, C. (2006). Improved convergent heuristics for the 0-1 multidimensional knapsack problem. *Annals of Operations Research*. doi:doi:10.1007/s10479-009-0546-z

Hansen, P., Labbe, M., & Schindl, D. (2005). *Set covering and packing formulations of graph coloring: algorithms and first polyhedral results* (Tech. Rep. No. G-2005-76). GERARD, Universite de Montreal, Quebec, Canada.

Hansen, N., & Ostermeier, A. (2001). Completely derandomized self-adaptation in evolution strategies. *Evolutionary Computation, 9*, 159–195. doi:10.1162/106365601750190398

Hansen, P., Brunswick, N., & Jaumard, B. (1990). Algorithms for the maximum satisfiability problem. *Computing, 44*, 279–303. doi:10.1007/BF02241270

Hardy, C., & Latane, B. (1986). Social loafing on a cheering task. *Social Science, 71*, 165–172.

Haro-García, A., & García-Pedrajas, N. (2009). A divide-and-conquer recursive approach for scaling up instance selection algorithms. *Data Mining and Knowledge Discovery, 18*, 392–418. doi:10.1007/s10618-008-0121-2

Harren, R., & van Stee, R. (2009). Improved absolute approximation ratios for two-dimensional packing problems. In I. Dinur, K. Jansen, J. Naor, & J. Rolim (Eds.), *Approximation, Randomization, and Combinatorial Optimization* (LNCS 5687, pp. 177-189). Berlin: Springer.

Hartmann, A. K., & Weigt, M. (2005). *Phase Transitions in Combinatorial Optimization Problems: Basics, Algorithms and Statistical Mechanics*. New York: Wiley. doi:10.1002/3527606734

Hartmann, S., & Kolisch, R. (2000). Experimental evaluation of state-of-the-art heuristics for the resource-constrained project scheduling problem. *European Journal of Operational Research, 127*(2), 394–407. doi:10.1016/S0377-2217(99)00485-3

Hart, P. E. (1968). The condesed nearest neighbour rule. *IEEE Transactions on Information Theory, 18*(3), 431–433.

Hertez, A., & Kobler, D. (2000). A framework for the description of evolutionary algorithms. *European Journal of Operational Research, 126*, 1–12. doi:10.1016/S0377-2217(99)00435-X

Hertz, A., & de Werra, D. (1987). Using tabu search techniques for graph coloring. *Computing, 39*(4), 345–351. doi:10.1007/BF02239976

Hertz, A., Plumettaz, M., & Zufferey, N. (2008). Variable space search for graph coloring. *Discrete Applied Mathematics, 156*, 2551–2560. doi:10.1016/j.dam.2008.03.022

Hingston, Ph., & Kendall, G. (2004). *Ant colonies discover knight tours*. Berlin: Springer Verlag.

Hogg, T., Huberman, B. A., & Williams, C. P. (Eds.). (1996)... *Artificial Intelligence, 81*(1-2).

Holland, J. H. (1975). *Adaptation in natural and artificial systems*. Ann Arbor, MI: University of Michigan Press.

Hoos, H. (2002). An adaptive noise mechanism for Walk-SAT. In *Proceedings of the Eighteenth National Conference in Artificial Intelligence* (pp. 655-660).

Hopper, E., & Turton, B. (2001). An empirical investigation of meta-heuristic and heuristic algorithms for a 2D packing problem. *European Journal of Operational Research, 128*, 34–57. doi:10.1016/S0377-2217(99)00357-4

Ho, S.-Y., Liu, C. C., & Liu, S. (2002). Design of an optimal nearest neighbor classifier using an intelligent genetic algorithm. *Pattern Recognition Letters, 23*(13), 1495–1503. doi:10.1016/S0167-8655(02)00109-5

Hosoda, T., & Disney, S. M. (2006). On variance amplification in a three-echelon supply chain with minimum mean square error forecasting. *Omega, 34*(4), 344–358. doi:10.1016/j.omega.2004.11.005

Householder, A. (1958). Unitary triangularization of a nonsymmetric matrix. *Journal of the ACM, 5*, 339–342. doi:10.1145/320941.320947

Hu, X., & Eberhart, H. (2002). Multiobjective optimization using dynamic Neighborhood Particle Swarm Optimization. In *Proceedings of the Congress on Evolutionary Computation (CEC' 2002)*, Picataway, NJ (Vol. 2, pp. 1677-1681). Washington, DC: IEEE.

Huang, C.-F., & Rocha, L. M. (2005). Tracking extrema in dynamic environments using a coevolutionary agent-based model of genotype edition. In *Proceedings of the 2005 Conference on Genetic and Evolutionary Computation* (pp. 545-552). ACM Publishing.

Hughes, J. B., Macbeth, I. C., & Pattullo, D. M. (1990). Second generation switched current signal processing. In *Proceedings of the IEEE international symposium on circuits and system* (pp. 2805-2808).

Hughes, J. B., Worapishet, A., & Toumazou, C. (2000). Switched capacitors versus switched-currents: a theoretical comparison. In *Proceedings of the IEEE international symposium on circuits and systems* (pp. 409-412).

Hull, C. L. (1943). *Principles of behavior: An introduction to behavior theory*. New York: Oxford University Press.

Hung, W. N. N., Song, X., Yang, G., Yang, J., & Perkowski, M. (2006). Optimal synthesis of multiple output Boolean functions using a set of quantum gates by symbolic reachability analysis. *IEEE Transactions on Computer-Aided Design of Integrated Circuits and Systems, 25*(9), 1652–1663. doi:10.1109/TCAD.2005.858352

Hu, T. C. (1982). *Combinatorial Algorithms*. New York: Addison-Wesley.

Hutter, F., Hoos, H. H., & Stützle, T. (2007). Automatic algorithm configuration based on local search. *AAAI*, 1152-1157.

Hutter, F., Tompkins, D., & Hoos, H. (2002). Scaling and probabilistic smoothing: Efficient dynamic local search for SAT. In *Proceedings of the Eight International Conference of the Principles and Practice of Constraint Programming* (pp. 233-248).

Hutter, F., Hoos, H. H., Leyton-Brown, K., & Stützle, T. (2009). ParamILS: An automatic algorithm configuration framework. *Journal of Artificial Intelligence Research, 36*, 267–306.

Hvattum, L. M., Lokketangen, A., & Glover, F. (2004). Adaptive Memory Search for Boolean Optimization Problems. *Discrete Applied Mathematics, 142*, 99–109. doi:10.1016/j.dam.2003.06.006

Ibaraki, T., Imahori, S., & Yagiura, M. (2008). Hybrid metaheuristics for packing problems. In C. Blum, M. B. Aguilera, A. Roli, & M. Sampels (Eds.), *Hybrid Metaheuristics: An Emerging Approach to Optimization* (Vol. 114 of Studies in Computational Intelligence, pp. 185-219). Berlin: Springer.

Imahori, S., Yagiura, M., & Ibaraki, T. (2003). Local search algorithms for the rectangle packing problem with general spatial costs. *Mathematical Programming, 97*, 543–569. doi:10.1007/s10107-003-0427-1

Imahori, S., Yagiura, M., & Ibaraki, T. (2005). Improved local search algorithms for the rectangle packing problem with general spatial costs. *European Journal of Operational Research, 167*, 48–67. doi:10.1016/j.ejor.2004.02.020

Imahori, S., Yagiura, M., & Nagamochi, H. (2007). Practical algorithms for two-dimensional packing. In Gonzalez, T. (Ed.), *Handbook of Approximation Algorithms and Metaheuristics* (*Vol. 13*). London: CRC Press.

Iori, M., Martello, S., & Monaci, M. (2003). Metaheuristic algorithms for the strip packing problem. In Pardalos, P., & Korotkikh, V. (Eds.), *Optimization and Industry: New Frontiers* (*Vol. 78*, pp. 159–179). Berlin: Springer.

Ishibuchi, H., & Nakashima, T. (1999). Evolution of reference sets in nearest neighbor classification. In *Selected papers from the Second Asia-Pacific Conference on Simulated Evolution and Learning on Simulated Evolution and Learning* (LNCS 1585, pp. 82-89).

Ishibuchi, H., Nakashima, T., & Nii, M. (2001). Learning of neural networks with GA-based instance selection. In *Proceedings of the 20th North American Fuzzy Information Processing Society International Conference,* Vancouver, Canada (Vol. 4, pp. 2102-2107).

Ishtaiwi, A., Thornton, J., Sattar, A., & Pham, D. N. (2005). Neighborhood clause weight redistribution in local search for SAT. In *Proceedings of the Eleventh International Conference on Principles and Practice Programming* (LNCS 3709, pp. 772-776).

Jackson, J. M., & Harkins, S. G. (1985). Equity in effort: An explanation of the social loafing effect. *Journal of Personality and Social Psychology*, *49*, 1199–1206. doi:10.1037/0022-3514.49.5.1199

Jakops, S. (1996). On genetic algorithms for the packing of polygons. *European Journal of Operational Research*, *88*(1), 165–181. doi:10.1016/0377-2217(94)00166-9

Janis, I. (1971). Groupthink. *Psychology Today,* 43-46.

Jansen, K., & van Stee, R. (2005). On strip packing with rotations. In H. Gabow & R. Fagin (Eds.), *Proceedings of the Thirty-Seventh annual ACM symposium on Theory of computing* (pp. 755-761). New York: ACM Press.

Jin, Y., & Branke, J. (2005). Evolutionary optimization in uncertain environments - a survey. *IEEE Transactions on Evolutionary Computation*, *9*, 303–317. doi:10.1109/TEVC.2005.846356

John, S., Naim, M. M., & Towill, D. R. (1994). Dynamic analysis of a WIP compensated decision support system. *International Journal of Manufacturing System Design*, *1*(4), 283–297.

Johnson, D. E., Aragon, C. R., McGeoch, L. A., & Schevon, C. (1991). Optimization by simulated annealing: an experimental evaluation; Part II, graph coloring and number partitioning. *Operations Research*, *39*, 378–406. doi:10.1287/opre.39.3.378

Johnson, D. S. (2005). The NP-Completeness Column. *ACM Transactions on Algorithms*, *1*(1), 160–176. doi:10.1145/1077464.1077476

Johnson, D. S., Mehrotra, A., & Trick, M. A. (2008). Special issue on computational methods for graph coloring and its generalizations. *Discrete Applied Mathematics*, *156*(2), 145–146. doi:10.1016/j.dam.2007.10.007

Kado, K., Ross, P., & Corne, D. (1995). A study of genetic algorithm hybrids for facility layout problem. In *Proceedings of the Sixth International Conference on Genetic Algorithms* (pp. 498-505).

Kaelbling, L. P., Littman, M., & Moore, A. (1996). Reinforcement learning: A survey. *Journal of Artificial Intelligence Research*, *4*, 237–285.

Karp, R. (1972). Reducibility among combinatorial problems. In Miller, R. E., & Thatcher, J. W. (Eds.), *Complexity of computer computations* (pp. 85–103). New York: Plenum Press.

Kavsek, B., & Lavrac, N. (2006). APRIORI-SD: Adapting association rule learning to subgroup discovery. *Applied Artificial Intelligence*, *20*(7), 543–583. doi:10.1080/08839510600779688

Keller, R. E., & Poli, R. (2007). Cost-benefit investigation of a genetic-programming hyper-heuristic. In *Proceedings of the 8th International Conference on Artificial Evolution (EA'07),* Tours, France (pp. 13-24).

Kendall, G., & Hussin, N. M. (2005). Tabu search hyper-heuristic approach to the examination timetabling problem at university of technology MARA. In E. K. Burke and M. Trick (Eds.), *Proceedings of the 5th International Conference on the Practice and Theory of Automated Timetabling (PATAT'04)* (LNCS 3616, pp. 270-293).

Kendall, G., & Mohamad, M. (2004). Channel assignment in cellular communication using a great deluge hyper-heuristic. In *Proceedings of the 12th IEEE International Conference on Network (ICON'04)* (pp. 769-773).

Kenmochi, M., Imamichi, T., Nonobe, K., Yagiura, M., & Nagamochi, H. (2009). Exact algorithms for the two-dimensional strip packing problem with and without rotations. *European Journal of Operational Research*, *198*, 73–83. doi:10.1016/j.ejor.2008.08.020

Kennedy, J., & Eberhart, R. C. (1995). Particle swarm optimization. In *Proceedings of the IEEE International Conference on Neural Networks* (pp. 1942-1948). Washington, DC: IEEE Computer Society.

Kennedy, J., Eberhart, R. C., & Shi, Y. (2001). *Swarm intelligence*. San Francisco: Morgan Kaufmann Publishers.

Kerntopf, P. (2004). A new heuristic algorithm for reversible logic synthesis. In *Proceedings of the Design Automation Conference* (pp. 834-837).

Kerr, N. L. (1983). Motivation losses in small groups: A social dilemma analysis. *Journal of Personality and Social Psychology*, *45*, 819–828. doi:10.1037/0022-3514.45.4.819

KhudaBukhsh. A. R., Xu, L., Hoos, H., & Leyton-Brown, K. (2009). SATenstein: Automatically Building Local Search SAT Solvers from Components. In *Proceedings of the 25th International Joint Conference on Artificial Intelligence (IJCAI-09)*.

Kibbler, D., & Aha, D. W. (1987). Learning representative exemplars of concepts: An initial case of study. In *Proceedings of the 4th International Workshop on Machine Learning*, Irvine, CA (pp. 24-30).

Kim, H., & Ryan, J. (2003). The cost impact of using simple forecasting techniques in a supply chain. *Naval Research Logistics*, *50*(5), 388–411. doi:10.1002/nav.10065

Kim, K. (2006). Artificial neural networks with evolutionary instance selection for financial forecasting. *Expert Systems with Applications*, *30*, 519–526. doi:10.1016/j.eswa.2005.10.007

Kirkpatrick, S., Gelatt, C. D., & Vecchi, M. P. (1983). Optimization by simulated annealing. *Journal of Science*, *220*(4598), 671–680. doi:10.1126/science.220.4598.671

Kloks, T. (1994). *Treewidth (LNCS)*. Berlin: Springer Verlag. doi:10.1007/BFb0045375

Kochenberger, G., Glover, F., Alidaee, B., & Rego, C. (2004). A unified modeling and solution framework for combinatorial optimization problems. *Operations Research Spectrum*, *26*(2), 237–250.

Kochol, M., Lozin, V., & Randerath, B. (2003). The 3-colorability problem on graphs with maximum degree four. *SIAM Journal on Computing*, *32*(5), 1128–1139. doi:10.1137/S0097539702418759

Kohonen, T. (1990). The self-organizing map. *Proceedings of the IEEE*, *78*, 1464–1480. doi:10.1109/5.58325

Komorita, S. S., & Barth, J. M. (1985). Components of reward in social bargaining. *Journal of Personality and Social Psychology*, *48*, 364–373. doi:10.1037/0022-3514.48.2.364

Krasnogor, N., & Smith, J. (2000). MAFRA: A Java memetic algorithms framework. In Freitas, A. A., Hart, W., Krasnogor, N., & Smith, J. (Eds.), *Data Mining with Evolutionary Algorithms* (pp. 125–131). Las Vega, NV.

Kravits, D. A., & Martin, B. (1986). Ringelmann Rediscovered: The Original Article. *Journal of Personality and Social Psychology*, *50*, 936–941. doi:10.1037/0022-3514.50.5.936

Krivelevich, M., & Sudakov, B. (2006). Pseudo-random graphs. In Gyori, E., Katona, G. O. H., & Lovász, L. (Eds.), *More sets, graphs and numbers* (*Vol. 15*, pp. 199–262). Berlin: Springer. doi:10.1007/978-3-540-32439-3_10

Kroll, P., & Krutchten, P. (2003). *The Rational unified process Made Easy*. Reading, MA: Addison-Wesley.

Krzakała, F., Pagnani, A., & Weigt, M. (2004). Threshold values, stability analysis, and high-q asymptotics for the coloring problem on random graphs. *Physical Review E: Statistical, Nonlinear, and Soft Matter Physics.*. doi:10.1103/PhysRevE.70.046705

Kubat, M., & Matwin, S. (1997). Addressing the course of imbalanced training sets: One-sided selection. In *Proceedings of the 14th International Conference on Machine Learning*, Nashville, TN (pp. 179-186).

Kubat, M., Holte, R. C., & Matwin, S. (1998). Machine learning for the detection of oil spills in satellite radar images. *Machine Learning*, *30*(2-3), 195–215. doi:10.1023/A:1007452223027

Kuncheva, L. I. (1995). Editing for the k-nearest neighbors rule by a genetic algorithm. *Pattern Recognition Letters, 16,* 809–814. doi:10.1016/0167-8655(95)00047-K

Kuncheva, L. I., & Bezdek, J. C. (1998). Nearest prototype classification: Clustering, genetic algorithms, or random search? *IEEE Transactions on Systems, Man, and Cybernetics, 28*(1), 160–164. doi:10.1109/5326.661099

Landauer, R. (1961). Irreversibility and heat generation in the computing process. *IBM Journal of Research and Development, 5,* 183. doi:10.1147/rd.53.0183

Larsen, A. (2000). *The dynamic vehicle routing problem.* Copenhagen, Demark: Technical University of Denmark.

Latane, B., Williams, K. D., & Harkins, S. G. (1979). Many hands make light the work: The cause and consequences of social loafing. *Journal of Personality and Social Psychology, 37,* 822–832. doi:10.1037/0022-3514.37.6.822

Laurikkala, J. (2001). Improving identification of difficult small classes by balancing class distribution. In *Proceedings of the 8th Conference on Artificial Intelligence in Medicine in Europe,* Cascais, Portugal (pp. 63-66).

Lavrac, N., Kavsek, B., Flach, P., & Todorovski, L. (2004). Subgroup discovery with CN2-SD. *Journal of Machine Learning Research, 5,* 153–188.

Leahey, T. H. (1997). *A history of psychology: Main currents in psychological thought* (4th ed.). Upper Saddle River, NJ: Prentice- Hall.

Lee, K., & Geem, Z. (2005). A new meta-heuristic algorithm for continuous engineering optimization: harmony search theory and practice. *Computer Methods in Applied Mechanics and Engineering, 194*(36-38), 3902–3933. doi:10.1016/j.cma.2004.09.007

Leighton, F. T. (1979). A graph coloring algorithm for large scheduling problems. *Journal of Research of the National Bureau of Standards, 84*(6), 489–503.

Leo, H. W. Y., & Wallace, K. S. T. (2004). Strip packing using hybrid genetic approach. *Engineering Applications of Artificial Intelligence, 17,* 169–177. doi:10.1016/j.engappai.2004.02.003

Li, C. M., & Huang, W. Q. (2005). Diversification and determinism in local search for satisfiability. In *Proceedings of the Eight International Conference on Theory and Applications of Satisfiability Testing (SAT-05)* (LNCS 3569, pp. 158-172).

Li, C. M., Wei, W., & Zhang, H. (2007). Combining adaptive noise and look-ahead in local search for SAT. In *Proceedings of the Tenth International Conference on Theory and Applications of Satisfiability Testing (SAT-07)* (LNCS 4501, pp. 121-133).

Li, W., & Alidaee, B. (2002). Dynamics of local search heuristics for the traveling salesman problem. *IEEE Transactions on Systems, Man, and Cybernetics - Part A, 32,* 173-184.

Li, X. (2003). A non-dominated sorting particle swarm optimizer for multiobjective optimization. In *Proceedings of the 2003 international conference on Genetic and evolutionary computation*: Part I, Chicago (pp. 37-48).

Li, X., Branke, J., & Blackwell, T. (2006). Particle swarm with speciation and adaptation in a dynamic environment. In *Proceedings of the 8th Annual Conference on Genetic and Evolutionary Computation* (pp. 51-58). ACM Publishing.

Liaw, H.-T., & Lin, C.-S. (1992). On the OBDD-representation of general Boolean functions. *IEEE Transactions on Computers, 41,* 661–664. doi:10.1109/12.144618

Liu, H., & Motoda, H. (Eds.). (2001). *Instance selection and construction for data mining.* New York: Springer.

Liu, H., & Motoda, H. (Eds.). (2007). *Computational methods of feature selection.* New York: Chapman & Hall.

Liu, H., Hussain, F., Lim, C., & Dash, M. (2002). Discretization: An enabling technique. *Data Mining and Knowledge Discovery, 6*(4), 393–423. doi:10.1023/A:1016304305535

Liu, H., & Motoda, H. (2002). On issues of instance selection. *Data Mining and Knowledge Discovery, 6*(2), 115–130. doi:10.1023/A:1014056429969

Lodi, A., Martello, S., & Monaci, M. (2002). Two-dimensional packing problems: A survey. *European Journal of Operational Research, 141,* 241–252. doi:10.1016/S0377-2217(02)00123-6

Loulou, M., Dallet, D., & Marchegay, P. (2000). A 3.3V switched-current second order sigma-delta modulator for audio applications. In *Proceedings of the IEEE international symposium on circuits and systems* (pp. 409-412).

Loulou, M., Dallet, D., Masmoudi, N., Marchegay, P., & Kamoun, L. (2004). A 3.3V, 10 bits, switched-current second order sigma-delta modulator. *Journal of analog integrated circuits and signal processing, 39*(1), 81-87

Lozano, M., Sotoca, J. M., Sánchez, J. S., Pla, F., Pekalska, E., & Duin, R. P. W. (2006). Experimental study on prototype optimisation algorithms for prototype-based classification in vector spaces. *Pattern Recognition, 39*(10), 1827–1838. doi:10.1016/j.patcog.2006.04.005

Luh, L., Choma, J. J., & Draper, J. (1998). A 50-MHz continuous-time switched-current $\Sigma\Delta$ modulator. In *Proceedings of the IEEE international symposium on circuits and systems* (pp. 579-582)

Lung, R. I., & Dumitrescu, D. (2007). Collaborative evolutionary swarm optimization with a Gauss Chaotic Sequence Generator. *Innovations in Hybrid Intelligent Systems, 44*, 207–214. doi:10.1007/978-3-540-74972-1_28

Lung, R. I., & Dumitrescu, D. (2008). ESCA: A new evolutionary-swarm cooperative algorithm. *Studies in Computational Intelligence, 129*, 105–114. doi:10.1007/978-3-540-78987-1_10

MacAllister, W. (2009). *Data Structures and algorithms using java.* New York: Jones & Bartlett publishers.

Macionis, J. J., Clarke, J. N., & Gerber, L. M. (1997). *Sociology* (2nd ed.). Scarborough, Ontario, Canada: Prentice Hall Allyn and Bacon.

Maffray, F., & Preissmann, M. (1996). On the NP-completeness of the *k*-colorability problem for triangle-free graphs. *Discrete Mathematics, 162*(1-3), 313–317. doi:10.1016/S0012-365X(97)89267-9

Magazine, M., Polak, G., & Sharma, D. (2002). A multi-exchange neighborhood search for integrated clustering and machine setup model for PCB manufacturing. *Journal of Electronics Manufacturing, 11*, 107–119. doi:10.1142/S0960313102000448

Mahdavi, M., Fesanghary, M., & Damangir, E. (2007). An improved harmony search algorithm for solving optimization problems. *Applied Mathematics and Computation, 188*(2), 1567–1579. doi:10.1016/j.amc.2006.11.033

Malaguti, E., & Toth, P. (2010). A survey on vertex coloring problems. *International Transactions in Operational Research, 17*(1), 1–34. doi:10.1111/j.1475-3995.2009.00696.x

Marin, H. T. (1998). *Combinations of GAs and CSP strategies for solving examination timetabling problems.* Unpublished PhD thesis, Instituto Tecnologico y de Estudios Superiores de Monterrey.

Marín-Blázquez, J., & Schulenburg, S. (2005). A hyper-heuristic framework with XCS: Learning to create novel problem-solving algorithms constructed from simpler algorithmic ingredients. In T. Kovacs, X. Llorà, K. Takadama, P. Lanzi, W. Stolzmann, & S. Wilson (Eds.), *Proceedings of the 8th International Workshop on Learning Classifier Systems (IWLCS'05)* (LNCS 4399, pp. 193-218).

Markowitz, H. M. (1952). Portfolio selection. *The Journal of Finance, 7*, 77–91. doi:10.2307/2975974

Marseguerra, M., & Zio, E. (2000). System design optimization by genetic algorithms. In *Proceedings of the IEEE reliability and maintainability symposium* (pp. 222-227)

Martello, S., Monaci, M., & Vigo, D. (2003). An exact approach to the strip packing problem. *INFORMS Journal on Computing, 15*(3), 310–319. doi:10.1287/ijoc.15.3.310.16082

Maslov, D., & Dueck, G. W. (2004). Reversible cascades with minimal garbage. *IEEE Transactions on Computer-Aided Design of Integrated Circuits and Systems, 23*(11), 1497–1509. doi:10.1109/TCAD.2004.836735

Maslov, D., Dueck, G. W., & Miller, D. M. (2005). Toffoli network synthesis with templates. *IEEE Transactions on Computer-Aided Design of Integrated Circuits and Systems, 24*(6), 807–817. doi:10.1109/TCAD.2005.847911

Maslov, D., Dueck, G. W., & Miller, D. M. (2007). Techniques for the synthesis of reversible Toffoli networks. *ACM Transactions on Design Automation of Electronic Systems, 12*(4). doi:10.1145/1278349.1278355

Maslov, D., & Miller, D. M. (2007). Comparison of the cost metrics through investigation of the relation between optimal ncv and optimal nct 3-qubit reversible circuits. *IET Computers & Digital Techniques, 1*(2), 98–104. doi:10.1049/iet-cdt:20060070

Maslow, A. H. (1962). *Towards a psychology of being.* Princeton, NJ: Van Nostrand.

Maslow, A. H. (1970). *Motivation and personality* (2nd ed.). New York: Harper & Row.

Masmoudi, S., Fakhfakh, M., Loulou, M., Masmoudi, N., & Loumeau, P. (2007). A CMOS 80 MHz low-pass switched-current fourth order sigma-delta modulator. In *Proceedings of the international multi-conference on systems, signals and devices. Conference on sensors, circuits and instrumentation systems.*

McAllester, D., Selman, B., & Kautz, H. (1997). Evidence for Invariants in Local Search. In [Cambridge, MA: MIT Press.]. *Proceedings of AAAI, 97,* 321–326.

Medeiro, F., Perez-Verdu, B., & Rodriguez-Vasquez, A. (1999). *Top-down design of high-performance sigma-delta modulators.* Dordrecht, The Netherlands: Kluwer.

Medeiro, F., Rodríguez-Macías, R., Fernández, F. V., Domínguez-Astro, R., Huertas, J. L., & Rodríguez-Vázquez, A. (1994). Global design of analog cells using statistical optimization techniques. *Analog Integrated Circuits and Signal Processing, 6*(3), 179–195. doi:10.1007/BF01238887

Mellouli, A., & Dammak, A. (2008). An algorithm for the two-dimensional cutting-stock problem based on a pattern generation procedure. *International Journal of Information and Management Sciences, 19*(2), 201–218.

Mendes, R., & Mohais, A. (2005). DynDE: A differential evolution for dynamic optimization problems. In *Proceedings of the 2005 IEEE Congress on Evolutionary Computation* (pp. 2808-2815). Washington, DC: IEEE Computer Society.

Mendez-Diaz, I., & Zabala, P. (2008). A cutting plane algorithm for graph coloring. *Discrete Applied Mathematics, 156,* 159–179. doi:10.1016/j.dam.2006.07.010

Merkle, R. C. N. (1993). Reversible electronic logic using switches. *Nanotechnology, 4,* 21–40. doi:10.1088/0957-4484/4/1/002

Merlot, L. T. G., Boland, N., Hughes, B. D., & Stuckey, P. J. (2002). A hybrid algorithm for the examination timetabling problem. In E. K. Burke & P. De Causmaecker (Eds.), *Proceedings of the 4th International Conference on the Practice and Theory of Automated Timetabling (PATAT'02)* (LNCS 1153, pp. 207-231).

Merriam-Webster. (1997). *Merriam-Websters's Collegiate Dictionary.* Merriam-Websters.

Michalewicz, Z. (1992). A modified genetic algorithm for optimal control problems. *Computers & Mathematics with Applications (Oxford, England), 23*(12), 83–94. doi:10.1016/0898-1221(92)90094-X

Michalewicz, Z. (1996). *Genetic algorithms+ data structures.* New York: Springer.

Michel, L., & Van, P. (2001). *Hentenryck. Localizer++: An open library for local search* (Tech. Rep. No. CS-01-02). Providence, RI: Department of Computer Science, Brown University.

Miller, D. M., Maslov, D., & Dueck, G. W. (2003). A transformation based algorithm for reversible logic synthesis. In *Proceedings of the Design Automation Conference* (pp. 318-323).

Minner, S. (2003). Multiple-supplier inventory models in supply chain management: A review. *International Journal of Production Economics, 81,* 265–279. doi:10.1016/S0925-5273(02)00288-8

Mir, M., & Imam, M. (2001). A hybrid optimization approach for layout design of unequal-area facilities. *Computers & Industrial Engineering, 39,* 49–63. doi:10.1016/S0360-8352(00)00065-6

Monasson, R., Zecchina, R., Kirkpatrick, S., Selman, B., & Troyansky, L. (1999). Determining computational complexity from characteristic 'phase transitions'. *Nature, 400,* 133–137. doi:10.1038/22055

Montgomery, D. (2005). *Design and analysis of experiments.* New York: Wiley.

Morago, R. J., DePuy, G. W., & Whitehouse, G. E. (2006). A solution methodology for optimization problems. In A. B. Badiru (Ed.), *Metaheuristics* (pp. 1-10, 13). New York: Taylor & Francis Group.

Moser, I., & Hendtlass, T. (2007). A simple and efficient multi-component algorithm for solving dynamic function optimisation problems. In *Proceedings of the 2005 IEEE Congress on Evolutionary Computation* (pp. 252-259). Washington, DC: IEEE Computer Society.

Mühlenbein, H., & Mahnig, T. (1999). FDA-A scalable evolutionary algorithm for the optimization of additively decomposed functions. *Evolutionary Computation, 7*(4), 353–376. doi:10.1162/evco.1999.7.4.353

Mukhopadhyay, A., Roy, A., Das, S., & Abraham, A. (2008). Population-variance and explorative power of harmony search: an analysis. In *Proceedings of the Second National Conference on Mathematical Techniques: Emerging Paradigms for Electronics and IT Industries (MATEIT 2008)*, New Delhi, India.

Nanni, L., & Lumini, A. (2008). Particle swarm optimization for prototype reduction. *Neurocomputing, 72*, 1092–1097. doi:10.1016/j.neucom.2008.03.008

Narendra, K. S., & Thathachar, M. A. L. (1989). *Learning Automata: An Introduction*. Upper Saddle River, NJ: Prentice Hall.

Nareyek, A. (2003). Choosing search heuristics by nonstationary reinforcement learning. In *Metaheuristics: Computer decision-making* (pp. 523-544). Dordrecht, The Netherlands: Kluwer Academic Publishers.

Nediak, M., & Eckstein, J. (2007). Pivot, Cut, and Dive: A Heuristic for Mixed 0-1 Integer Programming. *Journal of Heuristics, 13*, 471–503. doi:10.1007/s10732-007-9021-7

Nelder, J., & Mead, R. (1965). A simplex method for function minimization. *The Computer Journal, 7*, 308–313.

Neveu, B., Trombettoni, G., & Araya, I. (2007). Incremental move for strip-packing. In N. Avouris, N. Bourbakis, & I. Hatzilygeroudis (Eds.), *Proceedings of the Nineteenth IEEE International Conference on Tools with Artificial Intelligence* (Vol. 2, pp. 489-496). Washington, DC: IEEE Computer Society.

Neveu, B., Trombettoni, G., Araya, I., & Riff, M.-C. (2008). A strip packing solving method using an incremental move based on maximal holes. *International Journal of Artificial Intelligence Tools, 17*, 881–901. doi:10.1142/S0218213008004205

Newell, A., & Simon, H. A. (1972). *Human problem solving*. Upper Saddle River, NJ: Prentice-Hall.

Newman, D. J., Hettich, S., Blake, C. L., & Merz, C. J. (1998). *UCI repository of machine learning databases*. Irvine, CA: University of California, Irvine, Department of Information and Computer Sciences. Retrieved from http://www.ics.uci.edu/~mlearn/MLRepository.html

Nielsen, M., & Chuang, I. (2000). *Quantum Computation and Quantum Information*. Cambridge, UK: Cambridge University Press.

Norsworthly, S. R., Schreier, R., & Themes, G. C. (1997). *Delta sigma data converters: theory, design and simulation*. Washington, DC: IEEE Press.

Nowicki, E., & Smutnicki, C. (1996). A Fast Taboo Search Algorithm for the Job Shop Problem. *Management Science, 42*(6), 797–813. doi:10.1287/mnsc.42.6.797

O'Connor, I., & Kaiser, A. (2000). Automated synthesis of current memory cells. *IEEE Transactions on Computer-Aided Design of Integrated Circuits and Systems, 19*(4), 413–424. doi:10.1109/43.838991

Oh, I., Lee, J., & Moon, B. (2004). Hybrid genetic algorithms for feature selection. *IEEE Transactions on Pattern Analysis and Machine Intelligence, 26*(11), 1424–1437. doi:10.1109/TPAMI.2004.105

Oliaei, O., Loumeau, P., & Aboushady, H. (1997). A switched current class AB delta-sigma modulators. In *Proceedings of the IEEE international symposium on circuits and systems* (pp. 393-396)

Oliaei, O., & Loumeau, P. (1996). Current mode class AB design using floating voltage-source. *Electronics Letters, 32*(17), 1526–1527. doi:10.1049/el:19961065

Omran, M., & Mahdavi, M. (2008). Global-best harmony search. *Applied Mathematics and Computation, 198*(2), 643–656. doi:10.1016/j.amc.2007.09.004

Ong, Y. S., Krasnogor, N., & Ishibuchi, H. (2007). Special issue on memetic algorithms. *IEEE Transactions on Systems, Man and Cybernetics. Part B, 37*(1), 2–5.

Oommen, B. J., & Hansen, E. R. (1987). List organizing strategies using stochastic move-to-front and stochastic move-to-rear operations. *SIAM Journal on Computing, 16*, 705–716. doi:10.1137/0216047

Oommen, B. J., & Ma, D. C. Y. (1988). Deterministic Learning Automata Solutions to the Equipartitioning Problem. *IEEE Transactions on Computers*, *37*(1), 2–13. doi:10.1109/12.75146

Oommen, B. J., Misra, S., & Granmo, O.-C. (2007). Routing Bandwidth Guaranteed Paths in MPLS Traffic Engineering: A Multiple Race Track Learning Approach. *IEEE Transactions on Computers*, *56*(7), 959–976. doi:10.1109/TC.2007.1045

Oommen, B. J., & St. Croix, E. V. (1996). Graph partitioning using learning automata. *IEEE Transactions on Computers*, *45*(2), 195–208. doi:10.1109/12.485372

Ouelhadj, D., & Petrovic, S. (2008). A cooperative distributed hyper-heuristic framework for scheduling. In *Proceedings of the IEEE International Conference on Systems, Man, and Cybernetics (SMC'08)* (pp. 2560-2565).

Özcan, E., & Ersoy, E. (2005). Final exam scheduler – FES. In *Proceedings of the IEEE Congress on Evolutionary Computation (CEC'05)* (Vol. 2, pp. 1356-1363).

Özcan, E., Bykov, Y., Birben, M., & Burke, K. E. (2009). Examination timetabling using late acceptance hyper-heuristics. In *Proceedings of the 2009 IEEE Congress on Evolutionary Computation (CEC'09)* (pp. 997-1004).

Özcan, E., Bilgin, B., & Korkmaz, E. E. (2008). A comprehensive analysis of hyper-heuristics. *Intelligent Data Analysis*, *12*, 3–23.

Papadopoulos, A. N., & Manolopoulos, Y. (2004). *Nearest neighbor search: A database perspective*. Berlin, Germany: Springer-Verlag.

Paquete, L. F., & Fonseca, C. M. (2001). A study of examination timetabling with multiobjective evolutionary algorithms. In *Proceedings of the 4th Metaheuristics International Conference (MIC'01)* (pp. 149-154).

Pardalos, P. S., & Shylo, O. V. (2006). *An algorithm for Job Shop Scheduling based on Global Equilibrium Search Techniques. Computational Management Science. DOI: 10.1007/s10287-006-0023-y Patel, J., & Chinneck, J. W. (2006). Active-Constraint Variable Ordering for Faster Feasibility of Mixed Integer Linear Programs*. Mathematical Programming.

Paredes, R., & Vidal, E. (2006). Learning prototypes and distances: A prototype reduction technique based on nearest neighbor error minimization. *Pattern Recognition*, *39*(2), 180–188. doi:10.1016/j.patcog.2005.06.001

Parsopoulos, K. E., & Vrahatis, M. N. (2002). Particle swarm optimization method in multiobjective problems. In *Proceeding of the 2002 ACM Symposium on Applied Computing (SAC' 2002)*, Madrid, Spain (pp. 603-607). New York: ACM Press.

Patel, K., Markov, I., & Hayes, J. (2008). Optimal synthesis of linear reversible circuits. *Quantum Information and Computation*, *8*(3-4), 282–294.

Patterson, D. J., & Kautz, H. (2001). Auto-Walk-sat: A Self-Tuning Implementation of Walk-sat. *Electronic Notes in Discrete Mathematics*, 9.

Pedroso, J. P. (2005). Tabu search for mixed integer programming. In Rego, C., & Alidaee, B. (Eds.), *Metaheuristic Optimization via Memory and Evolution: Tabu Search and Scatter Search*. Dordrecht, The Netherlands: Kluwer Academic Publishers. doi:10.1007/0-387-23667-8_11

Pelikan, M., & Mühlenbein, H. (1999). *The bivariate marginal distribution algorithm* (pp. 521–535). Advances in Soft Computing-Engineering Design and Manufacturing.

Peres, A. (1985). Reversible logic and quantum computers. *Physical Review A.*, *32*(6), 3266–3276. doi:10.1103/PhysRevA.32.3266

Petford, A. D., & Welsh, D. J. A. (1989). A randomized 3-colouring algorithm. *Discrete Mathematics*, *74*(1-2), 253–261. doi:10.1016/0012-365X(89)90214-8

Petrovic, S., Patel, V., & Yang, Y. (2005). Examination timetabling with fuzzy constraints. In E. K. Burke & M. Trick (Eds.), *Proceedings of the 5th International Conference on the Practice and Theory of Automated Timetabling (PATAT'05)* (LNCS 3616, pp. 313-333), Springer.

Petrovic, S., Yang, Y., & Dror, M. (2007). Case-based selection of initialisation heuristics for metaheuristic examination timetabling. *Expert Systems with Applications: An International Journal*, *33*(3), 772–785. doi:10.1016/j.eswa.2006.06.017

Pillay, N., & Banzhaf, W. (2008). A study of heuristic combinations for hyper-heuristic systems for the uncapacitated examination timetabling problem. *European Journal of Operational Research*. doi:.doi:10.1016/j.ejor.2008.07.023

Pongchairerks, P., & Kachitvichyanukul, V. (2005). Non-homogenous particle swarm optimization with multiple social structures. In V. Kachitvichyanukul, U. Purintrapiban, & P. Utayopas (Eds.), In *Proceedings of the Simulation and Modeling: Integrating Sciences and Technology for Effective Resource Management, the international conference on simulation and modeling*, Asian Institute of Technology, Bangkok, Thailand.

Pongchairerks, P., & Kachitvichyanukul, V. (2009). Particle swarm optimization algorithm with multiple social learning structures. *International Journal of Operational Research*, 6(2), 176–194. doi:10.1504/IJOR.2009.026534

Prasad, A. K., Shende, V. V., Markov, I. L., Hayes, J. P., & Patel, K. N. (2006). Data structures and algorithms for simplifying reversible circuits. *Journal on Emerging Technologies in Computing Systems*, 2(4), 277–293. doi:10.1145/1216396.1216399

Prestwich, S. (2004). Local Search on SAT-encoded Colouring Problems. In *Theory and Applications of Satisfiability Testing* (LNCS 2919, pp. 105-119).

Prestwich, S. (2005). Random walk with continuously smoothed variable weights. In *Proceedings of the Eight International Conference on Theory and Applications of Satisfiability Testing (SAT-05)* (LNCS 3569, pp. 203-215).

Provost, F. J., & Kolluri, V. (1999). A survey of methods for scaling up inductive learning algorithms. *Data Mining and Knowledge Discovery*, 2, 131–169. doi:10.1023/A:1009876119989

Puntambekar, A. A. (2009). *Analysis of algorithm and design*. New York: technical publications pune.

Pyle, D. (1999). *Data preparation for data mining*. San Francisco: Morgan Kaufmann.

Quinlan, J. R. (1993). *C4.5: Programs for machine learning*. San Francisco: Morgan Kaufmann.

Qu, R., Burke, E. K., & McCollum, B. (2008). Adaptive automated construction of hybrid heuristics for exam timetabling and graph colouring problems. *European Journal of Operational Research*, 198(2), 392–404. doi:10.1016/j.ejor.2008.10.001

Qu, R., Burke, E. K., McCollum, B., Merlot, L. T., & Lee, S. Y. (2009). A survey of search methodologies and automated system development for examination timetabling. *Journal of Scheduling*, 12(1), 55–89. doi:10.1007/s10951-008-0077-5

Raquel, C. R., & Naval, P. C. (2005). An Effective use of distance in multi-objective particle swarm optimization. In *Proceedings of the genetic and evolutionary computation conference* (pp. 257-364).

Raquel, C., Prospero, C., & Naval, Jr. (2005). An effective use of crowding distance in multiobjective particle swarm optimization. In *Proceedings of the 2005 conference on Genetic and evolutionary computation*, Washington, DC.

Rardin, R. L., & Uzsoy, R. (2001). Experimental evaluation of heuristic optimization. *Journal of Heuristics*, 7(3), 261–304. doi:10.1023/A:1011319115230

Rattadilok, P., Gaw, A., & Kwan, R. (2005). Distributed choice function hyper-heuristics for timetabling and scheduling. In *Proceedings of the 5th International Conference on the Practice and Theory of Automated Timetabling (PATAT'2004)* (pp. 51-67).

Rechenberg, I. (1973). *Evolutionsstrategie: Optimierung technischer Systeme nach Prinzipien der biologischen Evolution*.

Redl, T. A. (2003). *Graceful graphs and graceful labelings: two mathematical programming formulations and some other new results* (Tech. Rep. No. TR03-01). Houston, Texas: Rice University, Department of Computational and Applied Mathematics.

Reinelt, G. (1991). TSPLIB: a traveling salesman problem library. *ORSA Journal on Computing*, 3, 376-384. Retrieved from http://softl ib.rice.edu/softlib/tsplib/

Rennera, G., & Ekart, A. (2003). Genetic algorithms in computer aided design. *Computer Aided Design*, 35, 709–726. doi:10.1016/S0010-4485(03)00003-4

Resende, M. G. C., & Feo, T. A. (Eds.). (1996). *A GRASP for satisfiability, cliques, coloring, and satisfiability: Second DIMACS implementation challenge* (Vol. 26). Providence, RI: American Mathematical Society.

Resende, M. G. C. (1998). Computing approximate solutions of the maximum covering problem using GRASP. *Journal of Heuristics, 4,* 161–171. doi:10.1023/A:1009677613792

Reyes-Sierra, M., & Coello-Coello, C. A. (2006). Multiobjective particle swarm optimizers: a survey of the state-of-the-art. *International journal of computational intelligence research, 2*(3), 287-308.

Ridge, E. (2007). *Design of experiments for the tuning of optimization algorithms.* Unpublished doctoral dissertation, Department of Computer Science, University of York, UK.

Rinaldi, F., & Franz, A. F. (2007). A two-dimensional strip cutting problem with sequencing constraint. *European Journal of Operational Research, 183*(3), 1371–1384. doi:10.1016/j.ejor.2005.12.050

Riquelme, J. C., Aguilar, J. S., & Toro, M. (2003). Finding representative patterns with ordered projections. *Pattern Recognition, 36*(4), 1009–1018. doi:10.1016/S0031-3203(02)00119-X

Robertson, I. (2001). *Problem solving.* Philadelphia: Psychology Press.

Robertson, N., & Seymour, P. D. (1986). Graph minors II: Algorithmic aspects of tree-width. *Journal of Algorithms, 7,* 309–322. doi:10.1016/0196-6774(86)90023-4

Rosa, A. (1967). On certain valuation of the vertices of a graph. In *Theory of Graphs, International Symposium,* Rome (pp. 349-355). New York: Gordon and Breach.

Rosenberg, A. (1986). DIOGENES. In *Proceedings of the Aegean Workshop on Computing VLSI Algorithms and Architectures,* Loutraki, Greece (LNCS 227, pp. 96-107). Berlin: Springer.

Ros, F., Guillaume, S., Pintore, M., & Chretien, J. R. (2008). Hybrid genetic algorithm for dual selection. *Pattern Analysis & Applications, 11,* 179–198. doi:10.1007/s10044-007-0089-3

Ross, P. (2005). Hyper-heuristics. In: E. K. Burke & G. Kendall (Eds.), *Search methodologies: Introductory tutorials in optimization and decision support techniques* (Ch. 17, pp. 529-556). New York: Springer.

Rossi, C., Barrientos, A., & Cerro, J. D. (2007). Two adaptive mutation operators for optima tracking in dynamic optimization problems with evolution strategies. In *Proceedings of the 9th Annual Conference on Genetic and Evolutionary Computation* (pp. 697-704). ACM Publishing.

Rossi, C., Abderrahim, M., & Diaz, J. C. (2008). Tracking moving optima using Kalman-based predictions. *Evolutionary Computation, 16,* 1–30. doi:10.1162/evco.2008.16.1.1

Rudell, R. (1993). Dynamic variable ordering for ordered binary decision diagrams. In *Proceedings of the International Conference on CAD* (pp. 42-47).

Ryu, S., Duggal, A., Heyl, C., & Geem, Z. (2007). Mooring cost optimization via harmony search. In *Proceedings of the 26th ASME International Conference on Offshore Mechanics and Arctic Engineering.*

Saka, M. (2007). Optimum geometry design of geodesic domes using harmony search algorithm. *Advances in Structural Engineering, 10*(6), 595–606. doi:10.1260/136943307783571445

Saka, M. (2009). Optimum design of steel sway frames to BS5950 using harmony search algorithm. *Journal of Constructional Steel Research, 65*(1), 36–43. doi:10.1016/j.jcsr.2008.02.005

Sanchez, J. S., Barandela, R., Marques, A. I., Alejo, R., & Badenas, J. (2003). Analysis of new techniques to obtain quaylity training sets. *Pattern Recognition Letters, 24,* 1015–1022. doi:10.1016/S0167-8655(02)00225-8

Schiermeyer, I. (1994). Reverse-Fit: A 2-optimal algorithm for packing rectangles. In J. van Leeuwen (Ed.), *Proceedings of the Second Annual European Symposium on Algorithms* (LNCS 855, pp. 290-299). Berlin: Springer.

Schuurmans, D., & Southey, F. (2000). Local search characteristics of incomplete SAT procedures. In [Menlo Park, CA: AAAI Press.]. *Proceedings, AAAI-2000,* 297–302.

Schuurmans, D., Southey, F., & Holte, R. C. (2001). The exponentiated sub-gradient algorithm for heuristic Boolean programming. In [San Francisco, CA: Morgan Kaufman Publishers.]. *Proceedings, IJCAI-01*, 334–341.

Schwefel, H. (1981). *Numerical optimization of computer models*. New York: John Wiley & Sons, Inc.

Schwefel, H.-P. (1994). On the Evolution of Evolutionary Computation. In Zurada, J., Marks, R., & Robinson, C. (Eds.), *Computational Intelligence: Imitating Life* (pp. 116–124). Washington, DC: IEEE Press.

Sebban, M., Nock, R., Chauchat, J. H., & Rakotomalala, R. (2000). Impact of learning set quality and size on decision tree performances. *International Journal of Computers. Systems and Signals*, *1*(1), 85–105.

Selman, B., & Kautz, K. A. (1993). Domain-Independent extensions to GSAT: Solving large structured satisfiability problems. In R. Bajcsy (Ed.), *Proceedings of the international Joint Conference on Artificial Intelligence* (Vol. 1, pp. 290-295). San Francisco, CA: Morgan Kaufmann Publishers Inc.

Selman, B., Kautz, H. A., & Cohen, B. (1994). Noise Strategies for Improving Local Search. In [Cambridge, MA: MIT Press.]. *Proceedings of AAAI*, *94*, 337–343.

Selman, B., Levesque, H., & Mitchell, D. (1992). A New Method for Solving Hard Satisfiability Problems. In [Cambridge, MA: MIT Press.]. *Proceedings of AAA*, *92*, 440–446.

Seshadri, A. (2009). *Multi-Objective Optimization using Evolutionary Algorithm*. Retrieved from http://www.mathworks.com/matlabcentral/fileexchange/10351

Shakhnarovich, G., Darrel, T., & Indyk, P. (Eds.). (2006). *Nearest-neighbor methods in learning and vision: Theory and practice*. Cambridge, MA: MIT Press.

Shannon, C. E. (1938). A symbolic analysis of relay and switching circuits. *Transactions of the AIEE*, *57*, 713–723.

Shende, V. V., Prasad, A. K., Markov, I. L., & Hayes, J. P. (2003). Synthesis of reversible logic circuits. *IEEE Transactions on Computer-Aided Design of Integrated Circuits and Systems*, *22*(6), 710–722. doi:10.1109/TCAD.2003.811448

Shi, Y., & Eberhart, R. (1998). A modified particle swarm optimizer. In Proceedings of the Evolutionary Computation *World Congress on Computational Intelligence* (pp. 69-73). Washington, DC: IEEE.

Shylo, O. V. (1999). A Global Equilibrium Search Method. *Kybernetika I Systemniy Analys*, *1*, 74–80.

Siarry, P., Berthiau, G., Durbin, F., & Haussy, J. (1997). Enhanced simulated annealing for globally minimizing functions of many-continuous variables. *ACM Transactions on Mathematical Software*, *23*(2), 209–228. doi:10.1145/264029.264043

Siau, K., & Halpin, T. (2001). *Unified Modeling Language: system analysis, design and development issues*. Hershey, PA: IGI Global.

Sierra, B., Lazkano, E., Inza, I., Merino, M., Larrañaga, P., & Quiroga, J. (2001). Prototype selection and feature subset selection by estimation of distribution algorithms. A case study in the survival of cirrhotic patients treated with TIPS. *Artificial Intelligence in Medicine* (LNAI 2101, pp. 20-29).

Silberholz, J., & Golden, B. (2010). Comparison of metaheuristics. In Gendreau, M., & Potvin, J.-V. (Eds.), *Handbook of metaheuristics*. Heidelberg, Germany: Springer. doi:10.1007/978-1-4419-1665-5_21

Silver, E. A., Pyke, D. F., & Peterson, R. (1998). *Inventory Management and Production Planning and Scheduling*. New York: John Wiley & Sons.

Silver, E., Peterson, R., & Pyke, D. F. (2000). *Decision Systems for Inventory Management and Production*. New York: John Wiley & Sons.

Simoes, A., & Costa, E. (2008). Evolutionary algorithms for dynamic environments: Prediction using linear regression and Markov chains. In *Parallel problem solving from nature* (pp. 306-315). Springer.

Simon, H. A. (1952). On the application of servomechanism theory in the study of production control. *Econometrica*, *20*(2), 247–268. doi:10.2307/1907849

Skiena, S. S., & Revilla, M. A. (2003). *Programming challenges: The programming contest training manual*. New York: Springer.

Smith, R. E. (1993). *Psychology.* St. Paul, MN: West Publishing Co.

Soh, T., Inoue, K., Tamura, N., Banbara, M., & Nabeshima, H. (2008). A SAT-based method for solving the two-dimensional strip packing problem. In M. Gavanelli & T. Mancini (Eds.), *Proceedings of the Fifteenth International RCRA Workshop on Experimental Evaluation of Algorithms for Solving Problems with Combinatorial Explosion.* Aachen, Germany: RWTH Aachen University.

Soke, A., & Bingul, Z. (2006). Hybrid genetic algorithm and simulated annealing for two-dimensional non-guillotine rectangular packing problems. *Engineering Applications of Artificial Intelligence*, *19*, 557–567. doi:10.1016/j.engappai.2005.12.003

Somenzi, F. (2001). *CUDD: CU Decision Diagram Package Release 2.3.1.* Boulder, CO: University of Colorado at Boulder.

Soyster, A. L., Lev, B., & Slivka, W. (1978). Zero–one programming with many variables and few constraints. *European Journal of Operational Research*, *2*(3), 195–201. doi:10.1016/0377-2217(78)90093-0

Spielberg, K., & Guignard, M. (2000). A Sequential (Quasi) Hot Start Method for BB (0,1) Mixed Integer Programming. In *Proceedings of the Mathematical Programming Symposium*, Atlanta.

Srinivas, N., & Deb, K. (1994). Multiobjective optimization using nondominated sorting in genetic algorithms. *Evolutionary Computation*, *2*(3), 221–248. doi:10.1162/evco.1994.2.3.221

Stadler, P. F. (1995). Towards a theory of landscapes. In R. Lop'ez-Pe~na, R. Capovilla, R. Garc'ıa- Pelayo, H. Waelbroeck, & F. Zertuche (Eds.), *Complex Systems and Binary Networks* (Vol. 461, pp. 77-163). Berlin: Springer.

Stadler, P., & Schnabl, W. (1992). The landscape of the traveling salesman problem. *Physics Letters. [Part A]*, *161*, 337–344. doi:10.1016/0375-9601(92)90557-3

Sterman, J. (1989). Modelling managerial behaviour: Misperceptions of feedback in a dynamic decision making experiment. *Management Science*, *35*(3), 321–339. doi:10.1287/mnsc.35.3.321

Sternberg, R. J. (1998). *In search of the human mind* (2nd ed.). New York: Harcourt Brace.

Sutton, R. S., & Barto, A. G. (1998). *Reinforcement learning: An introduction.* Cambridge, MA: MIT Press.

Swell, E. C. (1996). An improved algorithm for exact graph coloring. In Johnson, D. S., & Trick, M. A. (Eds.), *Cliques, Coloring, and Satisfiability: 2nd DIMACS Implementation Challenge* (pp. 359–373). Providence, RI: American Mathematical society.

Tajbakhsh, A., Rahmati, M., & Mirzaei, A. (2009). Intrusion detection using fuzzy association rules. *Applied Soft Computing*, *9*(2), 462–469. doi:10.1016/j.asoc.2008.06.001

Talbi, E.-G. (2009). *Metaheuristics: From design to implementation.* New York: Wiley & Sons.

Talbi, E. (2006). *Parallel combinatorial optimization.* Hoboken, NJ: John Wily & Sons. doi:10.1002/0470053925

Talbi, E. G. (2002). A taxonomy of hybrid meta-heuristics. *Journal of Heuristics*, *5*(8), 541–564. doi:10.1023/A:1016540724870

Tan, N. (1997). *Switched-current design and implementation of oversampling A/D converters.* Berlin: Springer Verlag.

Teghem, J. (1996). Programmation linéaire. *Editions Ellipses*, 51-62.

Terashima-Marin, H. T., Moran-Saavedra, A., & Ross, P. (2005). Forming hyper-heuristics with GAs when solving 2D-regular cutting stock problems. In *Proceedings of the 2005 IEEE Congress on Evolutionary Computation* (Vol. 2, pp. 1104-1110).

Terashima-Marin, H. T., Ross, P., & Valenzuela-Rendon, M. (1999). Evolution of constraint satisfaction strategies in examination timetabling. In *Proceedings of the Genetic and Evolutionary Computation Conference (GECCO '99)* (pp. 635-642).

Terashima-Marín, H., Flores-Álvarez, E., & Ross, P. (2005). Hyper-heuristics and classifier systems for solving 2D-regular cutting stock problems. In *Proceedings of the 2005 Conference on Genetic and Evolutionary Computation* (Vol. 2, pp. 637-643). New York: ACM Press.

Tereshima-Marin, H. T., Zarate, C. J. F., Ross, P., & Valenzuela-Rendon, M. (2007). Comparing two models to generate hyper-heuristics for the 2d-regular bin-packing problem. In *Proceedings of the 9th Annual Conference on Genetic and Evolutionary Computation (GECCO'07)* (pp. 2182-2189).

Tfaili, W., & Siarry, P. (2008). A new charged ant colony algorithm for continuous dynamic optimization. *Applied Mathematics and Computation, 197*, 604–613. doi:10.1016/j.amc.2007.08.087

Thathachar, M. A. L., & Sastry, P. S. (2004). *Network of Learning Automata: Techniques for On line Stochastic Optimization*. Dordrecht, The Netherlands: Kluwer Academic Publishers.

Thierens, D. (2008). From Multi-start Local Search to Genetic Local Search: a Practitioner's Guide. In *Proceedings of the 2nd International Conference on Metaheuristics and Nature Inspired Computing (META'08)*. Tunisia: Hammamet.

Thompson, J. M., & Dowsland, K. A. (1998). A robust simulated annealing based examination timetabling system. *Computers & Operations Research, 25*, 637–648. doi:10.1016/S0305-0548(97)00101-9

Thornton, J., Pham, D. N., Bain, S., & Ferreira, V., Jr. (2004). Additive versus multiplicative clause weighting for SAT. In *Proceedings of the Nineteenth National Conference of Artificial Intelligence* (pp. 191-196).

Tinos, R., & Yang, S. (2007). A self-organizing random immigrants genetic algorithm for dynamic optimization problems. *Genetic Programming and Evolvable Machines, 8*, 255–286. doi:10.1007/s10710-007-9024-z

Tlelo-Cuautle, E., & Duarte-Villaseñor, M. A. (2008). Evolutionary electronics: automatic synthesis of analog circuits by GAs. In Ang, Y., Yin, S., & Bui, L. T. (Eds.), *Success in Evolutionary Computation* (pp. 165–187). Berlin: Springer Verlag. doi:10.1007/978-3-540-76286-7_8

Toffoli, T. (1980). Reversible computing. In de Bakker, W., & van Leeuwen, J. (Eds.), *Automata, Languages and Programming* (p. 632). New York: Springer.

Toffoli, T. (1980). Reversible computing. In de Bakker, W., & van Leeuwen, J. (Eds.), *Automata, Languages and Programming* (p. 632). New York: Springer.

Toumazou, C., Hughes, J. B., & Buttersby, N. C. (1993). *Switched currents an analogue technique for digital technology*. London: Peter Peregrinus.

Tsetlin, M. L. (1973). *Automaton Theory and Modeling of Biological Systems*. New York: Academic Press.

Tufte, E. R. (2001). *The Visual Display of Quantitative Information* (2nd ed.). Cheshire, CN: Graphics Press.

Ursulenko, A. (2006). *Notes on the Global Equilibrium Search (Tech. Rep.)*. Al Paso, TX: Texas A & M University.

Ursulenko, A. (2006). *Notes on the global equilibrium search*. College Station, TX: Texas A&M University.

Vaughn, N., Polnaszek, C., Smith, B., & Helseth, T. (2000). *Design-Expert 6 User's Guide*. Stat-Ease Inc.

Vazquez-Rodriguez, J. A., Petrovic, S., & Salhi, A. (2007). A combined meta-heuristic with hyper-heuristic approach to the scheduling of the hybrid flow shop with sequence dependent setup times and uniform machines. In P. Baptiste, G. Kendall, A. Munier-Kordon, & F. Sourd (Eds.), *Proceedings of the 3rd Multi-disciplinary International Scheduling Conference: Theory and Applications (MISTA'07),* Paris (pp. 506-513).

Veeramachaneni, K., Peram, T., Mohan, C., & Osadciw, L. A. (2003). *Optimization Using Particle Swarms with Near Neighbour Interactions* (LNCS 2723). New York: Springer. ISBN:0302-9743

Voss, S., & Woodruff, D. L. (2002). *Optimization software class libraries*. Norwell, MA: Kluwer.

Voudouris, C., Dorne, R., Lesaint, D., & Liret, A. (2001). iOpt: A software toolkit for heuristic search methods. In *Proceedings of the International Conference on Principles and Practice of Constraint Programming* (LNCS 2239, pp. 716-729). Berlin: Springer.

Vredeveld, T., & Lenstra, J. (2003). On local search for the generalized graph coloring problem. *Operations Research Letters, 31*, 28–34. doi:10.1016/S0167-6377(02)00165-7

Wall, M. (1996). *GAlib: A C++ library of genetic algorithm components (Tech. Rep.)*. Mechanical Engineering Department, Massachusetts Institute of Technology.

Wang, Y. (2002a). Keynote: On cognitive informatics. In *Proceedings of the 1st IEEE International Conference on Cognitive Informatics (ICCI'02)*, Calgary, Canada (pp. 34-42). Los Alamitos, CA: IEEE CS Press.

Wang, Y. (2003). On cognitive informatics. *Brain and Mind: A Transdisciplinary Journal of Neuroscience and Neurophilosophy, 4*(3), 151-167.

Wang, Y. (2007a). *Software engineering foundations: A software science perspective: CRC series in software engineering II.* Boca Raton, FL: Auerbach Publications.

Wang, Y., & Chiew, V. (2009). On the cognitive process of human problem solving. *Cognitive Systems Research: An International Journal, 10*(4).

Wang, F., & Harjani, R. (1997). *Design of modulators for oversampled converters.* New York: Springer.

Wang, Y. (2002b). The real-time process algebra (RTPA). *Annals of Software Engineering, 14*, 235–274. doi:10.1023/A:1020561826073

Wang, Y. (2007b). The theoretical framework of cognitive informatics. *International Journal of Cognitive Informatics and Natural Intelligence, 1*(1), 1–27.

Wang, Y. (2007c). On laws of work organization in human cooperation. *International Journal of Cognitive Informatics and Natural Intelligence, 1*(2), 1–15.

Wang, Y. (2007d). On the cognitive processes of perception with emotions, motivations, and attitudes. *International Journal of Cognitive Informatics and Natural Intelligence, 1*(4), 1–13.

Wang, Y. (2007e). The OAR model of neural informatics for internal knowledge representation in the brain. *International Journal of Cognitive Informatics and Natural Intelligence, 1*(3), 68–82.

Wang, Y. (2008a). On contemporary denotational mathematics for computational intelligence. *Transactions of Computational Science, 2*, 6–29. doi:10.1007/978-3-540-87563-5_2

Wang, Y. (2008b). On concept algebra: A denotational mathematical structure for knowledge and software modeling. *International Journal of Cognitive Informatics and Natural Intelligence, 2*(2), 1–19.

Wang, Y. (2008c). RTPA: A denotational mathematics for manipulating intelligent and computational behaviors. *International Journal of Cognitive Informatics and Natural Intelligence, 2*(2), 44–62.

Wang, Y. (2009a). On abstract intelligence: Toward a unified theory of natural, artificial, machinable, and computational intelligence. *International Journal of Software Science and Computational Intelligence, 1*(1), 1–17.

Wang, Y. (2009b). On cognitive computing. *International Journal of Software Science and Computational Intelligence, 1*(3), 1–15.

Wang, Y. (2009c). A cognitive informatics reference model of autonomous agent systems (AAS). *International Journal of Cognitive Informatics and Natural Intelligence, 3*(1), 1–16.

Wang, Y. (2010). A Sociopsychological Perspective on Collective Intelligence in Metaheuristic Computing. *International Journal of Applied Metaheuristic Computing, 1*(1), 110–128.

Wang, Y., Kinsner, W., Anderson, J. A., Zhang, D., Yao, Y., & Sheu, P. (2009). A doctrine of cognitive informatics. *Fundamenta Informaticae, 90*(3), 203–228.

Wang, Y., Kinsner, W., & Zhang, D. (2009). Contemporary cybernetics and its faces of cognitive informatics and computational intelligence. *IEEE Transactions on System, Man, and Cybernetics (B), 39*(4), 823–833. doi:10.1109/TSMCB.2009.2013721

Wang, Y., Wang, Y., Patel, S., & Patel, D. (2006). A layered reference model of the brain (LRMB). *IEEE Transactions on Systems, Man and Cybernetics. Part C, Applications and Reviews, 36*(2), 124–133. doi:10.1109/TSMCC.2006.871126

Wang, Y., Zadeh, L. A., & Yao, Y. (2009). On the system algebra foundations for granular computing. *International Journal of Software Science and Computational Intelligence, 1*(1), 64–86.

Wascher, G., Haussner, H., & Schumann, H. (2007). An improved typology of cutting and packing problems. *European Journal of Operational Research, 183*(3), 1109–1130. doi:10.1016/j.ejor.2005.12.047

Wegener, I. (2000). *Branching programs and binary decision diagrams: theory and applications*. Philadelphia: Society for Industrial and Applied Mathematics.

Westen, D. (1999). *Psychology: Mind, brain, and culture* (2nd ed.). New York: John Wiley & Sons.

Weyland, D. (2010). A Rigorous Analysis of the Harmony Search Algorithm: How the Research Community can be Misled by a 'Novel' Methodology. *International Journal of Applied Metaheuristic Computing, 1*(2), 50–60.

Wiggins, J. A., Eiggins, B. B., & Zanden, J. V. (1994). *Social psychology* (5th ed.). New York: McGraw-Hill.

Wikipedia. (2009). *Metaheuristic*. Retrieved from http://en.wikipedia.org/wiki/Metaheuristic.

Wilbaut, C., & Hanafi, S. (2009). New convergent heuristics for 0-1 mixed integer programming. *European Journal of Operational Research, 195*, 62–74. doi:10.1016/j.ejor.2008.01.044

Wille, R., & Drechsler, R. (2009). BDD-based synthesis of reversible logic for large functions. In *Proceedings of the Design Automation Conference* (pp. 270-275).

Wille, R., Große, D., Teuber, L., Dueck, G. W., & Drechsler, R. (2008). RevLib: an online resource for reversible functions and reversible circuits. In *Proceedings of the International Symposium on Multi-Valued Logic* (pp. 220-225). Retrieved from http://www.revlib.org

Wille, R., & Drechsler, R. (2010). Effect of BDD Optimization on Synthesis of Reversible and Quantum Logic. *Electronic Notes in Theoretical Computer Science, 253*(6), 57–70. doi:10.1016/j.entcs.2010.02.006

Wilson, D. R., & Martinez, T. R. (1997). Instance pruning techniques. In *Proceedings of the 14th International Conference on Machine Learning*, Nashville, TN (pp. 403-411).

Wilson, D. R., & Martinez, T. R. (2000). Reduction techniques for instance-based learning algorithms. *Machine Learning, 38*, 257–286. doi:10.1023/A:1007626913721

Wilson, G. C., McIntyre, A., & Heywood, M. I. (2004). Resource review: Three open source systems for evolving programs—Lilgp, ECJ and grammatical evolution. *Genetic Programming and Evolvable Machines, 5*(19), 103–105. doi:10.1023/B:GENP.0000017053.10351.dc

Wittig, A. F. (2001). *Schaum's outlines of theory and problems of introduction to psychology* (2nd ed.). New York: McGraw-Hill.

Wolpert, D. W., & Macready, W. G. (1997). No free lunch theorems for optimization. *IEEE Transactions on Evolutionary Computation, 1*(1), 67–82. doi:10.1109/4235.585893

Wong, T., Cote, P., & Gely, P. (2002). Final exam timetabling: a practical approach. In. *Proceedings of the IEEE Canadian Conference on Electrical and Computer Engineering, 2*, 726–731.

Worapishet, A., Hughes, J. B., & Toumazou, C. (1999). Class AB technique for high performance switched-current memory cells. In *Proceedings of the IEEE international symposium on circuits and systems* (pp. 456-459)

Worapishet, A., Hughes, J. B., & Toumazou, C. (2000). Low-voltage class AB two-step sampling switched-currents. In *Proceedings of the IEEE international symposium on circuits and systems* (pp. 413-416).

Wu, S., & Olafsson, S. (2006). *Optimal instance selection for improved decision tree induction*. Paper presented at the 2006 IIE Annual Conference and Exhibition, Orlando, FL.

Wu, Z., & Wah, B. (2000). An efficient global-search strategy in discrete Lagrangian methods for solving hard satisfiability problems. In *Proceedings of the Seventeenth National Conference on Artificial Intelligence* (pp. 310-315).

Xu, K., Dong, Y., & Evers, P. (2001). Towards better coordination of the supply chain. *Transportation Research Part E, Logistics and Transportation Review, 37*(1), 35–54. doi:10.1016/S1366-5545(00)00010-7

Xu, L., Hutter, F., Hoos, H., & Leyton-Brown, K. (2008). SATzilla: Portfolio-based Algorithm Selection for SAT. [JAIR]. *Journal of Artificial Intelligence Research, 32*, 565–606.

Yaguiura, M., & Ibaraki, T. (1999). Analyses on the 2 and 3-flip neighborhoods for the MAX SAT. *Journal of Combinatorial Optimization, 3*, 95–114. doi:10.1023/A:1009873324187

Yaguiura, M., & Ibaraki, T. (2001). Efficient 2 and 3-flip neighborhood search algorithms for the MAX SAT: Experimental evaluation. *Journal of Heuristics*, *7*, 423–442. doi:10.1023/A:1011306011437

Yang, S. (1991). *Logic synthesis and optimization benchmarks user guide* (Tech. Rep. No. 1/95). Durham, NC: Microelectronic Center of North Carolina.

Yang, S. (2003). Non-stationary problem optimization using the primal-dual genetic algorithm. In *Proceedings of the 2003 IEEE Congress on Evolutionary Computation* (pp. 2246-2253). Washington, DC: IEEE Computer Society.

Yang, S. (2006). A comparative study of immune system based genetic algorithms in dynamic environments. In *Proceedings of the 8th Annual Conference on Genetic and Evolutionary Computation* (pp. 1377-1384). ACM Publishing.

Yang, Q., & Wu, X. (2006). 10 challenging problems in data mining research. *International Journal of Information Technology and Decision Making*, *5*(4), 597–604. doi:10.1142/S0219622006002258

Yang, S., & Yao, X. (2005). Experimental study on population-based incremental learning algorithms for dynamic optimization problems. *Soft Computing - A Fusion of Foundations. Methodologies and Applications*, *9*, 815–834.

Yeung, H. L. W., & Tang, W. K. S. (2004). Strip-packing using hybrid genetic approach. *Engineering Applications of Artificial Intelligence*, *17*, 169–177. doi:10.1016/j.engappai.2004.02.003

Yeung, L., & Tang, W. (2004). Strip-packing using hybrid genetic approach. *Engineering Applications of Artificial Intelligence*, *17*, 169–177. doi:10.1016/j.engappai.2004.02.003

Yıldız, A. R. (2009). A novel hybrid immune algorithm for global optimization in design and manufacturing. *Robotics and Computer-integrated Manufacturing*, *25*, 261–270. doi:10.1016/j.rcim.2007.08.002

Yin, P. Y. (2010). *MetaYourHeuristic V. 1.3, Intelligence Computing Laboratory, National Chi Nan University, Taiwan.* Retrieved from http://intelligence.im.ncnu.edu.tw

Yin, P.-Y. (2010). Editorial. *International Journal of Applied Metaheuristic Computing*, *1*(1), 1.

Zander, A. (1979). The psychology of the group process. *Annual Review of Psychology*, 418.

Zarei, O., Fesanghary, M., Farshi, B., Saffar, R., & Razfar, M. (2009). Optimization of multi-pass face-milling via harmony search algorithm. *Journal of Materials Processing Technology*, *209*(5), 2386–2392. doi:10.1016/j.jmatprotec.2008.05.029

Zdeborová, L., & Krzakała, F. (2007). Phase transitions in the coloring of random graphs. *Physical Review E*.

Zeng, F., Low, M. Y. H., Decraene, J., Zhou, S., & Cai, W. (2010). Self-Adaptive Mechanism for Multi-objective Evolutionary Algorithms. In *Proceedings of the 2010 IAENG International Conference on Artificial Intelligence and Applications*.

Zhang, X. (2004). The impact of forecasting methods on the bullwhip effect. *International Journal of Production Economics*, *88*(1), 15–27. doi:10.1016/S0925-5273(03)00128-2

Zhirnov, V. V., Cavin, R. K., Hutchby, J. A., & Bourianoff, G. I. (2003). Limits to binary logic switch scaling – a gedanken model. *Proceedings of the IEEE*, *91*(11), 1934–1939. doi:10.1109/JPROC.2003.818324

Zhong, J., & Muzio, J. C. (2006). Using crosspoint faults in simplifying Toffoli networks. In *Proceedings of the IEEE Northeast Workshop on Circuits and Systems* (pp. 129-132).

Zipkin, P. H. (2000). *Foundations of Inventory Management*. New York: McGraw-Hill.

Zitzler, E., Deb, K., & Thiele, L. (2000). Comparison of multi-objective evolutionary algorithms: Empirical results. *Evolutionary Computation*, *8*(2), 173–195. doi:10.1162/106365600568202

About the Contributors

Peng-Yeng Yin received his BS, MS, and PhD degrees in computer science from National Chiao Tung University (Hsinchu, Taiwan). From 1993 to 1994, he was a visiting scholar in the Department of Electrical Engineering at the University of Maryland (College Park, MD, USA) and in the Department of Radiology at Georgetown University (Washington D.C., USA). In 2000, he was a visiting professor in the Visualization and Intelligent Systems Laboratory (VISLab) in the Department of Electrical Engineering at the University of California (Riverside, USA). From 2006 to 2007, he was a visiting professor at Leeds School of Business, University of Colorado. From 2001 to 2003, he was a professor in the Department of Computer Science and Engineering, Ming Chuan University (Taoyuan, Taiwan). Since 2003, he has been a professor of the Department of information Management, National Chi Nan University (Nantou, Taiwan). Dr. Yin received the Overseas Research Fellowship from Ministry of Education (1993) and the Overseas Research Fellowship from National Science Council (2000). He has received the best paper award from the Image Processing and Pattern Recognition Society of Taiwan. He is a member of the Phi Tau Phi Scholastic Honor Society and listed in Who's Who in the World, Who's Who in Science and Engineering, and Who's Who in Asia. Dr. Yin has published more than 100 academic articles in reputable journals and conferences including IEEE Trans. on Pattern Analysis and Machine Intelligence, IEEE Trans. on Knowledge and Data Engineering, IEEE Trans. on Education, Pattern Recognition, Annals of Operations Research, IEEE International Conference on Computer Vision, etc. He has been on the editorial board of the International Journal of Advanced Robotic Systems, the Open Artificial Intelligence Journal, the Open Artificial Intelligence Letters, the Open Artificial Intelligence Reviews and served as a program committee member in many international conferences. His current research interests include artificial intelligence, evolutionary computation, metaheuristics, pattern recognition, content-based image retrieval, relevance feedback, machine learning, computational intelligence, operations research, and computational biology.

* * *

Bahram Alidaee received the B.S. degree from the University of Tehran, Iran, the M.B.A. degree from the University of North Texas and the Ph.D. degree from the University of Texas at Arlington. He is currently a professor of operations management at the School of Business Administration, the University of Mississippi. His research interests include applied optimization, applied graph theory, heuristic programming, complex systems, game theory and cost allocations. He is member of INFORMS, DSI, POMS, APICS, ISM, and IEEE Computer Society.

Noureddine Bouhmala was born in Casablanca, Morocco. He obtained his MSc degree from the Swiss Federal Institute of Technology at Lausanne in 1994 and his PhD in Computer Science from the University of Neuchatel, Switzerland, in 1998. He is presently an Associate Professor at Vestfold University College and Associate Professor II at the University of Agder. His research interests include Meta-Heuristic Algorithms for Combinatorial Optimization, Parallel Computing, and Data Mining. He is also an Associate Professor II in the Department of ICT, University of Agder, Norway.

Professor Edmund Burke is Dean of the Faculty of Science at the University of Nottingham and he leads the Automated Scheduling, Optimisation and Planning (ASAP) Research Group in the School of Computer Science. He is a member of the EPSRC Strategic Advisory Team for Mathematics. He is a Fellow of the Operational Research Society and the British Computer Society and he is a member of the UK Computing Research Committee (UKCRC). Prof. Burke is Editor-in-chief of the Journal of Scheduling, Area Editor (for Combinatorial Optimisation) of the Journal of Heuristics, Associate Editor of the INFORMS Journal on Computing, Associate Editor of the IEEE Transactions on Evolutionary Computation and a member of the Editorial Board of Memetic Computing. He is also the Research Director of EventMAP Ltd. and a Director of Aptia Solutions Ltd, both of which are spin out companies from the ASAP group. Prof. Burke has played a leading role in the organisation of several major international conferences in his research field in the last few years. He has edited/authored 14 books and has published over 180 refereed papers. He has been awarded 47 externally funded grants worth over £11M from a variety of sources including EPSRC, ESRC, BBSRC, EU, Research Council of Norway, East Midlands Development Agency, HEFCE, Teaching Company Directorate, Joint Information Systems Committee of the HEFCs and commercial organisations. This funding portfolio includes being the Principal Investigator on a recently awarded EPSRC Science and Innovation award of £2M, an EPSRC grant of £2.6M to investigate the automation of the heuristic design process and an EPSRC platform grant worth £423K.

Yann Cooren, was born in Bordeaux, France in 1982. He received his engineering degree and his master from the École Nationale Supérieure d'Électronique, d'Informatique et de Radiocommunications de Bordeaux (ENSEIRB). In 2008, he obtained his PhD from the Laboratoire d'Images, Signaux et Systèmes Intelligents (LiSSi) of the University of Paris 12. His main research interests are metaheuristics and, particularly, the Particle Swarm Optimization method.

Joaquín Derrac received the M.Sc. degree in computer science from the University of Granada, Granada, Spain, in 2008. He is currently a Ph.D. student in the Department of Computer Science and Artificial Intelligence, University of Granada, Granada, Spain. His research interests include data mining, lazy learning and evolutionary algorithms.

Rolf Drechsler received his diploma and Dr. phil. nat. degree in computer science in 1992 and 1995, respectively. Before he became full professor at the University of Bremen in 2001, he was with the Corporate Technology Department of the Siemens AG, Munich. His main research areas are in the development and design of data structures and algorithms with a focus on circuit and system design. He published over 150 scientific papers and more than 10 books in the areas of testing, verification, synthesis and reasoning technology. He was a member of the program committees of numerous international conferences including DATE, DAC, ICCAD, VLSI Design, ASP-DAC and served as topic chair for formal verification for the Design, Automation and Test in Europe (DATE) and the Design Automation Conference (DAC). He received best paper awards from the Haifa Verification Conference (HVC) in 2006 and from the Forum on Specification and Design Languages (FDL) in 2007 and 2010.

Kourosh Eshghi is Dean of Industrial Engineering Department at Sharif University of Technology, Tehran, Iran. He received his Ph.D. in the field of Operations Research from University of Toronto in 1997. His research interests include graph theory, integer programming and combinatorial optimization. He is the author of 2 books and over 50 journal papers.

Mourad Fakhfakh was born in Sfax-Tunisia in 1969. He received the engineering and the PhD degrees from the national engineering school of Sfax Tunisia in 1996 and 2006 respectively. From 1998 to 2004 he worked in the Tunisian National Society of Electricity and Gas (STEG) as a chief of the technical intervention service. In September 2004, he joined the higher institute of electronics and communications (ISECS) where he is working as an assistant professor. Since 2002 he has been with the electronics and information technology laboratory (LETI/ENIS) where he is currently a researcher. His research interests include current mode techniques, symbolic analysis techniques, analog design automation, and optimization techniques.

Salvador García received the M.Sc. and Ph.D. degrees in computer science from the University of Granada, Granada, Spain, in 2004 and 2008, respectively. He is currently an Associate Professor in the Department of Computer Science, University of Jaén, Jaén, Spain. His research interests include data mining, data reduction, data complexity, imbalanced learning, statistical inference and evolutionary algorithms.

Dr. Zong Woo Geem is an academic advisor and faculty of a newly established academic institute named iGlobal University located at Annandale, Virginia, USA. He is an inventor of music-inspired meta-heuristic algorithm, Harmony Search, which has been successfully applied to various optimization problems in many fields such as computer science, electrical engineering, civil and environmental engineering, mechanical and chemical engineering, bio and medical applications, real world applications, etc. He has researched at Virginia Tech, Johns Hopkins University and University of Maryland at College Park, publishing nearly one hundred technical papers including three edited books from Springer. Dr. Geem is also a concert soloist, who has sung at Washington National Cathedral and Basilica of the National Shrine in Washington DC.

Dr. Fred Glover is the Chief Technology Officer in charge of algorithmic design and strategic planning initiatives for OptTek Systems, Inc., heading the development of commercial computer software systems currently serving more than 80,000 users in the United States and abroad. He also holds the title of Distinguished Professor at the University of Colorado, Boulder, where he is affiliated with the Leeds School of Business and the Department of Electrical and Computer Engineering. Dr. Glover is widely known for his work in the applications of computer decision support systems, including industrial planning, financial analysis, systems design, energy and natural resources planning, logistics, transportation and large-scale allocation models. He has authored or co-authored more than 370 published articles and eight books in the fields of mathematical optimization, computer science and artificial intelligence. He is also the originator of Tabu Search (Adaptive Memory Programming), an optimization search methodology of which more than 200,000 Web pages can be found with a simple Google search.

Dr. Glover is the recipient of the highest honor of the Institute of Operations Research and Management Science, the von Neumann Theory Prize, and is an elected member of the National Academy of Engineering. He has also received numerous other awards and honorary fellowships, including those from the American Association for the Advancement of Science (AAAS), the NATO Division of Scientific Affairs, the Institute of Operations Research and Management Science (INFORMS), the Decision Sciences Institute (DSI), the U.S. Defense Communications Agency (DCA), the Energy Research Institute (ERI), the American Assembly of Collegiate Schools of Business (AACSB), Alpha Iota Delta, the Institute of Cybernetics of the Ukrainian Academy of Science, and the Miller Institute for Basic Research in Science.

Ole-Christoffer Granmo was born in Porsgrunn, Norway. He obtained his M.Sc. in 1999 and the PhD degree in 2004, both from the University of Oslo, Norway. He is currently an Associate Professor in the Department of ICT, University of Agder, Norway. His research interests include Intelligent Systems, Stochastic Modelling and Inference, Machine Learning, Pattern Recognition, Learning Automata, Distributed Computing, and Surveillance and Monitoring. He is the author of more than 45 refereed journal and conference publications.

Mohamed Haddar was born in 1963 (in Tunisia). PhD in applied Mechanics (1991). Professor at the National School of Engineers of Sfax in Tunisia. Director of the Mechanics Modelling and Production Research Unit. The topics of the research activities deal with the dynamic behaviour of machine elements (gears, bearings, belts...) and the manufacturing process simulation.

Jean-Philippe Hamiez was born in June 1970 in Amiens (France). He received a Master degree in Fundamental Computer Science from the University of Picardie Jules Verne (Amiens) in 1996 & a Ph.D. in Computer Science from the University of Angers in France (supervised by Pr. Jin-Kao Hao) in 2002. Since 2003, he is Associate Professor at the University of Angers in the LERIA Lab. ("Metaheuristics, Optimization & Applications" Research Group). Its research activities concern the analysis & resolution of (theoretical or practical) combinatorial optimization & constraint satisfaction problems (NP-hard or NP-complete) of large sizes: Graph vertex coloring, sports league scheduling, & two-dimensional strip packing in particular. To tackle these problems, he used various (sometimes hybrid) methods including e.g. greedy algorithms, enumerative schemes, metaheuristics (especially tabu search), or population-based strategies.

Dr. Saïd Hanafi holds a Full Professor position in Computing Science at Institute of Techniques and Sciences, University of Valenciennes and is currently in charge of the team Operations Research and Decision Support. His research lies in the design of effective heuristic and metaheuristic algorithms for solving large-scale combinatorial search problems. His is interested in theoretical as well as algorithmic modelling and application aspects of integer programming and combinatorial optimisation and has published over 30 articles on the topic. His current interests revolve around the integration of tools from hybrid methods mixing exact and heuristics for solving hard problems.

Jin-Kao Hao holds a full Professor position in the Computer Science Department of the University of Angers (France) and is currently the Director of the LERIA Laboratory. His research lies in the design of effective heuristic and metaheuristic algorithms for solving large-scale combinatorial search problems. He is interested in various application areas including bioinformatics, telecommunication networks and transportation. He has co-authored more than 120 peer-reviewed publications and edited four books. He has served as an Invited Member of more than 130 Program Committees of the Conferences and is on the Editorial Board of four International Journals.

Jianing He is an instructor of logistics in the Department of Economics & Management, Nanhai Campus at South China Normal University. Dr. He had visited and studied in Texas A&M International University for one year. She earned a Ph.D. in Logistics Engineering and Management in South China University of Technology. Dr. He has publications in such outlets as Industrial Engineering Journal, Science Technology and Engineering, Journal of Transportation Engineering and Information, and some international conferences and proceedings.

Francisco Herrera received the M.Sc. degree in Mathematics in 1988 and the Ph.D. degree in Mathematics in 1991, both from the University of Granada, Spain. He is currently a Professor in the Department of Computer Science and Artificial Intelligence at the University of Granada. He has published more than 150 papers in international journals. He is coauthor of the book "*Genetic Fuzzy Systems: Evolutionary Tuning and Learning of Fuzzy Knowledge Bases*" (World Scientific, 2001). As edited activities, he has co-edited five international books and co-edited twenty special issues in international journals on different Soft Computing topics. He acts as associated editor of the journals: IEEE Transactions on Fuzzy Systesms, Mathware and Soft Computing, Advances in Fuzzy Systems, Advances in Computational Sciences and Technology, and International Journal of Applied Metaheuristic Computing. He currently serves as area editor of the Journal Soft Computing (area of genetic algorithms and genetic fuzzy systems), and he serves as member of the editorial board of the journals: Fuzzy Sets and Systems, Applied Intelligence, Knowledge and Information Systems, Information Fusion, Evolutionary Intelligence, International Journal of Hybrid Intelligent Systems, Memetic Computation, International Journal of Computational Intelligence Research, The Open Cybernetics and Systemics Journal, Recent Patents on Computer Science, Journal of Advanced Research in Fuzzy and Uncertain Systems, International Journal of Information Technology and Intelligent and Computing, and Journal of Artificial Intelligence and Soft Computing Research. His current research interests include computing with words and decision making, data mining, data preparation, instance selection, fuzzy rule based systems, genetic fuzzy systems, knowledge extraction based on evolutionary algorithms, memetic algorithms and genetic algorithms.

Imed Kacem was born in 1976. He received his "Diploma of Engineer" from ENSAIT (French High School) and his MS degree from Lille 1 University, both in 2000; his PhD degree in Computer Science in 2003 from the Ecole Centrale de Lille and his Habilitation Degree (HDR) from Paris-Dauphine University in 2007. He is a Full Professor at Paul Verlaine University of Metz (UPVM). His research interests include combinatorial optimisation and scheduling. He is the author of nearly 100 publications in refereed journals, conferences, books and chapters of books. He is Area Editor for *Computers & Industrial Engineering*. He is on the editorial boards of *European Journal of Industrial Engineering, International Journal of Advanced Operations Management, Advances in OR, IJAMC, JSCI, JPAM* and *JISE*. He was the Organisation Chairman of CIE39, ICSSSM06 and WAC/ISIAC06. He is listed in *Who's Who In the World*.

Voratas Kachitvichyanukul is a Professor in Industrial and Manufacturing Engineering at the School of Engineering and Technology, Asian Institute of Technology, Thailand. He received his PhD from the School of Industrial Engineering at Purdue University in 1982. He has extensive experience in simulation modelling of manufacturing systems. His teaching and research interests include planning and scheduling, high performance computing and applied operations research with special emphasis on large-scale industrial systems.

Mohammad Rahim Akhavan Kazemzadeh is a MSc. Student in Rail Transportation Engineering, School of Railway Engineering, Iran University of Science and Technology. His research interests are metaheuristics optimization methods, parameter tuning of metaheuristics, multicommodity network design problems, and optimization in rail transportation problems. He has one under-publishing book in the field of metaheuristics and some published papers in the field of network design and metaheuristics.

Gary Kochenberger has a degree in electrical engineering a Ph.D. in Management Science from the University of Colorado. He taught at Penn State for many years and since 1989 has been a professor of Operations Management at the University of Colorado at Denver. In recent years, his focus has been combinatorial optimization. He has published three books and more than seventy articles. Moreover, he has been actively engaged in several journals including positions as part of the editorial boards for INTERFACES, POMS, and IJMOR.

Julien Lepagnot was born in France in 1982. He received the Master degree in Computer Sciences in 2008 from the University Evry-val-d'Essonne. Now, he is pursuing a PhD degree in computer engineering at the University Paris 12. His main research interests include image segmentation and compression, stochastic global optimization heuristics and multi-agent systems.

Mourad Loulou was born in Sfax, Tunisia in 1968. He received the Engineering Diploma from the National School of Engineers of Sfax in 1993. He received his Ph.D. degree in 1998 in electronics system design from the University of Bordeaux France. He joined the electronic and information technology laboratory of Sfax "LETI" since 1998 and he has been assistant Professor at the National School of Engineers of Sfax from 1999. Since 2004 he obtained his HDR from the University of Sfax and he has been an associate Professor. Currently he supervises the Analogue, Mixed Mode and RF Design Group EleCom of LETI Laboratory. His current research interests are on Analogue, Mixed and RF CMOS integrated circuits for communications and design automation of analogue CMOS Integrated Circuits. He is senior member IEEE; he is currently the IEEE Tunisia Section and CAS Chapter chair.

Houra Mahmoudzadeh is currently a Ph.D. Student in the field of Operations Research at the Mechanical and Industrial Engineering Department at University of Toronto, Canada. She received her M.Sc. degree in the field of Operations Research from Sharif University of Technology under the supervision of Professor Kourosh Eshghi in 2007. Her research interests include metaheuristics, graph theory, combinatorial optimization, and robust optimization.

Siwar Masmoudi was born in Sfax- Tunisia in 1977. She received her 'Diploma of Maitrise' in 2004 and her Master degree in 2006, both in Electronics from the Faculty of science of Monastir, and the National Engineering School of Sfax, respectively. Since 2006, she is a Phd student in the Electronic and Information Technology Laboratory of Sfax "LETI". She joined the Higher institute of Electronics and Communication of Sfax (ISECS) in 2007, where she is working as a contract assistant. Her current research interests are on Switched current technique, Sigma Delta Converters.

Ahmed Mellouli was born in 1977 (in Tunisia). Engineer in electromechanical from the National School of Engineering of Sfax (2000),received his master degree in Operations Research & Production Management from the Faculty of Economics and Management Sciences in Sfax. He is a PhD student working in the National School of Engineering of Sfax. His main fields of research include: Cutting stock, Mathematical Programming, and Heuristic Methods.

Mustafa Misir received his B.Sc. and M.Sc. degrees in Computer Engineering from Yeditepe University in 2007 and 2008, respectively. He was awarded as a student assistant during his undergraduate study. He worked as a teaching and research assistant during his graduate study in the Artificial Intelligence research group at Yeditepe University. Currently, he is studying towards PhD in the Department of Computer Science (Informatics) at Katholieke Universiteit Leuven as a research fellow. He is also working as a researcher in the CODeS Research Group, Katholieke Universiteit Leuven, Campus Kortrijk and IT Research Group, KaHo Sint-Lieven. His research interests include combinatorial optimization, hyper-heuristics, meta-heuristics and reinforcement learning.

Amir Nakib was born in Algeria in 1977. He received the Magister in signal processing in 2003 and a second M.S. degree in image processing in 2004 from the University Paris 6. He received in December 2007 a PhD degree in computer engineering at University Paris 12 (France). His main research interests include image segmentation and compression, signal compression, and stochastic global optimization heuristics.

Su Nguyen is a research associate in Industrial and Manufacturing Engineering at the School of Engineering and Technology, Asian Institute of Technology, Thailand. His research interest includes discrete-event simulation, and applied metaheuristics in large-scale optimization problems.

Gabriela Ochoa is a Senior Research Fellow with the Automated Scheduling, Optimisation and Planning (ASAP) research group in the School of Computer Science at the University of Nottingham, since October 2006, where she coordinates a project on 'Automated Heuristic Design'. She received her PhD in Computer Science and Artificial Intelligence from the University of Sussex, UK, in 2001. Gabriela Ochoa has been involved with inter-disciplinary research, and foundations and applications of evolutionary algorithms since the mid 90s, and more recently with meta-heuristics and hyper-heuristics. She has published over 30 refereed research articles, serves on the program committees of major conferences in evolutionary computation and meta-heuristics, and has refereed for reputable journals in these fields. Gabriela Ochoa has recently dictated a tutorial on hyper-heuristics, and proposed and co-organised two workshops on hyper-heuristic methodologies held as part of reputable evolutionary computation conferences. She is the guest co-editor of the first special issue on hyper-heuristics (Journal of Heuristics, 2009).

Hamouche Oulhadj was born in Algeria in 1956. He received the B.S degree in Electrical Engineering at the Polytechnic School of Algiers, the DEA and the PhD degree in Biomedical Engineering from the University Paris 12 in 1985 and 1990 respectively. Now, he is an Associate Professor at the same University. His main research interests are pattern recognition, biomedical image segmentation and information extraction.

Ender Ozcan is a science and innovation lecturer with the Automated Scheduling, Optimisation and Planning (ASAP) research group in the School of Computer Science at the University of Nottingham, UK. He received his PhD from the Department of Computer and Information Science at Syracuse University, NY, USA in 1998. He worked as a lecturer in the Department of Computer Engineering at Yeditepe University, Istanbul, Turkey from 1998-2007. He established and led the ARTIficial Intelligence research group from 2002 and awarded two research grants from TUBITAK. He served as the Deputy Head of the Department from 2004-2007. Dr Ozcan joined the ASAP group as a senior research fellow in 2008. He has been serving as an executive committee member for the LANCS initiative, which is one of the largest Science and Innovation Rewards given by EPSRC (Engineering and Physical Sciences Research Council, UK). His research interests and activities lie at the interface of Computer Science and Operational Research. He has been leading studies in the field of metaheuristics focusing on evolutionary algorithms (memetic algorithms, PSO), hyper-heuristics, and their applications to the real-world and theoretical problems. Dr Ozcan has published over 55 refereed papers. He has been a member of the program committees in major international conferences and refereeing for reputable journals. He has co-organised five workshops on hyper-heuristics and metaheuristics and he is the guest co-editor of the forthcoming first special issue on hyper-heuristics (Journal of Heuristics, 2009).

Patrick Siarry was born in France in 1952. He received the PhD degree from the University Paris 6, in 1986 and the Doctorate of Sciences (Habilitation) from the University Paris 11, in 1994. He was first involved in the development of analog and digital models of nuclear power plants at Electricité de France (E.D.F.). Since 1995 he is a professor in automatics and informatics. His main research interests are computer-aided design of electronic circuits, and the applications of new stochastic global optimization heuristics to various engineering fields. He is also interested in the fitting of process models to experimental data, the learning of fuzzy rule bases, and of neural networks.

Giglia Gómez-Villouta graduated in 1997 from the Pontificia Universidad Católica de Valparaíso, Valparaíso, Chile and received in 2002 a Master degree in Computer Engineering from the Universidad Técnica Federico Santa María, Valparaíso, Chile. She obtained her Ph.D. degree in Computer Science at the University of Angers in France 2010. She holds currently an Associate Professor position at the Universidad de Valparaíso, Chile. She has been working on the 2D strip packing problem and is interested more generally in intelligent computing for optimization.

Haibo Wang is an assistant professor of decision science in the Division of International Business and Technology Studies, A.R. Sanchez Jr. School of Business at Texas A&M International University. He earned a Ph.D. in Production Operations Management. Dr. Wang has provided consulting services to organizations in China and US. Dr. Wang has publications in such outlets as the European Journal of Operational Research, IEEE transactions on Control System Technology, Journal of Operational Research Society International Journal of Flexible Manufacturing Systems, Communications in Statistics, Journal of Heuristics, Journal of Combinatorial Optimization and Journal of Optimization Letters and International Journal of Information Technology and Decision Making.

Yingxu Wang is professor of cognitive informatics and software engineering, Director of International Center for Cognitive Informatics (ICfCI), and Director of Theoretical and Empirical Software Engineering Research Center (TESERC) at the University of Calgary. He is a Fellow of WIF, a P.Eng of Canada, a Senior Member of IEEE and ACM, and a member of ISO/IEC JTC1 and the Canadian Advisory Committee (CAC) for ISO. He received a PhD in Software Engineering from The Nottingham Trent University, UK, in 1997, and a BSc in Electrical Engineering from Shanghai Tiedao University in 1983. He has industrial experience since 1972 and has been a full professor since 1994. He was a visiting professor in the Computing Laboratory at Oxford University in 1995, Dept. of Computer Science at Stanford University in 2008, and the Berkeley Initiative in Soft Computing (BISC) Lab at University of California, Berkeley in 2008, respectively. He is the founder and steering committee chair of the annual IEEE International Conference on Cognitive Informatics (ICCI). He is founding Editor-in-Chief of *International Journal of Cognitive Informatics and Natural Intelligence* (IJCINI), founding Editor-in-Chief of *International Journal of Software Science and Computational Intelligence* (IJSSCI), Associate Editor of IEEE Trans on System, Man, and Cybernetics (A), and Editor-in-Chief of *CRC Book Series in Software Engineering*. He is the initiator of a number of cutting-edge research fields and/or subject areas such as cognitive informatics, cognitive computing, abstract intelligence, denotational mathematics, theoretical software engineering, coordinative work organization theory, cognitive complexity of software, and built-in tests. He has published over 105 peer reviewed journal papers, 193 peer reviewed conference papers, and 12 books in cognitive informatics, software engineering, and computational intelligence. He is the recipient of dozens international awards on academic leadership, outstanding contribution, research achievement, best paper, and teaching in the last 30 years.

Dennis Weyland studied computer science at the University of Dortmund, Germany, and received the diploma degree in 2006. Currently he is working as a PhD student at IDSIA (Istituto Dalle Molle di Studi sull'Intelligenza Artificiale) in Lugano, Switzerland. Additionally he is finishing his studies in mathematics at the FernUniversität in Hagen, Germany, for a second diploma degree. His main research interests are search heuristics and complexity theory.

Robert Wille received the Diploma degree and Dr.-Ing. degree in computer science from the University of Bremen, Bremen, Germany, in 2006 and 2009, respectively. He is currently with the Group of Computer Architecture at the University of Bremen. His research interests include reversible logic and quantum computation, techniques for solving satisfiability problems, as well as verification of circuits and systems. Dr. Wille was a recipient of the Young Researchers Award from the International Symposium on Multiple-Valued Logic (ISMVL) in 2008 and of the Best Paper Award from the Forum on Specification and Design Languages (FDL) in 2010.

Li Xianglu received the B.S., M.S. and the Ph.D.in 1985, 1987, and 2002, respectively, from the Mathematics Department at the Zhengzhou University in mathematics. She is currently working at Economics and Management School, Zhongyuan University of Technology, Zhengzhou, China. Her research interests are combinatorial optimization, approximation algorithm design and multiple objective optimization.

Masoud Yaghini is Assistant Professor of Department of Rail Transportation Engineering, School of Railway Engineering, Iran University of Science and Technology. His research interests include data mining, optimization, metaheuristic algorithms, and application of data mining and optimization techniques in rail transportation planning. He published several books and papers in the field of data mining, metaheuristics, and rail transportation planning. He is teaching data mining, advanced operations research, and metaheuristic algorithms postgraduate courses.

Index